Secret Chamber

The Quest for the Hall of Records

Robert Bauval

CENTURY · LONDON

First published by Century in 1999

Copyright © Robert Bauval 1999

Robert Bauval has asserted his right under the Copyright,
Designs and Patents Act, 1988, to be identified as the author of this work

First published in the United Kingdom in 1999 by
Century, 20 Vauxhall Bridge Road, London SW1V 2SA

Random House Australia (Pty) Limited
20 Alfred Street, Milsons Point, Sydney,
New South Wales 2061, Australia

Random House New Zealand Limited
18 Poland Road, Glenfield,
Auckland 10, New Zealand

Random House (Pty) Limited
Endulini, 5a Jubilee Road,
Parktown 2193, South Africa

The Random House Group Limited Reg. No. 954009

A CIP catalogue record for this book
is available from the British Library

Papers used by Random House UK Limited are natural, recyclable
products made from wood grown in sustainable forests.
The manufacturing processes conform to the environmental
regulations of the country of origin.

ISBN 0 7126 8048 9

Typeset by MATS, Southend-on-Sea, Essex
Printed in Great Britain by Clays Ltd, St Ives plc

Contents

PART TWO: EXPLORATION

To Michele: my beautiful companion, my friend and my wife.
Thank you for saving my life.

Acknowledgements

Putting together *Secret Chamber* with its complex and varied topics has not been an easy task. And even though I thoroughly enjoyed the experience of piecing together this huge historical puzzle, I honestly believe that it would not have been possible without active support, help and love from numerous friends and colleagues.

First and foremost I want to thank my wife, Michele, who, for the fourth time round, has had to endure the traumas of a household in which a writer is hatching a manuscript. As always, she has done so with true grit and good cheer – especially that this time she has also had to cope with other troubles and difficulties. She is the rock upon which our home stands, and I am immensely grateful to her. I also am hugely grateful to my daughter, Candice, and my son, Jonathan, who put up with a father who is never 'with them'. Perhaps not, but Candice and Jon, you are always in my heart.

Along with my family comes my dear friend, companion-at-arms and valued colleague Graham Hancock, with whom I have gone through thick and thin, down into the Underworld and back as well as having co-authored two number one bestsellers with him so far. We have held fast in the face of bitter opposition over the years and are now proud to enjoy our new battle cry: 'We're still here!' To Graham I owe much, not least his unyielding loyalty, great generosity and staunch support.

Special thanks go, in priority, to film director and producer Diana Lucas of Johannesburg, South Africa. A film on the Giza conundrum that Diana has directed and produced is, in my opinion, a landmark in television actuality programmes. Thanks and praise also go to M-Net's presenters Derek Watt and Ruda Landman, director Joy Wilson-Price and manager Erika Alberts. Also in the world of television, press and publishing I would like to express my warm thanks to the following friends and colleagues: Nancy Stern and Lee Miller of Fox TV; my dear friend and film-maker Roel Oostra; Karim Wissa and Samir Rafaat; Jean-

Claude Bragard and Petra Collier of the BBC's *Ancient Voices* team; Julian Hudson and Chris Hale of the BBC's *Horizon* team; Stephen Johnson of Random House South Africa; Roy Bird of *Quest for Knowledge* magazine; Graham Birdstall of Quest Publications and J. Douglas Kenyon of *Atlantis Rising* magazine.

There are, of course, my many friends, old and new, towards whom I feel a special sense of gratitude and affection for their advice, support and for simply being there when I needed them: Dennis and Verena Seisun; Jean-Paul and Pauline Bauval; Geoffrey and Therese Gauci; Linda and Max Bauval; Yuri Stoyanov; Michael Baigent; Robert and Olivia Temple; Mohamad Nazmy, Methat Yehya, Ihab Rashad and all the Quest Travel team in Cairo; Mohamad El Kirsh my loyal taxi-driver and friend in Cairo; Uri Geller; my great-cousin Fedora Campos in Alexandria; the intrepid architect Mimi Awad; John and Josette Orphanidis; Bob Lomas; my solicitor and friend Nigel Brain; Colin Wilson; John Anthony West; the versatile Paula Tsaconas; Bill and Carol Cote; my New York 'buddy' Demetria Daniels; the unsinkable Dr Zahi Hawass; the peripatetic Mary Lumando and Vanda Osmon; the 'Falconer' Peter Whitehead; 'darling' Ann Mokhtar Kortam of the Mena House Oberoi; Chris O'Kane; Viviane Vayssieres; William Horsman; Toby and (Santa) Theresa Weiss; The 'Lady Morgana' Sylvie Moulaert-Glanz; Ed Meltzer; Kele Baker; Princess Madeleine and Prince George of Bentheim; Mark and Sabrina Borda; Ruth and Gloria; Andy Collins; James Holland; Jean Kerisel; philosopher extraordinaire John Lash; Dr Archie Roy; Dr Mary Brück; Robert Speight; Greg Taylor; Mustapha Abdel-Aziz; Bianca Gauci; 'Frank' El Farag; 'Zarzoor'; David and Christiane Joury; Tony and Florence Alexander; Gamal Mohamad, Charlotte Ames, and all the staff at the Movempick, Victoria and Mena House hotels.

I would also like to acknowledge and thank the many individual researchers and organisations for the use of quotations from their books and other publications. Because of the extensive and varied nature of this present thesis, and for the sake of thoroughness and quality of presentation, it has been necessary to bring into the discussion many points of view in quotation form to avoid distortion and misrepresentation. This not only has added cogency and scholarly value to the debate, but also has provided the readers with a good source of links with these works. The individuals and organisations I wish to pay tribute to in this respect are: John Anthony West; Michael Baigent and Richard Leigh; John Van Auken; Edgar Evans Cayce and Douglas Richards; The Edgar Cayce Foundation; A. Robert Smith; Dr Zahi Hawass; Peter Tompkins; Garth

Acknowledgements

Fowden; George Hart; Murry Hope; Dr Miriam Lichtheim; Dr I. E. S. Edwards and his estate; Dr Mark Lehner; Dame Frances Yates and her estate; Jeremy Naydler; David Ovason; R. T. Rundle Clark and his estate; Dr R. O. Faulkner and his estate; Dr Joseph Schor and Joe Jahoda; Graham Hancock; Simon Cox; Andrew Collins; Colin Wilson; E. A. Wallis Budge and his estate; The German Archaeological Institute in Cairo; Rudolf Gantenbrink; The BBC; The Supreme Council of Egyptian Antiquities; *The Times* of London; the *Daily Mail*; the *Daily Telegraph*; the *Al Ahram* and the *Egyptian Gazette*.

Thank you so much to my editor Mark Booth at Century/Random House UK whose persistent ways and true professionalism turned this book into a much better read than it would have been. To Liz Rowlinson at Century whose good humour and dedication to this project made it a real pleasure to put this book together; to Kelly Todd at Random House for her tireless efforts; to my agents Bill Hamilton and Sara Fisher and 'Betty' at A.M. Heath & Co. whose constant support and friendship is always greatly appreciated. And last but by no means least, my acknowledgement and deep thanks to Simon Cox for his excellent research on the 'Sokar' material in Part One of this book and his help in the editorial work. Simon's good humour and hard labour have been a great asset to this project and I look forward to seeing his first book, *The Makers of Time*, on my bookshelves soon.

Finally, a huge thanks to all my readers around the world who, during my hours of darkness in 1997, sent their love and positive energies that saw me through my trials and tribulations. It is your warm support that makes all of this effort worth the while.

Robert G. Bauval, Buckinghamshire, 1999

Prologue

The Symbol of the Records

'There shall appear and shine the sign of the Son of Man in the Heaven . . .'

Matthew 24:30

'Only an initiate may understand . . .'

Edgar Cayce on the Great Pyramid of Giza, 'reading' 5748-5

A MYSTERY WHOSE TIME HAS COME

The story that I am about to tell is as strange as it is controversial. It is the story of an age-long mystery. A mystery which has haunted the imaginations of seekers from generation to generation. A mystery which has, in recent years, split the archaeological establishment and has caused debate around the world. To some it is a figment of the imagination, a myth without historical basis. To others it is an obvious possibility, a near-certain historical reality, a fact that will soon be confirmed at the turn of a spade. For deep inside the oldest, the largest, the tallest, the most tremendous and sacred monument on this planet, is a heavily guarded secret. Inside the Great Pyramid of Giza, wrapped in unearthly darkness and standing in hallowed stillness, could lie a secret chamber, waiting any minute now to be opened. It could be the supreme archaeological prize. Since March 1993, an entrance which may lead to such a chamber has been known.

Yet there is more.

The Giza necropolis, it seems, has finally decided to discharge all its secrets at once. For not far from the Great Pyramid, in a shallow enclave to the east, is the Great Sphinx. It, too, may be guarding a treasure-trove under its belly: a 'Hall of Records' of a civilisation long lost in the mist of time. There, too, with amazing synchronicity, an entrance to such a vault has been known since 1993.

Why have these 'chambers' not yet been opened?

What could be within them?

Could the Egyptian authorities know more than they are letting on?

Is there a 'conspiracy' here, one that might involve not just Egyptology but other, more sinister, institutions? Or is there 'something else'?

When I first started to plan this book, my original premise was to write an historical account on the inside story of the expeditions and people involved in this drama. The last seven years has seen a huge confusion generated in the international media and on the Internet as to what was happening at Giza, and now it was time I set the record straight. For the previous twenty years, I had been steeped in the mysteries of this place. Since 1992, I have been investigating the behind-the-scenes activities and have collated a mass of damning evidence. I now felt that the responsibility was on me to expose the story to the public with objectivity and without bias. But the more I pondered on how to structure this book, the more I became convinced that there was something else, something far more important that was unfolding at Giza. Something subtle, almost subliminal. Something which I am now convinced is of immense relevance to us as a species on this planet. An event whose time has come. To understand it, to 'see' it, to fathom its meaning, a type of intellectual archaeology was required. A gigantic historical puzzle needed to be pieced together, and I set myself the daunting task of undertaking this.

TRUTH AND FICTION

The lure of a 'secret chamber' or Hall of Records at Giza has fired the imagination of the general public and has drawn into this history-long quest a horde of unusual seekers. Ranging from sedate scientists to armchair speculators, from eminent academic institutions to dubious psychic societies, from reputable archaeologists to innocuous Walter Mitty characters, and from staunch sceptics to New Age gurus, a bedazzling assortment of followers have rubbed shoulders at Giza. In trying to make an intelligent assessment of all these goings on, the innocent bystanders will have to sieve through a bewildering pile of conflicting rumours and 'official' information poured into the media and the cybernet news machine. Periods of eerie silence from the Egyptian authorities as well as the Egyptological establishment, when coupled with some rather erratic behaviour from the main players, inevitably caused the great rumour mill of the Internet to hatch a series of global conspiracy theories involving foreign governments, the CIA, powerful business moguls and Egyptian government officials as well as myself.[1] The result is that truth has been mixed with fiction, blurring and distorting the reality of the drama which is unfolding there on the eve of the new millennium. For on this dusty plateau of Giza is being played history's most exciting and most meaningful game: the quest, no less, for the spiritual and cultural origins of civilisation, and its true destiny.

THE STAKES ARE HIGH

One of the principal objectives of *Secret Chamber*, therefore, is to put into a concise and clear perspective the events behind this quest. To this end, I have taken every step to ensure that only documented evidence and reliable information are used. There has been close on a decade of careful collection and collation of data as a result of my direct involvement in this incredible historical conundrum. The extraordinary story that unfolds, however, is an ancient one, spanning from the dawn of human awareness to the present, and, as we shall see, with a grand finale (or new beginning, as the case may be) awaiting us at the closure of this second millennium. The telling of this story, however, is not by any means the sole objective of this book. There is another, far more profound goal for *Secret Chamber*. In the many years of being exposed to this curious affair, I have gradually become convinced that there is something else at play here, something extremely powerful connected with 'prophecy' and involving strange synchronicities. As much as I have disciplined myself to stay within the bounds of scientific investigation, I could not help sensing at times an invisible influence at work, a subtle and indefinable energy that gave this quest a momentum of its own.

The quest for the Hall of Records is unlike any other. By its very nature, it is a path charged with powerful archetypal and mythical forces. One constantly gets the feeling that some ancient plan has been reactivated and is rushing head-first toward an apotheosis at Giza. There is a peculiar sense of urgency, as well as a sense of enchantment and magic that engulfs the players, as if at any moment something momentous will be revealed. In order to make proper sense of all this, and more importantly, in order to understand what could be in the hatching there for the new millennium, one must, by necessity, undergo a type of intellectual initiation. Only then will the greater picture emerge. *Secret Chamber*, therefore, has been designed for precisely this purpose. Part I will provide the reader with all the necessary background information. Legends, myths and ancient texts will be explored; ancient traditions will be tracked across the ages. A picture will then begin to emerge of what the elusive Hall of Records might actually be and, more intriguingly, what it might contain. Part II will then take the reader back to Giza. Now fully 'equipped', the reader is ready to follow the recent expeditions, to understand their motives and agendas, and to become aware of the great implication of the events that are about to be unleashed there.

PYRAMID FOR THE SECOND COMING

In an unprecedented display of openness, the Egyptian Supreme Council of Antiquities through its principal spokesman, Dr Zahi Hawass, has boldly announced to the world that on the 31st December 1999, at the stroke of midnight, a military helicopter will carry a golden pyramid-shaped icon made of durable alloys and place it on the top of the Great Pyramid of Giza.[2] At approximately the same time, within the Great Pyramid itself, a small mechanised robot equipped with a video camera linked to TV networks around the world will proceed to lift open the small trap-door at the end of the southern shaft of the Queen's Chamber.[3] These two events, as we shall see, are laden with religious and esoteric significance of the highest magnitude. At the heart of this is the oddity of a fundamentally Muslim country staging what is essentially a Christian event. The role of Coptic esotericism remains a mystery. Moreover in the last forty years or so various esoteric groups which mix Christian with pagan elements, and the AMORC Rosicrucians have installed themselves at Giza to play their part in the millennial 'celebrations' planned for December 1999. All these organisations seem to share a common motive, namely to bring about a reformation of the world order. And some of these organisations, as we shall see, perceive these events taking place at Giza as the prelude to the 'Second Coming'.

One of the most active of these groups, and certainly the most successful in establishing itself at Giza, is the Association of Research and Enlightenment (ARE). Based in Norfolk, Virginia in the USA, this society is also known to its many thousands of members world-wide as the Edgar Cayce Foundation (ECF). In our previous book, *Keeper of Genesis* (*Message of the Sphinx* in the USA), Graham Hancock and I have shown how the ARE, since 1973, had put into practice a bizarre and daring plan to find the fabled Hall of Records at Giza. It was their founder, the so-called 'Sleeping Prophet' Edgar Cayce (1877-1945), who had predicted in 1932 that this Hall of Records would be re-discovered by the year 2000. The ARE, either directly or fronted by another group, has been able to secure several official exploration licences to probe the Giza plateau with radar and other sonar equipment. The ARE's presence at Giza is controversial to say the least. Other than its obvious motives to vindicate the 'prophecies' of Edgar Cayce on the Hall of Records and its 'Atlantean' origin, the ultimate motives may be far more bizarre. As author and researcher John Anthony West points out:

> Of those who predict an enlightened new age arising out of the demise of the old, the American psychic Edgar Cayce is the best known and the most specific. Cayce predicted that in 1998 a secret chamber between the paws of the Great Sphinx of Giza would be opened and would reveal the lost history of Atlantis. This event would be the harbinger for the Second Coming, he said, and the signal that the new age would soon begin. Two independent scientific investigations have verified the existence of what appears to be a chamber between the paws of the Sphinx, but at present, Egyptian authorities have no plans to investigate further.'[4]

The two 'independent' scientific investigations that John West is alluding to took place in 1991 and 1996. In both instances, the ARE was involved, financially and practically. One of the ARE's principal funders for these expeditions was Dr Joseph Schor, a Jewish businessman from New York. Schor is the vice-president of Forest Laboratories Inc., a multi-million-dollar pharmaceuticals and drugs manufacturer. Schor is also a registered life-member at the ARE and staunch believer in the Cayce prophecies. The 1996 expedition, for example, was fully funded by Dr Schor. And although the expedition was fronted by the Florida State University, Schor maintained full financial and managerial control. As we shall see later, two other expeditions, also funded by Dr Schor, took place in 1997 and 1998.

Related to the search for the Hall of Records are other 'prophecies' by Edgar Cayce, the most relevant to the millennium events being, oddly enough, the placing of a gilded capstone on top of the Great Pyramid of Giza:

> The apex (capstone), the crown or apex, was of metal; that was to be indestructible, being of copper, brass and gold with other alloys . . . it became very fitting that there should be the crowning or placing of this 'symbol of the records' . . . by one who represents both the old and the new . . .

Is the gold-encased capstone which will be placed on top of the Great Pyramid fulfilling Cayce's prediction?

Dr Zahi Hawass is a Ph.D. in Egyptology specialising in the Old Kingdom period or Pyramid Age. He thus in a sense represents ancient Egypt and, more particularly, the ancient Pyramid Age. He is also an Under-secretary of State for the Giza Monuments, and as such represents the new regime of that country responsible for the Pyramids and the Sphinx. As official keeper of the Giza monuments, Dr Hawass has been chosen to oversee the millennium ceremony and the placing of the gilded capstone. But could the 'choosing' have been made long before? Back in 1978 the ARE collaborated with the Stanford Research Institute (SRI) and Dr Hawass to have a 'direct shot at finding the Hall of Records' at Giza. The operation had been masterminded by Hugh Lynn Cayce, the eldest son of Edgar Cayce and also the president of the ARE at the time. His official biographer, A. Robert Smith, reported this rather unorthodox connection with Hawass:

> When the funding ran out, SRI packed up and returned to the United States. Like the Cayce Petroleum Co., SRI and the (Cayce) Foundation had nothing but dry wells when they ran out of money. Discouraging as these inconclusive results were, Hugh Lynn had no sense of defeat. He would stay with the search as long as it took, building alliances with other groups and individuals. One of the latter was the Egyptian inspector at Giza, (Zahi) Hawass, whom he had met through Lehner (ARE's Egyptologist) in 1975. In 1980 Hawass accommodated the ARE by conducting an excavation in front of the sphinx temple. A core drilling through fifty feet of debris struck red granite instead of the natural limestone bedrock from which the sphinx had been carved. Since the granite had to have been imported, this discovery raised questions why it was placed there and what more might be found if a dig were permitted. Such an operation would require approval at a higher government level. If Zahi Hawass was to advance within the government, to further his own career and open doors for Hugh Lynn's project, he could best do it on the wings of higher education at an American Ivy League college. His Patron (Hugh Lynn) cleared the way: 'I got him a scholarship at the University of Pennsylvania in Egyptology to get his Ph.D. I got the scholarship through an ARE person who happens to be on the Fulbright scholarship board. He has aided Mark (Lehner) to work on the sphinx, and I am very appreciative.'[5]

Just before his death in 1984, Hugh Lynn announced a long-term action plan for the quest of the Hall of Records at Giza in a rather cryptic tone, and which was passed on to his successors:

> I'm never giving up there. It is very important. If we get to the Old Kingdom there, it is going to make history look like . . . We are looking for the records.

This is what the readings say, of the Pyramids themselves and the Sphinx. We are looking for the Atlantean records which are buried there. We are looking for Hermes' records and his prophecy of his next reincarnation as Jesus. I think they are there, in front of the Sphinx. The Sphinx is guarding them. We are playing for all the marbles.[6]

However, Dr Hawass has hotly denied that his liaison with the Edgar Cayce Foundation and Hugh Lynn was anything other than a casual friendship and that in no way had the latter participated in obtaining Hawass an 'Ivy League' education in the USA.[7] Indeed, when a statement to this effect was made by John Anthony West in a circular letter to the investors of an expedition at Giza,[8] Dr Hawass immediately threatened to contact his lawyers should West not immediately retract his statement:

As to the statements contained in Mr West's letter to his investors, let me make emphatically clear that I have never had any connections with the Edgar Cayce Foundation. It has not sponsored me, nor financed my post-graduate studies at the University of Pennsylvania. The record is clear that I was able to attend the University of Pennsylvania as a Fulbright Fellow and Scholar, not through any aid, effort, or help to me, or through any connection with the Cayce Foundation.[9]

Having known Dr Zahi Hawass personally over the last few years, and after discussing this matter with many of the people involved, I have arrived at the conclusion that there is no evidence to support the claim made by A. Robert Smith. The matter is reported here because it raises an important aspect of the involvement of the ARE in Egypt which is of interest to the public.

Today the post of executive president for the ARE is held by John Van Auken, a long-time member of the Cayce Foundation who has known Dr Hawass for many years. John Van Auken, not surprisingly, is a keen Cayce enthusiast. For years he has been advocating a 'Second Coming' scenario based on the Cayce prediction and biblical passages interpreted as prophecies of the same. In the *San Diego Union Tribune* of 13th January 1995, for example, Van Auken was quoted as saying that:

I believe the changes prophesied by the Bible are very close upon us . . . In the next three years, by 1998, I think we will see the beginning of the next major Earth changes. A seven year purging and cleansing of the Earth, most likely will be completed by 2002, marking the end of the Tribulations and the beginning of Jesus' 1000-year reign.

Van Auken is the author of several ARE publications, including six books on the Cayce prophecies and teachings. His most recent book is *The End of Times: Prophecies of Coming Changes* in which the Second Coming is promoted in connection with the finding of the Hall of Records.[10] Oddly, there is another Cayce 'prophecy' that also seems to relate to the ceremony of the placing of the 'symbol of records' i.e. the capstone on the Great Pyramid. In one of his so-called 'readings', Cayce described the celebrations that would take place during this ceremony:

> . . . hence there has arisen from this ceremony many of those things that may be seen in the present: as the call to prayer (Muslim?), the church bells in the present (Christian?) . . . the sounding and the trumpets (Jewish?) . . . the sounding as of ringing in the New Year (millennium?) . . . the old record in Giza is to . . . 1998 from the death of the Son Of Man (Jesus) . . .' [Reading 378-14] (words in closed brackets are my inclusion)

In recent interviews, Dr Hawass has described his version of the celebrations for the events planned at Giza for the millennium. Speaking to a German-Austrian TV crew in February 1999, for example, Dr Hawass stated that 'when the golden capstone will be lowered by the helicopter, the people from all over the world will cheer and dance like in the old day'.[11] According to an interview with Dr Hawass published by *The Irish Times* of 18th April 1999:

> The idea for the (millennium) celebration came from Pharaonic reliefs at Abu Sir, site of yet more pyramids (albeit ruined ones) about 15 km south of Giza. There Dr Hawass, the ebullient archaeologist in charge of the Giza plateau, discovered a scene depicting workers dragging a capstone with the hieroglyphic word for 'white gold' written underneath. He also found a relief showing women dancing . . . explained Dr Hawass: 'My interpretation is that when the king finished building the pyramid they put a capstone on top and after the people sang and danced because the nation's project was finished. This is what we are doing at the millennium.'

In the Cayce lore, the finding of the 'records' is directly associated with Christ and a supposed connection between Christ and the Great Pyramid. In a 'reading' given in 1932, for instance, when asked about the 'records of the Christ', Edgar Cayce replied that:

> those records that are yet to be found . . . of the Christ, of the tomb, in those of the tomb, or those yet to be uncovered in the Pyramid. [Reading 5749-2]

These 'records', furthermore, were programmed to be found beginning in1998.[12] As we shall see later, the figure of Christ is often also associated with that of Osiris, the ancient Egyptian deity. In 1998 Dr Hawass announced the discovery of the 'Tomb of Osiris' at Giza. In that same year he made the announcement that the 'chamber' inside the Great Pyramid would be opened.[13]

Coincidence?

Or are we seeing prophecies in the making?

Or, more likely, the making of prophecies?

But if so, to what end?

In what way could the 'fulfilment' of these strange 'prophecies' possibly serve modern Egypt?

EYE OF VIGILANCE

On the 3rd October 1998, a press conference was organised in Cairo for Minister of Culture Farouk Hosni and the French composer Jean Michel Jarre. The latter has been an international household name since the 1970s due to the enormous success of his electronic high-tech music compositions 'Oxygène' and 'Equinox'. Jean Michel Jarre is also an ambassador for UNESCO and has, since the 1980s, been organising extravaganzas of laser lights and music for historical events. One of these was for the bicentennial of the French Revolution in 1989, where more than two million spectators gathered in the Champs-Élysées in Paris, from the Place de la Concorde all the way to the new 'Paris 2000' Place de la Défense. This show, which was televised around the world, featured a pyramid structure erected in front of the Grande Arche de la Fraternité, literally the 'Arch of the Brotherhood'. From the high-tech pyramid, laser images were projected on to the high-rise buildings nearby, including at one stage the so-called 'eye of vigilance', a symbol commonly used by Freemasons.[14] During the press conference the Egyptian Minister of Culture stated that an opera composed by Jarre, entitled 'The Twelve Dreams of the Sun', would be performed to coincide with the unveiling of the golden capstone for the Great Pyramid at the end of the millennium, and Jarre himself declared that 'since the pyramids are linked to the sun' he had decided to stage a 'modern, multimedia opera that will last twelve bows and accompany the sun from the second millennium to the third millennium in the tradition of Ra, the pharaonic sun god'.

Farouk Hosni then explained that this event was also connected to another similar event that had recently taken place in Paris in May 1998, when a gilded capstone was placed on the Egyptian obelisk of the Place de la Concorde.[15] There is a strange history attached to this obelisk. It had originally stood as one of a pair outside the Temple of Luxor in Upper Egypt. In 1827 it was commissioned by Charles X to be brought to France, but it arrived in Paris in 1836 and was erected at the Place de la Concorde by Louis-Philippe. Interestingly, both these monarchs were prominent members of the Grand Orient, the body that regulates Freemasonry in France.[16] Other Egyptian obelisks were also erected in New York's Central Park and London's Victoria Embankment in the 1870s. These events, too, were under the auspices of the Masonic Lodges.[17] All stand as symbols of Freemasonry's alleged roots in ancient Egypt. The main symbol, in fact, is not the whole obelisk; in Masonic lore the golden pyramidion or capstone that crowns its top is a symbol with many layers of meaning. At one level it represents the so-called Supreme Being under whom all religious systems can unite.

SKULL AND BONES

In 1998 rumours were circulated on the Internet and in esoteric magazines[18] that ex-President of the United States George Bush was somehow involved in the millennium activities that were planned for Giza. It seems that as early as 1989, the Millennium Society of America, a body that promotes projects and activities for the year 2000, announced that George Bush was 'committed to ushering in the next millennium at the Great Pyramid of Cheops at Giza'.[19] Conspiracy theorists began to see links with this curious announcement and an ultra-elitist fraternity to which Bush belonged. This fraternity, which goes under the name of 'Skull and Bones', is based at Yale University. George Bush's link with the 'Skull and Bones' goes back to his father, Prescott Bush, who was initiated into the fraternity in 1917. George Bush himself was initiated in 1948. The name 'Skull and Bones', for those familiar with esoteric symbolism, conjures up the Order of the Freemasons (as well as the Knights Templar) who employ the same insignia in their higher initiation rituals of the Master Mason Degree.[20] Several CIA high officials, including George Bush, have been associated with the 'Skull and Bones' and it has long been known that several US presidents were Freemasons, and that most of the signatories of the Declaration of Independence in 1776 also belonged to the Masonic Order.[21] It is recognised that the Masonic ideal is the establishment of a 'New World

Order', the latter said to be symbolised by a glowing capstone on top of a pyramid, as can be seen on the American one-dollar bill.[22] Bush himself has been a great advocate of a 'New World Order' during his presidential career.[23] It was also pointed out that, whether by coincidence or design, George Bush Jr. announced his candidature for the presidency on 2nd March 1999, the same day that Dr Zahi Hawass presented, on a much hyped Fox TV special, the newly found 'Tomb of Osiris' to the American public.[24] Another possible link that has been made with the Bush family and the Giza affair is the alleged affiliation of George Bush Jr. with Florida State University.[25] This, as we shall recall, was the institution which collaborated with Dr Joseph Schor and the ARE in their quest to find the Hall of Records at Giza in 1996-98. Although I do not much subscribe to these sort of far-fetched 'conspiracy theories', all this goes to show the potential energy that this millennial ceremony can cause. We shall examine this particular issue more closely in the closing chapters of this book.

Although opinions vary as to the meaning of the glowing pyramid and eye symbol in Freemasonry, what some of the ARE followers may have in mind is vented in a recently published book by the ARE Press which is entitled *The Second Coming 1998*:

On the back of every US dollar bill is a pyramid with an eye in the middle of it. The 'eye in the pyramid' symbolises the pineal or third eye of the body in beautiful mystical fashion. The eye also represents the seven stones above the empty sarcophagus (of the Great Pyramid), making one of the United States' most common symbols a very esoteric one.[26]

This 'esoteric' symbol is also seen on the 'Great Seal of the United States', whose origin is often said to be Masonic.[27] On the back of the Great Seal, however, is also found another powerful esoteric symbol. Peter Tomkins, author of *Secrets of the Great Pyramid*, explains:

The reverse of the Seal of the United States of America . . . according to M.P. Hall, not only were many of the founders of the US government Masons, but they received aid from a secret and august body existing in Europe, which helped them to establish the United States for 'a peculiar and particular purpose known only to the initiated few'. The Great Seal, says Hall, was the signature of the exalted body, and the unfinished pyramid on its reverse side 'is a trestleboard setting forth symbolically the task to the accomplishment of which the US Government was dedicated from the day of its inception'. The eagle was apparently intended to represent a phoenix, or symbol of immortality of the human soul. Great currency has been given to the pyramid and phoenix symbols by placing them upon a one dollar bill . . .[28]

The phoenix symbol, as we shall see later, was also associated with the Egyptian sun god Ra, as well as Osiris, and in Christianity, the phoenix is often used to denote Jesus and his return or 'Second Coming'. In the Masonic Order the phoenix is the insignia of the so-called 18th Degree, one of Freemasonry's most important titles.[29] Returning to the Great Seal of the United States, on the top of the glowing capstone can be seen the words 'Annuit Coeptis', and below it are the words 'Novus Ordo Seclorum' i.e. 'The New World Order'. The Latin words 'Annuit Coeptis' apparently mean 'he is the beginning', yet the similarity of the word 'Coeptis' with 'Copti', which means 'ancient Egyptians', and which also denotes the nine million modern-day Christian Egyptians, is striking.[30]

Joseph Jochmans, author of the book *Time-Capsule: The Search for the Lost Hall of Records in Ancient Egypt*, suggests that in Masonic tradition 'the Freemasons predict that some day a man will locate this buried vault and that he will be an initiate "after the order of Enoch"'.[31] The prophet Enoch and his association with the Great Pyramid of Giza was the subject of an extremely controversial book written by Dr James Hurtak in 1977.[32] Dr Hurtak, whose far-out views are open to serious scrutiny, has been involved in several expeditions to Giza in the 1970s and 1980s and, more recently, in the 1996-97 expedition with Dr Schor and the Florida State University. Hurtak is also the founder of the Academy for Future Science in Los Gatos, California, which, among other things, promotes the existence of UFOs and the imminent fulfilment of the biblical prophecies in Revelations, and his name has been linked with Dr Mark Lehner, the representative of the ARE in Cairo during the early 1970s.[33]

It is not clear whether there are any significant connections between the Freemasons and the ARE. Nonetheless, some links are worth noting. For example, it appears that the first ARE headquarters at Virginia Beach were originally purchased from the Shriners, an elite Masonic group operating in the USA which claims extensive links with Egypt.[34] Also, as with the Cayce readings, in Masonic lore the Great Pyramid of Giza is often regarded as a temple in which specially selected men were initiated into the mysteries. For example, in a speech delivered by a British Freemason, Bertram A. Tomes, to the Masonic Temple in Swansea in 1922, the author speaks of 'the Pyramid of Ghizeh: the Masonic Temple of Ancient Egypt' and identifies the King's Chamber as 'the chamber of Osiris, the raised Master', who vanquished death through the ancient Egyptian system of initiation.[35] Edgar Cayce also refers to Jesus as the 'raised Master' of Christianity. As author Richard H. Drummond reviewed in his Edgar Cayce guidebook, *A Life of Jesus the Christ from Cosmic Origins to the Second Coming*:

> The initiation of Jesus in Egypt is said to have involved a literal passage through the chamber in the Pyramid - evidently the Great Pyramid on the Giza Plateau . . . A number of the Cayce readings refer to Jesus as the Great Initiate, who took 'those last of the Brotherhood degrees with John, the forerunner of Him, at that place', that is the Great Pyramid of Giza.[36]

Indeed, so close is Cayce's terminology to that of 'Masonic' rituals that Drummond felt the need to add:

> These references to initiation and brotherhood degrees may be distasteful to some readers, given the centuries-long tensions between some of the Christian churches and various non-ecclesiastical religious orders such as the Masonic and the Rosicrucian . . .

A reading given by Edgar Cayce in the 1930s is far more specific about the Masonic world view for the coming new age:

> A great number of individuals formulated into groups who have declared specific or definite policies will be questioned as to purpose and as to the ideal. Some of these groups will be drawn into coalition with questionable groups. Hence this is not, in the immediate, the time for the joining definitely with any individual group's activity other than that which stands alone on Christ's principles. For, with those changes that will be wrought, Americanism with the universal thought that is expressed and manifest in the Brotherhood of man into group thought, as expressed by the Masonic Order, will be the eventual rule in the settlement of affairs in the world. Not that the world is to become a Masonic Order, but the principles that are embraced in same will be the basis upon which the new order of peace is to be established . . . [reading 1152-11]

Although the Rosicrucians, who we shall encounter later on, are today tolerated in Egypt and indeed often given privileged access to the Great Pyramid by the authorities, the Freemasons, on the other hand, have been officially banned from Egypt since 1964. The 'Egyptianised' strain in Masonic symbolism and rituals is, of course, well-known. Less well-known, however, is the deep involvement that the modern Egyptian monarchy once enjoyed with the Freemasons. We shall see later how the 'founder of modern Egypt', Muhamad Ali, was part of a secret Masonic fraternity and how several of his descendants, including the Khedives Tewfik Pasha and Ismail Pasha, were initiated into the Masonic Orders.

We shall also see how under the British (1882-1956) Egypt was ruled by High Commissioners and Egyptian monarchs who were initiated into the Brotherhood through the United Grand Lodge of England, the Grand Orient of France, and the specially formed Masonic order known as the United Grand Lodge of Egypt and the Sudan.

A NEW WAY OF THINKING

There is little question that the events planned for the new millennium at Giza are highly charged with powerful ideologies. There is little question, too, that these ideologies, as we have briefly seen so far, invoke the 'Second Coming' of some Messianic figure as well as that of a Masonic 'New World Order'. It should be evident, therefore, that the placing of a gilded capstone on the Great Pyramid at the stroke of midnight on the eve of the new age is not merely a 'millennium celebration' for Egypt, but could be the result of a carefully planned, carefully manipulated long-term strategy.

But if so, then by whom?

And for what motives and agendas?

In one of his many trance sessions Edgar Cayce was once asked to explain the meaning and purpose of the Great Pyramid and the ceremony of the placing of the gilded capstone. His cryptic reply was that 'only an initiate may understand'. *Secret Chamber*, therefore, will, in a way, 'initiate' the reader so that he can 'understand'. One of its principal aims, therefore, is to provide the reader with all the 'scientific' as well as the 'esoteric' knowledge required for this task. In the ancient Egyptian initiatory tradition the neophyte who successfully underwent the process of acquiring such knowledge was said to be 'equipped'. In this way, we will appreciate that the Great Pyramid and the Giza necropolis as a whole are not 'tombs' or 'temples' in the conventional sense of the words, but rather are instruments that were designed to service powerful rituals of initiation. Although these monuments and structures are much damaged, weatherworn and somewhat incomplete today, they can still produce the potent subliminal effect on the human psyche which they were primarily intended to do. In Hermetic and Alchemical tradition such an instrument is known as a 'device', and the Great Pyramid of Giza is perhaps the most powerful of such Hermetic devices. I truly believe that the Great Pyramid and the Giza necropolis as a whole have the innate energy to cause a powerful transcendental shift in thinking on a massive, even global scale provided that the right buttons are pushed at the right time.

There is not much doubt that we are heading for a radical reformation in the way we perceive ourselves on this planet. The excessive, almost abusive rationalistic and 'scientific' thinking of the last few centuries is about to give way to a new and much-needed spiritual and intuitive way of thinking that best befits our human condition. As Joseph Ritman, founder of the Bibliotheca Philosophica Hermetica in Amsterdam, so well put it, 'it is the application of that life goal which in ancient Egypt was called "thinking with the heart and feeling with the mind"'. The question is no longer whether such a consciousness shift will take place, but whether we, as individuals or groups, will choose to promote or oppose this shift or, as is bound to be the case with many, exploit it for personal gains.

I am convinced that the Giza necropolis has been designed for precisely such a purpose. I am convinced, too, that the time has come for that purpose to re-activate itself. I am also convinced that some sort of bizarre plan is being implemented at Giza to 'hijack' this all-powerful device in order to promote something else, something that the monuments of Giza were never intended to do. A great call to gather at Giza on the eve of the new millennium has been made by the Egyptian government. Through the international media, an open invitation has been sent all over the world to witness the crowning of the Great Pyramid with the golden capstone and, it is hoped, experience the opening of the secret chamber. On that night of nights, while TV networks send images of this event to hundreds of millions of viewers by satellite throughout the world, an estimated crowd of two hundred and fifty thousand will gather on the many sandy knolls and hills that surround the site of Giza. While the Great Pyramid and the Sphinx are illuminated with projectors, laser beams will project images and symbols onto the sky. Starting at 11.00 p.m., the great constellation of Orion and the star Sirius, which, as we shall see, is much inbued with Christic lore symbolic of the 'Second Coming', will slowly make their way to the meridian and align with the passage system of the Great Pyramid. In the eastern horizon, the zodiacal constellation of Leo will align itself with the Great Sphinx. At the stroke of midnight, as mankind enters the new age of Aquarius, a military helicopter will hover over the Great Pyramid and lower in place the gilded capstone.

While within the monument a tiny robot deep inside the narrow star-shaft of the Queen's Chamber will shine its beams of light on a small 'door', ready to take its first glance into the unknown. The channels to the collective subconscious will be flung wide open, and the world will be readied and primed to receive a powerful subliminal message. *Secret*

PART ONE: THE TRADITION

Chapter One

Robot, Radar and Drills

'It's a sarcophagus! . . . We found a sarcophagus!'

from video film allegedly taken during the live discovery
of the 'Tomb of Osiris' at Giza – Schor Expedition, November 1997

'In December 1999 a robot will climb up the shafts of the
Pyramid . . . and this will be Egypt's gift to the millennium.'

Dr Zahi Hawass, M-Net TV interview November, 1998

SENTINEL OF THE MYSTERIES

There is nothing more awesome or more provocative than the sight of the
Giza necropolis. Home of the Three Pyramids and the Great Sphinx,
Giza personifies the mysteries of our remote past. To many, Giza also
symbolises that universal yearning and age-old expectation that one day
a great discovery will be made, one that will totally alter our perception
of who we really are and where we have come from. The Giza necropolis
is an elevated rocky plateau situated approximately nine miles west of
modern Cairo. To get there today will take you half an hour by bus from
central Cairo. The necropolis is best approached from the east through
the village of Nazlat El Samman. Flanked by busy coffee bars, souvenir
shops and restaurants, the high street of Nazlat is a bustling array of
donkeys, camels, horses and street vendors. Upon reaching the extremity
of this street, the humdrum of modern Egypt suddenly switches itself off
as you are confronted with an alien landscape and the gaze of the
venerable sentinel of the ancient mysteries, the human-headed lion-
bodied statue universally known as the Sphinx.

3

The Sphinx has been deliberately made to face due east, the place of the rising sun at the equinoxes. Hoary and laden with age, weather-beaten by the elements and scarred by vandals and thieves, the Sphinx testifies to the passing of three great civilisations: Pharaonic, Greek and Roman. It may well see ours through yet. Carved as a monolith from the living rock, the Sphinx is sixty-five feet tall and forty-five feet wide. From its rump to its front paws you could easily string together four full-sized tennis courts. It sits, with front paws outstretched, in a U-shaped pit. On the walls of the pit today can be seen the deep, vertical erosion fissures that bear witness to a prehistoric time when heavy rainfalls may well have scarred the exposed limestone. In 1991, Boston geologist Robert Schoch and Egyptologist John Anthony West created a huge controversy over the age of the Sphinx. They pointed out that the vertical erosion suggested an age for the statue of more than 8000 years.[1] In 1996, Graham Hancock and myself showed, with the use of precessional astronomy, that the Sphinx is linked to the date of 10,500 BC.[2]

To the left, or south, of the Sphinx lies the so-called Valley Temple, a large rectangular structure constructed with massive square columns and beams. The peripheral load-bearing walls of this temple are fashioned with immense blocks, some weighing more than one hundred family-size cars. The roof has long disappeared, the stones probably used for modern construction work in Cairo. The Valley Temple is totally free of any inscriptions, making it very difficult to know its function or its age. A few wide gullies are still embedded in the upper walls, again suggesting that this temple was built at a time when heavy rainfalls were experienced.

Immediately in front of the Sphinx is yet another temple, this one appearing even more antiquated than the Valley Temple. Dubbed the Sphinx Temple by Egyptologists, no one is sure of the purpose it served, nor when it was built. Twenty-four columns within the central courtyard and the fact that the east-west axis is aligned with the Sphinx, suggest an astronomical function related to the equinox sunrise and sunset. South of the Sphinx, and running west up the natural escarpment, is the so-called causeway that leads to the main pyramid plateau. Today only part of the pavement remains.

MANSIONS OF ETERNITY

At the western extremity of the causeway is the Second Pyramid of Giza. Allegedly built by the pharaoh Khafre in c.2500 BC, this pyramid is 447 feet tall and is the only one at Giza which still retains part of the original casing stone on its apex. To its left, and some 450 yards away, is the Third (and smallest) Pyramid of the famous triad. It stands 204 feet high and was allegedly built by the pharaoh Menkaure, a son of Khafre. To the left of the Second Pyramid, some five hundred yards to the north-east, is the Great Pyramid, the largest of all the pyramids in the world. Weighing as much as six million tons and towering 480 feet above the ground, the statistics of the Great Pyramid are mind-boggling: more than two and a half million blocks, each weighing an average of two tons, were needed; the construction is perfectly set out and perfectly aligned to the four cardinal directions, and all this, according to Egyptologists, without the use of iron tools, the wheel or even the simple pulley. As if this was not enough, the builders flaunted further their engineering prowess by incorporating within the Pyramid a complex system of inclined passages, tunnels, galleries and chambers. There are three chambers in the Great Pyramid, one subterranean and two within the superstructure, the latter two being known as the Queen's Chamber and the King's Chamber. Some of the blocks and beams that make up the King's Chamber weigh as much as seventy tons, jointed so tightly that even a razor blade cannot be passed through them.

When the Great Pyramid was first opened in AD 820 by the Arabs, they found nothing except an empty sarcophagus inside the King's Chamber. It has the peculiar distinction, as the English Egyptologist Sir William Plinders Petrie pointed out, of being slightly larger than the entrance to the chamber, proving that it was placed within the chamber before it was closed from the roof. This fact, as well as the austerity and simplicity of its design, makes it difficult to imagine that it was used for a royal burial, and many researchers today agree that the pyramid was probably used for a ritualistic purpose. Shooting upwards from the south and north walls of both the King's Chamber and Queen's Chamber are two narrow shafts, with a cross section of eight inches by eight inches. Those from the King's Chamber run right through to the outside of the pyramid, whereas those from the Queen's Chamber stop within the core (the southern one after a little over sixty yards). Thought at first to have been ventilation shafts, these strange devices are now recognised to have been aligned to important star systems and thus probably used for ritualistic purposes.

Since the ninth century, when the Arabs took an active interest in the Giza necropolis, all efforts to find a secret chamber have met with frustration. From treasure hunters with battering rams in the Middle Ages to the use of gunpowder by Colonel Howard-Vyse in 1837 and more recently with radar and seismographs, no secret chamber has been found.

Egyptologists became convinced that no such chamber existed, and anyone who did was pilloried by his peers and the Egyptological establishment.

Then in 1993, on 22nd March, everything suddenly changed. A team working under the German Archaeological Institute in Cairo sent a small robot into the unexplored southern shaft of the Queen's Chamber. Equipped with headlights and a video camera, the robot managed to reach the end of the shaft some sixty-five yards from the Queen's Chamber and sent images of a mysterious small 'door' embossed with two copper handles. Although strongly suggestive of a concealed chamber beyond, Egyptologists were opposed to this idea and the huge debate that ensued caused the Egyptian authorities to ban any further exploration. In that same year, an American expedition, under the aegis of a Boston University geologist, conducted a seismographic survey around the Great Sphinx and discovered a large rectangular anomaly under the paws of the statue. Again, the authorities, averse to the possibility of a secret chamber, promptly banned further exploration. Then, three years later in May 1996, a team led by Dr Joseph Schor investigated the area around the Great Sphinx with ground-penetrating radar equipment and discovered another large rectangular cavity, this time under the rump of the statue. Yet again, the Egyptian authorities stopped the exploration. In November 1997, however, Dr Schor somehow managed to get another chance at finding a secret chamber. This time his radar picked up a tunnel leading out and westward from the rectangular cavity behind the Sphinx. Following the direction of this tunnel, the Schor team believed it was leading to an ancient well-shaft some 200 yards behind the Sphinx. Again the work was halted by the authorities.

DISTURBING DENOMINATORS

There are, as we shall see, some disturbing common denominators at play here. First, of course, there is the systematic halting of the explorations each time they seem to be on the verge of finding a way to a possible secret chamber. All the explorations, too, were conducted either in secrecy or were allocated official explanations as to their purpose that had nothing or little to do with the main objective of the explorations. For example, the investigation of the shafts in the Great Pyramid by the Germans was registered as a 'cleaning job', and in the case of the King's Chamber, to improve the internal *ventilation* of the monument. Although it is true that this was one of the objectives, nothing was said at the time of any *exploration* by robot of the unfathomed shafts of the Queen's Chamber. It was common knowledge that these shafts did not pierce through to the outside of the Pyramid and, quite obviously, could not be of any use for 'ventilation', unlike the shafts of the King's Chamber. What were the Germans really up to? Why the misinformation?

Also, when the Schor exploration was under way in 1996, the official reason given was to repair 'faults and chasms' in the bedrock of the Giza Plateau for the 'safety of tourists'. Whereas the team had secretly focused their radar around the Sphinx, seeking evidence of a secret chamber there.

Circumstances were such that I found myself involved indirectly with all these expeditions. In April 1993 I exposed the inside story of the Germans' exploration of the shafts. Then in April 1996, with Graham Hancock, I blew the cover off the Schor expedition to reveal their clandestine search for the Hall of Records near the Sphinx.[3] A campaign ensued in the international press for the Egyptian authorities to have a more open policy at Giza. Finally, in early 1998, the Egyptians caved-in under pressure and promised to keep the public informed. Yet on two further occasions, as we shall see, Schor and his team managed to conduct more research at Giza on the quiet, and were even allowed to drill near the Great Pyramid in their search for the Hall of Records.

BEHIND THE SCENES

Investigating behind the scenes of these strange explorations and events, I fell upon a web of intrigue and confusion. These matters will be fully exposed in Part Two of this book. A brief review, however, is called for here. In *Keeper of Genesis*, Graham and I reported that as early as 1976, an expedition was mounted at Giza to find the Hall of Records. This expedition was headed by the Stanford Research Institute (SRI), America's second largest think-tank and research facility who undertake work on behalf of many of America's covert government agencies. This was a front. Behind the SRI was another organisation, one whose backstage entry at Giza would mark the start of rumours of weird connections, conspiracy plots and archaeological machination. This organisation was the Association of Research and Enlightenment (ARE), a psychic establishment based in Virginia Beach, in Norfolk, USA.

The ARE was founded in 1931 to promulgate the teachings of their founder, the 'Sleeping Prophet' Edgar Cayce (1877-1945). Represented in Egypt from 1974 by Mark Lehner, who is today one of Egyptology's foremost experts on Giza, and with the help and collaboration of Dr Zahi Hawass (who was then Chief Inspector at Giza), the ARE financed the SRI in 1976–77 to use seismographic equipment in an attempt to find the Hall of Records. The latter, as we have already seen, was said by Edgar Cayce to be concealed beneath the bedrock near the Great Sphinx by 'Atlanteans' in 10,500 BC, and which he predicted would be rediscovered between 1998 and the year 2000. The executive director of this project for the ARE was Virginia-born businessman Joseph Jahoda. It was Jahoda who had put up most of the financing for Mark Lehner's expenses in Egypt. It was also Jahoda who had represented the ARE during the 1991 expedition. On this occasion, Jahoda was accompanied by Dr Joseph Schor.

In 1996 Joseph Jahoda appeared again at Giza, this time as executive director for the Schor expedition. Like Joseph Jahoda, Dr Schor has long-term links with the ARE. He is a life member of this organisation and one of its principal funders. During the 1996 expedition Dr Schor had commissioned a Los Angeles film maker called Boris Said to document the activities on site and, more importantly, to have the TV cameras handy when, and if, the Hall of Records was located. A promotional film of the expedition was made with the intention of selling a two-part documentary to Fox TV. In April 1996 I managed to obtain a copy of this film, and found out that they planned to open a secret chamber 'live' on camera before 1998, just as Edgar Cayce had predicted. A copy of this film was passed to the Egyptian authorities for comment, and the matter was exposed in the international press.

The result was predictable but also surprising. Dr Hawass denied any knowledge of Schor's connections with the ARE, and merely announced that he had now stopped the expedition because 'they had not followed the rules'.[4] There was a strange paradox here. On the one hand it was evident that Jahoda and Schor were extremely well known in Egypt and were old acquaintances of Hawass. It was also clear that they were favoured for licences to explore the Giza necropolis in their quest to locate the Hall of Records. Yet on the other hand Dr Hawass, who was their ally and friend, openly denied any involvement with the ARE and what it stood for. He also publicly stated that he had been the only member in the Antiquities Committee who was against granting a licence to Dr Schor, and he now seemed to imply that no further licences would be granted to him.

Something did not quite fit here. All this rhetoric made it clear that neither the Schor Foundation nor the Cayce Foundation would be permitted to conduct searches at Giza or make more films. Against all odds, however, the Schor team did in fact return to Giza a year later, in November 1997, this time with more clout than ever before. More equipment and more personnel were brought in, and they were granted special access to the monuments to conduct ground-penetrating radar searches.

In August 1998 I managed to obtain films shot during this expedition. Strange experiments appeared to have been carried out in the Great Pyramid, and the team was filmed investigating an ancient well shaft located one hundred and eighty yards behind the Great Sphinx. The film showed Dr Schor and Joseph Jahoda controlling the operation from above with walkie-talkies and a TV monitor. Several men, including a cameraman, descended with climbing gear down a vertical shaft to reach a large grotto or chamber partially submerged with water. Trying to find a suitable place to put the camera tripod, the crew unearthed the lid of a massive sarcophagus fixed into the bedrock. Radar and seismographic equipment was lowered. Careful readings revealed a tunnel heading east from under the sarcophagus toward the rump of the Sphinx. At this cliff-hanging stage the Egyptian authorities intervened and the exploration was halted. This was the last time anyone would be allowed to search for hidden chambers at Giza.

Except Dr Hawass.

In early 1998, Dr Hawass conducted a preliminary archaeological investigation of the well shaft. The entrance of this underground complex is under the limestone platform of the causeway that runs between the Valley Temple near the Sphinx and the Second Pyramid. The whole complex consists of three chambers set at different levels. The first chamber, which is only twenty feet below the causeway, seems to be of no special significance. The second chamber, which is a further forty-five feet lower, has seven niches carved into the side walls. In two of these niches are empty sarcophagi, apparently dated to the Sait Period c. 600 BC, a strangely late date that we will come back to. The third chamber is a further thirty feet lower. In the middle of this chamber lies the black granite sarcophagus discovered by Schor and his team. Dr Hawass pumped the water from the chamber to reveal a small perimeter wall around the sarcophagus, which apparently supported four pillars at each corner. Ironically, these findings were first presented by Dr Hawass at an ARE convention in Virginia Beach in August 1998. Hawass appeared to claim the discovery for himself even though many in the audience were well aware that it was Schor and his team that had discovered the room with the sarcophagus months earlier. Amazingly, Dr Hawass also informed the audience that this chamber represented the symbolic 'Tomb of Osiris'. Later, in November 1998, Hawass also announced that he planned to open the 'door' at the end of the southern shaft in the Great Pyramid, and suggested that this would be done on the day of the new millennium.

December 1998 saw Dr Hawass inviting Fox TV to prepare for a two-hour 'live' broadcast, which was scheduled for transmission on 2nd March 1999 (Graham Hancock, John West and I were also invited to take part). It was during the live transmission that Dr Hawass dropped a bombshell. Standing in the 'Tomb of Osiris' near one of the walls, Dr Hawass revealed the entrance to a tunnel: '. . . to be fair,' he said, 'I have not excavated this tunnel yet, then really I do not know where it leads us. But I always say you never know what the sands and the tunnels of Egypt may hide of secrets . . .'[5]

Meanwhile an 'entente cordiale' was struck between Dr Hawass and myself. This enabled me, on the one hand, to get deeper behind the scene, and on the other to take a wider view of these odd activities at Giza. Slowly a veil began to lift. Fleeting and faint but nonetheless perceptible, a picture began to emerge.

What a strange picture it was.

We shall return in Part Two and examine in greater detail what really went on during all these recent expeditions at Giza, what was really found there and why the public was kept at bay. Before we can do this, we must first undertake a journey into the past. We must trace the origin of the Hall of Records and track through the ages the mysterious tradition which kept its memory alive, and which is now leading us back to it.

Chapter Two

The Prophecy of Monte Libyco

How perfect are your Laws, O Life . . . they guide the mind aright, for the heavens declare the glory of God; and the starry sky sheweth his handiwork . . .

19th Psalm

In that day there shall be a monument to the Lord in the midst of the land of Egypt, and a pillar at the border thereof to the Lord. And it shall be for a sign and for a witness unto the Lord of hosts (stars) in the land of Egypt . . .

Isaiah 19; 19-20

THE HERMETIC PROPHECY

According to the book of the Kore Kosmou[1], a first-century tract belonging to the Hermetic writings, the great goddess Isis informs her son, Horus, how the Egyptian god of wisdom and magician of words, Thoth, known to the Greeks as Hermes, revealed 'the great mysteries of the heavens' by inscribing them in sacred books which he then concealed somewhere in Egypt, with the intent that one day they will be discovered by 'the fully worthy':

Is it not fitting, my son, that I should leave this report unfinished; I must tell you what Hermes (Thoth) said *when he deposited the books*. Thus did he speak: 'Ye holy books, which have been written by my perishable hands, they have been

11

anointed with the drug of imperishability by Him who is master over all, remain ye undecaying through all ages, and be ye unseen and undiscovered by all men who shall go to and fro on the plains of this land (Egypt), until the time when the heavens, grown old, shall beget men (of soul and body) worthy of you.' Having spoken this prayer over the works of his hands, Hermes (Thoth) was received into the sanctuary of the everlasting zones (i.e. 'he died, and went into Heaven')[2]

Elsewhere in the Kore Kosmou the 'books of Hermes' are referred to as being 'accurate knowledge of the truth . . . the secret things of Osiris . . . these holy symbols of the cosmic elements' (i.e. books written in Egyptian hieroglyphs).[3] This prophecy of Hermes-Thoth is clear in its meaning: there will be born men that are worthy to read the books that he concealed in the land of Egypt. Attached to this strange message is another important proclamation by Hermes-Thoth, one that gives us not only clues and indications of where the place of concealment might be, but also provides us with a stunning motive: the great expectation of a massive 'Second Coming' event that is to take place there in Egypt at a prescribed time in the future when the earth has been 'purified by flood, fire and plague'[4]:

> Those gods who ruled the earth will be restored, and they will be installed in a city at the furthest threshold of Egypt (in summo initio Augypti) which will be founded towards the setting sun and to which all human kind will hasten to by land and by sea . . .[5]

This proclamation appears in another tract, the so-called books of Asclepius. Here Hermes-Thoth is asked by one of his pupils the precise whereabouts of this magical city of the gods, to which Hermes-Thoth replies: 'in a very great city, in Monte Libyco'. In his detailed analysis of this mysterious text, the historian Garth Fowden, a fellow at the Centre for Greek and Roman Antiquities at the National Hellenic Foundation in Athens, points to another passage in Asclepius which alludes to the 'tomb of Asclepius' in this strange and special place called Monte Libyco. The actual passage reads:

> . . . Asclepius who was the first inventor of the art of healing, and to who a temple has been dedicated in Monte Libyco . . . There lies the material man, that is, the body . . . [Asclepius III, 37]

It is well-known in Egyptology that the Greeks identified Asclepius, the god of healing and medicine, with the great 'wise man' par excellence of ancient Egypt, the high-priest, astronomer and master architect

Imhotep.[6] Imhotep is believed to have lived in the Old Kingdom period (c. 2600 BC), known to Egyptologists as the Pyramid Age. His reputation as a high-priest of Heliopolis (the *On of the* Bible and the 'City Of The Sun' of the Greeks), and also as a great magician-healer, was so immense that eventually it spread to the far corners of the known world, deep into the Hellenic and Roman empires under his classical name of Asclepius. His emblem, the entwined snake on the stem of the apothecarian's cup, is still used today by pharmacists throughout the world. It was, however, Imhotep's great genius in the royal art of architecture that earned him immortality among the Egyptians, for it was he who was responsible for the planning and design of the world's oldest known major architectural structure, the impressive stepped-pyramid complex of Memphis, which still stands almost intact today some seven-and-a-half miles south of Cairo near the village of Saqqara.[7] Saqqara derives its name from the very ancient god of the dead, Sokar, with whom Osiris was closely identified, the supreme god of resurrection and the afterlife. Thus, Imhotep not only introduced the art of building and construction to the world, but was also attributed the invention of the 'pyramid' complex and, by extension, the great Giza pyramids. In a study of the legendary figure of Imhotep, Egyptologist George Hart of the British Museum quotes the full epithets given to Imhotep as found on an inscription carved on the limestone bust of the pharaoh Zoser, the Pharaoh for whom Imhotep, in fact, designed the stepped-pyramid complex at Saqqara:

> Seal-Bearer of the king of Lower Egypt; one who is near the head of the king; Director of the Great Mansion; Royal Representative; High Priest of Heliopolis; Imhotep . . .[8]

On stone vessels discovered in a maze of tunnels under the stepped-pyramid of Zoser, Imhotep is mentioned as 'Chief Lector Priest'[9], and elsewhere Dr I.E.S. Edwards, in his classic book *The Pyramids of Egypt*, provides yet another telling epithet for Imhotep, that of 'Chief Of The Observers', one which, Edwards concludes, 'may in itself suggest an occupation connected with astral . . . observation'.[10] Thus we can deduce from these titles that Imhotep not only occupied the highest religious office after the king, namely that of High-priest of Heliopolis, but also that Imhotep's initiation and erudition was specifically related to the observation of the stars, i.e. astronomy. This correlation between the initiation process and astronomy is particularly interesting and, I believe, the key to understanding the ancient Egyptian system of initiation. It is also interesting, as was noted by George Hart, that on a papyrus in the

British Museum we read that Imhotep belonged to 'those wise men who foretold the future . . .'[11] and that he compiled 'writings' and 'books' which are deemed to be 'of more value than the house of master-builders or a tomb in the western desert'.

Now the direct symbolic connection with the pyramid complex (that Imhotep is the designated 'inventor') and the pattern and motion of the stars (of which Imhotep was the chief observer) has already been fully expounded in my previous books, *The Orion Mystery* and *Keeper of Genesis*. We will review again from a new viewpoint these stellar connections in Part Two, as they now have particular relevance to the Hermetic prophecy we are investigating here. Meanwhile, what clearly emerges concerning Imhotep is that we are dealing with a master-architect and super-initiate who not only was attributed the gift of foretelling the future by the stars, but who supposedly also left behind valuable 'books' and 'writings' as an intellectual legacy or memorial of his skills and knowledge. In the corpus of the Hermetic writings, three of the most important tracts are wholly devoted to Asclepius. Since, as we have already seen, Asclepius was identified with Imhotep by the ancient Greeks and Egyptians of the Graeco-Roman period, it is justified to wonder whether there is some connection between the Hermetic writings and those unknown 'writings' and 'books' of Imhotep.

MONTE LIBYCO

The region where all the large pyramid complexes or 'fields' dating from the Old Kingdom stand is spread along a wide strip of desert land adjacent to the western shoreline of the River Nile. It runs some forty-three miles from the pyramid field of Abu Ruwash in the north to the pyramid field of Meidum in the south. To Egyptologists this region is known as the Memphite necropolis, on account of it having serviced the city of Memphis (the 'White Wall'), the ancient capital of the Pyramid Age. Memphis was still a bustling royal city when Julius Caesar came to Egypt in 50 BC. There are ten pyramid 'fields' in the Memphite necropolis containing some twenty-five 'great' pyramids allocated by Egyptologists to the Old Kingdom (c. 2600–2200 BC) spanning from the Third Dynasty to the Seventh Dynasty. These are, counting from the north, Abu Ruwash, Giza, Zawyat Al Aryan, Abusir, Saqqara north, Saqqara south, Dashour, El Lisht, Meidum and Hawara. The central part or node of the Memphite necropolis is, without doubt, the Giza necropolis, allegedly built by the great pharaohs of the fourth Dynasty,

Khufu, Khafre and Menkaure, also known to the modern world as Cheops, Chephren and Mycerinos. Although the location of Imhotep's tomb has never been found, many Egyptologists agree that he would have almost certainly been buried somewhere in the Memphite necropolis, either at Saqqara or perhaps at Giza.

In his huge multi-tome opus which he modestly titled *Excavations at Giza*, Cairo-born Egyptologist Selim Hassan discussed at length the location of 'Monte Libyco', the so-called Libyan Mountain or mount. In his investigation Hassan first drew attention to the fact that ancient Egyptian scribes, in their graphic depiction of the central region of the Duat, the afterworld or 'underworld' of the dead, known as the Fifth Division, 'imagined a long black tunnel running through the thickness of the earth, each end of which terminated in a sphinx or lion', the latter known under the name of Aker. This was an idea, explained Hassan, that had 'originated in the Old Kingdom', or the Pyramid Age (c. 2500 BC). Thus in line 1014 of the Pyramid Texts, found inscribed inside fifth and Sixth Dynasty pyramids at Saqqara, we read that:

> The Earth speaks, the gate of Aker is opened . . . may you remove yourself to the sky upon your iron throne . . .

Hassan also intimated that in Chapter XCIV of the Book of the Dead, the initiated person proudly proclaims that he is 'supplied with the Books of Thoth (Hermes) in order that I may be purified when I enter Aker (Sphinx-Lion)'. We thus can deduce, wrote Hassan, that:

> It was necessary for the dead (or initiate) to be equipped with the Books of Thoth (Tehuti) which contain powerful magic spells, in order to traverse Aker. This may have been necessary partly to overcome the dangers of the way . . . [12]

Hassan then pushed his investigation further in order to determine the actual location of Aker. According to Hassan, the Giza necropolis was in all likelihood perceived by the ancients as the physical representation of the Fifth Division of the Duat. The Duat, as many of the ancient texts affirm, contained twelve divisions or 'hours' and Hassan pointed to the curious fact that the Fifth Division was given the name of Rostau, which was also the name of the Giza necropolis in ancient times.[13] In the many depictions of the Fifth Division, as seen in tombs and on papyrus of the New Kingdom period, there are always shown two huge recumbent lions or sphinxes, the so-called Aker, partly buried in sand. Between the two Aker-sphinxes, looming high above them, is often shown a large 'mount' or pyramid. This whole ensemble, noted Selim Hassan, is not only extremely reminiscent of the Giza necropolis as seen looking north, but also the way the image is sloped from west to east provides a correct stylised image of the manner in which the actual Giza plateau slopes gently from west to east at an incline of about ten degrees. In the Pyramid Texts the Aker Sphinx-Lion is closely identified with the 'Akeru', the 'Lion People', who are said to be among the primeval or original inhabitants of Egypt.[14] We shall return to the mysterious 'Akeru' later. Meanwhile, and bearing all this in mind, here is Selim Hassan's vivid interpretation of the Fifth Division of the Duat and its correlation to the Giza mount or plateau:

> Thus it would seem that Aker is not the Underworld itself, but part of it, where this is clearly seen in the book of the Imji Duat as inscribed in the tomb of Seti I, where the double sphinx has its place in the centre of the Fifth Division called Rostau. Above Aker in this scene is a large pyramid which, in connection with Aker in sphinx form and the name Rostau, which was also applied to the Giza necropolis, suggests that this division was originally a complete version of the Underworld according to the Memphite beliefs. In The Two-Way Book we have a mention of the 'highland of Aker' which is the dwelling place of Osiris: 'Osiris who is in the highland of Aker'. This may be a reference to the sandy Libyan plateau (Monte Libyco) where is the earthly Rostau . . .[15]

We shall return to Osiris and his 'dwelling place' at Giza in a later chapter of this book. As for the correlation of Monte Libyco to the Memphite necropolis (whose epicentre is Giza), the same conclusion is also arrived at by the scholar Garth Fowden. In his book *The Egyptian Hermes*, Fowden comments that the

> subsequent reference (in Asclepius III, 37) to the temple and tomb of Asclepius-Imhotep in Monte Libyco establishes that the allusion in Ascl.27 ('in a very great city, in Monte Libyco') is to the ancient and holy Memphis necropolis, which lay in the desert jabal (mount) to the west of Memphis itself . . . [16]

Thus it is clear that the Giza plateau or 'Libyan mount' is none other than the Monte Libyco alluded to in the Hermetic writings and to which, according to the prophecy of Hermes-Thoth, will one day return the gods, and on that special day people from all over the world will come and gather to witness this event. But how valid is this Hermetic prophecy? Does it draw from older Egyptian sources?

THE CORPUS HERMETICUM

Although we have reserved a full chapter for the Hermetic writings and their influence on modern esoteric thinking, a brief treatment on the problems they have raised is, I think, necessary at this stage.

There is much debate amongst academics on the actual origins and age of the Hermetic writings and thus, by extension, the Hermetic prophecy related to Giza or Monte Libyco. Most scholars agree that the Hermetic texts (also known as the Corpus Hermeticum or Hermetica, for short) were finally written down in their present form by unknown 'Hellenised' Egyptians or, as the case may be, 'Egyptianised' Hellens (Greeks) in the ancient city of Alexandria sometime between the last century BC and the second century AD. There are two groups of texts, one known as the 'philosophical' texts and the other known as the 'technical' or 'alchemical' texts.[17] It is the 'philosophical' texts which concern us most in our investigation. Most were written in Greek but some, probably older texts, are in the ancient Egyptian Coptic language. These were found in 1945 at Nag Hammadi in Upper Egypt.[18]

The *Hermetica* contains some twenty-one books; there are eighteen so-called Libelli that form part of the main corpus, as well as three so–called Latin Asclepius. There is also a collection of short 'excerpts' and 'fragments' which are generally considered part of the *Hermetica*.[19] It is not clear how many authors contributed to the *Hermetica*, as all the books are ascribed to Hermes Trismegistus (Hermes the Thrice Great). Hermes, as we have seen, was equated by the Greeks with the Egyptian wisdom god Thoth (Tehuti in Egyptian). It is important to realise, however, that in the Hellenistic world (and later in Renaissance Europe), Hermes Trismegistus was not quite the same figure as his Egyptian prototype, whom we shall discuss in greater detail shortly. Hermes Trismegistus, in actual fact, is an *Egyptian* Hermes, a syncretism or coalition, as it were, between Thoth and the Greek Hermes but also with a pedigree not unlike the biblical Enoch or the Arabian Idris, a legendary figure recording the wisdom and knowledge of the pre-Flood era and preserving it for the benefit and future of mankind. As for his epithet 'The Thrice Great', it probably does come, however, from the ancient Egyptians who, as early as the third century BC, often referred to Thoth as 'Great-Great', 'Very Great' or 'Thrice Great'.[20] The motive for attributing their works to this semi–divine, mythical character, according to the scholar Walter Scott, 'must have been similar to that which made a Jew write a Book of Daniel, or a Book of Enoch, instead of a book of his own'.[21] In those times there was a tendency, says Scott, 'to lean on the support of authority and tradition'; the god Thoth of the Egyptians had, for thousands of years before, been attributed divine knowledge and wisdom from the gods which he then imparted to humans in his famous 'Books'. According to ancient Egyptian tradition, there were some forty-two books belonging to Thoth. In his study of the Egyptian gods, Egyptologist George Hart provides a series of titles for Thoth that defines the paramount role of this god as the protector of 'Truth' and as the emissary of the sacred wisdom of the gods.[22] These titles or epithets are 'mightiest of the gods'; 'lord of the sacred words'; 'Thoth the Great, the Great, the Great', i.e. Hermes-Thoth the Thrice Great. Thoth, writes Hart, as the 'lord of the sacred words',

> gave to the Egyptians the knowledge of how to write by picture symbols, hence hieroglyphs could always possess a magical force. Scribes regarded themselves as 'followers of Thoth'. Thoth represented to the Egyptians the embodiment of all

Fig. 1. Hermetic Silence. Engraved by G. Bonasone, 1555, Bologna.

scientific and literary attainments, being in command of all 'the sacred books in the House of Life'. The 'House of Life' (Per Ankh) was a revered resource centre accessible only to scribes, containing a wealth of knowledge . . . all under the protection of Thoth . . .[23]

This 'knowledge' and 'wisdom', Hart says, was deemed too secret for profane eyes, and was only accessible to a few initiates. Indeed, a knowledge that was so powerful was harboured in the sanctuary-library or House of Life of Thoth and, according to one ancient papyrus dated to the Pyramid Age, it was 'not even possessed by the pharaoh himself'.[24] Lucie Lamie, the daughter of the famous Egyptologist and symbolist R. A. Schwaller de Lubicz, gave a vivid description of this mysterious 'House of Life' allocated to Thoth and his wisdom-books:

> Is the 'House of the Seat of Life' mentioned on one of the vases of the First Dynasty Serpent King, the prototype of the 'House of Life', the 'University' of the late dynastic period? It was in the 'House of Life' that the young scribes learned the meaning of the hieroglyphs, mathematics, geometry, astronomy, medicine and all that concerned the ritual and maintenance of the temples – in short everything necessary for life on earth and in the other world. The stone vases of the first two dynasties, heaped in the galleries under the stepped pyramid of Zoser, along with ivory tablets and clay seals, reveal an elaborate system of administration. Writing was by this time completely constituted. This implies a long previous development; yet this development, as well as the origins of the written language, remains mysterious.[25]

Author and historian Peter Tompkins offers some tantalising glimpses on what the 'mysterious' quality of the hieroglyphs might be in the foreword he wrote to John Anthony West's book *Serpent in the Sky*:

> (Schwaller) de Lubicz was well versed in Hermetic wisdom . . . [and] soon found the same wisdom built into the glyphs, statues and temples of Egypt. By interpreting the ancient Egyptian hieroglyphs as symbolic carriers or a Hermetic message, de Lubicz discovered in Egypt the earliest known source of Sacred Science which forms the basis of what has become known as the Perennial Philosophy, fragments of which have been kept alive among Gnostics, Sufis, Cabalists, Rosicrucians, and Masons, but primarily by a series of enlightened and clairvoyant masters.[26]

It is very clear, therefore, that by attributing the Hermetic writings to Hermes the Thrice Great, i.e. Thoth, the ancient writers – or more likely the compilers – of these texts grafted upon them the highest possible pedigree: that of being directly linked to the divine and supreme wisdom

*Fig. 2. Hermes Trismegistus handing the Tablets of the 'Law' to the Egyptians
(Cathedral of Siena).*

and 'Word' of God. Now for a long time the Hermetic writings were lost to history. From about the fourth century AD till the late fifteenth century AD little was heard of them in Western Europe, and they were assumed lost for ever.[27] However in 1460, by one of those propitious and strange synchronicities of history, an almost intact copy of the full Hermetica was found and delivered to Cosimo di Medici, the Doge of Florence and 'Father of the Italian Renaissance'.[28] The first of the Libelli, known under the mysterious title of *Poimandres*, was soon translated by Cosimo's protégé, the scholar and linguist Marsilio Ficino. So powerful was the effect of the Hermetica on the scholars of that epoch that many modern students of the Renaissance, notably the late Dame Frances Yates of the Warburg Institute, became convinced that these texts, with the philosophy and 'magic' that they extolled, gave a new impetus to the Renaissance whose reverberations were still strongly felt in the Enlightenment of the seventeenth century.[29]

By the late fifteenth century Hermes Trismegistus's popularity as a teacher of divine wisdom[30] was, among the intellectuals, the merchants, the bankers and even the clergy, beginning to rival that of Jesus. Indeed, were it not for fear of persecution by the Papal Inquisition, some scholars have conjectured that the *Hermetica*'s fame would have surpassed that of the New Testament.[31] The authority and driving force that buttressed the *Hermetica* was that divine revelations, akin to those received by Moses on Mount Sinai, had been handed to Hermes Trismegistus. Cyril of Alexandria quotes a fine example to illustrate this approach from a Hermetic text that he says was written in Athens. In it the author presents 'our Hermes as seen through the eyes of an Egyptian priest'. In this tract the anonymous Athenian Hermetist depicts Hermes in the same unmistakably Egyptian terms as those in which Artapanus had envisaged Moses (Cyril of Alexandria – *Contra Julianum* i548ac). So convinced were the Renaissance scholars of this that some went as far as to petition the Pope that the Hermetica should be canonised and be made part of the Christian teachings of the Church. One such erudite scholar was François Foix de Candalle, better known as Flussas. In 1574 he published a Latin version of the *Poimandres* and dedicated it to the Holy Roman Emperor Maximilian II. In his dedication Flussas wrote that 'Hermes Trismegistus attained to a knowledge of divine things surpassing that which was revealed to the Hebrew Prophets, and equalling that of the Apostles and Evangelists'[32]:

> What more is made known to us by those who were instructed by our Saviour Himself? And yet this man (Hermes) was anterior in time, not only to the disciples of our Lord, but also to all the prophets and teachers of our Law and, as the ancients say, to Moses himself.[33]

Another who risked the papal dungeons for his outward support of the Hermetica was the Italian scholar Francesco Patrizi, who published the Libelli of the Corpus Hermetica with a preface addressed to Pope Gregory XIV. After extolling the virtues of the *Hermetica* and the supreme wisdom and 'philosophy' of Hermes Trismegistus, Patrizi then makes this extraordinary request to the Pope:

> I would have you, then, Holy Father, and all future Popes, give order that some of the books which I have named (prominent among these was the *Hermetica*) shall be continually taught everywhere, as I have taught them for the last fourteen years at Ferrara . . .[34]

Amazingly, Patrizi went on to make a further, most daring suggestion to the Pope for a wider and more 'practical' application of the *Hermetica*, namely to bring back to the Catholic fold all the Protestants in Germany:

> You will thus make able men in Italy, Spain, and France friendly to the church; and perhaps even the German Protestants will follow their example, and return to the Catholic faith. It is much easier to win them back in this way than to compel them by ecclesiastical censures or by secular arms. You should cause this doctrine (of Hermes) to be taught in the schools of the Jesuits, who are doing such good work. If you do this, great glory will await you among men of future times.[35]

Modern scholars of the Hermetic tradition, such as Dame Frances Yates, have even suspected that at least one of the Popes had practically adopted Hermeticism. In 1492, a prominent member of the Borgia Family became Pope. Under the name of Alexander VI, the 'Borgia' Pope was 'one of the most publicised and colourful characters of the Renaissance'.[36] Alexander VI was deeply interested in astrology and magic, and demonstrated this unusual papal trait by giving his support to the famous Hermetic Christian-Cabalist Pico Della Mirandola. So steeped was the Pope in Hermeticism and its 'Egyptian' magic that he commissioned the painter Pinturicchio to decorate the ceiling of the Borgia apartments in the Vatican with 'Egyptianised' scenes showing Hermes Trismegistus with Isis and Osiris. The frescoes were studied in great detail by the Renaissance scholar F. Saxel of the Warburg Institute in London. Dame Frances Yates, also of the Warburg, explains how in the first two rooms of the Borgia apartments there are scenes of the twelve sibyls proclaiming the coming of Christ, along with twelve Hebrew prophets, with Hermes Trismegistus as a central figure under the signs of the zodiac. There are also scenes of the Twelve Apostles with the Virgin announcing the arrival of Jesus, followed by depictions of the 'seven liberal arts', one of the prominent tenets of Freemasonry[37], with astrology as the most prominent. It is, so far, says Yates, a perfectly orthodox programme:

> But very strange are the Egyptian scenes in the Room of the Saints. The emblem of the Borgia family was the bull, and the Borgia bull becomes identified in this series with Apis, the bull worshipped by the Egyptians as the image of Osiris . . . The Egyptian series begins with the story of Io, turned into a cow by Juno, who sets Argus to watch her. Argus was killed by Mercury (Hermes) . . . Having been rescued by Mercury from Argus, Io escapes into Egypt where she became the goddess Isis . . . There follows in the frescoes a scene where Io–Isis is seated on a throne with a figure on the left identified by Saxel as Moses. The figure on her

Fig. 3. Pinturicchio, Isis with Hermes Trismegistus and Moses, Room of the Saints, Apartamento Borgia, Vatican.

right is obviously the same person as shown with the zodiac in the Room of the Sibyls . . . Hermes Trismegistus . . . Why did the Pope have such a programme painted early in his reign, a programme which glorifies the Egyptian religion, shows the Egyptian Apis Bull worshipping the Cross, associates Hermes Trismegistus with Moses?[38]

The answer to this question, concludes Yates, was because the Borgia Pope wished to proclaim a reversal of the policy of his predecessors and, under the influence of Pico Della Mirandola and his Hermetic disciples, implement a programme using Hermetic magic and Cabala as tools to religious reformation and conversion. The situation, then, had reached a curious and dangerous position for the Catholic Church and, quite clearly, something had to be done about it.

On the Campo de' Fiori in Rome, on 17th February of the year 1600, Giordano Bruno, probably the Renaissance's most notorious erudite and

'Heremetic' magus, was dragged by monks of the Papal Inquisition, gagged, tied to a wooden stake and burnt alive. Bruno had, in the eyes of the Papal Inquisition, committed heresy by advocating that the sign of the cross was not original to Christianity but was venerated long before by the Egyptians. Bruno was alluding to the so-called Ankh symbol, also known as the 'cross' or 'key' of the Nile or of 'life'. Bruno's death effectively marked the abrupt end of the Church's precarious tolerance for the Hermetic-Egyptian 'religion' and this caused the movement to go deep underground. It was not to resurface openly for many decades to come. We shall return to Bruno and this dramatic episode of history later. Meanwhile we need to consider briefly the scholastic arguments of those who see, on the one hand, Hermes Trismegistus as an Egyptian magisage, and those who see him as an historical fraud and the figment of the devious imagination of unknown writers in the first century AD in Alexandria.

HERMES TRISMEGISTUS UNDER TRIAL

In 1610, some ten years after the burning of Giordano Bruno, James I of England invited to London the scholar Isaac Casaubon whom Frances Yates described as 'one of the most brilliant scholars of his time, profoundly erudite in all branches of classical learning and also in the Church'.[39] Casaubon's mission: to mount an 'attack on the legend of the hoary antiquity of the Hermetica' and discredit its authors for having 'plagiarised' from the Bible and the works of Plato.

Casaubon was born in Geneva in 1559 of Protestant parents. By the time he reached the age of manhood, the great persecution of 'heretics', from both the Protestant and Catholic sides, was in full swing. On the one side the papal secular army, led by the Hapsburg Holy Roman Emperor, had caused havoc in Germany and the Low Lands. On the other side, the Protestant princes, such as James I of England and Frederick IV of the Palatinate and other princes of Germany, were mounting a resistance among the continental populace. One of the effective 'weapons' used, apart from the more common brutal force of the sword and the mass burnings at the stake, was an array of subliminal symbols and slogans. A sort of sixteenth- and seventeenth-century equivalent of propaganda warfare was masterminded by an assortment of super-magi: John Dee, Giordano Bruno, Andrea Valentinus, Tomasso Campanella, Michael Maier and others. Theirs was the subtle deployment of powerful manipulative techniques involving a mixture of Hermetic, Cabalistic, and Alchemical 'magic', making up what the scholar Joseph Ritman would later call 'the silent language'. We shall examine thoroughly these curious manifestations of psychological religious warfare, but suffice to say at this stage that in the strange battle that ensued over a century or so, one of the by-products was the formation of speculative Freemasonry that spread across Europe and ultimately found its way into the New World.

Isaac Casaubon, although undoubtedly a true scholar of his time, was not working in a vacuum but within a highly charged atmosphere of religious intolerance. It must be remembered, for example, that at the time he was undertaking his investigation into the *Hermetica*, Casaubon was under the direct patronage of James I of England, whose notorious and rather unhealthy paranoia with 'magic' and 'demons' was to degenerate into a horrific nation-wide witch-hunt with mass burnings at the stake. In this charged climate of antipathy for the occult 'philoso-phies' and 'arts', it would have been unwise, not to say unsafe, to extol the virtues and validity of the Hermetic writings, and Casaubon's con-clusions must, therefore, be evaluated in the light of such a context. Space does not permit us here to review all the finer points of Casaubon's attack on the *Hermetica*. In brief, then, the brunt of Casaubon's attack on the *Hermetica* was essentially on linguistic technicalities, style, and syntax, as well as historical anomalies. All this led Casaubon to conclude, with the full weight of his scholarly reputation, that the *Hermetica*, far from being of great Egyptian antiquity and the source of divine revelations preceding or contemporary with Moses, had to be dated to the post Christian era, and that it was the fabrication of 'semi-Christian authors' and, therefore, must be regarded as nothing less than 'forgeries made for a good purpose, yet detestable because untrue'.[40] Even though Casaubon conceded that the personage of the Egyptian Hermes Trismegistus might have indeed existed in antiquity, he concluded that this personage could not be the author of the *Hermetica*. The effect of this rationalisation was tremendous. In the words of Frances Yates:

> Some discoveries of basic importance for the history of thought seem to pass relatively unnoticed. No one speaks of the 'pre-Casaubon era' or of the 'post-Casaubon era' and yet the dating by Isaac Casaubon in 1614 of the Hermetic writings as not the work of a very ancient Egyptian priest but written in post-Christian times, is a watershed separating the Renaissance world from the modern world. It shattered at one blow the build-up of Renaissance Neoplatonism in the basis of the *prisci theologi* (the supreme theology) of whom Hermes Trismegistus was the chief. It shattered the whole position of the Renaissance magic with its Hermetic-Cabalistic foundation, based on the ancient

'Egyptian' philosophy and Cabalism. It shattered even the non-magical Christian Hermetic movement of the sixteenth century. It shattered the position of an extreme Hermetist, such as Giordano Bruno had been, whose platform of a return to a better 'Egyptian' pre-Judaic and pre-Christian philosophy and magical religion was exploded by the discovery that the writings of the holy ancient Egyptian (Hermes Trismegistus) must be dated, not only long after Moses but also long after Christ. It shattered, too, the basis of all attempts to build a natural theology on Hermetism . . .[41]

It is not our objective to argue about the authenticity or the origin of the *Hermetica*. It must be pointed out, however, that many modern researchers and authors today have now recognised, in spite of Casaubon's views, that the Hermetic writings not only contain a genuine strain of ancient Egyptian influence, but that they may indeed be the actual ancient Egyptian initiatory and 'philosophical' religion rehashed and modified to suit the predominantly Greek 'gentile' population of Alexandria during the first century BC to the second century AD. At the very least, it is clear that a detailed translation in Greek of the temple literature which was written in the old-style Egyptian hieroglyphics would require much more than a scant involvement from the Egyptian temple priests.[42] The fourth-century Platonist philosopher Iamblichus of Apamea makes it clear to us, for example, how an Egyptian priest named Bitys translated some of the hieroglyphic texts of Thoth into the Greek language.[43] These particular texts, apparently, were from the temples in Sais – the place where the Greek philosopher Solon had encountered 'Egyptian priests more learned in the history of Greece than any Greeks'[44] and whose story on Atlantis was later imparted by Plato in his *Timaeus*.[45] Indeed Iamblichus tells us that Pythagoras and Plato, during their long stays in Egypt, would be assisted by Egyptian priests in order to 'read through the stelae of Hermes' written in the ancient Egyptian hieroglyphic language.[46] Manetho, an Egyptian high priest who wrote a 'history of Egypt' in Greek for Ptolemy I Soter in the fourth century BC preserved in fragments of narratives in the works of Josephus (AD 38-100) and Africanus (AD 180-250), is considered by Egyptologists today to have drawn from original native sources. In the manuscript known as Ps-Manetho,[47] it is reported that this famous Egyptian scribe and high-priest, after making reference to the original books of Thoth, went on to assert that 'after the Flood they were translated from the sacred language (Egyptian hieroglyphs) into Greek, and deposited in books in the sanctuary of Egyptian temples . . .'[48]

More interesting still, there exists an ancient Egyptian text written on papyrus and dated from the Ptolemaic era which tells of the strange story of the Prince Setne 'who had studied to good purpose the manuscripts in the . . . Library of Magical Books'.[49] It seems that Prince Setne had learnt of the existence of a fabulous book written by Thoth and which possessed great 'magical powers' and could enable a 'man to see Re rising in heaven with his cycle of gods'.[50] This marvellous book was apparently kept in a tomb of a nobleman named Nefer-Ka-Ptah in the necropolis of Memphis at Saqqara. After an epic search Prince Setne found the tomb and descended into its vault. There, inside the sarcophagus, Setne saw the book which 'illuminated the place so brilliantly' that Prince Setne did not need any torches to light his way. In the tomb Prince Setne encounters the spirit (ka) of the dead man's wife, who recounts to Setne how the magical book came to be found by her husband Nefer-Ka-Ptah:

> The book was contained in an iron chest sunk in the middle of the river at Coptos; in the iron box was a bronce box; in the bronce box a box of palm tree wood, which contained a gold box, the true recepticle of the book'.[51]

The book, we are told, was guarded by 'swarms of serpents and noxious reptiles of all kinds'. After opening the various boxes, Nefer-Ka-Ptah took out the mysterious book and started to read the first magical spell which 'acquainted him with all the secrets of Heaven and Earth' and allowed him to see the splendour of the sun-god rising with all his retinue of gods.[52] The story of Prince Setne is, undoubtedly, a fictional tale. But it demonstrates, nonetheless, that during the times of the Greeks in Egypt, there existed a popular belief that some fabulous and magical books of 'hermes' (the Greek 'Thoth') were concealed in the region of Memphis where today stand the many pyramic-fields of the Old Kingdom. Such a tradition was almost certainly known to the Greeks scholars who frequented the ancient temples of Memphis and received their teaching and initiation from Egyptian priests. It would seem likely, if not certain, that it was translations in Greek of such temple books of 'Hermes' which formed the basis, if not the actual corpus, of the philosophical Hermetica.

It is, of course, tempting to see the craze for the Hall of Records as a modern, New Age fad which it is anachronistic to attribute to the ancient Egyptians. But in fact ancient Egypt was saturated with notions of magical records and books lost and found again in propitious circumstances. For example, W. Marsham Adams in *The Book of the Master*, published in 1898, referring to inscriptions on the walls of Denderah, writes:

'the same records tells us how that original building was erected by Pepi, a monarch of the Sixth Dynasty, and the plan upon which Pepi religiously carried out the ancient design did not originate in his own mind, but was brought to light by him from a crypt or secret chamber being written "in archaic characters", say the records, by Khufu himself and buried by him on the spot eight hundred years before the days of Pepi'. The majority of such references to records are related to Thoth, who was believed to have left a considerable quantity of texts in secret hiding places on earth. A book placed under the side of the god Khnum came to the knowledge of mortals, no one knows how. The gods themselves did not hesitate to pass some of their secrets on to people by letting a providential manuscript fall from the heavens.[53]

All this alone should be sufficient evidence that the Greek 'version' of the 'Books of Thoth' – albeit with a strong dose of Greek Neoplatonic ideologies – are none other than prototypes of the *Hermetica*. But there are, in fact, even more specific reasons for seeing in the Hermetica a distinct Egyptian influence. For example, in his extensive study on the *Hermetica*, the scholar Garth Fowden points out that the *Kore Kosmou*, which is grouped with the 'philosophical' Hermetic texts:

> treats Hermes straightforwardly as a god, and surrounds him with an unashamedly mythological narrative. The figure of Thoth, the divine author of the Egyptian temple literature, lurks only just below the surface of the Kore's Hermes, all-knowing revealer of wisdom to mankind – and in general Egyptian ideas are particularly prominent in this text.[54]

> The Hermetica are presented as revelations of divine truth, not as the product of human reason; and in the philosophical as in the technical texts those who do the revealing are typical deities of Graeco-Egyptian syncretism – in other words, even allowing for the presence of some characteristically Greek elements . . . the overall atmosphere is Egyptian. Alongside Hermes Trismegistus himself and Isis, who had long been associated in the Egyptian as well as the Greek tradition, we find Asclepius, identified with the Egyptian Imhotep/Imouthes; Ammon, the Egyptian god Amun [and] . . . Horus the son of Isis . . . And their presence indicates a more than superficial familiarity with the native (Egyptian) milieu.[55]

Interestingly, Fowden also alludes to the principal and supreme divinity in the philosophical texts, 'Poimandres', as being 'unique to the Hermetica', but goes on to say that 'the origin and meaning of Poimandres is unclear, though it may well be Egyptian'.[56] The figure of Poimandres, which we will also encounter later on in Chapter 6, is of particular interest. In the Hermetica, right from the very opening of the first tract, Poimandres is said to be the 'divine intellect', i.e. the 'mind' of

God, who imparts the divine wisdom and knowledge to none other than Hermes-Thoth himself. He is, as Fowden shows, the same as the Greek concept of *Nous*, which loosely translates as the 'divine intelligence' or 'intelligence of the supreme authority'.[57] The fourth-century alchemist Zosimos of Panopolis, who almost certainly had read and studied the Hermetica,[58] after the full initiation of one of his pupils, exhorts the latter to 'hasten towards Poimenandres (sic)', implying here the same concept of *Nous*.[59] But who really was 'Poimandres'? And what does his mysterious name mean?

In 1993 a major breakthrough in the etymology of the name 'Poimandres' and the very origins of the *Hermetica* came from within the Warburg Institute of the University of London, the hub of modern Hermetic studies today. The scholar Peter Kingsley, in a landmark article published in the *Journal of the Warburg Institute*, delivered a heavy broadside to the entrenched academic view that the *Hermetica* was a mere fabrication of Greek and neo-Platonic ideologies and 'that there is hardly anything of which it can be asserted without doubt that is of native Egyptian origin'.[60] After reminding his peers that 'there has been a growing awareness over the past thirty years of the need to approach the Corpus Hermeticum . . . by viewing it against its Egyptian background', Kingsley presents a twenty-five-page detailed dissertation which proved, beyond any doubt, that the name 'Poimandres' is not only ancient Egyptian in origin but, through the full appreciation of Greek and Egyptian etymology, stood for 'P-eime-neter-Re', i.e. 'The Knowledge of Re', the ancient Egyptian sun-god and supreme manifestation of the creative forces.[61] Kingsley's full argument is far too technical and lengthy to be repeated here, but his carefully and ingeniously constructed case is beyond reproach. Bearing in mind that in ancient Egyptian religion Thoth had received the divine wisdom and knowledge from the supreme god Re, the opening scene of the first book of the Hermetica (Libellus I 'Poimandres'), which has Hermes seeing a divine apparation that proclaims 'I am Poimandres, intelligence of the Supreme authority', is clearly derived from an ancient Egyptian original which can be loosely translated as 'I am the supreme divine wisdom and knowledge of Re'[62]

At any rate, the issue is now in a sense academic, for Hermeticism has, in fact, survived in one form or another through various esoteric societies such as Freemasonry and Rosicrucianism, and also in the occult traditions of alchemy and Cabala and, as we shall see later, as a growing movement in its own right. Our objective is to determine whether there is a basis and a validity to the essential message of the Hermetic prophecy, namely the re-discovery of a cache of 'sacred' writings which will

Chapter Three

The Language of the Gods

'The practice of magic was regarded as fundamental to the state of Egypt. The books of magic are not the scribbling of fantasists but rather the work of official institutions such as the House of Life, and form part of the royal archives . . .'

Christian Jacq, *Magic and Mystery in Ancient Egypt*, p.18

'To the people of antiquity Egypt appeared as the very mother of magic . . .'

Lewis Spence, *Egypt*, p. 252

THE MAGICIAN AND THE PYRAMID

The oldest and most authentic document that speaks of a secret chamber at the Giza necropolis which might contain the records or 'books' of Thoth is the so-called Westcar Papyrus, labelled No. 3033, which is today kept in the underground vaults of the Antiquities Museum in East Berlin.

The Westcar Papyrus, which bears the name of an English traveller, was discovered in 1824. The papyrus itself is dated to about 1650 BC, but the style and language used is classical Middle Kingdom c.2000 BC. Yet its context and content relates to the Pyramid Age and, more especially, the reign of Khufu, the supposed builder of the Great Pyramid of Giza. In the winter of 1995, I obtained permission to examine the original Westcar Papyrus at the Berlin Museum. I wanted to see for myself this important document, and particularly the section which speaks of King Khufu. After going through the red tape that such ventures typically require, a young Egyptologist was instructed by the curator of the Egyptian Department, Dr Helmut Wildung, to take me to the underground vaults. Going through the dimly lit corridors of the extensive storehouses of the museum, I was astounded to see so many ancient Egyptian artefacts still wrapped in the packets that were used for their transportation out of Egypt. How many items, I wondered, may still shed clues on this mysterious civilisation and its secrets?

The pages of the Westcar Papyrus measure about twenty inches by twenty-eight inches and are kept in a wooden chest of drawers, each sheet carefully covered with protective glass. Dr Miriam Lichtheim, the renowned American philologist, who published an English translation of the Westcar Papyrus in 1975, comments on the narrative aspect of this crucial document:

> This important papyrus, the beginning of which is lost, contains a series of tales woven together by a narrative frame. The whole cycle consists of at least five tales. Of the first, only the last words are preserved. The second has large lacunae, while the third, fourth and fifth are complete, except for the abrupt ending of the fifth tale . . . The setting of the tales is the Old Kingdom, specifically the time of the Fourth Dynasty: King Khufu is being entertained by his sons. First each son in turn tells a marvellous event that happened in the past. Then, when it is the turn of Prince Hardedef, instead of telling stories of past wonders, he asks permission to introduce a living magician . . .[1]

The scribe who compiled the text on the extant papyrus is unknown, but it is clear that the narrator of these extraordinary tales was very familiar with the genealogy of the family of King Khufu. Like most of these 'magical' tales, Egyptologists have concluded that the narrative is a sort of Pharaonic fiction story, merely written for entertainment and effect. But although the tales are magical in their nature, it may well be that they reflect historical events embellished in prose style. At any rate, the particular tale that is of interest to us is the fourth one, for it clearly offers a tantalising set of clues to the existence of a possible 'secret chamber' concealed either in the Great Pyramid itself or somewhere on the Giza necropolis. In view of the importance of this manuscript, it is translated here in its entirety, although with some minor editing for ease of comprehension:

> Now Prince Hardedef stood up to speak: 'So far you (King Khufu) have heard examples of the skills of those who have passed away, and one cannot tell the truth from the false. But there is a subject of your majesty in your own time, unknown to you, which involves a great magician.' Said his majesty: 'What is this about, Hardedef, my son?' Said Prince Hardedef: 'There is a man named Djedi

who lives in Djed–Snefru (probably Dashour, some twelve miles south of Giza). He is a man of a hundred and ten years, who eats five hundred loaves of bread, half an ox for meat, and drinks one hundred jugs of beer to this very day. He can join a severed head. He can make a lion walk behind him, its leash on the ground. *And he knows the number of the secret chambers of the sanctuary of Thoth.'* (My italics.) Now the majesty of King Khufu had been spending much time searching for the secret chambers of the sanctuary of Thoth in order to copy them for his 'Horizon'(i.e. Pyramid). Said his majesty: 'You, yourself, Hardedef, my son, shall bring Djedi to me.' (Prince Hardedef then proceeds to collect the magician Djedi by ship, up-river. Djedi takes along his 'books' and two ships carry him and his retinue to the palace.) After he had reached the residence, Prince Hardedef entered in to report to the majesty of King Khufu. Said Hardedef: 'O King, my Lord, I have brought Djedi.' Said his majesty: 'Go, bring him to me.' When Djedi had been ushered in to him, his majesty said: 'How is it, Djedi, that I never got to see you?' Said Djedi: 'He who is summoned comes, O King, my Lord, I was summoned and I have come.' Then the majesty of King Khufu said: 'It was also said that you know the number of the secret chambers of the sanctuary of Thoth.' Said Djedi: 'Please, I do not know the number, O King, my Lord, but I know where the place is.' His majesty said: 'Where is that?' Said Djedi: 'There is a chest of flint in the building called "Inventory" in On (Heliopolis). It is in that chest . . .'

Then Djedi pronounces a rather strange prophecy. For when King Khufu commands him to bring the 'flint chest' to him, Djedi states that he is not the one ordained for this task, but someone who is yet not born:

It is the eldest of the three children who are in the womb of Ruddedet who will bring it to you . . . She (Ruddedet) is the wife of a priest of Re, Lord of Sakhbu, who is pregnant with the three children of Re, Lord of Sakhbu. He has said that concerning them that they will assume this beneficent office in this whole land, and the eldest of them will be high priest in On.' His majesty's heart grew sad at this. Djedi said: 'What is this mood, O King, my Lord? Is it because of these three children? I say: first your son (as King) then his son, and then one of the three children.' Said his majesty: 'When will Ruddedet give birth?' Said Djedi: 'She will give birth on the fifteenth day of the first winter month.' Said his majesty: 'Just when the sandbanks of the Two Fish Channel (the start of the Nile Delta) are dry! I would have crossed over myself, so as to see the temple of Re, Lord of Sakhbu.' Said Djedi: 'Then I shall make four cubits of water over the sandbanks of the Two-Fish Channel (so that the King can cross).'

In recompense for this, King Khufu ordered that the magician Djedi be assigned to the palace and under the jurisdiction of his son, Hardedef. Although most Egyptologists attribute such a story to the realm of fiction (George Hart, the British philologist, describes such narratives as 'tales of fantasy'[2]) there are elements in it that have the ring of authenticity. One of them is the curious prophecy by Djedi that the oldest of the triplets of Ruddedet, wife of the priest of On, will be the one chosen to bring to King Khufu the mysterious flint chest that is in the 'Inventory' building and which, according to Djedi, contains the 'number' of the secret chambers of the sanctuary of Thoth. If the story was entirely fictional then surely the writer would have made either Djedi or Hardedef the hero of the tale, i.e. to be the one to deliver the secrets of Thoth to King Khufu. An analogy in this line of reasoning can be made about the story of Jesus in the Gospels. Although many historians of the Gospels question the story of the miracles and other far-fetched events in these texts, few doubt that Jesus was tried for dissent and suffered the penalty of crucifixion. This is because if this story had not been such a well-known historical fact at the time the Gospels were written, then surely the authors would not have admitted to such a humiliating end for their Messiah. The same reasoning applies to the author or authors of the Westcar Papyrus. They, too, were obliged to report the authenticity of the finding of the 'number' of the secret chambers of Thoth, namely by the 'eldest son' of the wife of the priest of On, quite simply because it was a known fact at the time. Even though such an argument may not be taken as proof of authenticity, it shows that elements of the narrative have the ring of truth. What seems certain, though, is that by the Middle Kingdom, that is two or three centuries after the construction of the Great Pyramid, there was still a memory of a 'secret chamber' or 'chambers' being planned for Giza by Khufu and modelled, as it were, on those of Thoth.

Where were the 'secret chambers' of Thoth?

And what could they have contained?

WORDS OF POWER

Every alchemist or magician knows that one of the great secrets of their art is in the power of words. Or more precisely, the way certain words can be charged with power and effect. In the early stages of World War II the British had been suffering defeat after defeat and morale was low. There had been the fall of France, Italy, Belgium and the Netherlands, and then the humiliating retreat at Dunkirk. Churchill needed one decisive 'victory' to change the tide of war. He had it with the Battle of El Alamein in Egypt, with the devastating blow that the 8th Army, under Montgomery, inflicted on Rommel and the Afrika Korps. This gave him the long-awaited opportunity to deliver his famous words: 'This is not the end. But it is the beginning of the end . . .' The sheer alchemical power of these words changed the mood in Britain. They had begun to believe that the German army was invincible, but the mood changed overnight. They could win this war, and eventually they did.

In 320 BC, when Alexander the Great faced the 'Invincible' Persian army of Darius III, King of Kings, at Issus in Syria, he was outnumbered ten to one. Alexander, when informed that Darius III's chariot had been sighted near the front line, decided to lead a charge personally on his famous black stallion, Bucephalus. Ptolemy, a seasoned general with many victories to his name, advised Alexander against such folly. 'If I were Alexander,' said Ptolemy, 'I would not carry this act of madness!' 'If I were Ptolemy,' replied Alexander, 'I, too, would not do this. But I am Alexander.' The impact of these words, so charged with immense confidence and bravado, impressed the other generals present at the scene, and within minutes the word got around Alexander's army that their young and daring king would lead a charge directly against the Persians in an attempt to 'check mate' its king. Wearing a golden breastplate and helmet, with Bucephalus snorting like a demon from hell, Alexander charged. He managed to break through the Persian defence line, and went straight for Darius. The 'King of Kings' panicked, turned his chariot and left the battlefield. The rest is the history of our modern civilisation.

When Mary Magdalene fell at the feet of Christ after being hotly pursued by a Jewish mob ready to stone her, Jesus picked up a stone and handed it to the crowd; he then spoke the words of magic: 'Let the one among you who is without sin cast the first stone.' The effect was electrifying. A great truth was delivered with stunning effect, and the desired alchemical reaction took place within the hearts of the crowd as they dispersed in shame. The power of words, when linked to a dramatic act of courage, defiance or 'wisdom', can generate a form of magic that will cause a massive and irreversible reaction in the mind or psyche of the receiver. As was noted by Christian Jacq, one of the rare breed of Egyptologists who appreciate that aspect of Egyptian wisdom, '. . . magic can perhaps be defined as the essential energy that flows through the divine and human spheres . . . Learning hieroglyphs, "the words of the gods", is the way to acquire knowledge of those names (of the gods) and the energy they hold . . .'[3] In other words, Jacq recognised that the 'language' of the gods is the hieroglyphic language. The intellectual and intuitive ability to learn and apply this 'language' is what it takes to become a magician[4] and Wallis Budge noted that Thoth:

had the knowledge of the 'divine speech' . . . that he was the 'lord of the books' and the 'scribe of the gods' and 'mighty in speech', i.e. his words took effect, and he was declared to be the author of many of the funerary works by which the deceased gained everlasting life . . .[5]

There is a great deal of misconception about magic in the modern world. The established religious bodies have, apparently for our own salvation, made it their business to persecute it and now, after two millennia of battle, have, or so we are led to think, all but eradicated this supposedly 'demonic' practice. In effect, however, magic is still around, except it is used as a means for exploitation under the guise of 'marketing', 'publicity', 'advertising' and, in its most dangerous cloak, 'politics'. Magic, in other words, has become a commercial and political, rather than a spiritual, tool. Oddly enough, the very bodies that practise it most, the religious institutions, are those who condemn it with the most virulence and severity. As Christian Jacq noted:

> It is not possible to separate magic and religion. Can we imagine a ritual without the influence of magic? Don't the religions of the book – Christianity, Judaism, Islam – however much they may sometimes deny it, exert a magic over the human soul, enabling it to reach out to the realities that our senses cannot grasp?[6]

The most potent delivery of magic requires an ambience in which powerful rituals, symbols and evocative liturgy are combined with the use of words to cause an effect on the human mind. The most vivid example of this is the Catholic Christian mass dispensed within the magical and 'sacred' ambience of the church or cathedral. Archetypal symbols abound, and the eucharistic liturgy, with the carefully chosen magical words and rituals evoking blood rituals, death, resurrection and redemption, is closely related to that of pagan 'dying and resurrecting' sons of gods, such as Adonis, Dionysis, Mithra and Osiris and their religions practised in ancient times. Indeed, as many researchers have shown, the Christian rituals and myths are practically modelled on these more ancient religious systems.[7] Yet, ironically, the Church has, for the last fifteen centuries or so, embarked on a global policy of suppression, condemnation and eradication of magic. In a recent study on the origin and meaning of magic, author and researcher Jeremy Naydler wrote:

> There are formidable obstacles to approaching magic as it was practised in ancient Egypt. Most obviously there is the heritage of European religious thought that, conditioned by the theology of the Christian Church, has created a spiritual atmosphere in which magic is viewed with fear and distrust. The

attitude of the Church to magic has been, and remains, hostile and condemnatory. At the beginning of the century, the *Catholic Encyclopaedia* defined magic as 'The art of performing actions beyond the power of man and with aid of powers other than the Divine', and condemned it and any attempt at practising it as 'a grievous sin against the virtue of religion, because all magical performances, if undertaken seriously, are based on the expectation of interference by demons or lost souls'. For centuries in the Christian West any relationship to the spiritual world other than that sanctioned by formal religion has been discouraged. And so magic – along with its 'occultism' in general – has been widely regarded as a dangerous deviation from the norms of beliefs and worship established and promulgated by the Church . . .[8]

Naydler also points out that the division of magic and religion is a product of the Christian era, and that prior to the formation of the Church of Rome in the fourth century AD, such a division was unknown. In short, Naydler says, 'religion and magic were not separated: religion was magical'.[9] We shall see later how 'magicians' of the Renaissance not only advocated the return of the 'Egyptian' magical religion, but took terrible personal risks by trying to induce the Pope to replace the orthodoxy of the Church with the Hermetic 'magical' religion of Hermes Trismegistus, the Egyptian Thoth.

The modern term 'magic' comes from the Greek 'magos' which denoted priests and seers from the East, notably Persian, Indian, Babylonian and Egyptian. Thus in the Greek Gospel of Matthew, for example, the Magi from the east that follow the star of Bethlehem are to be perceived as 'magicians' who, in accordance with their art, were in contact with a supernatural power beyond. Although we generally speak of the ancient Egyptian religion, the ancient Egyptians themselves had no concept of religion as such, and indeed no word exists in the hieroglyphic language that can be translated as 'religion'. 'From the Egyptian point of view,' wrote the eminent philologist A.H. Gardiner, 'we may say that there is no such thing as "religion"; there was only *Heka*, the nearest English equivalent of which is "magical power".'[10] Naydler wrote:

> To understand, to harmonise with, and then to activate Heka in given situations is the sacred science and practice of magic. It follows, therefore, that a path of inner development is a prerequisite for the ability to wield magical power . . . So the magician is one who has made him or herself a clear channel for transmitting Heka . . . [11]

In ancient Egypt the prerequisite for holding a position of high office – and ultimately the supreme office of Pharaoh – was that the individual should be in possession of Heka, i.e. magical power. All matters of state, being the dispensation of royal decrees, censuses, inventories, laws and even war, were administered through the medium of magic. As we have pointed out, the ability to activate magic required a sacred ambience, as well as sacred words, signs and rituals. It took a magician to do so. The magician, therefore, was an indispensable entity in the Pharaonic household, one who had to be proficient in the highest degrees of magic. This may partly explain why, in modern esoteric societies such as the Freemasons, individuals who are likely to hold a high office of state – like many of the US presidents, for example – underwent a ritualistic initiation into the higher degrees, such as the much written about 33rd Degree of Freemasonry.[12]

In the Pharaonic theocracy, the training and initiation process of a magician-neophyte was carried out in a special 'school' attached to the temple complex. These 'schools', as we have seen earlier, were known as the 'House of Life' and in here a stringent learning process was implemented. Only a handful became adepts, and it was these special men, or women, who were highly prized for their skills and ability to perform magic. These adepts were known as 'scribes of the House of Life', a title which conferred upon them the highest degree of magical power. Thoth, according to the ancient Egyptian tradition, was the actual 'inventor' or 'father' of such magic. Thoth was thus called the 'Master of Words of Power'; 'Thoth Great One of Spells'; 'Thoth Master of the Divine Word'; 'Thoth the Magician'. All these titles are thus encapsulated in the famous epithet 'Thoth the Thrice Great'. So great was Thoth's wisdom and ability to deliver words of magical power, that he held the highest office in the Egyptian pantheon, that of 'Judge of the Gods'. He was also the 'Messenger of the Gods' and was assigned the supreme office of 'Scribe of Osiris', i.e. the magician of Osiris.[13] We have already made the distinction between Thoth and Hermes Trismegistus, i.e. the syncretised 'Egyptian Hermes' of the Hellenistic period, that quintessential sage or wise man of the Western esoteric traditions. It is now clear to see why Thoth was his model and prototype. Indeed, in a sense Thoth can be regarded as the prototype wise-man and magician, the supreme archaic equivalent of a Merlin, a John Dee, a Francis Bacon and an Albert Pike[14] all rolled into one. Unlike some of these historical characters, however, Thoth was deemed to place 'truth' above all other considerations, and that in the application of magic it was imperative that the words spoken were filled with 'truth'. As such, Thoth's integrity was beyond question or reproach. It was Thoth who was called upon to judge the great battle of succession between Horus, the son of Osiris, and Seth, brother and murderer of Osiris. It was also Thoth who was in charge of the navigation and the course of the celestial 'ship of a million years' on which the retinue of the supreme God, Atum-Re, travelled across time and space, and it was Thoth who was the keeper of divine time as defined by the motion of the stars.[15] All these required a total commitment to the 'truth'. Thus, the magician was the ultimate practitioner of truth and of Heka, i.e. true magic or, better still, magical truth. The word, Heka, in its connotation of 'truth' has in fact survived in Egypt. In the pure, Arabic dialect, Egyptians still say 'Hake' to mean what is 'right' or 'true'. To be of 'hake' means to be both wise and truthful. One cannot exist without the other.

SACRED SCIENCE

Thoth was depicted sometimes as an ibis, other times as a baboon, and his celestial counterpart was the moon. His most common form is of a man with the head of an ibis. To understand this strange and curious symbolism, it is important that we cut beyond the orthodox veil of contemporary Egyptology and delve deep into the symbolist approach pioneered by the likes of R. A. Schwaller de Lubicz and John Anthony West.[16] In his book, *Serpent in the Sky*, West explains an inherent problem with modern Egyptology:

> When it comes to symbolism, we find a free-for-all, with little unanimity of opinion anywhere. At best, a symbol is recognised as a subconscious representation of archetypal concepts, perhaps experienced in dreams. At the more common worst, symbols are regarded as arbitrary devices invented by aggrandising priesthoods to cloak their activities in secrecy and buffalo the masses. The symbol in ancient Egypt is neither. It is a scrupulously chosen pictorial device designed to evoke an idea or concept in its entirety. It is a means of bypassing the intellect and talking straight to the intelligence of the heart, the understanding. The heart synthesises, the mind analyses. A true symbol is neither primitive or subconscious. It is a deliberate means of evoking understanding, as opposed to conveying information. Words convey information; symbols evoke understanding . . .[17]

In November 1998, John West and I organised a special guided tour of Egypt which we called 'Stars and Signs'. Several authors who had studied ancient Egypt and its 'sacred science' of symbols, including Colin Wilson, Michael Baigent, Graham Hancock, Robert Temple and Yuri Stoyanov, were invited to participate in the event. Among the guests was my brother, Jean-Paul, an architect and keen adept of ancient Egyptian architectural style and its symbolic function. During one of the sessions where symbolism was discussed, I asked Jean-Paul to narrate how, as young boys, we used to trap a certain bird in the Western Desert of Alexandria. Here, in brief, is the story he narrated:

> There is a small bird, a type of wagtail, known to the Egyptians as Abu Deil, 'Father of Tails', which comes from Central Africa. Each year, in late September, this bird migrates north to the Egyptian shore of the Mediterranean. On its long journey, the Abu Deil takes rest in the desert west of Alexandria in order to feed and replenish its energy stores for the long and dangerous crossing of the sea – a sort of refuelling transit. Sought for its delicate flesh, the Bedouin of the western deserts have, since time immemorial, learnt the complex techniques of trapping this elusive and highly intelligent bird. And it is from the Bedouin that, as young boys in our teens, we learnt the art of trapping the wagtail. Late September is, of course, the time of the autumn equinox, when the sky is clear and the air very still. The waters of the Nile are receding after the flood period in August, and there is a feeling of renewal of the vegetation and the thick and rich alluvial soil of the Nile Valley. The Abu Deil appears, as if by magic, at dawn, with the equinoctial sun rising due east. It likes the open desert, perching always on small rocks, watching, and communicating with the environment with the constant wagging of its tail. The art of trapping lies in the knowledge that it feeds solely on a cockroach called the Abu Defess, a sort of soft, rounded creature that lives in the hot sand. The bait is hooked on a small, metallic trap carefully placed in the sand near a rock. The game is now to lure the wagtail to the rock. This is done with immense patience and skill. By making a gurgling noise – achieved by rubbing your hand over your throat – you 'speak' to the bird, telling it, as it were, to go to the rock . . .

If one is not 'initiated' into all this, the image of the wagtail as a hieroglyphic sign cannot be properly understood. At best it will be interpreted as a 'bird' indicating the motion of 'wagging'; at worse it will be read as being merely a phonetic, i.e. alphabetic, glyph. In actual fact as we have seen, the full knowledge of the appearance of the wagtail in Egypt should evoke the idea and moods of the autumn equinox, the receding waters of the Nile, the rich soil of the valley, the purity of the western deserts, and the stillness and calm of the weather at this time of year. Possibly more, such as the idea of 'migration' from the south, the daring crossing of the sea, the knowledge of navigation of birds, and so on. A hieroglyph, therefore, encapsulates the knowledge of the image in the fullest sense. Without such knowledge or 'initiation' the reader cannot possibly decipher the true messages and the whole range of ideas locked in the image. This system of knowledge is the Q-basics of the mysterious hieroglyphic language of images. Imagine the display of a 'wagtail' icon on your Windows 98 computer screen which, when you 'click' it, opens, or unzips, to use the correct jargon, up into a large file full of information and rich in photographs and illustrations. Then imagine this icon in your mind, so that when you think of it, the same data begins to unfold. The icon does not necessarily have to be that of a 'wagtail'; it can be some image that symbolises a wagtail. This appreciation that one image can be represented by, or grafted onto, another image or sign or word, and the knowledge of how to perform this, is the art of the true alchemist or magician. In Christian symbolism Jesus is the 'lamb', the 'phoenix', the 'saviour', the 'redeemer', the 'crucified' and so on. A 'cross', a 'lamb' or a 'phoenix', therefore, are icons to convey the vision and many subtle aspects of his nature. Thus to be privy to the secrets of hieroglyphs and symbolic sign language of the Egyptians you must, by necessity, be in possession of this knowledge. By definition, so should all modern Egyptian philologists and Egyptologists. Sadly, nothing is further from the truth. As Lewis Spence once wrote:

> Most of what has been written by Egyptologists on the subject of Egyptian magic has been penned on the assumption that magic is either a degraded form of religion, or its foundation. This is one of the results of the archaeologist entering a domain where he is usually at a loss . . .[18]

As Henri Frankfort and, of late, Jane B. Sellers have pointed out, the modern Egyptological establishment, since the 1940s or so, has cut itself away from the magical and mystical tradition of ancient Egypt.[19] Regarding themselves as 'scientists', they feel uneasy and somewhat polluted when confronted with the intense esoteric aspects of the very 'science' they have declared themselves the custodians of. As 'scientists' they must conform with its rigorous rules, which demand strict objectivity towards the analytical process of investigation. A recent example of this is the heated debate that has been generated over the discovery of a small 'door' at the end of the long, narrow shaft of the Queen's Chamber within the Great Pyramid of Giza. Its discoverer, the German robotic engineer Rudolf Gantenbrink, is the epitome of the modern 'scientist' cast. Pragmatic to the core, sceptical and rigorous in his analytical approach, he systematically rejects the persistent suggestion that the shafts in question, as well as the 'door' he has discovered, are, in all likelihood, 'magical devices'[20] intended to assist the soul of the departed king to reach the astral realm of the gods. On his new official Internet website,[21] Gantenbrink presents a thoroughly analytical treatise on the design and meaning of the Great Pyramid and the shafts within it. There is, amazingly, not one word or reference to the esoteric aspect of the monument, the belief system of its builders, the Pyramid Texts that relate to it or even the intense astronomical qualities and alignments of its design. In spite of the overwhelming evidence to support the stellar alignments of the shafts,[22] these are practically ignored by Gantenbrink. To him, the design and construction of the Pyramids and the shafts must be brought down to the nuts-and-bolts of modern architectural rules of measurement and dimensional units, which he sees as the key to solving the 'problem' of the Great Pyramid. Feeding into AUTO-CAD software the data and measurements derived from Petrie (1881), Maragiolio and Rinaldi (1960), as well as those measurements he had made himself in 1992-93, Gantenbrink undertakes a mathematical analysis of the design of the Pyramid by comparing the principles of its architecture to that of a modern town house.[23] Here is a sample of Gantenbrink's analysis:

> It is interesting that the shifting of the lower construction point of the shafts from the pyramid axis amounts to exactly 22 cubits, i.e. 2 x 11 cubits. This shift resulted in quite substantial problems during execution of the works, because the exit points clearly had to lie at equal height. For this, not only had two angles to be determined but so had the ratio of the two angles to each other and to the axis of the pyramid, in order for them to be precisely executed structurally. A grid of 11 x 11 cubits was placed above the pyramid. The grid therefore corresponds to a scale of 1:40 referred to the pyramid base. This grid is irrelevant to the height of the pyramid. In actual fact, the Cheops grid, as I ascertained during my ongoing work, is not square but rectangular, in a ratio of 7 to 11 cubits, i.e. one 40th of the height to one 40th of the base. We are using the square grid here only to clarify the design process more effectively. The right northern shaft is clearly designed in a ratio of 11:7 grid points and the left southern one in a square ratio of 7:7 grid points. By reversing the ratio of 11:7 to 7:11, I obtained the counter-angle in the diagonal, which lies at 90° to the northern shaft. The angle, the counter-angle and the square counter-ratio can therefore be geometrically determined . . .

And so on. This is like a surgeon trying to find the soul of a person by dissecting his body. Sadly, this is the very thing that has been happening to the scholarship of ancient Egypt – and indeed to other ancient cultures – when left in the hands of 'scientists' alone. Egyptology is not a 'science', it is a *sacred science*. The Great Pyramid is not only an engineering structure conforming to clear geometrical rules, but a sacred temple of initiation into the mysteries of cosmic existence. To be sure, the ancient architect-priests used a geometrical canon to design their monuments, but this canon was an intrinsic part of the sacred science of initiation. Geometry was sacred. Art was sacred. Architecture was sacred. Hieroglyphs were sacred. Astronomy was sacred. They were all part and parcel of a sacred science taught to high initiates in the temple. The mind of man, which they deemed the most sacred thing of all creation,[24] was to be made adept to this science or knowledge in order to find God. Those who planned and designed the Great Pyramid were not architects in our modern definition of the word. These men, however, were magicians, supremely initiated into the sacred science of symbols and cosmic ambience. The Great Pyramid is not just a masterpiece of architecture, it is a masterpiece of sacred science.

THE NATURE OF THOTH

The identity and nature of Egyptian deities is a matter of much misunderstanding among Egyptologists. As pointed out by one recent researcher:

> It is not uncommon amidst conversation about ancient Egypt to hear people refer to 'the Egyptian pantheon'. Yet most Egyptologists will tell you quite categorically that there is no such single pantheon, but rather several – all of them very confusingly cross-related in a manner which defies a universal coherent, hierarchical classification. The fact that several of the gods have half a dozen or more alter egos with different animal heads or crowns or other headgear and apparel to match is itself a source of endless confusion to the uninitiated. It is also an endless fascination to the Egyptologists whose forte lies in the field of unravelling such mysteries and classifying everything as neatly and as tightly as possible. To date, this has been done by either grouping the related god-figures themselves together, or otherwise relating them to the city or 'Nome' specifically dedicated to their worship. Unfortunately, neither of these two approaches provides any real sense as to why such a complex approach to their religion should have been adopted by the Egyptians. In fact, even eminent Egyptologists have so far given up trying to resolve the problem, that they have in most cases opted for a choice between animism or the idea that a specific deity must have been named after a real historical figure whose personality and exploits only subsequently became 'mythologised'. From such limited vision and real understanding historical chaos is derived . . .[25]

A good example of such tagging is provided by Egyptologist George Hart, an expert in Egyptian deities. In his *Dictionary of Gods and Goddesses* Hart defines Thoth as:

Thoth-'Dejeheuti' in ancient Egyptian – can be represented under two forms:
   (a) Sacred Ibis . . .
   (b) Baboon (Papio Cynocephalus) . . .

Thoth can be depicted as the ibis or baboon appear in nature or, in the case of the ibis, anthropomorphic with the bird's head superimposed on his shoulders. In each instance the god wears a crown representing the crescent moon supporting the full moon disk. Both his sacred creatures can be interpreted in terms of lunar symbolism. Thoth as moon-god could manifest himself as the sacred ibis whose long curved beak hints at the crescent new moon and whose black and white feathering could be seen as indicating the waxing and waning of the moon. Baboons make agitated chattering sounds at dawn and consequently this could be understood as a greeting to the rising sun by creatures of the moon-god . . . [26]

On first impression, such an interpretation seems reasonable. Closer scrutiny, however, reveals the flaws in this over-simplistic analysis. And no wonder. According to George Hart, Egyptian 'scribes did not concern themselves with the historical or logical development that might have led to the adoption of these creatures as sacred to Thoth'.[27] This sort of oblique logic that passes for scientific Egyptology these days is at best confusing, at worst actually misleading. Today there are virtually no royal ibises to be found in Egypt. As for baboons, these have long disappeared. So one wonders about exactly which observations Egypto-logists such as Dr Hart derive their interpretations from. In order to observe these creatures in a natural habitat similar to Egypt, one has to travel upriver to Sudan. In 1979 I had the opportunity to work in the Jabal El Fau region, some 186 miles from Khartoum. Our base camp was sited at the foot of a rocky mount which was populated by baboons. The first thing I noticed about these creatures is their human-like features. This forces the mind to ponder on the primitive state of humans. In short, the sight of a baboon acts as a subliminal device to trigger the idea of 'origin' and remote 'ancestors'. The other thing which is striking about baboons is their power of observation. They sit, perched on the rocky hilltops for hours, especially at dawn and sunset, and watch intently what is happening around them. With sharp, piercing eyes that reflect a wisdom evolved through millions of years, the baboon notes, records and analyses every move, every change with infinitely finely tuned intuition and instincts.

One of the technicians working on the project had developed a curious rapport with one of the creatures. A large male baboon had taken to coming down at dawn and sitting calmly on a rock, watching the man go about his work. Finally, after weeks of such ritual, the baboon approached the man. There was no threat in the baboon's mannerism or in his eyes. What the man felt was a strange sense of communion and familiarity. It was as if he and the creature had become one, brought together by an invisible interface, a sort of ancient link that flowed between them. For weeks the baboon would come at dawn, and each time the same magical mood would take over. Here were two creatures, one still in the 'primordial' state, the other 'evolved'. Yet, in a strange way, it was the man who seemed to be the pupil, and the creature the teacher. A teacher of what? The man became aware of his own great ancestry, and of an ancient legacy that seemed locked in the depths of his instinctive and intuitive self. He realised that the creature was showing him how to communicate again in the 'silent language' of nature and of the cosmos. He remembered that he was, after all, natural man, cosmic man, made from the same stuff as the baboon, moulded and forged in this form by billions of years of mutation and evolution. A baboon, therefore, is an ideal symbol to denote such cosmic awareness.

As for the ibis, this bird is the Nilotic creature par excellence. It seems to know every cycle, every variation, every current of the sacred river. The cycles and rhythms of the Nile closely follow the four colures (main stations) of the year. In the summer solstice the river swells and overflows with the flood waters coming from the far off south. At the autumn equinox they are at mid level. At the winter solstice they are at their lowest. At the spring equinox they are again at mid-level. In the sky the sun exhibits the same cycle, finely tuned by the moon and the stars.[28] To be like the royal ibis, therefore, is to know the secrets of the Nile and of the sky; and by extension, the very forces that regulate Egypt itself. The combined symbol of baboon and ibis, therefore, denotes divine knowledge of the 'silent language' of the gods, as well as a mediator between animal-man and his divinity. Thoth, later Hermes Trismegistus of the Renaissance, was that magical entity, endowed with the knowledge and wisdom of the divine, and inventor of the sacred science of ancient Egypt. Egyptologist Christian Jacq, in his book *Magic and Mystery in Ancient Egypt*, calls Thoth the 'patron of Egyptian magicians'[29] and says that he served as 'model for all his disciples', i.e. the scribe-magicians[30]; Thoth was the 'master of hieroglyphs and magic . . . the guardian of wisdom, ineventor of the sacred language, astronomer, mathematician . . . the measurer of all things . . . "equipped" with magical power'.[31] To acquire the secrets of Thoth's magic, the candidate must pass through the high initiation process practised in the 'House of Life'. In his book *Freemasonry of the Ancient Egyptians*, Manly P. Hall provides a glimpse of the immensely powerful cerebral abilities that high-initiates, even in later times, would acquire through this initiation. Hall speaks of the initiation of Plato and Pythagoras which, according to many accounts, took place in Egypt.[32] It was said of Pythagoras that when perfect strangers met him on the road they 'fell upon their knees before him, overcome by some mysterious force which he emanated'. A similar story is reported of Appolunius of Tyana who, when hearing of a riot among the people, stood silently in front of them and, by the sheer forceful presence of his charismatic personality and carefully chosen words of power, quelled the agitated crowd. The patriarch Moses, who also underwent his initiation into the Egyptian mysteries at Heliopolis, was such a man.[33] The point that is being made here is that there existed a sacred science in Egypt that could only be imparted to gifted individuals with a strong predisposition for intuitive learning – the type of learning that is done with the human apparatus of perception, with the fine tuning of the five senses such that they functioned jointly as super receivers and transmitters of messages. Thus the initiation or training of natural magicians was to fine-tune the sensory perception. Anyone can fine-tune his sense to 'read' the messages of nature. However, to be a magician is to be able to reverse the process, i.e. to transmit the messages to others by using the 'language of the gods'. This is the *arcana arcanorum*, the ultimate secret of the magician. Thoth, the inventor of this magic, was supreme in its application. Equipped with such a cognition of Thoth, we can now examine the purpose of his divine mission as 'messenger' of the gods.

MEMORY DEVICE

There is a most telling passage in Plato's *Phaedrus* in which a 'King of Thebes' called Thamus expresses his deep concern to Hermes-Thoth. Thamus fears that by introducing 'writing', i.e. a means of recording things and events, men will no longer use their great and natural capacity of memory, and this will foster 'forgetfulness and sloth' and alienate men from the inner world which links them to God and to nature:

> The story is that in the region of Naucratis in Egypt there dwelt one of the old sacred gods of the country, the god to whom the bird called Ibis is sacred, his own name being Thoth. He it was that invented number and calculation, geometry and astronomy, not to speak of draughts and dice, and above all writing. Now the king of the whole country at that time was Thamus, who dwelt in the Great City of Upper Egypt which the Greeks call the Egyptian Thebes, while Thamus they call Ammon. To him came Thoth, and revealed his arts,

saying that they ought to be passed on to the Egyptians in general. Thamus asked what was the use of them all, and when Thoth explained, he condemned what he thought the bad points and praised what he thought the good. On each art, we are told, Thamus had plenty of views both for and against; but when it came to the writing Thoth said: ' Here, O King, is a branch of learning that will make the people of Egypt wiser and improve their memories; my discovery provides a recipe for memory and wisdom.' But the King answered and said: ' O man full of arts, to one it is given to create the thing of art, and to another to judge the measure of harm and of profit they have for those who shall employ them. And so it is to you, by reason of your tender regard for the writing that is your offspring, have declared the very opposite of its true effect. If men learn this, it will plant forgetfulness in their souls; they will cease to exercise memory because they rely on that which is written, calling things to remembrance no longer from within themselves, but by means of external marks. What you have discovered is a recipe not for memory but for reminder. And it is no true wisdom you offer your disciples, but only its semblance, for by telling them many things without teaching them you will make them seem to know much, while the most part they know nothing, and as men filled not with wisdom, but with the conceit of wisdom, they will be a burden to their fellows . . .'[34]

The hieroglyphic language that Thoth-Hermes had invented was, in fact, a conversion of the silent 'language of gods' into a system of signs and symbols which could more easily be stored in the memory and then released at will. Yet 'King Thamus' also feared that this system would be misused, and could fall into the hands of evil manipulators. A good example of this is how in the 1930s highly talented and cultivated Germans were converted en masse to Nazi ideologies through the manipulation of symbols and slogans.

In order to make use of symbols in the most effective way, it is important to first realise that a symbol is imbued with primordial or archetypal connotations, as well as culturally based ones. Take the symbol of the Red Cross, for example. The primordial element is the red colour itself, evoking the most powerful and magical substance in nature: human blood. The latter comes tagged with powerful connotations of life, death, pain, suffering, rejuvenation, sacrifice, individual identity, family bond, racial caste and so on. The higher the degree of knowledge of this particular symbol, the more effective it becomes. For example, knowing that the Red Cross was once the emblem of the crusades and the Knights Templars, and also that it is a symbol of the Rosicrucian Order and was painted on the sails of the ship in which Columbus discovered the New World, adds to the power of the symbol and the ideologies it can evoke. Yet to a non-Christian and non-western culture such as the Arabs, the Red Cross can evoke strong negative perceptions. It is for this reason, for example, that the Saudi Arabian authorities were opposed to the Red Cross Organisation and Swissair and to the use of their logos in the country.[35] Indeed, matters can go much further than this, as we shall see.

HERMETIC DEVICE

A very curious incident happened in Saudi Arabia in 1982 while I was working there. I had sent my Sudanese secretary, Abu Bakr, to collect an airline ticket for me at the Saudia (airline) office in downtown Riyadh. He returned with strange news: the Saudia office, he was told, was temporarily closed and all flights were grounded around the world. The rumour was quickly circulating in town that something dramatic had occurred while King Khaled was about to board the royal carrier in Riyadh that morning. The king was accompanied, as was the custom, by a Mutawa, a holy man who, upon seeing the aircraft, suddenly began to pray and beg the king not to board the flight. The problem, it seemed, was that the Mutawa had seen a Christian cross on the fuselage of the aircraft, a very disturbing omen in those days. Stare as they might, neither the king nor his entourage could see this 'cross'. Where was it? The Mutawa had been the victim of a phenomenon known as 'image in background effect'. His eyes, quite simply, had focused on the white background between the letter 's' and 'a' (**sa**) of the SAUDIA logo, which formed in his mind a white cross. The very minute he pointed this out, everyone began to 'see' this cross. Everywhere, on tickets, airline uniforms, Saudia offices, travel agents, posters and so on. It was as if the whole country had been suddenly hit by a malignant virus that had spread its infection everywhere. The 'cross' spread like wildfire. It was, of course, impossible to tell whether this had been a deliberate trick or just coincidence. This was now academic. The 'device', whether put there intentionally or through hazard, had been detonated by the Mutawa and the whole country was now awash with white 'Christian' crosses. Rumours of plots and conspiracies against Islam began to circulate. Left unattended, they would contaminate the psyche of the nation like a plague. A royal decree was thus issued to have all the Saudia logos changed.

Another well-known example of a deliberately planted 'Hermetic device' was brought to light in 1982 by authors Michael Baigent, Richard Leigh and Henry Lincoln in their best-selling book *The Holy Blood and the Holy Grail*. This involved a painting by the seventeenth-century French artist Nicolas Poussin known as 'Les Bergers D'Arcadie'. In this painting, which depicts a pastoral scene in the fictitious land of Arcadia,[36] a group of shepherds are crouching over a sarcophagus on which is inscribed the Latin words ET IN ARCADIA EGO, 'And in Arcadia I'. The authors suspected this apparently incomplete phrase to be a sort of anagram. When they rearranged the letters in a coherent Latin phrase, it produced 'I TEGO ARCANA DEI' which translates as 'I Conceal the Secrets of God'.[37] The profile of the mountain peaks and other features of the painting were then matched to an actual landscape in the south of France where a similar sarcophagus had once existed. Gradually other clues led them to an ultra-secret society known as the Prierie de Sion and, through them, a whole mystery involving the bloodline of Jesus and the lineage of the French monarchy emerged.[38] Poussin's 'magical' or 'Hermetic' device had worked. Although it had remained dormant for nearly four centuries, it was, as intended, inevitably picked up by inquisitive and initiated minds who pursued its message to its full conclusion. There are strewn around the globe hundreds, perhaps thousands of such powerful magical Hermetic devices. The big question, of course, is whether they were deliberately designed to unleash Hermetic ideologies at some time in the future, or whether they were merely put there for artistic, decorative or functional purposes.

Take, for example, the glass pyramid that was constructed in Paris in the Palais du Louvre's courtyard in 1984 by architect Ming Pei.[39] The choice of a fifty-two degrees angle for the slopes, which is the same as the Great Pyramid of Giza, is a strong indication that the architect, or those who commissioned him, had a certain ideology in mind that relates to Egypt or its esoteric tradition. This line of thought is supported by the fact that at the other extremity of the Louvre is the famous Egyptian obelisk which was brought to Paris from the Temple of Luxor in Upper Egypt in 1836, and known to have had Masonic connotations at the time.[40] The head of the Commission Des Grandes Travaux which commissioned the glass pyramid at the Louvre was French president François Mitterrand, whose brother at the time was the Grand Master of the Grand Orient, the body that regulates Freemasonry in France.[41] The glass pyramid, in fact, was to be a memorial for the bicentenary of the French Revolution. Now it is well-known to French historians that one of the principal philosophical themes of the French Revolution was the installing of the so-called *Etre Supreme* or 'Supreme Being' as the new godhead for France. This 'god' was associated with the so-called 'Eye of Vigilance' set in a blazing triangle or pyramid. This emblem is clearly Masonic, a reminder of the fact that many of the revolutionary leaders, including Danton, Robespierre and Murat, were linked to Masonic lodges. Oddly, in the reign of Louis XIV, the Sun King, the artist

François Dubois, proposed the raising of a giant pyramid in the courtyard of the Louvre which would be crowned with an 'eternal flame' to the glory of the 'Roi Soleil', the Sun King.[42] It may be relevant that Francois Mitterand was often dubbed the 'new Sun King' by the French media, a comparison with Louis XIV that may not be entirely jocular. Several architects during the French Revolution, for reasons that still remain unclear, proposed the raising of massive 'Egyptian' pyramids for the city of Paris, notably Etienne Louis Boullée, who was in charge of the highly symbolic demolition of the Bastille in 1784. He proposed to use the stones of the Bastille to erect his giant pyramid and, had it been built, it would have towered today in the very heart of Paris.[43] It may not be a coincidence, therefore, that when the French composer Jean-Michel Jarre was commissioned by François Mitterrand to organise the celebrations of the bicentennial in 1989, the musician chose to raise a huge metallic pyramid in front of the Grande Arche at La Défense, the latter known as the Arch of the Brotherhood, a name, needless to point out, that reeks of Masonic connotations. We shall return to these issues later, when we examine the millennium ceremony planned by Jean-Michel Jarre for Giza and the Great Pyramid.

Meanwhile we hope that it has become obvious to the reader that the glass pyramid at the Louvre is very likely another of those Hermetic devices, that, if its symbolism and links were investigated, would unravel the high ideals of the French Revolution, its esoteric connection with the Masonic ideals of a New World Order and, by extension, its origins in the ancient initiation cult of Egypt. In short, the device is intended to 'recruit' the right individual whose mind is predisposed to undergo the process of the Masonic–cum–Egyptian initiation path. Monuments such as the Louvre pyramid or the Concorde Obelisk are quite simple yet most ingeniously function as self-activating devices that draw into their fold the unsuspecting yet primed individual in an attempt to self-initiate him (or her) into what may be termed the Masonic ideals. Whether or not Ming Pei intended this to happen, the structure he created is, by virtue of its shape, design and location, a highly charged Hermetic device.

The 'books' of Thoth–Hermes, the manuals of this ultimate Hermetic system of knowledge, are, if we accept the ancient prophecies, concealed somewhere in Egypt, somewhere in a place called Monte Libyco, somewhere near, or even within, the Great Pyramid of Giza.

Finding them, therefore, could be the ultimate prize – or weapon.

THE 'NUMBER' OF THE SECRET CHAMBERS

In late October 1925, the world of Egyptology celebrated the seventieth birthday of Adolf Erman, the famous German philologist. It was Erman who, in 1890, provided the first extensive translation of the Westcar Papyrus, a task which apparently had taken five years to complete. As is customary in Egyptological circles, the occasion of Erman's landmark birthday prompted a special edition of an academic journal, in this case the *Zeitschrift für Ägyptische Sprache*, where a variety of eminent peers presented articles in honour of their elder colleague. It was thus that Alan H. Gardiner, the well-known British Egyptologist and expert grammarian of Middle Kingdom hieroglyphs, presented an article on the Westcar Papyrus entitled 'The Secret Chamber of the Sanctuary of Thoth', which appeared in the prestigious academic publication *Journal of Egyptian Archaeology*.[44] This article was published in its entirety as an appendix in my book *The Orion Mystery*, but no commentary or discussion was given due to the lack of space.

The Westcar Papyrus, which we have already reviewed at the start of this chapter, is regarded by Egyptologists as a sort of parchment version of the Rosetta Stone, meaning that it was from it that much of our contemporary knowledge of ancient Egyptian grammar and syntax was derived. For many years after Erman's epic translation no substantial new evidence was extracted from it, and the exciting reference to a secret chamber and the mysterious haul it may contain was taken as fiction. Gardiner felt, however, that he had now, in 1925, detected ' the solution of an old *crux interpretum* in the Westcar Papyrus'.[45] This *crux interpretum*, or crucial interpretation, concerned the hieroglyphic words 'ipwt' and 'wnt' which, according to Gardiner, stand for 'secret chambers' and 'sanctuary' respectively. In the Westcar Papyrus, in the story of the magician Djedi, the latter informs King Cheops (Khufu), the builder of the Great Pyramid of Giza, that he, Djedi, knows 'the number of the ipwt and of the wnt of Thoth', which Cheops had long sought for in order to 'do the same for his pyramid'.[46] The statement by King Cheops, which incidentally is one of the few attributed to this enigmatic pharaoh, reads in full: 'Then the Majesty of King Cheops said: "It is also said that you (Djedi) know the number of the secret chambers of the sanctuary of Thoth." To which Djedi replied: "Please, I do not know the number, O king my Lord, but I know the place where it is."' After careful reflection on the words and statement by King Cheops, Gardiner pointed out that the 'nature of the *ipwt* and of the *wnt* mentioned in this passage present a

51

problem', for the word *wnt* contained the determinative sign representing a 'building' or 'structure' of some sort. Gardiner thus argued that

> the resemblance of its name (wnt) to the name of the city where Thoth was particularly worshipped, namely *Wnw* (Hermapolis Magna, also known to the Arabs as Ashmunein) would seem to indicate that it was the primeval sanctuary of Thoth, or else his tomb.[47]

Adolf Erman had concluded earlier that the similarity between the two names was 'fortuitous', but Gardiner did not think so. It was clear to him that the *wnt* was to be seen as a special building dedicated to Thoth, and offers that it may well be the sanctuary either at Hermapolis Magna or another known to have existed in the Delta region north of modern Cairo. Gardiner also contested the notion that King Cheops was not, in fact, looking for the sanctuary itself, but rather for the *ipwt*, i.e. the 'chambers' of the *wnt*, i.e. the 'sanctuary' of Thoth. This was suggestive that the 'chambers' were no longer in the sanctuary of Thoth but that somehow they had been removed and concealed elsewhere. It is these 'chambers' that Cheops wished to find, so that he could do the same for his pyramid at Giza. There is, quite obviously, an illogical situation here, for how could the 'chambers' be removed from the sanctuary? Perhaps they were not chambers at all, but portable shrines, similar to those, for example, found in the tomb of Tutankhamun. There, in this king's sepulchre, were found four wooden 'chambers' which were plated in gold. They were removed in 1922 and are now displayed in the Cairo Museum, along with the rest of the Tutankhamun relics. Could the 'secret chambers' of the sanctuary of Thoth be such contraptions? Was it these 'chambers' that Cheops wanted to find in order to use them for his pyramid?

Reading the statements of Cheops and Djedi more closely, it also becomes apparent that the king was specifically asking for the 'number' of the 'secret chambers', and not the chambers themselves. In this respect Djedi states that he does not know the 'number', but rather knows where it may be found. 'There is a box of flint in a room in Heliopolis called "Revision" . . . it is in it.' What was that mysterious black box? And what was the even more mysterious 'number' that was in it? Why was Cheops so eager to obtain it so much so that the king had 'long been searching' for it? Examining the syntax of the word 'sipty', meaning 'revision', or 'inventory', Gardiner points out that it also stood for 'taking stock' of the property of a temple, and thus concludes that the *wnt* was a sort of archive room, a 'hall of records' if you will, that contained, among other things, the 'number' that Cheops so desperately needed for his pyramid in order to construct 'secret chambers' within it.[48]

THE INVENTORY ROOM

Following Gardiner's interpretation of the Westcar Papyrus, another British Egyptologist, F.W. Green, came up with a radical new interpretation of his own that provides us with a tantalising insight as to what may have been the nature of the enigmatic 'number' that was so highly prized by the builder of the Great Pyramid. In an article also entitled 'The Secret Chambers of the Sanctuary of Thoth',[49] Green rejects Gardiner's idea that all that King Cheops wanted was simply to know the number of the secret chambers of the sanctuary of Thoth, merely to design his own pyramid in the same manner. Green felt that one should look more closely at the story itself, rather than only at the philology. He first pointed out that in the story, the writer seems to confuse two words, 'pdwt' ('something that stretches', like a rope or a line) and 'ipwt' ('account', 'archive' or 'plan'), which, says Green, is 'of somewhat similar sound which may also have conveyed to him somewhat similar ideas, such as a stretched string for marking a wall, and a succession of lines in list form'. Green thus ventures that the 'room' called 'Revision' (archives) 'may be a "chart room" or perhaps a "drawing room" where plans were made and stored'.[50] Green then turns to the rest of the story where Djedi the magician informs King Cheops that he, Djedi, is not the one who can bring the 'flint box' or its mysterious and precious contents to the king, but rather one of the three children of a high-priestess called Rewdedet, who is destined to become pharaoh. Rewdedet is said to be the wife of the high-priest of Heliopolis, where the 'flint box' is kept. Now it is an historical fact that the Fifth Dynasty which succeeded Cheops and his son, Khafre, and his grandson, Menkaure, builders of the other two pyramids at Giza, were three brothers born from the union of a priest and priestess of Heliopolis. I.E.S. Edwards, in his classic book *The Pyramids of Egypt*, nominates them as follows:

A papyrus in the Berlin Museum, known as the Papyrus Westcar, has preserved a legend concerning the origins of the Vth Dynasty which may embody a kernel of truth. The papyrus itself probably dates from the Second Intermediate Period, but it was certainly a copy of an older document. According to this legend, the first three kings of the dynasty – Userkaf, Sahure, and Neferikare – were triplets begotten of Ra (the Sungod) and born of the wife of a priest of Ra.

Userkaf may well have sprung from a priestly stock, and it seems likely that he himself held the office of high priest of Heliopolis before ascending the throne . . . Sahure and Neferikare were possibly brothers . . .[51]

These first three kings and three of their successors built pyramids at Abusir and Saqqara; the last king of this dynasty, Unas, errected his pyramid south of the stepped pyramid of Zoser. It is in this last sepulchre that suddenly the tradition of keeping the interior of pyramids bereft of any inscriptions is broken; for in Unas's pyramid the walls of the main chambers and corridors are inscribed with texts, the so-called Pyramid Texts, which are considered to be the oldest body of religious inscriptions in history.[52] The Pyramid Texts have been discussed at length in my previous books, *The Orion Mystery* and *Keeper of Genesis*. Until their rediscovery in 1881 by Gaston Maspero, these texts had remained a secret for nearly five thousand years. In brief, then, the Pyramid Texts, which are best described as magical texts, were intended to somehow cause the transfiguration of dead pharaohs into astral beings in the celestial realm of Osiris near or within the constellation of Orion, and their decoding recently[53] has indeed proved to be the key to unravel the mysterious purpose and function of the great pyramids of Giza.[54] We shall return to this matter in a later chapter. Meanwhile Green, in his analysis of the Westcar Papyrus, felt that it was highly likely that the prophecy made by the magician Djedi that the mysterious *ipwt* would be somehow 'brought' to Cheops by a future king of the Fifth Dynasty, might indeed relate to the introduction of writings in the chambers of royal pyramids, in an attempt to replicate the 'secret chambers' of Thoth. Green pointed out that the thousands of lines that constitute the bulk of the Pyramid Texts are arranged according to a fixed and sacred system. Green thus suggested that this sacred system of lines – which are also known as 'utterances' – and not the design of the chambers themselves, were, in fact, the mysterious *ipwt*:

> These long lines of religious texts, set out in certain order, were something quite out of the way, and the report of them and of their magical value must have impressed those who were living at the time of their execution, and a rather hazy account was handed down to the compiler of the Westcar text. He could not have seen the Pyramid texts himself; they were closed up . . .[55]

Green then goes on to assume 'that Khufu did not embellish his "Horizon" (i.e. his Pyramid) with these magical formulae as he doubtless would have done' had he found the sealed 'flint box' and its content. But what if he had? What if that mysterious black box with its precious cargo did, in fact, end up inside the Great Pyramid? Where could it be?

In March 1993, as we have already seen, a German team explored the narrow shafts which emanate from the so-called Queen's Chamber. At its end, some sixty-five yards deep into the central core of the pyramid, the miniature robot discovered a mysterious door apparently locked with two copper handles from the inside. Could the enigmatic black box from Heliopolis be concealed in a small chamber behind this door?

Frustratingly, as we have seen, the Egyptian authorities have put a clamp on any further exploration since then. We shall return to this event and its serious implications. Meanwhile let us take a look at the textual evidence of another possible 'secret chamber' at Giza, this time not inside the Great Pyramid but deep within the natural bedrock of the plateau – underneath the belly of the Great Sphinx.

Chapter Four

The Tomb of Osiris

'This is the Place . . . the burial of Osiris in the House of Sokar . . .'

Memphite Theology c. 2000 BC, Shabaka Stone, British Museum

SECRETARY OF OSIRIS

Other than his attributes as the supreme magician and inventor of the sacred science, Thoth, above all else, was the messenger of the gods. As such, his word was beyond reproach and his wisdom unquestioned. So much so, that the ancient Egyptians allocated to Thoth the role of 'secretary' to Osiris, the legendary founder of pharaonic civilisation and god of the afterlife. According to Diodorus, a Roman historian who lived in the first century BC:

> Osiris held Hermes (Thoth) in high honour, because of his ingenuity and power of quick invention. Hermes taught men to speak distinctly, he gave names to things which possessed none before, he invented letters, and instituted the worship of the gods, he invented arithmetic, music, and sculpture, and he formulated a system of astronomy. He was the confidential scribe of Osiris, who invariably accepted his advice upon all matters.[1]

But who really was Osiris, this man-god whom Thoth so diligently served? Could such a figure have actually existed?

When the Egyptologist Sir Wallis Budge set about compiling a study of Osiris, he ended up with an 800-page thesis which he titled 'Osiris and the Egyptian Resurrection'.[2] In spite of this, Budge had to concede that his study was not exhaustive.[3] One does not have to search too far to

Fig. 4. The god Thoth.

know the reason why. The cult of Osiris preceded Christianity by at least 3000 years and, furthermore, survived alongside it as a serious opponent for over three centuries. Indeed, the Osirian cult would have survived even longer had not the Church systematically destroyed its temples and outlawed its practice in AD 391.[4] (We shall see later, however, how the cult of Osiris may have indeed reached our modern era, not just through the secret societies and esoteric groups that evoke his name each day, but actually within the very heart of Christian religion itself.) With such an expanse of time to contend with, space allows us only a cursory view of this remotely ancient and all–powerful deity. There are literally thousands upon thousands of ancient texts inscribed in temples and pyramids, on the walls of tombs and coffins, on papyrus, tablets, stele, and amulets that speak of Osiris and the trinity he formed with his sister-wife, Isis, and their divine son, Horus. Yet in spite of such a mass of texts, it is a well-known peculiarity of Egyptology that no complete narrative of his life, mythical or historical, has ever been found from ancient Egyptian sources. However, through various apocryphal versions from Greek and Roman sources, as well as from the Egyptian texts available, it has been possible to reconstruct an acceptable version of the myth of Osiris. In brief this is as follows:

> Osiris was the eldest son of the Sky-goddess, Nut, and the Earth-god, Geb. He was born on the first of the so-called 'five epagomenal days', that is five days before the summer solstice. His birth was followed by that of his brother, Seth, and of his two sisters, Nephtys and Isis. Osiris and Isis married and became, in effect, the first pharaonic couple to rule Egypt. They established a kingdom of the *First Time* in the Memphis area (near modern Cairo) under divine rule.

Osiris was said to have introduced civilisation to the inhabitants of Egypt and brought a system of cosmic order and law. His brother, Seth, who was jealous of Osiris, killed the latter and cut his body into fourteen parts and cast them all over the land of Egypt. Isis, after an epic search, brought the parts together (except the phallus which she could not find) and revived Osiris through the magical rites she had learnt from the god Thoth. She then placed an artificial phallus on the body of Osiris, and thus became pregnant with his seed. Meanwhile Osiris departed into the sky to establish a cosmic kingdom of the First Time (the Duat) among the stars of Orion on the banks of the celestial Nile, i.e. the Milky Way. Isis gave birth to a son, Horus, in the marshes of the Delta. Horus grew up and challenged his evil uncle, Seth, to a duel. After a great battle that took place in the Memphis region (at the legendary Kher-Aha, 'Place of the Battle') Horus defeated Seth, and won back, with the aid of Thoth, the throne of Egypt. All subsequent kings of Egypt were deemed to be the

Fig. 5. Sokar-Osiris.

reincarnation of Horus. When a Horus-king died, he, too, would be brought to life through the magical rituals of Isis and, like Osiris, would impregnate the womb of the goddess (the queen or a high-priestess) with his seed, and then depart into the sky to join Osiris in the constellation Orion (the Duat).

Although Egyptologists are adamant that Osiris was a mythical character, the ancient Egyptians themselves had no hesitation in asserting that Osiris had actually lived on earth in a remote golden age, and had established civilisation in their land. Indeed the whole system of pharaonic theocracy, its religious festivals, its calendars, its laws and even its codes of social behaviour, rested on this very belief.

If Osiris did exist, then surely such a king to whom, as we shall see later, was attributed messianic virtues by the ancient Egyptians would have been buried in a magnificent sepulchre, as all other subsequent kings of Egypt had been. Let us, then, indulge for a while in such a hypothesis by asking where could the tomb of Osiris be?

THE HOUSE OF SOKAR

When the Greek writer and historian Herodotus visited Egypt in the fifth century BC, he was taken to the Giza necropolis by an Egyptian priest.[5]

It is probable that at this time the Great Sphinx was totally covered in sand, for Herodotus does not mention this monument at all, which would be an unlikely omission for one who has come to be known to the world as the 'father of history'.[6] Herodotus, on the other hand, does mention the Great Pyramid in much detail, and also made this tantalising comment:

> as I said . . . the *mound* upon which the pyramid stands, and the *underground chambers* which Cheops intended as vaults for his own use – these last were built on a sort of island surrounded by water which was introduced from the Nile by a canal . . . [7]

Egyptologists generally discount Herodotus's story as being the result of gossip that the gullible Greek might have picked up from an uninformed priest or dragoman. French pyramid researcher and engineer Jean Kerisel, however, is not so sure. Kerisel is a senior consulting engineer in his late eighties and president of the Franco-Egyptian Society in Paris. He has been decorated with the Croix de Guerre and the Legion d'Honneur, France's highest recognition for services rendered to the nation. Kerisel has recently been appointed as senior adviser for the Tower of Pisa Restoration Project in Italy.[8] In 1991, after participating as a senior consultant on the Cairo Underground project, Kerisel became interested in ancient Egypt and the Great Pyramid. Convinced that there was substance in Herodotus's story about the 'island tomb' under the Great Pyramid, Kerisel applied to the Egyptian authorities for permission to investigate the so-called Subterranean Chamber of the Great Pyramid. This chamber deemed by Egyptologists abandoned while in the process of construction lies some 400 feet underneath the Pyramid, and is reached by a low tunnel cut into the natural rock and sloping at an angle of a little more than twenty-six degrees which is maintained with gun-barrel precision. Normally such permissions as sought by Kerisel are gained with the utmost difficulty. Kerisel, in spite of his impressive academic and civil credentials, had to wait until 1996 before being given the opportunity to verify his theory. Engineering calculations had convinced Kerisel that a secret chamber underneath the bedrock of the Subterranean Chamber of the Great Pyramid might exist just as Herodotus had reported. His objective, therefore, was to drill a small hole in the horizontal tunnel that led to the Subterranean Chamber at a specific spot where he thought he had detected an 'anomaly'. Kerisel's exploration, unfortunately, yielded no conclusive evidence to support his theory, and he has now, due to his age and health, abandoned the hope of any further exploration. He remains adamant, nevertheless, that somewhere under the Great Pyramid or under the bedrock of the Giza plateau would one day be found the mysterious 'tomb of Cheops' reported by Herodotus.[9] I have known Jean Kerisel since 1993, when we both participated in a BBC documentary about the Great Pyramid.[10] In July 1999 I met Kerisel again in Paris, where we both participated in a new documentary that the BBC was making for the Discovery Channel.[11] Kerisel reiterated his belief to me, and was as convinced as ever that some day a secret chamber would be found under the bedrock at Giza. All his engineering instincts and vast experience in subterranean engineering projects[12] had made him the best expert to pass a good educated guess on this matter, and I could not help feeling that this highly learned and seasoned engineer was right. Time, however, will tell.

Meanwhile another interesting and somewhat similar theory has recently been put forward by author Andrew Collins in his book *The Gods of Eden*.[13] Collins points out that the Giza necropolis, which is in fact a large rocky *mound*, might have represented the 'Mound of Creation' often mentioned in Egyptian texts. In some narratives this 'Mound' was said to have been the first solid land mass to emerge from the waters after a great 'deluge', in others from the 'primeval ocean' of creation.[14] Collins therefore postulates that the Giza necropolis as a whole might have originally been landscaped in such a manner so that it was surrounded like some gigantic moat by water brought down by canals from the Nile in order to *emulate* the 'Mound of Creation'.[15] We shall return to this intriguing 'Mound' and what it might have truly represented to the ancients later on. Meanwhile let us examine another intriguing theory presented by a Scottish researcher, Steuart Campbell. Referring to French Egyptologist Alexandre Lenoir, Campbell writes:

> . . . In an article in *FMR* ('A dissertation on the Pyramids of Egypt' No.39. 1989) he (Lenoir) boldly claimed that educated travellers and antiquaries are generally in agreement on the nature of the Great Pyramid: 'all considered it to be the tomb of Osiris . . . it was therefore his simulacrum, as are all tombs that have been raised in honour of mythological personages' . . . an essential belief of the religion, especially the cult of Osiris, was that man consisted both of body and spirit, and that the latter lived on after death. Indeed it was believed that one could provide a 'tomb' (in effect a cenotaph) for the spirit . . . similarly the Great Pyramid might have been intended as a dwelling place for the spirit of Osiris . . .[16]

Campbell's idea, based on Alexandre Lenoir's thesis, is not as far-fetched as it may first appear. It is well known that several pharaohs did, indeed, have cenotaphs, i.e. 'false' tombs for their 'spirits', built for them at different places and away from their actual resting place. Good examples of this strange practice are the many tombs and cenotaphs of the early Dynasties kings, where the physical remains of these kings were buried in mastabas in Lower Egypt near Memphis, whereas their cenotaphs were at Abydos in Upper Egypt, 1000 miles further south.[17] Also in the Pyramid Age, for example, the pharaoh Sneferu had at least one cenotaph-pyramid erected for his 'spirit' in the region of Dashour in the Memphite necropolis, and probably another one at Meydum.[18]

Writer and researcher Simon Cox[19] has also postulated on the idea of a 'secret chamber' styled cenotaph under the Giza necropolis, though this time not beneath the pyramid itself but in a place he refers to as 'the missing piece of Giza'. Cox theorises, however, that it is *actually* the tomb of the god Sokar (whom Cox regards as the archetype or role-model of Osiris) that should be sought, and not that of Osiris himself. Cox's theory has much merit, and I have asked him, therefore, to present it here in his own words:

In the archaeological season 1906-07, Petrie was digging in the desert between Giza and Zawiyet el-Aryan, about one-and-a-quarter miles south of the Plateau, when he discovered a hoard of *ushabti* figures. The exact spot is hard to pinpoint as Petrie only states that he found the figures in the plain beyond a rocky ridge that rose half a mile south of the Great Pyramid. The *ushabti* figures were found in pits about ten feet deep that were filled with sand and rubbish. To all intents and purposes, these figures were what are known as extrasepulchral *ushabtis*, in other words, they were left by pilgrims and were unrelated to any original tomb or burial. More of these figures were excavated in 1919 by an antiquities inspector called Tewfik Boulos, on a small hill about three-and-three-quarter miles south of the Petrie find. Some of the *ushabtis* found by Petrie belonged to an individual called Khamwase, a son of Rameses II. However, Petrie found no tomb as such, but he did find some limestone building blocks that he could not explain. Why were the extrasepulchral *ushabtis* left at Giza? Is there a correlation between these figures and the extrasepulchral finds at Abydos? Was there a 'tomb of Osiris' at Giza/Rostau? To answer these questions we must take a closer look at the deity that predates even Osiris and whom Osiris actually assimilates in the late Old Kingdom. That deity is Sokar.

The falcon-headed deity, Sokar, has gained popular notoriety because of his place in the fourth and fifth hours of the Duat. Many authors and researchers in this field have highlighted the fourth and fifth hours without fully understanding the role of the deity whose realm it is. Many have assumed that this figure is just another side of Osiris and have therefore ignored him altogether. Sokar, however, deserves better. In our opinion, Sokar was the oldest deity known in Egypt, far older than Osiris and responsible for many of the later god figures of

Dynastic times. Sadly, textural and archaeological evidence for the cult of Sokar is sparse but from what we have we can piece together a picture of how the deity was revered and worshipped in Archaic and quite probably Pre-Dynastic times as well. By the time of the New Kingdom, the cult of Sokar had appropriated many of the ritual, mythological, and ideological elements of the cult of Osiris. But who was Sokar?

Sokar was originally a god of the Memphite necropolis, and indeed his name is echoed in the place today called Saqqara. His sanctuary was at Rostau which, as we shall demonstrate, was at south Giza and at where certain parts of his festival were held. The primary objects of his cult were a mound and his sacred boat called the Henu-barque, which carried the dead king to heaven. During the Old Kingdom, Sokar is seen as a patron of craftsmen and specifically of metal workers, and in the book of the Duat, Sokar inhabits a strange land of the dead, a land that even Ra has no access to. Sokar can be seen in the representations of the fourth and fifth hours of the Duat standing upon his mound within what seems to be a hill topped by a black conical symbol of some sort, possibly a stone. In this place the barque of the sun god, Ra, assumes the form of a snake in order to crawl along the sand and so traverse the realm of Sokar safely, whilst the souls of the dead cry out from the darkness around him. The realm of Sokar is guarded by the two Aker lions and by a plethora of snakes and strange beings.

Sokar is the god of death, as Osiris is later the god of the dead and resurrection. Within the Pyramid Texts there is such a close connection between these two gods that their actions and roles are often interchangeable, indicating that there was an early tradition for Sokar's role in the Underworld. Indeed, in utterance 532, stanza 1256, we read, ' . . . they have found Osiris, his brother Seth having laid him low in Nedil when Osiris said "Get away from me," when his name became Sokar . . .' It seems clear from this reference that the Egyptians, as early as the Pyramid Texts, were justifying the assimilation of Sokar by Osiris, and looking at the age of the texts, we must conclude that Sokar is an already archaic deity by this time. We believe that from the textual and iconographic evidence, Sokar was seen as much more 'real' than later deities. As we shall demonstrate, Sokar was also the original archetype for the god Horus and we believe that the legendary 'Followers of Horus' should in fact be renamed 'The followers of Sokar', highlighting the possible eastern origins of this most ancient of characters.

This means that it is necessary to re-evaluate the idea that there was a tomb of Osiris at Giza mirroring the tomb of Osiris at Abydos. Surely, our references must now be to the tomb of Sokar. Sokar is also assimilated with the Memphite god Ptah by the time of the Old Kingdom and it would seem that his assimilation had been going on for some time. Further evidence of his assimilation with Osiris can be seen in certain similarities between some of the ceremonies enacted in Sokar's festival and some episodes in the Khoiak festival of Osiris at Abydos. As we have seen, the character of Sokar is intimately associated with his Henu-barque, possibly echoed by the various boat burials found within the pyramid fields. At the Festival of Sokar there were, at some point in the ten-day festival, ceremonies at a Sokar-Osiris tomb known as the Shetayet, in the Memphite necropolis, specifically at Rostau.

Fig. 6. The Boat of Sokar on the back of the Aker Lion. Under the Aker is the dead god Osiris under the mound-pyramid formed by the daily circuit of the sun.

The French Egyptologist Christine M. Zivie believes that Rostau is located in the region of Gebel Gibli, about half a mile south of the Great Pyramid and the site of the so-called southern hill at Giza. This prominent hill is the only point on the Plateau where all nine pyramids can be seen from, and where, in my opinion, the Fifth Division can be found. It is interesting to note that in this area Petrie found 'many pieces of red granite, and some other stones scattered about the west side of the rocky ridge, as if some costly building had existed in this region'.

This would place a possible structure just to the west of the southern hill, in direct line with a most intriguing feature of the Plateau, the Wall of the Crow (Heit el-Ghourab). Could it be that Howard-Vyse was right in thinking that the wall was indeed a causeway, leading from an as yet undiscovered structure? If not a causeway, then maybe an enclosure wall for the Shetayet of Sokar and the Henu-barque sanctuary. Egyptologist Mark Lehner has stated that the Wall of the Crow is quite possibly the oldest structure on the plateau and a close inspection of this feature reveals it to be of cyclopean construction, with huge blocks used in the body of the wall and three truly enormous limestone blocks used to form the roof of the tunnel that runs through it from north to south (or vice versa). It is also interesting to note that the name Rostau was applied to an ancient village, later known as Busiris, which stood approximately on the site of the modern village of Nazlet-Batran. It was in the desert to the west of this village that Petrie found the extrasepulchral *ushabtis* mentioned above. It is tempting to speculate that these pieces of granite could have belonged to the Henu-barque sanctuary of Sokar. If this was the case, then the tomb of Sokar (Osiris) could not be far away. The eminent British Egyptologist I.E.S. Edwards noted that the Shetayet must have been a separate edifice, although undoubtedly close to the sanctuary of the Henu-barque.[20]

The idea that the Great Pyramid, or indeed the Giza necropolis as a whole, might have been regarded as the 'dwelling place' for the soul or spirit of Osiris (or the combined deity Osiris-Sokar) is, interestingly enough, much supported by ancient texts. As Egyptologist Selim Hassan pointed out, there are several statements made to that effect in the so-called Book of the Two Ways, dated to c. 2000 BC.[21] For example, there is a reference to the 'Highland of Aker which is the Dwelling Place of Osiris', and also of 'Osiris who is in the Highland of Aker'.[22] Aker, as we have already seen, was an ancestral deity who had the shape of a huge lion or sphinx and which, according to Hassan and others,[23] may have represented the Great Sphinx of Giza.[24] Hassan consequently concluded that the 'Highland of Aker' must, by necessity, be the elevated plateau of Giza – the 'Monte Libyco' of the Hermetic texts.[25] In late 1997, as we have already briefly mentioned, Dr Hawass announced the discovery of a large underground tomb some two hundred and twenty yards behind the Sphinx, i.e. in the 'Highland of Aker'. This tomb, which was totally submerged in water when Hawass found it, fitted in some respects the description given by Herodotus. It had, for example, a large sarcophagus surrounded by water, giving the impression that it was lying amidst a small island. Dr Hawass implied that certain inscriptions found in the tomb showed that this sepulchre was not that of Cheops, as Herodotus had reported, but a tomb dedicated to Osiris – in short, a cenotaph as postulated earlier by Alexandre Lenoir and Steuart Campbell. After careful examination of the tomb, however, Dr Hawass concluded that it was to be dated to the Saite Period c.665-525 BC, thus nearly two millennia after the construction of the Great Pyramid. We shall return to this mysterious tomb in detail in Chapter 12.

Meanwhile certain questions need asking about this new find and its alleged symbolic purpose. Firstly, why build a 'symbolic' tomb so deep into the bedrock? Indeed, why have it submerged in water where no one could possibly visit it? Does it not defeat the whole purpose of a cenotaph or shrine, where pilgrims and visitors are actually meant to pay homage? Could it not be possible that Hawass is wrong in his conclusions, and that the well–shaft and the 'tomb' are, in fact, much older than he presently thinks? Is it not also possible that what we have here is neither a 'tomb' nor a 'cenotaph' but something else? Could it not be, for example, an antechamber or an entrance of some sort leading elsewhere, perhaps to the true location of the 'tomb of Osiris'? What evidence in ancient texts exists to support such an idea?

The place of the burial of Osiris

There are many tantalising indications in ancient Egyptian texts that the region near the Giza pyramids was somehow regarded by the ancients not only as a 'gateway to the Afterworld' but that it had served as *the burial place of Osiris*.[26] One of the oldest documents that makes direct reference to the burial place of Osiris and the vicinity of Giza is the so-called Shabaka text dated from c. 750 BC and preserved today in the British Museum on a slab of black granite stone. As was the case with the Rosetta Stone, the Shabaka Stone was acquired in rather dubious circumstances. It seems that for a long while it was in the hands of Arab farmers who, not knowing what it was, used it as a millstone on which they ground corn and wheat. Whether due to this or other causes, the central portion of the inscribed text has been totally erased. The stone then somehow came into the possession of the Earl Spencer who, in 1805, 'donated' it to the British Museum.[27] It is today displayed in the main Egyptian hall on the ground floor, fixed on the eastern wall by metal brackets. The importance of the Shabaka Stone, in my opinion, exceeds by far that of the Rosetta Stone, not only by virtue of its antiquity but more so by the weighty revelations it contains. It is simply marked exhibit No. 498, and sadly many visitors today pass by it without much notice. Yet within its textual content this much neglected black stone could very well hold the clue to the real burial place of Osiris.

The Shabaka Stone measures about three feet by four-and-a-half feet, and has two main horizontal lines of texts written at the top and running the whole width of the slab, and sixty-two columns of text running down its height which are meant to be read from left to right. Interestingly the ancient scribe who carved these hieroglyphs in c. 700 BC gave us the reason why he did so and thus, deliberately or otherwise, has shed a faint beam of light on the possible great antiquity and importance of the textual material:

This writing was copied out anew by his majesty (King Shabaka) in the house of his father Ptah-South-of-his-Wall (Memphis), for his majesty found it to be a work of the ancestors which was worm-eaten[28] so that it could be understood from beginning to end. His majesty copied it anew so that it became better than it had been before . . .[29]

How long King Shabaka had reigned after these mysterious 'ancestors' is not known, but Miriam Lichtheim, the American philologist at UCLA, who studied the inscriptions of the Shabaka Stone, was of the opinion that the original version may date as far back as the Pyramid Age.[30] The Shabaka Stone has suffered the same fate as the Westcar Papyrus, namely that Egyptologists have placed upon its literary content a tag of fiction. Thus according to the German philologist Kurt Sethe, for example, the Shabaka text is nothing more than a 'dramatic play' and thus implies that its narrative carriess absolutely no historical value whatsoever.[31] These sort of hasty and sweeping statements, however, are, unfortunately, very common in Egyptology and, although perhaps valid in some cases, tend to put a stop to further interpretations. Graham Hancock and I have discussed the contents of the Shabaka texts, which is also known as the Memphite Theology, in great detail in our previous books, so a full discussion here is not necessary.[32] The specific passage that concerns us in this present investigation, however, is found between the horizontal lines fifteen and twenty-three, and reads as follows:

> **This is the land [of] the burial of Osiris in the House of Sokar**. [Arrived] Isis and Nephtys without delay, for Osiris has drowned in his water [the Nile]. Isis and Nephtys looked out, beheld Osiris and attended to him. Horus speaks to Isis and Nephtys: Hurry, grasp him . . . Isis and Nephtys speak to Osiris: We come, we take you [to the place]. They heeded in time, and brought him to [the land]. Osiris entered the hidden portals . . . thus came Osiris into the earth . . . to the north of the land to which he had come . . .[33]

If Miriam Lichtheim's conclusion that the Shabaka text could have its origin in the Pyramid Age is right, as I believe it is, then what we have here is a crystal-clear allusion that at about the time the Giza necropolis was developed, there was a belief that the 'body of Osiris' had been buried in a mysterious place called 'The House of Sokar'. In a similar vein, the Egyptologist Selim Hassan, in his study of ancient Egyptian texts,[34] notes that there is often mention of a place called Rostau as being 'the kingdom of Osiris in the Tomb',[35] while Adolf Erman, the German philologist, demonstrated that

Fig. 7. The stele of the Sphinx. Note the 'Sanctuary Under the Aker Sphinxes'.

. . . the celebrated shrine of Rostau, the gates of the ways, led directly to the Underworld [of Osiris] . . . [and] it is possible that part of this shrine has survived in the so-called Temple of the Sphinx . . .[36]

Is there a connection between this 'House of Sokar' and the 'Shrine of Rostau'?[37] Could both be the same place? The place where, as the ancient texts say, is to be found the 'body of Osiris'?

THE WATERY ROAD TO ROSTAU

In the pyramid of Unas, where are found the bulk of the Pyramid Texts, there is a telling passage, denoted as line 445, which has the departed Osiris-king state: 'I am Sokar of Rostau . . .'[38]; and yet another passage that virtually echoes the Shabaka texts by stating: 'They [Isis and Nephtys] have found Osiris . . . when his name became Sokar . . .'[39]

These two statements alone should leave us without any doubt that the so-called 'House of Sokar' is in a place called Rostau, and that it was there

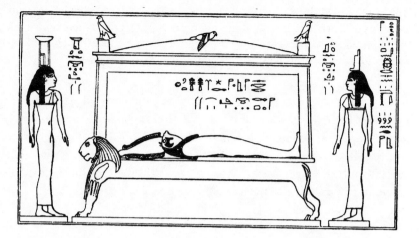

Fig. 8. Sokar–Osiris of Busiris. The Temple of Denderah.

that the defunct Osiris was supposedly put to rest. Now we shall recall
that in our discussion on the Hermetic prophecy of Monte Libyco, we
have demonstrated that Rostau was in fact the Giza necropolis and that it
was there, according to the prophecy, that the 'return of the gods' would
one day take place. This conclusion, which was also reached by Selim
Hassan, adds cogency to the postulation made by Adolf Erman that the
'Shrine' or 'House' of Sokar in the place called Rostau is in the close
proximity of the Great Sphinx of Giza. Also in her study of ancient
Egyptian texts, Miriam Lichtheim was able to conclude that Rostau was,
indeed, 'the necropolis of Giza' itself.[40] Further support of the Rostau-
Giza connection comes from the philologist R.O. Faulkner who wrote
that 'Rostau was another name for the Giza necropolis as well as the
(gates) of the Underworld[41] (i.e. the Duat of Osiris)'.[42] While the
mythologist R.T. Rundle Clark goes even further by saying that not only
was Rostau the modern Giza, it specifically was: 'the home of a form of
Osiris known as Sokar'.[43] There is, too, textual evidence still extant near
the Sphinx, namely in the inscriptions on the New Kingdom stela that is
housed between the front paws of the statue. There, in line seven of the
stela, it is clearly stated that the Sphinx is located '. . . beside the House
of Sokar . . . in Rostau . . .'[44]

Another confirmation from an ancient source can be found in the so-
called 'Coffin Texts' dated c. 1800 BC.[45] In these texts there is not only a
clear connection made between the so-called 'efflux' or bodily remains of
Osiris and the region of Rostau, but here we are also given an intriguing
clue of what might be found at this strange and mysterious place:

This is the sealed thing which is in darkness, with fire about it, which contains the efflux of Osiris, and it was put in Rostau. It has been hidden there since it fell from him, and it is what came down from him onto the desert sand; it means that what belongs to him (his body) was put in Rostau . . .[46]

In this context, the 'efflux' means that which is expelled from the living body. Efflux was seen by the Egyptians as having life of its own; indeed they saw anything that was discharged from the living body as having life. It seems that efflux, as opposed to the Ka (spiritual double), or the Ba (soul), was seen as the physical reality of the spiritual being, for instance, in Pyramid Text, utterance 32 we read:

This cold water of yours, O Osiris, this cold water of yours, O King, has gone forth to your son, has gone forth to Horus. I have come and I bring to you the Eye of Horus, that your heart may be refreshed possessing it; I bring it to you under your sandals. *Take the efflux which issued from you*; your heart will not be inert, possessing it . . .

And in utterance 33 we see:

O king, take this cold water of yours, for you have coolness with Horus in your name of Him who issued from cold water; take the efflux which issued from you . . .

Osiris was the ruler of the 'Land' or 'kingdom' of the dead, a place that was known to the ancient Egyptians as the Duat.[47] We have already seen how, during the Pyramid Age, the Memphite region where stand the great pyramid fields was regarded as the terrestrial counterpart of the Duat, and that Giza is to be correlated to the 'Fifth Division' or 'Fifth House' of the Duat known as the 'House of Sokar' in Rostau.[48] This mysterious place, as the Shabaka Stone and the Pyramid Texts inform us, was also supposed to contain the body of Osiris. So let us take a closer look at the so-called Fifth Division or House of the Duat and see what else it may reveal.

THE PLACE OF TRANSFIGURATION

The extensive funerary literature known as the 'Shat-ent-Am-Duat', which loosely translates as the 'Book of what is in the Duat', is found written on papyrus and also inscribed on the walls and ceilings of tombs

Fig. 9. The god Thoth recoding the weight of the heart.

from the New Kingdom (c.1500 BC) onward. A translation of this strange work, along with vignettes and illustrations, was published in 1905 by Wallis Budge in a three-tome work entitled *The Egyptian Heaven and Hell*. In this work Wallis Budge provides an excellent description of the Fifth Division or House of the Duat, along with a pictorial from one of the Rameside tombs in Thebes.[49] He notes, as Selim Hassan also did,[50] that the apotheosis of the whole transfiguration ritual of the deceased during his traumatic journey through the Duat takes place in the deepest and most central part of the afterworld topography, namely in the Fifth Division known as the House of Sokar in Rostau. In the pictorial of the Fifth 'Division' (see Fig. 10), we are shown a tunnel filled with water that leads, from east to west and rising uphill, towards a large sphinx whose hind parts are covered with sand. This sphinx, known as the 'Aker', seems to be protecting the entrance to a curious, elliptical chamber in which stands Sokar, here depicted as a hawk-headed man holding a pair of large wings belonging to a huge double-headed serpent. Behind and above this scene is seen a huge 'pyramid' or mound on top of which is a goddess's head, apparently that of Isis, and above the head is a sort of bell-shaped object flanked by two hawks or kites (see Fig. 11). According to historian and mathematician Livio Stechini,[51] this bell-shaped object is an omphalos, a sort of navel-shaped sacred stone similar to the one in Delphi (and at the oracle of Zeus-Ammon at the Egyptian oasis of Siwa). These stones, as the Orientalist and author Robert Temple showed in his fascinating book *The Sirius Mystery*, were often used by the ancients to denote important geodetic centres.[52] Many Egyptologists, including Selim Hassan as we have seen earlier, have noted the uncanny similarity of the Fifth Division of the Duat with the Giza necropolis as seen from the south side of the Sphinx.[53]

We have seen how the Aker lion figure is identified with the Great Sphinx of Giza and also how in the Book of the Two Ways[54] it is said that 'the Highland of Aker' (the Giza plateau) is the 'Dwelling Place of Osiris'.[55] It is thus self evident that there is an inseparable link between the 'House of Sokar', the 'Dwelling or Burial place of Osiris' and the

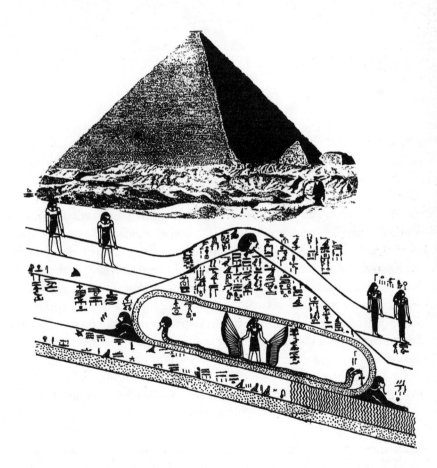

Fig. 10. The 'Fifth Division' of the Duat, i.e. The House of Sokar at the centre of the Duat. Note the giant Sphinx-like Aker guarding the entrance of the hermetically sealed capsule located under the 'pyramidal-mound'. Compare this symbolic imagery with the Great Sphinx and Great Pyramid profile seen from the south-east.

Fig. 11. The House of Sokar in the 5th hour-division of the Duat. Note the omphalos on top of the pyramid flanked by two birds. The falcon-headed god Sokar is standing with the hermetically sealed room spanning the wings of the multi-headed serpent. The sealed room is protected by the Aker Lions facing the east and west.

region of 'Rostau'. It is also evident that all these supposedly mythical locations were in some mysterious way to be associated with the Giza necropolis in a time frame known as the 'First Time' and which, interestingly, was also often said to be the 'Time of Osiris'[56]. In a detailed study of the ancient Egyptian Book of the Two Ways, Egyptologist and archeo-astronomer Jane B. Sellers discussed yet another important aspect of Rostau, and points to the fact that certain statements in those scriptures strongly indicate that 'Rostau' is somehow to be sought in the night sky:

> I have travelled by the roads of Rostau on water and on land . . . these are the roads of Osiris and they are in the sky . . . [57]

As the above passage indicates, the ways to Rostau are to be imagined in the sky and also on 'water' and on 'land'. For example, in the Coffin Texts (c.2000 BC) we read that:

> I shall not be turned back at the gates of the Duat. I ascend to the sky with Orion . . . I am one who collects for himself his efflux in front of Rostau . . .[58]

I am Osiris, I have come to Rostau in order to know the secret of the Duat . . . I have come equipped with magic, I have quenched my thirst with it, I live on white emmer, filling the Winding Waterway . . .[59]

. . . on the day of concealing the mysteries of the deep place in Rostau . . . I am he (Osiris) who sees the the secret things in Rostau . . . O you who open up ways and open up paths for the perfected souls in the House of Osiris . . .[60]

. . . Sokar . . . (is) happy and content when (he) sees that this mansion of mine is founded among the waters . . . while Sokar belongs to Rostau . . .[61]

I will recite the words of those whose places are secret, who are in Rostau . . .[62]

I have passed over the paths of Rostau, whether on water or on land, and these are the paths of Osiris; they are at the limit of the sky . . .[63]

The paths are in confusion . . . it is those who know them who will find (their way) their path; they are high on the flint walls which are in Rostau, which is both on water and on land . . .[64]

Perhaps the most mysterious, evocative and revealing reference to Rostau and what it meant to the ancient Egyptians is found in spell 1087 of the Coffin Texts:

This is the word which is in darkness. As for any spirit who knows it, he will live among the living. Fire is about it, which contains the efflux of Osiris. As for any man who shall know it, he will never perish there, since he knows what shall be in Rostau. Rostau is hidden since he fell there, for he is one who has come down from upon the desert, *and he possesses writing material* . . . Rostau is (another name) for Osiris. As for any man who is there, he will see Osiris every day, his breath will be in his nose, and he will never die . . .

Let us now return to Jane Sellers' thesis on Rostau. In order to make cogent sense of the notion that there is a place called Rostau in the celestial landscape, Sellers proposed that the most likely explanation for such a celestial journey to reach Rostau on 'water' was that the ancient priests who composed these texts were referring to the region of the sky we know today as the Milky Way. There are, in fact, in the Pyramid Texts as well as the Coffin Texts and the Book of the Dead, many allusions to a large celestial waterway invariably called the 'Winding Waterway' or, simply, the 'Waterway'. We have previously shown in *The Orion Mystery* how this was imagined to be the celestial 'Nile' and was identified with the shimmering band of stars we call the Milky Way.[65]

The celestial Rostau, therefore, was imagined to be located somewhere near the Milky Way. But where exactly?

Giza, the earthly Rostau, is located on the west bank of the River Nile. Thus by transposition, we can deduce that the celestial Rostau is a region of the starry sky on the west 'bank' of the Milky Way. Furthermore Giza, as expounded in *The Orion Mystery* and *Keeper of Genesis*, is a counterpart of a portion of the sky near the Milky Way which contains Orion, Sirius and the constellation of Taurus and Leo.[66] Everything thus strongly points to the idea that we are invited to consider this celestial region as a sort of 'guide map' – one, perhaps, that may lead us to the 'tomb' or 'burial place' of Osiris. Could the mysterious 'House of Sokar', which reputedly contained the 'efflux' of Osiris, also be marked on this 'star map'?

STARS AND SIGNS

There is a great paradox in Egyptology that so far has not been properly explained. Although the earliest reference to Osiris is found in the Pyramid Texts which date from c.2300 BC, a cursory study reveals that the mythology, doctrines, liturgy and rituals which they contain could not possibly have developed overnight, but would have required a long process of intellectual and religious evolution long before that date. Although all Egyptologists seem to agree to this, none can agree, however, on how long before that date this process would have begun. A tentative date of around 6000 BC was suggested by Jane B. Sellers on astronomical grounds, but an even earlier date of around 10,500 BC also based on astronomical considerations is, in my opinion, more likely.[67] Furthermore, the Egyptologists are also at a loss to explain why in the large quantities of inscriptions that predate the Pyramid Texts, not one single mention of Osiris has been found.[68] It is as if the cult of Osiris, with its rituals, doctrines, liturgies and mythology, suddenly materialised out of nowhere and, almost overnight, was readily adopted as the principal religion of the pharaonic state. Faced with this paradox, Dr I.E.S. Edwards argues:

> In remote antiquity, before the union of Upper and Lower Egypt under Menes (i.e. prior to c. 3300 BC), Osiris had been probably first the king and then the local god of the ninth lower Egyptian Nome with its capital at Busiris. Subsequently his influence spread until he became the chief god of a group of Nome's in the eastern Delta . . . Horus, later regarded as the son of Osiris, was at this time a completely independent god, ruling a group of Nome's in the

western Delta. Isis, who figures in Pyramid times as the wife of Osiris, seems also to have been a Delta goddess, but nothing is known with certainty about her origin. After the cult of Osiris became linked with that of Horus, its influence began to extend southwards until, by Pyramid times, *Osiris had become identified with Sokar* (my italics), the god of the Memphite necropolis . . .[69]

Even if such views are accepted, they still do not explain how the cult of Osiris was integrated so swiftly into the religion of the state. Something surely must have happened to cause the Pyramid kings to adopt it with so much conviction and zeal. An analogy can perhaps be drawn with the events that fired the Hebrews in Palestine during the time of Jesus. Around the end of the first century BC there was a widespread and fervent expectation for the coming of the messiah as foretold in the Scriptures. A new 'star' appeared in the east, which was interpreted as a sign of a divine birth. Prophets such as John the Baptist began to proclaim the imminent coming of this messiah. Finally the appearance of Jesus during a baptism ritual by John the Baptist in the Jordan River triggered the belief that the prophecies had been fulfilled and thus prepared the way for Christians.

Was the sudden introduction of the Osirian cult the result of a similar 'messianic' display of stars and signs?

SYMBOL OF THE RETURNING MESSIAH

Egyptologists tend to agree that whatever else it was that launched the Egyptians of the Old Kingdom into a frenzy of pyramid building, it had much to do with a mysterious relic kept in a small temple at Heliopolis.[70] Known originally as Ounu or Anu (the biblical On), Heliopolis was the major religious centre of Egypt – and probably the known world – during the Pyramid Age. Although it is generally accepted that Heliopolis long predated the Pyramid Age, how long before is the subject of much debate among researchers.[71] From various ancient texts Egyptologists have deduced that in the city of Heliopolis there had existed a small temple known as 'the temple of the Phoenix' in which was housed a cult object known as the 'Benben'. The oldest reference to this mysterious object is found in the Pyramid Texts:

O Atum-Khoper (the rising sun), you became high on the heights, you rose up as the Benben-Stone in the mansion (temple) of the 'Phoenix' (Bennu) in On (Heliopolis) . . . O Atum, set your arms (the sunshine) about this king (the dead, mummified king), about this construction, about this pyramid . . . that the king's essence may be in it, may endure forever . . . O Atum, set your protection over this king, over this pyramid of his, over this construction of his, prevent anything from happening evilly against it for ever . . . O Horus (the son of the king), this king is Osiris, this pyramid of the king is Osiris, this construction of his is Osiris, betake yourself to it . . . [72]

The phoenix, called the 'Bennu' by the ancient Egyptians, was said to have been a magical fire-bird that had alighted on the 'primeval mound of creation' at the beginning of time. By uttering the first cry or 'Word', the phoenix had set in motion 'time' and the 'new age'. As R.T. Rundle Clark explains:

Underlying all Egyptian speculation is the belief that time is composed of recurrent cycles which are divinely appointed: the day, the week of ten days, the month, the year – even longer periods – determined according to the conjunctions of sun, moon, stars and inundation. In a sense when the Phoenix gave out the primeval call it initiated all these cycles, so it is the patron of all divisions of time, and its temple at Heliopolis became the centre of calendrical regulation. As the herald of each new dispensation, it becomes, optimistically, the harbinger of good tidings. During the Middle Kingdom the Bennu Bird became the 'soul' of Osiris . . . [73]

Clark also expounds on the place of origin of the Bennu-Phoenix and its strange connection with Heka, the 'vital essence' of the gods[74]:

The Egyptians had two ideas about the origins of life. The first was that it emerged in God out of the Primeval Waters; the other was that the vital essence – Heka – was brought hither from a distant magical source. The latter was the 'Isle of Fire', the place of everlasting light beyond the limits of the world, where the gods were born and revived and whence they were sent into the world. The Phoenix is the chief messenger from this inaccessible land of divinity . . . So the Phoenix came from the far-away world of eternal life . . . to land, at last, in Heliopolis, the symbolic centre of the earth where it will announce the new age . . . [75]

Thus the 'call' of the phoenix to 'announce the new age' was made through the power of Heka[76] and it is that 'call' or 'Word' that brought light and life to the world. First there was the 'Word', then the 'Light' and then finally 'Life'. Interestingly, there is a passage in the Coffin Texts which has the soul of the deceased proclaiming:

I come from the *Isle of Fire*, having filled my body with Heka, like that Bird (the Bennu-Phoenix) who came and filled the world with that (Heka-magic) which it had not known . . . [77]

It is thus from the 'Isle of Fire' that the 'magic' came, 'brought hither' to our world by the agency of the Bennu-Phoenix bird.[78] But what exactly did the Bennu-Phoenix bring to the world at the moment of creation? What could have been its precious cargo? A clue, perhaps, may be found the *Histories* of Herodotus:

> They (the Heliopolitan priests) tell a story about this bird which I personally find incredible: the Phoenix is said to come from Arabia (east), carrying the (dead) parent bird encased in myrrh; it proceeds to the temple of the sun (Heliopolis) and there buries the body. In order to do this, they say it first forms a ball as big as it can carry, then, hollowing out the ball, it inserts its dead parent, subsequently covering the aperture with fresh myrrh. The ball is then exactly the same weight as it was at first. The Phoenix bears the ball to Egypt, all encased as I have said, and deposits it in the temple of the sun . . . [79]

Although Herodotus's account is probably a somewhat obscured version of the original Egyptian myth, it very likely follows the essential outline, and from this account, along with snippets from the Pyramid Texts, Coffin Texts and other Egyptian religious writings, we can piece together a coherent image of that magical bird – Bennu or phoenix – and its role in the creation myth of ancient Egypt. The 'ball' that the phoenix 'deposits in the temple of the sun' at Heliopolis which Herodotus reports is almost certainly an allusion to the magical substance, the 'Heka', that the Bennu brought to Egypt from that faraway mythical land of the gods called the 'Isle of Fire' (i.e. the 'Arabia' of Herodotus, that is the land in the east). The placing of the 'dead parent' in the 'ball' followed by the sealing with myrrh is also very reminiscent of the sealing of the casing or coffin of a swathed mummy (the dead parent) with similar glue-like substances. There is, too, much in the ancient Egyptian texts that implies that the Benben Stone was also seen as a 'cosmic egg' which was brought to Egypt in cycles by the phoenix after long periods of absence for the purpose of 'hatching' a new cosmic age.[80] At any rate, when we equate all this to the 'mound of creation' upon which the phoenix alights, we are provided with an even more complex and powerful symbolism that needs careful elucidation. For as R.T. Rundle Clark points out:

> The appearance of Atum . . . on the Primeval Mound was not the only way of expressing the first event (of creation), even in Heliopolis. Since the waters (the primordial sea) were in absolute darkness the emergence of God meant the coming of light, the first morning. For the Heliopolitan morning was marked by the shining of light on an erect pillar or pyramidion on a support which could reflect the rays of the rising sun. At the beginning a light-bird, the Phoenix, had alighted on the sacred stand. Known as the Benben, to initiate the great age of

the visible God (the sun). The rising of the Mound and the appearance of the Phoenix are not consecutive events but parallel statements, two aspects of the supreme creative moment . . . Creation was also repeated in the rebirth of the soul (of Osiris) after death and provided theme in the installation ceremonies of the kings. In fact most solemn religious rites derived their power or authority from the pretence that they were in some way a return to the original event of creation. The temple which enclosed the Benben Stone was the centre of calendrical rites as well as the scene of the rising of the High God. It was the place where the mysteries of creation were ceremoniously repeated . . .[81]

As we shall now see, all these powerful ideologies brought together by the symbol of the Benben Stone are intimately related to the idea of a monumental pyramid or, more precisely, to the act of placing *a gilded capstone upon its apex*. It is when we fully appreciate this fact that the true significance of the Benben and its relation to the 'Mound of Creation' become clear. But how can the cosmic attributes of the phoenix and the opening of a new age be related to the Benben *and* the Pyramid?

THE 'PYRAMID' THAT FELL FROM HEAVEN

In 1989 I published an article in the Oxford periodical *Discussions in Egyptology* in which I reviewed the nature and origin of the Benben Stone and its powerful connection with the pyramid cult.[82] I was aware at the time that various depictions of the Benben Stone seen in the many vignettes of the Book of the Dead showed that this object was shaped like a cone or *pyramid*.[83] Also there had been hints by the Egyptologists Wallis Budge and Jean-Philippe Lauer that the Benben Stone was likely to have been a sacred meteorite akin to the so-called 'Black Stone' of the Muslims kept encrusted on the wall of the Ka'ba shrine at Mecca in Saudi Arabia.[84] Such clues provided me with the basis for my own investigation into this strange object. I discovered that most meteorites are composed of almost pure iron, containing only a small percentage of nickel and almost imperceptible traces of other elements such as zinc and carbon. There is, however, a rare variety of large meteorites known as 'oriented meteorites' which attracted my attention: these were *shaped like pyramids*! This was because such meteorites, due to the uniform direction of flight as they plunge through the earth's atmosphere, have the front moulded by the frictional heat causing them to be shaped like a cone or pyramid. An excellent example of such a meteorite is the one known as 'Willamette' displayed at the Smithsonian Institute in New York.

Another very good example is 'Morito' displayed at the Institute of Metallurgy in Mexico City.[85] Bearing in mind this and the iron composition of these meteorites, I was naturally very intrigued to find out that in the Pyramid Texts there were numerous references to the 'bones' of the dead kings being made of a substance called 'bja' which Egyptologists translated as 'iron':

> I am pure, I take to myself my iron bones, I stretch out my imperishable limbs . . .[86]

> My bones are iron and my limbs are the imperishable stars . . .[87]

> the (dead) king's bones are iron, and his limbs are the imperishable stars . . .[88]

Now equating the 'bones' of dead kings to 'iron' does not make much sense until one realises that the transfigured body of a departed monarch was imagined to become a 'star':

> The king is a star . . .[89]

> The king appears as a star . . .[90]

> Behold, the king arises as this star . . .[91]

> [O king] . . . be a soul like a living star . . .[92]

> I [the king] am a soul . . . I am a star of gold . . .[93]

We shall return to the significance of this later in the chapter.

Even today, the streaking of a meteorite across the dark sky is often referred to as a 'falling star' or 'shooting star'. Now the phoenix – and thus by extension the Benben Stone – was often identified with the 'soul' of Osiris and the 'soul' of Osiris was, in turn, identified with the constellation of Orion.[94] It is reasonable to conclude that the Benben Stone was, among other things, symbolic of the 'star-soul' of Osiris – and, perhaps more specifically, Osiris's cyclical return as the 'phoenix' to mark the opening of a new age. Interestingly, Egyptologists also agreed that it was probably the pyramidal-shaped Benben Stone which had inspired the actual design of monumental pyramids and, more specifically, the shape of the capstones or pyramidions that were commonly placed on their summit.[95] By extension, therefore, these capstones could thus be regarded as being symbolic of the star 'soul' of

79

Osiris. Furthermore, in the Pyramid Texts there appears to be no distinction between the deceased king and the god Osiris. It is as if these two entities had merged into one. Thus, for example, in the texts-bearing Pyramids of the pharaohs Unas, Pepi or Teti their names are always compounded with that of Osiris as 'this king Osiris-Unas', 'this king Osiris-Pepi' and so on. Indeed, the compounded name of Osiris with the dead king is intermingled with the Pyramid itself, as if to tell us that all three entities are to be regarded as one and the same thing:

> . . . this king (Unas) is Osiris, this pyramid of the king (Unas) is Osiris, this construction of this king (Unas) is Osiris . . .[96]

The conclusion was unavoidable: the capstones, once placed on top of monumental pyramids, were to be regarded not only as representative of the Benben Stone and the phoenix but, in their deeper layer of symbolism, they were also meant to evoke the idea of the astral 'soul' of Osiris and his cyclical return to the world to announce a new age. Furthermore, Egyptologists such as I.E.S. Edwards had deduced that these mysterious capstones were almost certainly covered with gold leafing. In his book *The Pyramids of Egypt*, Dr Edwards brings to our attention an inscription found by French Egyptologist Gustave Jequier at the pyramid of Queen Udjebten which 'refers to the gilded capstone of her pyramid'.[97] This would suggest, wrote Edwards, 'that these stones were, at least sometimes, overlaid with gold'.[98] It is thus not surprising that the Pyramid Texts not only stated that the 'bones' of the astral king were made of iron, but that his flesh was made of 'gold', i.e. *covered in gold*:

> O king, raise yourself upon your iron bones and golden members, for this body of yours belongs to a god; it will not grow mouldy, it will not be destroyed, it will not putrefy . . .[99]

Such a description is clearly a metaphor for the sight of a royal mummy encased in its golden, human-shaped coffin. A wonderful example of such a king with 'flesh of gold' is, of course, that of the boy-king Tutankhamun which today can be seen at the Museum of Egyptian Antiquities in Cairo. Adorned in this manner the dead king's body was deemed to be transfigured into that of a god.[100] By equating such symbolism to the statement in the Pyramid Texts which reads 'I am a soul . . . a star of gold',[101] then it can be deduced that the reappearance or 'return' of 'the soul of Osiris', i.e. the phoenix, *was enacted by the actual*

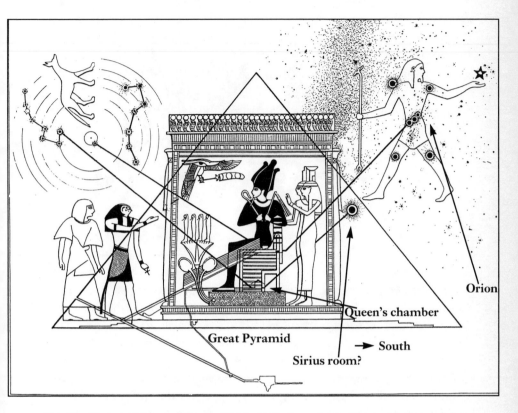

Fig. 12. Allegorical drawing showing Osiris on his throne in the King's chamber and the southern shaft of the Queen's chamber passing between the thighs of Isis.

placing of a gilded capstone on the 'mound of creation' – the latter, I believe, being either the actual mound at Heliopolis or the Great Pyramid of Giza.

One of the best surviving examples of such a symbol is the capstone or pyramidion of Amenemhet III (c. 1800 BC) which is today displayed in the central hall of the Antiquities Museum in Cairo. This capstone was intended for Amenemhet's pyramid at Dashour, located some twenty-eight miles south of Giza. It was discovered in 1902 by Gaston Maspero.[102] Cut as perfect as a diamond from a single piece of black granite, it weighs a staggering four tonnes. In April 1995 I had the opportunity to take along with me to the Cairo Museum Robert McKenty, a Canadian researcher.[103] Robert had brought along a high-quality steel rule that could highlight errors in flatness of surfaces down to a fraction of a millimetre. As we placed the instrument all over the sculpture, hardly any variation could be recorded: the stone, amazingly,

Fig. 13. Osiris on his throne receiving the Eye of Horus on the Mound-Pyramid of Creation. The god Sokar lies inside the Mound-Pyramid receiving the solar energy from the summit. The symbols of north and south flank the mound.

seemed to be 'machine-polished' to perfection.[104] Such meticulous, almost obsessive, craftsmanship was suggestive that the stone had been so prepared in order to receive a thin metallic surface, in this particular case probably gold sheeting. Interestingly, the 'Benben' of Amenemhet III has two large 'eyes' carved on one of its sides. The inscriptions below the 'eyes' and at the bottom of the pyramidion do not make clear whether these are to be regarded as the 'eyes' of the sun-god Ra, or those of Osiris.[105] Egyptologists are generally of the opinion that they belong to the former.[106] This, in my view, is probably incorrect. There are many other reasons, as we shall soon see, to show that the 'eyes' on the Benben should be allocated not to Ra but to Osiris or, to be more specific, to the 'soul of Osiris'.

THE EYE AND THE IRON THRONE OF OSIRIS

There is a great deal of debate and confusion concerning the etymology of the name Osiris and the mysterious symbols attached to it. It may surprise the reader to learn that the name is not Egyptian but Greek. The true and original name of the god in its most ancient form was As-Ar or Ausar, composed by two hieroglyphic signs of the 'throne' and the 'eye'.

It is only much later, around 500 BC or so, that the Greeks gave it its classical pronounciation. The 'throne' almost certainly symbolises the 'throne of Osiris' or, more generally, the 'throne of divine kingship' – and in its other-worldly connotation, it may also stand for the 'throne of Osiris in the Duat'. Such a conclusion conforms with the role and function of Osiris as 'Lord of the Duat' and, at any rate, is confirmed by the many depictions in funerary art showing Osiris sitting on a throne in the so-called 'Judgement scene' where the god dispatches his verdict on the souls of the dead. There is an interesting variation of this depiction, however, in which Osiris is seen sitting on his throne placed on the summit of a pyramid or mound (see Fig. 13).[107] Concerning this last, Rundle Clark had this to say:

> In this version (depiction) the central object is a mound which is approached by steps. Inside is either the recumbent figure of Osiris *or a figure which represents him* illumined by the night sun during its underworld journey. The stepped hill is, of course, the Primeval Mound, but this time it is given directions. The goddesses of North and South, and sometimes signs for East and West, decorate the outside of the steps . . . .Above the mound Osiris sits enthroned, protected sometimes by a goddess, and approached by Horus and Thoth and a peculiar being carrying two stiff serpents arranged in an X. The first god (Horus) to approach Osiris presents him with the Horus Eye – the old motif of the recovery of Osiris which is as old as the Pyramid Texts . . . The figure with the crossed serpents is probably the Divine Word . . .[108]

One of the most potent symbols of ancient Egypt is the *Udjet* sign, which is depicted by an 'eye'. So ingrained was this symbol that it has survived to this day, generally used as a talisman to ward off evil and danger.[109] Although the term *Udjet* is of the feminine gender, the 'eye' is that of a falcon and is clearly associated with primitive falcon gods such as Horus and Sokar.[110] In his detailed study of the *Udjet* symbol, R.T. Rundle Clark shows that the 'eye' was also associated with the sun and the moon that represented the two eyes of the cosmic falcon.[111] Since one of these 'eyes', the moon, wanes and waxes in a cycle of one month, the ancients used numerical fractions of the value one to design the Udjet symbol; the act of 'putting together' the Udjet-eye symbolised the return of the full moon which, according to Clark, signalled the idea 'that all is well' and that 'Maat', the cosmic order, is undisturbed[112]:

> I am seeking the Eye of Horus, that I might bring it back and count it . . . I am Thoth who brings back Maat . . . I am he who returns the Udjet Eye, I am he who abolishes its dimness, when its brightness was damaged . . . in the House of the Moon . . . [113]

Egyptian literature is full of references to the 'bringing back of the Eye'. This strange motif, for example, is repeated no less than four hundred times in the spells and incantations of the Pyramid Texts and many scores more throughout the whole corpus of these ancient texts. The thematic myth associated with the 'eye of Horus' revolves around an epic battle that supposedly took place between Horus and his uncle Seth, with these two deities quarrelling over the throne of Osiris. After a raging fight that went on for several years, Horus lost his left eye and Seth lost his testicles.[114] The battle finally ends when Thoth intervenes and persuades the contenders to put their case for arbitration before the council of the gods, known sometimes as The Great Ennead.[115] The outcome is in favour of Horus, who is crowned as the first legitimate divine king of the Osirian Kingdom. As soon as his coronation is over, Horus journeys into the realm of the Underworld-Duat in search of the 'body' of his father, Osiris. He then presents to the listless body of Osiris the 'Eye', whence Osiris is immediately revived:

> O Osiris the king, I bring to you the Eye of Horus . . . O Osiris the king, Horus has put his Eye on your brow in its name of Great-of-Magic . . . Live, O my father Osiris the king, for I set for you the Eye of Horus on you.[116]

> O Horus who is (also) this Osiris the king, take the uninjured Eye of Horus. O Horus who is this Osiris the king, I paint it on your face for you, for Horus painted his uninjured Eye. O king, I attach your eyes to your face for you intact, so that you may see with them . . .[117]

> O my father the king, the doors of the sky are opened for you . . . stand up and see this, stand up and hear this which your son Horus has done for you: he smites him (Seth) who smote you . . .[118] . . . may you remove yourself to the sky upon your iron throne . . .[119]

> Stand up for me, O my Father; stand up for me, O Osiris the king, for I am indeed your son, I am Horus . . . I have installed you, of my father Osiris the king, upon the throne . . .[120]

In these passages from the Pyramid Texts we are thus provided with a potent link between the 'Eye' and 'Throne' symbols, both now merging with the resurrection or reawakening of Osiris in his tomb. Let us hold this strange imagery in our mind while we return to the depictions in Fig. 10 showing the Primeval Mound and the House of Sokar. In this depiction it is obvious that the throne is intended to represent the 'Benben' symbol, for it was the latter that was deposited by the Bennu-Phoenix on the summit of the original Primeval Mound when the new age was

Fig. 14. Pyramid texts. Note five-painted stars.

announced. And this imagery, of course, takes us to the monumental pyramids themselves, for as we have noted for many researchers including Dr I.E.S. Edwards the stepped pyramids of the third Dynasty were almost certainly representative of the Primeval Mound.[121] Indeed, the hieroglyphic sign of a stepped pyramid was often used to denote the Primeval Mound.[122] It is also known that the true, smooth-faced pyramids of the Fourth Dynasty, which include the Giza group, incorporated within their structural core a stepped pyramid, a fact that is very suggestive that they, too, were to be regarded as symbolic of the Primeval Mound.[123] In Fig. 13 showing the Primeval Mound on which Osiris is seated on the throne, the Mound itself is fixed along the four astronomical directions, again a strong clue that it is meant to represent a classical pyramid monument whose four sides were always aligned towards the four astronomical (or cardinal) directions. This notion is further strengthened by the analysis made by Dr Edwards for the word 'Mr', which stood for 'pyramid'. This word is formed by three signs, an 'eye-shaped' symbol, an 'owl' and a 'standard or post', all forming the phonetic word 'M(e)r'. Edwards showed that the determinative for the word 'r', which means 'to ascend', is, in fact, the sign to denote a stepped pyramid or Primeval Mound.[124] He then pointed out that the 'm' sign, which means 'place', has led him to conclude that the word 'Mer', therefore, could mean 'the place of Ascension'.[125] Now it is unquestioned that the only physical objects that could literally be said to have 'ascended' to the summit of monumental pyramids were, of course, the Benben pyramidions, the symbols of the astral 'soul' of the transfigured Osiris-king. Thus in Fig. 13 we have the symbols of Osiris (or his 'soul'), the 'eye' and the 'throne', all meeting together at the summit of the Primeval Mound or pyramid – which should now make it clear to us that, on the one hand, the symbol of a Benben Stone with the Eye, especially when placed on the top of the 'Primeval Mound' or Pyramid, is fully interchangeable with, on the other hand, the symbol of 'the throne with the eye' – the latter forming the name of Osiris. Algebraically then, Benben with Eye = Throne with Eye = Osiris.

The reader is now asked to recall how, in the Pyramid Texts, the original Benben Stone was said to be made of iron ('star' matter, i.e. meteoritic iron). It is, therefore, very significant to note that in the Pyramid Texts the 'throne' of Osiris is frequently said to be made of 'iron', the same cosmic stuff from which the 'bones' of the astral souls were also made:

I [the Osiris-king] ascend to the sky . . . I sit on this iron throne of mine . . .[126]

May you [the Osiris-king] remove yourself to the sky upon your iron throne . . .[127]

You will ascend to the sky . . . you being seated upon your iron throne . . . you have traversed the Winding Waterway in the north of the sky as a star . . . the Duat has grasped your hand at the *place where Orion is* . . . (the celestial 'Giza'?)[128]

Now here is the consequence of all this: the idea of the returning phoenix coming to 'the place where Orion is' (i.e. the celestial Giza[129]) in order to announce a new messianic age is symbolised by the act of placing a capstone on top of a monumental pyramid. An idea, of course, that is also applicable to the return of a messianic figure at the opening of a new age which, in Christian lore, suggests similarities with the 'Second Coming' of Christ.

Fig. 15. Pyramid texts. Note 'throne and eye' name of Osiris compounded with the name of the pharaoh Unas (in the cartouche).

The reader will notice, however, that in Fig. 13 there is within the Pyramid/Mound itself another figure, that of a hawk-headed mummified man lying on its back. Rundle Clark described this mysterious entity as the 'recumbent figure of Osiris or a symbol which represents him'. But what symbol could that be? A clue is given by Wallis Budge in his description of the combined god Osiris-Sokar 'in which he appears as a hawk-headed mummy'.[130] There is, too, an almost identical recumbent hawk-headed figure depicted on the wall of the temple of Denderah in Upper Egypt which is also referred to as Sokar-Osiris of Busiris[131] (see Fig. 8). Here we see Sokar-Osiris lying on a catafalque or bed the base of which is shaped like the Aker lion; on one side of the bed stands the goddess Isis, and on the other side Nephtys.[132] It is clear that by equating this imagery to the statement made in the Shabaka Stone quoted on page 66 we get, in fact, the very same imagery in words.

Bearing all this in mind, let us now compare Fig. 1 showing the Fifth Division and the House of Sokar with Fig. 10 showing the stepped pyramid/Mound and Osiris on his throne. In Fig. 13 we see the god Sokar holding the plumes of the giant serpent in the House of Sokar surmounted by a Pyramid/Mound, and in Fig. 13 we see the same entity lying within or under a stepped-pyramid/Mound. The 'Mound' in Fig. 13 is, as Rundle Clark pointed out, a representation of the 'Creation Mound'. But what of the 'Mound' in Fig. 10? Let us examine this

87

'Mound' more closely. At the top of the Mound in Fig. 10 are two symbols, one a human head and the other a bell-shaped object (identified, as we have seen earlier, as an omphalos or sacred geodetic marker) which is flanked by two kites.[133] The two kites, according to Egyptologist George Hart, symbolise the goddesses Isis and Nephtys[134] – again a pictorial depiction of what is in the Shabaka text. Rundle Clark explains further by saying that the omphalos-shaped object is yet another hieroglyphic sign to denote the Primeval Mound.[135] As for the human head that crowns the Pyramid/Mound, the hieroglyphic texts that accompany it state that this is 'the flesh of Isis who is above the sand of the land of Sokar'.[136] Now the name of Isis, like that of Osiris, is a Grecian derivative. The true name of the goddess in the ancient Egyptian language is Ast, which in its oldest form was written with two signs, one of which was a 'throne'. We can now see that the 'throne' of Isis, the omphalos-shaped object and the 'throne' and 'eye' of Osiris all merge in the complex symbolism of the Primeval Mound and, by extension, also of the original Benben/Pyramidion capstone. The star *sirius*, as we shall see later, is also representative of Isis, and could also be interchanged with these symbols at the top of the 'Mound'. But there is more. according to George Hart again, the Pyramid/Mound is representative of the desert 'tomb of Osiris', i.e. the 'burial place of Osiris' in the 'House of Sokar' in Rostau (i.e. Giza).[137] it thus follows that the stepped-pyramid/Mound in which lies the recumbent hawk-headed figure is representative of the 'tomb of Osiris-Sokar' at giza. As for the huge recumbent sphinx called Aker which protects this 'tomb', we have already seen how many agree that it represents the Great Sphinx of Giza (i.e. Rostau). The overall conclusion is thus inevitable: the Egyptians, from the earliest of times, believed that somewhere underneath the bedrock of Giza, and more specifically somewhere underneath the area where the Great Sphinx stands, was to be found the 'tomb of Osiris'.

Intriguingly, however, all these depictions and interchanging symbols are also extremely suggestive that this tomb is in the form of a pyramidal structure or 'Mound'. Could it not be that the various connections between the 'throne of Isis', the idea of a 'star' and the symbol of the Benben may, in themselves, also point to *another* secret chamber concealed within the core of the Great Pyramid or Simon Cox's 'Mound'? We shall review the evidence which leads to such an exciting conclusion for the Great Pyramid later on. Meanwhile the reader should also bear in mind that we shall also later see how [1] the goddess Isis was herself identified with the star Sirius whose hieroglyphic name, 'Sept', is composed of the signs denoting a Benben and a 'five-pointed star'; [2]

how the Benben and the five-pointed star meet up in the 'missing' capstone of the Great Pyramid of Giza; and [3] how the southern shaft of the Queen's Chamber in the Pyramid was not only directed to Sirius but that at its end, two hundred feet deep into the heart of the Pyramid, lies a small 'door' which many believe could lead to a secret chamber.

In the meantime I was faced with a web of tantalising and complex ideas which although they were floating next to each other in my mind, nonetheless lacked that catalyst I needed to bring them together. Yet at the same time I could not shake off the strong feeling that here, in this strong brew of symbols, was the rudiments of an arcane 'message' which, like the proverbial X on a treasure map, seemed to mark the location of the Fifth Division of the 'Duat', i.e. the House of Sokar, somewhere in the Giza necropolis. As strange as it seemed, it was as if I was being 'guided' by the star Sirius whose rays, as it were, illuminated the deep and dormant recesses of my memory. But how could this be? Why did such strange and 'far out' ideas trouble my mind? And why, too, was I making an almost unconscious association of that star with the 'missing' capstone of the Great Pyramid? It did not make any sense. Yet to another side of my mind, a side that responded not with the limitation of the rational process but rather with the intuitive and creative faculties, it did seem to make 'sense'. Was I perhaps being made receptive, in some strange and inexplicable way, to some powerful subliminal message that was locked in the symbolic stellar lore of the ancient Pyramid builders and their cultic images? A 'message' which was not primarily intended for me or indeed for anyone else today, but had been long ago aimed at primed initiates of the Heliopolitan cult? Was I the unsuspecting victim – or beneficiary – of a devastatingly powerful Hermetic device?

It was at that point of impasse in my investigation that I suddenly remembered the so-called 'wider plan' of the star correlation theory presented in my first book, *The Orion Mystery*. In a section of that book termed 'Signpost to the Benben Stone', I had shown how the vast region which encompassed the Giza necropolis, the temple of Heliopolis and a third site known as the Khem (the Letopolis of the Greeks)[138] together defined over the landscape a huge 'Pythagorian' right-angled triangle (see Figs 16 and 19).[139] Let us note in passing that the name Khem is extremely reminiscent of the name 'Khemmis', the latter being the place on the west bank of the Nile in the Delta region where, according to Egyptian mythology, Isis gave birth to Horus.[140] I had also suggested that the three corners of this 'Pythagorian' triangle were probably specifically and deliberately marked by [1] the apex of the Great Pyramid; [2] the apex of the Heliopolitan 'Mound' (the Benben); and [3] the apex of a

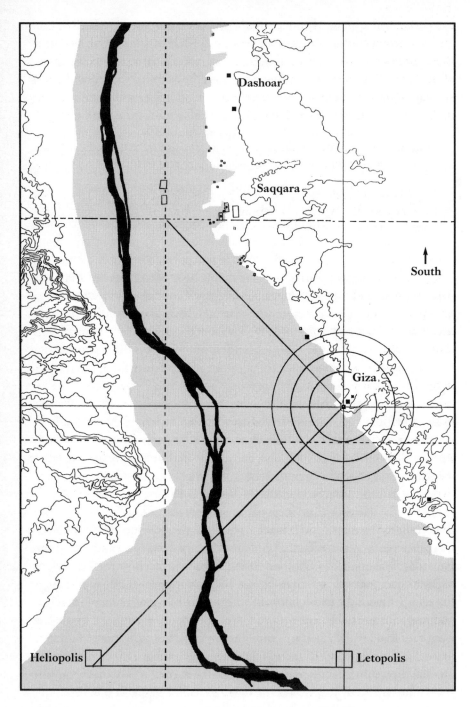

*Fig. 16. Schematic map of the Mephite necropolis 'The Land of Sokar'
with main geodetic point marked by the Giza site.*

tower that had apparently once stood at Khem-Letopolis.[141] Much in this curious geometrical arrangement was suggestive that the link between these three sites provided a sort of giant 'signpost' that led to the entrance of the Great Pyramid and, ultimately, through the narrow shafts shooting skywards toward 'the place where Orion is' which the Pyramid Texts tell us is where the 'gates of the Duat', i.e. Rostau, could to be found[142]:

> I shall not be turned back at the gates of the Duat. I ascend to the sky with Orion . . . I am one who collects for himself his efflux in front of Rostau . . .[143]

> You will ascend to the sky . . . you being seated upon your iron throne . . . you have traversed the Winding Waterway in the north of the sky as a star . . . the Duat has grasped your hand at the place where Orion is . . .[144]

In this ground plan, furthermore, I had shown how the Great Pyramid itself represented a star in Orion's belt, Zeta Orionis, and how Khem-Letopolis probably represented the corresponding position of the star Sirius near the west banks of the Milky Way.[145] With these thoughts in mind, I also recalled a statement made by the French Egyptologist George Goyon in connection with the Great Pyramid which now, in the light of what has just been said, took on a new and eerie significance. 'The monument,' Goyon had written, 'was placed under the stellar protection of the god Horus . . .'[146] We shall see later how the 'star' of Horus was, in actual fact, also the star Sirius. Suffice at this stage to mention that in the ancient Pyramid Texts, as well as in all other religious literature of ancient Egypt, the stellar Horus was said to have been born from the 'womb of Sothis', the name given by the Greeks of Egypt to Isis-Sirius.[147] In *The Orion Mystery* there is an appendix entitled 'The Survival of the Star Religion' where I presented a detailed analysis on how in ancient Egyptian texts – such as the Carsberg I Papyrus, for example – the apparent nine-months (273 days) cycle of the star Sirius measured from its meridian passage was likened to the gestation cycle of the human foetus – which led me to conclude that the 'seeding of the womb of the goddess Sirius-Isis' mentioned in the Pyramid Texts was probably imagined to take place when Sirius was observed at the south meridian at dawn.[148] During the Pyramid Age this important event occurred, incidentally, some twenty days before the autumn equinox when the sun was right on top of the 'scales' of the zodiacal constellation of Libra.[149] The zodiacal constellation of Libra was almost certainly associated with the cosmic 'scales' often seen in funerary vignettes depicting the so-called Judgement Scene of the 'weighing of the heart' and where Osiris is shown seated upon his throne flanked by Isis and Nephtys.[150] The alignment of Sirius with the meridian axis of the Great Pyramid and also the southern shaft of the Queen's Chamber thus created a powerful sky-ground ritualistic setting for the 'seeding of the womb of Isis' with the embryo of the future Horus-king.[151] I thus postulated that this was a powerful king-making ritual which during the Pyramid Age may well have been enacted inside the Queen's Chamber of the Great Pyramid with an ithyphallic statue of the king (or perhaps even his mummy) placed in front of the opening of the southern shaft.[152] And it was this very shaft, as we have said, that led to a 'door' deep within the core of the Pyramid . . .

The probability for the existence of a secret chamber – or even a second one – at Giza, under the Sphinx or inside the Great Pyramid, is very high indeed. But assuming that secret chambers do exist at Giza, concealed there by the original builders of that site, then what would be their purpose? What cargo could be so precious, so obsessively important to preserve, which could induce a people to undertake such a vast and mind-boggling construction enterprise? What could possibly have been considered so valuable, so meaningful, so vitally necessary to posterity, to have it guarded by such a mighty memorial?

One word springs to mind: 'knowledge'. The knowledge of Thoth.

According to the most conservative estimates, there are 4500 years that separate us from the supposed construction of the Giza necropolis. Could the system of knowledge of those ancients who planned Giza have somehow survived through this immense period of time? And was it inscribed, as all the ancient texts suggest, on tablets and slabs by the hand of the god Thoth himself? Are these safely preserved in hermetically sealed rooms? And, more importantly, is there tangible or scientific evidence to verify such a hypothesis? Has anyone tried? Who? And what have they found?

Yet before we tackle these provocative questions, we need to see how a substantial portion of this legendary 'knowledge' might have been transmitted across the ages through another route – one so well concealed that it has hitherto escaped the attention of the Egyptologists and historians altogether. Concealed, I will suggest, in a 'place' that no one can reach with spade, scalpel or radar, but only through an initiatory process that the 'knowledge' was designed for. Because not all knowledge, as the ancient master initiates knew so well, is something that one merely recorded in books and inscriptions; rather, true knowledge was better 'deposited' in a much vaster crucible and far more sophisti-cated device at their disposal: *the memory of man.* As we shall now see, such powerful ideas may, indeed, have been preserved by inserting them, like some archaic intellectual microchip, deep into the body of new belief systems and promising religious and intellectual movements, in order for them to be carried forward through periods of danger and tribulations. And when the 'time was right and good', these ancient ideas could be reawakened from their millennial slumber.

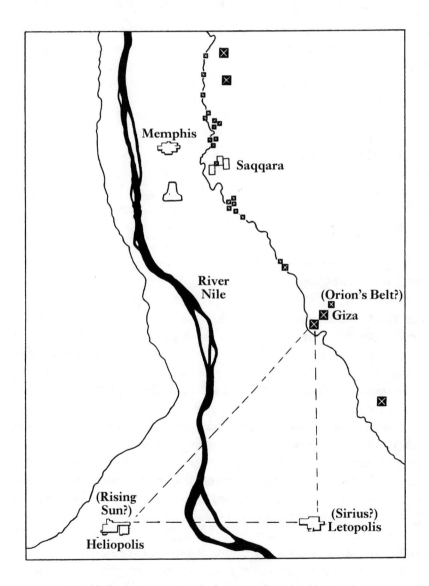

Fig. 17. Pythagorean triangle formed by Temple of Heliopolis, Temple of Letopolis and the Great Pyramid.

Chapter Five

The Knowledge

'The Kingdom of Heaven is within you . . .'

'The basis of this knowledge (Gnosis), the fundamental principles on which all the teachings rested, was the essential inherent divine nature of man, and the consequent possibility of becoming by self-knowledge a god-like being . . .'

William Kingsland[1]

IN THE BEGINNING

All tenets, doctrines, laws, beliefs, rituals, ceremonies, temples, pyramids, tombs – in short, the very foundations and edifices upon which the Pharaonic state and theocracy rested – were based on the immutable conviction that the king was permanently linked via his divine lineage to the distant golden age of the gods called Zep Tepi, The First Time.[2]

The notion of the First Time is a complex one. As far as the ancient Egyptians themselves were concerned, the First Time was emphatically believed to be an historical time during which the gods had lived on earth, when the life and passion of Osiris had taken place, and when the miraculous birth of Horus instigated the divine lineage of Pharaonic kingship. Thus the First Time was invariably known as the 'Time of Osiris' or the 'Time of Horus'. The principal tenets of the ancient temple cult and the Pharaonic state that administered it were that during this golden age of the gods a system of 'cosmic law' called Maat had been established by Osiris, and that it was the duty and function of his son Horus and all successive Horus-kings to ensure that Maat was upheld and kept unchanged throughout the ages. As the ancient texts proclaim:

Great is Maat, enduring is its effectiveness, for it has not been changed since the Time of Osiris (i.e. the First Time) . . .[3]

There is much speculation among scholars of religion and philosophy as to what exactly Maat was to the ancient Egyptians. Maat was personified by a winged-goddess on whose head was affixed a large plume or feather which, according to many researchers, symbolised 'Truth' or the 'lightness' of a truthful and righteous heart. Wallis Budge describes the goddess Maat as

. . . the personification of law, order, rule, truth, right, righteousness, canon, justice, straightness, integrity, uprightness and of the highest conception of physical and moral law known to the Egyptians.[4]

Perhaps the best way to perceive Maat is for it to be the combination of all these ethics which are encapsulated in the principle of 'Divine Truth', or simply 'Truth'. Maat, in short, is the 'code of practice' of the gods to which a human being must adhere in his earthly existence in order to progress towards a god-like state. Maat is that divine microchip within our heart that tells us what is right or wrong, and guides us through life in accordance with the Divine Will. Obey Maat, and you tread on the paths of godliness; ignore it or obey other 'laws' that in your heart you know are wrong, and you deviate from the divine path. However, Maat in itself was not sufficient for achieving immortality of the soul. It was merely the essential prerequisite to right of entry into the heavenly kingdom of Osiris. The deceased must first successfully overcome all the ordeals and tribulations which he had to face during his frightful journey through the Duat, and the road that leads to the court of Osiris. In order to do so, the deceased must be 'equipped', i.e. initiated, into that system of magical knowledge of Thoth known as Heka. It is Heka that gets the deceased through the Duat, and Maat that ensures his entrance to the heavenly kingdom of Osiris. Both Maat and Heka, in a sense, go hand in hand, and together provide the individual with both the *quality of character* and the *knowledge* to achieve immortality. Not surprisingly then, the goddess Maat is often said to be the companion or wife of Thoth.[5]

The apotheosis of the soul's journey through life and death is reached in the so-called Hall of Judgement of Osiris. Here, sitting on his cosmic throne, Osiris is presented with the spiritualised deceased after his journey through the Duat. This dramatic scene, also known as 'the weighing of the heart' ceremony, is beautifully depicted in the celebrated

Papyrus of Ani displayed in the British Museum (see Fig. 19).[6] On the far right of the scene is Osiris on his throne within an open shrine. He is wearing the white crown of kingship and the 'two plumes' of 'great magic', and holds the flail and crook, symbols of Pharaonic royalty. Behind him, standing in protection and adoration, are the goddesses Isis and Nephtys. In front of Osiris is an open lotus flower from which emerge the so-called 'four sons of Horus', the personification of the cardinal directions and who, in the Pyramid Texts, assist Osiris on his heavenly ascent into the starry world with their 'iron fingers'.[7] Outside, the shrine of Osiris is being brought by Horus a spiritualised dead person who has successfully passed the final tribulation of the 'weighing of the heart' and, consequently, is now entitled to meet the god and enter his heavenly kingdom. Further to the left of the scene is the god Thoth, standing upright with his hands holding a palette and a pen, and about to record the reading on a large set of scales manned by a priest with a jackal's mask. The scales symbolise Maat, whose image can be seen on the top of the vertical arm of the instrument. In one tray is the feather of Truth, and in the other the heart or essence of the deceased. Holding the symbol of life and rebirth in his hand, the god Anubis or Upuaut, the 'opener of the ways', brings in the next deceased whose heart is ready for weighing. Above the scene is a row of deities representing the forty-two judges that assist Osiris in his final verdict of who is and who is not worthy of entry into the heavenly realm.

Students of comparative religion have, quite naturally, drawn attention to the striking similarity of this process of attaining immortality of the soul with the doctrines and dogmas of Christianity. In the Bible, for example, a similar concept and system of cosmic order and divine law is encapsulated in the so-called Ten Commandments given to Moses on Mount Sinai. They are supposedly the righteous tenets that an individual must abide by in order to gain approval from God and, eventually, access to heavenly immortality. In the Canonical Gospels this is spelled out by Jesus in the so-called Sermon on the Mount.[8] But in order to explain his own intervention in the Divine Law, Jesus speaks further to the gathering of followers by saying:

> Do not suppose that I have come to abolish the Law and the Prophets; I did not come to abolish, but to complete. I tell you this: so long as heaven and earth endure, not a letter, not a stroke, will disappear from the Law until all that must happen has happened. If any man therefore sets aside even the least of the Law's demands, and teaches others to do the same, he will have the lowest place in the kingdom of heaven, whereas anyone who keeps the Law, and teaches others to do so, will stand high in the kingdom of heaven. I tell you, unless you show

Fig. 18. The Pharos Lighthouse of Alexandria (compared to George Washington Masonic Monument in Alexandria, Washington DC).

yourselves far better men than the Pharisees and the doctors of the law, you can never enter the kingdom of heaven.[9]

There is, however, a marked distinction between modern esoteric Christianity and the Osirian religion. In the Osirian religion, abiding by the Divine Law is not all that is required from the individual; the latter must also acquire 'knowledge' which is achieved through the process of initiation established by Thoth and set forth in his magical 'books'. Christianity demands not 'knowledge' but 'faith'. It is this that demarcates the fundamental difference, between the Church and the old Osirian religion as well as an early form of Christianity know as 'Gnosticism'.

The word 'gnosis' in Greek, the language of the early founding Church, simply means 'knowledge' or, in the context that it is applied here, 'knowledge of the Divine'.[10] In this respect it is extremely relevant to our line of investigation to realise that Gnosticism was born in Egypt, in those formative years when Christianity was dragging its heels in the wake of 3000 years of the Osirian religion that was still to prevail in that land until the fifth century AD. It is not the purpose or task of this book to go into the complex scholarship of Gnostic studies, but a brief overview is, at this stage, imperative to our investigation. However, let us begin by saying that the latest research shows that this early form of Christianity was rooted in the ancient mystery and initiatory religions of Egypt, Greece and the East, and that it was through Gnosticism that these ancient systems were carried across the ages to finally discharge themselves, albeit much mutated and distorted, in the modern mystery schools of Rosicrucianism and Freemasonry. In his comprehensive and rather daring study entitled *The Gnosis or Ancient Wisdom in the Christian Scriptures*, the scholar William Kingsland argues that:

> . . . the (Christian) scriptures are not always to be taken literally as biographies of the life of Christ but that they also contain allegorical and symbolical levels of meaning as well. The figure of Christ that emerges is not much one of a suffering saviour, pouring out his life's blood for the redemption of the world, but rather of a guide to the essential 'gnosis' that the 'kingdom of heaven lies within' . . .[11]

The crux of Kingsland's thesis is that the teachings of Jesus have much in common with other mystery religions associated with teachers such as Hermes Trismegistus, Buddha and Zoroaster, and that they also form part of a system of enlightenment involving initiation into the so-called Mysteries, and that the rudimentary basis of these secret ceremonies have survived today in the rituals of modern initiation societies such as the Freemasons.[12] In the author's own words:

> The existence of the ancient Mysteries in Egypt, Greece, and elsewhere is of course well-known as a matter of history; and many of the more esoteric ceremonies in connection with these have survived to this day in the rituals of Freemasonry and the Church itself . . . In all ages of which we have any literary records we find the tradition of a recondite knowledge which could not be disclosed to any save to those who had undergone the severest tests as to their worthiness to receive it. This knowledge was generally known under the term of the Mysteries, and it was concerned with the deepest facts of Man's origin, nature, and connection with super-sensual worlds of beings, as well as with the 'natural' laws of the physical world. It was no mere speculation; it was real knowledge, Gnosis, knowledge of 'the things that are', knowledge of Reality; a knowledge that gave its possessor powers which at one time or other have been regarded as pertaining only to the gods . . . The basis of that knowledge, the fundamental principle on which all the teachings rested, was the essential divine nature of man, and the consequent possibility of becoming, by self-knowledge, a

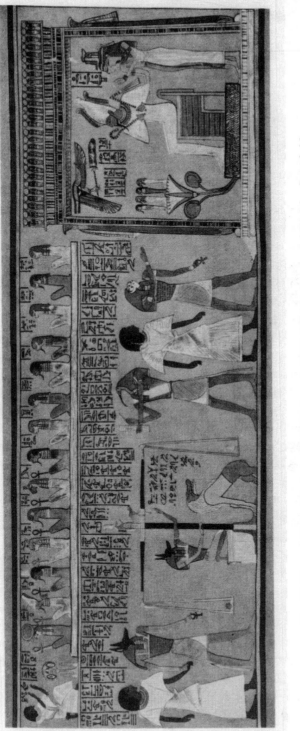

Fig. 19. The weighing of the heart in the Judgement Hall of Osiris. Papyrus of Hunifer, British Museum.

god-like being. The final goal, the final objective of all the Mysteries, was the full realisation by the initiate of his divine nature in its oneness with the Supreme Being . . .[13]

What exactly is Gnosticism? Where did it develop? Why did it disappear? And what connection could it have with our quest for the secret chamber at Giza?

THE SON OF GOD

In the winter of the BC, on a rocky limestone platform near the fishing hamlet of Rhakotis, on the Mediterranean coastline of Egypt, the exhausted army of Alexander the Great set camp. Here, Alexander had decided to raise a city in honour of the gods. Barely a few months before, he and his intrepid companions at arms had faced the 'invincible' Persian army on the narrow littoral of Issus in Syria and, against all the odds and rules of strategic warfare, Alexander had won the day.

It is said that the two armies had passed each other like ships in the night, and the next morning Alexander realised that he was on the wrong side of the narrow land strip, with no option of retreat and with his supply line cut off. He had no other recourse but to face the Persian army head on. Outnumbered by more than ten to one (40,000 on Alexander's side, 600,000 on the Persian side), Alexander had to come up with a daring strategy. He personally led a charge directly towards the Persian king. Riding at full gallop on his black horse Bucephalus, yelling fierce battle cries along with his companions, Alexander crossed the narrow river that separated him from the Persian army's left wing, broke through the archers and infantry, and headed for the chariot of Darius. In a moment of fear and panic, the Persian 'king of kings' turned his chariot and fled into the hills. Hearing of this, the Persian army lost its will to hold, and was virtually annihilated. Were it not for the hour of nightfall when this happened, Darius, too, would either have perished or been taken prisoner. As it turned out, he abandoned his heavy chariot, threw off his heavy armour, jumped on a horse and managed to escape. But the victory was total for Alexander. He was only twenty-three at the time.

News began to reach the corners of the known world that this young hero, with golden locks and piercing dark eyes, had become the ruler of the world. It was probably then that Alexander began to truly believe in his invincibility and, more importantly, in his own divinity. According to Plutarch, who wrote the biography of Alexander,[14] Olympias, the mother of the future conqueror, had been an Ipiriot princess who traced her descent from the Homerian hero, Achilles. A wild and mystical woman by nature, Olympias was appointed by her father as a priestess of the Oracle Temple of Zeus at Dodona, where she often partook in the orgiastic ceremonies of Dionysos, where snakes were used in strange sexual rituals. Dionysos (literally 'son of god' in Greek) was a hero–deity who had been born from the union of Zeus with a mortal, Semele. He was nursed by the nymphs of the mountains of Nysa, and when he reached manhood, travelled to Syria, Egypt, Asia and all the way to India teaching the secrets of wine cultivation and bringing civilisation to these regions of the world. Now the Oracle of Zeus at Dodona had a strange connection with Egypt. It was said that in far-off times, two black birds had flown out of the temple of Karnak in Upper Egypt, one alighting at the oasis of Siwa in the great western desert of Egypt and Libya, and the other reaching Dodona in Greece. There the twin oracles of Zeus and Ammon were founded. Plutarch reports that on her wedding night, Olympias dreamt that the thunderbolt of Zeus-Ammon had penetrated her womb and made her pregnant with Alexander. This was to have a profound effect on Alexander who, it is said, had inherited from his mother her strange and mystical nature. After the death of his father, Philip, in 336 BC, Alexander ascended the throne at the age of twenty-one. Twelve years later, when he died of a mysterious fever in Babylon, Alexander had conquered the whole known world of his epoch, and changed the course of history like no man had before or after him. Groomed and educated by Aristotle himself, Alexander was set to become the archetype of the philosopher-hero king and whom later many admirers, including Caesar, Louis XIV and even Napoleon, sought to imitate.

Plutarch, who consulted the work of earlier writers, said that Eratosthenes, the famous Alexandrian astronomer who was the first man to calculate the circumference of the earth in c. 255 BC,[15] reported that when Olympias sent forth Alexander on his epic expedition she revealed to him the secrets of his divine birth and how he was the seed of Zeus-Ammon, whose oracle centre was at Siwa.

Two years after the battle of Issus, Alexander made his triumphal entry into the land of the pharaohs. News of his arrival spread through the temples of Egypt and, more especially, to the priests of Ammon at the Oracle Temple of Siwa. Leaving his army on the site of the future Alexandria, and entrusting the plans of the new city to the architect Deinokratis, he assembled a small group of friends and set off for the oasis of Siwa. This journey was destined to enter history as one of the most mysterious and magical pilgrimages of all times. Among those who went with Alexander to Siwa were Ptolemy, future king of Egypt and founder of the enlightened Ptolemaic dynasty, and Callisthenes, the nephew of Aristotle. The journey, which involved going west along the Mediterranean coastline for 190 miles then cutting south and inland at Paraitonion, the modern Marsa Matruh, for another 190 miles to Siwa, would have taken at least two weeks. So arid and barren was this last stretch of desert that it is said that in c. 525 BC the Persian king Cambyse had lost a whole army of 50,000 men in a sandstorm in this area.[16]

In the spring of 1999, I finally took a trip to the fabled oasis of Siwa. Since my early teens, when we lived in Alexandria, I had always wanted to visit Siwa. In those days, in the early 1960s, it was quite common for young boys and girls of the cosmopolitan community of Alexandria to go in the summer months to Marsa Matruh, the small beach resort 190 miles west of Alexandria, and the site of the ancient Paraitonion where Cleopatra and Mark Antony had bathed in the wonderful blue lagoons that distinguished this enchanted place. There we would camp with the boy scouts and girl guides from the Alexandrian English, French, Italian and Armenian schools, and some of us would dream of going inland to the oasis of Siwa, another four hours' drive due south through the empty western desert. Lack of funds and the dangerous track that led to Siwa somehow prevented us from going. Now, in that warm week in April, all was in place for the journey.

I had been staying in Alexandria since November 1998 in order to research and write this book. Michele, my wife, and my children, Candice and Jonathan, had come for the Easter holidays, and were keen to see some desert landscape once again. Readers of *The Orion Mystery* will recall that my little family was with me in Saudi Arabia back in 1982, when the rudiments of the star-correlation theory were developed. Candice was three years old then, and Jonathan was not yet born. Since then we had lived short spells in Spain and Australia, to finally settle in England in 1989 in Buckinghamshire. There, in collaboration with Adrian Gilbert and Graham Hancock, I wrote *The Orion Mystery* (1994) and *Keeper of Genesis* (1996). For *Secret Chamber*, the last in this trilogy on Giza, I decided to write the book on location in Egypt. I rented a flat near the beach in Agami, a small resort just outside Alexandria, adopted two local mongrel dogs, Coco and Macedonia,[17] two rabbits, three turtles, and bought a new Pentium II computer with Word 97. I then shipped from England all the books and research data I would need, an old 1987 Mercedes-Benz 300 E for transport, and declared myself a recluse, well almost, until July the next year, when the completed manuscript had to be delivered. Needing a break from the intensive writing, I arranged for the family to come over for two weeks in April. With the Mercedes packed to the brim, and with a good supply of water and fruits for the journey, we set off early in the morning for Marsa Matruh. Stopping only for lunch, we then headed south on the newly tarmaced Siwa highway and into the unknown. After nearly three hours of driving on an almost straight and flat road, with only flat desert and the occasional hill as far as the eye could see, we began to wonder if the oasis existed at all. Some twelve miles before we reached the oasis, and now with nightfall upon us, the front wheel flung a small rock that hit the under-carriage of the car and damaged the fuel pump. Losing fuel like a hit World War II Spitfire, we barely made it to the little village of Siwa. Tired and confused, we booked into one of the small hotels in town and slept till dawn.

We decided to wander into the bustling village centre, and after a quick breakfast of broad beans and sweet tea, we climbed a small rocky knoll in the centre of the village to get a better look at the place. Nothing can prepare you for the sheer magic and beauty of this oasis. A huge flat bowl of palm groves rimmed by mounds, mesas and dunes. Two huge lakes, shimmering gold and blue in the morning light, flanked the east and west sides of the oasis. And far to the east, on top of another rocky mound, we could see the Oracle Temple of Zeus-Ammon.

When Alexander the Great and his small retinue reached the oasis, they immediately made their way to the temple. A contingency of Greeks from Cyrene, near modern Tripoli in Libya, had travelled to join Alexander's cortege. On their approach to the Oracle they were greeted by priests and priestesses, and temple dancing girls who threw petals and perfumes on Alexander and his companion, singing and shouting praise and welcome to the young hero. At the foot of the mound upon which the Oracle Temple stood, the Hierophants and high-priests greeted Alexander with shouts of 'Dionysos! Dionysos!', literally 'Son of God! Son of God!' A king-messiah was in the making.

It was no exaggeration when the eminent scholar Ulrich Wilcken wrote that 'the whole subsequent course of history, the political, economic and cultural life of after times, cannot be understood apart from the career of Alexander'.[18] The French historian Paul Faure went much further. In his biography of Alexander, Faure demonstrated how Alexander, or rather the myth of Alexander, had paved the way and set the scene some three centuries later for a new 'Son of God', a 'Filius Dei', one whose modest Nazarene mother, somewhat like Olympias before her, also claimed to have become pregnant through divine intervention.[19]

For centuries after his death, his embalmed corpse, mummified in the ancient Osirian tradition and kept in a golden sarcophagus, was venerated in the city of Alexandria. Among those nobles who paid homage at his shrine were Julius Caesar, Octavian and Hadrian. Even during early Christian times, when the body had been transferred into a glass coffin, crowds of devotees would parade through his shrine during the feasts of his birth (September) and death (June), and celebrate his 'resurrection' as the god Dionysos.[20] It seems that Alexander is also mentioned in the Koran as Iskander Dul El Qarnein, Alexander the 'two horned', i.e. the horns of the ram-god Ammon. It is reported that at the legendary place where the tomb of Alexander had stood, today in the busy street of Nebi Daniel,[21] pious Muslims would come to pray to the 'prophet-king', 'instrument of divine will', and later in the fifteenth century, roughly at the same spot, was raised the mosque of the prophet Daniel, the legendary founder of the Arab city of Alexandria.[22]

THE 'SECOND' HALL OF RECORDS?

In the first century AD, the legacy of Alexander's conquest had reached its peak. The city of Alexandria, now a huge metropolis rivalling Rome and Athens, was the learning and cultural centre of the known world, and home of the famous library where scholars from all parts of the Graeco-Roman empire came to learn, teach and exchange ideas. In their recent study on the tradition of magic and alchemy, *The Elixir and the Stone*, best-selling authors Michael Baigent and Richard Leigh place the city of Alexandria as the node or nucleus from which Gnosticism and Hermeticism evolved and flourished. They also showed that it was in Alexandria that the ancient principles of alchemy and magic were absorbed and injected into western culture to find their way to Europe and the Renaissance and, ultimately, the modern world.[23] In their section on Alexandria the authors give a vivid and colourful picture of the city as it must have been in the first century after Christ:

> If Egypt as a whole had prospered (under the Ptolemies), the supreme manifestation of that prosperity was the city of Alexandria . . . During the first century of the Christian era, Alexandria was the wealthiest, most urbane, most cosmopolitan, cultured and civilised city of the Graeco-Roman world, and the unrivalled centre of world trade. The population has been estimated at 500,000, far exceeding that of any other Mediterranean metropolis. The city was renowned for its architecture. Among its chief attractions was the famous lighthouse of Pharos, numbered among the seven wonders of the ancient world . . . According to one account, the city itself encompassed more than 800 taverns,

more than 1500 bathhouses, more than 2400 temples and more than 24,000 houses. There were also theatres, a stadium for games, a forum, a large market, an immense gymnasium, numerous public parks and sacred groves. There were innumerable monuments. At the entrance of the temple of Augustus stood two columns (obelisks) subsequently known as 'Cleopatra's Needles', one of which now stands on the Embankment in London, the other in New York's Central Park. In all these constructions, there was so prolific a use of white marble that the eyes, in sunlight, were said to be dazzled.[24]

As I have said, one of the city's chief attractions was the golden sarcophagus of Alexander the Great. It stood in its Doric shrine well into the third century AD, and its last appearance in recorded history was during the visit of the Roman Emperor Caracalla in AD 215.[25] Surpassing by far the fame of all other monuments, temples and building of that city was the Bibliotheca Alexandrina, the world-famous Library of Alexandria, whose fabled collection of ancient books and texts has fired the imaginations and dreams of scholars and researchers throughout the ages, and whose senseless destruction deprived humanity of the largest and most priceless intellectual treasure-trove of history. 'By dint of its bibliographical collections,' write Baigent and Leigh, 'the city had outstripped other centres of study, such as Athens and Corinth, and emerged as the supreme seat of learning for the classical world.' Alexandria's Library, known as the 'Museion', i.e. 'temple of the Muses', was the ancient world's Oxford and Cambridge, Harvard and Yale, Sorbonne and the Beaux Arts all rolled into one. It was one of the first truly 'universal' seats of learning, where scholars were fully subsidised with free accommodation, meals and were exempt from paying taxes. The original Museion was founded by the first of the Ptolemy 'pharaohs', Ptolemy-Soter, the 'Saviour', in c. 295 BC. He gave orders that all books found on ships that sailed into Alexandria were to be copied, and the originals stored in the Museion. He also commissioned copies from other libraries from around the world. At the height of its glory the Library of Alexandria contained some 500,000 books or scrolls, all kept neatly in shelves and niches, carefully catalogued and labelled. It was at the Alexandria Library that Eratosthenes calculated the dimensions of the earth; that Euclid wrote books on geometry that were still used in schools until quite recently; that Hipparchus predicted the creation of stars, worked out the rate of stellar precession and produced the first catalogues of star magnitudes and co-ordinates; and where Galen wrote books on medicine and healing that were still in use in sixteenth-century Europe.

There were many others who came to study at the Library and who, collectively, 'established the foundations for the systematic study of mathematics, physics, astronomy, literature, geography and medicine'.[26] We may wonder, however, what suddenly triggered this age of enlightenment in Egypt. The answer seems to be rooted in the very context and location of the Library itself. For although most of the material stored in the Library was written in Greek, there were, almost certainly, many works from ancient Egyptian sources written in Coptic and hieroglyphic. We must recall that here, in Egypt, for the last three thousand years before the Ptolemies came to power, there was a wealth of material, thousands upon thousands of texts, that had been compiled on papyrus, tablets, stele, palettes, tomb and temple walls, palaces, shrines and pyramids: a sort of gigantic 'hall of records' strewn all over Egypt. According to St Clement of Alexandria (AD 150-215) who coined the phrase 'Egypt was the Mother of magicians', the Egyptians had forty-two books of wisdom reputedly written by the god Thoth which were stored in secret chambers in temples.[27] These books were reputed to be divine revelations dealing with subjects such as law, astronomy, medicine and geography. This is backed up by the many statements made by the Greeks themselves in respect to the superior knowledge of the ancient Egyptian priests and wise men. The great scholar and historian Strabo, writing in c.25 BC during his stay in Egypt, made, for example, this telling statement:

> The Egyptian priests are supreme in their knowledge of the skies. Mysterious and reluctant to communicate with strangers, they sometimes let themselves be persuaded, on the long term and after much supplication, to reveal some of their knowledge; nonetheless they keep to themselves the bulk of their secrets. They revealed to the Greeks the secret of the full year – which the Greeks ignored like many other things – until the modern astronomers got to know of them by those who translated into Greek the knowledge of the Egyptian priests . . .[28]

The Egyptian priests, however, above all were the keepers of a very ancient system of magic, secret initiations and rituals which, for lack of better words, we have called 'the science of immortality'.[29] St Clement of Alexandria who, as first president of the Christian Catechetical school of Alexandria and leader of the Christian community in Egypt, was in an excellent position to know such things, wrote that 'the Egyptians entrusted their Mysteries of Initiation to future kings and to priests selected for their education, learning and background',[30] and Plutarch, who was an eye witness to what he wrote, reported that 'the priests of Isis who died were dressed in sacred costumes symbolising the different

106

aspects of the goddess, which were the same costumes placed on statues to show that the divine speech, the holy discourses, the initiations, are with them and that they are crossing into the afterlife carrying nothing else but this "word",[31] while Synesius simply stated without hesitation that 'the learned Egyptian priests are the keepers of the highest wisdom and knowledge'.[32] At any rate, it should become evident to the reader that the Library of Alexandria had become the repository not only of books from all over the known world, but perhaps more importantly, a storage, at least in papyrus form, of ancient Egyptian texts and, quite possibly, a collection of copies of the fabled books of Thoth.

These last, acting as a potent intellectual and spiritual catalyst, not only caused the Greek scholars to come up with various 'discoveries' in the sciences of astronomy, mathematics and geography (more likely re-discoveries) but created the alchemical reaction in the minds of some erudite people that was to coalesce in the secret teachings we loosely call Gnosticism and Hermeticism.

HERMES MEETS JESUS

In the middle of the first century AD the intellectual and spiritual conditions in Alexandria were absolutely perfect for the seed of Christianity to spawn and flourish. For three millennia or more, the land of Egypt had practised a mystery religion which was based, as we have seen earlier, on the figure of Osiris, who had undergone a sacrificial death, resurrected, and went on to establish a 'kingdom of heaven' in the afterlife realm. Osiris was the 'Son of God' par excellence, a man-god who had been sent by the Creator to earth in order to teach men the divine law and, more importantly, provide them with a means to achieve salvation and immortality of the soul. For generation upon generation, the pharaohs of Egypt were emphatically believed to be the reincarnated 'sons' of Osiris, and each year their 'divine birth' was celebrated with the rising of the star Sirius, the star of the Divine Mother, Isis, which occurred around the time of the summer solstice.[33] During the Ptolemaic period under the enlightened Greek-pharaohs, Alexandria became a hotbed for religions of all kinds. Large numbers of Jews settled in Alexandria, and the city was full of 'preachers' and 'teachers' expounding this or that religion or cult. The Greeks, quite naturally, had imported with them the Olympian religion and mystery cults, particularly that of Dionysos and Demeter. Prominent above all these was the cult of Serapis, the official religion of the Ptolemies. We have already seen how Ptolemy I Soter had asked his Greek and Egyptian theologians to create the ideal deity for Alexandria, resulting in the god Serapis modelled on Ausar-Hapi, 'Osiris of the Nile'. The general idea was to merge the ancient Egyptian Osirian mysteries with those from Greece, a process that is technically known as 'syncretism'. When Egypt fell to Rome in 30 BC and became a Roman Province, other cults were brought in, notably the cult of Mithras, another dying and resurrecting 'son of God' whose birthday was celebrated on 25th December, near the winter solstice.[34] The Romans, and the Greeks before them, were quite accommodating to virtually all cults, and thus syncretism, in a sense, was a natural process of mutation and integration that took place in the melting pot of Alexandria.

When the first of those Jewish immigrants who called themselves 'followers of Jesus'[35] came into Egypt, none of the Church's doctrines and dogmas were yet in place. Indeed there was no Church, or at least no elaborate establishment as we know it today. Legend has it that St Mark the Apostle and Evangelist came to Egypt and founded the first Church in Alexandria. The site of his martyrdom at the hands of the Romans is said to be where today stands the Protestant church of St Mark in Mohamad Ali Square.[36] A curious story accompanies the coming of Mark that probably provides the basis for the Gnostic movement that ensued. According to a letter allegedly written by Clement of Alexandria to an unknown person, St Mark also wrote, in addition to the canonical gospel which we attribute to him today, in Alexandria a 'secret gospel' which appears to be directed to adepts of the Mysteries. Clement reports that after St Peter was martyred in Rome

> . . . Mark came over to Alexandria bringing both his own notes and those of Peter (concerning the teachings of Jesus), and from which he transferred to his former book (the canonical gospel) the things suitable to whatever makes progress towards gnosis (divine knowledge). He (thus) composed a more spiritual Gospel for the use of *those who were being perfected* . . .[37]

This story, of course, raises a crucial question with regard to the true teachings of Jesus and, more specifically, whether these 'secret' teachings were intended for only 'those who were being perfected'. This curious terminology used by St Clement very much implies that he was thinking of high 'initiates', i.e. those who were groomed and trained to receive the gnosis of the Christ. This supposition is confirmed further in Clement's mysterious letter when he writes that before Mark died

... he left his composition to the church in Alexandria, where it even yet is most carefully guarded, being read only by those who are initiated into the Mysteries ...[38]

What 'church'? St Clement states that Mark came over to Alexandria after the martyrdom of Peter which, according to most historians, occurred in AD 64 in Rome under the Emperor Nero. The latter is known to history as the crazed persecutor of the Christians, but although Nero's mental instability is not contested by any (he murdered his mother and wife, and was prone to severe delusions of himself as a poet and charioteer), it is an historical fact that there were very few 'Christians' in Rome at the time. St Paul had just arrived in the city, and from all accounts the Jewish slaves of Rome were all 'anxious to learn from him the nature of his new sect' indicating that no one had yet told them about it. As for Nero's role as the proverbial Anti-Christ this, as many historians agree, was a propaganda job by the Church after the advent of Constantine the Great.[39]

It is also doubtful whether 'Christianity' had any serious foothold in Egypt, and those who followed the teachings of Jesus did so in very small groups with no 'church' as such to report to. If and when St Mark came to Alexandria, he must have found among his most likely converts those Greek-Egyptians or Egyptian-Greeks who, for the last three centuries, had become adepts of Serapes, the syncretised divinity of the city. It must have seemed pretty obvious to anyone who wanted to promote the religion of 'Jesus' in Egypt that the image of a humble Nazarene carpenter who had been crucified as a slave by the Roman procurator in Jerusalem had to be presented as something else – something that would at least match the pedigree of Serapis or, even better, his prototype, Osiris. The idea of a 'Son of God' to the Alexandrians, as we have seen, was nothing new. The combined Horus-Osiris pharaohs had fulfilled this role for several millennia, and since 320 BC Dionysos-Alexander had provided the Alexandrians with a golden effigy of their own of such a 'Son of God'. Also the promise of salvation or resurrection was old hat to the natives of Egypt, whether Egyptians or Greeks. It would have been unthinkable to the followers of Serapis, Osiris or Dionysos that such salvation could be guaranteed by 'faith' alone, and that no initiation in the Mysteries would have been required.

The letter we have quoted above from St Clement of Alexandria, who we should not forget was the leader of the Christian community of Alexandria nearly two centuries after the supposed arrival of St Mark in Egypt, makes this quite clear, and thus speaks of a 'secret gospel' of Mark which was intended for adepts of the Mysteries. Were there such teachings of Jesus that could be construed as being part of an initiatory process towards gnosis? And if so, where are they? Before we tackle this intriguing question, there is, too, something else about St Mark mentioned in Clement's letter which suggests an initiation system known by Mark much akin to those practised in the pagan Mysteries. Authors and researchers Robert Lomas and Christopher Knight, in their best-selling book *The Hiram Key* analysed the content of St Clement's letter and brought to attention the curious reference to Jesus performing a ritual on a young man which, in their view, much resembled the rituals of Freemasonry.[40] A woman's brother had died while Jesus was in the neighbourhood, and he was beseeched by her to help:

> And Jesus . . . went off with her into the garden where the tomb was, and straightaway a great cry was heard from the tomb. And going near, Jesus rolled away the stone from the door of the tomb. And straightaway, going in where the youth was, he stretched forth his hand and raised him, seizing his hand. But the youth, looking upon him, loved him and began to beseech him that he might be with him. And going out of the tomb they came into the house of the youth . . . And after six days Jesus told him what to do and in that evening the youth comes to him, wearing a linen cloth over his naked body. And he remained with him that night, and Jesus taught him the mystery of the kingdom of god . . .[41]

Lomas and Knight draw attention to the fact that in Masonic rituals, which they also found have striking similarities with those practised by early Christian 'Gnostic' sects, the so-called Third Degree of the Brotherhood involves the 'raising' of a candidate wearing a white linen cloth after a symbolic 'death' and also 'the mantle of the Templar (who performed a similar ritual) was originally plain white linen'.[42] It struck Lomas and Knight that a similar 'naked youth in white linen' was also mentioned in the Gospel of Mark. The scene is in the garden of Gethsemane when Jesus is about to be arrested by the Roman soldiers:

> And a certain young man followed them, having linen cloths cast about his naked body. And they laid hold of him. But he, casting off the linen cloth, fled from them naked . . .[43]

All this suggested to Lomas and Knight 'that there was a secret tradition' concealed in the Testaments in certain parables that can only be understood by those initiated in the Mysteries,[44] and that this 'tradition', in turn, was openly flaunted in the Gnostic writings. As many authors before them had shown, including eminent scholars such as

Elaine Pagels, this Gnosticism posed a serious threat to the Orthodox and Catholic Churches, because it suggested to the followers of Jesus that enlightenment and the path to salvation and everlasting spiritual life could be achieved without the need for priests and bishops. Indeed the Gnostics went further: they have Jesus himself branding the Orthodox Church as 'an imitation church' in one of their better known codeces, the so-called Apocalypse of Peter:

> And there shall be others who are outside our numbers who name themselves bishop and also deacons, as if they have received their authority from God. These people are dry canals. They do business in my word. They praise the men who propagate falsehood . . .[45]

Such 'heresy' was not only dangerous to the Church, it revealed an image of Jesus as a 'pagan' sage or teacher of the Mysteries. From the end of the second century AD, a systematic smear campaign by the Church began to be launched against the Gnostics and 'pagans' of Egypt. By the end of the fourth century AD, the matter came to a head. Ancient shrines were violated and destroyed, some converted into Christian churches, and 'innumerable books were piled together, many heaps of volumes . . . to be burnt under the eyes of the judges as prohibited'.[46] The final act of destruction came in Alexandria, when in AD 391 Emperor Theodosius issued a decree to have all pagan temples closed. Encouraged by such imperial support from Constantinople, the Alexandrian Christians went on a wild rampage. Incited by the local Patriarch Theophilus, a Christian mob attacked the great temple of Serapis at Karmuz, and razed it to the ground. All that remains today are two small sphinxes on pedestals and the foundation of the temple. They then turned against other temples and shrines in the city, and eventually attempted to do the same to ancient Egyptian temples all over Egypt. Theophilus then personally led troops to destroy the desert monasteries of 'heretic' Christian monks. He was subsequently made a saint of the Coptic and Syrian Churches. Theophilus was succeeded by his nephew, St Cyryl, who carried on with his uncle's religious ethnic cleansing. The horror of it all came in a disgusting finale in AD 415 on a bright sunny day in Alexandria. The beautiful Hypatia, the first woman mathematician and head of the Neo-Platonist School of Philosophy in Alexandria, who was the daughter of the scholar Theon, was stalked by Cyryl's Nitrian monks, a sort of proto-Nazi youth gang, dragged from her chariot to a nearby church, stripped naked and had her flesh scraped off her bones with broken abalone shells. Her crime: being a mathematician (which the Church equated with 'paganism'). This violent act of senseless and gruesome cruelty brought to focus the determination of the Church to stamp out non-Christian factions, and from then on Alexandria quickly declined as a major centre of learning.[47]

Perhaps the worst act of vandalism committed by the Church in Alexandria was the deliberate destruction of the famous Library and Museion, an act which is still today described as the biggest crime against the intellectual development of humanity. 'It was as if the entire civilisation,' lamented the eminent American scientist Carl Sagan, 'had undergone some self-inflicted brain surgery, and most of its memories, discoveries, ideas and passions were extinguished irrevocably. The loss was incalculable.'[48] With the slate of history seemingly wiped clean, the Church began to rewrite its own history and, by and large, the history of the world. Gnosticism, however, was not totally eradicated, at least not in spirit. It re-emerged, for example, albeit in much mutated forms, in the twelfth century with the Cathars of southern France, but they, too, were viciously stamped out by a papal army sent to their stronghold in Montsegur. [49] In the early fourteenth century the mass eradication of the Order of the Knights Templar by the Church was also, in a sense, a genocide against a form of Gnosticism, in that the Templars were Christians who are said to have practised initiation rites akin to those of the ancient Mysteries. [50] It can also be argued that the Sufis of Islam were, in more ways than one, the carriers and perpetuators of Hermeticism, Gnostic thought and, more especially, alchemy. And it has been shown that 'many Sufi texts run perfectly parallel to those of the Hermetic corpus'.[51] Indeed, according to authors Michael Baigent and Richard Leigh: 'Hermeticism can now be seen as having emphasised, if not established, many key points of contact between Islam and Judaism. Such as shared views of Old Testament prophets.'[52] Moreover we shall encounter in the next chapter the mysterious Sabians of Harran and the early traditions among the Arabs of an ancient knowledge being preserved in 'Books of Hermes' in a repository most reminiscent of the Hall of Records. And we shall also see how, in the tenth century, the Arabs of Andalusia not only practised a hybrid form of Hermeticism, but also had developed it into a form of 'astral magic' much akin to that of the ancient Egyptians. But more of that later. Meanwhile, there are many who have argued, and not without justification, that the nearest sect to Gnosticism in modern times is the Masonic Order and that of the AMORC Rosicrucians.[53] It is well known, for example, that these organisations have graded systems which include a medley of pseudo-Egyptian and other pagan rituals, as well as maintaining a strong sense of Biblical mystic. But more of that later on.

THE GNOSTIC 'HALL OF RECORDS'?

In 1947 the Gnostic heresy was to make a comeback with a vengeance. With a story that has the hallmark of an Indiana Jones movie plot, a secret haul of Gnostic writings was unearthed in Upper Egypt near the little hamlet of Nag Hammadi in the winter of 1945. A young Egyptian boy called Mohamad Ali El Samman, and his brother Khalifa, were by chance digging into the soft soil near a large boulder on the edge of the Jabal El Tarif. The boulder, 'shaped somewhat like a stalagmite',[54] had broken off in prehistoric times, and it was there that, in c. AD 350, some unknown Gnostic priest buried a large earthenware jar in which were carefully stored 'books' made from rolls of papyrus. There the jar lay undisturbed for over 1500 years. Mohamad and his brother, by one of those strange synchronicities of history, had come, as other villagers had come since time immemorial, to collect nitrate-rich soil from the foot of the Jebel to use as fertiliser, and, on that propitious day, dug precisely where the ancient jar was buried. The lads broke the jar, wrapped the precious books in their gallabeyas,[55] and took the cargo back to their village of Al Kasr.

It so happened that in the preceding months a terrible feud had erupted between the Al Samman family and that of the Hawara of a nearby village, and the local police paid unannounced visits to Mohamad and Khalifa's home to search for illegal arms. Fearing that the police would confiscate the ancient books, and somehow realising that they may interest the local Coptic priest, Basilius Al Messihi, Mohamad asked the latter to safeguard them for him. The Nag Hammadi Library, as it is today called, comprises thirteen books or 'codices' (plural for 'codex', an ancient name to denote a wad of documents making up a 'book'), with the thirteenth badly damaged and much of its content missing. Each 'codex' includes various tracts, the total of the whole library being fifty-two such tracts. After a convoluted saga with one of the books being used as fuel for cooking by the Coptic priest's wife, and others ending up being sold on the black market in Cairo, in 1949 Codex I was exported out of Egypt by a Belgian antiquities dealer called Albert Eid who first tried to sell it in auction in New York. In 1952 Eid's widow presented Codex I to the Jung Institute in Zurich. There Professor Gilles Quispel quickly realised the importance of the find. Upon examining the other codices, which meanwhile had all been collected by the Egyptian authorities and stored at the Coptic Museum in Cairo, Quispel realised that many of the documents he was seeing were previously unknown texts covering a period that was vital in understanding the formation of the Christian

Church. Eventually Codex I, now named the 'Jung Codex', was returned to Egypt. In 1960 the Egyptian Ministry of Culture in collaboration with UNESCO formed the so-called Nag Hammadi Library Project and by 1979 an English translation was on the market.

In the autumn of 1995 the author Graham Hancock[56] and I had the opportunity meeting Professor Quispel in Amsterdam. After the BBC documentary *The Great Pyramid: Gateway to the Stars* was shown in Holland in 1994, I was contacted by Joseph Ritman, owner and founder of the celebrated *Bibliotheca Philosophica Hermetica* in Amsterdam. Ritman had been impressed by the Orion-Giza correlation theory and felt it was a vital key in understanding the mysteries and origin of Hermetic and Gnostic thinking.[57] After visiting the library, which is truly an Ali Baba's cave of books on Hermeticism, Gnosticism, mysticism, alchemy, Freemasonry and Rosicrucianism, we made our way in the early evening with Mr Ritman to his house in the lovely flowery street of Bloemstraat, where we were introduced to Professor Quispel. Also present were Professor F. Janssen, Mrs Ritman and her daughter. At dinner we discussed the terrible loss of the Alexandria Library and, of course, the dramatic recovery of the Gnostic Library of Nag Hammadi. Could another, perhaps older, treasure-trove of ancient texts still exist in the sands of Egypt, waiting to be found by the lucky turn of a spade? Graham Hancock and I were at the time working on the manuscript for *Keeper of Genesis* and we informed our Dutch host that we strongly suspected that somewhere under the bedrock of Giza might lie such a cache. We spoke of the legendary 'Hall of Records' and the result of the recent seismographic work of John Anthony West and Dr Robert Schoch near the Sphinx, and how a possible secret chamber had been detected by their instruments somewhere under the front paws of the statue.[58] The Gnostic texts of Nag Hammadi, which were already having an immense effect on our perception of Christianity and its links with the ancient Mysteries, were offering a tantalising glimpse of what much older, and purer writings might reveal.

But the Nag Hammadi Library was not the only latter-day 'Hall of Records' that had found its way from ancient Alexandria to present times. Another collection of codices had, in sort, been 'unearthed' in 1460 by the Medicis of Florence – codices, furthermore, that pertained to be written by the hand of the god Thoth himself.

Chapter Six

The Return of the Magicians

'It is probable that Hermes Trismegistus is the most important figure in the Renaissance revival of magic . . .'

Frances Yates, *Giordano Bruno and the Hermetic Tradition*, p. 18

'Once on a time, when I had begun to think about the things that are, and my thoughts had soared high aloft while my bodily senses had been put under restraint by sleep – yet not such sleep as that of men weighed down by fullness of food or by bodily weariness – methought there came to me a Being of vast and boundless magnitude, who called me by my name and said to me, 'What do you wish to hear and see, and to learn and come to know by thought?' 'Who are you?' I said. 'I am,' said he, 'Poimandres, the Mind of the Sovereignty.'

Corpus Hermeticum, Libellus I – 1-2

THE POIMANDRES

Throughout the Middle Ages and, more especially, during the early Renaissance period in Europe, erudite men continued to be haunted by the idea that ancient Egypt had been the possessor of a secret system of knowledge handed down to them by the Creator. Such belief, of course, was regarded as heresy by the Church, and was a crime that could lead to punishment and death. It is thus a measure of the power of this belief that any writings on this subject have survived at all. Yet they did. They were to change the course of the intellectual history of the world.

In 1460 the Duke of Florence, Cosimo de Medici, the founder of the famous family that ruled Florence until 1537 and a man dubbed the 'Father of his Country', was seventy-one years old and in poor health.[1] A keen supporter of the humanities and avid admirer of Plato and the ancient Athenian academy, one of Cosimo's ardent passions was the collection of ancient manuscripts. This, in part, was to furnish the Medici Library which Cosimo had created for the benefit of scholars and the public.[2] Cosimo had heard of the legendary books of Hermes Trismegistus (Thoth) from the writing of St Clement of Alexandria, and became obsessed in acquiring a set for his library.[3] His dream was fulfilled when a monk found an almost complete set, written in Greek, in Macedonia and brought it to the Florentine court. The Corpus Hermeticum that reached Cosimo de Medici comprised fourteen volumes, the fifteenth one being missing.

The Florentine scholar Marsilio Ficino had recently been appointed as 'high-priest' to Cosimo's Platonic Academy modelled on the Athenian Academy of Plato. Dozens of manuscripts by Plato had been assembled and were now awaiting translation, but Ficino was ordered by Cosimo to leave these works aside and rather focus his time and energy on the translation of the Corpus Hermeticum. Why? What could have so compelled the Duke of Florence to give such a bizarre instruction? After all, Cosimo's Platonic Academy had been created in honour of the great Plato, not to mention that scholars around Europe had been waiting for almost 700 years for a translation of the great man's works since the closing down of the Athenian Academy by the Church in AD 529. This amazing behaviour by Cosimo is reported by the eminent Renaissance scholar Dame Frances Yates (1899-1981) in her landmark book *Giordano Bruno and the Hermetic Tradition*:

> It is an extraordinary situation. There are the complete works of Plato, waiting, and they must wait whilst Ficino quickly translates Hermes, probably because Cosimo wants to read him before he dies. What a testimony this is to the mysterious reputation of [Hermes] the Thrice Great One! . . .[4]

The motive behind Cosimo's decision seems to have been rooted in his rapidly failing health. It was well-known to Renaissance erudites such as Cosimo that the ancient Egyptians were reputed to have possessed the secret of immortality and that these secrets had been safeguarded in the so-called Books of Thoth-Hermes. Cosimo, as we have said, was well-read in the works of Clement of Alexandria. He would have almost certainly been familiar with Clement's *Stromata*, in which the author speaks of a sacred temple library, and also where he gives a detailed eye-witness account of an elaborate procession of Egyptian priests during which the fabled forty-two books of Thoth were displayed to the populace.[5] Also it was commonly believed that Plato, and before him Solon and Pythagoras, had spent many years with the priests of Egypt and had been initiated into their Mysteries.[6] Indeed, Plato states as much about Solon in the *Critias*. Cosimo's wish was granted. Ficino managed to complete the translation of the first book of the Corpus, classified as Libellus I and entitled the *Poimandres*.

The Corpus Hermeticum is essentially a series of 'discourses' and exchanges between a teacher and his pupil or, more specifically, between a master that has acquired gnosis and a neophyte who is being tutored or initiated into this mystical system of divine knowledge. The teacher is generally Hermes, but other tracts also have the goddess Isis instructing her son, Horus. The first of the Hermetic tracts, the Libellus I, however, opens with Hermes himself first receiving the divine knowledge from an entity called Poimandres, while in a state of trance or semi-sleep. There has been much debate in scholarly circles on who or what Poimandres is. The most likely identification is that Poimandres is Egyptian in origin and represents 'the knowledge of Ra', i.e. the knowledge that the Creator passed on to Thoth.[7] At any rate, from the text itself, it is clear that this entity is to be regarded as the 'Supreme Mind', i.e. the Mind of God, and that by uniting or merging with this Mind, one acquires gnosis. Hermes, while in that state of trance or slumber, is asked by Poimandres what he, Hermes, wishes to 'hear and see, and to learn and come to know by thought', to which Hermes answers:

> I would fain learn the things that are, and understand their nature, and get knowledge of God. These are the things of which I wish to hear.

To which Poimandres replied:

> I know what you wish, for indeed I am with you everywhere; keep in mind all that you desire to learn, and I will teach you.

Hermes then has an ecstatic vision of light filling the space all around him, with a part of this space becoming a spiralling abyss of darkness which changes into a watery substance with fire and smoke, and from which could be heard 'an indescribable sound of lamentation'. Finally from the light came forth 'a holy Word which took its stance on the watery substance, and methought this Word was the voice of the Light'. At this stage what Poimandres says to Hermes after this ecstatic experience surely must have sent a chill down Cosimo's back as he read Ficino's translation in his deathbed:

> That Light is I, even Mind, the first God, who was before the watery substance which appears out of the darkness; and the Word which came forth from the Light is the Son of God . . .[8]

To both Ficino and Cosimo, the similarity of these statements with those found in the Book of Genesis in the Bible was striking. Had not Moses, like Hermes, seen 'a darkness over the face of the abyss and the Spirit of God brooding over the waters'? Had he not, too, announced the creation by the powerful Word of God? Yet had Ficino and Cosimo also been familiar with the ancient Egyptian creation myth they would have seen there, too, some eerie similarities. For, as we have already seen, this creation myth speaks of the 'Word' that Thoth brought forth from the gods at the time Atum-Ra, the sun god, the god of 'light', appeared over the dark watery abyss.[9] In other parts of the *Poimandres* Ficino noted more similarities with the Book of Genesis: man is made in the image of God; Hermes, like Moses, is the 'Law-Giver'; and in the Libellus I the author 'actually uses almost the same words as Moses when describing God's command to mankind to increase and multiply'.[10] Yet Hermes is better still than Moses, for he actually states that the 'Word', which illuminates all things, is, in fact, the 'Son of God'. In the minds of the Renaissance scholars this term could only mean Jesus Christ. But how could it be that in ancient texts, reputed to predate the Gospels by several centuries, such an event is foreseen? Slowly but surely, the idea began to seed in the mind of the Renaissance scholars that Hermes must have received divine revelations in the same way the prophet Moses had on Mount Sinai; Hermes, therefore, just like Moses, was to be regarded as a prophet of Christianity.[11] Very much in the same way that the Nag Hammadi texts were to affect the collective perception of those who read them in modern times, so too did the Hermetic texts affect the Renaissance scholars and all who came into contact with them. Like the Nag Hammadi texts, the overall effect was to seriously put into question the authority of the Roman Catholic Church. As authors Baigent and Leigh noted:

> Hermetism is a mystical tradition, a mystical body of teaching, a mystical mode of thought. Like other such traditions, bodies of teaching and modes of thought, it repudiates simplistic belief and blind faith. It repudiates codified dogma and the interpretative necessity and authority of priests. It also refuses to accept the rational intellect as the supreme means of cognition, the supreme arbiter of reality. Instead it emphasises and extols the mystical and numinous experience – direct and first-hand appreciation of the sacred, direct knowledge of the absolute.[12]

Unlike the Gnostic texts, however, the links of the Hermetic texts with ancient Egyptian religion are clear. All the figures and deities, for example, that are represented in the Hermetic texts are of Egyptian origin: Thoth-Hermes, Osiris, Isis, Horus, Tat,[13] Ammon or Amun, and Asclepius-Imhotep. And although there has been endless debate in scholastic and academic circles as to the extent of direct influence on the *Hermetica* by Egyptian mystical ideas and belief systems, with some scholars even claiming hardly any connection at all,[14] the best way to view the content of the *Hermetica* is provided by Egyptologist Geraldine Pinch:

> Many of the ideas in these [Hermetic] texts could be developments of Egyptian religion, but they are probably blended with elements of Persian, Gnostic and perhaps Jewish mythology, all translated into Hellenic philosophy . . .[15]

Such syncretism, as we have seen, came together in the city of Alexandria during the first two centuries of Christianity. Furthermore it is precisely this Alexandrine syncretism which, after the rediscovery of the *Hermetica* by the Italian scholars, acted as a powerful intellectual device that detonated in the rich minds of the Platonic Academy a great revival or Renaissance: the revival of 'natural' and 'sympathetic' magic,[16] the revival of the quest for gnosis, and finally the revival of alchemy and the search for 'words of power' which, like in ancient Egypt, could be packed and charged with puissant ideas and deep meaning:

> In Hermeticism, as in Hebrew and in the later Judaic Kabbala, sounds, words, even individual letters can be the equivalent of storage cells, repositories charged with a form of divine or magical power as a battery is charged with electrical energy . . .[17]

> In Alexandria . . . cults, sects, religions, philosophical schools and systems jostled against each other, contended with each other, cross-fertilised each other, nourished each other in a dynamic, constantly mutating intellectual bouillabaisse. The modes of thought resulting from this interaction are today referred to collectively as 'syncretism'. Alexandrian syncretism was to exercise a determined influence on the evolution and development of Western consciousness, Western attitudes, Western values. And among the most important of Alexandrian syncretism was the amalgam that would subsequently coalesce into Western magical tradition . . . This tradition can most conveniently be called Hermeticism, or Hermetic thought.[18]

A 'magic' for what purpose? And how can this 'magic' relate to the Great Pyramid and Sphinx of Egypt? Or to the belief in a 'Second

Coming'? How can all this possibly lead the seekers of gnosis to a secret chamber or 'Hall of Records' at Giza?

A MAGICAL RELIGION

A century or so after the rediscovery of the Corpus Hermeticum, a strange regeneration of 'Egyptian' mysticism was taking place in Western culture. The *Hermetica* was being circulated among scholars, the educated classes and even royalty.[19] A new breed of 'Hermetic' philosophers, cabalists, alchemists, magicians, seers and wizards of all sorts began to emerge.[20] In Chapter 2 we saw the bizarre involvement of the Papacy with Hermeticism and how some misguided scholars attempted to convince the Church not only that Hermes-Thoth was a prophet of Christianity, but also that his 'books' should be canonised and embraced as 'gospels' of the Roman Catholic Church. Others, more radical in their demands, went as far as to preach the return of the 'Egyptian' religion as the true religion of the world. Among the most forceful and influential of these new Hermetic activists was a mysterious Italian scholar from the Nolan region called Giordano Bruno.

Before the late 1960s very few people indeed, except within a tight academic circle, had even heard of Giordano Bruno.[21] It was not until the British scholar Frances A. Yates took up the task of understanding Bruno's role and motives in the Italian Renaissance and, more importantly, his strange contacts in the French and English courts, that the true picture of Bruno's bizarre mission began to emerge. In her turning-point work, *Giordano Bruno and the Hermetic Tradition* (first published in 1962 in London), Yates performed a sort of intellectual archaeological feat by discovering the rudiments of a powerful esoteric tradition which had hitherto gone undetected. This tradition, as we shall see, almost certainly caused the formation of speculative Freemasonic and Rosicrucian movements and ultimately, as I shall also show, set up the conditions that were to lead seekers to look for the fabled 'Hall of Records' at Giza. To give a name to this mysterious 'tradition' Yates was to coin the phrase 'the Hermetic Tradition'.[22]

Giordano Bruno's mission began in 1581, when he set himself the task of persuading the monarchs of Europe to install, no less, the 'magical religion of the Egyptians' as the new religion of the world. That year, Bruno had arrived in the city of Paris after wandering out of Italy and through Europe for several months. In Paris he gave public lectures which eventually got him noticed by the French king, Henri III. Bruno, by then, had developed an extremely high level of proficiency in the classical art of memory called mnemonics and had already published two books on the subject. Yates writes:

> This classical art, usually regarded as purely mnemotechnical, had a long history in the Middle Ages . . . In the Renaissance it became fashionable among Neoplatonists and Hermetists. It was now understood as a method of printing basic archetypal images on the memory . . . a kind of inner way of knowing the universe . . . The Hermetic experience of reflecting the universe in the mind is, I believe, at the root of Renaissance magic memory, in which the classic mnemonic with places and images is now understood, or applied, as a method of achieving this experience by imprinting archetypal, or magically activated, images on the memory. By using magical or talismanic images as memory-images, the Magus (magician) hoped to acquire universal knowledge, and also powers, obtained through the magical organisation of the imagination – a magical powerful personality, tuned in, as it were, to the power of the cosmos. This amazing transformation, or adaptation, of the classical art of memory in the Renaissance has a history before Bruno, but in Bruno it reaches culmination. The De umbris idearum and the Cantus Circaeus . . . are his two first works on magic memory. This reveals him as a magician . . .[23]

The human memory has a natural system of selecting images, colours, scents or sounds in order to store vast amounts of information, moods, ideas, feelings and sensations. Imagine a day at the beach with friends and family, full of activities, full of fun and full of wonderful sensations. That day, however, something unusual happens. You are stung by a blue-bottle jellyfish. Years later you are visiting an aquarium somewhere else in the world, and in one of the displays floats a little blue-bottle jellyfish. Suddenly that 'image' unleashes the memories of that day on the beach. The blue-bottle is the 'icon' or 'archetypal image' in which was stored all the memories of that special day. Your mind will most certainly work out why the memory came to the surface by relating the jellyfish to the events remembered. It could have happened in a far more subtle way. You could have seen something totally unrelated, say, a postage stamp, whose colour very closely resembled that of the blue-bottle jellyfish. The unconscious mind makes the association, and the memories of that day will again flash in your mind. Except this time you may not be able to work out why this has happened, i.e. your conscious mind may not have registered what exactly it was that triggered the memory. This phenomenon is what the Hermetic scholars would have called the 'silent language' and what the ancient Egyptians would have called the 'language of the gods'.

The classical art of mnemonics is to learn how to create such an icon yourself and store it in the mind; then, at a later date, unleash it at will to bring back the desired memory stored in it. A very simple example of this is when you tie a string on your finger in order to remind you of something later on. This works so long as the item you wish to remember is simple and straightforward. What if the subject matter involved remembering a complex chain of events such as a Shakespeare play or a lecture on atomic physics? A far more sophisticated method would be needed, and that is where the art of mnemonics can be applied. One of the techniques is to imagine a house that you are familiar with, and allocate in chronological order the memory of each event to a room or item in this house. Later you can visualise yourself walking around the house along a predetermined route, entering the rooms and, as you encounter each item or 'icon', the memory that it 'stores' begins to unfold. It takes many years of practice to become a master of the art of memory, and those few who have the ability and intellect to become adepts will develop tremendous insight, which in turn can be converted into enormous power of influence and manipulation. Vast memory that can be controlled, like that of a powerful computer, translates into vast reservoirs of knowledge. Knowledge, as we all know, is power. The greater the memory and the more refined the means to store and control it, the greater the power of the magician.

Recognising such immense abilities in Giordano Bruno, Henri III appointed him as a spy to the French court, a sort of Renaissance version of James Bond, and dispatched him to the English court of Elizabeth I. The year was 1583. Commenting on this mission, Frances Yates writes that

> . . . Henri III, who, by sending Bruno into England on some mission . . . changed the course of his life from a wandering magician into that of a very strange kind of missionary indeed . . .[24]

The 'strange kind' of mission that Bruno set out for himself was the extraordinary task of persuading the Elizabethan court, and through it eventually the whole of Europe, to adopt the 'true religion of the world'. That Bruno's intention was to attempt this is confirmed by a letter written by the English ambassador in Paris, Sir Henry Cobham, to Francis Walsingham in England to warn him of Bruno's hidden motives: 'Doctor Giordano Bruno Nolano, a professor in philosophy, intends to pass into England, whose religion I cannot commend.'[25] This is a wonderful English understatement. For the religion that Cobham 'cannot commend' and which Bruno is bringing to England, as we shall see, is none other than the ancient Egyptian religion or, more precisely, that magical religion that he, Bruno, has discovered in the Hermetic texts.[26] Bruno, in this ambitious and daring mission, is trying single-handed to seed the idea of a total general reformation of the world, a sort of intellectual and spiritual 'Second Coming' which he believes can be brought about by the revival of ancient Egypt's magical religion. To do this, Bruno is applying his own magical powers, that is the 'words of power' which are made the more devastating by linking them to talismans and archetypal images.[27] Making use of a mixture of alchemical and cabalistic techniques, Bruno's brand of magic using words and images is clearly 'Egyptian' in style. This is made evident when he wrote:

> . . . the sacred letters used among the Egyptians were called hieroglyphs . . . which were images . . . taken from things of nature, or their parts. By using such writings and voices, the Egyptians used to capture with marvellous skills *the language of the gods* (my italics). Afterwards when letters of the kind which we use now were invented . . . they brought about a great rift both in memory and in the divine and magical sciences.[28]

This statement alone demonstrates the amazing perceptive ability this sixteenth-century magician had. For we must remember that Bruno was writing these words more than three centuries *before* the Frenchman Champollion deciphered hieroglyphics.[29] From the time he began his visit to England in 1583, Giordano Bruno went about proclaiming the imminent return of the magical religion of Egypt. As Frances Yates pointed out:

> The works in the form of dialogues written in Italian which Bruno published in England are usually classified as moral and philosophical . . . both Bruno's proposed reform and his philosophy are related to his Hermetic religious mission . . . a mission [which] . . . becomes expanded into a projected full restoration of the magical religion of the pseudo-Egyptians of the Asclepius (a major tract on the Hermetica) . . .[30]

Yet Bruno was no New Age ranter. In Bruno we have the perfect example of how a powerful intuition can know what scientific minds have trouble perceiving. It was Bruno, for example, who introduced Copernicus's ideas of heliocentricity to the Oxford scholars by using his own intuitive vision of the planets and the sun.[31] It was also Bruno who was among the very first to imagine a cosmos populated by innumerable other worlds.[32] We may thus wonder if his unusual intuition will not one day prove correct when he spoke of a revival of the 'magical Egyptian religion' in the Western world. In his major work *Spaccio della Bestia Trionfante*, which was written in England in 1584, Bruno's central theme is 'the glorification of the magical religion of the Egyptians'.[33] In this work Bruno correctly detected in this ancient religious system that the worship of the Egyptians was the worship of 'God in things' and that communication with the divine could thus be achieved through all things in nature, by the application of a special magic which the Egyptian priests were the masters of:

> . . . for as the divinity descends in a certain manner inasmuch as it communicates itself to nature, so there is an ascent made to the divinity through nature. Thus through the light which shines in natural things one mounts up to the life which presides over them . . . And in truth I see how the wise men (of Egypt) by these means had power to make familiar, affable and domestic gods, which, through the voices which came out of the statues, gave counsels, doctrines, divinations and superhuman teachings. Whence with magical and divine rights they ascended to the height of the divinity by the same scale of nature by which the divinity descends to the smallest things by the communication of itself . . . Those wise men, then, in order to obtain certain benefits and gifts from gods, by means of profound magic, made use of certain natural things in which the divinity was latent, and through which the divinity was able and willing to communicate itself for certain effects. Whence those ceremonies were not vain fancies, but living voices which reached to the very ears of the gods . . .[34]

Bruno was living in a time of great expectation for some major religious reformation. A sort of 'Second Coming' frenzy was about to take hold of the European masses. Signs in the heavens were eagerly awaited. Rumours ran wild that soon a messianic-like child would be born and would unite Europe and the world under a fully reformed Christianity. Hermeticism, according to many, was the ideal tool in an attempt to activate this religious reform.[35] As the Parisian scholar J. Dagens noted, 'the end of the sixteenth century and the start of the seventeenth century have been the golden age of the Religious Hermetism'.[36] Using complex mathematical calculations, some astronomers and religious reformers worked out that the coming of such a messianic 'child' would take place at the end of the sixteenth century,[37] and this would be made manifest with signs in the heavens. Amazingly, the heavens were to oblige with the sudden appearance of a supernova star in 1604.[38]

This spectacular phenomenon took place in the constellation of

Cygnus. This event, among others, was to trigger a bizarre religious reformation movement in Europe known as Rosicrucianism with its strange figurehead called Christian Rosecroix.[39] We shall return to the Rosicrucian movement later on. Meanwhile, let us see how much of the Corpus Hermeticum concerned the stars and the ability of Egyptian magicians to draw their power down to earth. This principle is encapsulated in the famous Hermetic dictum 'As Above, so Below' and is disclosed in the book of Asclepius in a lengthy passage known as the Lament. The Lament opens with a haunting statement about the relationship between the cosmos and Egypt:

> Do you not know, Asclepius, that Egypt is made in the image of Heaven, or so to speak more exactly, in Egypt all the operations of the powers which rule and work in heaven have been brought down to Earth below? Nay, it should be said that the whole Cosmos dwells in this our land and its temples . . .[40]

The text then goes on to describe the departure of the gods from Egypt back to heaven, and the great calamities that this will cause to Egypt:

> . . . and yet, since it is fitting that wise men should have knowledge of all events before they come to pass, you must not be left in ignorance of this: there will come a time when it will be seen that in vain have the Egyptians honoured the deity with heartfelt piety and assiduous service; and all our holy worship will be found bottomless and ineffectual. For the gods will return from Earth to Heaven; Egypt will be forsaken, and this land which was once the home of religion will be left desolate, bereft of the presence of its deities. This land will be filled with foreigners . . . O Egypt, Egypt, of thy religion nothing will remain but an empty tale, which thine own children in time to come will not believe; nothing will be left but graven words, and only the stones will tell of thy piety . . . no one will raise his eyes to heaven, the pious will be deemed insane, and the impious wise; the madman will be thought a brave man, and the wicked will be esteemed good. As to soul and the belief that it is immortal by nature, or may hope to attain immortality, as I have taught you, all this they will mock at, and will even persuade themselves that it is false . . .

Then, as we have seen, with amazing premonition,[41] comes the great Hermetic prophecy that the gods will return to Egypt in some distant future:

> But when all this has befallen, Asclepius, then the Master and Father, God, the first before all, the maker of that god who first came into being, will look on that which has come to pass and will stay the disorder by the counterworking of his Will . . . He will call back to the right path those who have gone astray, he will

cleanse the world from evil . . . Those gods who ruled the earth will be restored, and they will be installed in a city at the furthest threshold of Egypt (*in summo initio Augypti*) which will be founded towards the setting sun and to which all human kind will hasten by land and by sea . . .[42]

We have already seen in Chapter 2 how the 'city on the furthest threshold of Egypt' was named Monte Libyco in the *Hermetica*, and that it turned out to be that plateau on the edge of the Libyan desert which today we call Giza and where stand the three Great Pyramids and the Sphinx. Although this conclusion could not have been known to Giordano Bruno in the sixteenth century, Bruno nonetheless saw himself as the herald of the 'holy and awe-striking restoration' of the magical religion of Egypt by proclaiming its triumphant return in a magical 'city of the sun' as mentioned in the texts. In a curious way Bruno, with his highly tuned perception, seems to have intuitively worked out that one of the most important aspects of the Egyptian gnosis involved a profound understanding of the stars, and how these could be used to create powerful talismans and memory devices in the mind. His book, *Spaccio della Bestia Trionfante*, is full of allusions and explanations of such 'astral memory' systems which, according to Bruno, were vital in the cultivation of a super-memory and a means to tune oneself into the Universal Mind or Cosmos. In this respect Bruno came extremely close to a very similar system of initiation that was indeed actually used by the Heliopolitan priesthood of the Pyramid Age in conjunction with the monuments on the Giza Plateau in order to induce or awaken 'astral memory'.[43] We shall return in due course to these strange memory mechanisms of the ancient pyramid builders of Egypt. Meanwhile let us find out what 'city' Bruno had in mind and when and where the magical Egyptian religion would make its long awaited return.

THE HERMETIC CITY OF THE SUN

There exists an obscure medieval manuscript whose relation to Bruno's Hermetic religious mission has somehow escaped attention. This manuscript, copies of which are kept in various libraries in Europe, is generally known as the 'Picatrix'.[44] The title, however, is a misnomer. It seems that the Renaissance scholars mistranslated the Arab author's name and used it as the title.[45] The Picatrix was almost certainly composed in the middle of the eleventh century by an Arab scholar who lived in Andalusia in Spain, and its original title was *Ghayat El Hakim*, which means 'The Aim of the Sage'.[46] The Picatrix was first written in Arabic, using as its source a collection of 'two hundred and twenty-four books' on Hermeticism, astrology, magic and alchemy.[47] Although it is known to have circulated among scholars in medieval and Renaissance times, it was not until 1933 that the Arabic version was made available to modern academics through the efforts of the German scholar Hellmut Ritter, and it took until 1962 for a German translation to be made. It was this last translation that Frances Yates studied at the Warburg Institute in London. The American scholar David Pingree, working closely with the Warburg, produced a Latin translation in 1986 and now an English translation is being readied by J.B. Trapp, also of the Warburg.[48]

The Picatrix deals essentially with a form of Hermetic magic known to scholars as 'Celestial Magic' or 'Astrological Magic'.[49] As we have seen, this sort of magic attempts to 'draw down' to earth the power and influence of the stars and the planets. The idea is to select a special object or monument, which is called a talisman, and through rituals, ceremonies and magical incantations induce the astral energies of 'spirits and angels' to dwell in it.[50] David Pingree, a renowned expert on the Picatrix, explains the rudiments of this strange yet powerful form of magic:

> . . . all magical acts . . . are sanctioned and even effected by the power of God acting through his angels and spirits who dwell above the sublunar world, that is in the celestial spheres; these angels and spirits are the highest beings that can be reached by man and who can intervene on earth. In this celestial purification lies the principal conceptual difference between classical magic and that of the *Ghayat* (Picatrix). The ostensible object of one branch of celestial magic is to draw these celestial spirits down to earth to induce them to enter into a material object (a talisman) which thereupon possesses well-defined magical powers . . . Normally the ritual is performed at an astrologically determined time; in its most advanced form, the theory is that only at such moments does the ray of the celestial body penetrate directly into the talisman and permit the spiritual power to travel along it . . .[51]

The Picatrix is a sort of manual of how such talismans can be created. It finally ends, however, with a most ingenious concept for the design of a mega or super-talisman. The author of the Picatrix proposes, no less, the design of a *whole city* as a 'talisman', a sort of magical city set along special astronomical and astrological alignments, with monuments, statues, shrines and buildings carefully designed along sacred geo-metrical schemes and 'images of the stars'.[52] In the Latin version of the Picatrix, such a magical talismanic city is said to have been designed by Hermes-Thoth, and was called Adocentyn. It was situated near 'abundant water' in which Hermes also built 'a temple to the sun'.[53] It was built in 'the east of Egypt' and was an amazing 'twelve miles long', with figures of a lion, an eagle or hawk, a bull and a dog set at each of its four gates which were directed toward the four cardinal points on the horizon.[54] In the original Arabic version of the Picatrix, however, the city is called Al Ashmunain, which is the Arabic name for Hermapolis Magna, where once had stood the most celebrated shrine to Thoth.[55] Yet the mention of a twelve-miles-long city clearly suggests something else, something that would also befit the astronomical and astrological system of magic that was indeed practised in Egypt by the legendary Thoth-Hermes. This, I postulate, is none other than the vast twelve miles or so strip of desert near Cairo in which are found the great pyramid fields of the Memphite necropolis. In support of this hypothesis are the following comments by Frances Yates in her study of the magical city of Adocentyn in the Picatrix:

> There was a big influence of Hermetic and gnostic literature and ideas on the Arabic world and particularly among the Arabs of Harran. Talismanic magic was practised by these Arabs, and influence came through the Sabaens who were immersed in Hermetism, in both its philosophical and religious, and its magical aspects. Picatrix is by an Arabic writer under strong Sabaen, that is to say Hermetic, influence . . . The city of Adocentyn in which virtue is enforced on the inhabitants by magic helps to explain why, when the magical Egyptian religion decayed, manners and morals went to rack and ruins, as is so movingly described in the Lament. And in the prophecy in the Asclepius, after the Lament, of the eventual restoration of the Egyptian religion, it is said: '*The gods who exercise their dominion over the earth will be restored one day and installed in a City at the extreme limits of Egypt, a City which will be founded towards the setting sun, and into which will hasten, by land and by sea, the whole race of mortal men . . .*' In the context of the Asclepius, the City of Adocentyn might thus be seen both as the ideal Egyptian society before its fall and as the ideal pattern of its future and universal restoration.[56]

We have seen in Chapter 2 how in the book of Asclepius, the location of this magical city is given as 'Monte Libyco' which we subsequently identified as being the Memphite necropolis, the central feature of which is the Giza plateau.[57] A further clue lies in the mention of the 'Sabaens' in connection with this magical 'city'. Who were the mysterious Sabaens, or Sabians, from whom the author of the Picatrix drew his ideas? And how could these Sabians lead us to Giza Plateau?

THE PILGRIMAGE OF THE SABIANS

Unknown to Bruno and his contemporaries, there had once existed elsewhere in the world a religious sect that had, in fact, adopted the Hermetic or magical religion of the Egyptians that Bruno was so determined to restore to the world. This sect was known as the Sabians, whose stronghold was the mystical city of Harran in south-east Turkey. Harran is mentioned in the Book of Genesis where it has the distinction of being the place God first spoke to the patriarch Abraham.[58] The city of Harran was apparently sacred to the moon-god Sin, a tradition that was still upheld well into Christian times.[59] There is a strange story by an Arab, Am Nadim, written in AD 987 in which he quotes from a book entitled 'The disclosure of the Doctrine of the Harranians, who in our time are known as the Sabians'[60]:

> . . . in AD 830 (the Caliph) Al Mamun setting out of Baghdad, his capital, on a campaign against the Byzantines, passed through Harran, and noticed, among those who there presented themselves before him, some people strangely dressed, asked them: 'To which of the people protected by law (people of the Scriptures) do you belong?' They answered, 'We are Harranians.' 'Are you Christians?' 'No.' 'Jews?' 'No.' 'Magians?' 'No.' 'Have you a holy scripture or a prophet?' To this they gave an evasive answer. 'You are infidels and idolaters then.' Said the Caliph, 'And it is permitted to shed your blood. If you have not, by the time when I return from my campaign, become either Moslems or adherents of one of the religions recognised in the Koran, I will extirpate you to a man.'

Under this threat, many of them, in outward profession at least, went over to Islam, and others to Christianity. But some of them held out, and consulted a Moslem jurist, who, in return for a large fee, gave them this advice:

> When Al Mamun comes back, say to him 'We are Sabians'; for that is the name of a religion of which God speaks in the Koran.

The Caliph Al Mamun never returned. Al Mamun had, in actual fact, been to Egypt ten years before his encounter with the Sabians. He is distinguished in the history of pyramid exploration for having been the first to enter the Great Pyramid in modern times.[61] According to the scholar Walter Scott, the Harranians, now called 'Sabians', had to make good their claim by stating officially to the Moslem authorities that the 'book' to which they belonged was the 'book of Hermes' and that their prophet was Hermes Trismegistus.[62] Scott argues that some of the Harranian scholars must have been acquainted with the Hermetica and other Neoplatonic works and in view of the supposed great antiquity of the Hermetic writings chose these as the scriptures acceptable to the Moslem authorities.

There is, however, another explanation. The tenth-century Arab historian Al Masudi reported that 'under Omar son of Abdel Aziz (AD 705-710) the chief seat of knowledge was transferred from Alexandria to Antioch; and later on in the reign of Al Mutawaqil, it was transferred to Harran . . .'[63] Al Mutawaqil reigned from AD 847 to 861. This means that the reputation of Harran as a 'chief seat of knowledge', and ranking in par with Alexandria and Antioch, preceded their supposed deceptive conversion to Hermeticism. The truth may well be that the Harranians were not only considered scholars and erudite men from much earlier times, but that they had probably adopted the Hermetic religion long before the visit of the Caliph Al Mamun in AD 830. One suggestion is that the tutelary deity of Harran being the primitive moon-god Sin was readily transferable to that of the moon-god Thoth (Hermes) of the ancient Egyptians. Although the city itself was dedicated to the moon, the author of the Picatrix strongly indicated that the Sabians of Harran were essentially magicians who practised that special celestial or astrological magic devised in ancient Egypt. This form of magic was specifically associated with the stars, and thus as Frances Yates pointed out, a better name for it would be 'astral magic'[64] or 'star religion'[65] since the Sabians were, in effect, star-worshippers.[66] In 1946 the Egyptologist Selim Hassan, while studying the star religion of the ancient Egyptians, came across a passage in the Geographical Dictionary compiled by the eleventhcentury Arab historian and geographer Yakut El Hamawi, where the Giza Pyramids were mentioned. Perplexed by what he saw, Hassan was to write:

> The association of the Giza Pyramids with the stellar cult was long maintained by tradition, and those of Khufu and Khafre retain the reputation of being connected to star-worship as late as the Arab Period. In the Geographical Dictionary, (called the) *Mo'agam El Buldan* by Yakut El Hamawi,[67] it is said, after giving the measurements of the two largest of the Giza Pyramids: 'To both of them the Sabians made their pilgrimage.'[68]

Hassan pointed out that the Arabic name for 'Sabians' was *Al Sabi'a*, meaning the 'people of Sab'a'. Hassan was aware of the tradition that associated the Sabians with star-worship, and this led him to make this interesting connection with ancient Egypt:

> Now, of course, the Sabians were star-worshippers, and if I guess rightly they had derived their name from the Egyptian word S'ba . . .[69]

In the ancient Egyptian hieroglyphic language, the word *S'ba* means 'star'.[70] In hieroglyphs there are no vowels; it is generally difficult to know how a certain word would have been pronounced. In the case of the word *S'ba*, it is likely that it was pronounced 'saba'.[71] Let us recall that the Harranians, according to Arab tradition, associated their name with 'people of the book', i.e. from the Scriptures or Bible.[72] Hassan thus pointed out that the name chosen by the Harranians denoting a 'star' is also found in the Bible, where the word 'saba' means 'hosts', usually to denote 'heavenly bodies' i.e. stars.[73] Another clue as to why the Sabians may have performed their pilgrimage to the Giza Pyramids is given by various Arab authors who, as early as AD 670, report a persistent legend that the Great Pyramid of Giza was built by Hermes 'before the Flood' in order to preserve an ancient system of knowledge.[74 & 75] In the Picatrix there is a clue as to what the Sabians might have been looking for at Giza, one that strangely echoes the notion of a secret subterranean chamber. For in one of the passages an adept of the talismanic astral magic makes this eerie declaration:

> When I wished to bring to light the science of the mystery and nature of Creation, I came upon a subterranean vault full of darkness and winds . . .[76]

At any rate, all this implies, if not explicitly, that the magical city proposed by Giordano Bruno is one and the same as [1] the city of Adocentyn in the Picatrix; [2] the Hermetic city founded 'towards the setting sun' in the Asclepius;[3] and the magical pyramid 'city' of 'Monte Libyco', i.e. the Memphite necropolis and Giza. We shall later return to Giza and its strange connection to astral magic. Meanwhile let us probe the Hermetic, a little further for more clues.

THE SIGN OF THE CROSS

In 1591 Bruno made the fatal mistake of returning to Italy. Blinded by his own convictions and deep sense of mission, Bruno unwisely had hoped to convince the bishops of Rome of a great reformation plan for Christianity through the revival of the Egyptian Hermetic religion. In May 1592, Bruno was arrested by the Papal Inquisition and put into a dungeon in Rome. After a lengthy trial and opportunities to recant his 'heresy', on the morning of 17th February 1600 he was taken to Campo de' Fiori

(Place of the Flowers), a wedge stuffed in his mouth to prevent him from speaking, tied to a wooden pole and burnt alive. Thus the last of the 'Egyptian' magicians died in silence, his head turned away from the crucifix that was brandished to his face by a Dominican monk.

During his bogus trial at the Vatican, a bishop had asked Bruno to explain his claim that the Egyptians knew the sign of the cross long before Christianity. To this Bruno first cautiously explained that he had come across this statement in Ficino's translation of the Hermetica. But then, in an extraordinary act of defiance, he infuriated his inquisitors by speaking of the sign of the cross in connection to astral magic:

> . . . and that the planets (and stars) and their influences have more efficacy . . . when they are at the beginning of the cardinal signs, that is when the colures intersect the ecliptic or the zodiac in a direct line, when two circles intersect in this manner is produced the form of such a character (i.e. a cross) . . .[77]

Astronomically speaking, Bruno's statement is indeed correct. The event actually occurs twice a day, although at different times of the day as the seasons change. The sign of the cross is produced when the prime meridian is directly above an observer, such that the meridian line forms one arm of the cross and the latitude line forms the other. As Bruno stated at his trial, the ideal 'astrological' times of the year for the influences of astral magic to be at optimal efficacy would be during the solstices or the equinoxes, i.e. at the colures. The 'cross' thus formed on the ground at these times will occur either at sunrise or sunset, or at noon or midnight. Now Ficino, who translated the *Hermetica* for Cosimo de Medici in 1463, commented that the Egyptian cross thus formed by the colures was not only a 'testimony to the "gift of the stars" (i.e. astral magic) but also as a *presage to the coming of Christ*.'[78] These statements regarding the cross and the colures made by Bruno and Ficino are, in fact, lifted from the *Hermetica* in a tract known as the Kore Kosmou.[79] In this tract the goddess Isis discourses with her son, Horus, who asks her why men who are born outside Egypt lack the refined intelligence of the Egyptians. To this Isis replied:

> The Earth lies in the middle of the Universe, stretched on her back as a human might lie . . . her head lies toward the South, her right shoulder toward the East, her left shoulder toward the West and her feet lies beneath the Great Bear constellation (i.e. North) . . . But the right holy land of our ancestors (Egypt) lies in the middle of the Earth; and the middle of the human body is the sanctuary of the heart, and the heart is the headquarters of the soul, and that, my son, is the reason why the men of this land . . . are more intelligent . . .[80]

Thus the huge 'crucifix' formed on the earth, i.e. when the colures intersect the ecliptic and are on the horizon, has 'Egypt' as it epicentre, where the east-west and north-south axes of the earth intersect. Thus in Egypt, at a place the Hermetic adepts called 'the sanctuary of the heart', the epicentre or 'headquarters of the soul', was imagined to pass a prime meridian and a prime latitude. Since 1860 it has been argued by some researchers that the prime meridian of Egypt, as well as for the whole planet, should, in fact, be made to pass through the apex of the Great Pyramid.[81] The reasoning behind this is that not only does the Great Pyramid sit at the centre of the Earth's land masses, but it is alsoaligned to the four cardinal directions with such uncanny precision that it compelled a French astronomer, for example, to call it the 'perfect meridional instrument.'[82] Indeed, when in 1884 the International Meridian Committee met in Washington DC to decide where the world's prime meridian should pass, the Astronomer Royal of Scotland 'took the view that if there had to be a prime meridian, then it should be set on the Great Pyramid in Egypt.'[83]

We shall recall that at midnight on 31st December 1999, the Egyptian authorities will place a gilded capstone on top of the Great Pyramid, an event that will be televised live around the world. Now close to midnight on that date the colures will be ideally set, such that the vernal equinox colure (through Leo) will be in the east, the autumnal equinox colure (through Aquarius) will be in the west, the winter solstice colure (through Orion) will be in the south and the summer solstice colure (through Draco) will be in the north. In *Keeper of Genesis* we have shown that it was when such a perfect conjunction occurred that at Giza the ground and sky locked in perfect correlation.[84] More on this in due course.

Meanwhile the burning of Giordano Bruno had sent a gruesome signal of intolerance across Europe. The Hermetic tradition, as it had done once before, took a nosedive and went deep underground. It was to resurface eventually in a strange disguise. The thread is picked up by Frances Yates in the 1960s. After reviewing Bruno's reckless appeal for religious tolerance, his philanthropy and his call for the reformation of Christianity through the revival of the Egyptian gnosis, Yates asked herself 'where is there such a combination of this?':

> The only answer to that question that I can think of . . . is Freemasonry, with its mythical links with medieval masons, its toleration, its philanthropy and its Egyptian symbolism.[85]

Yates, of course, could have added several other similarities: Freemasonry's initiation systems based on the ancient mysteries; its preoccupation with symbolic architecture and sacred geometry in city developments and plans; and finally its epic feud with the Roman Catholic Church. Although Freemasonry does not emerge as an organised secret society in England before the early part of the seventeenth century, Frances Yates felt compelled to drop this bombshell:

> One cannot help wondering whether it might have been among the spiritually dissatisfied in England, who perhaps heard in Bruno's 'Egyptian' message some hint of relief, that the strains of the Magic Flute (a synonym for Freemasonry) were first breathed in the air . . . We are told that Mozart's Magic Flute embodies some of his beliefs as a Freemason. If so, we might have in this opera a translation into poetic and musical imagery of the theme of the good religion of the Egyptians, of the mysteries of Isis and Osiris into which the good are initiated, of the magical atmosphere through which human souls make their way to a Hermetic-Egyptian salvation . . . It was, of course, with continental Freemasonry that Mozart was in contact. But all continental Freemasonry ultimately derived from England; and it was in Elizabethan England that Giordano Bruno had so fervently preached the revival of the Egyptian religion . . .[86]

But there was something else, something far more subtle and amazingly ingenious that was brewing in the minds of some 'Hermetic' scholars immediately after Bruno's death . . .

THE OPENING OF THE TOMB

In the closing decade of the sixteenth century, Europe was locked in the effervescence of a millennial mood, and of great expectations for a new age that would bring radical reformation in Christianity and unify the war-torn continent under one messianic-like prince.[87] Astrologers, using various computations and charts, had earmarked 1604 as being the most propitious year, when the signs of the long anticipated new world order would manifest in the sky.[88] As if by divine intervention, 1604 saw the appearance of two new stars: one in the constellation of Serpentarius and the other in Cygnus.[89] The Oxford scholar Christopher McIntosh, who studied the effect of these strange events, wrote:

> At the time the new stars appeared in the sky, Jupiter and Saturn were in conjunction in the 9th House (of the Zodiac). As Jupiter was considered a good planet and Saturn a bad one, there was some speculation as to which was dominant. The general consensus, however, was that, as the 9th House is

Jupiter's House and Jupiter rules Pisces, the sign which was in the ascendant at the time of observation, Jupiter was the dominant planet. Both planets were also favourably placed, in relation to the other planets. When Saturn is well placed it brings forth thoughtful, serious men. The combination, therefore, promised the advent of a prophet or prophets who would be wise, just and righteous. It was believed, moreover, that these astrological positions corresponded to the position present at creation . . . thus the signs and the appearance of the new stars in 1604 were the same as those for the beginning of the world, proving that 1604 would also see a great new beginning . . .[90]

Around 1604, a group of Hermetic scholars met in Germany. Capitalising on this fervent messianic mood, they hatched a sort of intellectual *coup d'état* by planning to detonate a powerful 'Hermetic device', one that involved hoaxing a sort of huge messianic stunt in the very heart of central Europe. This mysterious group[91] claimed to belong to a secret and 'invisible' society known as the Meritorious Order of the Rosy Cross, the Rosicrucians for short .[92] 'The Rosicrucian movement,' wrote McIntosh, 'is part of a way of thinking whose roots go far back into antiquity and which can be described as the Western esoteric tradition.'[93] The 'tradition' which McIntosh is speaking of is, of course, none other than the Gnostic-Hermetic tradition of ancient Alexandria, of the Sabians, of Ficino and of Bruno. As Frances Yates was to explain this mysterious 'new way of thinking':

> . . . Rosicrucians represent the Hermetic-Cabalistic tradition of the Renaissance in some form . . . It may therefore be suggested that Rosicrucian aspirations after a universal reform in a Hermetic context may well owe something to Bruno . . . (but) . . . is there, or is there not, a connection between the Rosicrucians and the origins of Freemasonry? Some people think there is . . . It is not impossible that the influence of the importation of Rosicrucian ideas into England (in c.1614) . . . may have crossed with an earlier courtly stream, perhaps influenced by Bruno, to produce Freemasonry . . .[94]

The Rosicrucian hoax of 1604 was almost certainly masterminded by a learned pastor from the city of Tubingen in south-west Germany. Working in secret with a small group of colleagues,[95] a book was produced anonymously and distributed widely around Germany and other parts of Europe. Under the ostentatious title of *A Discovery of the Fraternity of the Most Noble Order of the Rosy Cross,* also known as the *Fama Fraternitatis* or simply the Rosicrucian Manifesto, this book announced the discovery of the tomb of a magician-sage called Christian Rosencreutz and the launching of a new spiritual age for mankind.

We are informed that the latter had acquired some very secret knowledge during his travels in the Middle East. This knowledge, or gnosis, was to be used somehow to bring about a great religious reformation. To this end Christian Rosencreutz was said to have recruited three helpers whom he called 'Brothers' and thus, the authors say, was born the Fraternity of the Rosy Cross. Soon they grew in numbers. The principal occupation of the 'Brothers' was to heal the sick and similar acts of philanthropy, as well as to spread the 'knowledge' around the world. The 'Brothers' were bound to meet once a year at their headquarters known as The House of the Holy Spirit. Apparently the first of the original fraternity to die was buried in England. When Christian Rosencreutz himself died, we are told he was buried in an underground vault. The finding and opening of this vault now, 120 years after his death, was to mark the beginning of the new age and the long awaited reformation of the world. The date of the opening of the tomb was deduced to be 1604.[96] Much of the mysticism of the Rosicrucian Manifesto revolves around the opening of this mysterious tomb. The hoax was specifically intended to be perceived as the dawn preceding the first sunrise of the new age. As the Rosicrucian Manifesto proclaims:

> We know . . . that there will now be a general reformation, both of divine and human things, according to our desire and the expectations of others; for it is fitting that before the rising of the Sun should break forth Aurora, or some clearness of divine light in the sky.[97]

'The opening of Christian Rosencreutz's tomb', wrote Christopher McIntosh, 'whether an actual event or a symbolic movement, sent forth a spectre that was to haunt Europe almost as persistently as would the spectre of Communism two and a half centuries later.'[98] This ploy or 'Hermetic device' worked beyond expectations. Rumour of an ultra-secret fraternity working behind the scenes to bring about a general reformation of Europe spread like wildfire among the learned of Germany, France, Holland and England. Like some sort of intellectual virus, Rosicrucian 'thinking' began to affect the best minds of the seventeenth century. In England it is almost certain that characters such as Francis Bacon, Robert Fludd, Robert Boyles, Elias Ashmole and Sir Christopher Wren all got involved in one way or another with the Rosicrucian movement.[99] Even the great Isaac Newton, and René Descartes in France, seem to have fallen under its magical spell.[100] Amazingly, many historians today seem to agree that not only might the Rosicrucian movement have provided the esoteric strain that created 'speculative' Freemasonry in England, but it might also be indirectly responsible for the foundation of the Royal Society in England in 1660.[101] We shall later see how the same esoteric 'strain' eventually played a major role in the formation of the Egypt Exploration Society in 1882 and the creation of the prestigious 'Petrie' Chair of Egyptology at University College London. More interestingly, we shall also see how the latter-day 'Rosicrucians' have been promoting, since the early 1930s, the search for a secret underground vault at Giza akin to, perhaps even modelled on, the notions of the legendary Hall of Records.

In 1798, Napoleon invaded Egypt. It was then that the first Masonic Lodge was installed in Egypt. Known as the lodge of Isis, it was inaugurated by General Kleber, the leader of the French military occupation.[102] Throughout the nineteenth century lodges were established across Egypt under the auspices of the central Masonic bodies of Europe, such as the Grand Orient of France and United Grand Lodge of England. In 1876 the Grand National Lodge of Egypt was founded, boasting as one of its members the Khedive Tewfik Pasha, who had received his Masonic initiation in London. In 1882 Britain landed its naval forces in Alexandria, invaded Egypt and set up a High Commission, with Tewfik as its puppet ruler. In 1883 the United Grand Lodge of Egypt and the Sudan was formed.

Since then strange things had been going on at the Great Pyramid.

Chapter Seven

The Parent Country

'According to Plato, the first characteristic of the philosopher is that he must be prepared to follow the answers wherever the argument goes . . .'

Anne Freemantle, *The Age of Belief*

THE ISIS LODGE

Masonic historians have long debated the origin of Freemasonry. As an institution, there is little doubt that this secret society originated in the early seventeenth century in England and Scotland, and that with the exile of the Stuart monarchy in France and Holland, it is believed that it took root on the European continent.[1] It was, at first, an elitist fraternity appealing particularly to the aristocracy and the monarchy. Many British kings, princes and noblemen were initiated into the Brotherhood and still are to this day.[2] The same applied to continental Europe, where it was especially rife in France and Germany.[3] 'Speculative' Freemasonry, which simply means Freemasonry as an esoteric, mystical society, did not just spring up from anywhere, and there have been many attempts to claim as its source the ancient mystery religions of Greece and the East and, more particularly, the ancient Egyptian religion and cult of Osiris.[4] In his controversial *Inside the Brotherhood*, author Martin Short writes that:

Today Freemasons may deny that any part of their cult hearkens back to the pagan gods of the Nile. Yet in Freemason's Hall, Dublin, home of the world's second oldest Grand Lodge, the Holy Arch Room contains two large sphinxes and other sculptures aping Ancient Egypt. In Philadelphia, USA, the Masonic

Fig. 20. Napoleon inside the Great Pyramid c. 1798.

Temple boasts 'the finest specimen of Egyptian decoration outside Egypt'. Even London's Great Eastern Hotel at Liverpool Street station has a magnificent Egyptian Temple for lodges to rent for their ritual nights out.[5]

I have visited the Masonic 'Egyptian' Temple, Philadelphia on several occasions. The temple was completed in 1889. It is fifty-one feet by forty-three feet, and there are twelve huge columns which support the four sides of the temple, with each column apparently being a replica of an original in Egypt. On the east wall can be seen the 'all-seeing eye of Horus' with colour panels representing Osiris, Isis and various other Egyptian deities. Philadelphia in Greek means 'Brotherly Love' or 'Love of the Brotherhood', and Philadelphia is, to many, the hub of American Freemasonry.[6] It boasts, for example, of having been the place where Benjamin Franklin installed one of the first Masonic lodges in the USA,[7] and the University that bears his name has a fraternity called 'Sphinx', to add to the 'Egyptianised' folklore and symbolism.[8] Interestingly, as we have seen in the prologue, it was at this university that the education of Dr Hawass, Director-General of the Giza Pyramids, was allegedly arranged by the Edgar Cayce Foundation.[9] But more of that later. Philadelphia is by no means the only Masonic city which displays a blatantly Egyptianised temple. Washington DC, the Masonic 'capital' par excellence,[10] was apparently planned along Masonic principles[11] and today has a massive Masonic monument in the fashionable suburb of Alexandria whose design evokes the Pharos or ancient light-house of Alexandria in Egypt.[12] This is the so-called George Washington Masonic National Memorial, which was erected on the spot where the legendary Masonic lodge No. 22 once stood, where apparently George Washington himself was initiated into the Brotherhood in 1753.[13] The Alexandria Masonic memorial took fifty-two years to build. When it was completed in 1923, the building was consecrated with the well-known Masonic ceremony of 'placing the corner stone', an event that was attended by many notables and presided over by Chief Justice William Howard Taft, a prominent Freemason and US President from 1909 to 1913. Taft, a former Yale student and professor of law, was also a prominent member of the Skull and Bones fraternity.[14] The building was fully inaugurated in 1931 by President Herbert Hoover.[15]

The Alexandria George Washington Masonic National Memorial has a floor dedicated to one of Freemasonry's most bizarre and high-ranking societies, the so-called 'Ancient Egyptian Arabic Order Noble of the Mystic Shrine'. Known simply as the 'Shriners', the order is governed by an Imperial Council and boasts approximately 550,000 members in the USA alone. It has the peculiarity among Masonic fraternities of allowing women members in to their lodges. The men wear the fez or red cap (hence their nick-name, the 'Red Shriners') and the women members are referred to as the 'daughters of Isis'.[16] Like most of these Masonic groups, their official role appears purely philanthropic, although it is far from clear why the Shriners entertain such an obsessive fascination with ancient Egypt and its mysteries. However, they are by no means the only Masonic order with such a curious trait.

One of the oldest and most mysterious of 'Egyptian' Masonic orders was known as the 'African Architects'. It was founded in Germany in 1767 by Frederick Von Koppen, an officer in the Prussian army.[17] Von Koppen is often said to be the author of a strange work known as the *Crata Repoa*, which purported to be authentic reproductions of initiation rituals performed in the Great Pyramid by ancient Egyptian priests.[18] As odd as it may seem, this bizarre 'Egyptian' secret society received the sponsorship of Frederick II of Prussia, who had built for its members a magnificent library in the region of Silesia in south Poland.[19] Yet the most intensely 'Egyptianised' Masonic orders were created in France. The largest and most active is the so-called 'Masonic Order of Memphis and Misraim', headquartered in the city of Paris. This order is a fusion of two Masonic orders, Memphis and Misraim. Misraim is the ancient

Fig. 21. An opening of a Masonic lodge of Memphis-Misraim in Belgium.

Hebrew name for Egypt, and Memphis is the name of the oldest
Pharaonic capital near the Memphite pyramid necropolis.[20] Presided
over by a 'Great Hierophant', the Memphis-Misraim Order was
originally very elitist. Today it has dwindled to an estimated 8500
members world-wide, the majority being, for some unexplained reason,
in South America.[21] The spark and impetus behind these 'Egyptian'
Masonic orders in France was the Napoleonic campaign in Egypt, which
was not only to fire the imagination of the popular esoteric movement in
Europe but also imported the seed of Freemasonry into Egypt and the
rest of the Arab world.[22]

In 1798 Napoleon Bonaparte invaded Egypt with a force of 40,000
men. Much has been said about the true motives of Napoleon's
'expedition' to Egypt, some having a kernel of truth, others falling into
the realm of fiction. The 'expedition', there is no doubt, reeked of
mythical and archetypal connotations. As French Masonic historian

Gerard Galtier noted, Napoleon was perceived, like Alexander the Great and Augustus Caesar before him, as the 'warrior-king and pacifist, who was recreating the universal empire, and bringing into contact the wisdom of the east with the scientists of the west'.[23] It seems almost certain that Napoleon was fired by a vision far beyond military expansionism.[24] In this respect, his motives have often been linked to the strong possibility that Napoleon was a Freemason, and was probably even initiated during his 'expedition' to Egypt, either in Malta, where his fleet took anchor, or, as some would have it, in Egypt itself and even within the Great Pyramid of Giza.[25] There is also some evidence, albeit circumstantial, that Napoleon belonged to a lodge called 'Egyptian Hermes'.[26] Although it cannot be proved with certainty that Napoleon was a Freemason, it is nonetheless a fact that he had a very intimate relationship with the Brotherhood. Several members of his family were initiated into the Masonic order, including his father and his brother, Joseph, the latter making Grand Master of the Order in 1805.[27] Even his wife, Josephine, was the Grand Mistress of the so-called Adoption Lodges, established by women of the aristocracy and using the pseudo-Egyptian rituals brought into France in 1784 by the enigmatic Count Cagliostro.[28] Most of the officers in Napoleon's army were Freemasons, including several of his top generals such as Murat, Kleber, Augereau, Kellermann, Massena and Macdonald[29] – Kleber, as I've already mentioned, is reported to have founded the first Masonic lodge in Egypt.[30] In 1798 Admiral Horatio Nelson, also a Freemason, tracked down Napoleon's pristine fleet at Abukir, a bay to the east of Alexandria, and destroyed it.[31] This left the French forces trapped inland. In 1801 the French army in Egypt surrendered to a British military expedition led by General Ralph Abercromby, the latter also a Freemason.[32]

In 1805 the British, in collaboration with the Sultan of Turkey, installed an Albanian, Mohamad Ali, as ruler of Egypt. By that time a few Masonic lodges had been established in Alexandria by French officers.[33] Masonic historian Gerald Galtier reports the existence of a secret document found by the Austrian police in 1818 which implicates Mohamad Ali with a Masonic group known as the 'Egyptian Secret Society'.[34] Apparently this society, 'which professed a great veneration for Napoleon',[35] differed from traditional Freemasonry in that it allowed women to join. It had bases in several ports of the Mediterranean, particularly in Italy and Greece. It is probable that Mathieu de Lesseps (father of the famous Ferdinand de Lesseps who built the Suez Canal) was involved with this secret society.[36] Mathieu had been consul for France in Alexandria from 1803 and 1806, and was a personal friend of

Mohamad Ali. Another ex-consul of France in Egypt, Domenico Drovetti, was reported to be the leader of the 'Egyptian Secret Society', bearing the title of Grand Copt.[37] It was about this time that the Khedive Mohamad Ali offered as a 'gift' to the British and the Americans the two ancient obelisks that had stood, since the days of Cleopatra, near the eastern port of Alexandria.

THE PILLARS OF SAINT MICHAEL

The two obelisks of Alexandria, dubbed Cleopatra's Needles by the British forces, had in fact originally stood in the great sun-temple of Heliopolis near Cairo. There, too, during the Pyramid Age, had existed the sanctuary of the Phoenix which housed the sacred Benben Stone.[38] Cleopatra had the obelisks transported down the Nile to Alexandria and placed outside a temple, the Caesarion, which was built in honour of her son, fathered by Julius Caesar.[39] In Christian times this temple was converted into a church and dedicated to the archangel Michael, and a golden winged effigy of St Michael (akin to Hermes) was probably placed on top of one of the obelisks.[40] According to Aubrey Noakes, author of *Cleopatra's Needles*, the pair of obelisks were first noticed by Sir John Moore, a Freemason, while he was riding along the coast after the battle of Alexandria.[41] During the course of 1801-02, his successor, the Earl of Cavan, organised the removal of one of the obelisks to be shipped to England, this being abandoned when the Earl received orders from London to stop all activities because, apparently, the Khedive Mohamad Ali had not given formal permission for its removal.[42] Mohamad Ali had offered the obelisk as a 'gift' to George IV in 1820, some fifteen years after the defeat of Napoleon in Egypt. This is confirmed by a letter written to *The Times* by Sir James Bloomfield, one of King George IV's ministers.[43] Interestingly, George IV was also a Freemason.[44] The 'gift' was then extended in 1931 to King William IV, also a Freemason.[45] The matter, however, remained in limbo until 1868, when another prominent Mason, Sir James Alexander, began to campaign in England to bring the obelisk to London.[46]

At about that time in Egypt, various Masonic lodges were being set up in Alexandria. The first lodge to get a warrant from United Grand Lodge in England was the St John Lodge No. 919 of Alexandria.[47] It was followed by the Hyde Clark Lodge in Alexandria, established in 1865.[48] That same year the first lodge in Cairo was created, the Bulwer Lodge No. 1068, at the Kasr El Noozah Palace on Shoubra Road.[49] It was in this lodge that one of the sons of the Khedive Mohamad Ali, Prince Halim Pasha, was initiated. Halim was then made Masonic District Grand Master for Egypt, his installation taking place in England during a short visit there.[50] It is also reported that Halim Pasha became Grand Master of the Order of Memphis in 1867.[51] In 1875 Sir Alexander went to Alexandria to see the obelisk for himself and to solicit permission from the Khedive, Ismail Pasha, to export it to England. Ismail, a grandson of Mohamad Ali, had also been initiated into the Masonic orders, including that of Memphis.[52] The Khedive immediately reconfirmed his grandfather's wish to see that the obelisk was handed to the British.

It was during this visit to Egypt that Sir Alexander was introduced to Waynman Dixon, a structural engineer working in Cairo. Dixon drew plans of how to remove the obelisk in a specially designed metal container that could float, an engineering idea that much appealed to Sir Alexander. Back in England Sir Alexander met Waynman Dixon's elder brother, John. The latter was a Freemason and, most probably, so was his younger brother, Waynman.[53] It was then that Sir Alexander was contacted by Sir Erasmus Wilson, a wealthy dermatologist and keen Freemason.[54] Wilson offered to put up £20,000 to cover the cost of bringing the obelisk to London and, at the recommendation of Sir Alexander, signed a contract to that effect with John Dixon. The first meeting between the two men is described in a letter by Sir Erasmus Wilson, in which Wilson makes this revealing statement: '. . . I soon found that Mr Dixon was a Freemason, hence, all formality and ceremony were at once banished.'[55] After agreeing to work together on this project, Wilson then asked Dixon a 'favour':

> . . . which is to give an interview to my friend, H.P. Stephenson, who is a civil engineer and will influence with his opinion; (he is) also a Freemason . . .[56]

Since 1871, that is four years before they met Sir Alexander, the Dixon brothers had been implicated in another, even more intriguing affair in Egypt, this time involving not only Freemasonry but another fraternity in Britain, the so-called Anglo–Israelites.[57] In brief, the Anglo–Israelites, founded in the 1840s, believe that the Anglo–Saxon people are direct biological descendants from the ancient Israelites and, by definition, God's chosen people.[58] Also known as the 'Identity Movement', the theory behind the Anglo–Israelite movement was first formulated in the early 1800s by Richard Brothers, a deranged Canadian who ended up in an asylum. Brothers's mission was taken up by a man called John Wilson who published a book, *Our Israelitish Origin*, in 1840. This publication was soon to gain immense support in evangelical and Biblical groups in Britain and also in the USA. Among these were the so-called Adventists, the Church of God and the Jehovah's Witnesses.[59]

One bizarre offshoot of the Anglo-Israelite movement was Pyramidology.[60] This quirky pseudo-science purports that the Great Pyramid of Giza is a prophetic monument, and that in the dimensions of its internal passage system it gives the dates for the fulfilment of Biblical prophecies leading to the Second Coming of Christ.[61] Interestingly, it is reported that the founder of the Jehovah's Witnesses, Charles Taze Russell (1852-1916), was a Pyramidologist.[62] Apparently his successor, Judge Rutherford, advised the Witnesses in 1928 to reject such ideas, causing a huge split within the organisation.[63] Pyramidology was also to infiltrate the so-called Worldwide Church of God (WCG). This 'Church' was formed in the 1930s, and one of its fundamental tenets, based on prophetic doctrines, was the imminent Second Coming of Christ. Its teachings were based on the views of Herbert Armstrong, a newspaper advertiser and staunch supporter of the Anglo-Israelites.[64] At its peak in the 1940s, the WCG had over 100,000 members, ran a TV programme and owned a magazine with eight million copies in circulation. Today its membership, however, is on the decline.[65] Armstrong's Pyramidology was influenced mostly from the works of Charles Piazzi Smyth (1819-1900), the Astronomer Royal of Scotland and author of *Our Inheritance in the Great Pyramid*.[66] An accomplished astronomer of the highest calibre, Smyth nonetheless succumbed to the spell of the Anglo-Israelite movement. His book, backed by his immense scientific reputation, not only fully endorsed their theories, but was the principal cause that launched this bogus movement to greater heights world wide.[67] The movement, like that of the Adventists and the Jehovah's Witnesses, is essentially millennarian in that it advocates the imminent Second Coming of Christ and the start of his 1000 years' reign.[68]

Professor Hermann Bruck, a retired Astronomer Royal for Scotland, and his wife Dr Mary Bruck, a lecturer in astronomy at Edinburgh University, are the authorities on the life and works of Charles Piazzi Smyth.[69] I met the Brucks in 1993, a few months before the publication of my first book, *The Orion Mystery*. The Brucks live on the Penicuik Estate outside Edinburgh, and are now both retired. Mary was assisting me in an investigation I was conducting to trace the whereabouts of ancient relics that had been taken out of the shafts of the Queen's Chamber in the Great Pyramid by John and Waynman Dixon back in 1872.[70] I knew that these relics had made their way to Scotland where they had been examined by Piazzi Smyth.[71] Mary had access to the private letters of Smyth as well as his diary. In the archives of the Royal Observatory of Edinburgh, Mary Bruck found further private correspondence of Piazzi Smyth, from which it was ascertained that the Dixon brothers had been involved with Piazzi Smyth as early as 1871 and that, in 1872, they had been acting on behalf of Piazzi Smyth in a rather strange exploration inside the Great Pyramid.[72] Waynman Dixon, who was based in Cairo, spent several months exploring the Great Pyramid in the hope of finding a secret chamber and the 'records of the ancient founders'.[73] In a letter sent to Piazzi Smyth dated 25th November 1871, for example, John Dixon wrote that:

> I am more then ever convinced of the probability of the existence of a passage and probably a chamber containing possibly the records of the ancient founders . . . as soon as I have a decent plan drawn I will send it to you . . .[74]

It was Waynman who, in September 1872, discovered the two mysterious narrow channels which emanate from the Queen's Chamber.[75] A few small relics were also found in these shafts which, after having apparently vanished for over 120 years, caused a huge controversy when, in 1993, Mary Bruck and I eventually traced them to the British Museum in London.[76] In his 1880 edition of *Our Inheritance in the Great Pyramid*, the meaning of these channels is discussed in the context of Biblical prophecies, and the uncanny proposal was made to Smyth that these shafts may be symbolic of the Second Coming and that their opening will take place at 'the time of the end'.[77]

Returning to the obelisks, the idea of bringing the Alexandria obelisk to London had, in fact, first occurred to the Dixon brothers long before they met Sir James Alexander and Sir Erasmus Wilson. This was explained by Waynman Dixon in an open letter to the *Newcastle Daily Chronicle* soon after the obelisk eventually arrived in England in January 1878 and was about to be placed into position on the Victoria Thames Embankment in London:

> The origin of the cylindrical plan (for the transport of the obelisk) was in this wise. My brother, Mr John Dixon C.E., came out to Egypt in October 1872 for the opening of the Ghizeh Bridge near Cairo (a project supervised by the Dixons) which he had just completed, and when in Alexandria we went one morning to inspect the site of the fallen obelisk, and discussed together the possible means of transport, and I there and then suggested the idea to him of enclosing it as it lay in a cylindrical iron pontoon . . .[78]

While in Egypt, John Dixon had been handed a cigar box by Waynman in which were stored the relics from the shaft in the Queen's Chamber of the Great Pyramid. These ended up being sent to Piazzi Smyth in November 1872 by parcel post.[79] It was also about that time that the Dixon brothers managed to extract a piece of the original casing stone of the Great Pyramid and dispatch it to Piazzi Smyth in Edinburgh. This was to serve as evidence for Piazzi Smyth's 'prophetic' theory and the Anglo-Israelite connection.[80] The crux of the Biblical prophecy theory of Piazzi Smyth rested on two factors, one being that the Pyramid contained in its design the value of 'pi'; the other that the unit of measurement used was the so-called 'Pyramid Inch' and 'Sacred Cubit'.[81] Thus the piece of casing stone was to serve as evidence to support Smyth's calculations and conclusions, namely that the Great Pyramid had been built under divine guidance by the Israelites during their captivity in Egypt. It was Piazzi Smyth's reasoning that, due to the similarity between this 'primitive' 'Pyramid Inch' and the British inch, the Anglo-Saxon race must be the direct descendants of the Israelites whom he claimed had built the Pyramid.[82]

Amazing as it may seem, this outrageous theory, or at least some aspects of it, captured the interest of the Egyptologists at the British Museum, including the curator, Samuel Birch.[83] Smyth was invited by Birch to join the Society of Biblical Archaeology, which was also connected to the Palestine Exploration Fund.[84] The latter was formed in 1865 under the patronage of Queen Victoria and was chaired by the Archbishop of York. These organisations had, as a main objective, the validation of Biblical history, and the work at first was mostly carried out by the Royal Engineers, many of whom were prominent Freemasons.[85] One of the founding members of the Society of Biblical Archaeology, and also a close friend of Birch and Piazzi Smyth,[86] was William Simpson, an artist and journalist. Eighteen seventy-one saw Simpson being initiated into Freemasonry and he joined the famous Quatuor Coronati lodge in 1886, eventually becoming its Senior Warden.[87] The founder of this immensely powerful Masonic lodge was Sir Charles Warren who, also as an active member of the Palestine Exploration Fund, made quite a stir in 1884 by claiming to have located the remains of Solomon's Temple in Jerusalem.[88]

Another prominent Freemason involved with the Palestine Exploration Fund was Lord Kitchener, who became a Senior Grand Warden of the National Grand Lodge of Egypt in 1895.[89] A close associate of Warren and Kitchener, and also a fellow explorer with the Palestine Exploration Fund, was Sir Charles Wilson, who was in charge of a major survey of the Temple Mound in Jerusalem in 1865.[90] Both Wilson and

Warren have managed to associate their names with the very fabric of the Temple Mound, with two architectural features, the so-called 'Warren Gate' and the 'Wilson Arch' found in an underground gallery of the site. Interestingly, Sir Charles Wilson, who was also a colonel with the Royal Engineers, was later to become a founding member of the Egypt Exploration Fund under the presidency of Sir Erasmus Wilson.[91] At their very first annual meeting in July 1883, M. Naville, one of the first Egyptologists to work for the Egypt Exploration Fund, presented a paper on the Biblical city of Pithom, which the Scriptures associate with the Israelites during their captivity in Egypt. The whole presentation reeked of Biblical-Israelitism, and the Earl of Wharncliffe, who was present at the meeting, enthusiastically commended the progress of Naville's works 'and the great importance of their results in illustration of Bible history'.[92] On the board of directors was Amelia Edwards, a rich and intrepid Victorian lady who had travelled extensively in Egypt, and who acted as honory secretary along with Reginald Poole of the British Museum.[93] According to Erasmus Wilson's official biographer, Dr R.M. Hadley, 'it was entirely due to him that a Chair of Egyptology was founded at University College' in London.[94] When in 1892, after his death, Amelia Edwards created the Chair, she chose Wilson's old college out of all the London colleges.[95] By 1869 Erasmus Wilson had accumulated a vast wealth from his investments in gas and railway shares. With an endowment of £5000, which he donated to the Royal Dermatology College, the first Chair of Dermatology was created and Wilson became its first professor. Further donations and his own important status eventually secured him the presidency of the college and a knighthood from the Queen in 1881.[96] After the death of Wilson's widow, the bulk of his fortune, some £209,000, went to the Royal College of Surgeons, who used it to extend their building.[97]

Opposite the Royal College of Surgeons, on the south side of Lincoln's Inn Fields, is the famous Sir John Soane's Museum, which houses one of the largest private collections of ancient Egyptian artefacts. At the time when the Alexandrian Obelisk (Cleopatra's Needle) was being erected in London, the director of the museum, Joseph Bonomi, was acting as a consultant to Erasmus Wilson and the Dixon brothers.[98] Bearing this in mind, as well as the intense 'Masonic' involvement in this operation, there is a rather curious communication between Bonomi and Piazzi Smyth, in which attention is brought to the strange fact that the area of Lincoln's Inn Fields is roughly the same as that of the base of the Great Pyramid.[99] Such a strange coincidence may be just that, a coincidence, were it not for the fact that the north-west corner of Lincoln's Inn

Fields leads into Great Queen's Street in which is found Freemason's Hall, the seat of the United Grand Lodge of England. Freemason's Hall is itself designed as a crude replica of Solomon's Temple, having its directional axis towards the east, commemorating the so-called 'Star of the East', with its strange association with both the star of Bethlehem, the Magi, and the star of ancient Egypt, Sirius, personified by the goddess Isis, consort of Osiris.[100]

In the pseudo-science of Pyramidology instigated by Piazzi Smyth, there is much ado about the so-called 'angle of Bethlehem' of about twenty-six degrees which extends from the Great Pyramid toward Bethlehem in the east.[101] It is also often pointed out that twice that angle, which is fifty-two degrees, gives both the latitude of London as well as the angle of slope of the Great Pyramid.[102] Interestingly, the 'Star of the East' was also the name allocated to an important Masonic lodge in Egypt, in which Lord Kitchener was initiated into the order in 1883.[103] The 'Star of the East' lodge was founded in 1871, and eventually became one of the four senior lodges of Egypt.[104] The other three were Bulwer Lodge, Grecia Lodge and Zetland Lodge.[105] The 'Star of the East' lodge had, at first, the peculiarity of 'working' in Arabic; the lodge was known as Kawkab Al Sharq[106] and was reserved mainly for the Egyptian elite.[107] In 1908 it was taken over by an English officer, Bro. P. Delanoy, and moved into the headquarters building of the District Grand Lodge of Egypt and the Sudan. Delanoy was a high-ranking Freemason in Egypt and at the time was District Warden of Egypt and Sudan. In 1905, at the dedication ceremony of the new Masonic Hall in Alexandria, he presided over the ceremony.[108] In a speech which reeked of Anglo-Israelism and Masonic pseudo-history, Delanoy made certain telling remarks that give us an inside view on the sort of ideas being circulated in Masonic circles in Egypt at the time. After extolling the virtues of Freemasonry and how it was practised in ancient Egypt through the lineage of the Biblical patriarchs Abraham, Jacob, Joseph and 'our Grand Master Moses', Delanoy commented to the eminent Masonic congregation present, which included Sir Reginald Wingate, the British High Commissioner, that:

> ... Your attendance tonight in such numbers, and the interest you take in our fascinating science, convinces me that you are implanting Masonic principles on such a sure and solid foundation, that a new era must be predicted for our interesting work which for ages has now been dormant in this wonderful and parent country of Freemasonry ... Freemasonry would almost appear to have left Egypt by way of the Delta (with Moses and the Israelites), but from the education and instruction given to Moses, acquired afterwards by Pythagoras

and others, our science was happily preserved and handed on to worthy representatives in Palestine, and . . . by Pythagoras himself to England. Singularly from England it is returning again to its ancient stronghold, the land of Goshen (Egypt). Thanks to such men as those I have already named of this lodge . . . to the District Grand Master, General Sir Reginald Wingate, whose interest in his district is very sincere, aided by his deputy, Crookshank Pasha, Freemasonry, I firmly believe, has this time come to stay . . .[109]

Freemasonry, in fact, stayed in Egypt until 1964. It is not clear how much the order had infiltrated into Egyptian society, but according to Masonic researcher Gerard Galtier, Freemasonry, and especially the 'Egyptian' order of Memphis and Misraim, enjoyed 'an immense success' among the high society from various nationalities and religious groups until the epoch of King Farouk in 1952. After the Egyptian officers ousted the British-manipulated monarchy in 1952, the Masonic lodges were viewed with great suspicion and began slowly to fade away. After the Suez War of 1956, Egypt's first president, Gamal Abdel Nasser, expelled many resident foreigners, many of whom were Freemasons, and the lodges began to lose members who were afraid of being regarded as being against the new regime. In 1964, after a huge scandal involving the Israeli master spy Eli Cohen, who had belonged to a Masonic lodge in Egypt,[110] the Egyptian government banned Freemasonry from Egyptian soil altogether.[111] A number of Egyptian journalists and researchers, such as the writer Samir Raafat for example,[112] have recently questioned whether Freemasonry has not merely disguised itself in the many Rotary and Lion's clubs that still operate in Egypt.[113] This, however, seems highly unlikely. For one, it is well-known that Mrs Susan Mubarak, the wife of Egypt's latest president, is a staunch supporter of the Rotarian and plays a prominent role in the society's international activities.[114] Nonetheless, the recent bout of Masonic accusations in Egypt reflect the extremely sensitive and suspicious way the Brotherhood is viewed in the Arab world.[115]

In an extensive study on the subject of Freemasonry in Egypt and, more specifically, on its influence during the formative years of the modern Egyptian state, author and researcher Karim Wissa, a senior civil servant in the Foreign Affairs Ministry, brings to light some extraordinary implications that had hitherto been ignored or covered up.[116] In 1986 Wissa became fascinated with the subject of Freemasonry and its curious links with Egypt, and after several years of research in the various archives of Egyptian newspapers and Masonic lodges in France and Englandhe presented his findings to the prestigious Centre

Nationale De Recherches Scientifiques (CNRS) in Paris. His work was published in a detailed article titled 'Freemasonry in Egypt: From Bonaparte to Zaghloul' in the CNRS's journal, *Turcica*.[117] In this study, Wissa brings forth the strong hypothesis that many of the early political parties that were formed the turn of the century and which served as the backbone for the 1952 revolutionary movement in Egypt and as prototypes to the formation of an independent republic in Egypt, were either para-Masonic organisations or, at the very least, highly influenced by Masonic principles and ideals. Wissa clearly recognised in such Masonic influence the strong rivalry between French and British Masonic groups. The British brand of Freemasonry, regulated in Egypt by the United Grand Lodge in London, was of a more traditionalistic style, with religious tolerance and no political overtone to it. The French brand, regulated by the Grand Orient in Paris (and to a lesser extent by the Orders of Memphis and Misraim), was distinctly 'anti-clerical' and 'anti-monarchy' with extremely political overtones, especially in the spreading of ideals of revolution and republicanism.[118]

Under the French revolutionary, quasi-Masonic tricolour motto of 'Liberty, Equality and Fraternity', the Egyptian new elite and intelligentsia saw in French Freemasonry and its lodges in Egypt an ideal breeding ground and meeting place for the revolutionary movement that was slowly brewing in Egypt, a movement that, by virtue of the politico-military context of the nation, was, by necessity, anti-monarchy and anti-British.[119] Wissa identifies an incredible assortment of important Egyptian personalities who were directly involved with the Masonic lodges in Egypt prior to its outlawing in 1964. These include several members of the Royal Family from Ismail Pasha (known to the West as the 'Khedive') to the last monarch of Egypt, the exiled King Farouk.[120] Interestingly, Wissa also points out the Masonic affiliations of Egyptian political leaders such as Ahmad Orabi, who headed the foiled *coup d'état* against Tewfik Pasha in 1882, and Mohamad Farid and Saad Zaghloul, who headed the powerful National and Wafd Party which started the popular uprising against British imperialism in Egypt. After the 1952 revolution organised by the 'Free' officers movement led by Gamal Abdel Nasser and Mohamad Naguib, the tide turned against the Masonic lodges in Egypt. They came to be looked upon with suspicion, with accusations of harbouring 'strong Zionist affiliations'.[121]

In Israel a strange Judeo-Zionist movement had sprung up known as the B'nai B'rith, which resembled the Masonic movement with lodges and elite, secret members.[122] Although the B'nai B'rith lodges in Cairo and Alexandria were shut down after World War II, there was much suspicion that its members had moved into the more traditional Masonic lodges in these cities. With the important role that Britain played in the establishment of the Jewish State of Israel in 1948, with the so-called Balfour Declaration[123] (Lord Balfour was also a prominent Mason,[124] this suspicion became uncontrollable and the Masonic lodges began to fold or, to coin a Masonic phrase, were put 'into hibernation'. In April 1964 the Egyptian Ministry of Social Affairs ordered the closing of the largest of the Masonic lodges, the so-called Masonic Temple in Alexandria at No.1 Toussoun Street, because 'associations with undeclared agendas were incompatible with rules covering non-profit organisations'.[125] A scare ran across the lodges in Egypt, and within weeks they had all disappeared, documents had been burnt and Masonic paraphernalia destroyed or hidden.[126] In spite of this dissolution, there are many who believe, as we have already seen, that the Brotherhood is still active in Egypt through its infiltration into elite societies and 'clubs' such as the Rotary and the Lion's.[127]

In a recent article in a popular glossy periodical in Egypt, independent journalist Samir Rafaat published a provocative article titled 'Free-masonry in Egypt: is it still around?'[128] In a dramatic opening paragraph Rafaat reports the various rumours that the many ex-US presidents, including George Bush, attended the funeral of King Hussein in Jordan because the latter held the high Masonic title of 'Prince of Jerusalem'; a full review of the Masonic influence in Egypt, past and present, is presented by the author.[129] In early August 1999 I contacted Samir Rafaat and Karim Wissa, and we agreed to meet in Cairo to exchange notes and ideas. The meeting took place in the elegant open coffee hall of the Nile Hilton Hotel, one of the favourite haunts of Egyptian high society. I was extremely impressed by the erudition and high level of culture that these two men exhibited. Both spoke perfect English and French, and more than likely other European languages, as is customary among the highly educated Egyptians. I was interested in telling these men of the connec-tions between the Edgar Cayce Foundation and the Egyptian Antiquities at Giza, but as it turned out Samir Rafaat was a close acquaintance of Dr Zahi Hawass and the conversation became rather strained and contrived. Rafaat, who was the more forthcoming of the two men I was facing, gave a lengthy exposition on how he was 'sick of conspiracy theories' and simply wanted nothing to do with them. After his 'Masonic' article in the press he was swamped, he said, by e-mails from all over Egypt and around the world, many raising the issue of the 'Temple of Solomon' and its connection with the Masonic myth. He saw nothing odd in the Egyptian authorities' decision to celebrate the millennium with the gilded capstone over the Great Pyramid although he did recognise the strong Masonic symbolism of the emblem. I left the two men with a distinct impression that I was touching upon a very taboo subject in Cairo.

Samir Rafaat is a Copt. It is a curious misconception that the Copts are often regarded as the true descendants of the pharaohs. This is not quite correct. When Alexander the Great invaded Egypt in 332 BC, all those native Egyptians who lived along the banks of the Nile were, quite obviously, the descendants of the ancient Pharaonic people. Indeed even after that their genetic origin remained virtually unchanged as few native Egyptians intermingled with the Greeks and other foreigners who, at any rate, were based mostly in Alexandria. In 30 BC Egypt became a Roman province and by the fourth century AD its official religion became Christian Roman Catholicism. Christianity had, in fact, taken root in Egypt since at least the second century AD, but because of the large number of Greeks in Egypt, it was originally much flavoured with Hellenic ideologies, rituals and, especially, iconography. This brand of 'Greek' Christianity became known as Greek Orthodox Christianity. By the fifth and sixth century AD, most of the native Egyptians were converted into the Christian faith. However, in the seventh century AD the Muslims invaded Egypt and many Christians were then converted into Islam, mostly by force. Those few who remained Christians became known as 'Copts'. Today the Copts number about eight million against the fifty-eight million strong Muslim population.

When Freemasonry was introduced in Egypt in the early 1800s, it is not clear whether the recruits coming from the local populations were predominantly Copts or Muslims. Samir Rafaat jocularly told me how, after he had begun to research the origins of Egyptian Freemasonry, his mother casually informed him that his own grandfather had been a Freemason. Indeed, Samir felt that the more he investigated this subject, the more it began to appear as if everyone in Egypt has either a grandfather or a great-uncle who had been involved in one way or another with the Masonic lodges.[130] Certainly, the Copts, with their religious and ethnic origins harking back to the Gnostic roots of Christianity (and almost certainly at one time much influenced by Hermeticism and the Ptolemaic Sarapis religion), would, on face value, seem an ideal breeding ground for any new – or remnant – Masonic movement in Egypt. Yet the syncretist aspirations of Freemasonry are incorrectly perceived today in Egypt – and indeed elsewhere – as anti-religious, which, of course, is quite untrue.[131] Nonetheless, this misconception and other cultural considerations would make it almost impossible, in my opinion, for Freemasonry to operate in Egypt – at least not openly. Yet certain paradoxes remain. For how are we to explain the large membership influx into the Lodges prior to 1952 of Egyptian officials, notables and even monarchs, all of whom where either Muslims or Copts? Could there be any validity in the apparently unsolicited accusations that sometimes appear in the Egyptian press that the Masonic brotherhood is still active in Egypt through such organisations as the Rotary and Lions Club? Unlikely, *but not impossible*. Further investigation into this fascinating subject, however, is beyond the scope of this book.[132]

Oddly, even though Freemasonry is clearly a dubious subject in Egypt, the Rosicrucian order, which has many of the 'speculative' aspects of Freemasonry,[133] i.e. a sort of hybrid Hermeticism and Gnosticism injected into its teachings, symbolism and rituals, is extremely well tolerated in Egypt today. It is even allowed to perform rituals and ceremonies inside ancient temples and the Great Pyramid itself.[134] The modern Rosicrucian order (as opposed to the 'older' original fraternity that emerged in seventeenth-century Germany), known as AMORC,[135] has its roots in America. The scholar Christopher McIntosh of Colgate University in the US, who wrote extensively on the subject of Rosicrucianism, places AMORC's American origins with a man called H. Lewis Spence. Space does not allow us to give a full review here of Lewis Spence's work and the subsequent development of AMORC into a world-wide organisation with American headquarters in San Jose in California and European headquarters in Tremblay in France, plus numerous bases and lodges throughout Europe and Britain and as far removed as India and South Africa. In brief, in 1921 Lewis Spence received a 'charter' from Theodore Reuss, the head of an occult organisation in Germany, who founded in 1906 the famous OTO, the Ordo Templi Orientis. This 'charter' allowed Lewis to create AMORC which first had its headquarters in Florida then moved to California. Its teachings, according to McIntosh, incorporate elements of the Golden Dawn of the occultist Aleister Crowley[136] as well as those found in alchemy, Cabalism and Hermeticism.[137] In 1933 AMORC merged with FUDOSI (Fédération Universelle Des Ordres Initiatiques) and amalgamated a whole range of initiatory orders in Europe. Particularly active in Belgium, AMORC and FUDOSI stressed that the origin and true source of Rosicrucianism was ancient Egypt.[138] According to AMORC:

> The Rosicrucian movement, of which the Rosicrucian Order, AMORC, is the most prominent modern representative, has its roots in the mystery, tradition,

philosophy and myths of ancient Egypt dating back to approximately 1500 BC. In antiquity the word 'mystery' referred to a special gnosis, a secret wisdom. Thousands of years ago in ancient Egypt selected bodies or schools were formed to explore the mysteries of life and learn the secrets of this hidden wisdom. Only sincere students, displaying a desire for knowledge and meeting certain tests, were considered worthy of being introduced to these mysteries. Over the course of centuries these mystery schools added an initiatory dimension to the knowledge they transmitted . . . Rosicrucian tradition relates that the Great Pyramids of Giza were most sacred in the eyes of the initiates. Contrary to what historians affirm, our tradition relates that the Giza Pyramids were not built to be tombs of pharaohs, but were actually places of study and mystical initiation . . . Pharaoh Thutmose III, who ruled Egypt from 1500 BC to 1447 BC, organised the first esoteric brotherhood initiates founded upon principles and methods similar to those perpetuated today by the Rosicrucian Order, AMORC. Decades later Pharaoh Amenhotep IV was initiated into the secret brotherhood . . .[139]

This pseudo or mythical history, known as 'traditional' history, is typical of such esoteric schools. So potent is it in the minds of their members that no reasoning or logic will dissuade them. Our interest in the Rosicrucians, however, is in their fervent belief in the existence of a Hall of Records at Giza. Indeed, the organisation claims to be in possession of ancient maps which show the underground network of tunnels and chambers under the Sphinx, as revealed in 1936 by their founder, H. Lewis Spence.[140] These alleged 'ancient maps', which are often reproduced in simplistic, childlike drawings by many psychics and clairvoyants such as the well-known mystic H. C. Randall-Stevens of the so-called Knights Templar of Aquarius based in the Channel Islands,[141] generally show a series of descending steps in front of the Sphinx leading down into an entrance hall which opens into a large, circular 'temple' or room beneath the bedrock some thirty yards behind the Sphinx.[142] Further back, some 180 yards or so west of the Sphinx, is shown a deep shaft also serving as an entrance to the 'circular temple' and from which emanate tunnels leading to the three Pyramids at the western extremity of the site.[143] Such maps are worth mentioning solely because they bear an uncanny resemblance to the reality of what is being deduced today. For as we shall see in Part II and in the Epilogue, radar and seismographic equipment, as well as recent excavations behind the Sphinx, have shown that roughly such an underground scheme most likely does exist.[144] Interestingly, Randall-Stevens refers to this underground scheme at Giza as 'The Masonic Centre', claiming that Masonic-like initiation rites were performed there and, especially, in the Great Pyramid.[145]

Chapter Eight

The Hall of Records

'It is a legacy that will soon be discovered, and will bear profound determination not only for the history of dynastic Egypt but for the entire physical and spiritual epic of our evolution on this planet, up to the present, and for the years yet to pass . . .'

Dr Mark Lehner, *The Egyptian Heritage*, 1974, p. viii.

'The Hall of Records . . . it's a fantasy! Imagination and hallucination . . . !'

Dr Zahi Hawass, Carte Blanche M-Net TV, September 1996

THE SLEEPING PROPHET

Edgar Cayce was born on a farm on 18th March 1877 near the small town of Hopkinsville in the state of Kentucky, USA. His father, Leslie B. Cayce, was a small-time businessman with a string of failures. His mother, Carrie Majors, came from a well-to-do family of farmers, from whom she inherited three of the largest farms in Kentucky.[1] Leslie unfortunately squandered most of his wife's farming inheritance by borrowing heavily on her properties to set up stores, and ran into heavy debts. He eventually ended up selling door-to-door life insurance targeted especially for Freemasons.[2]

Raised in the heartland of the Christian county, at the early age of ten, Edgar Cayce served as a sexton in the local church and by the age of sixteen he had already read the Bible twelve times over.[3] From a very early age Edgar Cayce was prone to visions and apparitions. As a child he had witnessed the death of his grandfather being trampled by a horse. Later he often claimed to have experienced apparitions of his grandfather who spoke to him.[4] In 1890, at the age of thirteen, he saw a vision of an entity 'of radiant light' that promised that his wish to help others would be fulfilled.[5] Immediately afterwards Cayce developed an ability to memorise books by apparently inducing himself to sleep over them, a feat that consequently led him to excel in schoolwork and to impress his elders.[6] In 1892, following an injury caused by a baseball hitting him on his head, Cayce fell into a coma and then, as if in some kind of trance, 'dictated' random information to his parents on various matters including trends in the financial and political scene.[7] The next year Cayce began working at a local bookstore. Several years later, in 1898, he impressed the owner of a wholesale bookstore by memorising, word by word, their catalogue, an accomplishment that earned him a new job at the wholesale bookstore. Two years later, now at the age of twenty-three, Cayce was suddenly seized by violent headaches and lapses of 'being briefly out of his head', and then mysteriously lost his voice.[8] For months he could not speak. Specialists examined him but could find no cure to this affliction. Then, on 31st March 1901, Cayce was encouraged by a local hypnotist, Al Layne, to try self-hypnosis, as he had done with his experience in memorising books, in a desperate attempt to cure his affliction.[9] It worked, and the strange career of Edgar Cayce as a healer began.

In 1902 he worked in another bookstore in Bowling Green, Kentucky. That same year, while in a trance-induced state, he prescribed a cure for the desperately ill six-year-old daughter of the highly respected superintendent of local schools in Hopkinsville.[10] The news of her miraculous recovery spread and, a few days later, an article in the local paper would begin the diversion of Cayce's strange gift into the realm of public life.[11] On 9th October 1910 Edgar Cayce was catapulted to national fame by a dramatic article published in the *New York Times*. Wesley Ketchum, a medical doctor from Hopkinsville, became impressed with Cayce's psychic abilities and sent a paper to the American Association of Clinical Research. There was an immediate and enthusiastic reaction from the international press, including the *Boston Herald* and the prestigious *New York Times*, which ran a full-page article with photographs. Here are extracts:

ILLITERATE MAN BECOMES A DOCTOR WHEN HYPNOTISED

Strange powers shown by Edgar Cayce puzzle physicians: The medical fraternity of the country is taking a lively interest in the strange powers said to be possessed by Edgar Cayce of Hopkinsville, Kentucky, to diagnose difficult diseases while in a semi-conscious state, though he has not the slightest knowledge of medicine when not in this condition ... Its presentation (Ketchum's paper) created a sensation, and almost before Dr Ketchum knew that the paper had been given to the press he was deluged with letters and telegrams inquiring about the strange case. It is well enough to add that Dr Wesley H. Ketchum is a reputable physician of high-standing and successful practice in the homoeopathic school of medicine ... Dr Ketchum is not the only physician who had opportunity to observe the workings of Mr Cayce's subconscious mind. For nearly ten years his strange powers have been known to local physicians of all the recognised schools ... In all, young Cayce has given more than 1000 readings, but has never turned his wonderful powers to his pecuniary advantage although many people have been restored to health by following out the course treatment prescribed in his readings while in a state of hypnosis. President James Hylsop of the American Psychic Society has made suggestions in regards the development of the subject's powers. Other psychologists in Europe and America are seeking information, and Dr Ketchum's plan is to have a committee of scientists of the highest standing come to Hopkinsville and investigate in a most rigid manner and make report as to the truth of what is claimed but not understood ...[12]

Thousands of enquiries began to pour in from desperate people seeking remedies for their incurable conditions. The situation got out of control. Overwhelmed, Cayce decided to give up his 'readings' and open a photographic studio in Selma, Alabama. After a series of business tribulations, one of which involved the bankruptcy of a petroleum prospecting company set up by Cayce and a couple of New York businessmen, he then settled with his wife, Gertrude, and their two children, Hugh Lynn and Edgar Evans, in the small town of Virginia Beach in the county of Norfolk, Virginia in 1925. With the help of friends and investors, a hospital was built, but this venture, too, failed and the hospital was closed in 1931. Cayce was now fifty-four years old.

THE ASSOCIATION OF RESEARCH AND ENLIGHTENMENT

In that same year of 1931, Edgar Cayce and his eldest son, Hugh Lynn, now twenty-four years old, along with a group of supporters, founded the Association of Research and Enlightenment. By that time, Edgar Cayce had developed another psychic ability when he induced himself into a trance or hypnosis: this involved giving so-called 'life readings' to members of his family, close friends and colleagues. Essentially, these life readings involved Cayce being asked questions concerning the 'past lives' of his subjects and giving 'prophecies' for the future.[13] In order to understand the fundamental tenet behind this curious phenomenon, we need to appreciate the belief system upon which Cayce operated.

It is important to remember that Cayce himself was a fervent Christian and was deeply involved with various church activities and teachings.[14] Throughout most of his life, for example, he taught Bible studies to children and adult groups, and he was of the conviction that he was chosen to do God's work and, more specifically, follow in the ministry of Jesus.[15] This, on the whole, was perceived as the 'Work'.[16] Yet this predominantly Christian 'Work' would become entangled in a curious and complex way with the material churned out in the life readings, the 'past lives' of various individuals and the predictions concerning the future of the human race and the world and, in a most curious way, the origin, function and destiny of the Great Pyramids and Sphinx of Giza.

The main idea behind the readings of Edgar Cayce is that there existed an immense, universal source of information, a type of cosmic library or super spiritual computer which contained all the information and thoughts of the history of the world and into which Cayce, when in trance or self-hypnosis, could connect. This, in esoteric jargon, is known as the 'Akashic Records'. Kevin J. Todeschi, who wrote a book entitled *Edgar Cayce on the Akashic Records*, explains:

> For ease of understanding, the Akashic Records or 'The Book of Life' can be likened to the universe's supercomputer system. It is the system that acts as the central storehouse of all information for every individual who has ever lived upon the earth. More than just a reservoir of events, the Akashic Records contain every deed, word, feeling, thought, and intent that has occurred at any time in the history of the world. Much more than simply a memory storehouse, however, these Akashic Records are interactive; they have tremendous influence upon our everyday lives, our relationships, our feelings and belief systems, and the potential reality we draw toward us. The Akashic Records contain the history of every soul since the dawn of creation. These records connect each of us to one another. They contain the stimulus for every archetypal symbol or mythic story which has ever deeply touched patterns of human behaviour and experience. They have been the inspiration for dreams and inventions. They draw us toward or repel us from one another. They mold and shape levels of human consciousness. They are a portion of the Divine Mind. They are the unbiased judge and jury that attempt to guide, educate, and transform every individual to become that which she or he can be.[17]

Cayce followers emphatically believe that he was capable of connecting to the Akashic Records or 'Book of Life' in order to have access to all knowledge, past, present and future.[18] The origin of the term 'Akashic' is somewhat uncertain though it is most often associated with the name of Rudolf Steiner, whose anthroposophical movement grew out of Blavatsky's the theosophis Helena therapy. According to the *Encyclopaedia Britannica* the Akashic Records are

> in occultism, a compendium of pictorial records, or 'memories' of all events, actions, thoughts. And feelings that have occurred since the beginning of time. They are said to be imprinted on Akasha, *the astral light*, which is described by spiritualists as a fluid ether existing beyond the range of human senses. The Akashic records are reputedly accessible to certain select individuals – e.g. a spiritualist medium who conducts a séance. Akasha allegedly transmits the waves of human willpower through feeling and imagination and is a reservoir of occult power, an ocean of unconsciousness to which all are linked, making prophecy and clairvoyance possible.'

The concept of the Akashic Records is in many ways a Gnostic one, since it also proposes the existence of a vast and divine body of knowledge that can be tapped into by gifted individuals and which will somehow bring them full enlightenment and unity with the universal mind of God. In short, it relates in some ways to what the ancient Egyptians would have called the 'Books of Thoth'; what the Hermeticists would have called 'Poimandres' (the 'Divine Mind'); and what the early Christian mystics of Alexandria would have called 'Gnosis'. Indeed, there is a passage in the New Testament from the Revelations of John which comes very close to this very same concept and is also extremely reminiscent of the Osirian Judgement scene depicted in the Book of the Dead:

> And I saw the dead, small and great, stand before God; and the books were opened; and another book was opened which is the book of life: and the dead were judged out of those things which were written in the books, according to their work.[19]

By the end of his life in January 1945, Edgar Cayce had given over 14,000 'readings' which, if one is to believe his followers, were drawn by him from the Akashic Records as well as from the subconscious of all the individuals that came to him.[20] In the words of his second son, Edgar Evans Cayce:

> The physical readings (dealing with cures and prescriptions) make up sixty percent of Edgar Cayce's 14,000 or so readings. There are a number of minor categories such as business advice and dream interpretation, but by far the next largest category, approximately twenty percent of the total, are life readings.

These readings dealt with psychological rather than physical problems. They attempt to answer questions people might have about vocational problems, their purpose in life, and marriage and human relations . . .[21]

The main objective of the formation of the ARE in 1931, as well as the establishment of a headquarters at Virginia Beach, known as the Edgar Cayce Foundation, was to house the extensive volumes of readings, kept in manuscript and typed format, in a library both for posterity and where they could be consulted by anyone who may care to do so. The secondary purpose was to create a kind of 'university' and learning centre where members, as well as the visiting public, could enlist on courses or attend lectures and conferences dealing with a variety of metaphysical, psychic and healing subjects. Out of the 2800 or so life readings there are about 1200 which deal directly or indirectly with what can at best be termed a 'mythical' history involving a remote prehistoric epoch in Egypt and the lost civilisation of Atlantis.[22] Within these are a group of readings that concern the Giza necropolis and, more specifically, 'records' that have been concealed there under the bedrock of the plateau.

'READING' THE GIZA PLATEAU

According to the Cayce readings, the final destruction of the highly technologically advanced civilisation of 'Atlantis' took place around 10,500 BC.[23] Following the cataclysmic destruction of their continent, groups of Atlantean survivors emigrated to various parts of the world, some to the Americas (Yucatan, Peru, Ecuador, Mexico, Ohio), some to the Pyrenees and other parts of Western Europe, and others to the Nile Valley in Egypt. Approximately 300 readings deal specifically with Egypt and how a sophisticated contingent of Atlanteans came to this land in 10,500 BC bringing with them their 'records'.[24] According to the Cayce readings, it was during this period that the Giza necropolis was developed:

. . . Hence there began the first preparation for what has later become that called the Great Pyramid . . .[25]

Then with Hermes and Ra . . . there began the building of that now called Gizeh, with which those prophecies that had been in the Temple of Records and Temple Beautiful were builded, in the building of this that was to be the Hall of the Initiates of that sometimes referred to as the White Brotherhood.[26]

The Cayce readings go on to say that in the design of the Great Pyramid 'prophecies' leading to the Second Coming of Jesus were incorporated:

> The rise and fall of the nations were to be depicted in this same temple that was to act as an interpreter for that which has been, that which is, and that which is to be . . .[27]

> This then receives all the records from the beginning of that given by the priests . . . to that period when there is to be the change in the earth's position and the return of the Great Initiate (Jesus) to that and other lands for the folding up of those prophecies that are depicted there . . .[28]

The readings also give the date of construction and the relationship of the Giza and the Great Pyramid to the stars and important geodetic positions on the earth:

> . . . (it was built) 10,490 to 10,390 years before the Prince (Jesus) entered into Egypt . . .[29]

> When the lines about the earth are considered from the mathematical precisions, it will be found that the center is nigh unto where the Great Pyramid, which was begun then, is still located . . .[30]

> At the correct time accurate imaginary lines can be drawn from the opening of the Great Pyramid to the second star in the Great Dipper, called Polaris or the North Star. This indicates it is the system toward which the soul takes its flight . . .[31]

Several of the Cayce readings state that the Great Pyramid was used for initiation purposes and that the last of those who received their higher degrees of initiation in this monument were Jesus and St John the Baptist:[32]

> . . . and then (he, Jesus, went) into Egypt for the completion of the preparation as a teacher . . .[33]

> He was with John, the messenger, during the portion of the training there in Egypt . . .[34]

> John first went to Egypt, where Jesus joined him and both became initiates in the Pyramid or temple there . . .[35]

> In the same Pyramid did the Great Initiate, the Master, take those last of the Brotherhood degrees with John, the forerunner of Him, at that place . . .[36]

. . . as indicated oft through this channel, the unifying of the teachings of many lands was brought together in Egypt, for that was the center from which there was to be radial activity of influence in the earth . . .[37]

The Cayce readings also claim that there are 'records' associated with or belonging to Jesus which will one day be uncovered in Egypt. For when questioned about the travels of Jesus in India and other places, Cayce replied while in trance that:

One year in travel and in Persia; the greater portion being in the Egyptian. In this, the greater part, will be seen the records that are set in the pyramids there; for here were the initiates taught.[38]

(Pyramid) yet to be uncovered.[39]

But in Egypt was the greater period of activity – in the compiling of data. And portions of that as may yet be uncovered in the pyramids . . .[40]

. . . and those records that are yet to be found of the preparation of the man, of the Christ, in those of the tomb, or those yet to be uncovered in the pyramid . . .[41]

In the readings, Edgar Cayce repeatedly states that the return or 'Second Coming' of Christ, whom he often calls the Great Initiate, will either take place, or its preparation will begin, in the year 1998:[42]

. . . For he must enter again in that period, or in 1998.[43]

. . . the entrance of the Messiah in this period: 1998.[44]

This date of 1998, oddly enough, is also associated with the most important aspect of the Cayce readings concerning Egypt, namely the rediscovery of the fabled 'Hall of Records' of Atlantis which, Cayce claimed, was concealed at Giza:

For here those that were trained in the Temple Sacrifice as well as in the Temple Beautiful were about the sealing of the Record Chambers. For these were to be kept as had been given by the priests in Atlantis or Poseidia when these records of the race, of the developments, of the laws pertaining to One were put in their chambers and to be opened only when there was the returning of those into materiality, or to earth's experience, when the change was imminent in the earth; which change, we see, begins in '58 and ends with the changes wrought in upheavals and the shifting of the poles, as begins then in the reign (of Jesus?) in '98 . . .[45]

As author Kirk Nelson, who specialises in Edgar Cayce and his readings, noted:

> According to the Cayce readings, during the last part of this century, probably coinciding with the Second Coming, humankind will make the greatest archaeological discovery of all time. This discovery will involve the Egyptian pyramids at Gizeh. The Great Pyramid and the Sphinx will yield treasures beyond the wildest dream of any Egyptologist . . . The rise and fall of nations are depicted in the Great Pyramid along with the changes in religious thought which will come about in the world. This can be seen by examining the passages. The first passage is descending, and this undoubtedly represents the fall of humankind from grace. The next passage is ascending, which represents our ascent from the birth of Jesus to the present day. The stone prophecies continue until the return of the Great Initiate, Jesus, at the end of this age, 1998 . . . The (Hall of) records will not be found until there is the 'breaking up . . . of selfish motives in the world', and 'time has set the mark'. Clearly the selfish motives of the world will not be broken until 1998, and so the opening of the Hall of Records will probably coincide with the Second Coming . . .[46]

But where, according to Edgar Cayce, is the 'Hall of Records' of Atlantis to be found? And what might it contain?

THE KEEPER OF THE RECORDS

There are some forty Cayce readings that deal directly with the so-called 'Hall of Records' allegedly concealed in Egypt.[47] From these it can be deduced that there are several 'tombs', 'pyramids', 'chambers' and 'tunnels' yet to be uncovered in the vicinity of, or directly under, the Sphinx of Giza and that in at least one of these underground cavities or vaults will be found the records of Atlantis.[48] For example, one reading specifically states that

> . . . many are the temples . . . that are yet to be uncovered near the Sphinx . . .[49]

> . . . there is a chamber or passage from the right forepaw to this entrance of the record chamber or record tomb . . .[50]

> . . . This position lies, as the sun rises from the waters, the line of shadow or light falls between the paws of the Sphinx, that was later set as the sentinel or guard, and which may not be entered from the connecting chambers from the Sphinx's paw (right paw) until the time has been fulfilled when the changes must be active in this sphere of man's experience. Between, then, the Sphinx and the river . . .[51]

It lies between, or along that entrance from the Sphinx to the temple – or the pyramid; in a pyramid, of course, of its own.[52]

So here we have it: the basis of the belief system of the fabled Hall of Records of Atlantis as imagined by Edgar Cayce. But where did Cayce get his ideas? If not from the so-called Akashic Records, then from where?

ISIS UNVEILED

We have seen earlier how the Anglo-Israelite movement, the Adventist and Jehovah Witness movement and finally the Pyramidology movement of Piazzi Smyth and others[53] had spread, mingled, and created a belief that the Great Pyramid was designed under divine inspiration and acted as a prophetic device for the Second Coming of Christ. Several books on these subjects were widely circulated at the time when Cayce began to give his readings, from 1926 onwards, and were particularly popular among evangelical movements in America's mid-west and south, and in the intensely 'Masonic' counties in the state of Virginia.[54] The reader will recall that Cayce had worked for many years in bookshops during the early and impressionable years of his life. It will also be recalled that he was endowed with an unusual photographic memory. It is thus not unreasonable to presume that Cayce was influenced, wittingly or unwittingly, by this type of literature and developed from it his strange ideas of the connection between the Great Pyramid and the Second Coming of Christ. As for the 'Atlantis' sections in his readings, this too can be similarly explained by the prolific circulation of books on Atlantis around that time, following the work of Ignatius Donelly, *Atlantis the Antediluvian World*, published in 1882 by Harper & Brothers in New York.[55]

In these works, too, the idea that the pyramids of Egypt were somehow related to Atlantis was made.[56] Donelly, for example, wrote that 'the pyramid is one of those marvellous features of that problem which confronts us everywhere, and which is insoluble without Atlantis'.[57] As for the idea that the entity Hermes was somehow involved in the construction of the Great Pyramid, this too, as we have already seen, was a common belief among the Arab writers which, in turn, were quoted in many of the new genre of books on Atlantis and Pyramidology available to Edgar Cayce. Even the strange dating of 10,500 BC for the Sphinx and the idea of secret records can be extrapolated from the popular works of

Gerald Massey published between 1883 and 1907. Massey, who is described as 'a poet, Shakespearean scholar, mythographer and radical Egyptologist', wrote this of the Sphinx of Giza:

> The great Sphinx as keeper of these secrets was couched in mountainous repose upon the horizon in the eastern equinox, when the gate of 'fair exit' was in the lion sign and the gates of 'fair entrance' was in Aquarius, the water sign, that is figured over the abyss of source on the celestial globe. The Sphinx then is a figure of the double horizon and the duality of Har-Makhu when the place of conjunction was at the point of precession in the lion sign. And if, as is the Egyptian way, the fact was registered forthwith, we may date the Sphinx as a monument which was reared by these great builders and thinkers, who lived so largely out of themselves, some *thirteen thousand years ago.*[58]

Other ideas in Cayce's readings, such as the 'Great White Brotherhood' and the initiatory function of the Great Pyramid of the 'last' or higher 'degrees', can be found in the popular literature of Helena Blavatsky and the Theosophical movement that was also widely circulating at the times Edgar Cayce gave his first readings on the pyramids in 1931. In two particular works by Blavatsky, *The Secret Doctrine* and *Isis Unveiled*, both published in the late 1870s, there is much talk of the 'root races' of the world, the White Brotherhood and the Masonic style by degree initiations in the Great Pyramid of Giza.[59] Blavatsky also claimed that the empty coffer in the King's Chamber of the Great Pyramid was 'a baptismal font upon emerging from which the neophyte was born again and became an adept', meaning that the neophyte experienced death and learnt of its mystery.[60] Blavatsky herself had apparently spent a whole night alone in the King's Chamber in 1886 where 'she had some remarkable experiences'.[61] This idea, too, is expressed in the Cayce readings; for when asked about the meaning of the empty sarcophagus in the King's Chamber and what could be learnt from it, the following answer was given:

> That there will be no more death. Don't misunderstand or misinterpret! But the interpretation of death will be made plain.[62]

There can be little doubt, too, that the ideas of 'past lives' and reincarnation were most likely lifted from Blavatsky's works and teachings. Blavatsky had arrived in the USA in 1873 where, two years later, along with Colonel Henry Steel Olcott, a lawyer and veteran of the Civil War, she founded the Theosophical Society. This was a body intended to teach and promote the belief in a 'Universal Brotherhood based upon the essential divinity of man'.[63] The essential teaching of the Theosophical movement was the doctrine of reincarnation which Helena Blavatsky claimed she had mostly learnt while journeying in Tibet.[64] It was Helena Blavatsky who, in the nineteenth century, was largely responsible for reviving the idea of lost sacred and magical books and great libraries waiting to be rediscovered. And in her book *Isis Unveiled*, published in 1877, Blavatsky speaks of the lost sciences superior to our own and mentions a work referred to by Theophilus, the patriarch of Antioch, entitled *The Divine Book* which reputedly gave secret biographies of all the gods of Egypt and their origins. 'Clearly,' Blavatsky wrote, 'two things are necessary. First, to find the missing books of Hermes; and second, the key by which to understand them. Truly the land of Egypt is another abode of mystery!' Blavatsky herself sought the secret key to understanding the mysteries of Egypt among the Copts whom she regarded as the guardians of the esoteric tradition in that land. It is perhaps significant, in this context, that Blavatsky's teacher, Paulos Metamon, has been described as a 'Coptic magician'.[65] Bearing in mind, therefore, this fact that the teacher of the very person who first popularised the idea of a lost 'Hall of Records' was a Copt, it may not be entirely irrelevant to note that today many influential figures in Egypt who are, directly or indirectly, in a position to influence the outcome of the search for the Hall of Records are, in fact, members of the Coptic community.[66]

Also it should be noted that Rudolf Steiner, who was originally a member of Blavatsky's Theosophical movement (and who later founded the famous Anthroposophical movement which claims to be the true inheritors of the original Rosicrucians), wrote widely on subjects such as reincarnation, Atlantis and the Akashic Records which, of course, much preoccupied Edgar Cayce. Significantly, in his book *Egyptian Myths and Mysteries* which he wrote in 1908, Steiner quite clearly alluded to the lost 'books of Thoth-Hermes' and the fabled 'Hall of Records' when he wrote: 'a great treasure of occult wisdom in the domain of medicine will be raised to light one day, wisdom that mankind formerly possessed'.

There can be no denying that the terminology of the ideologies on reincarnation used by Edgar Cayce in his readings are conspicuously similar to those used by Blavatsky and Steiner, and much suggests that he, or his subconscious, was affected by her teachings, even though there is no reference, by Cayce, to her at all. Such correlation between Cayce and the various popular movements discussed above are so visible that Cayce's own son, Edgar Evans, the executive president of the ARE today, could not ignore the suggestion that they appear to be an interpretation of earlier ideas instigated by the Theosophical movement, although he naturally defends the originality of the Cayce readings:

> A Theosophist listening to Cayce might at first have thought his material to be just another expansion on the basic Theosophist story. Yet beyond use of some of the same terms, the Cayce story bears little resemblance to the occultist story. A small amount of occult material did appear to be incorporated in the Cayce material. Whether this was because they were both tapping from the same source, or because Cayce was picking up material from his audience, we have no way of knowing. The occultists, however, were the first to mention high technology, such as flying machines, in conjunction with Atlantis. Cayce later followed this theme in many life readings. Likewise the occultists were the first to refer to multiple destructions of Atlantis, although Cayce disagrees with the dates and number of destructions.[67]

Edgar Evans Cayce is, of course, splitting hairs here. The comparison with the story of Blavatsky, when one considers it was housed in the subconscious of Cayce and dictated while in a state of trance, is uncannily similar and likely to be a reinterpretation, albeit an unconscious one, through the Cayce readings. But does all this, therefore, mean that Edgar Cayce was a hoax? I do not believe this is the case. Everything known about the man, and there are dozens of books and thousands of articles written about him, attests that he was an honest and genuine human being, a devout Christian with a strong sense of mission. So how do we explain his 'readings'? It all depends how much of a sceptic you are and whether you entertain the possibility, however remote, that such a phenomenon as the power of prophecy or clairvoyance is possible. My own view on the Cayce readings is that they can be attributed to a very fertile mind with an unusually powerful memory that, while in a trance or hypnotic state, operated automatically and blended into a new inner vision to respond to suggestive questions. Needless to say, there are thousands of Cayce followers who believe emphatically in the Cayce readings and to many of them the phenomenon of remembering 'past lives' is not a matter of open conjecture and doubt, but one of fact.[68] Such faith is attested by the constant publications that are churned out every year. To other devotees, the readings have been taken with sufficient seriousness to prompt them to contribute financially and give of their time in the hope of vindicating the Cayce prophecies and readings.[69] This, not unexpectedly, amounts to trying to find evidence of Atlantis and, more specifically, the so-called Hall of Records that Cayce said existed at Giza under the bedrock of the Sphinx.

A most extraordinary adventure has been taking place at Giza involving the ARE and its members for the last forty years. Sometimes in the open, sometimes on the quiet, an array of colourful and shadowy characters have installed themselves on the Giza plateau with baffling ease and remarkable success. Let us now retrace their footsteps from behind the scene. This is the story of the most daring archaeological treasure hunt of this century, and one that, apart from the huge public controversy it has already generated, is on the verge of culminating in an extraordinary, earth-shattering conclusion for the opening of the new millennium.

Part Two: Exploration

Chapter Nine

The Search

'Egypt was only a dream to the many individuals who were told they had past lives there. It was not until 1957 that anyone had the determination and drive to begin the search . . .'

Edgar Evans Cayce, *Mysteries of Atlantis*, p.129

'Of course, the final confirmation lies beneath the paws of the Sphinx at Giza . . .'

Dr Mark Lehner, *The Egyptian Heritage*, p. v

TRAVELLERS' CHEQUES FOR THE SPHINX

In 1957 a rather daring although amazingly whimsical expedition was undertaken to Giza by two Edgar Cayce devotees. A twenty-seven-year-old woman, known by the ARE under the pseudonym 'Rhonda James', proposed to undertake a journey to Egypt in search of evidence for the Hall of Records.[1] Her real name, we discovered, was Marjorie Hansen.[2] Apparently no funds could be made available to Hansen by the ARE, so she and another woman friend managed to collect up enough money to finance the trip themselves. The idea of two young American graduates trying to explore the Giza necropolis in the late 1950s without credentials, licences, introductions or financial sponsorship seems, on the face of it, absurd and utterly naive. A year earlier Egypt had been at war with Britain, France and Israel over the nationalisation of the Suez Canal by the new Egyptian United Arab Republic. Its colourful and charismatic president, Gamal Abdel Nasser, had roused intense anti-foreign feeling in the country which had provoked a mass exodus by the large foreign resident communities, most particularly the hundreds of thousands of Jews living in Cairo, Alexandria and other large cities in Egypt. I was twelve years old at the time, and I remember the drama very vividly. From the rooftop of the block of flats where my aunt and cousins used to live, we would gather at night to watch the British and French aircraft drop their bombs on the way to Port Said in the Canal Zone.

These were dangerous times when Arab mobs, fired by the new wave of nationalism and crazed by the military intervention of the Western world, went on rampages in the streets of Alexandria against foreign residents and their properties. Stories of beatings and even lynchings in the town were rampant. My twin sister and I were, of course, taken out of school and forbidden to go out into the streets unescorted. I have two very vivid memories of these chaotic times: the first is being on the balcony of my home looking down at an agitated public demonstration of Arabs burning an effigy of Sir Anthony Eden, the British Prime Minister, whom the Egyptians deemed personally responsible for the Suez War; the other memory is the black-out during the air-raids, something my sister and I loved as we gleefully played at 'chambre noire' with our parents and Mabrouka and Ali, our devoted servants.

Like most foreigners at the time, we were given orders to leave the country and our properties and goods were placed under sequestration by the Egyptian authorities. Because of my father's connections and the high degree of respect he enjoyed from his Egyptian colleagues, we managed to obtain a dispensation from the Egyptian government to remain in the country. The next few years were a mess. The reformed Egyptian civil service was totally overwhelmed by the huge void left by the departing foreigners, and a terrible corruption set in. The simplest of administrative requirements, such as the application for a driving licence or the acquisition of permits of any kind, became bogged down in an incredible morass of red-tape and confusion. Nothing worked without the proverbial 'backshish' (bribe or tip). Foreigners were regarded with the utmost suspicion. The secret police were everywhere, looking for imaginary Zionist plotters and spies. Many areas had been designated 'military zones' and the few tourists who were bold enough to visit the archaeological sites were advised not to take photographs of government installations (which sometimes extended to archaeological sites).

This, therefore, was the context in which Marjorie Hansen arrived in Egypt; 1957, to put it mildly, was very much the wrong year for any foreigners to visit this country, let alone two young American ladies with a secret agenda to find the Hall of Records on behalf of a dubious 'psychic' organisation. Yet in spite of this, Hansen and her friend were to have an amazing success with the Egyptian Antiquities Organisation (EAO). They managed to raise enough money to pay for their journey by ship from New York, which in those days was a month's crossing by sea. They arrived in Egypt in the autumn and made their way to Cairo, where they stayed at the YMCA. Once settled, the two women proceeded to the Giza necropolis to begin their search. In the words of Edgar Evans Cayce:

> Strange as it may seem, 'Rhonda' (Marjorie) eventually obtained permission to bore holes about three meters apart at the base of the Sphinx. They used hand-operated drills (augers), and after about eight feet they hit water.[3]

It is unclear how Hansen obtained a licence to undertake such a daring exercise. The Giza necropolis in those days was swarming with dragomen, donkey and camel riders, souvenir sellers, and all sorts of shady characters and hustlers mostly trying to buy dollars on the black market.[4] More worrying, there were dozens of badly paid security guards and soldiers extremely sensitive to foreigners behaving in a suspicious manner. Two young American ladies roaming about with hand-drills must have stood out incredibly. Even Edgar Evans Cayce was to express surprise at Hansen's undertaking: 'I don't know how they got per-mission, maybe their good looks.'[5] Hansen claims that the 'authorities' charged her $300 which she apparently paid in travellers' cheques.[6] This statement alone is suspicious. Payments even today for licences, permits and tickets are invariably made in cash, and usually in Egyptian currency. Was Hansen's 'authorities' a fixer? This is a possibility. But even so, and in spite of the chaotic and corrupt conditions Hansen and her friend must have found themselves in, such obviously suspect activities as drilling holes around the Sphinx would require an 'official' permit of some sort in order to appease the security guards and antiquities inspectors.

The drilling operations produced no significant results, since a few feet down through the limestone bedrock Hansen struck the water table. Autumn is the period of the so-called high Nile after the yearly flood, when the water level is at its maximum, and reaches a few yards below the natural bedrock on which the Sphinx is carved. In 1957, prior to the construction of the Aswan Dam, conditions for a high water table were at their peak. The local water and sewage drainage system of the nearby village of Nazlet Al Samman was, at that time, a shambles. A crude open drain had been cut into the natural bedrock and passed barely fifty yards from the Sphinx and Khafra Valley Temple, discharging its foul waters into the surrounding soil.[7] On her return to the USA, Hansen wrote a twelve-page report and handed it to the ARE. In the summary, Hansen stated that

... the evidence, though slight and not conclusive, is promising. The visual evidence alone is sufficient as a basis for a thorough examination of the Sphinx for there is no record of such. Dr Selim Hassan in his excavation cleared the sand from the Sphinx (in 1934-36) and repaired damaged parts, but he removed no stones. There is almost no contemporary information on the Sphinx. Who built it and why is mainly conjecture. Foundation deposits containing such information were usually placed under most temples; so possibly some such might be found under one of the large limestone blocks composing the paws. Nor is a complete study of the Sphinx, itself, available ...[8]

Hansen's observations, as it turned out, 'were a precursor to extensive later work by other individuals' backed by or acting in favour of the ARE.[9] Her implications were obvious. If records of the builders could perhaps be found under the limestone blocks, then the chances of also finding a Hall of Records as Cayce had predicted were good. Hugh Lynn Cayce, who was executive president of the ARE at the time, desperately wanted to believe this. Hansen's apparent ease at getting involved in actual field work at Giza encouraged Hugh Lynn, and it was about this time that he made up his mind that he would do everything within his means to vindicate his father's prophecies about the Hall of Records. But the ARE at the time did not have either the expertise or the funds to mount any substantial archaeological expedition. Furthermore the likelihood of being granted official permission for such a venture by the Egyptian Antiquities Organisation was almost nil. The Egyptological profession and its academics do not, as a rule, condone the ideas and motives entertained by the followers of the likes of Edgar Cayce, let alone allow them to undertake archaeological digs and experiments around Egypt's most ancient and most prestigious monuments, the Great Pyramid and the Sphinx. The foreign archaeological missions, such as the Egypt Exploration Fund, the German Archaeological Institute, Chicago House, the Institut Français D'Archaeologie Orientale and so forth were prestigious institutions backed by the top universities and museums in Europe and America. Their staff were eminent Egyptologists, archaeologists and scientists. Nearly all concessions for new projects, especially at Giza, were granted to one or other of these bodies. There would certainly have been much protestation and opposition if an official licence was to be granted to such an organisation as the ARE which, after all, was entirely founded on the beliefs of a mystic and psychic with no credentials whatsoever.

Following the huge controversies caused by Piazzi Smyth and the 'pyramidologists' whose presence was still felt as late as the 1970s through the popular writings of such authors as Peter Tompkins and Peter Lemesurier,[10] Egyptologists cringed away from anyone or anything having to do with such, in their opinion, despicable and outlandish beliefs.[11] Hugh Lynn, although inexperienced in matters related to Egypt and Egyptology, nonetheless realised quickly enough that a different approach had to be worked out if the ARE was to get its chance to locate the Hall of Records. The political situation in Egypt and throughout the Arab world had much deteriorated after the Suez War, and things began to escalate again in 1967 between Israel and Egypt, culminating in the famous Six Days' War and the humiliating defeat of the Egyptians in the Sinai. Anti-Egyptian and Arab feelings ran high in the West and especially America. The feeling was reciprocated by the Egyptians, who accused the US and the British of backing Israel. After the death of President Nasser in 1969, Anwar Sadat took over the leadership and a gleam of goodwill and hope for cordial relations between the West and Egypt began to be felt, only to be shattered by the 1973 Yom Kippur War between Israel and Egypt. This time Egypt was backed by Russia and the risk of a major international escalation of the events was very real indeed. A precarious cease fire was negotiated through the political and indirect military intervention of the Americans. But anti-Israel, anti-Zionist and anti-American feelings ran high in Egypt Muslim fundamentalism began to show its dangerous face in the area. Amazingly, in the midst of such political turmoil and anti-American mood, Hugh Lynn Cayce was about to launch a plan of action that was to have amazing consequences for the world of Egyptology.

THE SCHOLAR

In 1971 a young man by the name of Mark Lehner made his way to the Edgar Cayce Foundation headquarters in Virginia Beach. Lehner came from a very respectable family from Sacramento, California, and his parents, it seems, had been keen followers of Edgar Cayce. In his words:

> My parents joined an ARE Study Group in Sacramento, California, when I was fifteen years old. Edgar Cayce literature was always in the house, and I grew up with it. While attending an ARE conference in Asilomar, I met Hugh Lynn Cayce who invited me to headquarters – that was in 1968. I became a resident of the (Virginia) Beach in 1971, when I came to stay for two years.[12]

Hugh Lynn Cayce, who also recalls his encounter with Lehner in his memoirs, presents the story in a somewhat different format. In his official biography compiled by the ARE's press editor, A. Robert Smith, Hugh Lynn is quoted saying:

> Mark was a college student in California and was involved in a lot of student protest activity at Berkeley and around there. He was pursuing a girl at our Asilomar conference. She dragged him into a meditation class I was giving. It enabled me to look at him, and I saw somebody that I thought I recognised. So I asked him to come to Virginia Beach. He came right at the time in 1972 that Charles Thomas (Cayce, who had just joined the staff of ARE of youth activities) was taking a youth group to Egypt and Europe. Mark very much wanted to go, so I gave him the trip.[13]

Lehner immediately took to Egypt. While at Giza, he left the group one day and spent much time alone around the pyramids and Sphinx, and meditated for a while in the King's Chamber of the Great Pyramid. It was there and then that he decided to make some sort of career involving Giza.[14] Back in Virginia Beach Lehner devoted the whole year of 1972 and part of 1973 researching the Cayce readings on Egypt. His research was eventually published by the ARE press in a book entitled *The Egyptian Heritage*. Lehner, at the time, seemed utterly convinced that the Edgar Cayce story on Atlantis and Egypt was 'rooted in truth', and the purpose of the book was to provide a compelling case to support this view.[15] In a few years Lehner would make a full 180 degrees turn on his beliefs. But more of that later.

Hugh Lynn was convinced that Lehner was the right man to represent them in Egypt. 'This is the man who can find what we are looking for,' stated Hugh Lynn in his memoirs. Hugh Lynn was hoping that Lehner would find proof of the lost civilisation of Atlantis as described in the Cayce readings and, ultimately, the Hall of Records. And in doing so, in the words of Hugh Lynn's biographer, 'it would be proof positive that Edgar Cayce had been more than a good storyteller and medical diagnostician. He would be recognised at last as the greatest mystic of modern times.'[16] So Hugh Lynn set out to transform his young protégé and make it all come true. According to Hugh Lynn:

> He (Lehner) asked if I thought they'd take him at the (American) University in Cairo. He told me he had some good grades and some very bad grades, and he asked if I'd write a letter of recommendation. I wrote to the dean of admissions who turned out to be someone who had read all the ARE books. He said he'd love to have Mark.[17]

Hugh Lynn solicited the financial help of Arch and Ann Ogden, a wealthy couple who lived in Florida. Arch Ogden, who had once been president of the Edgar Cayce Foundation, offered to put up the money for Lehner's college expenses in Cairo for two years, estimated at some $3500 per year, a rather hefty sum for 1972. Another benevolent financer of this enterprise, which was dubbed the 'Egypt Project', was Joseph Jahoda, a businessman from Virginia and long time supporter of the ARE.[18] Lehner arrived in Cairo in the autumn of 1973 amid anti-Israeli and anti-US riots that plagued Cairo just a few weeks before the Yom Kippur War with Israel. As other Americans were fleeing Egypt, Lehner opted to stay even though the university had temporarily stopped classes. He somehow managed to get a job as an assistant to an NBC correspondent in Cairo.[19] Eventually Lehner resumed his studies at the American University.

Meanwhile Hugh Lynn went off to Iran with Arch Ogden and Rufus Mosely, a commercial airline pilot living in Virginia Beach. Mosely, who undertook weekly flights to Cairo for TWA, had developed connections there in high places within the archaeological scene.[20] We shall encounter Rufus Mosely again later on in our story. Hugh Lynn believed that in a previous life he had been the disciple of Jesus, Andrew, and that he had travelled with the Messiah to Persia.[21] He, along with Mosely and Ogden, had gone there to verify this possibility in the region of Shushtar, some sixty miles from the Iraqi border.

Meanwhile, still at the American University in Cairo, Lehner began to meet important figures in the archaeological world, in particular Zahi Hawass, who was then chief inspector of the Giza Plateau. In 1976 came the first opportunity to involve Mark Lehner in official archaeological work in Egypt. The Institute for Antiquity and Christianity at Claremont Graduate School and Brigham Young University in the USA were collaborating on a project involving the famous Gnostic library of Nag Hammadi. Hugh Lynn makes a rather strange statement regarding the Gnostic texts in a review he gave on the English translation:

> They contain the earliest writings of the earliest monk – the book of Melchizedek, the book of Enoch. The writings have been translated, a big project, in one book. I wrote a review on the book, and told everybody that it mentioned several reincarnations of Jesus, referring to Melchizedek and Hermes . . .[22]

It seems that Hugh Lynn's interest in the Nag Hammadi project of Claremont Graduate School and Brigham Young University was that 'the Coptic Gnostic Library . . . contains important parallels to the view of Christianity and its origins given in the Edgar Cayce readings'.[23] This alone is interesting in itself, for here we have a clear recognition from the leader of the ARE's early projects in Egypt that the Christian element in the Cayce readings is parallel to Gnosticism with the added belief in an imminent Second Coming of Christ. At any rate, the ARE donated some $2,500 to the Nag Hammadi project in order to get Lehner in on it. There Lehner made his debut in archaeological in-situ work and learnt the ropes of modern digs. On his return to Cairo in 1976, Lehner met an American scientist, Dr Lambert Dolphin. It was Dolphin who was to finally catapult the ARE on its archaeological quest to find the Hall of Records at Giza.

JERUSALEM AND THE SPHINX

In the early 1970s Lambert Dolphin was part of a team of researchers and scientists working with Stanford Research International, a high-profile cutting-edge organisation based in Menlo Park, California, USA. This organisation, better known as SRI, had once been part of Stanford University in California. Founded in 1946 for the purpose of establishing a commercial arm for the university in order to attract outside funds, the SRI (originally known as the Stanford Research Institute), after a slow beginning, soon gained big government clients such as the CIA, the US Military and the Atomic Energy Commission. In the late 1960s, however, in the midst of the anti-war movement, hippie flower-power and student protests, the extent of the SRI's involvement in military and intelligence classified projects shocked the academic world and the undergraduates of Stanford University, who put pressure on the university board for SRI's closure or expulsion. It chose the latter, and in 1969 SRI became an independent research contractor, with more than seventy percent of its income coming from defence and intelligence projects.

Today SRI is regarded as one of America's largest think-tanks with a budget exceeding two hundred million dollars, and its special management consultant division, SRI Consulting, has five branches in the USA and four around the world, two of which are in the UK, in London and Croydon. One of SRI's most controversial projects has been the so-called Remote-Viewing programme undertaken for the CIA in the early 1970s. This involved the recruiting, testing and training of 'psychics' in order to use their alleged paranormal powers for military and intelligence purposes. Their prize recruit was a New York artist, Ingo Swann, who also helped set up the testing and training programmes with SRI.[24] We shall meet Swann later on in connection with Giza. Another famous psychic who collaborated in the programme was Uri Geller, the notorious Israeli spoon-bender.[25]

At about the same time that the Remote-Viewing programme was being implemented at Menlo Park, the SRI's Radio-Physics Division used ground-penetrating radar equipment at Giza in the hope of finding hidden chambers under the bedrock. The project, which started in 1974, was funded by the National Science Foundation[26] and supervised locally in Egypt by Ain Shams University in Cairo.[27] This, apparently, was a follow-up to an earlier project begun by the Berkeley University called the 'Cosmic Ray Project' under the supervision of the eminent scientist Dr Luis Alvarez.[28] Cosmic rays, which come from outer space, can penetrate dense material such as stone to a great depth, but as they do so the intensity or energy of the rays decrease. Thus the quantity of remnant energy recorded in what he calls a 'spark chamber' enables the investigator with a certain degree of accuracy to determine if any voids exist with the solid core of the material under investigation. Alvarez, a Nobel Prize winner for physics, conducted his experiment in the Second Pyramid of Giza in the hope of locating secret chambers by passing cosmic rays through the solid core of the monument. His work was funded and sponsored by the US Atomic Energy Commission, the Smithsonian Institute, the Faculty of Science of Ain Shams University, and under licence from the Egyptian Antiquities Organisation. After taking over two million readings, Alvarez had to conclude that their experiment had failed to locate any secret chambers inside this monument. But there was a certain degree of doubt raised on the validity of the readings when a reporter from *The Times*, John Turnstall, investigated the matter with Alvarez's Egyptian counterpart at Ain Shams University, Dr Amr El Goneid. The latter apparently let out that he believed that there was some mysterious energy 'force' within the pyramid that 'defied all known laws of physics'.[29] This was vehemently denied by Dr Alvarez who accused the reporter of making it up. Lack of funds and other reasons prevented further exploration, and sadly no work with the cosmic ray equipment was undertaken in the Great Pyramid itself. According to Dr Dolphin, it was Dr Alvarez who encouraged him and the SRI team to direct their expertise towards finding 'hidden chambers' at Giza:

> Prof. Alvarez suggested to me and to my colleagues at SRI International that we should attempt to build a 'ground-penetrating radar' to explore the pyramids, and to search for hidden tombs . . . With the help of in-house SRI R&D funds we soon had assembled a crude radar system . . . we then obtained a small grant from the National Science Foundation, teamed up with scientists from Cairo's

Ain Shams University, and enthusiastically went to work at Giza in the spring of 1974 . . .[30]

To assist the SRI team with local administrative and logistic problems in Egypt was a Mr S.O. Buckingham, also from Berkeley. With their new types of remote sensing equipment such as seismographs, thermal infra-red imagery and magnetometers, SRI hoped to get better and more conclusive results than the cosmic ray experiments.

Before we examine these events it is perhaps noteworthy that the personal interest in Giza shown by Dr Lambert Dolphin has recently been put under severe scrutiny by a pair of British authors, Lynn Picknett and Clive Prince.[31] These authors have exposed Dolphin as a 'Christian fundamentalist' with a curious interest in Biblical archaeology and associations with a Jewish fanatical organisation calling itself the 'Jerusalem Temple Foundation' which advocates the urgent construc-tion of a 'Third Temple' in Jerusalem to mark a new era for the Chosen People.[32] It is, in fact, quite true that in May 1983 Lambert Dolphin attempted to undertake 'remote sensing experiments' on the Temple Mount in Jerusalem in the hope of finding 'a secret room where the Ark of the Covenant or ancient temple records' and other underground features such as tunnels and galleries. This ended up being thwarted by the Israeli police. The events of this strange adventure began when, early in 1982, Dolphin was contacted by Stanley Goldfoot, head of the Jerusalem Temple Foundation in Israel. Goldfoot had been impressed by the SRI's credentials and experience in remote sensing archaeology, and invited Dolphin and the SRI to undertake an exploration in the Temple Mount.

The funds were partially put up by two ministers of the Christian Church in the USA, Pastors Chuck Smith and Chuck Missler. In April 1983 a seven-man team from SRI headed by Dolphin arrived at Tel Aviv airport. They had brought with them the latest and most sophisticated remote sensing equipment including high-frequency seismic sounders, high-resolution resistivity electrodes, and cart-mounted ground-penetrating radar – the sort of state-of-the-art high-tech arsenal that would normally cause the Israeli security police at Tel Aviv airport to go on red-alert. The fact that SRI came with heavy US military credentials may have, however, eased the way. At any rate, for the first few weeks they conducted remote sensing tests at various archaeological sites to try the equipment out. In the area of Bethlehem Dolphin conducted a radar scan on a mound called the Herodium, and later it was claimed in the press that he and his team had found a 'secret chamber' which supposedly was the 'tomb of Herod'.[33] But Dolphin's main target was the Temple Mount in Jerusalem.

Needless to say the Temple Mount is a huge political time-bomb with the three major world religions, Judaism, Christianity and Islam, all laying some sort of historical claim to it. On it originally stood the so-called 'First Temple' which supposedly had housed the Ark of the Covenant in its holy of holies. It is from a sacred 'rock' platform on the top of Temple Mount that the prophet Muhammad is said to have ascended to heaven, with the spot now marked by the famous El Aqsa Mosque, known as the 'Dome on the Rock'. In 1967 during the Six Days' War the Israeli army stormed the Temple Mount and annexed it to the Israeli part of Jerusalem. Since then Arab extremists have vowed to regain the Mount. It has been ever since the cause of terrible riots, and understandably any archaeological work there is treated with the utmost security and political sensitivity. It was fairly obvious to Dolphin and Stanley Goldfoot that they would not be granted official permission to conduct exploration in the Temple Mount. But with the help of a Rabbi, Yehuda Getz, they managed to get permission of sorts to explore the so-called Rabbinical Tunnel near the Western Wall. Since 1967, Rabbi Yehuda had been in charge of excavations of this tunnel under the sponsorship of the Ministry of Religious Affairs. The works had been kept as secret as possible to avoid possible political clashes with the Muslim WAQF or high command in Jerusalem.

At about 10 p.m. on the night of 22nd May 1983, Dolphin and the SRI team made their way to the grilled gates of the Rabbinical Tunnel. The WAQF, however, had alerted the Israeli police and Dolphin and his team were arrested and escorted to the Security Department at the police headquarters in Jerusalem. The team was eventually released but forbidden to conduct any more work. The story broke in Israel in the *Jerusalem Post* to the embarrassment of everyone:

SLOUCHING TOWARDS ARMAGEDDON, LINKS WITH EVAN-GELICALS: There are significant, and to some minds worrisome links between a handful of American Evangelical leaders and right-wing Israelis like Goldfoot. Some of the personalities are important men. Lambert Dolphin heads a key-section of the world's most massive research conglomerate, the Stanford Research Institute, a $200 million a year concern whose main clients are the US government and corporations like Bechtel.[34] Before the Temple Mount plotters – both the Lifta Terrorists and the Gush Emunim terror group – were arrested, Goldfoot and Dolphin planned to hover one day just before dawn in a helicopter 300 meters above the Temple Mount and the Holy of Holies (where the Ark of Covenant was kept) and to X-ray and probe the innards of the mount . . . Along with Lambert Dolphin they (other Christian Temple Mount activists) condemned the abortive attempt (by the Lifta group) to blow up the Dome on the Rock . . .[35]

Lambert Dolphin retaliated by suggesting that the article in the *Jerusalem Post* was part of some conspiracy against him and his friend, Stanley Goldfoot.[36] In July 1983 he told the newspapers:

> I deeply regret the cheap attack on my good friend Stanley Goldfoot who has spent much time and taken much trouble to free me from anti-Semitism and ignorance of Jewish values and consciousness . . . I believe the covenant God made with the Jewish people through Abraham extends to all gentiles who come to the Holy One of Israel through the Messiah Jesus. I would like to see the Temple rebuilt, but am not a member of the Jerusalem Temple Foundation.[37]

A few years later, in 1987, Lambert Dolphin resigned from SRI to run a small independent consulting service and devote the bulk of his time to 'Bible teaching, writing and Christian counselling'.[38] Today he devotes much of his time Biblical teachings and maintaining a website focused on Biblical issues and, more specifically, the Temple Mount.[39] In this website Dolphin seems to be promoting the works of Stanley Goldfoot and another Temple Mount fanatic, Gershon Solomon, who is the founder and leader of a group called The Temple Mount and Land of Israel Faithful Movement. Solomon, an officer in the Israeli Defence Force, claims to have been personally instructed by God 'as a divine call to consecrate himself to the work of the Temple Mount'.

Let us, however, return to the SRI's involvement at Giza and the meeting between Lambert Dolphin and Mark Lehner in the first half of 1977. After some discussions between the two men, the SRI agreed to undertake some preliminary tests in the area of the Sphinx using resistivity equipment, although, according to Lehner, they were 'a little nervous about doing so', although Lehner does not say why.[40] These tests were to prove encouraging, showing some 'anomalies' that could prove to be chambers or voids below the bedrock.[41] The results of the tests were later published by Lambert Dolphin in a brief report entitled 'Application of Modern Sensing Techniques to Egyptology'.[42] A series of resistivity traverses had been laid in shallow trenches around the Sphinx which produced some interesting, although inconclusive, results:

> Several anomalies were observed as a result of our resistivity survey at the Sphinx . . . A very limited number of measurements were taken due to the time

schedule of the project. As a result of the survey, the team discovered five areas of interest. Behind the rear paws (northwest end) we ran two traverses (number 206 and 207). Both traverses indicate an anomaly that could possibly be a tunnel aligned northwest to southwest. Another anomaly exists in the middle of the south side . . . There are two anomalies in front of the front paws of the Sphinx . . . One anomaly occurs on large electrode spacing, suggesting a cavity or shaft as much as 10 m deep . . . The resistivity anomalies we found around the Sphinx are not defined sufficiently to allow us any absolute certain conclusions, and we feel that a more detailed survey should be conducted . . .[43]

Although detailed reports were written for the 1974 and 1976 field seasons of the SRI's geophysical work in Egypt, no formal report was ever written about the much 'more extensive and ambitious project' that was undertaken in the spring of 1978 for the ARE. It was many years later – in fact during the course of 1999 while I was in the middle of writing this book – that Lambert Dolphin finally yielded to the many requests[44] and wrote a brief report which was posted on his website in July 1999. Unfortunately, Dolphin informs us that he, along with John Tanzi and Patti Burns who did the 1978 resistivity work at the Sphinx, were 'unable to locate our logs and printouts'.[45] This is how Lambert Dolphin, however, remembers the events:

In 1978 further work using the high-frequency seismic sounder, resistivity, aerial photography was sponsored by a group of private investors (RSI) from Milwaukee. The leader of the field work for RSI was mining engineer Ken Wakefield (more on him below). The investors gifted to the Egyptian Antiquities Organisation a large four-inch drilling rig with compressor and accessories as part of this project. A downhole borehole television camera was also acquired and given to the AO at the close of the field season. The drill made it possible to drill holes in bedrock in and around the pyramids using only air (instead of water) to remove cuttings. As an add-on to the above project, the Association for Research and Enlightenment (ARE) in Virginia Beach, Virginia was under the leadership of Dr Hugh Lynn Cayce. ARE asked us to conduct special studies in and around the Sphinx. Some of the readings recorded by the late Edgar Cayce concerned the Sphinx. The resistivity work done in 1976 around the Sphinx was very brief and wide electrode spacings were used. The 1978 resistivity work was much more thorough and our team used (as I recall) one-foot electrode spacings. Patti Burns and John Tanzi of the SRI team did the 1978 resistivity work, however none of us has been able to locate our logs and printouts . . .[46]

Lambert Dolphin also explains his personal relationship with Hugh Lynn Cayce and Joseph Jahoda (a prominent member of the ARE) on this project in these terms:

Hugh Lynn Cayce was a very gracious sponsor and spent considerable time with us during the time the field work was being done. He mentioned that the Cayce Foundation had less confidence in Edgar Cayce's readings in archaeology as compared to his medical readings and healing work. Yet ARE had ongoing interest in and around the Sphinx. Ongoing work has in fact continued by Dr Joseph Jahoda . . . I had the distinct feeling Hugh Lynn was at the time satisfied there was no Hall of Records anywhere under the Sphinx. I liked Hugh Lynn, and respected him very much. Joe Jahoda has always been congenial, friendly, helpful to this day . . .[47]

The ARE's version of the story is somewhat different. According to ARE's editor, A. Robert Smith – also the official biographer of Hugh Lynn Cayce – in late 1977 Lambert Dolphin took a trip to Virginia Beach to meet up with top ARE executives.[48] There he negotiated the terms and agreements of a contract whereby the SRI would undertake to help the ARE to search for the Hall of Records. The ARE would fund the entire project with an initial budget of about $100,000 – a substantial sum in those days and certainly one that must have put a strain on the financial securities of the ARE. Hugh Lynn Cayce, who was responsible for raising the money, appointed Mark Lehner as 'our man in Cairo' to represent the Edgar Cayce Foundation.[49] Work began in early 1978. Hugh Lynn himself flew to Cairo and spent some time with the team, at times supervising the activities at Giza himself. The representative of the Egyptian Antiquities Organisation (EAO) on site was Zahi Hawass, who was then Chief Inspector for the Giza Pyramids. Hawass, who was thirty years old at the time, was a bachelors graduate from the University of Alexandria, and had been working for the EAO since 1969, where he began his career as an inspector in Middle Egypt for the sites of Tuna El Gebel and Mallawi. In 1974 he was appointed inspector to work with the University of Pennsylvania at the site of Malkata and also became Chief Inspector at Giza. This was about the same time the SRI had begun its first surveys there. In 1978, when the Edgar Cayce Foundation and the SRI were exploring the Sphinx area, Hawass was put in charge as director of excavation at the northeast corner of the Sphinx and other digs in the Nazlet Al Samman area.

Until Lambert Dolphin's brief report of July 1999, no detailed report was ever published on the Edgar Cayce Foundation funded project – called 'The Sphinx Exploration Project' – either by the SRI or the EAO. The Edgar Cayce Foundation, however, did produce a small internal report in 1983 entitled 'Edgar Cayce Foundation Egypt/Sphinx Research Project 1976-1982'. A copy of this report was passed to me by

Rufus Mosely, the TWA airline pilot who had assisted Hugh Lynn Cayce in this and other projects in Egypt.[50] In 1995, when Graham Hancock and I were researching for our joint book, *Keeper of Genesis*, we also managed to obtain from Mark Lehner a personal account of what went on at Giza in 1978 during the Sphinx Exploration Project.[51] But perhaps the most telling recording of this expedition came not from written accounts but from another source altogether. I discovered that the whole expedition had been covered by a film crew who shot long sequences in 8 mm colour and sound. Through connections in the USA I managed to get a full set of the rough cuts of the film as well as the sound tapes.[52] It is especially from these and from Lehner's account that the following story was culled.

The Sphinx Exploration Project, as Lehner put it with refreshing honesty, was nothing less than 'a direct shot at finding the Hall of Records'.[53] In other words, the whole exercise was not, as some would have it later,[54] a 'scientific' expedition or works focused on 'restoration', but rather an attempt, pure and simple, of vindicating the prophecies of Edgar Cayce. Such is made blatantly clear not only by the very presence and direct funding of the Edgar Cayce Foundation but also by the various statements made by Hugh Lynn Cayce and Mark Lehner while on location at Giza in 1978. Hugh Lynn, for example, narrated the origin and purpose of this expedition in the following manner to a film interviewer near the Sphinx. In this interview Hugh Lynn is seen seated on an ancient limestone block with the Sphinx in the background:

> Within a short time, perhaps, we will begin to discover just how accurate the Edgar Cayce readings may be, and if his information is established as being accurate, it is possible for us, perhaps, to make a small contribution to man's understanding of himself in a new dimension of time and for this new age. A new concept for man's purpose in the earth, and a much longer existence in the earth than history at present suggests. In November of 1977, we were able to introduce to SRI –the Stanford Research Institute – who were doing some surveys, electronic surveys in Egypt, introduce them to Mark Lehner, representative of the Edgar Cayce Foundation in Egypt. Mark suggested that the SRI team explore the area immediately around the Sphinx and specifically around the right paw where Edgar Cayce had in 1923 mentioned specific anomalies, possible passageways etc. Now, in February and March 1978, this work is going on.

When the interviewer asked Hugh Lynn, notwithstanding the scientific information, where he, Hugh Lynn, felt the drilling should take place, the latter gave this reply:

Any drilling now in relationship to the right paw (of the Sphinx) would for me possibly touch the entrance to a passageway to a chamber that would lead to distant passageways to places where the (Hall of) Records . . . He (Edgar Cayce) didn't say, actually, that it (the Hall of Records) would be found behind the right paw; he said that the entrance to the passageway was from the right paw. Now that leaves us a lot of room under that paw as to where that shaft might come out. And so that's what we've been looking for. We were excited when the SRI team found some anomalies under the right paw, connected with the right paw, and that is, of course, what we are drilling first. Now I'm interested also in pursuing other drilling under the right paw so that we cover as much of that area directly under the paw as possible. Picking up any possible shaft that might come up under it. It's my theory here, and it's only a theory after all, that the . . . because we have no specific information from the Edgar Cayce readings whether it's under the front of the paw, the middle of the paw, the back of the paw . . . that they built a record chamber then drilled or cut away a passage, probably a very deep passageway, that has not been picked up yet that would come up under the right paw, for this right paw would remain as one . . . , they felt as a monument down through the ages, something that man would not destroy, and would always be a point from which the records could be found . . .

The interviewer then put the same question to Mark Lehner, who had this to say:

. . . One wonders what kind of truth we're dealing with about the ancient past, we're now talking about Atlantis following his (Edgar Cayce's) lead, or . . . what kind of truth are we dealing with in the psychic account, the myth and the archaeological account? Perhaps we are dealing with some kind of difference between literal truth, literal hard material truth, and literary truth – and sometimes the line between them becomes very fine indeed. As we worked at investigating the Sphinx, and as I see it, the project is about probing ancient myths and riddles . . . (it's like) being caught between two different truth levels, two different realities. It's hard to expect anything . . . Either Edgar Cayce is right or he's wrong. Either the Hall of Records is there, or it is not. Either the Great Pyramid was built 2500 BC by Khufu or it was built 8000 years earlier. So there are, there are . . . we have to say come off it now! It's either there or it's not. And there is that aspect to it. But at the same time it's more complicated, more subtle then an 'either or' situation . . .

There is little doubt, judging from the above convoluted statement, that Mark Lehner was torn by his allegiance to Hugh Lynn Cayce on the one hand and the hard realities of archaeology on the other. He wanted, like all good Cayceites, to believe in the Hall of Records and hope that it might show up in their exploration. But he was also pulled towards the rigid scientific approach of archaeological works, where speculation of any kind must be put aside, and the investigator must stick to the available evidence pulled out from the sand and earth – the kind of evidence that Lehner would later term 'bedrock realities'. Nonetheless, he clung to the fact that the Edgar Cayce readings uncannily 'interfaced' with textual material as well as depictions from ancient Egyptian sources. He, too, could not avoid noticing that the ancient texts and depictions pointed to the possible existence of a 'Hall of Records' or 'tomb of Osiris' or 'secret chamber' much in the manner described by Cayce in his readings. In this respect, Lehner brought into evidence the many 'tablets' that were left by pilgrims at the Sphinx sanctuary in ancient times, and how these supported the Cayce view:

> . . . Interestingly . . . some of the tablets refer to the Sphinx and the Sphinx sanctuary as the 'chamber of Sokar' . . . the same god which appears in the secret chamber between the paws of the Sphinx in this tomb painting . . . (Thothmoses IV) calls the Sphinx the 'sanctuary of Sokar' . . . so you have the question: in the minds of the ancient Egyptians who composed this sacred book on the king's tomb wall – the Book of What is in the Underworld – when they show the secret chamber in the Sphinx in a place called Rostau, which is called the 'secret place', and when you think that this place (Giza) was called Rostau, and was also said to be the 'sanctuary of Sokar', the god of the secret chamber, did they know, or did they have the idea, that there was a secret chamber under the Sphinx as far back as 1500 BC? Is the legend, or the mystery, or the myth of the secret chamber under the Sphinx as old as that? In the tomb paintings, the Sphinx is also called Aker, the guardian of the entrance of the Underworld. Now Aker had his own book called the Book of Aker, and this also appears in some of the tombs of the kings of the New Kingdom down in the Valley of the Kings at Thebes. And the Book of Aker is also very interesting for what the ancient Egyptians may have conceived when they thought of the Sphinx. Because one scene of the Book of Aker shows the Sphinx again in double, but in this case now opened up, and there is a pair of arms lifting the sun out of the body of the Sphinx. The sun, of course, is the symbol of Ra. And on either side of these pair of arms lifting the sun out of the body of the Sphinx, the gods are lifting up the boats, the sacred boats. It's a sort of resurrection scene. Everything is opening up from the body of the Sphinx. And that scene is interesting when we compare it with another scene from the Book of Aker. In this scene Aker is shown as a double sphinx but closed up. One paw this way and another paw this way, and two heads. And underneath the Sphinx-Aker there's a mummy with a white head-dress and a white beard, and there are rays of energy going down from the body of the Sphinx down to this mummy. And the texts identify this mummy as the 'body of Osiris' or, in other versions, the 'body of Ra' that is hidden under the Sphinx-Aker. And yet another scene of the Book of Aker shows Aker again in double, as a double Sphinx, and on either sides, from the paw, emerge the gods . . . Well you see the myth, this is all myth, legend. But in this case when we talk about Rostau, when we talk about the Book of Aker, the legends from ancient Egypt

from 1500 BC, and the Edgar Cayce readings start to interface. Of course the Egyptologists and the experts will say you're stretching things a bit; they will say that these texts are mythological, only symbolic of the death process, they're funerary works. They would charge that we are stretching things a bit when we see in these texts literal references to secret chambers under the Sphinx. But the interface between these ideas, these paintings and the Edgar Cayce readings is very strong. There are other little clues that make one wonder. For example in the tablets that Selim Hassan found left by the pilgrims. They often show the worshipper standing in front of the Sphinx, in front of a depiction of the Sphinx of Giza here, and there are some sixty of these tablets found. And the majority show the Sphinx standing on a high pedestal with a door at the bottom. Just as the Thothmoses stela here (Lehner is sitting between the paws of the Sphinx) where the Sphinx is sitting on top of a pedestal with a door at the bottom. This prompted early Egyptologists in the 1800s to probe the Sphinx to find the pedestal and the door underneath. So you see that it's possible that a secret chamber under the Sphinx, or a door under the Sphinx has gone back from the present day, through the Egyptologists of the 1800s . . . in the Greek period it was believed there was a tomb of a certain king here . . . the idea goes back, perhaps, to the New Kingdom Egyptians of 1500 BC . . .[55]

As Lehner pointed out, there is a rather uncanny similarity between the Cayce readings and those ancient texts and paintings concerning the *Book of Aker* and, as we have seen, the *Book of What is in the Underworld*.[56] The idea of a 'body of Osiris' or a 'body of Ra' under the Sphinx is, eerily, brought out in the Cayce readings where it is said that the bodies of the 'entities' lay in tombs or chambers underneath the Sphinx near or within the Hall of Records. For when asked 'Where are those records or tablets made of that Egyptian experience?', Cayce, in a trance state, replied:

> In the tomb of records, as indicated. For the entity's tomb then was part of the Hall of Records, which has not yet been uncovered. It lies between, or along that entrance from the Sphinx to the temple, or the pyramid; in a pyramid, of course, of its own . . .

TO DRILL OR NOT TO DRILL

On the six hours or so of film footage that was made during this expedition, much of it is devoted to general meetings, interviews with other players such as Mark Lehner, Zahi Hawass and various SRI staff, as well as a well-documented section of drilling that eventually took place near and around the Sphinx and, more specifically, under the right paw. Regarding the drilling operations, the idea was only to drill where the resistivity tests had indicated an 'anomaly', then verify what was in the hole by lowering a bore-scope video camera. To conform with Hugh Lynn's wishes, the first drilling operation took place at the right paw of the Sphinx, on the southern flank of the monument. The drilling frame was adjusted so that the angle of boring would be about forty degrees to the horizontal in order to get not just under the paw but across to the other side of the paw. It seems that although many anomalies were detected by the SRI remote sensing equipment, only five of these were drilled and verified with the bore-scope camera. According to A. Robert Smith in his official biography of Hugh Lynn Cayce, the project ran out of funds, and 'SRI packed up and returned to the United States'.[57] But there seems to have been a more serious 'internal problem' at play here that the parties might have preferred to put behind them. This problem had to do with the other client of SRI who had contracted them for a remote sensing survey at the same time they undertook the work at the Sphinx for the Edgar Cayce Foundation. Who was this mysterious client? And what exactly was the problem that sent SRI packing? A clue was given in the internal report prepared by the Edgar Cayce Foundation, where it is stated that 'toward the end of the season, serious problems began to develop between the SRI team and *the other major patron* who contracted for the survey of the pyramids and who was, at the same time, the party heading the drilling operations'.[58]

No indication as to what the 'serious problem' was is made in this report, nor is the identity of the 'major patron' given. On the films of the expedition the drilling team is seen wearing helmets with the logo 'RSI'. At first I did not realise this, in view of the close resemblance with the logo of the 'SRI'. It was not until I contacted Mark Lehner in 1996 that it was revealed to me that RSI stood for 'Recovery System International' and that it was, according to Lehner, a company formed specifically for the purpose of this project.[59] This is an extraordinary situation involving exploration of the most intrusive manner on the most ancient, most universally known monuments in the history of man. A makeshift company calling itself Recovery System International comes from the USA, presumably obtaining licences and security clearances from the Egyptian authorities to undertake explorations inside the Great Pyramid and around the Giza necropolis, then somehow also acts as drilling contractors to the Edgar Cayce Foundation's Sphinx Exploration Project, and then is heard of no more except through fleeting references as 'major patrons' or the 'other party' in ARE literature,[60] and not at all in SRI reports and the Egyptian Antiquities Organisation files – at least not in any that have been made available or accessible to the public.[61] Yet the presence of Recovery System International at the Great Pyramid and the Sphinx was not kept a secret in 1978. In one of the films of the Sphinx Project Exploration, several officials of the Egyptian Antiquities Organisation, including Zahi Hawass, the Chief Inspector of the Giza Pyramids, are openly seen with Recovery System International engineers while drilling operations are under way. Indeed, Hawass is seen inspecting the drilling of the hole at the right front paw of the Sphinx. Concordant with what Lambert Dolphin has stated recently, Mark Lehner confirmed to me in 1995 that Recovery System International was represented on site by an engineer called Ken Wakefield.[62] This was also confirmed to Graham Hancock and to myself by Joseph Jahoda during a telephone conversation in February 1995.[63] Oddly, Joseph Jahoda further informed us that he, himself, had been behind the drilling company that called itself Recovery System International:

> Well, it was a poorly . . . it's a long story. But the bottom line is we organised an expedition, a sort of fortune-hunter came along, and he put up the money for the drill. It was a hundred thousand bucks. Then we hired a film crew, a woman and man, a husband and wife team who brought all fantastic camera equipment, and we were ready to go.[64] And we started drilling . . . By the time we started to get ready for the third drill which I had very carefully calculated to cut through all kinds possible . . . I wanted it to be at an angle, a compound angle and everything else . . . and I had it all figured out . . .

Mark Lehner, in contradiction to what the Edgar Cayce Foundation said regarding the 'serious problem' that broke out between SRI and RSI, claims that there was 'a serious falling out' between RSI – who did not appreciate at all the Cayce component on the project – and SRI, to the extent that SRI feared 'they would not receive payment from RSI for work already done'.[65] Joseph Jahoda, on the other hand, speaks of a much more grave incident:

> The army came with their guns and they made us stop. They said we were shaking the pyramid . . . one of the organisations was scared the whole thing would fall apart, so they made us stop . . . There was a political feud between the various groups and if they had hit something, who knows . . . I really can't read their minds. However I was not there. I was in the United States at this time yelling frantically over the phone, 'Don't stop! Keep drilling! Let them shoot!' I was threatening everybody. I really got excited . . .[66]

Apparently there was a 'big lawsuit' fought for many years concerning Ken Wakefield, the drilling supervisor working with Mark Lehner.

Apparently SRI claimed that RSI still owed them unpaid bills.[67] Mark Lehner totally denied that they were stopped by the army or anybody else. The problem, according to Lehner, was much more prosaic, and mainly to do with money. At any rate it was a great disappointment and, worse, a feeling of having been short-changed is expressed by Hugh Lynn Cayce following the announcement by the Egyptian Antiquities Organisation that no more drilling will be allowed at the Sphinx:

> I'm disappointed, of course, that we've only drilled one hole under the Sphinx's paw. I understood that we would be allowed to drill from the other side and pick up the anomaly that the instruments indicated was here. I can understand, however, the Egyptians' problem with this, and the drilling between the two paws . . . I wish we had gone further with it. Also, of course, I was interested in the possibility of drilling towards the back of the paw, northwest, because they found there some anomalies they feel they have explained, but I would like to have seen a hole there . . . This is only one hole that's been drilled under the Sphinx's right paw. I had hoped that they would be able to drill another one from between the paws. I was also very interested in the possibility of a hole being drilled toward the back of the right paw . . . and another one in the northwest corner at the back paw . . . Mark, did you think they went far enough with this hole?

> Mark Lehner: Well, they went down twenty feet which would have put them on the other side of the paw . . .

> Hugh Lynn: On the other side . . . ??! . . . You mean it went through the whole . . .?? . . . How wide is this paw?! . . .

> Mark: I'm not sure . . . but Roger (?) calculated it out and it went far enough to be on the other side, under the paw and on the other side . . .

When asked whether he thought the SRI had drilled enough holes within the area to find 'what he was looking for', Hugh Lynn replied:

> Well obviously they haven't drilled enough holes to find what we are looking for! . . . But they say they drilled out the anomalies that they found. I was under the impression that these anomalies were actually empty spaces! This one, for example . . . well, we'll have another briefing on this . . . but I understand it was just a different formation that they saw in the rock formation here. Is that true, Mark? . . . I don't know . . .

> Mark: Well . . . the conclusion is that there's some kind of fissure down here and that they feel it may have been producing the anomaly, the echo . . . both the resistivity anomaly and the echo . . .

Hugh Lynn: Do you mean a 'hole' by a fissure . . . ? . . .

Mark: I'm not sure what they mean by a fissure . . . a natural kind of vein of poor limestone, uh . . . maybe ferruginous, that is iron ore deposit.

Was Mark Lehner concerned, asked the interviewer, that the technology of SRI to pinpoint 'anomalies' had perhaps failed to some extent? Mark answered: 'It's hard to say until the project has been completed and the whole data has been processed.' But then, perplexed, he asked 'why are they getting anomalies, and then not getting any cavities' when they examine the location with the bore-scope camera? In any case, all this was becoming academic because the Egyptian authorities had just announced that no more drilling would be allowed. Hugh Lynn was not amused: 'I certainly would like to discuss this with them because I had hoped there would be, as they indicated earlier, more drilling!' But it was to no avail. The Egyptians did not change their minds. This and the internal problems that marred the team as well as the drying up of funds caused the expedition to fold. But not before a strange alliance was struck between Hugh Lynn Cayce and the Chief Inspector at Giza, Zahi Hawass. In the words of Hugh Lynn's biographer, A. Robert Smith:

> When the funding ran out, SRI packed up and returned to the United States . . . Discouraging as these inconclusive results were, Hugh Lynn had no sense of defeat. He would stay with the search as long as it took, building up alliances with other groups and individuals. One of the latter was the Egyptian chief inspector at Giza, Hawass, whom he had met through Lehner in 1975.[68]

As for the 'groups' that Hugh Lynn Cayce developed an alliance with, one was the American Research Centre in Cairo, better known as the ARCE.

Meanwhile something unusual happened involving Zahi Hawass. For reasons that are not clear he started a dig in front of the Sphinx temple, apparently in connection with the Institute of Underground Water of the Egyptian Ministry of Irrigation.[69] A drilling through some fifty feet of debris struck red granite instead of the natural limestone of the area.[70] Red granite or, indeed, any other form of granite does not occur naturally in this part of Egypt. The nearest place was some 375 miles to the south. The stone, quite obviously, had to have been put there by man. The matter was quickly reported to the Edgar Cayce Foundation executives who quite naturally must have wondered if it might be part of the underground complex that Cayce had predicted existed in front of the Sphinx, i.e. between the river and the statue. According to A. Robert Smith:

> Since the granite had to be imported, the discovery raised questions why it was placed there and what more might be found if a dig were permitted. Such an operation would require approval at a higher government level. If Zahi Hawass was to advance within the government to further his own career and open doors for Hugh Lynn's project, he could do it best on the wings of higher education at an American Ivy League college.[71]

Also, again according to A. Robert Smith, it seems that Hugh Lynn, as he had done with Mark Lehner a few years earlier to get him into the American University in Cairo, also pulled a few strings for Zahi Hawass. In his own words:

> I got him a scholarship at the University of Pennsylvania in Egyptology, to get his Ph.D. I got the scholarship through an ARE person who happened to be on the Fulbright scholarship board.[72]

Hugh Lynn, it would seem, was also very 'appreciative' to Hawass for having aided Mark Lehner, as representative of the ARE in Egypt, to work on the Sphinx. He also felt, according to A. Robert Smith, 'some past-life connections'.[73] Contrary to what Lambert Dolphin said recently about how Hugh Lynn felt about the existence of the Hall of Records, this is what Hugh Lynn said – or rather vowed – after he left Egypt:

> I'm never giving up there. It is very important. If we get back to the Old Kingdom there, it is going to make history look like . . . We are looking for the records – this is what the readings say – of the pyramids themselves and the Sphinx. We are looking for the Atlantean records which are buried there. We are looking for Hermes' records and his prophecy of his next reincarnation as Jesus. I think they are there, in front of the Sphinx. The Sphinx is guarding them. We are playing for all the marbles.[74]

Like I previously pointed out, Dr Hawass emphatically denies such a claim that he was sponsored in any way by the ARE, and I am inclined to accept his position in this matter. Meanwhile, after the SRI flop, two other projects were funded by the Edgar Cayce Foundation. It seemed that Claremont Graduate School offered to the ARE the use of instruments lent to them by the University of California. But the ARE knew very well that they could not use such equipment on their own, but needed to operate through other American agencies approved and licensed to operate in archaeological works in Egypt. They turned to the American Research Centre in Egypt (ARCE). Hugh Lynn was quoted as saying: 'I gave them a little money and Mark (Lehner) got attached (to the ARCE) . . .' [75] It seems that what Hugh Lynn Cayce hoped was that 'it would make Mark Lehner the world's leading expert on the Sphinx [and], more important to Hugh Lynn, it gave his man in Cairo the leverage to search for the evidence of Ra Ta and the legendary Hall of Records'.[76] Ra Ta was, according to the Cayce readings, the high-priest in Atlantean times who had helped in the construction of the Great Pyramid and, most intriguingly, the very same entity which Cayce believed himself to be a 'reincarnation' of.[77] As Lehner himself explained back in 1974: 'Ra Ta, the high-priest of those times, is the central character in the drama presented in the readings'; and then he set about to argue that 'there are good empirical reasons for believing that the Ra Ta story is, in fact, rooted in truth'.[78] For example, in *The Egyptian Heritage*, Lehner devotes a complete section of the book to 'Reflections of the Ra Ta Period in Protodynastic Remains'. Lehner writes: 'If we accept the Ra Ta story as a record of historical fact, one of the most interesting questions which arises is: what happened between the end of that period described in the Cayce readings and the beginning of dynastic Egyptian history as depicted by archaeology? He then proceeds to give numerous examples of how those readings can be matched to actual archaeological evidence, such as finding 'correlations' between First Dynasty scenes depicted in palettes and equating the name of Ra Ta to that of Rostau.[79] Many years later, in 1995, Lehner disagreed with such interpretations, and today much downplays his ARE role in Egypt. He wrote to me that 'the goal of my work at the Sphinx after the SRI project was not to explore for hidden chambers but to document the monument with accurate large-scale maps, profiles and elevations'.[80]

According to Edgar Evans Cayce, however, it was Mark Lehner who went to the ARCE with a proposal to investigate the Sphinx from a mapping viewpoint. The project received approval from the ARCE archaeological review committee, and eventually a licence was granted by the Egyptian Antiquities Organisation. Mark Lehner was appointed as field director under the responsibility of Dr James Allen. The director of the ARCE at the time was Dr Paul Walker.[81] The Edgar Cayce Foundation was the major financial sponsor for the Sphinx projects in 1982. Other small grants came from the Chase National Bank of Egypt and the Franzhein Synergy Trust, the latter putting up some $20,000.[82]

In short, the Sphinx project's personnel were directly under the payroll of the Edgar Cayce Foundation. It is not clear whether Lehner received other financial assistance from the ARE, but judging from the 1982-83 budget breakdown for this project made by the ARE, it is clear that they, at least, regarded Mark Lehner, as late as 1983, as directly under their payroll. Mark Lehner, in fact, was receiving a salary or stipend of $1200 per month, a fairly generous sum for Egypt in 1982, plus travel to the US and local expenses. The ARE budget for the whole project was $30,000 for 1982-83 and $61,950 for 1983-84.[83] As Lehner himself explained, the funds supplied by the Edgar Cayce Foundation were pooled by 'a small number of people with particular interest in Egypt and the Edgar Cayce readings'.[84] One of these people was Joseph Jahoda of Astron Corporation in Virginia, a life-long member and staunch supporter of the ARE. Jahoda would appear several times at Giza in connection with explorations looking for the Hall of Records.

After the ARCE Sphinx Mapping Project was completed in 1982, Lehner was retained as a field director for the Giza Plateau Mapping Project, also run by the ARCE. The main funds came from a variety of sponsors, principally from the Yale Endowment for Egyptology and the millionaires Bruce Ludwig of TRW Realties in Los Angeles, and David Koch, renowned for having bought the Jacqueline Kennedy Onassis furniture collection. The Edgar Cayce Foundation also contributed to some minor extent. In the official acknowledgement of the ARCE for this project the name of Joseph Jahoda also appears alongside other contributors such as the General Dynamics corporation and various other individuals from other corporations, including a certain Matthew MacCauley, a musician from Los Angeles.[85] Also in 1984 another fully funded project by the Edgar Cayce Foundation involving Mark Lehner was the so-called Carbon-14 Dating Project, which cost around $17,000. This involved an attempt to date the Great Pyramid and other pyramids using the radio carbon-14 dating process. Eighty-five samples including five from the Sphinx were collected by a small team led by Lehner. Tests were then undertaken by Dr Herbert Hass at the Southern Methodist University and by Dr Willy Wolfli at the Eidgennossische Technische Hochschule in Zurich, Switzerland.[86] The outcome was surprising, as Lehner himself remarked at the time:

> The dates run from 3809 BC to 2869 BC. So generally the dates are . . . significantly earlier than the best Egyptological date for Khufu . . . In short, the radiocarbon dates, depending on which sample you note, suggest that the Egyptological chronology is anything from 200 to 1200 years off . . . I imagine

it'll make a stink. The Giza pyramid is 400 years earlier than Egyptologists believe.[87]

Rather than make a 'stink', as Lehner suggested, the whole episode, like the proverbial debate over the Dead Sea Scrolls, got lost in the dusty archives of academia. The problem was that the carbon samples were taken from the outside of the Pyramid, from minute bits of straw and wood caught in the mortar used to join the blocks. Many have argued, however, that such mortar could have been contaminated with other more recent repairs. More recent carbon-dating was conducted in 1995 by an American team financed by David H. Koch, one of Lehner's sponsors, and the result somewhat 'improved' the date of the Great Pyramid by 200 years or so, which in turn was explained away by assuming that the builders used 'older culture material'.[88]

Let us return, however, to the Lehner story. By 1984 Mark Lehner was moving away from the ARE and injecting his energy and resources into mainstream Egyptology. As Hugh Lynn Cayce had predicted, Lehner is today regarded as the world's leading authority on the Sphinx and the Giza necropolis. He has lectured as a professor of Egyptology at Chicago and Boston universities, and he is currently the curator of the Harvard Semitic Museum. Lehner has appeared as an expert authority on the Sphinx and the Giza pyramids in numerous magazine and newspaper articles as well as on several major TV documentaries. Hugh Lynn Cayce died in 1982, and the presidency of the ARE went to his son, Charles Thomas Cayce. He is still president today.

After the Carbon-14 Dating Project it looked as if the search for the Hall of Records at Giza had been abandoned by the ARE. Yet true to Hugh Lynn Cayce's vow that they would 'never give up the search', other ARE members, as we shall see, with or without the full support of the Edgar Cayce Foundation, slowly took the matter into their own hands.

A new hunt for the fabled Hall of Records was about to begin. And this time it would draw me in with a strange synchronistic premonition.

Chapter Ten

Faults and Chasms

'We sort of have 1996 set up for our little expedition to the Sphinx, with underground radar. 1996 was when Zahi (Hawass) said we'd be able to go. We'll do more ground-scanning . . . and I figure that by 1998 we'll hit something.'

Joseph Jahoda, February 1995 .

'. . . Certain people . . . acted as if the Giza Plateau, which contains the three Great Pyramids and the Sphinx, was their private property . . .'

Dr Mohamad Ibrahim Bakr, President of the Egyptian Antiquities Organisation, *Sunday Times* July 1993

STRANGE SYNCHRONICITIES

In the early part of 1994, a few weeks after the publication of my book *The Orion Mystery*, I received a letter from my good friend, the author Colin Wilson. Wilson, who was researching for his next book, *From Atlantis to the Sphinx*, asked my opinion on John Anthony West's geological dating of the Sphinx to a period much older than accepted chronology, and was also curious to know more about the astronomical connection of the Giza Pyramids and the date of 10,500 BC which I had briefly touched upon in my book. Oddly, although I had heard of the John West controversy, I had not known much of the man or his work at Giza. My focus was on astronomy and the Pyramids, not the geology of the Sphinx. My linking the Giza Pyramids to a date of 10,500 BC through astronomical reasoning had, by necessity of its implications, thrown me into the arena of the 'Age of the Sphinx' debate that was raging in the United States and Egypt. In

199

a way, it was very much Wilson's letter which prompted me to turn my attention away from the Giza Pyramids for a while and take a closer look at the other, perhaps far more symbolic monument of the Giza Plateau: the Great Sphinx.

At about that same time Graham Hancock and I had agreed to co-author a book which was to be an investigation into the Hermetic tradition through the ages and I was waiting for Graham to finish his book, *Fingerprints of the Gods*, before starting on this new project. I knew that Hancock had met John West in Egypt, and therefore asked him for more information on West's work and how relevant it was to his own search for evidence of a lost civilisation. Hancock informed me that he was devoting a whole chapter to John West and his work, and offered to send me a proof. In brief, John West, with the collaboration of Dr Robert Schoch, a professor of geology at Boston University, had studied the geological erosion of the Sphinx and the walls of the enclosure around it. He had concluded that they were not caused by sand and wind, as archaeologists maintained, but by rainwater. The depth of the grooves and fissures cut by the flowing water suggested a date of at least 2000 years earlier for the carving of the Sphinx. And on the basis of geological and climatic evidence, John West had even implied that the age of the Sphinx could be as old as 15,000 BC. As extraordinary as it seemed, here was the hard science of geology, backed by an eminent Bostonian academic, that threatened to topple whole tenets of Egyptian chronology and the origins of civilisation as taught in schools and universities. It implied, of course, that a much older and far more technologically advanced civilisation had touched Egypt in prehistoric times – an implication that inevitably brought the 'Atlantis' issue back into the limelight. Schoch and West's conclusion sent a wave of anger and controversy around the academic world, and the Egyptological and archaeological 'experts' came out in droves to defend their coveted turf. One of the most outspoken critics of the West-Schoch hypothesis was none other than Mark Lehner, now a visiting professor at Chicago University and tagged a leading expert on the Sphinx. The other was Zahi Hawass, now a doctor in Egyptology with a Ph.D. from the University of Pennsylvania (and Director-General of the Giza Monuments for the Egyptian Antiquities Organisation).

The 'Age of the Sphinx' controversy started when John West, in the late 1970s, read in a book by R.A. Schwaller de Lubicz, *Sacred Science*,[1] that the body of the Sphinx appeared to be eroded by water. Schwaller had suggested that the Nile's flood, which apparently might have reached the Sphinx upper levels in very remote antiquity, might have been responsible. Calculations, however, showed that flood waters were unlikely to have been that high. When West took Robert Schoch to see the Sphinx in 1990, the latter quickly realised that the vertical fissures he saw were not the result of flood water at all, but rainfall flowing over the body of the Sphinx and the walls of its enclosure. Schoch and West presented their hypothesis to the Geological Society in San Diego, and within a few days the news hit the press and a huge academic storm began to rumble, its echoes still felt to this day. The upshot was that the academics and 'experts' on the subject of Egyptian chronology and archaeology rejected outright any suggestion that the Sphinx could precede dynastic Egypt, this in spite of the well-argued geological evidence presented by Schoch. Rather than review the thesis with a cool head, the Egyptologists in particular came out screaming and exhibiting to the media the hallmark of an orthodoxy and dogmatism that was long thought by the lay public to have been purged out of such scientific circles. The issue was not only whether Schoch and West were scientifically right, but whether they had the right to argue such 'heretical' matter as outsiders in terms of the Egyptological profession. Dr Peter Lecorvra of the Egyptian Department of the Boston Museum of Fine Arts put it this way:

> That's ridiculous! Thousands of scholars working for hundreds of years have studied this topic and the chronology is pretty well worked out. There are no big surprises in store for us.[2]

Dr Lanny Bell, an Egyptologist at Chicago University, declared that although Egyptologists weren't geologists, he nonetheless was 'not willing to admit that we've lost 1500 years or more in our chronology'.[3] The Egyptological world was incensed. No words of encouragement or any suggestion of further investigations to confirm or rebuff the West-Schoch geological claim were offered by the establishment. As far as this particular profession was concerned the West-Schoch thesis was beneath serious consideration. the *New York Times* interviewed Mark Lehner, who delivered this broadside:

> You don't overthrow Egyptian history based on one phenomenon like a weathering profile. That is how pseudoscience is done, not real science![4]

In February 1992 John West and Schoch decided to take their debate to the American Association for the Advancement of Science in Chicago, where Mark Lehner led a group of sceptics to debate against the hypothesis. Present was Canadian author and journalist Paul William Roberts,[5] who reported the event with his characteristic blend of humour and lucidity on human nature, calling it an 'academic Armageddon'.[6] The debate, entitled 'How Old is the Sphinx?', attracted a huge audience and members of the media. On one side were Dr Robert Schoch and Dr Thomas Dobecki, a seismographer who had examined the Sphinx area with Schoch and West in 1991. On the other side were Dr Mark Lehner and Dr K. Lal Gauri, a geologist who had worked under Lehner during the ARCE Sphinx Project in 1982. John West was not allowed a place on the panel due to his lack of appropriate academic credentials. The debate, which started on relatively amicable terms, degenerated into a heated débâcle which ended up with shouts and accusations and Lehner snapping at West that he had no right to meddle in matters only Ph.D.s were qualified to deal with.[7]

Meanwhile West was working with Robert Watt, a producing partner of Steven Spielberg, and Boris Said, a film-maker from Los Angeles, on a documentary to present his thesis to the general public. There was, however, another aspect of the Schoch-West expedition at the Sphinx that had even more dramatic consequences if correct. The seismographer Thomas Dobecki had conducted acoustic tests all around the Sphinx with the help of West and Boris Said, and had pinpointed a large rectangular anomaly under the right paw of the Sphinx – just as Edgar Cayce had predicted.[8] Dobecki described it as 'a fairly large feature; it's about nine metres by twelve metres in dimension, and less than five metres in depth'. He pointed out that the regular shape of this rectangular 'anomaly' was inconsistent with naturally occurring cavities and, in his opinion, there was 'some suggestion that this could be man-made'.[9] The news of this ran through the Edgar Cayce Foundation and its members world-wide like an electric current. But why was Dobecki looking for 'anomalies and cavities' with seismographs when the principal objective was to determine the age of the Sphinx by examination of the erosion of the limestone? The seismographic data taken in the rear of the Sphinx's terrace (the natural platform of limestone on which the Sphinx stands) proved useful for Dr Robert Schoch in his geological argument for dating the Sphinx,[10] but it was made clear by Dobecki himself that he was also looking for evidence of a 'lost civilisation' and a secret chamber under the paws of the Sphinx.[11]

It is perhaps interesting to note that much of the funds for the project were gathered from ARE members or supporters, including two individuals who not only had donated some funds, but were apparently appointed by the ARE to oversee their own interests at Giza. One individual we have already met: this was Joseph Jahoda, who had previously funded ARE projects at Giza and who was embroiled in the drilling fiasco of 1978. The other was the millionaire Dr Joseph Schor, a life-long member of the ARE and a top executive with Forest Laboratories Inc. of New York.[12] The latter was to be implicated in 1996 in a huge controversy over explorations at Giza which we shall review shortly.

Meanwhile John West and Boris Said managed to produce a full-length documentary which was commissioned eventually by one of America's largest national channels, NBC. The documentary was titled *Mystery of the Sphinx* and was broadcast in November 1993 to a record thirty-three million viewers; it earned West an Emmy Award for best research. The reaction by Egyptologists this time round was even more virulent. Dr Hawass was particularly furious, and mounted a major attack in the press. One particular article, which appeared in the *Akhbar Al Yom* newspaper in Egypt, was extremely scathing. With a banner title of 'Stealing of Egypt's Civilisation', the newspaper accused John West and Robert Schoch of being 'liars, science pretenders . . . adventurers playing with our antiquities and lifting their hands against our history'. Dr Zahi Hawass was quoted saying that he thought that this was 'a sort of Zionist penetration'.[13] The undertone of the attacks, quite clearly, had become very political and plainly bordered on hysteria. There was also a gross distortion of the facts. The newspaper, for example, insinuated that West and Schoch (calling them 'certain scientists') had claimed that 'someone had fallen from heaven to build the Pyramids and the Sphinx and created the civilisation of the Egyptians' and that their 'genuine owners are the founders of the elusive Atlantis civilisation . . .'[14] Neither Schoch nor West, of course, had ever said such a thing, nor indeed believed it.[15] Dr Gaber Barakat, a professor at the Faculty of Science at Cairo University, accused the officials who had granted the Americans permits to work at the Sphinx, saying they were as much to blame for this controversy. Even Allah was evoked by Barakat, who exclaimed with indignation: 'Thanks to Allah for not being involved in this crime which could have led to a horrible archaeological catastrophe!' Dr Hawass, in a curious display of blatant disloyalty to his superior, Dr Mohamad Ibrahim Bakr, who was president of the Egyptian Antiquities Organisation at the time of the Schoch-West expedition, passed the blame to him by saying:

> . . . A key official in the Antiquities Organisation accompanied the mission and entered the area. He helped them obtain a permit from the ex-chairman of the Antiquities Organisation to shoot a profit-making propaganda film . . .

attributing all the great antiquities of Egypt to other people. This is a sort of Zionist plot! . . . (furthermore) they indeed shot the film and recorded an interview by the ex-chairman of the Antiquities Organisation who said he was pleased the Sphinx is 10,000 years old, as he did in a similar statement given to a foreign newspaper in support of this thesis.[16]

Hawass then directed his attack on Edgar Cayce, telling the *Akhbar Al Yom* newspaper:

The film indicates an attempt by these pretenders to prove that the Sphinx dates back to 15,000 years . . . and consequently the Pyramids and the great antiquities were not of the ancient Egyptians but other people of higher culture and education who came from the continent of Atlantis after its destruction and placed beneath the Sphinx the records of their lost continent! It is evident that John West represents nothing but a continuation of this cultural invasion to Egypt's civilisation. Before him was Edgar Cayce in Virginia who pretended that he had lived in Atlantis 15,000 years ago and then fled with the records to Egypt which he buried near the Sphinx . . .

When reading these allegations regarding John West and Edgar Cayce, I was perplexed. My investigation on the Edgar Cayce Foundation's connection with the Egyptian authorities at Giza back in 1978, when Dr Hawass was Chief Inspector of the Giza Plateau during the SRI/ARE Sphinx Project, clearly indicated that not only had Hawass been very well aware of the motives of the Edgar Cayce Foundation, who were searching for the Hall of Records, but indeed had himself inspected the drilling operations that they had carried out towards that objective. On three occasions the Edgar Cayce Foundation had been the principal financial sponsors of explorations at Giza, two at the Sphinx area and one at the Pyramids – a fact that Dr Hawass would surely have been well aware of. Furthermore there was the question of both Mark Lehner's education in Cairo sponsored by the Edgar Cayce Foundation as well as their alleged sponsorship of Hawass's entry at the University of Pennsylvania. Dr Hawass, as we have said earlier, categorically denied this claim several times in public.[17] But more perplexing was the occasional presence on site during the Schoch–West expedition of Joseph Jahoda, whom Hawass and Lehner knew quite well, and Dr Joseph Schor, a well-known supporter of the Edgar Cayce Foundation. Both Lehner and Hawass had gone out of their way during 1978-84 to accommodate the Edgar Cayce Foundation in their search for the Hall of Records at Giza and their attempt to vindicate the 'Atlantis' connection. Now, however, it was more than clear that they went out of their way to do just the opposite.

I was intrigued. I decided to get in touch with John West in the hope that he could enlighten me on this strange affair. West was temporarily residing in White Plains near New York at his sister's home. As I was planning a trip to New York to see my US publishers in May 1994, West suggested a meeting with him in White Plains. He also offered to arrange a meeting with Joseph Jahoda and Dr Joseph Schor. At the time I was working with the author Adrian Gilbert, and we travelled together to New York. There we rented a car and drove to White Plains. The home of John West's sister is in a wonderful rural setting adjacent to a forest with tall trees. They had prepared a barbecue and my first sight of John West was seeing him cook the most enormous T-bone steak. We took to each other immediately and have been friends ever since. West was at the time planning to resettle in the small town of Athens on the Hudson River, two hours, train ride from New York City. We discussed, of course, the age of the Sphinx in terms of the geology and astronomy, but my main interest was to know more on the ARE's involvement in Egypt and the role of Jahoda and Schor. West had not much time for the Edgar Cayce readings and those who believed in them. He thought the ARE people were very nice but a little too much into weird ideas for his liking. He maintained a cordial and friendly relationship with them, but that was all. He was not too familiar with the events of 1978-84, but confirmed that the ARE was indirectly supportive of his expedition in 1991-93, and that Jahoda and Schor seemed to act as their representatives in this matter.[18] West informed me that Schor and Jahoda had arranged to meet us at the Edgar Cayce Foundation in Virginia Beach. Apparently the grandson of Edgar Cayce, Charles Thomas, would also be present at this meeting. Graham Hancock and his wife Santha had also decided to join us there. They were flying from Washington DC, while Adrian and I decided to drive along the coastal road.

THE TWO JOES

The drive from New York to Virginia Beach takes about eight hours, with a dramatic crossing of Delaware Bay and the Chesapeake just before entering the county of Norfolk in Virginia. In the small beach resort of Virginia Beach we booked into a motel, then made our way to the Edgar Cayce Foundation. The complex consists mainly of two buildings: one is a wonderful colonial timber mansion that is, in fact, the refurbished 'hospital' in which Edgar Cayce had worked back in the 1930s and which today serves as offices to the ARE executives as well as a massage and meditation centre; the other is a large, rectangular concrete structure – looking more like a blockhouse, really – which serves as library, bookshop and conference centre. The latter also has some classrooms where various subjects are taught to members and day visitors ranging from ESP, healing, meditation and dream interpretation to Gnostic studies and reincarnation. There was, we had to admit, nothing sinister about this place or the people that worked in it. Many were young and old volunteers who lived in the area. Adrian and I were greeted with a warm welcome by a group of young people who were assigned to show us around the centre. Graham and Santha were already there, browsing in the main library which is situated on the top floor.[19]

We were told that our meeting with Charles Thomas, Jahoda and Schor would be over lunch, at the Ramada Ocean-Front Hotel across the road. There was an hour to kill, so we decided to familiarise ourselves with the organisation. We discovered that the Edgar Cayce Foundation has about 100,000 members world-wide and offices or representatives around the USA, South America, Canada, Europe, Australia, New Zealand, South Africa and Japan. It runs a press, the ARE Press, which issues several monthly or bimonthly publications, magazines, newsletters and also publishes it own books. The bookshop is well stocked with most books, as to be expected, by the ARE Press, but also a wide selection of associated titles, including books on ancient mysteries such as ours. The conference hall is of professional standard with a seating capacity for 500 people. The prize of the ARE is the large library that fills most of the top floor. It stocks a comprehensive range of books on esoteric subjects, mostly on Hermeticism, Gnosticism, mysticism, religious studies, astrology, Egyptology, and a panoply of New Age literature on healing, divination, channelling, reincarnation, ESP and so on. There is a staff of about thirty people, mostly volunteers on stipends, and the whole is managed by a board of executives headed by Charles Thomas Cayce. The latter, a graduate in psychology, is a softly spoken man in his early fifties. He joined the ARE in 1970 and became its president in 1976. This was after his father, Hugh Lynn, had his first heart attack.

Charles Thomas Cayce met us in the reception of the ARE. With him were two couples. They were introduced as Joe and Sherry Jahoda, and Joe and Laura Schor. Then Charles Thomas grinned at the two men and simply said: 'The two Joes!' The way their women were dressed and that 'something' that rich people have in their ways told us that what we saw here was, as the American says, 'old money'.

Lunch at the Ramada was a pleasant and friendly affair. The two Joes were open about their activities at Giza. The way Jahoda referred to

'Zahi' made it clear that he was on very familiar terms with the Egyptian official. Jahoda explained that when Zahi had studied at the University of Pennsylvania, they used to see each other quite often and he had stayed here, at Virginia Beach, with the Jahodas when visiting the ARE. They referred to Mark Lehner affectionately as 'young Mark' and did not bear any grudge whatsoever about his changing of camps nor, surprisingly, over Zahi Hawass's media attack on Cayce and his beliefs. As far as they were concerned, it was all part of the unfolding 'Atlantis' story. Such tribulations were just temporary hitches which simply meant that the time was not yet right for the Hall of Records to be found. I was fascinated by these men's confidence in the role they were playing and the way they approached it with such good nature. Charles Thomas kept silent and simply let the two Joes do the talking. What intrigued me most, however, was their utter certainty that they would soon get another opportunity to find what they were looking for at Giza, perhaps in a year or two. They now had to wait for the dust to settle a little, and then Zahi would arrange things for them. It was not so much a question of 'if', but more a question of 'when'. As for us, they were intrigued at the astronomical dating we had derived for Giza. I offered to give them a little talk with slides back at the ARE complex. We then parted company with the understanding that although we, as authors, would remain impartial and reserved the right to report to our readers whatever we deemed fit, we nonetheless wished to maintain an open dialogue with the ARE and the two Joes on the matter of Giza and the Hall of Records.

Back in England I began to work on the manuscript for *Keeper of Genesis*. A few days later a letter arrived from Joe Schor dated 24th May 1994. It was addressed to 'All the attendees of the joint meeting held at ARE Headquarters in Virginia Beach on May 21, 1994'. Schor commended my astronomical work and how, he felt, it 'corroborated the Cayce records'. He then offered that he would like us 'to work together to further delineate' the civilisation Cayce had spoken of, and suggested we all kept in touch from now on. I sent a response through Charles Thomas Cayce thanking him for hosting the meeting, and stating:

> As you can see, archaeo–astronomy is likely to add further weight to the belief that 'something' did happen around 10,500 BC at Giza which, if understood properly, could be of paramount importance to world culture. With the recent geological evidence of John West and now the archaeo–astronomical evidence to give it support, I feel that the search for whatever that 'something' was must go on.[20]

A few weeks later I got a parcel from Douglas G. Richards from

Virginia Beach. Richards had co-authored a book, *Mysteries of Atlantis Revisited*, with the son of Edgar Cayce, Edgar Evans, and the latter's daughter, Gail Cayce Schwartzer. Enclosed was a copy of the book – and also a two-page letter which basically tried to show how some of my conclusions supported the Cayce readings.[21] Apparently they were publishing an update on their book and wanted to know if there was any further archaeo-astronomical material regarding 10,500 BC that could be useful to them. I did not hear from the ARE until a few months later, when they invited me to give a talk at their annual 'Egypt' conference at Virginia Beach scheduled for July 1995.

This time I decided to take my family along – Michele, my wife, my daughter Candice and my son Jonathan. I gave a talk on the Orion-Giza correlation theory and also narrated the latest events at Giza, especially the now famous discovery of the 'door' inside the Great Pyramid by Rudolf Gantenbrink (which we will discuss in the next chapter). The audience – about 500 people – were enthusiastic and very receptive. The two Joes had come with their wives and we all went out for dinner in one of the excellent fish restaurants of Virginia Beach. This time I broached the issue of Dr Hawass's education at the University of Pennsylvania. Both Jahoda and Schor confirmed that Hawass was helped by the ARE in some way, but did not elaborate much further. They seemed as confident as ever that they were going to return to Giza and be allowed to conduct explorations for the Hall of Records. Sometime soon, they thought. I wished them luck but told them that I felt sceptical about their chances after the adverse media campaign that was waged in the Egyptian and American press. There had also been a huge controversy over the discovery of the 'door' in the Great Pyramid.[22] No one, not even the ARE with its good connections, I felt, would be allowed near the Sphinx or the Pyramids to look for hidden chambers. But the two Joes simply smiled. I figured it was best to let them have their delusions. There was no harm in this.

In February 1995, Jahoda had a telephone conversation with Graham Hancock in which he repeated his conviction that Hawass would soon arrange for them to resume their search at Giza. This time, however, Jahoda provided a rough schedule for an event:

> We sort of have 1996 set up for our little expedition to the Sphinx, with underground radar. 1996 was when Zahi (Hawass) said we'd be able to go. We'll do more ground-scanning . . . and I figure that by 1998 we'll hit something.'[23]

In November 1995, just a few months after the ARE conference, I decided to go to Egypt with a group of friends. Graham and Santha also joined us there. We all stayed in the Movenpick Jolie-Ville hotel near the Pyramids. Everyone was in great spirits. In the early morning of our first night at the hotel we were rudely awoken by a strange rumble and shaking. It was an earthquake, and we heard later that it had caused some minor damage to the walls of the inner chamber of the Second Pyramid. Also a huge boulder had been dislodged from the Mokkatam Hills and had destroyed a small village, killing many of its inhabitants. Shaken by this experience, we all met in the breakfast room to plan the next few days ahead. There, to my surprise, were the two Joes. With them was also the film-maker Boris Said, as well as a few other people I did not know. They turned out to be the crew for a TV film that Boris and the two Joes were planning to shoot. Schor informed me that they had seen the day before the president of the Egyptian Antiquities Organisation, Dr Abdel Halim Nureldin, and had lodged an application for a licence to conduct a radar search around the Sphinx and the Pyramids.

With the recommendations of Hawass, the two Joes felt that their chances were very good for getting this licence. Apparently the licence would be granted to the Florida State University with full financial backing from the Schor Foundation, which Joe Schor had recently registered in the US to cater for this type of research activity.[24] Dr Nureldin had promised them a reply by early 1996 – just as Jahoda had informed us back in February. It was then that we realised that these men meant business.

We wondered about how much of this latest development John West was aware of. Back in England I called West to let him know of the encounter with the two Joes. He was surprised and dismayed for having been kept out of the picture. It was then that he revealed that he was in litigation with Boris Said over financial matters regarding their 1991-93 expedition and the NBC documentary. He felt now that Boris and the two Joes had decided to hijack his research and use his data for their own end. I had to agree with West that this seemed unfair. I told him that Graham and I would support him in this matter, and would try to make Jahoda and Schor see the good sense of joining forces with West and his own team. West then wrote a letter to Schor outlining such a proposal.[25] Other than the impressive academic credentials of Dr Robert Schoch and his affiliation with Boston University, West had also managed to get sponsorship from the prestigious Princeton University's Princeton Engineering Anomalies Research Laboratory, represented by Robert Jahn and Brenda Dunne, who were also executive members of the cutting-edge Society for Scientific Exploration (SSE).[26] He thus proposed that Schor's planned expedition and his own could pool their academic resources as well as their experiences. In fact John West, through the academic front of Dr Schoch at Boston University, had already lodged a licence application with Dr Mohamad Bakr, then president of the Egyptian Antiquities Organisation, as early as April 1993.[27] Dr Bakr, however, lost his job in July that year, and so a new application was lodged by the Dean of Boston University, confirming the university's full support for and co-operation with the proposal made by Dr Robert Schoch.[28]

Joe Schor, however, was not moved. Schor was well aware of West's eagerness to resume his research at the Sphinx; this had been made plain to him by West on several occasions, and at least once by Graham, West and myself during a dinner in New York with Jahoda also present. Schor sent a reply to John West which amounted to a polite rejection of his proposals.[29] West took this rejection badly and decided to vent his annoyance and complaints ono the original investors of the 1991-93 Sphinx expedition, of whom Joe Schor was one.[30] In this letter West did not mince his words regarding what he interpreted as a sort of 'covert hostile takeover'. West's words could have been a little more diplomatic, but then he, himself, would admit that this is by no means his greatest asset. Unfortunately a copy of West's letter ended up with Schor. This was to be the beginning of open hostilities between West and Schor. Inevitably, Hancock and I were drawn into it. Our first approach was to remain neutral. This way, we felt, would not only allow us to monitor the situation from both sides but also we would retain our freedom of action vis-à-vis our readers and the general public who, at that stage, relied on us for updates on the events taking place at Giza. We thus informed both Joe Schor and John West of our position.

Meanwhile the Society of Scientific Exploration invited Hancock, West and myself to speak at a major symposium called 'Return to the Source: Recovering Lost Knowledge and Ancient Wisdom' to be held at the University of Delaware. Other researchers, too, were invited to speak, including authors Colin Wilson, Paul Devereux, Rand Flem-Ath and Paul William Roberts, and mathematician Jay Kappraff and geologist Dr Robert Schoch. Little did we know that open warfare would take place there between us and the Schor team. It was around that time, too, that Hancock, West and I also received an invitation to participate in the ARE 1996 Egypt conference. There was something rather puzzling about the title of this conference, which boldly proclaimed the 'Opening of the Hall of Records: The Return of the Ancient Egyptians – 10,500 BC to AD 1998'. There was, too, a talk by Ahmad Fayed, an ARE guide who was well acquainted with Dr Hawass on a personal level, that baffled us even more. Fayed's talk was titled 'Searching for the Hall of Records: Current excavations at Giza'. Who, we wondered, was currently searching for the Hall of Records and Excavating at Giza? The only team we knew that might be doing that was the Schor Foundation/Florida State University, but this team was still awaiting approval of its licence from the Egyptian authorities. This strange certitude that such a search was going to happen before the July 1996 conference uncannily mimicked the same confidence expressed earlier to us by Joseph Jahoda, Dr Schor's right-hand man in such matters. There could be little doubt that both statements were either connected or were based on the same source. Frankly, at this point in time, neither Hancock nor I believed that any team, let alone West because of the previous adverse public attacks from the Egyptian Antiquities Organisation or, worse, Schor and Jahoda with their obvious Edgar Cayce affiliations, would be permitted to conduct explorations at Giza, especially if this involved a search for the vexed Hall of Records. We were soon in for a big surprise.

SECRET CHAMBER

In all this confusion I had forgotten a main player in the affair who, I already knew, was closely associated with Schor's proposed exploration at Giza. This was Boris Said, the film-maker who had directed West's 1991-93 expedition and whom we had met at the Movenpick hotel at Giza with Schor in November 1995. I had met Boris Said, in fact, in late 1994 at Giza when I was doing a documentary there with the ABC channel for the *60 Minutes* team.[31] Both Boris and I happened to be staying at the Mena House Hotel near the Pyramids, and we stumbled upon each other at the reception. We recognised each other from the various TV documentaries we had appeared in. Boris has unmistakable features: a tall, heavy man with a striking white beard and deep, blue eyes. The next time we met was in November 1995 with Schor. Boris Said is the owner of a film production company called Magic Eye. He started his career as a film-maker after he decided to drop his earlier involvement in Formula One car racing and also with the American Olympic bobsled team.

I decided to get in touch with him to try and make some sense of this strange situation involving the Schor Foundation and Florida State University. I managed to trace him in New York, where he was staying with a friend. Boris was open and forthcoming. He told me that he and

Schor had an excellent relationship with Dr Hawass and that they were told that a positive decision regarding the licence would be given soon after Ramadan, which would be towards the end of March 1996. His role in this affair was to act as official film-maker for the Schor Expedition. They were planning a two-part documentary which they hoped to sell to NBC or Fox TV. He then, surprisingly, asked if Graham Hancock and I would like to be in this film. They had already shot a promotional film in November 1995, and now they were planning to shoot the full-length footage in March 1996, as soon as the licence by the Egyptian authorities was issued. In fact two licences were required, one for the actual filming, which was called a 'commercial permit' and issued by the Ministry of Information, and the other was an 'exploration permit' issued by the Egyptian Antiquities Organisation. (Actually the latter had, since early 1994, changed its name to the Supreme Council of Antiquities (SCA)).

I agreed to meet Boris in March and be interviewed for his film. This would allow me to get inside information of what was really going on. It was an opportunity not to be missed. Meanwhile Boris offered to send me a copy of the promotional film he had shot for the Schor/Florida State University (FSU) proposed expedition in November 1995. This arrived by international courier early in February 1996. It was titled *Secret Chamber* and had a run of about seven minutes. I was stunned. Suddenly it began to occur to me what the Schor/FSU team might be up to – and why Boris Said was so much involved. From the short promotional film it was clear that the intention was to prepare a big-budget film for a major TV network essentially to promulgate the Cayce prophecies about the Hall of Records. But even more dramatic, the film proposed to have a 'secret chamber' – the possible subterranean room that was picked up by the seismographs of Dr Dobecki during the 1991-93 West/Schoch expedition – *opened live* for the cameras. At the end of the promotion film was an amazing, totally unexpected teaser. Dr Hawass was filmed going down a tunnel mumbling the words: 'Even Indiana Jones will never believe we are here! We are now inside the Sphinx in this tunnel. This tunnel has never been opened before. No one knows, really knows, what is inside this tunnel. But we are going to open it for the first time . . .'[32] The voice of a narrator dramatically stated:

> Edgar Cayce, America's famous Sleeping Prophet, predicted that a chamber would be discovered beneath the Sphinx – a chamber containing the recorded history of human civilisation. For the first time we'll show you what lies beneath this great statue (the Sphinx) . . . a chamber which will be opened tonight, live, for our television cameras . . .[33]

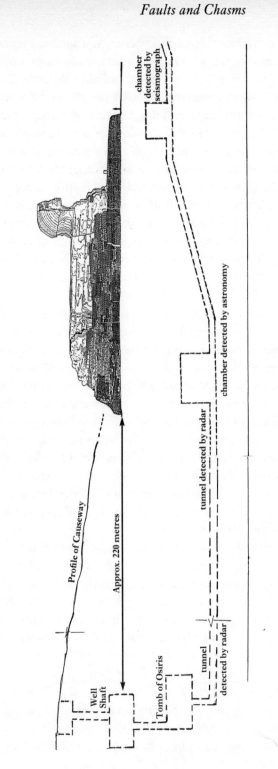

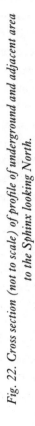

Fig. 22. Cross section (not to scale) of profile of underground and adjacent area to the Sphinx looking North.

I immediately called Graham Hancock. There was something else that was a little disturbing in this film, quite apart from the obvious stunt that was being prepared for a major television broadcast. Boris had used graphics to present our astronomical theory of 10,500 BC in order to add support to the claims of Edgar Cayce. This, in itself, was not our main objection. We had to concede that fate had it that our theories added support to the Cayce readings whether we liked it or not. Our concern was to be implicated in what was quite clearly a bizarre archaeological stunt of monumental proportions. No licences had so far been issued, and yet here was Boris Said being funded by Joe Schor – apparently to the tune of $100,000 for this short film alone – to announce a live opening on national TV of a yet-to-be-confirmed secret chamber and, to boot, the Edgar Cayce Foundation was announcing a conference in July with Ahmad Fayed's talk 'Searching for the Hall of Records: Current Excavations at Giza'.

We decided to investigate further. The first thing was to fax Joe Schor and probe him on how he saw our role in this matter. We also wanted to know whether he was willing to reconsider his position with regard to John West. We made it clear that although we had to remain neutral in this feud, we nonetheless strongly felt that John West deserved to be at least a participant in this proposed expedition.[34] We sent copies of this fax to John West, Boris Said and Joe Jahoda. On 14th March we received a reply from Boris Said extolling the virtues of Schor in this joint venture, as well as the merits of the proposed expedition. It was clear, at least as far as Boris was concerned, that John West was an unwelcome and troublesome element for this venture. The next day we got Schor's reply. It made clear to us that he had no intention of incorporating West in his plans. He did offer, however, that if the chamber under the Sphinx were opened, then he would 'give full credit (to John West) for having pointed it out'.[35] He also made it clear that, in view of our relationship with John West, this would 'preclude us from working with you . . . because it would require keeping confidences which would impinge on your policy of neutrality'.

Frankly, this decision by Schor suited us just fine. We were beginning to feel ourselves being drawn into a situation at Giza we did not approve of, and it was better for us to remain as independent observers in this unfolding drama. We nonetheless informed Dr Schor that we did not agree in keeping confidences on matters concerning Giza and the public, and took the opportunity to ask him not to make use of our ideas and material in the films that he had commissioned Boris to undertake.[36] The trip to Egypt in March promised to be very interesting. I was not to be disappointed.

A FAMILY GATHERING

I decided to turn this trip into a small holiday for the family as well. It was half-term for the children and so they came along with me, as well as my wife, Michele. We were also joined by a few friends from Oman, Linda and her son Max, and Jonathan Barker, an architect based in Muscat. We stayed at the Movenpick Hotel at Giza. John West was also there with some friends. John had managed to get hold of a copy of Boris's promotion film, and said that he had passed it on to Dr Hawass via an intermediary. Sparks were about to fly.

Word came to me that Boris, Schor and members of his team as well as Joe Jahoda were in Upper Egypt and would arrive at Giza on 1st April. I was also informed that with them was none other than Dr Thomas Dobecki, the seismographer who had discovered the possible chamber under the Sphinx during the 1991-93 West-Schoch expedition. I wondered what John West would make of this. It seems that they were bringing along sophisticated radar and seismographic equipment as well as filming equipment. Schor, Jahoda and Dobecki stayed in the Mena House Hotel at Giza. The rest of the team were booked at the Movenpick, where we were staying. Boris was staying at his flat in the village of Nazlet Al Samman. I stumbled on Schor and Jahoda in the reception of the Movenpick. They were surprised to see me and clearly uncomfortable. I tried to find out if they had been granted the exploration licence by the Egyptian authorities and how Dr Hawass fitted into all this, but the two men were not forthcoming. Boris, however, whom I met the next day, was friendly and outspoken. He came to our table at breakfast and was partly amused and partly concerned about an incident that had happened a few weeks ago as they were preparing for the expedition to Egypt. It seems that Joe Schor wanted everyone on his team to wear T-shirts with the Schor Foundation logo during the work at Giza. I remembered from the letter we had received from Schor back in 1994 that this logo comprised two large keys crossing each other. It was a little odd for Schor to want the crew to wear T-shirts with his logo, but what was the harm in that? The harm, according to Boris, was that in the centre of the logo there was also the well-known esoteric symbol of the double-pyramid, i.e. two triangles inverted into each other forming a six-pointed star. This was the so-called 'Seal of Solomon' and, Boris pointed out, could easily be mistaken for the Star of David, Israel's national emblem. I saw his point. Egypt was experiencing a wave of religious fundamentalism, and Boris and I both recalled how the Arab newspaper *Akhbar El Yom* had implied that the 1991-93 West-Schoch expedition at

Giza was a sort of Zionist plot, pointing out that both West and Boris were Jewish. Schor, who was also of the Jewish faith, apparently kept a residence in Jerusalem. With his expedition flaunting the 'Seal of Solomon' on their chest, this could certainly provoke more media accusations. Boris said that, luckily, he had talked Schor out of the idea. I took this story with a little pinch of salt.

Back in my hotel room, however, I decided to have a look at this logo on the 1994 letter I received from the Schor Foundation. But to my surprise it wasn't there. Had Boris made it up? No. For when I looked at the 1995 letter that the Schor Foundation had sent to John West, the 'Seal of Solomon' was, in fact, there where Boris had indicated. Sometime between May 1994 and January 1995 Schor had decided to add this sign to his logo. Although I felt sure that there was a simple explanation for this, this strange story nonetheless nagged my sub-conscious. I could not help recalling the saga involving Lambert Dolphin, the Temple of Solomon in Jerusalem and his search for the Hall of Records under the Sphinx with the Edgar Cayce Foundation back in 1978. It would not be the last time that the terms 'Zionist Plot' and 'Seal of Solomon' would be evoked in this strange story of Giza. But more of that later.

A new and rather glamorous character was about to enter this story. One morning, when the early spring sun was just right for a bit of sunbathing, I went to the pool of the Movenpick Hotel. Encircled with white and pink bougainvillaeas, it is one of my favourite places to read and enjoy the warm Egyptian sun. I was thinking of those youthful days in Alexandria by the sea, when my daydreaming was interrupted by a familiar voice. It was Mary Lomando, an American tour operator and good friend of mine, who was plagued with an acute penchant for the Giza mysteries. With her was a tall women in her thirties, slim and with long black hair. She was introduced as Corina. She had been, until lately, working for a German TV channel as their representative in Egypt. She was also a friend of Dr Hawass. Corina was interested in making a documentary of my work. I suggested, however, that perhaps Mary ought to introduce her to Boris Said, whom Mary also knew quite well. Two days later they were to announce their engagement not only to work together, but also to be married. On 3rd April Boris invited Mary to join him and Corina for a drink at his flat. We decided to meet in the bar of the Movenpick. I was first to arrive, then Boris. He then dropped the bombshell. He had just heard that Joe Schor had been granted a licence by the Supreme Council of Antiquities to conduct radar work at Giza. It was all supposed to be hush hush, but Boris felt I ought to know. He then suddenly remembered that he was to collect Corina from a restaurant, and rushed out. Mary arrived and then, to my surprise, Corina. She had taken a taxi from the restaurant. She then pulled out a visiting card, passed it to me, and asked me if I knew the person whose name was on the card. It was the visiting card of Joe Schor. Apparently Corina had just had dinner with him and his colleagues. They were celebrating the award of the licence with Dr Hawass. Boris then returned and took us to his flat. There he insisted that we see the promotional film, *Secret Chamber*, which he had made. The phone rang. It was Schor. Apparently he was furious that a copy of the film had been given to Hawass, and told Boris that I was trying to sabotage his expedition. Needless to say the evening ended there and then.

Back in England Graham Hancock and I had to prepare for the launch of our book, *Keeper of Genesis*. The *Daily Mail* had commissioned a serialisation in three parts, and we decided to expose in it the current situation at Giza. We felt the public had a right to know what was happening there, especially in the light of the somewhat unusual circumstances that the Schor Foundation and Florida State University were getting involved in the search for 'secret chambers' there. We first sent, however, an urgent fax to Dr Abdel Halim Nureldin at the Supreme Council of Antiquities in Egypt to give him the opportunity to comment on the matter before going to press. A copy of this fax was then sent to Dr Schor who was still in Egypt. This is what it contained:

Please be informed that our forthcoming book, *Keeper of Genesis*, will be serialised in a national British newspaper in the week starting Monday 15th April 1996 in three parts. Part three of this serialisation will report the recent events concerning newly proposed projects to be undertaken at Giza. In November 1995 the Schor Foundation, in collaboration with the Florida State University, has put in a formal application for a seismographic survey of the Giza necropolis. Also we understand that in November 1995 the Schor Foundation sponsored and financed the making of a promotional video film by Mr Boris Said of Magic Eye Inc. of New York. A copy of this promotional film was sent to us by Mr Said. In this film appears Dr Zahi Hawass, the Director-General of the Giza Pyramid Plateau, seen entering a tunnel under the Sphinx and stating that this said tunnel will soon be opened. Also in this film it is claimed by a narrator that a 'chamber' (possibly containing the 'recorded history of human civilisation' as predicted by the psychic Edgar Cayce in 1946) will be opened 'live' on a television programme. On 1st April 1996 a team comprising Mr Joseph Schor (president of the Schor Foundation), Mr Joseph Jahoda, Mr Thomas Dobecki, Mr Boris Said (and several members of a TV filming crew under the latter's responsibility) arrived in Cairo at the Jolie-Ville Movenpick Hotel and also at the Oberoi Mena House Hotel at Giza. Further to conversations with members of this team, we now intend to report in part three of the serialisation in the British national newspaper (as described above) that Mr Boris Said of Magic Eye Inc. is, since 1st April 1996, shooting a documentary film on the 'legends' of the Sphinx and also will cover on film the scientific work to be undertaken by the Schor Foundation/Florida State University. We also intend to report in the said part three of the serialisation that this latter team has brought to Egypt about 3.5 million dollars' worth of high-tech equipment for their forthcoming project at Giza. We also intend to report in the said part three of the serialisation that the latter team had been granted a five-year concession to work at Giza. We also intend to report that part of the motives and intentions of the proposed Schor Foundation/Florida State University project is to verify the possible existence of a chamber under the Sphinx as previously identified by the seismographic equipment of Dr Thomas Dobecki in 1990-91 while involved with Boston University/Dr Robert Schoch geological expedition at the Sphinx area (also involving Mr John Anthony West). This fax is to provide you with proper and fair forewarning of our intention to report the above events as from Monday 15th April in a British national newspaper. Should you have any comments you may wish to add or alteration to the above matter, please send such comments or alterations by fax to the number provided at the head of this document. These must reach us before noon on Saturday 13th April 1996.[37]

We never got a reply. But on 11th April we received a two-page fax from Schor. He went straight to the point by letting us know that 'your fax is filled with egregious errors of fact and is so replete with mis-statements, misinformation and innuendoes that should you proceed with publication of your serialisation that includes any reference to us and our work in Egypt we will bring suit for libel and damages resulting from your actions'. The 'egregious errors' that we had committed were as follows. Firstly, the promotional film that was shot by Boris Said in November 1995 was not, according to Schor, a promotional film at all. It was, he told us, 'made to test script and equipment and was made in November 1995 which was many months before we received approval for our expedition. We have abandoned its use because we have accrued much scientific information since then.' Secondly, the application for the licence was submitted in September and not November 1995. Thirdly, Schor had rented the equipment at $200,000, and not bought it for $3.5 million. Fourthly, the licence was for one year 'renewable' and not for five years. Well, we were glad to have such errors rectified, but that was precisely the purpose of our fax to Dr Nureldin in the first place. It was hardly a cause for a lawsuit. But there was more. Schor was indignant about the 'innuendoes' made about the Edgar Cayce Foundation and himself. 'Your reference to Edgar Cayce is misleading. We do not work for the Edgar Cayce Group, and we believe that the reference was intentionally made to mislead readers as to our scientific purpose.' Schor went on:

> Your fax erroneously ascribes certain motives and intentions to the parties involved in the exploration. The major purpose of the Schor Foundation and Florida State University is to aid in the preservation and restoration of the Pyramids and Sphinx. In addition, we are surveying the underground of the Giza Plateau to find faults and chasms that might collapse. This will increase the safety of the plateau because chasms and faults can be collapsed or roped off for the protection of tourists and plateau personnel.

The mention of John West in our fax brought, too, another legal threat:

> In addition to damaging the reputation of the parties involved in this project by publishing the series you seem to have intended to damage our relationship with Dr Nour El Din. Furthermore, in view of your reference to John West, your proposed publication may be part of a pattern of unlawful business practices. If you continue to attempt to publish the proposed serialisation or you engage in any further acts of harassment we will seek appropriate relief, including damages, from everyone involved.

We replied with a four-page fax, copy sent to Dr Nureldin. We told Dr Schor in no uncertain terms that we would not be intimidated by his legal threats and that we were going to publish our report, stating the facts as we understood them in good faith, in the British newspaper forthwith. We would, of course, take into account the technical errors he raised, such as the validity of the licence and the cost of the equipment. We also reasserted our rights and freedom to report matters concerning Giza to a wide public through the media of books and the press and television.

On 14th April 1996, just three days after Schor sent his fax, Dr Zahi Hawass was interviewed by the English language newspaper the *Egyptian Gazette*. In this interview he gave a rather different account of the current activities at Giza and, most curiously, made absolutely no mention of the Schor Foundation, Florida State University or their forthcoming exploration. According to Dr Hawass there were many 'tunnels' under the Giza plateau whose location and features are still unknown. He predicted that their discovery will 'bring many clues' regarding the establishment of the Giza Pyramids. He announced that the 'secret tunnels' in the Giza plateau will be the subject of a seminar that he was giving soon. The newspaper also said that Hawass would also 'reveal the secrets of the three tunnels inside the Sphinx' and also explain how he proposed to count the tunnels under the Giza plateau.[38] There was also an interesting reaction by Florida State University. They explained how they got involved in the Schor Foundation's exploration at Giza, and declared that in principle the mission of the joint venture was 'to address the current controversy over weathering, dating and construction of the Sphinx and other monuments on the Giza plateau'.[39] There were four members of Florida State University assigned to this project. These were Dr Daniel Pullen, Associate Professor of the Department of Classics; Dr Alan Zindler, Chair of Geology and head of the National High Magnetic Field Laboratory; Dr Leroy Odom, Professor of Geology; and Dr James Tull, Professor of Geology. Regarding the promotional film of Boris Said, the FSU stated that although they were invited to participate in the film, they declined:

> Unfortunately the promotional video used to invite our participation by in-
> cluding the name of the Florida State University in the credits was circulated
> without our authorisation.[40]

Much later Dr Schor did confirm to me in writing that he and his team at the Schor Foundation were 'archaeologists searching for ancient civilisations' and that they were also 'aware of the statements of Edgar Cayce'.[41] Apparently he also was interested in verifying the legends that the Ark of the Covenant was either under the Temple of Solomon or under the Sphinx of Giza.[42] Boris Said did, in fact, take sufficient film for a full-length documentary in April–May 1996, of which I was later given a copy and in which it is blatantly clear that Schor and his team were looking for a secret chamber under the Sphinx. But we shall return to this important film later on.

Meanwhile, the *Daily Mail* began our serialisation on 2nd May 1996, in spite of Schor's attempts to suppress it. This particular Giza alley cat was now out of the bag, and there ensued a huge reaction from the public, who swamped the Egyptian Supreme Council of Antiquities with letters and faxes. The controversy escalated. In July 1996 Dr Hawass announced that he had asked the Supreme Council to cancel the work of Florida State University which was sponsored by Schor because, he said, 'they were not following the correct steps'.[43] Inevitably all sorts of rumours began to circulate about what really had happened at Giza. One, allegedly emanating from Boris Said, claimed that nine cavities or tunnels had been detected by the Schor expedition's radar equipment which, apparently, had also detected metal.[44]

Meanwhile Graham Hancock and I attended the July 1996 ARE conference at Virginia Beach. It was at the precise time that Hurricane Bertha struck the coastline of North Carolina and Norfolk, Virginia, which ended up nearly disrupting the event. On the eve before his talk Graham had met with a group of twenty American senators in Washington DC, where the controversy over the Giza events was hotly discussed.[45] It was, of course, also brought up at the ARE conference.[46] But neither Schor nor Jahoda attended, so nothing new was said. I had the opportunity to have lunch with Charles Thomas Cayce and John Van Auken, a high executive of the ARE. I asked them what was the relationship they had with the Schor Foundation, and how the ARE was involved in this affair. They said that Schor and Jahoda, although life members of the ARE as well as sponsors, were operating on their own in Egypt. I asked, too, about Dr Hawass's education at Pennsylvania University, and they did acknowledge that the ARE had played a role in this matter. They were most concerned that Graham and I would turn the ARE conference into a political débâcle. I told them that we had no personal grudge against the ARE, and gave them my assurance that we had no intention of making any accusations but merely wanted to share our information and our concern with their members. We parted on amicable terms.

A month later, on 28th August 1996, I received a telephone call from Joseph Jahoda. He was calling from his office in Virginia, and wanted to see if there was a way of all of us patching up our differences. I took the opportunity to probe a little to see what was going on with the Giza exploration. I had assumed that their licence had been revoked, as Hawass said it would. But Jahoda confirmed that their licence was still active, although they were waiting for further approvals by the Egyptians for other specific explorations. I did not know it then, but according to Boris Said,[47] the team had applied for permits to conduct archaeological excavations. In this telephone conversation Jahoda re-confirmed that it was he who had controlled the drilling operation with Recovery System International back in 1978-79. Apparently the drill was a massive 100 horsepower piece of equipment, the sort used for oil wells. He repeated his story about the army coming in with guns and stopping the drilling operations. As we argued on who was to blame for the latest controversy related to Dr Schor, Jahoda began to speak of the 'Work' – a term used frequently by the Cayce followers – as if he was perceiving these activities at Giza as a very important spiritual mission for humankind. 'The Work is more important than our egos . . . and he (Schor) will do whatever it takes to have peace and harmony so that we can continue the Work . . .

And here we are on a sacred journey trying to find sacred knowledge of the whole universe, really . . . the world is at stake here.' When asked point blank whether they were looking for the Hall of Records, this was his reply:

> Well, I don't want to answer that question. I cannot speak for Joe, but I know what I want to do, I want to learn everything there is to learn about Egypt . . . whatever it is, whatever is there we'll find it . . . I can honestly tell you that this is a scientific project, we are there for five years or however long it takes, and we are going to find out everything we can learn about Egypt, project, everything, everything . . . whatever is there we will find it . . . whatever you think that means, that's what it is. We're scientists . . . if there is anything there I'm sure we will find it, if we are allowed to continue without interruptions from well-meaning . . . and people who lie! We are prepared to be there for as long as it takes to learn everything there is to know about the area, for mankind and knowledge which, according to Hoagland, I don't know how true he is, but what he's saying is the knowledge, whatever knowledge is there, is important to bring to the world . . .

A PUBLIC FORUM

In early September 1996 I was invited by the South African TV network M-Net to make a short film about the latest discoveries at Giza.[48] They had read the piece in the *Daily Mail*, and wanted to cover this controversy for their viewers. They wanted to film on location at Giza. The mood there was very tense, and they decided that it was best that Hawass and I were not to confront each other. They managed, however, to get a lengthy interview from Dr Hawass who spurted out again that my work was 'a sort of Zionist plot' trying to undermine Egyptian culture.[49] Asked about the promotional film of Boris Said where he appears in a tunnel under the Sphinx, Hawass claimed that his interview was taken out of context and that he was unaware of the full content of the film. He then denied any links with the ARE and Dr Schor, or that he had allowed them to look for the Hall of Records. He called such ideas 'imagination and hallucinations'. It was all getting very confusing for everyone.

In September 1996 I went with my wife, Michele, to the USA to the University of Delaware to attend the 'Return to the Source' symposium sponsored by the Society of Scientific Exploration. The evening before our talks, Graham Hancock and I were interviewed on the Art Bell radio show. Although we were no beginners in radio talks, this was quite a new experience for me. The Art Bell show is a very popular coast-to-coast radio broadcast with hundreds of thousands of listeners in nearly every state in the USA. It is designed to raise controversies, and interviews can run for several hours, and sometimes through the whole night. Ours was to run for over three hours. Art Bell announced that we would be joined by a surprise guest. It turned out to be Richard Hoagland. Hoagland is the author of the best-selling book *The Monuments on Mars*, and is a well-known figure in the controversial debate over the so-called 'Face on Mars' Hoagland had had a private meeting with Dr Schor who apparently had given him 'carte blanche' to represent him in this matter. Hoagland then said that Schor had admitted to him that he wanted to find the Hall of Records, and then Hoagland claimed to have been officially invited by the team for the opening of the 'underground chamber' which was scheduled to take place in early November 1996. A letter of invitation had been sent to Hoagland by none other than Boris Said. Art Bell, who had a copy of the letter, read it out loud on the air:

> I am happy to give you our invitation to join us on the Giza Plateau during the last week in October and the first week in November 1996, when we hope to be opening the first of the underground chambers which the Schor Expedition has discovered beneath the sands and limestone of the Giza Plateau. As discussed, we expect to be doing further exploration in the area in the course of the winter and will keep you advised of dates, in case you wish to be present at our future digs.[50]

Inevitably, there was an almighty reaction on the rumour mill of the Internet, whilst there was complete silence from the Schor and Jahoda side. In an interview given to Kenneth and Dee Burke of *Leading Edge Newspaper*, Boris Said later was to clear some of the confusion about the Schor expedition at Giza:

> I was over there for two years working in conjunction with a group called the Schor Foundation. It was about the search for Atlantis. There are a lot of published reports as to what the real purpose of the expedition was, but we were trying to find access to a room, which we believed we had identified under the front paw of the Sphinx. That room was identified by the exploration of geophysicist and seismologist Dr Thomas Dobecki in 1991, and it was later confirmed by ground-penetrating radar in 1996. The Egyptians have been very resistant to our suggestions that we drill a hole down into the room and excavate a tunnel at the back of the Sphinx which we think leads to that room . . .

Joseph Jahoda was also at the Delaware conference. He had come to attempt a reconciliation between all the parties involved. At the end of our talks, Graham Hancock and I were invited to answer questions from the audience. We asked John West and Robert Schoch to come on stage. Jahoda, who was also in the audience, was asked to join as well. Jahoda introduced himself as the 'director' of the previous 1978 ARE/SRI expedition and now also of the Schor expedition. He explained that the lack of release of data from the Schor Foundation was based on a requirement imposed on them by the Egyptian authorities. He announced that Dr Schor had invited Graham Hancock and myself to meet him in New York on the following Monday in order to clear matters.

Early that day Graham, Santha, Michele and I drove from Delaware to New York. There we first went to our mutual friend, Bill Cote. Bill had worked with Boris Said and John West on the making of the NBC film documentary, and we now wanted him to come with us to the meeting at Forest Laboratories with Dr Schor in order to act as witness. Forest Laboratories is on Manhattan's prestigious 3rd Avenue, on the twenty-third floor of a modern office block. Awaiting us was Dr Joe Schor and Joe Jahoda. The meeting started on the wrong foot when Schor insisted that it was to be 'off the record'. But we figured that 'off the record' information was better than no information at all, and reluctantly agreed to his request. All I can say here, therefore, is that we left satisfied that much of what we had deduced so far was correct. We also agreed to keep in touch but reminded the two Joes that we intended to maintain our role as independent observers and keep on informing the public with news from Giza, in spite of the moratorium on news related to their project imposed by the Egyptian authorities. Meanwhile Boris Said and Dr Schor parted company. According to Said, this was because Schor wanted to 'sell the show to Fox network, and Fox wanted absolute control of the subject matter'.[51] Boris objected, and the team split. There was the question of who owned the rights of the filming, and Schor and Boris ended up fighting the matter through the courts.

THE NEW AGERS

It was at about that time that Dr Hawass, as had been the case for John West in the early 1990s, began a press and public campaign against Hancock, West and myself. It all began on 10th February 1997 with an American independent reporter, Alexander Stille, who had gone to Egypt and had been escorted by Mark Lehner around Giza. Lehner lamented on the New Age movement which was causing much harm to professional Egyptology and Egyptian culture. Stille, on his return to the

US, decided to write an article for the *New Yorker* attacking Hancock, West and myself as being the main culprits of this supposed New Age movement threatening Egypt and its culture. Titled 'Perils of the Sphinx' and without as much as a phone call to any of us in order to at least get a balanced story, Stille's article went on a rampant soliloquy, accusing us of 'historical distortion' and of being 'New Agers'. According to Stille, here was the problem: 'making aggressive use of pseudo-scientific methods and the Internet, the New Agers are changing the way Egyptian monuments are seen by hundreds of thousands of tourists'.[52] Stille was also taken to Zahi Hawass who 'was in a dark mood about the New Agers'. Stille was of the opinion that Hancock and I had 'inflamed messianic hope' in the mass of New Agers around the world, causing them to batter Hawass with letters and faxes. It was, rather, the Egyptian and foreign press which got 'inflamed'. On 7th May 1997 Dr Hawass called a press conference in Cairo 'to vent his frustration with a group of pseudo-scientists whose personal attack, through television and other media, has recently escalated to the point where it has become threatening'.[53] He named his 'antagonists': Graham Hancock, John Anthony West and myself:

> I was silent for a year, but it (the pressure) increased and increased. I was laughing at their views two years ago . . . Years ago Anthony West somehow got permission to investigate (the Sphinx). I came upon him one day tapping all around the Sphinx and I stopped the work . . . We are not like Indiana Jones. We are scientists, and do everything carefully.

Dr Hawass seemed to be asking the international press to assist him in a 'counter attack' against what he saw as a subversive and dangerous threat to himself and, by extension, the Giza monuments. A sort of New Age paranoia was setting in. The result was an immediate campaign against us by the Egyptian press. Mug shots of the 'trio' were published in various newspapers and weekly magazines in Egypt, and we even made it in the hugely influential *Al Ahram* newspaper. There was, too, a full-page article in the *Egyptian Gazette* of 16th May under the incongruous banner 'Nauseating Headache over Great Pyramids, Monster Guard'. It was written by reporter Mohsen Arishie in that style that often typifies the hysteria of some Arab reporters when they think that 'national prestige' is being threatened:

> The ancient Egyptians are probably turning in their tombs following growing calls by some Western and Jewish scientists about the real builders of the Great

Pyramid and the world-famous monster, the Sphinx ... Some of these 'theorists' went so far in their zeal to excavate under and inside the Great Pyramids that they snapped at and insulted Dr Zahi Hawass, director general of the Giza antiquities, when he refused to listen to their lousy suggestions ... The Orion-inspired theorists scanned the Sphinx and the Pyramids with a special camera in 1992 and insisted that the extraterrestrial beings left data and secrets of their visit to Egypt in a room stationed between the monster's forelimbs ... The 'theorists' Graham Hancock and a colleague named Robert Bauval made a television movie and published a book *The Message of the Sphinx* to market their ideas ... Hawass was also attacked by unknown 'theorists' in Chicago and South Africa ... The Minister of Culture, Dr Farouk Hosni, explained that such ridiculous claims wanted to deprive Egypt of its glorious ancient history. He also mocked an Israeli attempt to attribute the ancient Jews as the real builders of the Great Pyramids and the Sphinx ... (Hawass) didn't exclude the possibility the commotion was suggested by Israel after its humiliation ...

It was fairly obvious that the *Egyptian Gazette* was drawing a very thin line between 'theorists' and 'terrorists'. At any rate, this press attack eventually escalated all the way to the normally sedate international edition of the *New York Times*[54] and the *Sunday Times* of London.[55] In the latter, reporter Steve Negus from Cairo reflected the growing hysteria with an article titled 'Egypt Plagued by New Age Pyramidiots':

As dawn breaks over the Pyramids, chanting New Age worshippers dance naked in the empty desert watched by a few incurious camel drivers. But other Egyptians are beginning to suspect that a sinister agenda lies behind the increasing numbers of outlandish foreigners who claim to be in search of pharaoh's ancient wisdom ... Hawass is particularly incensed by the writing of Robert Bauval, a Belgian architect, and Graham Hancock, British author of the best-selling *Fingerprints of the Gods*, and John West, an American tour guide, who all argue that the Pyramids were built by superior beings from Atlantis, extraterrestrial or angels. In response to growing concern about the activities of the New Agers, Egyptian authorities have vowed a public relations counter-attack. 'This is piracy', said Farouq Hosni, the culture minister. 'Our history and our civilisation must be respected.'[56]

A few weeks later on 10th August 1999 there appeared an even stranger article in the news section of the *Sunday Times* of London, which made me wonder at first whether it was not part of this 'public relations counter-attack' that Steve Negus was referring to. The article was written by Cherry Norton. I well knew, from previous experience, how difficult it was to get a sensational story past the stringent editorial of this prestigious newspaper without it being put to the utmost scrutiny for authentication and for verifying certain claims. Such were the responsibilities and standards of this world-wide newspaper which was read by millions and on whose authority so much was relied. Bearing this in mind, Norton's article at first struck me as either a hoax or a joke. It had the amazing title: 'Raiders of the Lost Archives find Pharaohs' Records':

> Two British Egyptologists believe they have found the site of an ancient underground chamber containing evidence of a lost civilisation. Nigel Appleby and Adam Child, already dubbed the 'raiders of the lost archives', are preparing an expedition to investigate a site near the great pyramids where they say the Hall of Records lies buried in the sand. They have been given permission by the Egyptian authorities to survey an area north of the Great Pyramid of Cheops using sensitive scanning equipment capable of detecting underground chambers. The Hall of Records, according to legend, is made of granite and sheathed with gold; it is said to contain artefacts and documents on the history of mankind whose discovery will herald a new dawn for civilisation. It is alluded to in the Bible and other ancient texts such as the Book of the Dead, Appleby said last week . . . According to Appleby, when the three stars of Orion's belt are lined up directly over the three of the great pyramids, the star Sirius is directly over the hall. By projecting its position on to the earth, its approximate position can be found . . .

The story read to me like an April Fool's scam that the newspapers often indulged in. But this was the month of August. The phone began to ring. First Graham, then West, then all sorts of people who wondered the same. No one had heard of Appleby or this bizarre expedition. The pattern fitted nicely with the previous scoops attacking us. There was the Hall of Records, the Orion theory, the messianic-come-new-dawn for civilisation and the claim of licences. It was too cranky and amazingly naïve to be true. Yet here we had it, in the news section of the world's most influential newspaper, the *Sunday Times*. We quickly checked with the correct authorities in Egypt, but as we expected, there was no licence issued for this or any other expedition at Giza or elsewhere in Egypt. We shall return to Nigel Appleby in our last chapter.

Meanwhile I just watched this strange press activity from a distance. The weight of ten years of stressful work and trooping around the world were beginning to take a serious toll on me.[57] I had been living on quick meals and bad diets, litres of coffee and tea, vitamin boosters and long hours of staring at my computer screen. My immune system was weak; I caught a series of viruses and infections that left me drained. I got depressed and began to suffer from serious insomnia. I was caught in a vicious circle and my doctor immediately ordered me to put on the brakes and take a few months off the job. I had, however, committed myself to several things. I had a book to finish with Graham Hancock, and dozens of conferences and talks booked till December 1998. Graham came to the rescue. He felt he could cope with the majority of the work, and suggested we bring in John Grigsby, our researcher, to take over the rest of my part in the new book. I cancelled as many conferences as I could. There was, however, one at the ARE in August 1997 that I couldn't put off. Both Dr Hawass and Dr Schor were invited as guest speakers, and I did not want people to think I was running away from the situation by cancelling my talk. It was not an easy decision. My kidneys and liver were playing up, and I was totally exhausted from the months of illness.

The ARE offered to pay for business class tickets for Michele and me, and assured me that they would make my stay as comfortable as possible. I shall never forget this trip. The east coast of the US was experiencing its hottest summer on record. The audience at the ARE was briefly told of my indisposition and I gave my talk as best as I could. But it was all worth the effort. For Dr Schor confirmed that, other than the hidden chamber under the front paw of the Sphinx located in 1991 by the West-Schoch expedition, the Schor expedition had now located a further hidden chamber, much larger than the first, somewhere beneath the rump of the monument. Schor said he was ninety-five percent sure that the readings they got with the radar indicated such a chamber. It was during this conference that Rufus Mosely, the pilot who had worked with Hugh Lynn Cayce back in the 1970s, called me up and offered to organise a private meeting between Hawass, Schor, Jahoda, John Van Auken (the ARE executive) and myself. I reluctantly agreed but insisted that it should be on neutral ground. We decided to hold the meeting in the Ramada Hotel's coffee shop restaurant. It was to be one of the strangest experiences of my life. I took a strong dose of painkillers and went down to the lobby to meet the men.

Entente cordiale

Zahi Hawass arrived impeccably dressed in a beige suite. He was accompanied by an Egyptian lady who was introduced as a journalist friend. With them was Jahoda, Schor, John Van Auken and Rufus Mosely. They had all come from Mosely's home where they had had lunch. They all seemed like old friends. Hawass scolded Schor in a friendly way for having misbehaved during the Giza expedition by letting the TV crew run around taking films all the time. He then expressed his anger at Hancock and me for having spread 'lies' about him. I replied that we simply had reported what we understood were facts, and that we intended to carry on doing so. We all felt, however, that we should not encourage the media to turn the debate and the conflict of ideas into a degenerating political smear campaign. In short, we agreed to disagree but at the same time to remain as civil as we could in the circumstances. We were promised access to the site and an open policy regarding information. There was an awkward moment when Boris Said suddenly appeared at the restaurant with a girlfriend. He had come for the conference and presumably had got a whiff of the meeting we were having. Everyone politely greeted him, and he left. The meeting took just over half-an-hour. We then all shook hands and parted. This was the beginning of a supposed 'entente cordiale' between the parties.

Back in my room, there was an urgent phone call from Graham Hancock in England waiting for me. Apparently Boris had telephoned him saying that he had video footage of the Schor expedition which showed that they were not only frantically looking for a secret chamber under the Sphinx, but that they had made an important discovery. He offered to send copies of these films to us. I stumbled on Boris outside the Ramada Hotel, who repeated the same offer. But as tempting as it was, we declined. We decided to give the entente cordiale a fair chance to work. It was not to work for very long.

THE ENTRANCE TO THE HALL OF RECORDS

Around September 1997, rumours began to circulate that Schor and his team, as well as Boris Said, had been back at Giza. Not just once, but several times. Furthermore they were planning a drilling operation sometime in 1998. Now prior to the strange encounter at the Ramada Hotel, I would have thought this very unlikely, if not impossible. Neither Hancock, West or I had been told of these events. As usual, there was the clampdown on information. I eventually discovered that the Schor and Boris Said team had been conducting experiments in November 1996 – that is six months after the controversy over the *Daily Mail* serialisation in May 1996 – and also in February 1997. It was not clear whether the Schor expedition licence had been reactivated or whether the team was working on a new licence altogether.[58] This time, however, the scope of their search and investigation would not be limited to the Sphinx but was extended to some curious experiments inside the Great Pyramid.

But what?

And what were they looking for?

I was not to find out the full details until late July 1998, through a very unexpected source. Meanwhile the entente cordiale received another boost of publicity in a place that could not have been more alien and further away from Giza: Alaska. An Egyptian living in Los Angeles called Abass Nadim had managed to persuade Dr Hawass to attend an open debate with Graham Hancock and myself, as well as other players that had entered the controversy over the dating of the Sphinx such as the eminent astronomer Dr E.C. Krupp. The debate was to take place in May 1998 on a cruise ship sailing from Vancouver to Alaska. Unfortunately at the very last minute I had to cancel my participation due to illness. John West decided to replace me. It was during this cruise that something rather unusual happened. The master of ceremonies had been Art Bell, of the 'coast to coast' radio show. Bell had met Dr Hawass in Egypt and had interviewed him on his show. A few weeks earlier, however, Bell had also interviewed Richard Hoagland and a man called Larry Hunter. The latter had been feeding Hoagland with controversial rumours about Giza, that supposedly secret excavations were taking place inside the Great Pyramid and, more intriguingly, that Dr Hawass had been demoted from his post and was about to be arrested by the Egyptian police.

Larry Hunter was running a website with a colleague, Amargi Hillier, which posted the most outrageous rumours and claims about Giza.[59] I had been paying mild attention to this website over the last few months because many such rumours concerned myself and Graham Hancock. Hawass was openly confronted by Art Bell with these accusations on the cruise while he was on stage in front of a large audience. Embarrassed, Hawass turned to Hancock and West for support. Although we had been at odds with Hawass for many years – and were still hotly debating the Giza issues – we knew that the accusations made by Hunter were untrue. Indeed, quite the opposite really; for there had been an official announcement made by the Supreme Council of Antiquities that Hawass, far from being demoted like Hunter said, had been elevated to the ministerial rank of Under-secretary of State for the Giza Monuments. This was a new posting created especially for Hawass, and which clearly showed that he was highly regarded by the Egyptian government. Hancock and West did the right thing. They condemned such irresponsible and malicious rumours, and put up a joint statement on the Internet to that effect.[60] When I got to hear of this, I, too, did the same.[61] I was not entirely persuaded that there had not been serious irregularities and odd 'goings-on' at Giza, and the matter of the ARE and the Schor involvement there was not fully cleared in my mind. Nonetheless, I was totally against the spreading of false rumours. Characters like Hunter and his colleagues, who confused an already confusing situation with wild rumours, simply had to be stopped.[62]

After the Alaskan conference I was contacted by Richard Hoagland, who kept on insisting that he had evidence of strange goings-on at Giza. Apparently Boris Said had provided him with video footage of the Schor expedition, as well as video film shot privately on Hi-8 by someone who had been there at the time. I told Hoagland that Boris had offered me this footage a year ago, but that I had turned it down. I was now coming out of my long illness and planned a holiday with the family to the US to stay with old friends in San Diego, California. I told Hoagland that perhaps we could meet then and he could show me the films.

We met at my friends' place on 22nd August 1998. Unfortunately Hoagland brought along the wrong video tapes. He thus suggested he make copies of the correct ones and have them mailed to me in England. Two video tapes arrived by FedEx two weeks later. I had them converted from NTSC to PAL and played the one marked '*Secret Chamber – Schor/Said un-aired video of Schor Expedition*'. What I was looking at was a fully developed TV documentary – complete with gaps left for commercials and titles – covering the events of the Schor expeditions from November 1995 to February 1997. The proposed title said it all. There was no doubt whatsoever that Schor and his radar crew had been focusing their efforts on finding an underground chamber under and around the Sphinx and, to a lesser extent, near the Pyramids. The film introduced Dr Schor as a man who was devoting his time and money to finding evidence of a lost civilisation and was now at Giza to search for clues and, more specifically, a secret chamber which might contain records and artefacts. The scientist who was manning the sophisticated scanning equipment was Dr Thomas Dobecki, recruited by Schor some-time after the aborted 1991-93 West-Schoch expedition. Using the new and more powerful equipment, Dobecki was able to re-confirm the existence of a 'chamber' under the front paw of the Sphinx, as well as a 'chamber' located under the hind part of the Sphinx. What was more exciting, however, was that there seemed to be a tunnel leading out from that last chamber and heading towards the Second Pyramid.

Could this tunnel be the entrance to the fabled Hall of Records that Cayce said was under the bedrock around the Sphinx?

Unable to get permits to excavate down to this tunnel, Schor and his team decided to look for an entrance somewhere between the Sphinx and the Second Pyramid. There was a rumour circulating at Giza that a deep well-shaft had been discovered recently under the causeway that linked the Sphinx complex with the Second Pyramid.[63] In fact, Boris Said had explored this well-shaft as early as 1992, and it was also well-known to Hawass and Mark Lehner for many years.[64] It was first discovered by the Egyptologist Selim Hassan in 1935, who was then the director of the Antiquities Department.[65] Hassan had recorded that the shaft descended deep into the natural bedrock and opened up into a sort of large man-made chamber in which were found two empty granite sarcophagi placed inside niches cut into the walls of the gallery. Hassan could see the well-shaft descending even further into another chamber below, but it was submerged in water. So clear was the water, however, that Hassan could discern a 'colonnaded hall' and other sarcophagi.[66] Since 1965 it had been used as a water well for the local area, but no one was tempted to explore it further.

Boris and Schor had a hunch that this well-shaft might in some way be linked to the tunnel that they had discovered at the rear of the Sphinx. Boris inspected the well-shaft again in 1996 and found that the water had been partially drained with a pump that had been left there. Hawass apparently had taken an interest in the shaft and was preparing for further excavations. In February 1997 Boris then went back, and this time could reach the lower 'colonnade hall' which had now been almost cleared from water. James Hurtak, the author of *The Keys of Enoch*, was also present with him, along with a small TV crew. They scraped the mud and dirt to expose the floor and, to their surprise, found the lid of a large sarcophagus fixed to the ground. It was made of black granite and weighed several tons. Unable to move it, they had Dr Dobecki use his scanning equipment to see what was underneath:

> According to our ground-penetrating radar, the lid was about 18 inches thick, and then about two and a half meters under it there was a space which was 2.5 meters wide with a domed ceiling, leaning down at an angle of 25 degrees in the direction of the Sphinx . . .[67]

Everyone was convinced that they had found an entrance to a tunnel leading towards the Sphinx and probably linking with the tunnel heading out from beneath the Sphinx toward the well-shaft. The team desperately tried to get permits to dig, but the Egyptians would not have it. Then a short while after, something odd happened. Dr Hawass announced that he had 'discovered' the 'tomb of Osiris' – which turned out to be none other than the 'colonnade hall' that Selim Hassan had in fact himself discovered back in 1935.[68] We shall examine this well-shaft in greater detail in Chapter 12, where I will narrate my own experience of going down into it in early August 1999.

Meanwhile Boris Said could no longer restrain himself. He told me and others that the discovery had been 'stolen' from him by Zahi Hawass and that he had lost trust in the man completely.[69] Needless to say relations between Boris and Hawass completely collapsed, with Boris apparently instigating a legal attack in Egypt against Hawass with the support of important people, while claiming that he had evidence that could much incriminate him.[70] I must say that I took all this accusation with a good pinch of salt, but I nonetheless felt that a certain degree of skulduggery had taken place at Giza, and it all centred on this obsession with finding the Hall of Records or a secret chamber of certain people while at the same time wanting everyone else to believe that they were involved in something else.

Around the middle of September 1998 I called Rufus Mosely at Virginia Beach. Rufus, we shall recall, is the airline pilot who worked with Hugh Lynn Cayce in Egypt. He also had been closely monitoring the various expeditions at Giza as well as the recent ones of the Schor Foundation. He informed me that a week earlier he had been at Giza with Dr Schor and his team where they were drilling between the second and third subsidiary pyramids – the so-called Queen pyramids – also known as G1C and G1D, which are located on the east side of the Great Pyramid. So far they had not found anything. What they were trying to do, according to Rufus, was prove to Zahi that the radar worked, then he would let them back to the Sphinx and check, with drill holes, the recent anomalies they had found in 1997. All this was news to me. I must confess that I was amazed that drilling had been allowed at all, considering the fuss that had happened back in 1977-78. Clearly the promise to let us know what was going on at Giza for our so-called 'entente cordiale' was not working. There was only one way to get to the bottom of this. I had to confront the main protagonists again. I phoned Dr Schor and asked him for an appointment.

NEW YORK NEW YORK

On 5th October 1998 I took a British Airways flight from London to New York. I booked in at the Madison Hotel on 44th Street. I had two days to spare over the weekend – Dr Schor was seeing me on the Monday. So I called John West who invited me to stay at his place in Athens, on the Hudson River. After a two-hour train ride from Manhattan, I arrived in the small, provincial town of Athens where John was waiting for me at the station. It was cold but wonderfully clear and sunny. John lives right on the river, in a wonderfully cosy timber house that is part of a country hotel. We talked of Giza and the Sphinx, and John was eager for me to meet with his new sponsor and mentor, Paula Tsaconas. Paula turned out to be a softly spoken lady in her early forties, with a remarkable sparkle in her eyes and that wonderful Californian zest for life, health and *avant-garde* ideas. She had amassed considerable financial wealth – something to do with telecommunication investments in the Far East. She was eager to listen to an idea that I had which I called 'Project Equinox 2000'. This entailed setting up a communication base in Cairo to be operational till the end of December 1999. The principal objective was to act as a contact point for all who wanted to follow the exciting events that we all hoped would take place in the next year or so, namely the opening of the 'door' in the Great Pyramid, perhaps even the return of a team to verify the claims of a possible chamber under the Sphinx, and finally the much hyped placing of a gilded capstone on top of the Great Pyramid on the eve of the new millennium and all the activities and festivities that will surround it. Another objective was to group prominent authors and researchers in the field of ancient Egypt and related subjects in order to give a series of conferences around the world, starting and ending in Egypt.[71] The idea much appealed to Paula Tsaconas, and she said that she would seriously consider sponsoring the venture.

On Monday I made my way back to New York to see Dr Schor. The meeting was friendly but, ultimately, fruitless. Schor repeated his obligation of confidentiality towards the Egyptian authorities and was reluctant to discuss his expeditions at Giza in any worthwhile detail. I told him that I had been commissioned to write *Secret Chamber*, and my objective was to tell the story of these events as best and as truthfully as I could. I also informed him point blank that I had actually seen the film that was shot by Boris Said, and would rely on what was in it unless he, Schor, was prepared to tell me his own version as well, which I would then also take into account.

Whilst in New York I decided to visit my friends Bill and Carol Cote. Bill had been part of the 1991-93 West-Schoch expedition and had been largely responsible for the making of the NBC *Mystery of the Sphinx* documentary. He was the owner of BC Video which specialised in this genre of films. Bill was also a close friend of the well-known psychic Ingo Swann, who had made a sensation in the 1970s as leader of the controversial Remote Viewing Program run for the CIA by the Stanford Research Institute. We shall recall that the Remote Viewing Program was run parallel with the SRI's Sphinx project, which had been sponsored by the Edgar Cayce Foundation. I had read somewhere that Hugh Lynn Cayce had asked Ingo Swann to 'remote view' the Sphinx area, and I wanted to know more about this connection.[72] Bill arranged for a meeting at Swann's home on 25th Street.

Ingo Swann lives in a typical artist's den, a basement flat decorated with his amazing surreal paintings and with wonderful exotic objects all over the place. A man in his early fifties, Ingo Swann is a funny, gentle and refreshingly honest man. I liked him immediately. His 'powers' had waned a little since the days of the Remote Viewing Program, and now he made a living from his paintings. Swann was not too keen to talk of those days back in the 1970s, but he was open about the matter of Giza and the Sphinx. It had not been the ARE who took him there, but the author Peter Tompkins.

They had spent a brief few days at the necropolis with Swann trying his psychic skill to locate underground chambers or tunnels. Swann was convinced that the 'Hall of Records', if it existed at all, was not at Giza. He said he 'saw' no hidden chambers around the Sphinx but rather plenty of tunnels and galleries which seemed to criss-cross each other all around the plateau. I offered the suggestiond that perhaps the legendary Hall of Records may not be a 'chamber' as such, but something else. Perhaps it would be something much smaller, and the 'records' not scrolls or tablets as everyone seemed to conjure. Swann was ready to give it another go, and I said that perhaps we could have this arranged. His 'work' was certainly non-intrusive and no permits would be required. Although I did not allocate much dividend to 'psychic' archaeology, there was, at least, no harm in it.

I returned to England feeling satisfied that I had tried all I could with Dr Schor. On 24th October 1998 I gave my first major public talk. This was at the annual Questing Conference in London run by the author Andrew Collins. I was in high spirits and decided to enjoy myself with the audience by giving a very informal talk where I also showed part of my collection of private slides and film linked to the Giza investigation. I also showed excerpts from the Boris Said/Schor expedition which I felt I should share with the public.[73] A few days later I took a flight to Cairo, this time to see Dr Hawass himself.

PROJECT EQUINOX

I arrived in Cairo late in the evening. As usual, my loyal taxi driver, Mahmoud Al Kirsh, was there to meet me with his tatty Peugeot 505. I told him that I was importing an old 1987 model Mercedes Benz 300 E to be used for my project in Egypt and that he could drive it, and his eyes gleamed with pride and expectation. A Mercedes car has much status value in Egypt, and this one, as I was to soon discover, would be the subject of an elaborate 'conspiracy theory'. Mahmoud drove me to Giza, where I was staying at the flat belonging to my friend Mohamad Nazmy. Mohamad had kindly offered the use of his working flat for the duration of the project, which was conveniently located only a few minutes away from the Pyramids and the Sphinx. Mohamad Nazmy is the owner of the travel group Quest, which is one of the most successful in Egypt. John West had been collaborating with Nazmy for years and, ironically, the latter was a very close friend of Zahi Hawass. Nazmy arranged the appointment with Hawass for me. The next day I made my way to Hawass's office to the north-west of the Great Pyramid. His staff immediately recognised me from the various TV appearances and, of course, the mug shots in the local press.

As offices go, Hawass's is typically chaotic. There is often a flurry of activities with secretaries barging in with papers to sign, messages to pass and visitors to usher in and out. Two or more visits may take place at the same time, with conversations mingling with Hawass's almost constant dialogues on the phone. On this occasion, to add a little humour, I brought along my local pet dog, Coco – a white mongrel female that looks like a cross between a British sheepdog and a cocker spaniel. Her amorous nature caused pandemonium, with Hawass's personal secretary refusing to enter the room. Coco had to wait outside in the garden. As much as he's formidable and sometimes rather fierce looking, there is something about Hawass that is disarmingly friendly. He can treat you as an old school friend with warmth and humour, or be as cutting and blunt as David Frost. We share a curious love-hate relationship that, I think, he finds hard to comprehend. He knew of my visit to Dr Schor; he could not tell me much of Schor's work, but said that he had instructed Schor to be as open as possible next time I saw him. We also discussed the Equinox 2000 project. He had no objections to the idea, but said that it would be impossible to arrange for a place in the precinct of the Giza necropolis. It was already all reserved for other activities and, in any case, the obtaining of permits for such an event would be very unlikely. He had another suggestion. He said that he could arrange with the Sound and Light people to allow us to place a small podium outside the necropolis, somewhere perhaps in front of the Sphinx area near the car park. That would do fine, I told him, and thanked him for his co-operation. Hawass then asked me if I, as well as Graham Hancock and John West, would consider joining him in a film that Fox TV was going to shoot at Giza in late November. I said I would discuss this with the others. I then discussed the possibility of having Rudolf Gantenbrink, the German robotic engineer, return to Giza in order to resume the exploration of the shafts in the Great Pyramid. It was clear from what Hawass said that the SCA was not keen to resume such work with Gantenbrink. He had caused too much disruption in the media. I expressed my views that no matter what the past problems, it was only fair to let him return, and that the public would see this as a proper resolution to the matter.

We shall return to Gantenbrink and the 'door' affair in the next chapter. Meanwhile I returned to England, where I was contacted by Joy Wilson-Price, the producer of the *Carte Blanche* programme for the South African M-Net TV channel. I had worked with Joy before, and she wanted to do a story on the recent events at Giza. Filming began in early November 1998, with Derek Watt, the well-known South African TV presenter, and Diana Lucas, the producer and director of this documentary. John West and Graham Hancock also happened to be in Egypt at the time, and were interviewed by the *Carte Blanche* team. They also managed to get Hawass to give a lengthy interview as well as show them around some of his new discoveries at Giza. Hawass also agreed to a joint interview with me in front of the Sphinx.[74] In this film Hawass openly discussed the Schor expedition, acknowledging that they were looking for the Hall of Records. He also confirmed the drilling and repeated what Rufus Mosely had said. Hawass said that he persuaded the committee at the SCA to allow the drilling in order to either prove or disprove Atlantis and the Hall of Records. Apparently nothing was found, thus proving the unreliability of the radar.

On 14th November we started filming with the Fox TV crew, led by Nancy Stern, a producer from New York. Nancy managed to organise a filming session in central Cairo at the famous Fishawi tea house in the Khan El Khalili bazaar. There Zahi Hawass, Graham Hancock, John West and myself smoked shishas (water pipes) and argued in a friendly manner the merits and faults of the various new theories on Giza. Hawass had arranged for Fox TV to film the 'live' opening of a tomb at Giza which belonged to an official called Kai of Fourth Dynasty as well as the so-called 'tomb of Osiris' in the well-shaft. Hawass also planned to open, for the first time, one of the small 'Queen' pyramids next to the Third Pyramid. The show was scheduled for 2nd March 1999 and would be presented by the TV personalities Maury Povich and Suzy Kolber.[75]

In early January 1999 I went again to New York to meet Dr Schor. It was bitterly cold, and New York was snowed under. Again, Schor received me very cordially but could and would not tell me much. He had apparently been told by Hawass to 'open his books' to me, but this time the reason he declined to do so was because he was reserving 'exclusivity' of his story to a film-maker and writer who was contracted by him to compile the events of his explorations at Giza. It was no use. I finally realised that I was not going to get much joy from this quarter. I gave Schor, however, some advice. I told him that the problem all along was that he and, more particularly, the Egyptian authorities had tried to perform a search for the Hall of Records under the guise of a 'restoration' or 'conservation' project. The public and the media had seen through this scam, and this, in my view, was the source of much of the demise of these expeditions. I said that the best way to approach a new expedition was for all parties to come straight out and declare their true intentions. My feeling was that this open-books strategy would work, and certainly Graham Hancock and I would support it.[76] Little did I know, however, that Schor was planning a new expedition at Giza and that, at long last, precisely such a strategy would be implemented. But more on this later.

While in the US, I was invited by John Van Auken of the Edgar Cayce Foundation to give a short talk on 22nd January. I drove via Washington DC, where I took the opportunity to visit the Washington Masonic Memorial in the Alexandria district. I wanted to take some photographs for a future book I had planned with Graham Hancock.[77] In Virginia Beach, John Van Auken took me out for lunch. With us was the film producer who had come to see John Van Auken about a possible documentary on the ARE. It was during this lunch that John Van Auken reconfirmed to me that the ARE had, in fact, contributed in some way to Dr Hawass's university education in the US back in the 1980s. From his viewpoint, I presumed he saw no harm in this. Dr Hawass, as we have said, hotly denies this, and it really now was a question of his word against theirs, although, as Hawass had pointed out earlier, he had categorical evidence which he could bring in support of his position.

It was not the first time that I had come across a 'their word against mine' situation involving Hawass. In fact one such situation was to end up in the High Courts of London. In what was possibly the most bizarre legal case in archaeology, the debate of a possible 'secret chamber' in the Great Pyramid found its way into a huge legal battle involving vast sums of money.

Chapter Eleven

Secret Chamber

'German scientists claim a hoax!'

(About the Upuaut Project), *Egyptian Gazette* 28th April 1993

'No one is allowed to use any results of this work for commercial business.'

(About the Upuaut Project), Dr Ali Hassan, Under-secretary of State for Pharaonic Antiquities, Egyptian Supreme Council of Antiquities, letter to BBC dated 27th January 1994

'I would hope that after payment of all expenses I will still receive an income of several million dollars.'

(About the Upuaut Project), Rudolf Gantenbrink, May 1994.

STARS AND SIGNS

My adventures with the shafts in the Great Pyramid date back to 1983. It was at that time that I had informed Dr I.E.S. Edwards, the eminent Egyptologist and world expert on the Pyramids of Egypt, of my Orion-Giza correlation theory.[1] It was a short while later that he referred me to the work of Dr Virginia Trimble and Dr Alexander Badawi in connection with these shafts.[2] Trimble and Badawi had shown that the southern shaft of the King's Chamber, which was angled at forty-five degrees, had been directed to Orion's belt, a constellation linked in the Pyramid Texts with the 'soul' of Osiris and that of the king. Later, in 1986, while I was living in Australia, I was to discover that the southern shaft of the Queen's Chamber was directed towards the star Sirius, identified with the sister-consort of Osiris, the goddess Isis.[3] This work was published in *Discussions in Egyptology* in 1990, an Oxford journal edited by the Egyptologist Dr Alessandra Nibbi. My article appeared under the title 'The Seeding of the Star-gods: A Fertility Ritual in Cheops's Pyramid?' in volume 16 of the journal. In this article I pointed out that the shafts in the Queen's Chamber, unlike those of the King's Chamber, did not pierce the pyramid throughout but, instead, stopped somewhere within the core of the structure. So far no one had explored these shafts to find out where they led, although some crude probing with rods had been undertaken by Flinders Petrie and the Dixon brothers back in the late 1800s.[4] It was a fair assumption, in my opinion, that the southern shaft of the Queen's Chamber should have the same 'astro-mythological' connotations as its counterpart in the King's Chamber. The star Sirius was an obvious contender. I proceeded to do the calculations and then had them verified by the astronomer Dr John O'Byrne of the University of Sydney.[5] Flinders Petrie had measured the slope of this shaft and given it as 38 degrees and 28 minutes.[6] I worked out, using the rigorous formula of precessional calculations, that the altitude of Sirius was very near to this angle around 2750 BC, a date that fitted within the estimated construction epoch of the Pyramid Age. I thus concluded that coincidence must be ruled out, and that the shaft had been deliberately aligned to this special star of ancient Egypt. The matter rested there until a fateful telephone call in December 1992.

Dr Iorweth Eiddon Stephen Edwards, better known as I.E.S. Edwards, was, in the opinion of many, the world's leading authority on the Egyptian pyramids. He started his career in 1934, when he joined the Department of Antiquities at the British Museum. During the War he was stationed in Egypt, where he collated the data and material which led to the 1946 publication of the classic book *The Pyramids of Egypt*.[7] In 1955 he became the Keeper of Egyptian Antiquities at the British Museum, a post that he held until his retirement in 1974. It was under Edwards's keepership that the famous Tutankhamun Exhibition in London took place in 1972. A member of the British Academy since 1962, and Vice-President of the Egyptian Exploration Society until 1988, Edwards's reputation was immense, and his word carried enormous weight.

We had been acquainted since 1984, and through the years we developed a friendship that was to last till his death in September 1996. He had been very interested in my work, and we held a frequent correspondence on the issue of the Giza pyramids. His phone call on 15th December 1992, however, came as a surprise. He first asked me if I had

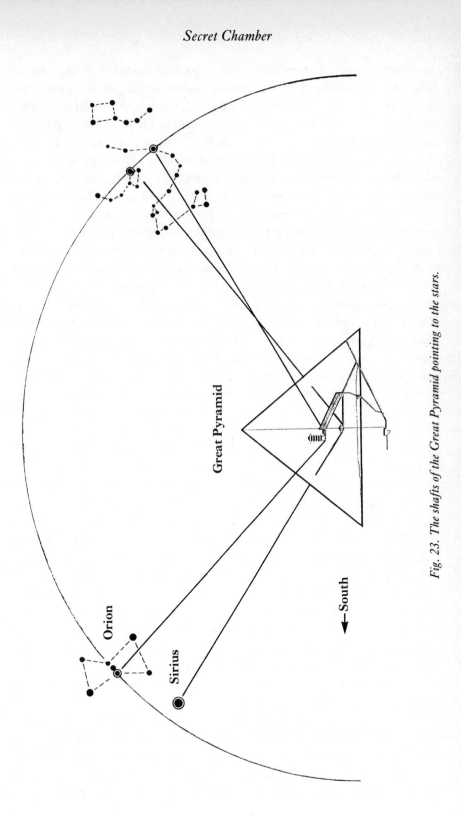

Great Pyramid

Orion

Sirius

←**South**

Fig. 23. The shafts of the Great Pyramid pointing to the stars.

done any studies on the shafts of the Queen's Chamber in the Great Pyramid. I referred him, of course, to my article in *Discussions in Egyptology*. It had been Edwards who had introduced me to its editor back in 1987. He then dropped the bombshell. He informed me that a German team had been exploring this shaft with a miniature robot since the beginning of 1992. The work was being carried out under the supervision and licence of the German Archaeological Institute in Cairo, whose director was Dr Rainer Stadelmann. According to Edwards, 'in their first attempt they were unable to go very far into the shaft and they had sent to Germany for a more powerful machine'.[8]

I informed Dr Edwards that I was planning a trip to Egypt for late February 1993, and asked him for an introduction to Dr Stadelmann. Apparently Stadelmann and he were not on good terms these days, and he suggested that his good friend Dr Henry Riad, an ex-director of the Antiquities Department in Cairo, could perhaps arrange this. It so happened that the husband of my cousin in Cairo, Dr John Orphanidis, was also acquainted with Dr Riad, and through him an appointment was finally arranged for me with Dr Stadelmann for early March 1993. Meanwhile I wrote a letter to Dr Stadelmann to explain why I wanted to see him:

> The purpose of my visit is to obtain the latest data on the shafts in both the King's and Queen's chambers in Khufu's pyramid for a future publication I am presently working on.[9]

I informed Dr Edwards that I had written to Dr Stadelmann, asking for an appointment. He replied[10] that he looked forward to hearing about the results of the German investigation into the Queen's Chamber ventilation shafts.[11]

Adrian Gilbert and his wife, Dee, came with me to Cairo. Adrian was then co-authoring with me *The Orion Mystery*, and Dee, a professional photographer, came along to shoot some photos for us. We arrived on 27th February. It was a tense time in Egypt, with terrorists setting off bombs in central Cairo. Adrian and Dee decided to visit Luxor in Upper Egypt, and I stayed in the Cairo area, waiting for my appointment with Dr Rainer Stadelmann. We met on 2nd March in his office at the German Archaeological Institute in the fashionable district of Zamalek. Dr Stadelmann was open and friendly, and informed me that the work in the shafts of the Queen's Chamber was being carried out by Rudolf Gantenbrink, a technician and specialist in robotics. Gantenbrink was in Munich completing the construction of a new robot to explore the southern shaft, which confirmed what Dr Edwards had told me back in London. Stadelmann told me that Gantenbrink was expected to return from Munich on 6th March in the evening. He was staying at the Movenpick Hotel at Giza and Stadelmann kindly offered to arrange a meeting for me that same evening. The meeting took place at eight o'clock in the evening in the restaurant of the Movenpick. I had taken along a good friend of mine, Marion Krause, a pharmacist from Berlin, in case an interpreter was needed.

Gantenbrink, however, spoke very good English. With him were two men, Jochen Breitenstein and Dirk Brakebusch. Breitenstein was introduced as a film-maker with offices in Munich and in Los Angeles. He had been brought here by Gantenbrink to shoot a film related to the exploration of the shaft. Brakebusch was a friend of Gantenbrink who was helping with the exploration and acted as assistant to Breitenstein. Gantenbrink explained that he had been involved with the German Archaeological Institute in Cairo since early 1992. He had sent them a proposal to explore the shaft with a mechanised robot in 1991, and they had agreed to incorporate his proposal into another scheme they had, which was to do with improving the ventilation of the Great Pyramid. The ventilation scheme entailed clearing the two shafts of the King's Chamber from debris and installing fans to increase the airflow through the internal system of the Pyramid and using the shafts as 'exhausts'. For this project Gantenbrink brought a group of sponsors from the German and Swiss industrial sector. These included the companies Hilti Bohrtechnik, Helios, Gossenbacher and Lufttechnische GmbH. The work was completed in early June 1992, and a press release to that effect was issued on 8th June jointly by Dr Stadelmann, Dr Hawass and Dr Mohamad Ibrahim Bakr, then the president of the Egyptian Antiquities Organisation, at a ceremony in the Boat Museum on the south side of the Great Pyramid.[12] After this event, Gantenbrink said he had returned to Germany to build a new and more powerful robot to explore the shafts in the Queen's Chamber. They were going to start the work the following day, 7th March 1993. He invited me to watch the operation. I told him that unfortunately I had to return to England. He promised to send me data and his new measurements for the slopes of the shafts, both for those in the King's Chamber and the Queen's Chamber. He also said he would send me some video films, so that I could see the inside of the shafts and how they were constructed. He said he would have all this ready for me within a few days. I thanked him and we parted company.

A PROMOTIONAL FILM

Back in England I resumed my work on the manuscript of *The Orion Mystery* and waited to hear from Gantenbrink. Meanwhile I reported the events of my visit to Egypt by letter to Dr Edwards:

> I would like to express my thanks again for the contact you have arranged for me with Dr Stadelmann. Through his own intervention, I met Dr Rudolf Gantenbrink and Herr Jochen Breitenstein. Dr Gantenbrink is leading the team who are working on the shafts in the Cheops pyramid, and Herr Breitenstein is a film producer. The latest data was this: the new equipment, appropriately termed 'Upuaut II', arrived in Egypt on Sunday 7th March, and work will now resume on the shafts in the Queen's Chamber. The Upuaut II, which is essentially a small video camera that is electronically monitored, will – within five days or so – give us a better picture of the shafts and, hopefully, tell us how far they go and what might be at the end of them. Perhaps some hieroglyphs, a cartouche or something of the kind. Dr Gantenbrink has promised to send me his data and a copy of the video. I will, then, from his measurements, work out a more accurate 'precession' dating of the Cheops pyramid. My calculation, of course, will be transmitted to you for your records.[13]

After waiting for nearly two weeks with no word from Gantenbrink, I decided to send him a fax in Cairo to remind him of the data on the shafts he had promised me.[14] By 26th March there was still no reply, so this time I sent a fax to Dr Stadelmann informing him that 'I was still waiting for the data and photos' Gantenbrink had promised so that I could use them in my book. On 31st March I got a reply from Dr Stadelmann but with no mention of Gantenbrink whatsoever. I was puzzled. Something did not seem right. I was either being given the cold shoulder in some polite Germanic way or something was wrong.

But what?

The next day, 1st April 1993, I heard on the news that an explosion had occurred inside one of the Pyramids at Giza and terrorists were suspected. I decided to telephone Dr Stadelmann in Cairo to find out what was happening. He was not there, but his secretary gave me some news. Apparently Gantenbrink had returned to Germany with his team. I asked why but she would not say. I pressed her a little and got Gantenbrink's telephone number in Germany. I phoned and he answered straight away. He said he had meant to contact me but that things had been very hectic in Cairo and that he had had 'some political problems' with Stadelmann and the Egyptian authorities, and he had thus 'resigned' from his commission. All this was very strange. Still, I was more interested in what he had found inside the southern shaft of the Queen's Chamber. Nothing could have prepared me for the big bomb-shell Gantenbrink was about to drop. Excitedly he said that he had managed to reach the end of the shaft some two hundred feet into the core of the Pyramid, and at the end had seen, through the video camera on his robot, what looked like a small 'portcullis door' on which were attached two small copper fittings.

Apparently he had filmed the whole discovery on video and was ready to send me a copy of the film. He would send the film by courier as soon as possible and meanwhile he promised to fax some information on the angle of the shafts so that I could use this for my work. This was very exciting news indeed. Unknown to me then, it was that very same day that Gantenbrink had sent a fax to the Egyptian Ministry of Culture. In this fax, which was dated 1st April 1993 and apparently transmitted at 1.30 p.m. that same day, Gantenbrink informed the minister, Dr Farouk Hosni, that the 'German Research Project Cheops Pyramid' had been successfully completed and that he was now poised to break the news in the international press, although he wanted to clear such a press release with the minister. He also offered to send a video film of the findings to the Minister.[15] Oddly, there was absolutely no mention of the German Archaeological Institute in this fax. No reply was forthcoming.[16]

Meanwhile Gantenbrink faxed the data on the angle of slopes of the shafts, and on 4th April the video film that he had promised arrived. Sure enough, on this film was shown the robot Upuaut II climbing the southern shaft of the Queen's Chamber and filming a small 'door' with copper handles. I was a little perplexed, however, about the style in which the film was made. It was, quite obviously, a promotional tape made by a professional. I looked again at the box in which the video tape was packed. On it was printed 'The Upuaut Project – Promotional Tape. High-tech Archaeology makes a sensational discovery in the Cheops Pyramid. Not for Broadcast. No public showing. 7 Min.' The person to contact was given as Rudolf Gantenbrink in Munich. There was no mention on the label of either the German Archaeological Institute or the Egyptian Antiquities Organisation. On the film itself, at the part when the 'door' was shown, the words 'Not for Broadcast' flashed on the screen. I decided to play the tape again and make a transcript. The male voice, which sounded American, was reading from a carefully worded script:

> With the Upuaut project archaeology has taken a giant step into the space age. After two years of preparation, a 200,000 dollars' investment and the

contribution of sponsors and volunteers, a German team under the auspices of the German Archaeological Institute in Cairo, and with the co-operation of the Egyptian Antiquities Organisation, will attempt to lift one of the last secrets of the Cheops pyramid. The man behind the project is Rudolf Gantenbrink, an engineer and specialist in robotics and computer analysis. He designed the Upuaut, the sophisticated robot especially designed for this project. Swiss precision miniature motion and specially designed gears are used to propel the robot. Even the cable, Upuaut's umbilical cord, was especially manufactured. The robot is provided with remote control that feeds the miniature video camera as well as the laser guidance system and a sensor capable of measuring the angle of incline accurately to one tenth of a degree. Mr Gantenbrink discussed the navigation technique with Ulli Kapp from the German Archaeological Institute. The plan is computer-generated and scaled to cubits, the ancient Egyptian measure. The shafts to be explored originate in the so-called Queen's Chamber. For the first time the robot enters the narrow shaft measuring twenty by twenty centimetres. First opened in 1872, its length a mystery, the shaft to date remains unexplored. No human has laid eyes upon the inside in over 4000 years. Upuaut begins its journey into the unknown. After two metres of horizontal travel, the robot masters a steep, almost forty-five degrees' incline by bracing its upper tracks against the ceiling of the shaft. Having negotiated the tricky bend, we're looking at a rather grim road ahead, full of sand traps and other surprises. Since the shaft is by no means constructed evenly, steering at times is a difficult task. It's been a long steep climb, a true test for the machine and the man at the controls. The surface of the shaft changes dramatically from walls which are extremely rough to a smooth almost polished appearance towards the end. Suddenly the sand is gone, and we are inside an area of fine Tura limestone. After two weeks of trial and error and numerous modifications to the vehicle and sixty-five metres of travel, on 22 March 1993 at 11.05 a.m., Upuaut reaches the end of its journey. Under the watchful eyes of the ever-present Egyptian government officials, the first sensation: a small piece of copper lying on the ground comes into view. Tension and excitement are mounting. This is the first metal found in the Cheops pyramid. What are these two dark spots at the end? Closer inspection reveals two copper fittings attached to the stone. The piece on the ground seems to have broken off from the fitting on the left. The diameter of the laser beam is five millimetres. Watch where it goes. As we can see, the stone is not firmly resting on the floor and there is virtually no damage to the bottom edge; there is no mortar present nor is there any build-up of debris in front of it. The triangular opening in the bottom right-hand corner reveals a slight recess in the wall. The only known elements comparable to this are the so-called portcullis slabs which were always placed in front of a tomb. The design worked by lowering the slab guided by grooves from the ceiling. What is the riddle the ancient master builders left for us to solve? What is still to be learnt? Only further research will tell.

There was something that I had seen and heard in the film that had made me uneasy, but I could not quite put my finger on it. Something that was not quite right. Something or someone that should not be there. It would take me quite a while to work it out. Meanwhile, just for a precaution, I decided from now on to be on my guard and keep a full record of what happened, both for its historical value and just in case there was trouble later on with this discovery. In my days in the construction industry I had trained as a claims engineer, and had learnt the hard way always to keep full records when I sensed something was not going quite right with a particular project. I had the same warning bells with this discovery in the Great Pyramid. My hunch and precaution were eventually to prove justified.

BREAKING THE NEWS

In the last few years there has been a constant stream of accusations that I somehow had 'hijacked' Gantenbrink's discovery and, contrary to his wish as well as the regulations of the Egyptian authorities, had rushed to the international media in order to use the discovery of the 'door' to promote myself and my books. More recently, such accusations have been loudly voiced in *The Stargate Conspiracy*, by Lynn Picknett and Clive Prince, where the authors stated:

> Gantenbrink's data had another use: it was seized upon by Robert Bauval, who saw it as a vindication of his theory, developed in the late 1980s, that the southern shaft from the Queen's Chamber was designed to align with Sirius . . . Bauval was so enthusiastic about Gantenbrink's discovery that he took it upon himself to make the announcement to the world's media in early April 1993 . . . Bauval's announcement to the world's media of the discovery of the door also attracted comment from Gantenbrink. Certainly, Bauval completely sidestepped the usual protocol. The news should never have been released without permission of the people whom Gantenbrink was working at the time, the German Archaeological Institute in Cairo and the Egyptian Supreme Council of Antiquities . . . What was the real reason for Bauval's haste in making the announcement to the world? Gantenbrink has no doubts about Bauval's motivation. 'This was a clever PR campaign. Without my discovery, we simply would not know a guy called Robert Bauval.' Gantenbrink goes further: he blames Bauval's premature and unauthorised release of his news to the press for the Egyptian authorities' refusal to allow him to continue his work in the Great Pyramid . . .[17]

In a similar vein, Rudolf Gantenbrink also made a statement to two other British authors, Chris Ogilvie-Herald and Ian Lawton, concerning a court case involving Gantenbrink versus the BBC that took place in 1994. Gantenbrink's statement was published in Ogilvie-Herald's EGYPTNEWS (a cybernetic news station) and subsequently in a book entitled *Giza: The Truth*[18]. Here is the full statement:

1. The first broadcast of filmed material from the shafts was done by a production called 'The Great Pyramid – Gateway to the Stars' which first presented the Bauval/Gilbert star correlation theory world-wide in public, shortly before their book came out.
2. This material was stolen from a home video sample tape.
3. The material was altered by stitching out the time code that had been copied on to this image for security reasons.
4. The material was released against a documented interdiction from myself and the German Archaeological Institute in violation of my copyright.
5. The material was released without any clearance of the Supreme Council of Egyptian Antiquities.
6. The material was illegally rebroadcast after an injunction issued by the High Court in London.
7. This world-wide 'first time' broadcast of shaft material, clearly linked our find to a highly controversial theory.
8. The broadcast led to a legal case at the High Court in London, and to heavy protests from the German Archaeological institute, the British Museum, and the Egyptian Supreme Council of Antiquities.
Remark:
The above claims to my statement are filed at the High Court in London, and at the offices of my lawyers Denton Hall/London.
München 20.1.99
Rudolf Gantenbrink

With such blatant accusations against the BBC and myself, I now feel obliged to break my long silence on this matter and put the record straight. It is something, however, that I take no pleasure in doing – not least because it also forces me to shed new light on other matters which were perhaps best left alone. So I will tell my story as it now must be told, not from memory but from documented evidence. All my intuitive senses tell me that a great find awaits mankind when the little 'door' in the Great Pyramid is finally opened. But this, I also believe, will never happen as long as there is confusion around its discovery. This, perhaps more than any other reason, is why my story needs telling.

First let me begin by saying that it is absolutely true that it was I who released the news of Gantenbrink's discovery to the British press. I have never denied that. But there is much more to this situation than meets the eye, as the evidence will now show. Secondly, it is also true to say that the discovery of the 'door' created a lot of attention towards my work and myself – attention that at first I was not unpleased to receive. Fate played an extraordinary hand here. In 1986 I discovered the 'Sirius' alignment of the southern shaft of the Queen's Chamber in the Great Pyramid; on 6th March 1993 I met Gantenbrink at Giza; two weeks later, on 22nd March, he discovered the 'door' at the end of the shaft. These are historical facts. For better or for worse, the paths of our separate destinies have crossed each other in a manner that no one could have foreseen. It is the stuff that strange synchronicities are made of. It is the way in which, perhaps, the gods amuse themselves. For two so dissimilar and disparate people as Gantenbrink and myself you will never meet. While I, on the one hand, was thrilled and proud of the connection with Gantenbrink, he, on the other hand, felt deeply embarrassed by the association his scientific work had with mine, which he saw as 'New Age' nonsense and 'virtual discoveries'.[19] While I, on the one hand, was open to healthy speculations and discussions on the question of a possible secret chamber at Giza, Gantenbrink was utterly repulsed by such ideas and was closed to any form of speculation. Whilst I regarded the BBC's interest in my work as a wonderful opportunity to share it with the public, Gantenbrink became convinced that the BBC wanted to 'steal' his footage and use it for their own purposes. Gantenbrink and I were, from the outset, a twain that simply never met. Still, I believed – and still do – that he has made a bold discovery in the Great Pyramid, and that our different outlook and work could be put aside. I opted, right from the beginning, to support him. It was to prove a mistake. But on with the story.

Immediately after receiving the Upuaut II project promotional video tape on 4th April 1993, I sent the following faxes to Gantenbrink in order to get some feel as to what he had in mind:

> Thank you for sending the promotion video of the Upuaut project which I received safely today by DHL . . . like I said on the phone, I will approach the top media on this. However, because this is such a sensational discovery, I will discuss this first with a very close friend who is a professional and specialist in production promotion, to see what is the best action that he advises for you in England. Please be assured that any action envisaged will be, of course, only through direct consultation with you and approval. The first thought that we had was whether you would be interested in a TV programme? This can be arranged quickly and we have very good contacts with the BBC . . .[20]

Gantenbrink informed me that he was now taking an extended skiing holiday in Austria. So having received the above fax, he called from the ski-resort on the morning of 5th April to explain how he wanted this matter played with the press and saying that everything had to be controlled and approved through him. I said that I fully understood this and would confirm all these points in writing to him immediately. This was done again by fax, but this time sent to the Hochgurgl Hotel in Austria where Gantenbrink was staying:

5th April 1993

Time 11.15 a.m. Thank you for calling from your hotel in Austria. I hope the skiing is going well and there is good snow. I would like to confirm that I understand the position with regards the promotion video tape on the Upuaut project as follows:
1. The story (in words only) can be given to *The Times* and they can describe or interpret only what they see or hear on the said tape. For this, which is seen as 'news', there are no copyrights involved.
2. Should they, or anyone, wish to show visual material from the said video tape, then they have to get the permission and discuss copyright with yourself at the address this present fax is now transmitted (and where you are till 13th April 1993).
I can also confirm that a contact has been made now, after your call, with *The Times* of London (Ms V. Brooman) and the 'Foreign News Desk' will be calling me shortly hopefully to arrange a viewing. I confirm that only a viewing will be permitted and that the tape will stay safely with me.

I then telephoned the hotel and told Gantenbrink that, in view of the delicate situation in breaking the news of the discovery to the press, I would like to have confirmation of this last fax which I sent to him in Austria. He agreed and promptly sent me a handwritten fax to my home:

5.4.1993

Dear Robert,

Thanks and snow is good. Indeed I can confirm to you that all your remarks from your fax today 11.15 a.m. are completely right.
Looking forward to hear from you.
Rudolf Gantenbrink

The contact with *The Times* proved problematic. The foreign news desk insisted that I send them a copy of the video tape before they could do anything. I told them I could arrange a viewing, but that Gantenbrink had issued very specific instructions that no copies should be handed to the press. I decided to try the *Daily Telegraph*. I was put in touch with their science and technology correspondent, Christine McGourty. Miss

McGourty was agreeable to have a viewing arranged, and suggested that I come to their main offices in Canary Wharf.

Situated on one of the higher levels in Canary Wharf tower, the *Daily Telegraph* office was buzzing with activity. It was my first inside view of the international press. Christine had set up a video player and TV monitor and, as Gantenbrink had instructed, I just showed her the film and told her that the idea was that she should 'report' what she had seen and heard from the voice-over in the film. She said that in order to make a proper article announcing the discovery, it was imperative that she speak to Gantenbrink. We telephoned Gantenbrink from Christine's office and she interviewed him at length. She then said that the story should appear in a day or two. To make sure that Gantenbrink was satisfied with the way this had been handled, I sent him the following fax that same evening:

5.4.1993

8 p.m.

Dear Rudolf,

Christine McGourty of the *Daily Telegraph* (technology-science correspondent) and whom you have spoken to on the phone today, wishes to express her thanks (to you) for speaking to her on the telephone and for the privilege to get the story that she saw in the promotion video. You can expect the story to be out either tomorrow or Wednesday at the latest. As you instructed I let the video speak for itself and have given no comments or speculation of my own. I was asked what was the cultic significance of the shafts and I directed Christine only to the King's shafts and to the consensus given in one of Dr I.E.S. Edwards's articles written in 1981. No comments were given on the Queen's shafts except, I presume, what you told Christine McGourty yourself on the phone.

It was then that I began to realise that no mention, as far as I could make out, was being made by Gantenbrink of the German (Deutsch) Archaeological Institute (DAI) to the press. I did not know how he was playing this card and I did want to meddle in this delicate issue. This was a matter between Gantenbrink and the DAI. Nonetheless I decided to clarify my position at least with Dr Stadelmann, the director of the DAI in Cairo. Stadelmann had been most cordial to me and I did not want him to think that I was acting behind his back. I therefore sent this fax to his office in Cairo to make him aware, at least, that I was now aware of the discovery and that more news was expected:

6th April 1993

Dear Dr Stadelmann,

. . . I must pass my congratulations to you for the find in a shaft of the Queen's Chamber which Mr R. Gantenbrink has told me about recently on the phone. We are all now waiting to hear more news on this.

Gantenbrink did not object to me showing the film to anyone. I felt that at least Dr Edwards and perhaps Dr Jaromir Malek, the Director of the Griffith Institute at the Ashmolean Museum in Oxford, should be privileged to see it. I thus telephoned Dr Edwards and also Dr Malek and arranged meetings with them as soon as possible. I then asked Adrian Gilbert to come and help me with this matter. On the morning of 6th April we drove together to Oxford and first saw Dr Malek. We had brought along a portable video and TV set, and he was shown the film in his office at the Griffith Institute. We then drove to the small village of Deddington where Dr Edwards lived, and we also showed him the film. Dr Edwards's eyesight was failing at the time, and his wife had to describe to him much that was being showed. He carried a large magnifying glass and when the part when the 'door' came up on the screen, Edwards practically jumped from his seat in awe. He wanted to congratulate Gantenbrink on the discovery, and I thus passed him the latter's telephone number in Germany. Dr Edwards felt that I should place the video tape in the custody of Dr Malek. I told him that I would check with Gantenbrink and let him know. I also told Edwards of the situation with the *Daily Telegraph* and he kindly offered to act as a consultant should they wish more official data on the pyramids. I thanked him and duly passed on the message to Christine McGourty:

6th April 1993

Christine McGourty – *Daily Telegraph*.

The video tape will be shown to two prominent Egyptologists this afternoon and, perhaps, they may agree to give their reaction etc . . . please call me if this of interest to you.

The story in the *Daily Telegraph* came out on 7th April. At first I could not find it but then saw it on page seven, in a tiny article that read:

Portcullis blocks robot in Pyramid
A tiny robot designed to investigate an air shaft of the Great Pyramid at Giza has been halted in its tracks by a stone portcullis, researchers said yesterday. Mr Rudolf Gantenbrink, leader of the research project of the German Archaeological Institute in Cairo, said they were very surprised by the discovery in a previously unexplored shaft leading from the Pyramid's so-called Queen's Chamber. The pyramid, about 4500 years old, contains four shafts, originally thought to have been for ventilation, but more recently thought to have been designed to serve as a passageway for the spirit of the dead pharaoh to ascend to the stars. The robot, which was sending video pictures back to a research team in the chamber, came up against the portcullis which has two copper fittings after a two-week, 70-yard journey along the shaft, which measures about eight inches in width and height.

The article attracted absolutely no reaction at all, at least as far as I could make out. Dr Edwards, I recall, could not even find it in the newspaper, and phoned me up to ask on which page it was. I then informed Gantenbrink by fax:

7th April 1993

9.25 a.m.

The story has come out on page 7 of the *Daily Telegraph* of 7th April 1993 . . . I am trying to contact Christine McGourty at the *Telegraph* to see if a more detailed story will follow, perhaps on the weekend. (Just received your call . . .) . . . I therefore confirm that you instructed that I remain the custodian of the tape until further instruction from you. I also confirm that the tape may be shown at my discretion.

Gantenbrink seemed satisfied with the *Daily Telegraph* article, but he, too, was a little disappointed with the apparent lack of reaction. I phoned Christine McGourty to see if they planned to do something bigger over the weekend. Without good and exciting photographs she felt it was not likely. Gantenbrink agreed to supply some photographs of the robot and the exploration, but insisted that he would not give photographs of the 'door'. I decided that the best thing was for me to take a quick trip to Munich to collect them, as well as any other data that could be used for an article.

KEYS TO THE WORLD

It was beautiful spring weather in Munich and Gantenbrink had come down from the Austrian ski-resort especially to meet me. He took me to his home in the fashionable street of Flemingstrasse in the east side of the city. There we watched various films of his exploration and discussed other projects that Gantenbrink wanted to organise. He told me that he had been in discussion with a large American television network, WQED in Pittsburgh, regarding a TV documentary series using the Upuaut project as a pilot. Jochen Breitenstein, who had shot the film of the discovery used for the Upuaut project promotional video, had introduced him to Dale Bell of Public Television International (PTI) from Los Angeles. Gantenbrink was planning to meet Dale Bell in Cannes for the MIP TV market convention. It all sounded very exciting. Gantenbrink was particularly stimulated about an idea he had of setting up a foundation that would sponsor archaeological works not only in Egypt but in other parts of the world. He would call it the Upuaut Foundation and would have it funded by big commercial sponsors and rich businessmen. Apparently Prince Albert of Monaco was very keen to participate. He would, of course, head the foundation himself and asked if I would be interested to join. At first I thought he was joking, but gradually realised that he was deadly serious. I said that I would gladly help, but only on an informal and independent basis. I had my own writing career to take care of, but I felt I could at least act as some sort of representative for Gantenbrink and his foundation in the UK.

It was during this first visit to Munich – and there would be several in the following months – that I learnt that Dr Hawass had been suspended from his post at Giza. It seems that there had been a huge row between him and Dr Bakr, the president of the Egyptian Antiquities Organisation (EAO), and that because of that Dr Hawass was asked to leave his post. This had apparently happened on the 21st March, the day before Gantenbrink's discovery. I tried to find out more about what actually had happened which prompted Gantenbrink to 'resign' from the German Archaeological Institute in Cairo a week after the discovery, but Gantenbrink was a little vague. He was mostly upset that Stadelmann had delayed a statement to the media about the discovery which he and Breitenstein wanted to have released to the press. Apparently Stadelmann did not agree on the wording.[21] Gantenbrink, however, was very concerned about Hawass's departure. They had struck up a good friendship while he had worked at Giza, and he felt that as a result of Hawass's sudden departure he had lost a good ally and supporter.

Gantenbrink then said something that struck me as most odd. He was adamant that Dr Hawass would soon be reinstated his post, and that it would be Dr Bakr's turn to be fired. I dismissed this remark as mere wishful thinking on Gantenbrink's part, and left it at that. It would, however, come to haunt me a few months later. Gantenbrink then supplied me with a set of colour photographs, as well as some documents that he said would be useful for a possible extended article in the newspaper. I tried to persuade Gantenbrink to release a photograph of the 'door', as this would not only bring the right attention to his discovery, but it was high time that this matter was made public through the media. But Gantenbrink was adamant – no photographs of the 'door' would be released.

On the flight back to London, I took out the documents that he had given me. They all seemed to be dealing with various discussions and negotiations about a big television documentary series. One document, which was written by Jochen Breitenstein, grabbed my attention. It was dated February 1992, although judging from the content, the date February 1992 was obviously a mistype and should have been February 1993, that is one month before the discovery of the 'door'. The document was titled 'Saving the monuments of Egypt: Aspects of a Television Series'. In this document Jochen Breitenstein explained how he had met Rudolf Gantenbrink in Munich in November 1992 and how they had decided to team up together to produce a film of the exploration. Through his extensive contacts in the entertainment business Breitenstein had been able 'to enlist the co-operation of one of the leaders in the television industry', public station WQED in Pittsburgh and was confident that 'a broadcast slot for the series thus is secured'. The multi-award-winning WQED network was well-known for its popular series *The National Geographic Specials* and *The Infinite Voyage*. Apparently WQED had assigned an 'Egypt specialist' called Miriam Birch as WQED producer for this particular TV series involving the Upuaut project. This was what the team had in mind:

> We will make use of the robot's quest for the Pyramid's 'Last Secret' and produce a television pilot hinging on this event. It will be designed to create awareness of the aforementioned tasks (i.e. 'saving' the monuments of Egypt) and will serve as a promotional tool for our supporters and allies. The TV series itself, at present 26 episodes are scheduled, will go into production in the fall of 1993. Public Television International (PTI), the marketing arm of QED Communications, will distribute the series either whole or on an episode-by-episode base to TV networks around the world.

Beginning 7th March, 1993, under the auspices of the German Archaeological Institute (DAI) and the supervision of its director, Dr Rainer Stadelmann, a specially designed remote control robot, equipped with a miniature TV camera, will enter the remaining two unexplored shafts of the Great Pyramid. A film crew will be on hand to cover the event.

Another document was faxed to me two days later by Gantenbrink. This one was dated 12th April 1993, that is three weeks after the discovery of the 'door', and was from Dale Bell of PTI International. Bell had laid down an elaborate business plan of how the project would be commercialised on various fronts. The plan had been presented to Pat Butler, a senior executive with the Washington Post and Newsweek Company, who was apparently keen to develop a home video market to rival their main competitors, Time-Life. Dale Bell, whom I was to eventually meet a few years later in connection with a TV documentary for the ABC network about the controversial Swiss-German author Erich Von Daniken,[22] had big ideas in mind. He saw the film footage of the Upuaut project as being the pilot that would launch the Washington Post and Newsweek Company into the home video market world-wide. Interestingly he quoted from a press release – which was presumably provided by Jochen Breitenstein – which announced the discovery of a 'yet-untouched blockage' inside the southern shaft of the Queen's Chamber equipped with 'two copper fittings, most likely locking devices'. Dale Bell mentioned the 'seven-minute promotional video tape edited from the more than twenty hours recorded' during Gantenbrink's two-week exploration in March 1993 and was of the opinion that 'we discern from the (film) release that the slab, with its two copper fittings, the one on the right extending further to the floor than the one on the left, is a stone portcullis, perhaps of polished alabaster, quite possibly shielding a burial site'. Here was what Dale Bell had in mind for a commercial deal:

We want to be able to produce a series of videos, in multiple languages, which will be sold over the air, throughout the world, even before a minute is actually broadcast. Think of the marketing of the *Titanic* as a prime example . . . Because *Newsweek* will be behind the sale of the videos on their 'label', their pages will serve as conduit for advertisers seeking 'sponsorship' to identify with the Upuaut exploration team. Think of 'The Cousteau Society' on sea, the Upuaut Team for land! . . . Once we finally broadcast the videos, domestically and internationally, we may do so on commercial network television, where *Newsweek* already has good access . . . Here lies the 'new frontier', uncovered by the application of science and ingenuity. The Upuaut robot, who with his clever name and hieroglyphics might become a model for merchandising later on, has just this potential . . . I see the Upuaut Team setting up a production company, for the production of the videos, the broadcast tapes, the books, the interactive, and the merchandising, then working out an arrangement with *Washington Post/Newsweek* which allows it first licensing access to much, if not all of our products, for an advance.

Dale Bell also saw the creation of a land-based equivalent of the Jacques Cousteau Society which he referred to as 'The Upuaut Project' that would begin with explorations in Egypt then expand world-wide, with PTI marketing its films, books, videos and general 'merchandising' on a permanent basis. All this, however, depended on having the exclusive usage of the discovery of the 'door' inside the Great Pyramid for a prototype or pilot documentary. The 'door', quite obviously, had acquired a vast commercial value in the mind of Dale Bell.

At any rate, back in England I set about trying to find the right newspaper which could do justice to the importance of the discovery. Again, I made sure that Gantenbrink was informed and fully aware of what was being done – especially now that I had seen those documents which Gantenbrink had handed to me. I thus sent the following telefax to Gantenbrink:

12.4. 1993

Dear Rudolf,

. . . I would like to say thanks again for the friendly welcome in your lovely home in Munich and a very informative session concerning the Upuaut II discovery . . . I am now in my home in England and am getting ready to meet the press and also Edwards tomorrow when everyone gets back to work. I think that you can expect a full feature in either *The Times* or the *Daily Telegraph* for Friday or the weekend edition (which is better, as there is plenty of space to do things more detailed). I will, of course, keep you fully informed.

Dr Edwards had said that he would speak to a friend at *The Times*, but nothing came of it. And Christine McGourty had by now lost interest. It was then that I thought of the *Independent*. I phoned their main office and they said that their archaeological correspondent would perhaps call me later. A few hours later a man called. He introduced himself as David Keys. He seemed very excited and wanted to see the video tape right away. I suggested that he come to my home. Keys, unlike McGourty before him, immediately realised the news value of the discovery and its dramatic implications. He was extremely puzzled, however, that neither the Egyptians nor, indeed, the German Archaeological Institute in Cairo had made a press announcement. It had now been almost two weeks since the discovery, and Keys felt that in view of the universal importance of the monument and the mind-boggling implications of an unopened 'door' deep within it, the news should have gone out within a few days, or a week at the most. He would, therefore, check with the German Archaeological Institute in Cairo to see what the score was on this matter. He nevertheless felt he could get a front-page article in the *Independent* which would, of course, produce a wide interest in the discovery. I decided, therefore, to make sure that everyone involved would be absolutely clear as to what was required. I drafted a sort of 'minutes of meeting' of my discussion with David Keys and faxed it to him. I then transmitted a copy of this fax to Gantenbrink and also to Dr Edwards:

14th April 1993

Dear Rudolf,

Enclosed is a fax sent to David Keys (archaeological correspondent of the *Independent*) which is self-explanatory. I chose the *Independent* because David Keys wants to make a big feature of your discovery. Call me if you need to know more.

(enclosed)

14th April 1993

8 a.m.

To: Archaeological correspondent for the *Independent*

Attention: David Keys

Following our conversation on the telephone today regarding the discovery of Mr Rudolf Gantenbrink in the Cheops Pyramid at Giza (officially called the Upuaut project), I would like to confirm the following:

1. We spoke on the phone at 5 p.m. on 13. 4. 1993.

2. A meeting took place at my residence in Beaconsfield at 9 p.m. to see the material available. You were shown the short video tape entitled 'The Upuaut Project' which witnesses the discovery of the unopened door inside the southern shaft of the Great Pyramid which emanates from the so-called Queen's Chamber.

3. You confirmed that you would very much like to do a feature on this discovery. I have therefore provided you with the following:

a) 6 (six) 8x6 colour prints:

–Exploded view of Cheops pyramid

–Upuaut II inside the shaft

–Upuaut II outside the Pyramid

–The project team working within the Queen's Chamber

–Rudolf Gantenbrink sitting outside the Pyramid

–Rudolf Gantenbrink at the top of pyramid with view over Giza

b) 2 (two) black and white photos showing the Upuaut II robot

c) 4 (four) 8x10 colour photos showing Upuaut II robot inside model shaft with feeding cable.

4. All the above is on loan to the *Independent* to be used, free of any cost, for an archaeological feature. They are to be returned when the feature is complete. Slides for item (a) above if you require them.

5. You were also given the following textual material:

Provided by R. Gantenbrink:

d) Press announcement (8th June 1992) Giza Plateau Egypt (2 pages): this gives background details of the Upuaut project.

e) List of technical sponsors for Upuaut I & II projects (2 pages).

f) Aspects of a (future) TV series (2 pages)

Provided by R. Bauval:

g) Article by Dr I.E.S. Edwards (1981) (2 pages)

h) Article by A. Badawi (1964) (16 pages)

i) Article by R. Bauval (1990) (8 pages)

(telephone numbers of R. Gantenbrink in Munich and Dr I.E.S. Edwards in Oxford also provided)

Before the publication of the article David Keys had conversations with Rudolf Gantenbrink over the phone. He also spoke to Dr Edwards. This is apparent from the content of his article.[23] I remember Keys also telling me that he had attempted to speak to someone at the German Archaeological Institute in Cairo and also with the Egyptian Antiquities Organisation, but I have no written record of this. At any rate, on the evening of the 15th April David Keys telephoned me to let me know that there was a good chance that the article would appear in the next morning's edition. He also was very hopeful of a front-page title, but would not know of this till much later in the night, just before the closing of the final editorial decisions. He read me the article over the phone, and I told him it sounded fine with me, but he needed to clear it with Gantenbrink. This, he said, he would do by reading it over the phone to Gantenbrink. He explained that it was not up to him as to what title the article would be under, as this was usually decided by the chief editor himself, especially in the case of a front-page story. Had we known what was in store, I think that both Gantenbrink and I would have objected, and asked for a different title. But as it turned out we did not have a say in this matter.

At about one in the morning Keys telephoned to say that he had just got the green light for the front page of tomorrow's edition. It was excellent news and we all waited with great anticipation. Adrian Gilbert was staying at my home, and we got up at six in the morning to get the papers. On the lower part of the front page was a diagram of the Great Pyramid showing the possible location of a 'chamber' behind Gantenbrink's door, and underneath it ran the following banner title: INTACT CHAMBER FOUND IN GREAT PYRAMID. It was, without doubt, a very provocative title which was stretching the speculation too far. It would have been far better for the newspaper to have added the word 'possible' and still get the same effect. But it was now too late to change things. Gantenbrink was not particularly upset, since he argued that it was David Keys and not him who had written the article. The article itself was fair and reasonable, although Keys had given it the necessary spark which the *Daily Telegraph* story had lacked. This time my name was also briefly mentioned in connection with the stellar significance of the shafts. Keys felt that this was justified. I had, after all, published the results in an academic journal, and my work had attracted the attention of eminent Egyptologists such as Dr Edwards. Later that day Keys phoned me to let me know that the *News at Seven* team at Channel Four wanted to cover the story that same evening. Keys also wanted me to participate, but I declined. This was Gantenbrink's moment of glory, and he should savour it alone. It was during that TV programme that Dr Edwards dropped the Egyptological bombshell by saying that he expected that behind the 'door' might be a statue of the king gazing towards the constellation of Orion. Naturally everyone wanted to know what he meant by this, and he, in turn, directed them to me, as he regarded me as the authority on this particular matter.[24]

Following the article in the *Independent* and the *News at Seven* TV broadcast, the story was picked up by the international press and a sort of media Chinese-whispers broke loose. The discovery of Gantenbrink hit the headlines in the top newspapers around the world, including *The Times* and the *Daily Telegraph* which had turned down the story a few days earlier. For three days it was total chaos as I was being chased by news-mongers who wanted to get hold of the Upuaut project video tape. Every TV network wanted footage of the robot finding the 'door', and every newspaper wanted a photograph of it. By not showing it, a huge 'demand factor' was being created. I informed Gantenbrink that I was getting angry calls from the press who were thinking that the visual material was being withheld to hype it for commercial reasons. Both Adrian Gilbert and I, as well as others such as David Keys and Dr Edwards, felt that a photograph of the 'door' should now be released to the press. I urged Gantenbrink to do so as soon as possible. But there was no changing his mind. He had his own views on this matter, and he would not be swayed. Meanwhile Dr Edwards advised that Gantenbrink should present his findings at a proper Egyptological conference. Dr Edwards suggested the British Museum as a venue, and a date was fixed for 22nd May 1993. Gantenbrink brought along his robot and was met at Heathrow Airport by my brother, Jean-Paul, who drove him to the British Museum. Meanwhile Adrian and I were organising the conference at the museum itself with Dr Edwards.[25]

At the start of his presentation, Rudolf Gantenbrink made an unexpected announcement: he offered, as a gift, the Upuaut robot to the British Museum.[26] He said, however, that he needed it for just one day to have it examined by a metallurgist in Surrey organised by David Keys before handing it to the British Museum for safekeeping. That night Rudolf, along with his robot, stayed at my home in Buckinghamshire. There, too, was Adrian Gilbert and my brother Jean-Paul. The next morning David Keys came by, and we all drove to Surrey. David Keys and Rudolf wanted a specialist in metal corrosion to examine some strange oxidisation that had formed on the robot. When this was done, my brother took Rudolf to Heathrow Airport and I was entrusted to deliver the robot to Dr Vivian Davies at the British Museum.[27]

It was at about that time that a huge dispute over the discovery began to be generated in Egyptological circles, particularly from the Germans. At first the debate was purely academic, namely whether the claim of a possible secret chamber was justified. According to *The Times*, the suggestion of a secret chamber had dismayed scientists at the German Archaeological Institute. There was, too, a rather confusing statement made by Dr Rainer Stadelmann, the director of the German Archaeological Institute in Cairo. Stadelmann was quite obviously upset at the way the news of the discovery had been handled in the media. He chose to downplay the find, arguing that the 'door' was merely a stone block leading nowhere.[28] Dr Gunter Dreyer of the German Institute also said to *The Times* that Rudolf Gantenbrink 'has got the idea that there is something big behind the door. But it's all imagination. No chamber has been discovered yet.'[29] Gantenbrink then replied in the *Independent* that 'the information that we have gathered so far does not exclude a chamber . . . it is indeed a possibility'.[30] Dr Edwards was even more bold on this issue: 'The presence of a door, complete with its copper handles, suggests that something important lies behind it.'[31] He also told *The Times* that he believed 'it is possible . . . that a secret chamber with a religious significance awaits discovery'.[32]

There was, too, the opinion of the Egyptian authorities to consider. The German Archaeological Institute in Cairo claimed that the Egyptians were upset about the 'unauthorised' release of the news, and feared this would cause problems.[33] Apparently the Egyptians had not been told of the intention to release the news to the press, and took this as an affront. Gantenbrink denied this, and told *The Times* that he had contacted various Egyptian officials but without response: 'It is purely their fault. If you try to hide a sensation you will have a big mess'.[34] The Egyptians expressed their anger in an inflammatory article that appeared in the *Egyptian Gazette* with the banner title: **German Scientists Claim a Hoax**. The article was written around interviews with Dr Mohamad Bakr, the president of the Egyptian Antiquities Organisation, and Dr Ali Hassan, director of Pharaonic Antiquities. Oddly, Dr Bakr accused the 'German scientist' of duping him and said that no permission had been granted for the exploration of the shafts. Indeed Bakr seemed to be rather perplexed as to how the discovery had been made in the first place since, he insisted, 'the EAO never granted its approval to this German'.[35] Dr Ali Hassan also expressed the very same view. According to Hassan:

> It has become clear that the foreign missions in Egypt have breached the limits controlling their activities in the country: the German Archaeological Institute

in Cairo had previously committed such a grave error when its officials launched self-determined studies inside the Great Pyramid although they (the EAO) had been told (that the work was) to clean out the ventilation openings there so as to replenish the airflow inside the burial room of this pyramid.

According to the *Egyptian Gazette*, Dr Ali Hassan 'strongly denied' that approval had been given to the 'German scientist' for this exploration. It was clear that as far as Dr Bakr and Dr Hassan were concerned, they had been kept in the dark as to what had happened there during those two weeks in March 1993, and that certain activities in the Queen's Chamber had taken place without their approval. But how could this be possible? If not under their approval, then under whose approval had Gantenbrink and his TV crew operated in the Queen's Chamber? I telephoned Gantenbrink to find out what had happened. Having aided him in bringing the news out in the international media, I now felt a little awkward to have been implicated in a scheme that had clearly very much incensed the high officials at the EAO. I urged Gantenbrink to make clear this matter. He explained that there had been three 'campaigns' that he had undertaken at the Great Pyramid.[36] The first was in January 1992 when he explored the lower part of the shafts of the Queen's Chamber with a robot under the direct responsibility and licence accorded to the German Archaeological Institute. The second 'campaign' was in May to June 1992, when he had cleared the 'air-shafts' of the King's Chamber and installed a ventilation system with electric fans; this too was under the direct responsibility of the German Archaeological Institute. The third 'campaign' was from 7th to 28th March 1993, which is when he had come with the television crew (Jochen Breitenstein and Dirk Brakebusch) to shoot a 'commercial' film. It was this last that Dr Bakr and Dr Hassan of the Egyptian Antiquities Organisation were referring to when they claimed that no approval had been granted.

The reason for their statements was probably this: after the second 'campaign' of May and June 1992, Gantenbrink had asked Dr Rainer Stadelmann, the director of the German Archaeological Institute in Cairo, for his assistance in obtaining the permits necessary for shooting a film with a television crew which he, Gantenbrink, intended to bring to Giza on 6th March 1993. Dr Stadelmann apparently agreed and offered to arrange for the necessary permits and security clearances for Gantenbrink and his television crew. But when Gantenbrink and the crew had turned up on 7th March 1993, they found out that Dr Stadelmann had not obtained these permits for them. So rather than abort the mission, Gantenbrink went to see Dr Hawass who, according to

Gantenbrink, gave him 'verbal permission' to carry on. The day before the discovery Hawass was suspended from his post at Giza following a scandal related to the loss of some valuable ancient artefacts from the store at Giza.[37] In spite of this, Gantenbrink carried on with his activities inside the Queen's Chamber, discovered the 'door' on the morning of 22nd March, and carried on with exploration of the northern shaft till 28th March.[38] He then 'resigned' and he and the television crew then packed their gear and left for Munich. It was four days after that, on 1st April, that he and I got in contact by phone.

What Gantenbrink called the 'third campaign' was in fact a commercial filming project that required a type of commercial licence of a quite different nature held by the German Institute. Such a licence was normally issued by the Egyptian Ministry of Information and formally approved by the Egyptian Antiquities Organisation. Hawass's 'verbal' permission was, of course, inappropriate and, strictly speaking, in contravention to the regulations of the Egyptian authorities. This breach was made the more serious because of the nature of what Gantenbrink was filming, namely an exploration work within a national monument under the jurisdiction of the Ministry of Culture and the EAO. No wonder, therefore, the public outcry in the *Egyptian Gazette* by Dr Bakr and Dr Hassan. Gantenbrink did not see it that way. He held Dr Stadelmann responsible for this mess and considered himself totally absolved of any misbehaviour since he had carried out his activities under the protection of Hawass's 'verbal permission'. I pointed out to him that although I could understand his viewpoint, the fact remained that, if what he had told me was correct, then it was clear that Gantenbrink had, unwittingly, carried out his activities outside the framework of the law in Egypt. At any rate Hawass had been suspended from his post and was no longer with the Egyptian Antiquities Department and was thus unable to validate his 'verbal permission'. This, of course, changed everything. I could now understand the reticence of Dr Stadelmann to participate in the release of the news with the discovery of the 'door' since, strictly speaking, it had been carried out outside the bounds of the German Archaeological Institute. I could also understand the anger and frustration expressed by Dr Bakr and Dr Hassan when they realised what had happened. In this light, then, it also became apparent to me that breaking the news in England had only antagonised the Egyptians even more. I certainly was not pleased with this turn of events. In any case, the damage had been done and nothing could change this. As I mentioned earlier, against all odds Gantenbrink was confident that Dr Hawass would very soon be reinstalled in his post at Giza, and that Dr Bakr would himself be dismissed. I did not share Gantenbrink's confidence in this matter, and felt it a most unlikely outcome.

Meanwhile the media continued to rumble, with Gantenbrink's discovery making it to various top international magazines such as the influential *Stern* and *Die Spiegel* of Germany, as well as many of the fringe periodicals.[39] It was in *Stern* that Gantenbrink decided to first release images of the 'door'.[40] Curiously, Gantenbrink also chose the magazine *Ancient Skies*, owned by the controversial Swiss-German author Erich Von Daniken, to later release photographs of the door and details of the explorations.[41] Apparently the two men had met at Giza prior to the discovery and had formed a cordial friendship. Another German cutting-edge magazine that ran the story in Germany was *GRAL* edited by Michael Hasse. The latter had previously edited Von Daniken's *Ancient Skies* magazine.[42]

In May 1993 Gantenbrink put me in touch with Dr Jean Kerisel, the French engineer who had also, before Gantenbrink, made detailed studies of the ventilation of the Great Pyramid and the idea of using booster fans in the shafts of the King's Chamber to lower the excessive humidity.[43] Kerisel was keen to organise a major presentation for Rudolf Gantenbrink in Paris to which he would invite top Egyptologists and academics. During the month of June Kerisel and I collaborated in preparing this conference, which took place on 21st June at the Fédération Des Travaux Publiques in Paris. Present were many eminent Egyptologists such as Dr Edwards, Jean Vercouter, and Jean-Philip Lauer.

It was right after this conference that I was contacted by Chris Mann of the BBC. What was to follow would eventually lead to one of the most exotic cases ever taken to the High Courts of England.

THE GREAT PYRAMID GOES TO COURT

Chris Mann is a senior producer with the BBC at the Religious Department, the largest in this legendary British institution. On a sunny day in early April 1993, sitting at an outdoor café in London, Chris fell upon the article in the *Independent* newspaper on Rudolf Gantenbrink's discovery in the Great Pyramid where my name was mentioned in connection with the religious significance of the shafts. At the time the Religious Department, which was under the control of John Blake, was looking for new ideas to expand its documentary programmes into new areas for their viewers. Chris immediately saw an opportunity with

Gantenbrink's discovery to launch this new concept. He, too, like many other television networks at the time, was fired by the idea of a 'live' broadcast of the opening of the 'door'. He called the British Museum who put him in touch with me. We eventually met in early July 1993. I invited him to my home for a showing of the Upuaut project promotional video. Chris was extremely excited and asked to be put into direct contact with Gantenbrink.

While I was trying to get Gantenbrink on the phone, Chris noticed a set of photographs on my office wall. One of them was an overhead of the three Pyramids of Giza and the other was an enlarged photograph of the three stars of Orion's belt. Chris asked why these two photographs were placed next to each other. I told him to look again more closely. He gasped, and began to pour out questions at me, seeing suddenly the centrepiece of a programme he could do on ancient Egypt and its mysterious pyramid cult. The 'door' began to take on a completely new perspective for him, and so did the shafts. Chris visualised a whole BBC evening on the Great Pyramid, part of which would deal with the archaeological aspect of Gantenbrink's work, and another part with the religious and symbolic meaning of the monuments and its mysterious shafts. Preliminary discussions with Gantenbrink were arranged for 20th July 1993. Unable to come himself, Gantenbrink sent his new 'public relations' representative, a man called Olaf Schroter, who was the director of a company called Media Design Consulting based in Hanover. I was surprised not to see Jochen Breitenstein, but I found out later that he and Gantenbrink had fallen out. The meeting between Olaf Schroter and the BBC took place at the BBC's London offices in Great Portland Street. Present at this meeting were Olaf Schroter, John Blake, Chris Mann, Adrian Gilbert and myself. Further to this meeting, and upon Schroter's request, the BBC sent a full proposal to Gantenbrink on 30th July 1993.[44] The idea at the time was to make a 'live' broadcast from the BBC studios integrating the Upuaut project and its discoveries with the star-correlation theory presented in my forthcoming book *The Orion Mystery*.

The next few months were spent in negotiations between Gantenbrink and Olaf Schroter on the one hand, and the BBC team on the other. Gantenbrink informed the BBC that he preferred to make his own documentary in Munich which he could then sell to the BBC. This documentary was to be called *Robot's Journey into the Past* and would be about fifty minutes long. As for the BBC, it was decided that they would produce their own documentary to be called *The Great Pyramid: Gateway to the Stars* as an *Everyman* special. For this documentary the

BBC offered to buy some footage – about two minutes – from Gantenbrink of the robot filming the discovery of the 'door'. With these two documentaries, the BBC thus planned a whole evening on Egypt for broadcast in early February 1994. The idea was to show Gantenbrink's documentary first, followed by the BBC's. According to Chris Mann, the BBC had agreed to pay Rudolf Gantenbrink £50,000 for his own film being made in Munich, and £80 per second for footage provided by Gantenbrink for their own film. The BBC planned to start filming for the latter on location in Egypt early in December 1993. Meanwhile, unknown to us some strange things were happening in Egypt.

In late June 1993 rumours began to circulate that Dr Hawass would soon be returning to his post at Giza. His arch-rival, Dr Mohamad Bakr, who was responsible for Hawass's departure back in March 1993, was himself fired from his post as president of the Egyptian Antiquities Organisation in late June 1993. Three weeks later, in a bizarre article headed **Egyptologist Claims 'Mafia' Link to Crime at Pyramids**, *The Times* correspondent in Cairo, Christopher Walker, reported:

> (Mohamad) Ibrahim Bakr, the expert removed from his post as chief of Egypt's vast archaeological heritage three weeks ago, has accused an official 'mafia' of controlling the Giza pyramids plateau for the last twenty years. Dr Bakr, who is highly respected among international Egyptologists, claimed that the plateau on the outskirts of Cairo has suffered widespread theft of antiquities and widespread financial malpractices which the 'mafia' wanted hushed up. 'This was the main issue,' Dr Bakr said of his resignation. 'I wanted these practices reported to the prosecution authorities, but my request was turned down.' In an interview with the *Al Ahram*, Dr Bakr disclosed that his departure came after personal differences with Farouk Hosni, the culture minister . . . Dr Bakr claimed angrily that 'certain people' whom he did not identify, acted as if the Giza plateau . . . was their private property. 'The exploitation ranged from entrance fees paid by visitors, to documentary films which they shot at Giza and sold abroad. Lately they even refused to register newly discovered antiquities.'[45]

Who was this 'mafia' that Dr Bakr was referring to? What 'personal differences' did he have with Farouk Hosni, the Minister of Culture, which caused his 'resignation'? And which 'documentary films' was he alluding to?[46] All this was very confusing. At this time, however, I had to put aside all this intrigue and concentrate on the writing of *The Orion Mystery* with Adrian Gilbert. Delivery was scheduled for August 1993, and we had much work to do. At any rate, not much happened on the matter of the 'door' till November 1993.

On 22nd November 1993, Gantenbrink paid his second official visit to the British Museum in London. This time he came to show more video films of the shafts, especially the northern shaft.[47] On this occasion Gantenbrink, Jean Kerisel and I were invited by Dr Edwards to London's prestigious Athenaeum Club in Piccadilly, where we all enjoyed an excellent meal and a long discussion on the Great Pyramid. After lunch I drove the little group to the British Museum, where Rudolf gave a one-hour audio-visual presentation to many eminent Egyptologists, including I.E.S. Edwards, George Hart, Richard Parkinson, Vivien Davies, T.G.H. James and Carol Andrews. After the presentation, Gantenbrink was interviewed on camera by the BBC for the programme they were making based on my book.[48]

On 10th December the BBC flew Adrian Gilbert and me to Cairo, where we joined Chris Mann and his crew at the Mena House hotel at Giza. A few days later we were joined by the television presenter Emma Freud, and filmed mostly at Giza till 20th December. On 21st December Chris Mann and I flew to Munich in order to attend a party organised by Gantenbrink to celebrate the completion of his documentary *Robot's Journey into the Past*. It was a very formal occasion, and among the guests were Jean Kerisel, my brother Jean-Paul, and the author Erich Von Daniken. Everyone was in high spirits and enjoying the evening. It was during this occasion that Rudolf distributed a very impressive glossy brochure entitled 'The Upuaut Project'. In it he presented the idea of a land-based 'Jacques Cousteau' style enterprise which would kick off with the film *Robot's Journey into the Past* followed by a ten-part television series on archaeology. A model of a huge, four-wheel base land vehicle, with 'The Upuaut Project' written across its body, was shown trekking over dunes in the desert. After the meal Rudolf gave a short speech and then his film was shown. It was a documentary, as expected, very much centred around Rudolf and his work at Giza. While watching I noted the exact angle of the southern shaft of the Queen's Chamber – 39.6 degrees – which was displayed on the monitor of his robot in a scene in the film.[49] Although the film was impeccably made, it clearly was made as a 'pilot' for an extensive series which would be related to the Upuaut project team, much like the one proposed earlier by Dale Bell of PTI. Gantenbrink insisted that the BBC had been aware of his intentions for this film to be a 'pilot' from the outset. On the other hand Chris Mann and John Blake of the BBC insisted that they had made it clear to Gantenbrink and Olaf Schroter that they reserved the right to adapt the film to suit the BBC's requirements. This difference in opinion was eventually to lead to a clash between Gantenbrink and the BBC.

In January 1994, just a few weeks before the scheduled broadcast for the BBC, Gantenbrink informed Chris Mann and John Blake that he now wished to stop his dealings with them, which also meant that he did not want to allow the BBC to use the two minutes of footage for their documentary.[50] Chris Mann and John Blake, understandably, were not amused. Not only was Gantenbrink blowing the opportunity of having his film aired on BBC prime time, but he was also putting into serious jeopardy the BBC's own documentary which was to be shown immediately after Gantenbrink's. Nothing, however, would sway Gantenbrink from this unfortunate decision. So in desperation the BBC decided to contact Dr Ali Hassan, the Under-secretary of State for Pharaonic Antiquities at the EAO. They were hoping somehow that he could have some leverage in this matter. It was then that a fundamental problem regarding the films shot by Gantenbrink at the Great Pyramid emerged for the first time.

Here is the sequence of events as they actually happened. On 20th January 1994 Romaine Lancaster, the assistant director to Chris Mann at the BBC, telephoned Dr Hassan in Cairo. It was then that Dr Hassan dropped his bombshell by saying to Romaine that the commercial filming rights that the BBC had been negotiating with Rudolf Gantenbrink since July 1993 did not belong to Gantenbrink at all. Perplexed, Romaine immediately informed Chris Mann. After several attempts to speak to Dr Hassan on the phone, Chris Mann decided to send him a fax asking him to explain this unexpected turn of events. Dr Hassan replied:

27 January 1994

Dear Dr Mann,

Answering your fax dated at twenty-six of January 1994.

I would like to inform you that the agreement between the Egyptian Antiquities Organisation (EAO) and the German Institute concerning the work in the Queen's Chamber of the Great Pyramid is a scientific and academic work, and in the agreement no one is allowed to use any results of this work for commercial business.

The Pyramid is in Egypt and the work has been done in Egypt and all the materials of this work belong to the EAO, and according to the agreement they (the German Institute) have the right to publish it but not to sell it.

Professor Dr Ali Hassan

It seems that not only had Gantenbrink been aware of this 'agreement' all along, but he had actually signed a 'statement' to that effect to Dr Rainer Stadelmann, the head of the German Archaeological Institute in

Cairo.[51] In this statement Gantenbrink had clearly recognised and accepted that he and all participants in the project related to the air-channels of the Great Pyramid were legally bound not to use any material such as films or pictures shot during the work for publicity or public showing or for commercial reasons without the written approval of the relevant Egyptian authorities. Furthermore Gantenbrink had signed this 'statement' in early September 1993 yet, amazingly, was still negotiating as late as January 1994 with the BBC's contracts manager, Andrea Ramsden-Cooke, to supply the BBC with his film plus the two minutes of footage to the BBC for a sum exceeding £50,000.[52] The logical thing to do now, in view of the urgency of the matter, was for the BBC to ask the EAO's permission to broadcast two minutes from the Upuaut project promotional video, a copy of which had been supplied to them by Gantenbrink early during the negotiations. They offered, of course, to pay any reasonable fees set by the EAO. According to the BBC, Dr Hassan gave the green light, and also stated that, because time was short (the BBC transmission date had now been fixed for 6th February 1994) the question of fees between the BBC and the EAO could be settled at a later date.

On 28th January 1994, a week before transmission of the BBC's *The Great Pyramid: Gateway to the Stars*, the BBC received a written warning from Gantenbrink's lawyers that should they make use of the film footage in question, the latter intended to take the matter to the High Court in London. The BBC was put in a very awkward position. The programme had already been announced to the media, and the *Radio Times* had prepared a cover feature coming out soon. It was too late to comply with Gantenbrink's request. At any rate, Dr Hassan had made it clear that all the material of this project – which included film commercial rights – 'belonged to the EAO'.[53] The BBC had not much choice but to go ahead with their broadcast as planned. On 6th February 1993 at 9 p.m. the documentary was aired by BBC 2. A week later, on 14th February, Gantenbrink instructed his lawyers, Denton Hall of London, to instigate legal proceedings against the BBC. The Great Pyramid, as incredible as it might sound, was to be taken to the High Courts of London.

GANTENBRINK VS THE BBC

This bizarre turn of events inevitably put a strain on my relationship with Gantenbrink. Adrian Gilbert and I had tried our best to prevent this clash between Gantenbrink and the BBC, but to no avail.[54] As much as I had admired Gantenbrink and his work, I was appalled by his litigious action against the BBC. The latter were, after all, going to ensure that he and his discovery of the 'door' in the Great Pyramid would receive world-wide recognition and acclaim. The BBC was also willing to pay the substantial fees for the rights of the films demanded by Gantenbrink. And now, ironically, they were being taken to task at the High Court. It was I who, after all, had introduced the BBC to Gantenbrink and, naturally, I did not feel pleased with the way things had turned out between them. I decided to remain neutral as much as I could.

On 17th March 1994, some ten days after the BBC's broadcast, I received an urgent telephone call from Tom Weldon, my editor at William Heinemann Books Ltd. Tom had just received a letter from Denton Hall, the lawyers of Rudolf Gantenbrink. It was a legal warning that no 'material' from the Upuaut project should be incorporated in my book, *The Orion Mystery*, without permission from Gantenbrink.[55] Since the book had already been published two weeks earlier on 7th February, Tom was naturally very concerned. I reassured him that all the 'material' we used – which amounted to one black and white 'official' photograph of the robot – had been approved by Gantenbrink. As for the narrative concerning the latter, I had actually shown a final proof of the book to Gantenbrink back in November 1993, and had accommodated some changes he had asked for, mainly on the episode dealing with the release of the news to the press in April 1993. He wanted to disassociate himself from this event and so, upon his request, the wording was adjusted accordingly.[56] I could not understand why Gantenbrink felt compelled to instruct his lawyers to take such action and, more annoyingly, had not informed me about it beforehand.[57] It was at this point that I felt a certain allegiance and responsibility towards the BBC. It was unfair that they be treated that way, and I decided I would try and help them clear this legal situation. My objective was to help all parties find an amicable – or at least a workable – solution instead of battling it out in court.

I contacted Chris Mann who welcomed my support and put me in touch with Roy Baker, the BBC lawyer dealing with this case.[58] I made it clear to Baker that my involvement was to be on a purely friendly basis. I wanted no part in this litigation but only wished to help and see if, perhaps, I could help bring the matter to a close with everyone involved receiving fair dues.[59] Here was the crux of the problem: Gantenbrink had submitted his affidavit to the High Court wherein, under oath, he claimed to have negotiated with Bo Carson Entertainment (who were involved with a film related to the discovery of the *Titanic* wreckage) for the exploitation of the commercial rights of his filming 'project' and who, with NBC backing, had, according to Gantenbrink, come up with figures of six million dollars for the US market, and ten million dollars for world-wide rights.[60] Much of the commercial value of the filming project depended, of course, on the potential filming of the opening of the 'door' by Gantenbrink. The latter was of the opinion that the BBC had jeopardised his chance to make such a film, and, deeming that since this potential project was worth at least as much as the *Titanic* project, Gantenbrink claimed damages in six figures from the BBC. At any rate, the big questions that needed resolving were these: [1] who exactly owned the legal rights to commercialise the films that were shot by Gantenbrink and his TV crew in the Queen's Chamber and in its shafts? [2] who owned the copyrights of these films?

The first question dealing with the commercialisation of the films should have been clear. A priori, the filming was done by Gantenbrink while conducting a scientific exploration on behalf of and under the legal responsibility of the German Archaeological Institute in Cairo. Gantenbrink, like all other participants in this project, was bound by the 'agreement' that existed between the German Institute and the Egyptian Antiquities Organisation (EAO). This 'agreement', as Dr Hassan had pointed out, apparently stipulated that the commercialisation rights were owned by the EAO. Gantenbrink, furthermore, had recognised and agreed to this condition in writing to the German Archaeological Institute.[61] There was one complication, though, that had been caused by an unusual statement made by Dr Rainer Stadelmann, the leader of the German Institute in Cairo. It seems that Dr Stadelmann confirmed to Gantenbrink's lawyers that the 'filming' taken by Gantenbrink 'ran parallel' to the scientific projects and thus was 'not encompassed' by the scientific work. That, on face value, would let Gantenbrink off the hook. And although Dr Stadelmann did not specifically make this clear, the implication was that Gantenbrink could, at least on principle, 'commercialise' the film since it was not shot, according to Dr Stadelmann, as part of a 'scientific work'. But if the film was not shot as part of the scientific work, then it was shot as part of what? The only reason would be as part of a documentary or documentaries intended for commercialisation. But if so, it was not up to Dr Stadelmann or the German Institute to grant such a commercialisation licence to Gantenbrink and his TV crew. So, strictly speaking, it did not matter how Dr Stadelmann wanted to interpret the manner in which the filming was carried out. As far as the EAO was concerned, they had not approved this, nor granted a commercial licence to Gantenbrink, and thus no matter the interpretation given by Dr Stadelmann to the lawyers, the

EAO had a legal right to claim that they owned the commercial rights since all the filming had been shot during the scientific work licensed to the German Archaeological Institute and thus, by law, all participants were bound by the 'agreement' signed between the EAO and the German Institute.

In Egypt, any TV crew wishing to make a commercial film of any antiquities must operate under a formal and written 'commercial licence' approved by the EAO and issued by the Ministry of Information.[62] Although Gantenbrink conceded that no such licence had been granted to him, he claimed that Dr Hawass had given him and his TV crew a 'verbal permission' to do the filming, and this was good enough for him and, by extension, the High Courts of England. He made this claim under oath and so did his two TV crew members, Jochen Breitenstein and Dirk Brakebusch. Dr Hassan, however, had told the BBC that Hawass had no right to do so and that in any case, Dr Hawass had not done so. Dr Hawass had, since early in 1994, been reinstated in his post of Director-General of the Giza Plateau with the EAO. Thus the best and only way to solve this matter was for the BBC to ask Dr Hawass himself. In person.

MEETING WITH THE 'KING' OF GIZA

In early May 1994, I flew to Cairo with Roy Baker, the BBC's lawyer. Roy had never been to Egypt and had asked me to assist him in this matter. I, too, wanted to get to the bottom of this strange story, and I wholeheartedly agreed to lend a hand. Although Dr Hawass had much commented on my work on radio and television,[63] I had never actually met the man himself. It proved to be quite an adventure. At first it seemed almost impossible to pin him down. He was either out of his office or busy with other visitors and guests. Finally, under the advice of some Egyptian friends in Cairo, we decided to drop in on him at the local coffee bar in central Cairo he and his colleagues hung about most evenings. He was most cordial and immediately apologised for all this delay. I remember being very impressed by this formidable man. Handsome and very presentable, he spoke with the self-confidence of an army general and with refreshing openness and directness.

Hawass is a man who does not mince his words. He obviously was upset with all this 'nonsense' and said he would be more than glad to assist the BBC with their enquiries. He gave us an appointment to see him the next day in his office at Giza. We turned up at 11 a.m., and after the customary waiting we were taken into his office. Hawass's daily job is to run the administration of the Giza necropolis. Under him are some dozen chief and junior inspectors, a varying number of archaeologists and students on work assignments, and the usual horde of secretaries and tea boys that no self-respecting public servant in Egypt would do without. Hawass put the phone down and explained that he had been talking to Gantenbrink. He was clearly miffed. Roy Baker explained that it was necessary to get a formal statement regarding this affair and, without much ado, asked Hawass whether it was true that he had given 'verbal permission' to Gantenbrink or his TV crew to shoot video films outside the jurisdiction of the scientific work carried out by the German. Hawass was totally indignant about such a question. Of course no such verbal permission had been given, he exclaimed, and had he known that such filming was taking place, he would have immediately put a stop to it. He then suggested that we deal with this matter with Dr Abdel Halim Nureldin, his superior and chairman of the EAO. Dr Hawass insisted that it was Dr Nureldin and the EAO permanent committee that dealt with matters of filming licences, not he. That was it. We thanked him and went to see Dr Nureldin. The latter had also asked Dr Stadelmann to come to his office at the same time. Dr Nureldin confirmed what both Dr Hassan and Dr Hawass had said: the commercial rights of the films belonged to the EAO, and the BBC must deal with them for matters of fees and permissions to broadcast. Affidavits were taken by Roy Baker and we returned to our hotel at Giza. Back in England Roy Baker informed Gantenbrink's lawyers of his findings in Cairo, and it was eventually decided among the parties to settle the issue out of court.[64] The battle over the Great Pyramid was over. At least for now.

POETIC LICENCE

In the course of the following months I was much occupied with the writing of my next book, *Keeper of Genesis*, which I was co-authoring with Graham Hancock. This book was looking into the controversy over the age of the Sphinx and we had decided to narrate aspects of the various explorations that had taken place at Giza in recent years. The Gantenbrink story was, of course, on our agenda. After the saga at the High Court with the BBC, Gantenbrink had cut communications with me. Eventually we began talking again, and I assured him that, no matter what our differences, he would have my support in his efforts to resume his explorations in the Queen's Chamber.[65] The German Institute, as well as the EAO, officially took the position with the media that the reason for not allowing Gantenbrink to return to Giza in order to resume the exploration of the shafts was because he had gone to the press with his discovery without the consent of the Egyptian authorities. I said that I would maintain my position – which I still do – that it was I who had, technically speaking, gone to the press with the news of the discovery of the 'door' back in April 1993. I took this position officially with Dr Helmut Kerieleis, president of the German Archaeological Institute in Berlin,[66] as well as with Dr Abdel Halim Nureldin, president of the EAO in Cairo.[67] I did the same with the public whenever I spoke at conferences or to the media.[68] Strictly speaking, it was true and I could say, hand on heart, that I did go to the British press back in April 1993. I was quite happy to take the blame. I believe in the total freedom of information of public interest and I had had, after all, no binding obligation with the German Archaeological Institute or the EAO not to release the news. But above all, by taking this position I felt this would at least increase the chances for Gantenbrink's return to Giza.

It was around that time that I decided to get more details from Gantenbrink about what actually had happened during the so-called 'third campaign' at the Great Pyramid which took place on 7th to 28th March 1993. One of the things that had nagged me was something that I had seen on the Upuaut project promotional video and which, later on, was broadcast also on the BBC film. Now, knowing the problems with the permits for the filming licences that had taken place, there was a particular scene in the promotional video which didn't quite add up. This was when Gantenbrink is seen making the discovery of the 'door' at 11.05 a.m. on 22nd March 1993. In this scene, just as the robot films the 'door' for the first time, we see Gantenbrink sitting on a chair gazing intensely at the monitor screen on which the images of the 'door' are displayed. Huddled around him are four men, three Egyptians and one European. The European was Ulrich (Ulli) Kapp, a representative of the German Archaeological Institute in Cairo. Ulli Kapp has been with the Institute for many years and the reader will recall that he had worked with Mark Lehner in 1982-84 during the Sphinx project collaboration between the American Research Centre in Egypt and the Edgar Cayce Foundation. He had a reputation for being very professional and reliable. Rudolf, however, eventually admitted that the scene shown in the video was not representative of what had actually happened that day in the Queen's Chamber. Ulli Kapp had not been present. In fact Dr Stadelmann had taken him off the job on 19th March, three days before the discovery. According to Gantenbrink there was an entirely different group of people with him in the Queen's Chamber on the day and time of the discovery.

But why had he shown the 'wrong' people on the film? I knew how meticulous and finicky he was with detail, so what could have induced him to do this? Apparently there was no actual footage of him and those people who had been in the chamber to use for the promotional film, so he applied 'poetic licence', i.e. made do with other imagery, even if not of the actual event. But surely a TV crew constantly on stand by – indeed a crew he had brought specifically to film this event – would have ensured that there would have been plenty of footage of this event to choose from? They had managed to film the 'wrong' people without too much problem, so why not film the 'right' people for future broadcasts and for historical posterity? At any rate, whatever the reason, this was an oversight that could throw much doubt on the authenticity and credibility of the piece. There was another problem here. The scene with the 'wrong' people had been aired not only on the BBC but also on many other channels around the world. Gantenbrink had also used it himself in his documentary *Robot's Journey into the Past* which had since been aired in the USA and other countries as well, and, I believe, also in Egypt.[69] Furthermore, I now remembered that Gantenbrink had also sent copies of the promotional video to the Egyptian Minister of Culture[70] as well as to many other government departments including the Ministry of Tourism.[71] It was, in fact, this very promotional film that he had sent to me to show to the press and had made a specific point that they must report only what they saw and heard on this tape. But why would he or anyone want the press to report what was clearly a fabrication? At the very least he should have made it clear to me and the press that what we were seeing on the video tape regarding the moment of discovery was 'poetic licence'. It was important that such a great event in the history of Egyptian archaeology involving the Great Pyramid be reported accurately – especially the circumstances of the discovery itself.[72] But, as it turned out, this oversight was but the tip of the iceberg.

ARCHAEOLOGICAL WATERGATE

To avoid further confusion, as well as to make sure that I reported the true facts in my forthcoming book, I asked Rudolf to answer in writing some important questions about his activities at Giza during his various campaigns. This, to my relief, he did.[73] In fact Gantenbrink now seemed more than eager to forward this information. I then asked the same questions to Dr Stadelmann of the German Archaeological Institute to compare notes.[74] To my astonishment, Stadelmann's replies disagreed, almost point by point, with those of Gantenbrink. Something was very wrong here. Here are my questions to Dr Stadelmann, with his replies and the comments given on them by Gantenbrink:

> *Question 1*: The exploration of the shafts in the Queen's Chamber by Mr Gantenbrink 'under the auspices' of the DAI (German Archaeological Institute) in Cairo began in January 1992 and by May 1992 his original mechanised robot (unnamed) had already penetrated some nineteen metres in both the southern and northern shafts of this chamber. Can you confirm this?
>
> **Stadelmann:** The shaft of the middle chamber, the so-called Queen's Chamber R was not penetrated before 1993 because the little robot which was used in 1992 had larger dimensions than the shafts of R.

'Under the auspices' of the German Institute is not quite correct. This research was a concession granted to the German Institute as a joint mission between the German Institute and the SCA (formerly the EAO).

> **Gantenbrink:** *This is incorrect.* The southern lower shaft (of the Queen's Chamber) was penetrated in 1992 up to a depth of 4.88 metres by the first robot. This robot, therefore, was obviously smaller in size than the opening of this shaft. In another campaign which took place in May 1992 the southern and northern shafts of the Queen's Chamber were both penetrated up to about nineteen metres with different equipment.
>
> *Question 2*: Was the work carried out the following year, that is from 7th March to 22nd March 1993, by Mr Gantenbrink in the same shafts of the Queen's Chamber with a new robot (named Upuaut II), also deemed to be 'under the auspices' of the DAI in Cairo? What does 'under the auspices' entail in this context? Does it mean that the work carried out by Mr Gantenbrink was under the direct responsibility of the DAI in Cairo?
>
> **Stadelmann:** Same as (question) Number 1 (i.e. re: 'under the auspices'). Mr Gantenbrink was technician and had prepared all the technical work and material. The concession was and is still owned (to date 11th October) by the German Institute.
>
> **Gantenbrink:** *This is incorrect.* I was formally nominated by the DAI as 'responsible project leader'.
>
> *Question 3*: Please confirm if Mr Gantenbrink's name was formally incorporated and/or recorded on the 'scientific licence' issued for this project. If so, in what capacity was Mr Gantenbrink operating, i.e. project director, field director etc.?
>
> **Stadelmann:** Mr Gantenbrink was working as a freelance technician within the frame of the German Institute's work. He paid for his expenses in Egypt and the technical material. He was responsible for all technical aspects; the project directors were Dr Zahi Hawass and myself.
>
> **Gantenbrink:** *This is incorrect.* I was formally nominated by the DAI as 'responsible project leader'. I have paid for all expenses (several hundreds of

thousand DM) excluding minor expenses like fuel for the DAI car or restoration mortar delivered by the EAO not exceeding a sum of 500 Egyptian pounds. Dr Zahi Hawass was throughout the campaign always presented to me as the EAO's official responsible for the Giza area and *not* as a project director. I must make it clear that it is only now, through the statement made by Professor Dr Stadelmann on 11th October 1995, that I have been made aware that Dr Zahi Hawass was also a project director for these campaigns in which I was involved. *Question 4*: Were the film-maker and producer Mr Jochen Breitenstein and his assistant, Mr Dirk Brakebusch, also considered to be officially members of this project? If so, in what capacity were they operating in the Queen's Chamber of the Great Pyramid and generally at Giza?

Stadelmann: Mr Jochen Breitenstein was introduced to me as a technician for the camera work within the project. Neither I nor Dr Hawass had any knowledge about the filming which apparently was done during non-working hours and outside the pyramid. Mr Breitenstein was duly listed on the security forms as assistant technician.

Gantenbrink: *This is incorrect.* Jochen Breitenstein was never introduced to Professor Dr Stadelmann nor to Dr Zahi Hawass as a 'technician' but repeatedly as a professional film-maker based in Los Angeles. Jochen Breitenstein was never involved in any filming of the inside of the narrow shafts in the Cheops Pyramid. This filming was carried out only by myself. Both Professor Dr Stadelmann and Dr Zahi Hawass were fully aware at all times of all the filming activities carried out by myself (inside the narrow shafts) and all activities carried out by Jochen Breitenstein and his camera assistant Dirk Brakebusch (inside the Pyramid and outside the Pyramid). No filming was ever carried out without the personal consent and approval of Dr Zahi Hawass and the full knowledge of Professor Dr Stadelmann. During all filming activities there was always either an EAO official or a member of the DAI. The only exceptions to this were some few shots with non-archaeological significance (like repairs in the hotel workshop etc.). Because only the Queen's Chamber was closed to the general public during working hours, filming sequences which involved other areas inside the Cheops Pyramid (namely the Grand Gallery, the King's Chamber, the descending corridor, and the Subterranean Chamber) were carried out (for obvious reasons) outside the general public's normal visiting hours. In any case, during this single occasion there was a EAO inspector and the DAI member Ulli Kapp present during the whole time. Also Professor Dr Stadelmann was duly informed about this 'early morning' filming activity which was also duly approved by Dr Zahi Hawass.

Question 5: Were you aware that Mr Breitenstein and Mr Brakebusch (as claimed by them) did not yet have – or ever did have – the required police clearance from the Egyptian authorities to work on this or any other scientific project in Egypt during March 1993?

Stadelmann: As far as I can tell Mr Brakebusch was never inside the Pyramid. He was a personal assistant for developing and cutting in the little laboratory which Mr Gantenbrink had installed at the hotel (Movenpick). He, too, was listed in the security form of the project.

Gantenbrink: Mr Brakebusch was always inside the Pyramid, whenever we were working there, on every single day of the campaign. Mr Brakebusch was the camera assistant of Jochen Breitenstein. Professor Dr Stadelmann was definitely aware of this fact. Mr Brakebusch was not at all a personal assistant for developing and cutting in the little workshop. In any case, no developing and cutting was made by him in the little workshop, or anywhere else in Egypt, either for films or for 'engineering matters'.

Question 6: Were you aware that Mr Gantenbrink, Mr Breitenstein and Mr Brakebusch were intending to shoot a commercial or 'pilot' TV documentary about the exploration of the shafts in the Queen's Chamber when they came to Egypt on 6th March 1993? And *Question 7*: Were you aware that they had no commercial licence from the Egyptian authorities to shoot such a documentary film?

Stadelmann: As I mentioned before, neither Dr Zahi Hawass nor we were informed that Mr Gantenbrink intended to shoot a commercial film. Mr Gantenbrink has later (in summer 1993) signed a paper that he would not use any film material without clearance with the Egyptian authorities.

Gantenbrink: *This is incorrect.* Both Professor Dr Stadelmann and Dr Zahi Hawass were fully aware of the fact that the filming of our campaign, performed using 'broadcast quality standard' equipment, was being made with a view to an eventual (commonly planned) commercialisation (with the proceeds not to be for personal profit but to serve to promote archaeology and especially to obtain further sponsorship for the protection and restoration of our cultural heritage). The document which I signed on 9th September 1993 stipulates an obligation to obtain the consent of the Egyptian authorities before the filming material could be used for broadcasting purposes, and it was, in any case, already confirmed verbally by myself as early as March 1993 to Dr Zahi Hawass. In June 1994 a Tomlin Order ratified by the High Courts of Justice of London transferred this obligation to the BBC who are since that date the owners of the commercial rights of the film *Robot Journey Into the Past*. No royalty fees have to be paid to me, or to anyone else from the BBC to obtain these commercial rights.

Question 8: Could you please confirm whether any member of the DAI was present in the Queen's Chamber during the exploration of the southern shaft between the dates 20th March and 22nd March 1993? If so, who?

Stadelmann: During the whole exploration there was always a member of our Institute (DAI), either me or the engineer Mr Kapp or our architect Nairi Hampikian present in the chamber. It goes without saying that there were always the representatives of the EAO present as well.

Gantenbrink: *This is incorrect.* There was no member of the DAI present during the last week of the March 1993 campaign.

Question 9: Could you please confirm who exactly was physically present inside the Queen's Chamber of the Great Pyramid on 22nd March 1993 when the discovery of the possible 'portcullis' was made? Could you confirm if any permanent DAI members were present at 11.05 a.m. on 22nd March 1993? If so, who?

Stadelmann: Portcullis exist in Egyptian tombs or pyramids only to block horizontal corridors. So the use of the word in this context and all the interpretations concerned with it are, technically speaking, incorrect. On 22nd March at 11.05 Mr Kapp and two representatives of the EAO, Mr Mohammad Shahy and Mr Mohammad Nuby, were present. I myself arrived shortly afterwards.

Gantenbrink: On 22nd March 1993 at 11.05 a.m. the DAI member Ulli Kapp was definitely not present, nor any other member of the DAI. Those present were myself, Jochen Breitenstein, Dirk Brakebusch and the EAO inspector Mohammad Shahy. Professor Dr Stadelmann did not arrive shortly afterwards at the site. He came some time later when I personally notified him, and in any case, directly to the Movenpick hotel in Giza. Dr Zahi Hawass also came directly to this hotel.

This was an amazing situation, and I really did not know what to make of it anymore, who to believe and how to handle this information. A major exploration inside one of the world's oldest monuments, the only surviving wonder of the ancient world, which resulted in a major archaeological find had taken place in conditions that, to say the least, raised suspicion. Being now privy to the conflicting statements made by Dr Stadelmann and Rudolf Gantenbrink, I had placed myself in a rather awkward situation. If I reported what Dr Stadelmann had said, then Gantenbrink would contest it as untrue and vice versa. After careful consideration, I decided that the first thing to do was to check some of the statements myself directly. One person who could certainly clarify this matter of whether Mr Ulli Kapp was in the Queen's Chamber at the time of the discovery was, quite obviously, Mr Kapp himself. I obtained his telephone number in Cairo from Gantenbrink and called Ulli Kapp. The following is from a full transcript of the telephone conversation. I publish it here for the sake of clarity and public interest:

RB: I'm trying to clear who was in the chamber at the time the discovery was made on 22nd March 1993. Were you in the chamber?

Kapp: No.

RB: You were not?

Kapp: No. But . . . Wait, wait, wait . . . do you speak German?

RB: No, I do not speak German. I'm sorry.

Kapp: OK . . . No, no . . . I was there one week before whatever it is . . . was discovered . . . then I had to leave.

RB: I know Rudolf very well and, as you probably know, I see him quite often. I'm writing a book on this matter and I need to be sure of the facts. What he's telling me is that for the last week or so you were not there.

Kapp: That's right.

RB: OK. That's what I wanted to check. And definitely not on the day the discovery was made. Well, thank you . . .

Kapp: No. No. Wait, wait, wait . . . What do you mean with 'discovery'?

RB: Well, the . . . the whatever he discovered. The slab, the block, the door, whatever you want to call it.

Kapp: No . . . This is the thing I saw! . . . We stopped . . . the robot stopped one metre before it . . . then I had to leave the job.

RB: Well, he's saying . . . Look, I want this clear because I'm very confused as to what I should say in my book. On 22nd March 1993 you were *not* there? Is that a fact?

(long pause)

RB: Well? It's either yes or no?

Kapp: . . . give me time to think! . . . well I mean . . . I don't know . . .

RB: Well, you told me before you were not there. I mean it's either you were or you were not.

Kapp: Well, I mean . . . you know, any detail which is already two or three years ago on a very certain day on a very certain moment . . . then you are a genius! . . . I'm not . . . so think about this!

RB: Well, I mean the information is known for a long time. Well I'm not being difficult. I just want to know this fact because I don't want to report that you were there when you were not there. It's an historical fact and it's embarrassing for me to write wrong things in my book. So . . . ?

Kapp: Well, OK. Then keep it like that. Yes.

RB: Keep what like that?

Kapp: As Ruddy (Gantenbrink) says.

RB: Fine. I mean, my information as far as I know, and that is why I'm trying to check with you, is that he says you weren't there during the last five or six days. And you certainly were not there . . .

Kapp: This is true. This is true.

RB: Fine. OK. Thank you Mr Kapp.

Kapp: Don't mention it. Bye bye.

This phone call to Mr Ulli Kapp was made on 10th November 1995, that is more than two and a half years after the discovery of the 'door'. Meanwhile, like I said, the 'poetic licence' in the various films shown on national and international television channels had been perpetuated to the public. There was no doubt that Mr Kapp, Dr Stadelmann, Dr Hawass, and indeed everyone else involved in this affair had seen one or more of these films. So why had they not come forward to point out that what was being shown was not actually what had happened on that historic day of 22nd March 1993? The same, of course, went for Gantenbrink. It is one thing using poetic licence for trivial or casual filming, but this was something else. This, to the world, was one of the most important potential archaeological discoveries of all times. There was, too, this confusing statement that Mr Kapp had made regarding the 'door'. After I had described the 'discovery' as being a 'slab', a 'block' or a 'door' to Mr Kapp, he had exclaimed that this was what he saw when the robot had stopped one metre before it, and *then* he, Ulli Kapp, had left the job. But both he and Gantenbrink had confirmed that he had left the job about one week before 22nd March 1993. So what was Mr Kapp trying to say when he concluded that the matter should be left 'as Ruddy says'?

I decided that my best course of action now was to inform the two official authorities of my findings and let them sort it out between themselves. I thus sent by fax a complete report to Dr Abdel Halim Nureldin, the president of the EAO, and also to Dr Helmut Kerieleis, the president of the German Archaeological Institute in Berlin.[75] Meanwhile I asked Gantenbrink to make matters a little clearer, in writing, concerning the circumstances in which the commercial filming was done at Giza during his campaign in March 1993. This he did right after the Christmas holidays of 1995.[76] This was a three-page report which explained, as he saw it, how and why the filming was made. He was adamant that both Dr Stadelmann and Dr Hawass were fully aware that he was making a commercial film to serve as a pilot for a television series. He insisted, however, that the proceeds were always intended to be for preservation and restoration of the monuments and not for personal profit. 'Indeed,' wrote Rudolf, 'before our March 1993 campaign started Dr Stadelmann was provided with a typed document entitled "Aspects of a Television Series" which I now attach.' Gantenbrink was thus outraged at what he called the 'false statements' made by Dr Stadelmann and offered to provide me with all the evidence required to back his own statements.[77] And although, he said, he did not agree with my own stellar theories on the Pyramids, he concluded:

> Nevertheless, I give you my full support, as I would anyone else, to correctly report the events related to our campaign. In this respect, and also because of the strange silence from the president of the DAI in Berlin, I can only encourage you to carry on with your investigation to expose this archaeological Watergate.

In May 1996 Gantenbrink managed somehow to convince the German Archaeological Institute to sign a 'declaration'. The purpose of this 'declaration' was to have all parties declare that the 'misunderstandings' that had occurred between the EAO and the DAI on the one hand, and Rudolf Gantenbrink on the other hand, were due to 'wrong representations in public'. To make sure, therefore, that this did not occur again, all the parties agreed to the following:

> 1. The campaigns conducted in 1992/1993 were joint undertakings of the German Archaeological Institute in Cairo, the Egyptian Supreme Council of Antiquities (formerly the EAO) and engineer Rudolf Gantenbrink.

2. The project partners were jointly responsible for the execution of the project.
3. None of the project partners reproaches another project partner for any misconduct during the execution of the works.
4. The first publication in the foreign press and, in particular, the statements of the press published after completion of the work have not been prompted by the direct participation of a project partner, but have been the result of an unfortunate chain of uncontrollable events.
5. Owing to the great efforts of all those involved in the project, the joint works in the years 1992/1993 were performed with great success. This applies, in particular, to the successful aeration of the Cheops Pyramid.
11th May 1996.

This declaration was signed in May 1996 by Rudolf Gantenbrink, Dr Stadelmann and Dr Kerieleis of the German Archaeological Institute. On 26th May 1996 Gantenbrink forwarded the same 'declaration' for it to be signed by Dr Nureldin, president of the EAO. I am not sure what happened then. 'History,' it seemed, had been 'written' – or, as the case may be, 'rewritten'.

For the whole of 1997 the Great Pyramid was officially closed. Rumour ran wild. The Internet was rife with stories of secret explorations, of secret chambers being found and, most of all, that the Egyptians were trying to see what was behind the 'door'. In fact the Pyramid had been closed for a much more mundane purpose altogether: to clean up the interior of the monument and install a new aeration (ventilation) system. Rudolf Gantenbrink's 'successful aeration' system was stripped down and replaced with a new one.[78]

WHEN WILL THE 'DOOR' BE OPENED?

The question I have been asked most frequently over the last six years is 'When will the "door" in the Great Pyramid be opened?' A closed 'door' inside one of the world's largest, oldest and most mysterious of monuments is powerful stuff, and it has triggered a sense of immense expectation in the collective subconscious. These expectations range from 'nothing will be found' to the most outrageous claims such as the remains of a UFO or an extraterrestrial being. It is one of those issues that has entered the mass psychosis of the new millennium and will be remembered as such in decades to come. At the time of writing these words (August 1999), the 'door' has not yet been opened.

To get the latest news before the closing of this chapter in this book, I took a quick trip to Egypt and went to see Dr Hawass at his office in Giza.

My objectives were many. I first wanted to hear from him, directly and at first hand, the latest news on what was happening and what was likely to happen at Giza in the next year or so. I also wanted to get his permission to inspect the 'tomb of Osiris' well-shaft and examine the mysterious tunnel that emanated from it towards the Pyramids. This last I will discuss in the next chapter. I raised, of course, the question of Rudolf Gantenbrink. Dr Hawass does not seem to be upset with Gantenbrink anymore, but still thinks that it will not be possible for Gantenbrink to resume the exploration of the shafts of the Queen's Chamber in view of the turmoil the March 1993 events had caused. I had another question. And although I knew what his answer would be, I asked Dr Hawass again whether he had been aware back in March 1993 that Gantenbrink and his colleagues were shooting a commercial film. His answer was an emphatic 'No!' Had he known of such an intention, he would have stopped their filming. He explained that at the time this filming was going on, he had been very busy 'fighting with Bakr' (the EAO president who had sacked Hawass in March 1993 then got himself sacked a few months later) and thus, in the confusion of this personal situation, was not paying much attention to what was happening with the German team. He had assumed that Dr Stadelmann had everything under control with this particular project.[79] All this was, at any rate, over and done with. I asked Hawass about the future. The opening of the 'door', he said, had to be postponed yet again. The event will not take place on the eve of the millennium, as he had previously announced, but sometime in the spring of the year 2000.

As for Gantenbrink, the last time I saw him was at Giza in February 1999.[80] He had come with a new sponsor from Germany to discuss the matter with Dr Hawass. Gantenbrink was staying at the Mena House hotel, where I had also booked, and we exchanged some pleasant conversation in the lobby with the writer and researcher Simon Cox, who was also in Egypt at the time. The next day Simon Cox and I dropped in at Hawass's office to give him our regards. Gantenbrink was there! The situation was electric. It was the first time that the three of us had met together. Just as I was about to open a discussion about the March 1993 'Gantenbrink' campaign at the Great Pyramid and the situation in general, a young Egyptian secretary brought a group of four visitors into Hawass's office – two men and two women in their fifties. They were all Americans. Their spokesman, a tall, distinguished man with white hair, turned out to be Bruce Ludwig, the realtor tycoon from Los Angeles. Ludwig had been financing Mark Lehner since 1984 at Giza and was obviously a close friend of Dr Hawass. I stood up and bid goodbye to

Hawass and Gantenbrink. It was probably the last time that I would see these two men together. But what is certain, however, is that both Hawass and Gantenbrink have entered the annals of archaeological history and, like the enterprising Dixon brothers, the infamous Colonel Howard-Vyse or the colourful Piazzi-Smyth before them, the names of these two men that I was now walking away from would always be entangled and entwined, for better or for worse, with the Great Pyramid of Giza.

But what of the 'door'? When will it be 'opened'? By whom?

Although Dr Hawass did not let out any news on this at the time, he must have had a pretty clear idea of when this task would be done – and who would do it. For in a short while Dr Hawass would officially reveal the identity of the 'team' selected to open the 'door' – and the venue he would choose to announce this would be the Ramada Oceanfront Hotel during the Edgar Cayce Foundation Conference at Virginia Beach.

Chapter Twelve

A Visit into the Underworld

'The search for the truth is too important to be ruined by a silly political game. My only hope is that they will soon reach the same conclusion.'

Rudolf Gantenbrink, the *Sunday Telegraph* 1st January 1995

'Dr Bakr says he was the victim of a campaign to have him removed because of his attempt to rid the EAO of what he terms "the rotten apples" . . .'

Middle East Times 19th–25th February 1995

WHAT NEXT?

The actual possibility of soon finding a secret chamber at Giza, as it stands in this month of August 1999, barely 140 days before the new millennium, is, from a statistical viewpoint, extremely high. There are three known locations where archaeological research has strongly indicated the possibility of hidden chambers yet to be discovered. The first is, of course, the area behind the 'door' that Gantenbrink discovered in March 1993 at the end of the southern 'shaft' or narrow tunnel emanating from the Queen's Chamber. There is about sixteen yards from the 'door' to the outside face of the Pyramid, which is more than ample space for a large chamber to have been concealed. The same applies, of course, to the northern 'shaft' or tunnel also emanating from the Queen's Chamber. In this shaft Gantenbrink was unable to take the robot to the end of the trail, for the shaft makes a sharp bend to the west after rising relatively straight for some twenty-six yards. Also, when the Dixon brothers explored this shaft in 1872, they seem to have pushed in a long

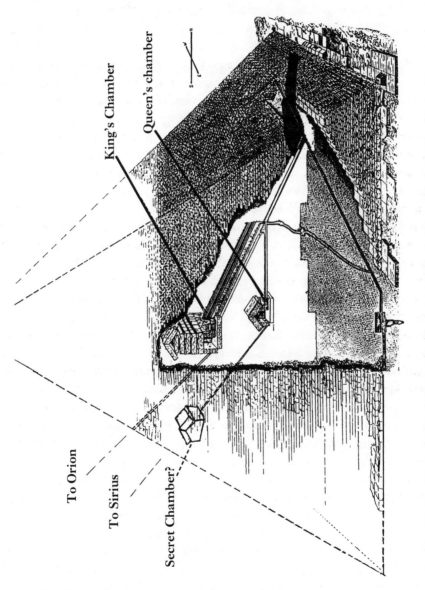

King's Chamber

Queen's chamber

To Orion

To Sirius

Secret Chamber?

Fig. 24. Possible chamber behind the 'door' at the end of the southern shaft in the Great Pyramid.

metal rod, which got stuck at the place of the bend, leaving a serious obstruction which, with his present equipment, Gantenbrink felt was too risky to overcome. It is reasonable to postulate, however, that perhaps the northern shaft, too, has a small 'door' at its end. If so, then the odds of finding a secret chamber will be much increased. Only further exploration, however, can resolve this issue.

Although all this appears to be a fairly straightforward situation which a few hours of exploration with a new robot might resolve, the technical considerations are not as simple as they may at first seem. Before I go any further into this discussion, I feel that it is important to make my position clear as to what I think we are dealing with here. My experience as a construction engineer, backed by a strong 'gut feeling', tells me that what we have here at the end of the southern shaft of the Queen's Chamber is, in fact, a small trap door. I believe – albeit without sufficient evidence at this stage – that we are looking at the entrance to a chamber, much like it would appear if we were able to look from inside the shaft into the Queen's Chamber itself. I shall get to what I also expect we might find behind the door later on. Meanwhile it must be emphasised that Rudolf Gantenbrink insists on calling the 'door' a 'slab' – in a bid to deflect any accusations that might be thrown at him by the Egyptologists for being too 'speculative' or rash about what might lie beyond this blockage. Having made this point, however, I will myself use the term 'door' in our discussion for the sake of uniformity.

On his well-designed website, Rudolf Gantenbrink has presented the various technical means at his disposal to undertake this challenge to find out what is beyond these narrow shafts or tunnels.[1] Gantenbrink suggests that a series of experiments carried out in steps should be undertaken, rather than 'comprehensive, far-reaching plans'. The 'door' or 'slab' appears to be of the portcullis type, meaning that it probably was slipped down into place along indentures or grooves on the side wall of the shaft. Such a technical closing and opening mechanism would be the logical way to control access to a possible chamber or storeroom on the other side, but there is no way to be sure of this, unless an attempt is made to see if the slab is loose. This could be achieved by either having the robot push against the slab and see what happens, or by attaching a series of flat, thin metal spatulas (such as those seen on forklift trucks) onto the front of the robot in an attempt to slip them under the thin gap at the bottom of the 'door' and lift it open, much like one would raise open a sash window or garage door. Thus Gantenbrink proposes that the first step should be an attempt to move or 'nudge' the slab and thus hopefully get some indication of how the ancient builders fitted it into place.

Now when the robot filmed the 'door' in March 1993, it was plain to see that there was a thin, five mm gap at the bottom of the 'door'. Also there was a tiny triangular cut on the bottom right-hand corner. Either of these openings might prove large enough to insert a fibre-optic lens and hopefully 'see' what lies beyond. Thus here, too, Gantenbrink proposes 'step two', which should entail inserting a fine probe with an optic-fibre lens through the five mm gap at the bottom of the slab to see what lies on the other side. As 'step three' Gantenbrink suggests the use of ultra-sound tests in order to determine the thickness of the 'door'. The thickness, of course, will dictate whether the 'door' can be lifted or whether other, more aggressive means may have to be used. Although Gantenbrink does not condone the latter, it may well be that the Egyptian authorities will have no other choice but to cut or break it open if the 'door' is to be opened at all. As 'step four' Gantenbrink favours the idea of using electricity to obtain more information on how the closing mechanism of the 'door' might work. He suggests that an electric current could be passed across the two copper fittings which are encrusted on the slab. An electrical connection might indicate that the fittings join up on the other side and which, in turn, might indicate whether the ancient builders used a 'clamp' as a grip or handle to operate the slab. If this proves to be the case, this would strongly suggest that the 'door' was closed from the other side where a chamber was built. Gantenbrink furthermore proposes that a special gas could be pumped under the 'door' to determine whether there is a void and, should there be one, how large it might be. This last test, however, has some drawbacks, for even if large voids are indicated, there is no telling whether these are fissures and large joints or a chamber. The element of doubt will, in my view, be too great.

If all or some of these tests prove positive and the 'slab' turns out to be a 'door', then, of course, attempts should be made to open it by the Egyptian authorities. The question now is not whether these tests and explorations are technically feasible, but whether the Egyptian authorities will eventually give Gantenbrink – or indeed anyone else – the green light to begin investigations in the shafts. From the various discussions I have had with Dr Zahi Hawass, however, it very much appears that Gantenbrink is unlikely to be involved.

On 21st August 1999, I met Dr Hawass at the ARE annual conference at Virginia Beach. We both were guest speakers, along with Graham Hancock, the authors Jeremy Naydler and Chris Dunn, as well as a few other speakers from within the ARE. There Hawass made two very important announcements concerning the 'door' and future exploration to find the Hall of Records. As far as the matter of the 'door' was concerned, Dr Hawass made it official that neither the German Archaeological Institute nor Gantenbrink will be involved in future exploration of the shafts because of 'political problems' which he did not wish to discuss again. The Egyptian Supreme Council had therefore decided to pass this commission to the National Geographic Society in the USA, and work was due to start in April or May 2000. The National Geographic had already worked at Giza on previous occasions, the last time being with Dr Farouk El Baz, the well-known Egyptian scientist, during which they investigated with fibre-optic cameras the second boat pit south of the Great Pyramid.[2] One thing would appear to be in no doubt: the team that performs the task of opening the 'door' will have to include a prominent Egyptian scientist. The most likely choice is again Dr Farouk El Baz. El Baz is one of Egypt's most popular and respected scientists and also a close friend of Dr Hawass. El Baz had previously worked for NASA in the 1960s and 1970s and was a key figure in the Apollo moon missions as well as with the early Mars probes and landings.[3] He has a penchant for geo–archaeology, the application of geological science to the field of archaeology, and is the instigator of the so-called Yardang theory, which suggests that the origin of Pyramids (and possibly the Sphinx) is rooted in the shape of wind-blown mounds in the deserts of Egypt.[4] There have been persistent rumours, however, which suggest that a Canadian company would be given the task of opening the 'door'. This rumour was made public back in March 1996 by the *Egyptian Gazette* when it announced that 'a multi-national archaeological mission' would undertake the exploration of the shafts of the Queen's Chamber which would involve a Canadian 'mission':

> The Great Pyramid differs from the norm in having two burial chambers within its structure and a third unfinished chamber underground . . . From each of the two upper chambers narrow, sloping tunnels were constructed, known as 'air-shafts'. However archaeologists believe they had little to do with ventilation, rather they suggest that they have some astronomical functions. In 1993, a German team led by Rudolf Gantenbrink and Rainer Stadelmann found a sealed door in one of the shafts from the Queen's Chamber using a robotic camera. The discovery led to speculation that a fourth chamber might be present . . . At an archaeological lecture in the United States which was attended by media representatives, diplomats and travel agents, Dr Zahi Hawass, chief of the Giza Antiquities authority, addressed this issue. He said that a joint archaeological mission involving Egypt, Canada and the German Institute for Archaeology will commence work on the Great Pyramid next September to follow up the discovery of the door. 'They will try to use another robotic camera to film what is behind that door.' He added that renowned Egyptian scientist Dr Farouk El Baz will also visit Cairo to assist the archaeological team.[5]

THE CANADIAN CONNECTION

The 'Canadian' connection that Dr Hawass was alluding to was, in fact, an outfit called Amtex Software Corporation based in Ontario, Canada. Amtex specialises in such things as air-traffic control training systems and other virtual reality software products. The company is owned and run by Mr Peter Zuuring, a Canadian with Dutch origins. Peter's involvement with the Great Pyramid began, in fact, when he read my book *The Orion Mystery* in October 1994. He immediately sent me a fax and suggested we meet to discuss a project that he would like me to get involved with, which entailed making a 3D replica of the Great Pyramid with a planetarium to show the stellar links.[6] It sounded interesting and we agreed to meet in New York in November 1994. Graham Hancock and his wife happened to be in New York at that time, and joined the meeting. Peter Zuuring was particularly interested in the 'door' discovered by Gantenbrink, and wanted to know how he could get involved with the exploration. This was in the middle of the High Court case with the BBC, and I told Peter that he would be better off dealing directly with the Egyptian authorities.

I frankly did not think that anything would come out of this and, back in England, I forgot all about it. A week later, however, Peter informed me that he was going to Egypt and then coming to Europe and asked if I could meet him in Amsterdam in early December.[7] We met there on 5th December 1994 at the Hotel Beethoven. He was excited and said that he had met Hawass at the Mena House hotel, and the latter had introduced him to his business 'agent'.[8] He now was planning a second trip to Egypt in March 1995 where he hoped to get permits from the Egyptian authorities for exploring the shafts. I could not believe that Peter had any chance of pulling this off, but he said that he was now extremely well introduced by the Canadian ambassador and he had struck up a good rapport with Dr Hawass. I was, myself, planning a trip to Egypt in March and so we decided to meet up there. Peter, however, cancelled his trip at the last minute. Instead he came later to London, where we met with a Dutch film producer, Roel Oostra, with whom I was working.[9] It was then that Zuuring told me that he was planning a preliminary scouting trip to Egypt in June where he hoped to probe the shafts with a specially designed metallic rod. I felt it was most unlikely to happen, but did not tell Zuuring.

In late June, however, after he had returned from his trip to Egypt, Zuuring informed me on the phone that he had visited Dr Stadelman of the German Institute and they had both gone to the Great Pyramid and there, in the Queen's Chamber, Peter had successfully used his metal probe and taken some pictures of the inside of the shaft. He said that he had discussed with Hawass the idea of making television documentaries hinged on this exploration and was thinking in big-money terms, with a figure of ten million dollars later mentioned.[10] It sounded all too familiar. I decided that it was only fair that Rudolf Gantenbrink be made aware of what was going on. Rudolf was at the time making a short documentary with Spiegel TV Reportage, headed by the German producer Tillman Schol. Schol got interested in this new development and decided to check for himself directly with Peter Zuuring and also with Dr Stadelman. Having confirmed with Zuuring and reported to me, Tillman Schol then decided to expose the story on the German television channel Sat-1.[11]

Just after the broadcast I met Peter one last time. The meeting took place at the Edgar Cayce Foundation in Virginia Beach. I had invited him to join me there, where I was giving a talk at their annual Egypt conference. I knew that Dr Schor and Joseph Jahoda would also be there, and Peter was keen to meet them in the hope that they could collaborate together in future exploration at Giza. We all stayed at the Ramada Oceanfront Hotel and shared a few meals together. This was the last time I saw Peter Zuuring. I did, however, speak to Peter a few more times on the phone in early 1996. He had apparently developed some good contacts with the Egyptian military as well as the Antiquities Organisation and was hoping to land some important software training contracts with them. The last time I spoke to Peter was in April 1996. He had called me from Canada to ask me if I knew Erich Von Daniken. Peter was very interested in talking to him about some project he was working on. I passed him Daniken's contacts, but I do not know what developed from this.[12] As for his meeting with Dr Schor and Joe Jahoda at Virginia Beach, nothing, as far as I know, came of it. I have recently heard that Peter Zuuring's company, Amtex, has gone into liquidation.[13] Also Dr Hawass has confirmed that the Supreme Council of Antiquities definitely has no dealings with Amtex or anyone else other than with National Geographic for the opening of the 'door' in 2000.

WHAT IS BEHIND THE 'DOOR'?

There is, of course, an irresistible urge to know what is behind the 'door' discovered by Gantenbrink. And this urge has almost reached breaking point in recent months, bringing with it the usual batch of Internet rumour and conspiracy theories. Some people, for example, are utterly convinced that the Egyptian authorities have already taken a peep to see what is behind the 'door'. This rumour was fuelled when the Great Pyramid was closed for restoration and cleaning in 1997.[14] However, the simple fact, I am afraid, is that no one yet knows what is behind the 'door' – that is if we accept the word of the Egyptian authorities on this matter per se. Certainly they have had plenty of time – and opportunities – to send a robot or probe up the shaft and attempt to see what is behind it by inserting a fibre-optic camera through the small triangular hole on the right-hand bottom corner of the 'door'. But have they? Many have asked point-blank questions to Dr Hawass and other Egyptian officials, including myself. The answer is an emphatic 'No'. It does seem inconceivable, though, that an attempt will be made by National Geographic to open the 'door' on 'live' TV without having had a 'dress rehearsal' for the event. So will National Geographic be allowed to have a mock attempt? I posed such a question to Dr Hawass in August 1999, and his reply was, 'Of course we will make sure that the event goes without problems.' But more than that, he would not say. Meanwhile we can, however, make some good educated guesses as to what may be behind it.

We have seen earlier on how the late Dr I.E.S. Edwards felt that the likely find would be a statue of the king gazing towards the constellation of Orion.[15] On the north side of Zoser's step-pyramid at Saqqara is a small shrine in which can be seen a statue of the king gazing upwards through peepholes towards the circumpolar stars. Was Dr Edwards's hypothesis based on this precedent? Unfortunately after having made his observation on the national news,[16] he was so ruthlessly pilloried by his peers that he refused to comment further on the matter, other than that it had been 'a wild guess'. Dr Hawass had also once suggested that there may be scrolls of papyrus but he, too, now refused to speculate. The fact is that the 'what's behind the door?' question has become an archaeological hot potato for the academics, and no one will venture any speculation – at least not publicly.

In *The Orion Mystery*, however, I put forward the suggestion that we might find the original Benben Stone of Heliopolis.[17] The logic behind this hypothesis was briefly reviewed in Chapter 4. My recent investigation into the ancient texts, however, has now made me lean more towards the idea that there could be a sort of 'sacred library' with books and 'instruction manuals' associated with the astral rebirth rituals of the Pyramid builders. This, of course, is also pure speculation. Nonetheless it is where I would put my money should it come to a wager. I base this intuitive guess on the written evidence in the Westcar Papyrus and other documents which we have discussed in a previous chapter. The reader will recall that in the Westcar Papyrus it is reported that King Cheops wanted to incorporate in the design of his pyramid a 'secret chamber' similar to that which was supposedly in the sanctuary of the god Thoth. We have also seen how at Heliopolis there was said to be a 'flint chest' which contained something so precious that it made King Cheops desperate to acquire it for his Pyramid. What could be in that mysterious 'flint chest'? The most precious cargo, in my view, that could – and should – be associated with both Heliopolis and Thoth would be the sacred writings of the 'gods' or, more specifically, those 'books' that were known as the 'books of Thoth'. This would explain why the Great Pyramid contains no inscriptions on the walls of its chambers or anywhere else on the monument. It would also explain why the shaft was only eight inches by eight inches, if only 'books' were intended to be hauled up to the top. But why build a shaft at all? Why not just place the 'books' in a small chamber within the core of the Pyramid then build solid masonry around it? This would surely make those 'books' totally inaccessible to intruders – indeed, no one would even suspect the existence of such a chamber. Whereas by linking such a possible chamber with a shaft that in turn connects with the Queen's Chamber further down the Pyramid, then should the entrance of the shaft be discovered (which it has) and should the shaft be probed (which it has) and finally should a 'door' be seen at its end (which it has), surely all this would act not as a deterrent but rather as an *invitation to find out what is behind it* (which it has). This implies to me that the ancient builders *actually wanted the 'door' to be found and, ultimately, what might be concealed behind it*. But not by anyone. Those who were worthy of finding it would not be barbarians; they would be advanced and sophisticated people not only having the means to reach the 'door' and open it, but to make proper use of the mysterious and precious cargo that might be behind it. As we shall see in the epilogue of this book, we are on the verge of finding out.

TUNNEL TO THE UNKNOWN

The hopes of Dr Schor and Joe Jahoda of ever finding the Hall of Records and vindicating Edgar Cayce's prophecies are, in my view, quite good, in spite of the political problems that surround this controversy. It has been my feeling all along that some sort of private agenda has been in the making since at least as far back as 1978 between the ARE and the Egyptian authorities, or perhaps just with Dr Hawass. I still feel the same. But my gut feeling is also that, in a strange way, our intervention in this matter by forcing this issue into the open has, in a roundabout manner, opened the way for a new and official expedition to at least have a fighting chance of success. My advice to Schor back in January 1999 was to do precisely that and, as we shall soon see, this strategy seems to have paid off. It was clear to me that by not coming out in the open about the true motive of his interest at Giza, it was very unlikely that either he or his associates would be granted any further permits to explore the bedrock around and under the Sphinx. Indeed, the impression I got from Dr Schor when I last saw him in New York was that he had arrived at the same conclusion. He seemed no longer to have the stomach for any adverse press reaction over this matter. He seemed to think that the next best thing to do was to write a book about his 1996–98 expeditions and then forget the whole thing. But I also knew that this, too, was unlikely. He had, after all, invested much energy and money in this quest, and he would see it through if he could.

We all knew that his claim of having found a large chamber under the Sphinx really depended on the accuracy and reliability of the radar he had used in 1996. And although he, himself, felt very confident about what his radar had picked up, and remains extremely hopeful that a chamber will eventually be found there, the Egyptian authorities – and especially Dr Hawass – seemed unconvinced. According to John Van Auken, the chief executive of the ARE at Virginia Beach, Dr Schor had provided them with the readings of his 1996 radar tests which they, in turn, had had verified with NASA. Auken told me personally in January 1999 that NASA had confirmed to him that Dr Schor's interpretation of the radar's readings was correct: there appeared to be a large cavity or chamber under the Sphinx's font paws. Still, Dr Hawass had remained sceptical and would not allow a drilling operation based on this evidence alone. The reader will recall that Dr Schor's radar readings had also shown an underground tunnel shooting from the rear of the Sphinx towards the so-called 'tomb of Osiris', i.e. the well-shaft located under the causeway, some 220 yards behind the Sphinx, and that the radar had also picked up another tunnel under the large sarcophagus lid that was in the lower chamber of that well-shaft which appeared to be directed towards the back of the Sphinx. The suggestion had then been made that these two tunnels could be linked. Also, in March 1999, when Dr Hawass took the Fox TV crew down into the 'tomb of Osiris', he revealed the existence of yet another tunnel, one that could actually be seen shooting from the north-west corner of the tomb towards the Great Pyramid.

In early August 1999 I decided to try and take a look for myself. As I had to go to Cairo to shoot a film with the BBC,[18] I decided to take this opportunity to ask Dr Hawass for permission to visit the 'tomb of Osiris'.

A SHORT JOURNEY INTO THE DUAT

On 3rd August I made my way to Dr Hawass's office on the north-west side of the Giza plateau. With me was the South African producer and director Diana Lucas. Diana had come to see Dr Hawass for a film she was planning based on my book. The sun was blazing hot but there was a nice breeze blowing from the north. A few clouds created an occasional relief from the intense ultraviolet glare that reflected from the Pyramids nearby. In the office it was cooler with the old-fashioned ceiling fans churning the air slowly. Dr Hawass was in excellent mood and looked relaxed and healthy. He greeted us in a friendly way and showed us the latest colour articles that had appeared in glossy periodicals such as *Paris Match* and *Le Figaro* about his excavation at the Oasis of Bahareya, where thousands of mummies had been unearthed in recent months. I told him of the film I was making with the BBC, as well as another film I was planning to do on the Pyramids with M-Net TV of South Africa. He seemed pleased and offered to help in any way he could. It was Diana Lucas who then seized the opportunity and asked him if he would kindly grant us permission to visit the 'tomb of Osiris'. He smiled and said, 'Yes, but no photographs, OK?' It was my lucky day. Hawass rang the bell located under his desk and his devoted secretary immediately came into the office. Hawass gave her some brief instructions and a few minutes later she returned with an inspector called Essam Shehab. Dr Hawass then gave the inspector a set of large keys and told him to take Diana and me to the 'Bir' (the 'well'). It was as simple as that.

Essam Shehab is a young man of thirty and, like most of the antiquities inspectors in Egypt, friendly and eager to please. We spoke in Arabic and we immediately struck up a little friendship. We went to the 'Bir' in a horse-drawn carriage which I negotiated for five Egyptian pounds. It was hot and humid, but Essam assured us that it would be cooler in the shaft. The entrance to the well-shaft is roughly one-third of the way up the ancient causeway coming from the Sphinx, and lies directly under the large limestone slabs which form the bottom of the causeway proper. We first had to go through a sort of underpass to reach a grilled gate securely closed with a heavy padlock. I asked Essam if we could take some photographs before entering. He agreed. Essam then opened the gate and started to go down a metal ladder to the first platform some twenty-one feet below. Essam was pretty strict about me taking photographs, but allowed one shot of me going down the ladder, which Diana Lucas took. I then packed the camera and left it in a bag near a rock on the floor of the first level.

So far we were receiving a good amount of daylight, and visibility was fine. But as I looked down the well-shaft heading towards the second level, it was like staring into an archaeological black hole. Essam tried the switch of the temporary lighting system. Nothing happened. There was no electricity. And we had brought no flashlights along with us. I told Essam to wait and rushed to the nearby village of Nazlet El Samman where I bought two cheap plastic flashlights with batteries. Back in the 'Bir' we resumed our descent to the second level. Essam said that this was his first time down the 'Bir', so none of us was quite sure what to expect. The metal ladder was extremely moist from humidity and very slippery, making the descent a somewhat hairy experience. It was now very dark, and even with the torches it was difficult to get a good perspective of this underworld environment.

Some thirty feet further down we finally reached the floor of the second level. It had seemed like forever. This turned out to be a large grotto, about twenty-five feet by sixteen feet with a ten-foot-high ceiling, which was quite obviously cut out by human hands. We shone little beams of light around. On the west and east walls were large niches cut into the natural bedrock. Essam let out a gasp of excitement as he pointed to a large, black granite sarcophagus that was in one of the west niches. Another sarcophagus, this one looking like it was made of red granite, was in an eastern niche. Their heavy lids had been pushed open. We looked inside but they were completely empty. The sarcophagi bore no inscriptions whatsoever. It was all very mysterious. Hawass had dated these artefacts to around the Twenty-sixth Dynasty, c.500 BC,[19] but I wondered why he was so sure of that conclusion, considering there were no inscriptions to go by. Although it was true that during the so-called Sait Period (c.600 BC) much tampering had taken place at Giza, and that the priests at that time seemed to favour the idea of tombs going deep underground in wide, rectangular shafts, such as those found at Saqqara for example, there was no hard evidence to associate the 'Bir' and the two sarcophagi with that period.

At best it was an educated guess. But even so, it was still possible – indeed likely – that the well or shaft was much older than Hawass thought. There was, in my view, no good reason yet to dispense with the possibility that it might date from the Pyramid Age, or even beyond. The ancient texts, as we have seen, were adamant that a vast underground system of tunnels and chambers existed at Giza, and the 'Bir' could, indeed, be part of such a network.

On the east side of this second level was another tunnel going directly downwards. We looked down. It was really like looking into the bowels of hell. We began our slow descent. Halfway down the air became stale and very humid, and we could hear water dripping down the walls and ceiling. I was reminded of a cave of stalagmites I had once visited in Spain. We finally reached the floor and emerged into a large grotto, also clearly hand-carved out of the natural rock. It measured about thirty feet by thirty feet and its ceiling height was about ten feet. It reminded me very much of the Subterranean Chamber in Khufu's Pyramid, with the same rough and 'unfinished' texture. In spite of the light from our electric torches, the room was cast in a tenebrous darkness that was cut only by the thin rays of orange light shooting from our small lamps. I panned the beam of light around the room and realised that much of the floor was submerged in water. The sense of mystery and a curious feeling of timelessness were overwhelming.

As our eyes became accustomed to the darkness we saw that at the centre of the room was a sort of 'island' measuring about sixteen feet by sixteen feet on which were strewn large blocks of stone, obviously the remains of pillars or columns that had once graced this place. At the centre of the 'island' we could see the dark, almost black lid of a large granite sarcophagus. It had been pushed sideways to reveal a totally submerged sarcophagus from which an eerie greenish glow emerged caused by the refraction of the beams from our torches. I stood on the lid of the sarcophagus and looked around. Hawass had dated this sarcophagus to an earlier period. According to him, this is how it was done: 'To derive the date of the shaft, a boy was lowered into the water-filled tomb on a rope to collect artefacts. From the objects retrieved (mostly broken pots), we dated the shaft to the New Kingdom, 1550 BC.'[20] My intuition told me that Hawass could be wrong. This place felt old, very old – perhaps as old as the Sphinx itself. Hawass had also claimed to have found

> . . . inscribed on the ground the hieroglyphic word 'pr', meaning 'house'. It is known that the Giza plateau was called 'pr wsir nb rstaw', or 'House of Osiris, Lord of Rastaw'. 'Rastaw' refers to the underground tunnels, and most likely the name of the plateau reflects the tunnels inside the Osiris shaft. The final chamber we found was most likely a symbolic tomb for the god Osiris; he was believed to control the underground tunnels and tombs of the kings . . .[21]

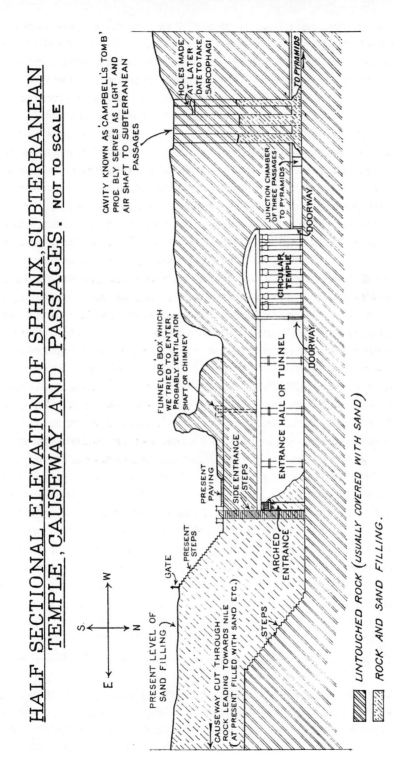

HALF SECTIONAL ELEVATION OF SPHINX, SUBTERRANEAN TEMPLE, CAUSEWAY AND PASSAGES . NOT TO SCALE

PRESENT LEVEL OF SAND FILLING

GATE

PRESENT STEPS

CAUSEWAY CUT THROUGH ROCK LEADING TOWARDS NILE (AT PRESENT FILLED WITH SAND ETC.)

STEPS

ARCHED ENTRANCE

PRESENT PAVING

SIDE ENTRANCE STEPS

ENTRANCE HALL OR TUNNEL

FUNNEL OR 'BOX' WHICH WE TRIED TO ENTER. PROBABLY VENTILATION SHAFT OR CHIMNEY

DOORWAY

CIRCULAR TEMPLE

JUNCTION CHAMBER OF THREE PASSAGES TO PYRAMIDS

DOORWAY

CAVITY KNOWN AS 'CAMPBELL'S TOMB' PROB BLY SERVES AS LIGHT AND AIR SHAFT TO SUBTERRANEAN PASSAGES

HOLES MADE AT LATER DATE TO TAKE SARCOPHAGI

TO PYRAMIDS

UNTOUCHED ROCK (USUALLY COVERED WITH SAND)

ROCK AND SAND FILLING.

Fig. 25.

299

Rastaw or Rostau, as the reader will recall, was predominantly considered to be that place in the Fifth Hour or House of the Duat – the Underworld – in which the transfiguration of Osiris had taken place. It was that 'sealed place', as the ancient texts say, that contained the efflux of Osiris.[22] Access to this mysterious place was from under the Aker Lion which, as we have seen in Chapter 4, can be identified with the Great Sphinx of Giza. In 1997 the seismographic and radar equipment of Dr Schor had detected a tunnel leading from the back of the Sphinx towards this location. They had also detected a tunnel leading out of this location towards the Sphinx. As I stood on top of the sarcophagus in this unlit and mysterious environment, it was very tempting to imagine that Schor might, after all, be correct in thinking that the two tunnels could be connected. I suddenly felt like Horus seeking the body of his dead father, Osiris.[23] Was this part of the underground 'kingdom of Osiris in Rostau'? The water surrounding the 'island' was like a small, medieval castle-moat glistening in the eerie glow. I did not dare go into it, for there was no telling how deep it might be. There was, too, the risk of scorpions and snakes lurking in the slime and mud.

Across the moat, on the north-west corner of the room, I could make out the opening of a tunnel. The opening was cut neat in a rectangular shape, about twenty inches by twenty inches. As I shone the beam of my torchlight into it, I could see that it ran some twenty to twenty-two feet then turned sharply to the right or east. It seemed to be blocked. According to Hawass, it led nowhere. He had sent a young boy through it 'only to find that it is closed off and does not lead to any more chambers'.[24] But then what was its purpose? Why bother to cut a tunnel in such amazingly difficult circumstances that leads nowhere? It was difficult to get a bearing in this hellish darkness, but to my estimation, the tunnel ran towards the south side of the Great Pyramid. For a brief moment I thought that if Gantenbrink's robot could *feel*, then it would have felt the same as I felt right now when its light beams shone on the strange little door that blocked its way.

Essam indicated that it was time to leave. I took a long look around, sighed, and made my way to the metal ladder that would take me back to the light, the world of the living.

Yet in the strangest of ways I was overtaken by a sense of sorrow, as if I had seen something – I know not what – which needed remembering. Giza, some visitors will surely attest, has that effect on you sometimes. As I climbed the long way up I could not help thinking of the weird AMORC maps that showed an underground system of chambers all meeting or emanating from somewhere not far from where we were now.

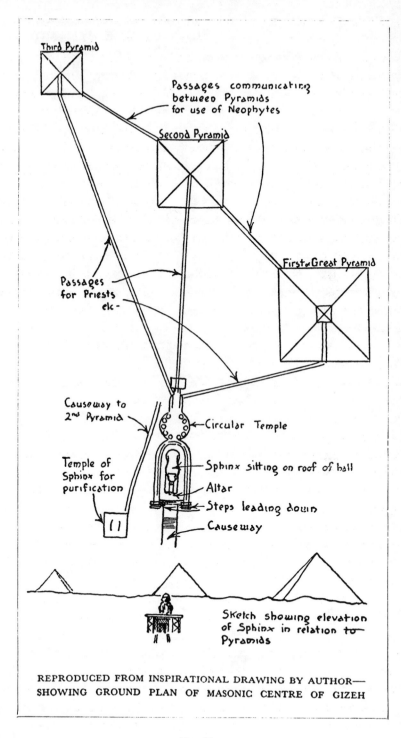

Third Pyramid

Passages communicating between Pyramids for use of Neophytes

Second Pyramid

First & Great Pyramid

Passages for Priests etc –

Causeway to 2ⁿᵈ Pyramid

← Circular Temple

Temple of Sphinx for purification

← Sphinx sitting on roof of hall

← Altar

← Steps leading down

← Causeway

Sketch showing elevation of Sphinx in relation to Pyramids

REPRODUCED FROM INSPIRATIONAL DRAWING BY AUTHOR—
SHOWING GROUND PLAN OF MASONIC CENTRE OF GIZEH

Fig. 26.

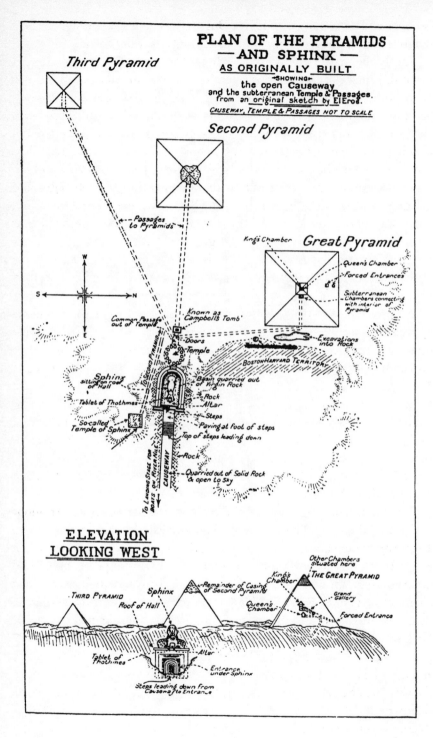

Fig. 27.

So near and yet so far, I thought. But from what? The mystery of this magical site had never gripped me as strongly as it did then.

Surely the matter could not be left at that. There was no question in my mind that what was now desperately needed to conclude this quest was another campaign by a team with sophisticated radar and remote-sensing equipment to conduct readings within the 'Bir'. The only team that was not only ready with the necessary equipment and expertise but also had the financial clout was the Schor Foundation. Although I had not approved of their style in the 1996–97 expeditions at Giza, I still felt that with a transparent approach to a new expedition here, the job could get done and we would perhaps all finally know, one way or the other, what was under the bedrock upon which stands the Sphinx. I was meeting Dr Hawass again in late August 1999 at the ARE Egypt Conference. Perhaps this matter could be broached again with him.

As it turned out, negotiations between Schor and Hawass had already begun and were well advanced for precisely such a new venture. Right before my talk on the morning of Saturday 21st August, Joe Jahoda approached me to let me know that the Schor Foundation had been granted a new licence to carry out a radar investigation at the Sphinx in November 1999. Hawass apparently was going to announce this news that very same evening at the ARE conference during his talk. Jahoda had wanted me to know this beforehand as he was a little worried that I might 'attack' Schor again in my talk, and thus jeopardise their latest – and probably only – chance. I said that I had no intention of doing so provided, of course, that Hawass made it clear that the matter was official, i.e. that the objective was to look for a secret chamber and not resort to those bogus motives as was the case back in 1996–97.

We shook hands and waited for Hawass's announcement. At about 7.45 p.m. Hawass made the historical announcement. He first went into a lengthy apologia about how he, himself, did not believe in a Hall of Records and that whoever did were quite simply wasting their time. 'I do not want to disappoint you,' Hawass said, 'but I am sure there is no secret chamber or Hall of Records of a lost civilisation,' he told the audience. And how was he so absolutely sure? Because, he said, he had worked at Giza for the last seventeen years and knew 'every grain of sand' on the plateau. That's how sure. But he wanted to settle this controversy once and for all. He was thus pleased to confirm that the Project Committee of the Egyptian Supreme Council of Antiquities had granted a licence to the Schor Foundation to have one last chance to find the legendary Hall of Records. Schor and Jahoda had assured him that they had acquired new and far more sophisticated radar equipment which he had agreed they could bring to Giza. Although he did not understand this type of technology, he nonetheless agreed that, for the sake of scientific curiosity, he was ready to let them use it around the Sphinx and, more especially, to re-examine that area under the front paw of the lion-statue where their previous radar had picked up what Schor believed was a hidden chamber. And so, at the eleventh hour of the millennium, the die was cast for one last try to locate the fabled secret chamber. This was wonderful news.

I remember later that evening looking at the image of the sky on Skyglobe 3.6 in my room at the new wing of the Ramada Oceanfront. In *Keeper of Genesis* we had shown how the sun's passage through the front paws of Leo was perceived by the priest-astronomers as the moment of entry through the Aker-Sphinx and into the mysterious Kingdom of Osiris in the Duat.[25] The monitor screen on my laptop PC showed that, at the time Hawass had made the announcement that evening, the sun had just entered the paws of Leo. The sky image also indicated that the coming dawn would witness the heliacal rising of Sirius in that part of the USA.[26] I called Michele, who was brushing her teeth. She came over with the electric toothbrush buzzing in her mouth. My talk that day had been all about the heliacal rising of that star and how it was the portent of historical events related to the Giza monuments. She turned off the electric toothbrush. In the silence of the night we gazed at the screen and smiled. Another strange synchronicity if ever there was one.

Epilogue

A Plot of Words

'It requires a very unusual mind to undertake the analysis of the obvious.'

Alfred North Whitehead

'Tis strange, but true; for truth is always strange – Stranger than fiction.'

Lord Byron, *Don Juan*.

HISTORICAL FACT, HISTORICAL FICTION

When, in July 1798, Napoleon arrived with his massive naval force on the shores of Alexandria in Egypt, he sent pamphlets to the Egyptians containing these words:

> People of Egypt! You will be told that I come to destroy your religion. Do not believe it . . . All men are equal before God; but it is wisdom, talents and virtues that make differences among men . . . Cadis! Sheikhs! Imams! Tell the people that we are the friends of the Moslems . . .[1]

It is then said that after Napoleon reached Cairo a few weeks later, he and General Jean-Batiste Kleber were taken to the Great Pyramid of Cheops and, under the guidance of a great Gnostic sage and master, were initiated into the fraternity of Freemasonry inside the King's Chamber.[2] Since no documented evidence[3] of the Masonic initiation of Napoleon in the Great Pyramid exists, the story cannot be proved. The reader will recall though that many members of Napoleon's family and close

305

entourage were Freemasons. Prior to Napoleon's occupation of Egypt, Freemasonry in France was gripped by an 'Egyptomania' introduced by the infamous Count Caliostro.[4] General Kleber, Napoleon's right hand man in Egypt, was himself a prominent Mason.[5] All this is very suggestive that the alleged initiation of Napoleon inside the Great Pyramid may actually be an historical truth. In his book on Egyptian Freemasonry, however, French Masonic historian Gerard Galtier reports that a certain Salutore Avventura Zola (apparently a relative of the great French writer, Emile Zola), who was Grand Master of the Masonic Order of Memphis in 1863 in Alexandria, stated:

> In August 1798, Napoleon the Great and Kleber, although the latter already a Freemason, were initiated into the Rites of Memphis by a man of venerable age, highly knowledgeable in the doctrine and customs, who was said to be a descendant of the ancient Egyptian sages. The initiation took place in the Pyramid of Cheops and they received, as only investiture, a ring, as a token of the dignity conferred upon them. Napoleon, as well as Kleber and various officers of his army, founded here the first lodge of Memphis in 1798-99.[6]

Galtier cites as his source the Masonic review, *Kneph*, of June 1883.[7] Did Mr Zola make this story up? Or was he reporting from another source? And was this source documented? Hundreds of Masonic scholars had searched in vain and the answer to these questions is that we shall probably never know. In this case we have to take into account that Freemasonry is sometimes accused of inventing a mythical history to give the fraternity 'symbolic' connections to important men and events in order to elevate its prestige. Mr Zola was the Grand Master of the Masonic Order of Memphis in Egypt. Having Napoleon as a member of the Brotherhood in Egypt was the highest honour possible. Mr Zola's unsupported statement must, therefore, be regarded as being possibly suspect. On the other hand we must also take into account that Mr Zola was a near contemporary of the Napoleonic occupation in Egypt and also belonged to the social circle that would have had direct contact with the great man. Zola was thus well placed in time and location to have had access to documented evidence that compelled him to write about Napoleon's initiation with such strong conviction and without the need to qualify his statement. To illustrate this peculiar phenomenon, let me cite one example that actually happened to me recently.

During the 1995 annual conference at the Edgar Cayce Foundation, I was staying at the Ramada Oceanfront hotel with my wife, Michele, and my two children, Candice and Jonathan. As we went into the restaurant for breakfast one morning, I saw Dr Schor, Joseph Jahoda and the Canadian businessman Peter Zuuring all having breakfast together. I went up to them to greet them. Michele was carrying a small camera with a built-in flash. We all smiled as she took a photograph. Later, in June 1996, Graham Hancock was touring the US giving talks on our new book, *Keeper of Genesis* (*Message of the Sphinx* in the US). During a talk in Los Angeles Graham projected a slide of this photograph. An Egyptian architect who was present at the talk thought he recognised Dr Farouk El Baz, the Egyptian scientist whom, as we have already seen, was nominated by Dr Hawass to oversee the opening of the Gantenbrink 'door' in the Great Pyramid. But instead of doing the obvious thing and verifying this with Graham Hancock – who would have immediately told him that the man he thought was Dr El Baz was, in fact, myself – the over-enthusiastic Egyptian architect reported what *he thought he had seen* to the author Richard Hoagland. This was exactly what the latter needed. Hoagland, who is well-known for his conspiracy theories involving NASA and US government intelligence agencies, was at the time concocting a complex conspiracy theory linking the Apollo moon mission and the Mars Global Surveyor missions to 'Masonic' ritual involving ancient Egyptian gods.[8] The news that 'Dr El Baz' had been seen with Dr Schor and Joseph Jahoda at the Edgar Cayce Foundation caused the proverbial penny to drop in Hoagland's mind. In a twist of poetic irony, he hastily telephoned me to tell me of his 'amazing breakthrough' in his investigation. You can imagine the expression on his face when I told him that the photograph he regarded as 'hard evidence' was taken by my wife, and that the man he thought was 'El Baz' was none other than myself. It took me a while to convince him of his mistake.

The plain truth is that as much as there is a pseudo-science that scourges the world today, there is, too, a rampant pseudo-history. Dozens upon dozens of books which belong to the science-fiction realm are unabashedly peddled as non-fiction by publishers who should know better. 'Giza and the Pyramids,' one honest film-maker told me recently, 'is hot stuff! Every network department is screaming for more.' I was reminded of the seventies film *Network*, in which the news department of a major US channel decided to put on the air 'live' the adventures of a radical terrorist group actually robbing banks and kidnapping people in order to improve its ratings![9] Anything goes as long as it sells. This is the strange and weird phenomenon that today is plaguing explorations and research at the Giza necropolis. In the course of my involvement with this place, I meet hundreds of individuals who are utterly convinced that they have a major role to play as well as 'something important to contribute' to this archetypal, quasi-mythical human drama. The majority of these characters turn out to be gentle and harmless people who are seekers of enlightenment and peace. Sometimes it is a refreshing and even rewarding experience to exchange ideas with some of them. A few are amusing 'Walter Mitty' type characters indulging in imaginary 'ancient Egyptian' roles they have created for themselves. But there are one or two who, wittingly or unwittingly, end up causing an incredible amount of trouble and confusion.

Take the case of Larry Hunter, a former US Navy intelligence officer who breeds prize cats in Los Angeles. Larry is a self-proclaimed 'independent Egyptologist' who frequently comes to Giza in search of the 'truth'. This amounts to gathering dubious 'confidential information' about 'secret excavations' in the Great Pyramid from equally dubious 'secret sources'. Most of the time it is harmless rumours, and as such Hunter is generally ignored by the Egyptian authorities who see him as part of the irksome 'Pyramid Groupies' that this site attracts. In July 1997, however, Larry Hunter and Richard Hoagland teamed up together and started a new rumour that was to cause an incredible amount of confusion and trouble.

Hunter had recently been to Egypt and had visited the inside of the Great Pyramid. At the top of the Grand Gallery, near the entrance of the first so-called 'relief chamber',[10] Hunter saw something that caught his attention: a rickety wooden ladder and a few electrical cables going into the dark entrance, and noted the presence of bags containing debris and rubble. This convinced him that something strange was going on. In a wild leap of imagination, Hunter concluded that Dr Hawass was secretly excavating a tunnel in order to gain access to the possible chamber behind the Gantenbrink 'door'. Excitedly, this was reported on the Internet. For months this rumour flowed from website to website and gradually began to be converted into a 'fact'. In April 1998 Hunter and Hoagland were given a huge opportunity to spread this story on Art Bell's 'Coast to Coast' radio programme.[11] The matter further escalated when Art Bell flew to Egypt to verify the story for himself. Amused by the whole bizarre turn of events, Dr Zahi Hawass decided to allow Art Bell unrestricted access to the Great Pyramid so that he could see for himself that what Hunter and Hoagland were saying was, quite simply, a pure fabrication or, at best, a witless mistake. After visiting the whole interior of the monument Art Bell was forced to concede that no secret excavation was taking place inside or outside the Pyramid. The 'relief chambers' were simply being cleaned.

The story, however, did not end there. In May 1998, during a major conference held on a cruise ship bound for Alaska and where Dr Hawass had come as a main speaker,[12] Art Bell read out a statement by Hunter and Hoagland which again accused Hawass of these goings-on in the Great Pyramid and claimed that, according to Hunter's 'informants', Hawass had been fired from his post. One of Hunter's 'informants' at Giza was a Canadian man going by the name of 'Amargi' Hillier, who had settled in the hamlet of Nazlet Al Samman near the Giza necropolis. Amargi runs a website and acts as a sort of 'Egypt gossip' clearing house.[13] Also as main speakers at this conference were my colleagues Graham Hancock and John Anthony West. I had been invited but had to cancel due to an illness. Although Graham, John and I were not regarded as best friends of Hawass by any means, we nonetheless felt sickened by such defamation. Clearly something drastic had to been done about Hunter et al. We really could not stay on the fence any longer and let these wild rumours infect the public domain. It so happened that we had just heard from official sources that Dr Hawass had been promoted to the ministerial status of Under-secretary of State for the Culture Ministry. Hancock and West decided to place a posting on the Internet condemning Hunter and Hillier for spreading such rumours.[14] I followed suit with a similar posting a few days later.[15] Hunter and Hillier then began to blame each other for their huge blunder, and ended up having a verbose war of words on the Internet.

The idea of a 'NASA' conspiracy at the Great Pyramid was too precious to give up for Hoagland.[16] In August 1998 Richard Hoagland came to meet me in San Diego, California. He wanted to show me some video footage he had got from Boris Said. This, he said, would persuade me that secret excavations were, in fact, going on inside the Great Pyramid – just as Larry Hunter had said. The meeting took place at my friend Dennis Seisun's place. The tapes, however, proved disappointing. All I was able to see was rough Hi-8 footage of a group of Americans inside the Great Pyramid's Grand Gallery and in the 'relief chambers'. The Grand Gallery was shored up with wooden scaffolding, which confirmed that the film was taken during the period when the inside of the Pyramid was being renovated. Nothing of notable value was shown. There was a young inspector from the EAO whom I knew who was accompanying the group. Other than that, I could see nothing suspicious. Hoagland realised he had brought the wrong tapes, and promised to send me copies of the 'right' ones through the mail. These arrived at my home in England a while later. There were two tapes. One was a repeat of what I had seen in San Diego but the other tape immediately grabbed my attention: it was marked 'Schor Expeditions at Giza – 1996-97'.[17] Although neither of the tapes proved Larry Hunter's claims, the 'Schor Expedition' tape, as we have seen in Chapter 10, provided me with a remarkable insight into the activities of Dr Schor and his team at Giza during the 1996-97 expeditions. It was after that that I decided to make a suggestion to Hoagland. I told him that I would see if Dr Hawass was willing to let him have unrestricted access to the Great Pyramid as he had done for Art Bell. The deal was that if Hoagland found no secret excavations then he would make this known publicly in a statement on the Internet. This would certainly put an end to all those rumours. I put the idea to Dr Hawass, who agreed, and a date was fixed for late November 1998 for Hoagland's visit. At the last minute, however, Hoagland pulled out.[18] He did not feel comfortable anymore with this plan.

The alleged secret excavations in the 'relief' chambers of the Great Pyramid were, of course, non-existent. The cables and bags of debris that Hunter had seen were the leftovers from the cleaning job that had been carried out in April 1997 when an Italian TV crew from RAI 3 had been taken to the 'relief' chambers by Dr Hawass to examine the graffiti left there by ancient workers.[19] The chambers were full of rubble which had to be cleared, and electrical cables were extended into them for the high-wattage lamps. Indeed, in December 1997 Graham Hancock had been escorted by Dr Hawass to these chambers and was also able to confirm that no excavations were taking place in there.[20]

The Larry Hunter affair, however, pales when compared to perhaps the most notorious case at Giza which involves a Territorial Army recruit, Nigel Appleby, and his merry band of Operation Hermes team members. With the Appleby affair, as it came to be called, a truly bizarre twist in the quest for the Hall of Records was about to take shape with disastrous consequences that would lead to an investigation by HM Crown Prosecution in London.

OPERATION HERMES: ASSAULT ON THE PYRAMIDS

We have already mentioned in Chapter 10 how the story of Nigel Appleby and his Operation Hermes first broke in the *Sunday Times* of London. The article, which was written by Cherry Norton, the reader will recall, had announced that Nigel Appleby had been granted a licence from the Egyptian authorities to excavate the Hall of Records at Giza.[21] Appleby's strange obsession with the Hall of Records began when he was a little boy in Cyprus. In his semi-autobiographical book Nigel recalls how in the small village where he lived there were many people who apparently 'claimed to see apparitions of ghosts and what looked like knights of the crusade'.[22] At the age of four, while playing with his sister, Nigel swallowed a massive dose of tranquillisers which almost killed him. He was rushed to the local hospital where he understandably had strange hallucinations. He dreamt he saw 'five wise men' who told him that he was destined for some very important mission later on in life. His miraculous recovery persuaded Nigel that he had been visited by some sort of angelic beings, and he thus decided to find out what his life mission was. Before he managed to do so, he was struck down by a rare ear infection that again temporarily affected his mind. While recovering in bed, he delved into books such as Erich Von Daniken's *Chariot of the Gods* and Robert Temple's *The Sirius Mystery*. These books so inspired Nigel that he began to devote all his free time to researching ancient mysteries, which eventually led him to believe that he had worked out where to find the fabled Hall of Records at Giza.[23] This, realised Nigel, was his life mission at last.

In Colchester, England, Nigel joined the Territorial Army. It was during a NATO exercise in 1993 that he met Bill Shirley, a fellow recruit who shared many of Nigel's interests. Nigel and Bill decided to found together Operation Hermes in order to find the Hall of Records. In 1997 they were joined by twenty other 'volunteers', many of whom were still active in the British armed forces. Apparently a training officer at the MOD's Colchester barracks agreed to provide them with various facilities and equipment.[24] From this military base Nigel and his team prepared for their 'expedition' to Giza. This entailed intensive training sessions in 'desert survival skills' and undertaking difficult treks in the forest in order to form strong 'bonding' between team members.[25] Other training sessions were organised through a specialist company called Outdoorlife Ventures based in Wales run by an ex-Royal Navy officer, David Nutt. Operation Hermes made contact with the British Embassy in Cairo with whom they were in 'close liaison' and apparently 'received a lot of help' while in Egypt.[26]

After the *Sunday Times* article the 'news' of the licensed expedition was circulated world-wide by Reuters, and Operation Hermes began to receive massive media attention.[27] This brought Nigel Appleby to the attention of a literary agent in London, Simon Trewin from Sheil Land Associates. Within days Nigel landed a big publishing deal with William Heinemann UK.[28] The book was published in early June 1998, but within days the publisher was obliged to pull it off the bookshelves and destroy all existing copies. The Egyptian authorities denied having had any dealings with Operation Hermes and said that no licence had been granted to them, and it also emerged that Nigel Appleby had used unauthorised material from over a dozen well-known authors, and was being threatened with legal action. The authors eventually settled for a formal apology, except one. Roger Ellis[29] was not satisfied with a simple apology, and decided to take the complaint to his local Member of Parliament and the Crown Prosecution. This amazing imbroglio ended up being raised at Westminster.[30] It is not clear whether Appleby was pursued for damages by his publishers, but the last I heard they had decided to drop this embarrassing affair and write off their losses. Nigel, however, was unrepentant. He keeps insisting that Operation Hermes is going to conduct an exploration in Egypt to find the Hall of Records in the near future.[31] His 'Foundation' now hands out impressive membership certificates and bestows merit titles for achievements in the arts and literature.[32] Nigel has recently announced his plans for a new and daring expedition. Not at Giza but in the remote regions of the Himalayas.[33]

Amazing as this may sound, the Appleby affair was followed by an even stranger story about Giza, this time involving the CIA, British MI5 and an extraterrestrial power group called the Council of Nine. Their aim? An 'insidious plot' to overthrow the religious order of the world . . .

THE STARGATE CONSPIRACY

Lynn Picknett and Clive Prince are two authors who specialise in a genre of books that balances precariously, as one critic put it, between non-fiction and the X-files.[34] Picknett and Prince have previously covered a wide variety of topics ranging from the mystery of the Turin Shroud to that of the elusive Knights Templar as well as the origins of Christianity.[35] In 1998 they decided to turn their investigation skills on Giza. A publishing deal was secured with Little Brown & Co. UK, and in July 1999 *The Stargate Conspiracy: Revealing the truth behind extraterrestrial contact, military intelligence and the mysteries of ancient Egypt* appeared in bookshops across the UK.[36] This book, whose title says it all, makes the claim that the CIA, MI5 and other military intelligence are using 'mind control' techniques and the work of some cutting-edge authors[37] to usher in a new religion involving extra-terrestrial beings passing as Egyptian gods known as the 'Council of Nine'. This insidious plot, according to the authors, also involves 'New

Age gurus to cutting-edge physicists, top-level scientists and multi-millionaires' as well as an assortment of 'alternative Egyptology' authors such as Graham Hancock, John Anthony West, Robert Temple and myself.[38] Thrown in, too, are colourful individuals such as the Israeli spoon-bender Uri Geller, the occultist Aleister Crowley, the psychic Edgar Cayce and the French 'Symbolist' Egyptologist R.A. Schwaller de Lubicz. Even the Nazi Party seems to have been somehow involved. Indeed, in *The Stargate Conspiracy* it is easier to work out who is *not* part of the plot. But there is, however, no use in protesting at their far-fetched claims; for as Picknett and Prince point out:

> This book is not an attempt to rally masses or create some kind of political backlash against the conspiracy. Perhaps, in any case, those with vested interest would ensure that such an attempt would be doomed to ignominious – and immediate – failure. Yet we believe that successful opposition is possible, beginning with the realisation that, perhaps like the Stargate itself, true resistance is in the mind.[39]

This sort of verbiage simply means that the authors want to have their cake and eat it. If there is no reaction to their book then, according to them, it is because the 'conspirators' have made sure that any 'political backlash' is 'doomed to ignominious and immediate failure'. *The Stargate Conspiracy* was hyped on the Internet months before its publication and received, presumably, the full backing of its publishers. This backing, in fact, came in the form of an unusually worded press release which associated all the supposed 'conspirators' with 'anti-black, anti-women and anti-Muslim' fundamentalist movements.[40] In the book itself the authors draw attention to the 'Magic 12'. The term, in actual fact, was coined by me when, in 1998, I brought together a group of popular authors for a millennium project – which I called Equinox 2000.[41] All the authors were researchers in the field of ancient mysteries and philosophies, and it was planned that we would give a series of conferences around the world, the last one being at Giza on the eve of the new millennium.[42] The objective was to symbolise the return of the Hermetic tradition to Egypt. A message of goodwill would then be delivered to the media. This, however, was far too straightforward for Picknett and Prince, who chose to see in this project some hidden and sinister CIA-linked agenda to pave the way for the return of the 'Council of Nine'. The author Colin Wilson, who reviewed *The Stargate Conspiracy* in the *Daily Mail*, was to write about this issue in the following manner:

SPACEMEN ARE COMING: On the eve of the millennium, a spectacular ceremony will take place on the Giza plateau, near Cairo. First, a magnificent gold capstone will be lowered into place on top of the Great Pyramid, to replace the old one which has been missing for thousands of years. Then, at midnight, the Egyptologist Robert Bauval will appear on a platform in front of the Sphinx, accompanied by a group known as the 'Magic 21' (sic) and will announce the return of the ancient gods to Egypt. Then, according to Lynn Picknett and Clive Prince, anything could happen. It may be the landing of a flying saucer full of duplicitous spacemen posing as ancient gods. It may be the announcement of the discovery of a secret chamber inside the Great Pyramid full of ancient texts proving the Egyptians knew far more than we do. Or it may be the announcement of a new religion, 'cynically exploiting the spiritual craving of the modern world' . . . What is the Stargate Conspiracy? On this vital matter, the book is slightly less than explicit. It begs the reader to follow the investigation like a detective story, working up to the grand denouement. But the climax never comes. Instead, we get dark innuendoes that a number of writers on ancient Egypt, such as Graham Hancock, Robert Temple and John Anthony West, are engaged in a sinister plot devised by the CIA . . .[43]

A website was set up to promote *The Stargate Conspiracy*, where members of the public were invited to contribute their views through something called 'The Stargate Assembly'.[44] A poll conducted on the Internet a few weeks after the publication of the book showed that over twenty percent of readers actually believed in this conspiracy.[45] Hardly a month after the publication of *The Stargate Conspiracy* came yet another book on the Giza conundrum. This was by Chris Ogilvie-Herald and Ian Lawton,[46] and carries the haughty title *Giza: The Truth*.[47] Here, too, the authors indulge in a bizarre acrimonious review of the work and activities of 'famous authors' and foul play at Giza. This book is more or less in the same line as *The Stargate Conspiracy* except that the CIA and MI5 are replaced by greedy authors and con-men duping the public and cashing in on the millennium frenzy surrounding Giza.[48] But it is really not my objective to pass further judgement on this strange publishing phenomenon.

In the Prologue I raised some troubling questions that now, with the hindsight of our research, can be carefully tackled. The stakes are high. Not just for the future of explorations at Giza, but also for the way we must perceive our lost past – and fragile future.

THE WIDER VIEW

I must confess that when I started writing *Secret Chamber*, I was somehow counting on my close and personal involvement with all the strange goings-on at Giza, in the hope of stumbling on some bizarre and perhaps even dangerous conspiracy. It was very difficult to see how so much smoke could exist without some sort of fire behind it. Indeed, it seemed extremely unlikely. But because something might look suspicious to some from the outside does not necessarily mean that there is some 'insidious plot' involved. In my investigation I have relied as much as possible on *documented evidence from primary sources*. And when on the few occasions where I had to depend on word of mouth, then I have used only recorded statements.[49] But perhaps most of all, through the years I have got to know personally many of the main players in this affair.[50] And although there are those whose personal motives and private agendas I still consider somewhat suspect and even dubious, they have nothing to do with the kind of 'insidious plot' imagined in *The Stargate Conspiracy* or the deceptive and tarnished motives derided by Ogilvie-Herald and Lawton or those 'secret explorations' hyped by Larry Hunter and Amargi Hillier.[51] One of the most potent powers in the human experience is the ability sometimes to see ourselves as others see us. I quote, therefore, from *The Stargate Conspiracy*, from a statement the authors made of themselves:

> We certainly considered the idea that we have developed into sad cases of paranoia – the thought was to recur several times as we plunged deeper into this investigation . . .[52]

I am not a sceptic and I have always encouraged a healthy opposition to orthodoxy and bigotry. I certainly believe in having an open mind, and encourage others to do so. But as someone wisely said – I think it was Gerald Hawkins – 'to have an open mind is one thing, but to have your brains drop out is another'. There will always be those who are ready to believe anything they hear or read. There will always be those who exploit such a phenomenon. All you have to do is read the history books – or indeed the modern tabloid press – to prove the point. Complacency, however, is not what I advocate either. I am not saying that all is well and above board at Giza and at the Supreme Council of Antiquities in Egypt. Far from it. My investigation leaves it clear in my mind that there has been – to put it as delicately as I can – some grave irregularities in the way certain explorations have taken place at Giza. There are still many questions to be cleared on how and why certain activities have been allowed to happen at all. Whether these can be classified as mistakes, political blunders, cover-ups or malpractice remains to be seen. The Giza monuments are a legacy to all humankind and the patrimony granted to UNESCO must be respected and applied. I believe that as long as there is no full transparency in all exploratory work at Giza, then rumours and wild conspiracy theories will persist and the trust in the keepers of this sacred site will become tainted and strained.

The Egyptologists and the Egyptian authorities have to recognise that the Giza monuments cannot be treated as any other ancient edifice in Egypt. They are unique not only in their architectural grandeur and precision, but also, and more especially, in the powerful spiritual, psychological and subliminal effect they have always exerted on people from all walks of life. They are, as I hope I have succeeded in showing in this book, powerful 'devices' that can have wide and far-reaching consequences on the collective unconscious. As such, these monuments must be handled with care. It is my conviction that the Giza monuments were deliberately designed to service a powerful initiatory process, that they are, therefore, highly energised spiritual tools that must not be tampered with lightly, or let into the wrong hands. Bearing this in mind, it is thus important that individuals or organisations with dubious agendas be kept away from direct exploratory work or, at the very least, carefully screened before licences are handed out.

This is especially important when it comes to explorations that may lead to the finding of a secret chamber. I remain convinced that such a find will be made sooner or later. I believe the evidence supporting such a notion is compelling – not to say overwhelming. Giza is a cipher, and if we have read its 'message' correctly, then there is 'something' underneath the Sphinx which, as we have shown in *Keeper of Genesis*, is directly related to the idea of the Egyptian 'genesis' or 'First Time', the 'transfiguration of Osiris' and the 'books of Thoth'. What that 'something' could be we can only guess. But my own gut feeling is that it will turn up to be a small, sealed casket containing perhaps relics attributed to Osiris and the 'books of Thoth'. Everything about the Giza necropolis compels me to conclude that it must be regarded as the major centre of the star-cult and magical initiatory tradition of ancient Egypt and, as such, would serve as a repository of all the original artefacts and books that were associated with Osiris, Thoth and their cult – much in the same way that the Vatican, for example, has served as a main repository of ancient books and relics associated with Christ and the Bible. As much as the Vatican clergy would want to ensure the preservation of not only artefacts and human remains but also written testimonies to the birth of Christianity for posterity and the benefit of the Church in future generations, so would the priests of the Pyramid cult want to ensure the preservation of the relics of Osiris and the 'books of Thoth'. Books with such a meritorious pedigree and believed to be of divine inspiration have a powerful hold on the collective psyche. I, myself, strongly believe that such relics and 'books', in some form or another, are preserved at Giza. The proof, of course, will be when Dr Schor and his team are allowed by the Egyptian authorities to verify this exciting possibility.[53]

We shall have to wait and see.

As for the placing of the gilded capstone on the Great Pyramid at midnight on the eve of the new millennium, I am not so sure how to regard this. On the face of it, it could be an innocent choice of celebration by the Egyptian authorities and the various organisers and committees who came up with this idea, or were part of the approval process. Yet I cannot dispel the nagging feeling that, in consideration of all the historical links that I have examined in this book, there lurks behind this affair a subtle, undetected force urging this powerful symbolic act forward. As I have already said, I am often haunted by the strong feeling that the Great Pyramids and Sphinx of Giza are powerful initiatory instruments that work subliminally and perpetually by their own innate energy. I am convinced that they are the crowning achievement of a powerful esoteric priesthood that intended them to be awakened at strategic moments in the evolution of mankind – with such awakenings brought about somehow by the majestic slow churning of the star-clock of precession. How exactly this phenomenon works, I cannot tell. All I know is that it *does* work. I see the handiwork of geniuses here – extraordinarily brilliant men who somehow seem to have understood something momentous about the human mind and how it 'works' with the rhythm of the stars and the silent 'language of the gods'.

Perhaps a curious event that happened to me in 1995-97 may shed a little light on this elusive phenomenon.

In October 1995 my old friend from Egypt, Dennis Seisun, came to visit me at my home in England. It is to Dennis, in fact, that I am indebted for being introduced to the Skyglobe 3.6 astronomical computer software. On this occasion I asked him to programme Skyglobe 3.6 in such a way so that an image of the eastern horizon would appear on the monitor screen of my computer when I switched it on every morning. I would thus be able to track the daily changes of the celestial bodies at sunrise. In short, I would follow the course of the sun and planets across the zodiacal belt throughout the year. Something odd then began to happen. I found myself thinking of certain things on certain days without knowing why or how. For example, in late May I would feel uneasy for no apparent reason, with an inexplicable sense of being drowned in a river. In mid-July I felt a sense of relief and, curiously, associated it with my twin sister. Then in late August I would have frequent thoughts of the Sphinx, and a strange sense of wanting to go between its paws. In late September I thought of a 'secret chamber' under the back of the Sphinx. It took me a long time to finally click that such thoughts were linked to watching Skyglobe 3.6 every morning. I was being affected subliminally by what I saw, namely the sun as it entered various stations along its yearly course. I had unconsciously identified myself with the solar disc, as the Horus-kings of Egypt and other high initiates had consciously done. As Graham Hancock and I have shown in *Keeper of Genesis*,[54] the same 'solar' journey was undertaken by the high-initiates during the Pyramid Age, the details of which are allegorically expressed in the astronomical-astrological rituals found in the Pyramid Texts.[55]

In late May the sun enters the Milky Way, hence the feeling of drowning in a river. In mid-July the sun emerges from the other side of the Milky Way, hence the sense of relief of having averted drowning. The association with my twin sister came from the fact that at that time the sun is in Gemini, the 'twin' sign. On 23rd August the sun is in conjunction with Regulus, the bright star between the 'paws' of Leo, the 'celestial Sphinx'.[56] A month later, on the equinox of September, the sun is directly under the rump of Leo. I was so deeply impressed by this subliminal 'astral influence' that I decided to test it on some friends, who curiously also responded to its strange effect.[57] This alone convinced me that one of the powerful tools of the initiatory process into the ancient mysteries was this blend of astronomy realities and astrological myth or – as we crudely refer to it today – astrology. Recently attention has been focused on this strange phenomenon by such authors as David Ovason, Robert Lomas and Christopher Knight and the Warburg Institute scholar Yuri Stoyanov in their studies on Masonic rituals in connection with astrology and astral magic.[58] As Ovason correctly points out: 'underlying the Masonic symbolism of initiation is a profound grasp of the cosmic bodies which are the subject of astrology'.[59]

THE MIDNIGHT HOUR AND THE MESSIANIC STAR

At midnight on 31st December 1999, as our planet straddles an old age and a new one, the star-clock of precession, as we shall now see, will chime a most remarkable and synchronistic 'midnight hour' for the new millennium and the star Sirius. To understand the inspiring sight that the hundreds of thousands of spectators at Giza will witness, as well as the hundreds of millions watching it 'live' on television, we need to go through a little lesson in observational astronomy.

From the earliest times, the star Sirius – the brightest star in the sky – has held a special fascination for man. Not only does its bluish-purple sparkle draw attention, like some exquisite cosmic gemstone, but its special position on the celestial landscape, as well as its unique motion, has given this star a mystique that caused it to be seen as the very centre of our universe.[60] Sirius is located immediately below the constellation of Orion, and together they form one of the best known navigational markers in the sky.[61] With one of the highest proper[62] motions among the visible stars, the position of Sirius relative to Orion and the Milky Way shifts at the rate of about one degree in every 3000 years as seen from the Earth – a relatively large distance in cosmic terms. Its strategic position in the sky coupled with its brightness created a very unusual phenomenon in the land of the Pharaohs in c. 3400 BC. Sirius would perform what is today known as a 'heliacal rising' (rising at the break of dawn for the first time after seventy days of invisibility) on the day of the summer solstice (21st to 24th June according to our Gregorian calendar). This phenomenon much impressed the ancient people of the Nile, more especially because at about the same time the waters of the Nile would begin to swell – another magical phenomenon which today we know is caused by the heavy tropical rains that fall in Central Africa at that time of the year. This rising of Sirius/summer solstice/Nile Flood con-junction quite understandably gave rise to much speculation among the ancient observers, and a powerful cult began to be formulated around this special star. It is known with certainty that the priest-astronomers of Egypt marked the New Year with the heliacal rising of Sirius as early as the Pyramid Age and probably even long before.[63] The celestial imagery they saw was this:

1. About one month before the summer solstice the constellation of Orion would be seen rising in the east, acting as a herald to the coming of Sirius and also the advent of the Nile's Flood.

2. On the day of the summer solstice, one hour before sunrise, the characteristic three stars of Orion's belt would rise in the east paving the way, as it were, for the 'birth' of the star Sirius after its long period of invisibility.

3. Minutes before the sun's light totally obliterates the starlight in the sky, the star Sirius emerges from the eastern horizon.

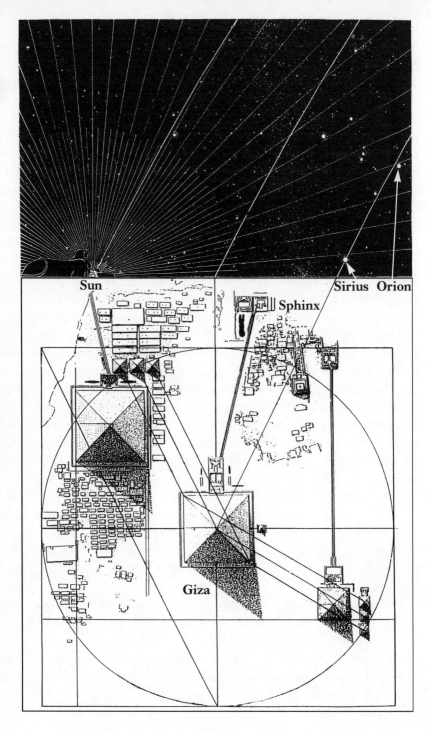

Sun

Sphinx

Sirius Orion

Giza

Fig. 28. Summer solstice in epoch 2500 BC: artist's impression of the 'Duat' region.

This unique cosmic spectacle, with its potent association with the yearly 'rebirth' of the Nile and, consequently, the rebirth of the whole of Egypt, gave rise to the myth of the Virgin-mother Star-goddess, Isis. It is a well-known fact that the legendary couple Osiris and Isis (who were also brother and sister), who founded the divine dynastic lineage of the Horus-kings of Egypt through the magical birth of their only son, Horus, were themselves identified with Orion (Osiris) and Sirius (Isis). In the Pyramid Texts the yearly heliacal rising of Sirius is dramatically presented as the moment when the womb of the Star-goddess Isis (know to the Greeks as Sothis) acted as a cosmic gate from which was 'reborn' the divine child Horus. As one such passage attests:

> (Osiris) . . . your sister Isis comes to you rejoicing for love of you. You have placed her on your phallus [belt] and your seed issued into her, she being ready as Sothis (Sirius), and Horus has come forth from her as 'Horus who is in Sothis'.[64]

The hieroglyphic sign that makes up the word 'Sirius' – 'Sepdt' in ancient Egyptian – is the combination of two symbols, namely the five-pointed star and the pyramidion or capstone of an obelisk or pyramid, i.e. a 'Benben'.[65] Although the five-pointed star symbol was used to represent any star in the sky, its combination with a triangle or pyramidion was specifically used to denote Sirius. This combined symbol was known as early as the Pyramid Age and may predate construction of the Great Pyramid by several centuries, if not millennia.[66]

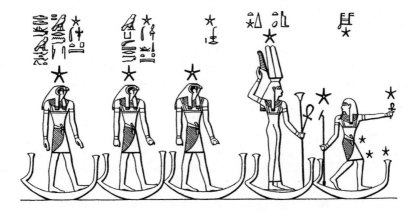

*Fig. 29. Orion-Osiris leading the way followed by Isis-Sirius
and the Horus-Kings as stars or planets.*

321

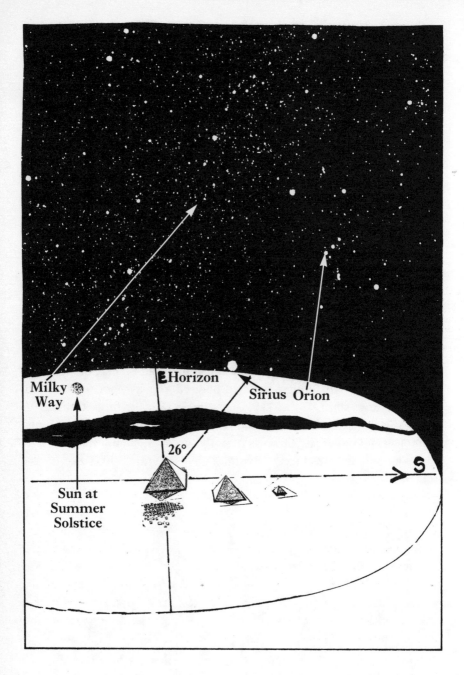

Fig. 31. Summer solstice in epoch 2500 BC: artist's impression of the 'Duat' region.

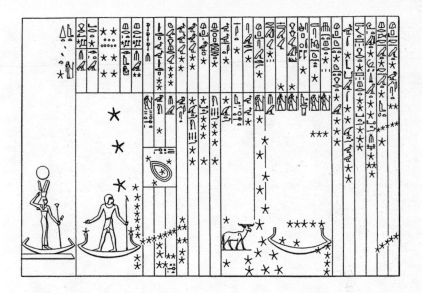

Fig. 31. Isis-Sirius and Orion-Osiris (far left), from the Tomb of Senmut c. 1450 BC) Note three stars of Orion's belt.

In 1990 I published a paper in the Oxford journal *Discussions in Egyptology* where I showed that the southern shaft of the Queen's Chamber in the Great Pyramid of Giza was directed, in c. 2500 BC, towards the star Sirius as it crossed the meridian (i.e. the north-south centreline axis) of the sky.[67] Since 1964 it had, in fact, been known that the southern shaft of the King's Chamber of the Great Pyramid was directed towards Orion's belt, also at the same date of c. 2500 BC.[68] In consideration of these facts, and also of the 'stellar' birth ritual described in the Pyramid Texts, I was compelled to put forward the hypothesis that some powerful ceremony was probably conducted in the Great Pyramid in conjunction with the motions of the star Sirius to mark the 'birth' of the divine child Horus.[69] Now there is, of course, another 'divine child' whose birth was also marked, some 2500 years later, by the appearance of a bright star in the east. This child was Jesus of Nazareth. It is only one of the Gospels – Matthew – that speaks of the Magi and the 'star in the east':

Jesus was born at Bethlehem in Judea during the reign of Herod. After his birth astrologers (Magi in the original Greek text) from the east arrived in Jerusalem, asking, 'Where is the child who is born to be king of the Jews? We observed the rising of his star, and we have come to pay him homage . . .'[70]

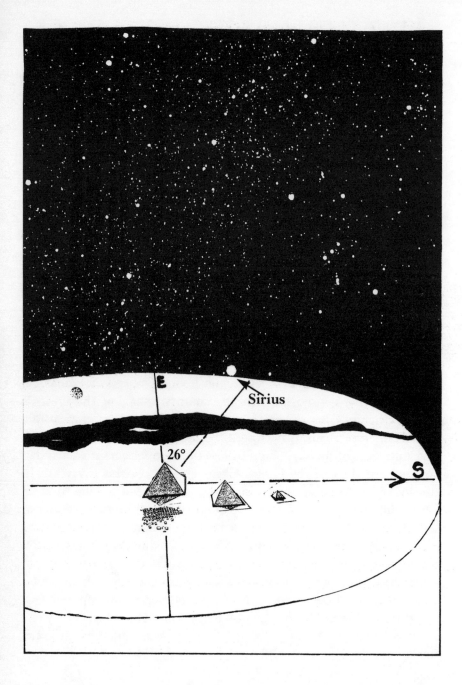

Fig. 32. Sirius rising just before the Sun near summer solstice c. 2500 BC. The same sky image was also seen at sunset at the time of Jesus during the winter Solstice near Chrismastime.

And the star which they had seen at its rising went ahead of them until it stopped above the place where the child lay . . .[71]

After they had gone, an angel of the Lord appeared to Joseph in a dream, and said to him, 'Rise up, take the child and his mother and escape with them to Egypt, and stay there until I tell you . . .' This was to fulfil what the Lord had declared through the prophet: 'I call my son out of Egypt.'[72]

The Matthew Gospel, according to some Biblical scholars, was probably written in the city of Alexandria in Egypt in the first century AD.[73] This was a place where, for over 3000 years, the 'birth' of a divine child was celebrated with the heliacal rising of the star Sirius at dawn, marking the beginning of a new day and, more specifically, the New Year. This special moment fell, as we have seen, around the time of the summer solstice in the middle of the third millennium BC. It is clear from the Matthew Gospel that the star of Jesus's birth was seen rising in the east, and that the Magi-astrologers followed this star – or rather its direction – in order to reach Bethlehem. It is important to place ourselves in the contexts where and when the Matthew Gospel was composed: first century AD Alexandria. The reader will recall from Chapter 5 that Alexandria was under Roman rule, and its tutelary deity was Serapes, the Hellenistic form of the Egyptian god Osiris. Now the son of Osiris was the 'divine child' Horus born from the womb of the virgin-star goddess Isis, whose star was Sirius. The appearance of Sirius at rising was thus in Roman times very much still a potent symbol of divine birth and, more especially, of the birth of a messianic-like 'king' of solar pedigree. The cult of Isis and the infant Horus was extremely popular in Graeco-Roman Egypt; the typical Egyptian iconography of the goddess holding the divine child Horus in her lap served as the prototype for the classical Madonna–like Isis holding the chubby-looking child known as Harpocrates, another name for 'Horus-the-child'. According to the eminent Egyptologist and orientalist E.A. Wallis Budge:

She (Isis) is represented in the act of suckling her child Horus (which) formed the foundation for the Christian figures and painting of the Madonna and Child. Several of the incidents of the wanderings of the Virgin with Child in Egypt as recorded in the Apocryphal Gospels reflect scenes in the life of Isis as described in the texts found on the Mettenich Stele,[74] and many of the attributes of Isis, the God-mother, the mother of Horus . . . are identical with those of Mary the Mother of Christ. The writers of the Apocryphal Gospels intended to pay additional honour to Mary the Virgin by ascribing to her the attributes which up to the time of the advent of Christianity they had regarded as the peculiar

325

property of Isis . . . and if parallels between the mythological history of Isis and Horus and the history of Mary and the Child be considered, it is difficult to see how they could possibly avoid perceiving in the teachings of Christianity reflections of the best and most spiritual doctrines of the Egyptian religion . . . (for example) the belief in the conception of Horus by Isis through the power given to her by Thoth, the Intelligence or Mind of the God of the universe, and in the resurrection of the body and of everlasting life, is coeval with the beginning of history in Egypt . . . Many of the heresies of the early Christian Church in Egypt were caused by the survival of ideas and beliefs connected with the old native gods which the convert to Christianity wished to adapt to their new creed. Be this, however, as it may, the knowledge of the ancient Egyptian religion which we now possess fully justifies the assertions that the rapid growth and progress of Christianity in Egypt were due mainly to the fact that the new religion, which was preached there by Saint Mark and his immediate followers, in all its essentials so closely resembled that which was the outcome of the worship of Osiris, Isis and Horus that popular opposition was entirely disarmed. In certain places in the South of Egypt e.g. Philae, the worship of Osiris and Isis maintained its own until the beginning of the fifth century of our era . . . speaking generally, at this period in all other parts of Egypt Mary the Virgin and Child had taken the places of Isis and Horus, and the 'God-mother' or 'mother of the god' was no longer Isis, by Mary . . .[75]

Dozens of the Mother-and-Child figurines which Wallis Budge alludes to are today preserved in the Graeco-Roman Museum in Alexandria as well as depicted in religious artwork from that period.

Another rival to 'Horus-the-child', however, was the Romanised cult of Mithras, a 'son of god' whose birthday, as we have seen in Chapter 5, was celebrated on 25th December, i.e. at around the winter solstice.[76] At sunset on that day, Roman families would light candles and adorn their homes with pine trees, a sort of early prelude to the idea of the Christmas-tree.[77]

It is well-known that Mithras was identified with Orion,[78] a fact made obvious not just from the ancient texts but also from the classical depiction of this god slaying the celestial bull. The association with the 'Bull of the Sky' is interesting, for Osiris, too, was often associated with the 'Bull of the Sky' and, of course, was identified with the legendary Apis bull of Memphis whose death marked the 'rebirth' of Osiris and from which the god later obtained his Grecian name of Serapis.[79] At the feet of Mithras can be seen the celestial 'dog', i.e. Canis Major, whose principal star is Sirius.[80] This picture is easily explained in astronomical terms: at sunset on 25th December during the early Graeco-Roman period, the picture afforded in the eastern side of the sky was that of Orion heralding the appearance of Sirius at its moment of rising in the

Fig. 33. Magi–astrologers on top of ziggurat.

horizon. Mithras, being originally a divinity from Persia (the 'East'), was connected with the cult of the Magi, a fact clearly confirmed by the depiction of the Nativity Magi in Renaissance Christian tradition donning the so–called 'Phrygian cap' worn by Mithras.[81] Thus it can be appreciated why the notion that Orion, i.e. three bright stars (Orion's belt), heralding the 'birth star' of the 'son of God' was symbolically transferred to the idea of 'three Magi from the east' heralding the birth of Jesus. Indeed, in some Western folklore traditions, the three Magi are called the 'three stars of Orion's belt'.[82] Now like the Romans, the early Judeo-Christians celebrated the transition of the new day (and year) not at dawn (sunrise), as the ancient Egyptians did, but at dusk (sunset). Bearing this in mind, and by reversing the dawn rising of Sirius to the 'dusk' rising of Sirius, we get a startling picture in the sky as seen from Egypt in the first century AD: *immediately after sunset, as the sky darkens, the first group of stars to appear in the east are those of Orion. These 'herald' the star Sirius that now is seen rising over the eastern horizon.*

There can be little doubt that the writer of the Matthew Gospel chose this immensely powerful astrological imagery to depict the Nativity story in astral terms to announce the coming of the new king-messiah. In the Pyramid Age, and throughout most of the pharaonic period, the star Sirius would rise close to 26 degrees 18 minutes south of east (azimuth 116 degrees 18 minutes) as seen from the Great Pyramid. Almost the same angle was formed to the north of east by the sun rising at the same time near the summer solstice, when in the sign of Leo. The latter 'solar' angle of 26 degrees 18 minutes gave the bearing of Bethlehem.[83] Bethlehem is located on latitude 31 degrees 42 minutes North and longitude 35 degrees 12 minutes East. At about the same epoch an observer at Bethlehem looking in the direction 26 degrees 18 minutes would see the setting of the star Sirius and, should he decide to 'follow that star', *would eventually reach the foot of the Great Pyramid of Giza.* Any first century AD astrologer in Egypt, especially one keen to link the town of Bethlehem with the place of divine birth and solar pedigree of the 'Lion of Judea' (David), would know this.

In their book *The Hiram Key,* authors Robert Lomas and Christopher Knight point out that the sect of the Mandeans of Iraq were the direct descendants of the Nasoreans of Judea, of which Jesus is said to have been a member.[84] It turns out that the Mandeans have an ancient tradition of a magical land in the west inhabited by spiritual beings and which they believed was under a special star. This star was apparently called 'Merica', and Lomas and Knight make the giant speculative leap of suggesting that was the basis of the name for 'America', the land in the west to which the Knights Templar supposedly sailed in 1303.[85] There is no need to go that far to explain the name of a land west of Judea which was under the tutelary of a special star – a star which, by extension, can be associated with the birth of a king-messiah. The name 'Merica' or 'Merika' sounds very Egyptian to me. It could be the composite of 'Meri-Ka', which would translate in ancient Egyptian as something like 'Spiritual Land of the Pyramids (i.e. Egypt)'.[86] This name would fit exactly the idea that under the star Sirius in the west, as seen from Bethlehem, was, in actual fact, the Great Pyramid. A pun, too, can be seen in the name 'Meri-Ka' and that of 'Mary Ka', i.e. 'The Spirit of Mary', which certainly would not have escaped the Christian mythmakers of Egypt and Judea.

Other links between Jesus and Egypt are also given in the Matthew Gospel when, immediately after the visitation of the Magi-astrologers, an angel instructs Joseph, in a dream, to leave Judea and direct himself to Egypt. By 'following' the direction of the star Sirius in the west, a traveller from Bethlehem would be on a course bearing straight to Heliopolis near the Great Pyramid. It cannot be a coincidence, therefore, that according to Christian tradition the Holy Family came to find sanctuary and rested under the tamarisk tree (sacred to Osiris) in the Cairo suburb of Matareya, the site of ancient Heliopolis. This was the solar city par excellence of the ancient world and where, since the dawn of civilisation, the solar 'king-priests' were ordained. Lomas and Knight show how the 'Star of David' was, in fact, a symbol of Jesus and how it is made up of two pyramids inserted into each other representing the idea of a 'king priest' messiah:

> The star of David is today fully accepted as the symbol of Judaism but the hexagram is actually two symbols superimposed to create a new, composite meaning, and its origin is not Jewish at all. The top and bottom points of this star are the apex of two pyramids, overlaid one upon the other. The upward pointing pyramid is an ancient symbol for the power of a king, with its base resting on Earth and its summit reaching to Heaven. The other represents the power of the priest, established in Heaven and reaching down to Earth . . . As such it is the only true sign of Jesus, and it carries the extra meaning as being representative of the bright star of David's line that arose in the morning. It is called the star of David, not because David invented it, but because Jesus used it and he positioned himself to be the 'Star of David' that had been prophesied . . .[87]

In actual fact, the predominant esoteric layer of meaning in the 'Star of David' symbol is that it symbolises the completion or fulfilment of the 'Work' which humanity must undertake in order to reunite with God. As such, Jesus the Messiah in the Christian mysteries is the epicentral figure who is deemed to have initiated the decisive turning point in the 'Work' for humanity to accomplish in His name. It can be thus appreciated why, in Masonic ideologies, such a role can, at least symbolically and at a lower though analogous level, be attributed to Messianic-like leaders such as Napoleon Bonaparte for the French and George Washington for the Americans. Perhaps worth noting in passing is that the same Hermetic tag was allocated by the English magician John Dee to Queen Elizabeth I, dubbed the Virgin Queen and the magical stellar maiden Astrae (Virgo), as Frances A. Yates has shown in her brilliant thesis *Astrae: The Imperial Theme in the Sixteenth Century.* [88]

At Heliopolis, as we have seen, was to be found the temple of the Phoenix in which was kept the Benben relic in the Holy of Holies. At the time of Jesus much of the remains of the sacred precinct still survived and the place of the Benben was marked by a free-standing obelisk dating from the time of Sesostris I.[89] The Benben, as we have seen in Chapters

Fig. 34. The 'G' in the blazing star.

4 and 5, was sacred to Osiris as well as to Ra, the sun-god, and was a symbol of divine birth. The star Sirius was associated with the idea of the Benben stone that crowns obelisks and pyramids. Thus in this imagery which brings together the star Sirius, the obelisk and the Benben capstone we have potent symbolism not only evoking divine birth but, more especially, the divine birth of Christ.

In 1995 I published an article which thus put forward the hypothesis that the Star of Bethlehem was none other than the star Sirius.[90] In that article I discuss the connection between the three Magi kings in Western and Eastern folklore with the three stars in Orion's belt which are also, by extension, the celestial representations of the three Pyramids of Giza.[91] Since in the Great Pyramid there are two shafts which were designed to point to Orion's belt and Sirius, then by transposition of religious ideologies and symbolism, the Great Pyramid becomes, in sort, a huge 'messianic time marker' – an idea, as we have seen, that was first nurtured by the Anglo-Israelites and commented on in my previous book, *Keeper of Genesis*.[92]

But that is not all.

The connection between the star Sirius and the gilded apex of an obelisk or pyramid crops up in the strangest of circumstances through the ages and, more intriguingly, in Masonic symbolism and Masonic astrological lore. Lomas and Knight, who are themselves Freemasons, describe the final stages of the Masonic ceremony of the 'raising' of the Master Mason, the ultimate level of initiation in craft Freemasonry. The general idea is that the initiate undergoes a symbolic death and then is 'raised' as an exalted Master. Lomas, who describes his own initiation, says that immediately after the 'raising':

> The Worshipful Master indicated upwards and to the left a glimmer of light in the East where I could see the small, illuminated shape of a star:
>
> . . . to that bright morning star whose rising brings peace and tranquillity to the faithful and obedient of the human race . . .[93]

According to Lomas and Knight, this 'Masonic star' is none other than the 'Star of David' which can be seen in profusion in Lodges and on Masonic regalia. But could this 'star' be the 'Egyptian' star Sirius?

THE FIVE-POINTED STAR, THE FREEMASONS AND WASHINGTON DC

In Masonic symbolism, one of the most potent symbols is the so-called glowing triangle or pyramid. This symbol is given prominence for it represents the idea of the 'Supreme Being' or 'Great Architect of the Universe' of the Freemasons.[94] In his controversial book *Inside the Brotherhood*, author Martin Short argues that this symbol was often associated with the term 'JAHBULON' used in the Master Mason degree ceremonies to denote the actual name of the 'Supreme Being'.[95] Short argues that in that strange name of Jahbulon there are three syllables – Jah (pronounced Yah), Bul and On – which seem to bring together the three principal Semitic names of God in ancient times: the Biblical 'Yahweh', the Semitic 'Baal' and the Egyptian sungod Ra, evoked by the name 'On', the ancient name of Heliopolis.[96] Martin Short thus concluded that:

> . . . if JAHBULON means anything, it probably means 'God, the Lord of On' (i.e. Heliopolis), or possibly 'He Who is the Lord of On'. Whether that god is the Sun God Ra or Osiris the God of the Dead depends on which period of history takes your fancy.[97]

Although this interpretation was hotly denied by the Freemasons in 1983,[98] there is another interpretation of Jahbulon which links this term directly with the sacred mound of Heliopolis where once stood the Benben and where today still stands the great obelisk of Sesostris I. Often in Freemasonry the glowing triangle contains the letter G which denotes both the Grand Architect as well as the belief that geometry lies at the root of sacred knowledge and architecture. This combined symbol is indeed the one most commonly found in Masonic iconography, and its origin can be traced to the so-called Old Charges of Freemasonry which date from the late fourteenth century AD. In these ancient documents we are told that the sacred art of geometry stands supreme among the 'seven liberal arts' or sciences:

> . . . The which seven liberal sciences be as it were all one science that is to say Geometry. For thus may a man prove that all science's in the world be Geometry . . . all is Geometry.[99]

The 'craft' of geometry, according to the Old Charges, was founded by a son of the Biblical Lamech called 'Jabal of Geometry'.[100] Now 'Jabal' in Semitic languages means 'Mound'. And if, through symbolic connotation, we replace 'Geometry' with 'On', i.e. Heliopolis, we have 'Mount of Heliopolis' on whose apex, the reader will recall, once stood the original Benben Stone. Also another symbol often associated or, indeed, combined with the glowing triangle and meant to replace the G is the so-called five-pointed star. This star, which is known as the blazing or radiant star (*L'etoile flamboyante* in French Freemasonry), appears almost always in connection with either the glowing triangle or the letter G. Author David Ovason,[101] in his extensive study into this subject matter, brought to our attention that the five-pointed star was modelled by Masons on the idea of the five-pointed star of the ancient Egyptians and, most particularly, the star Sirius whose hieroglyphic symbols, as we have already said, were the combined five-pointed star and the pyramidion of the obelisk or Pyramid.[102] As Ovason points out, the star Sirius, which rose with the midsummer sun throughout the Hellenistic period, was known to the Greeks and Romans as the 'Dog Star' partly because it was the dominant star in the constellation of Canis Major (the Great Dog) and partly because its rising at that time of year brought the 'Canicullis' or 'Dog Days' of June-July, so named because of the scorching heat they were associated with. Because of this association, some modern scholars have identified Sirius with the Egyptian dog- or jackal-headed god Anubis,[103] but the ancient Egyptians always identified

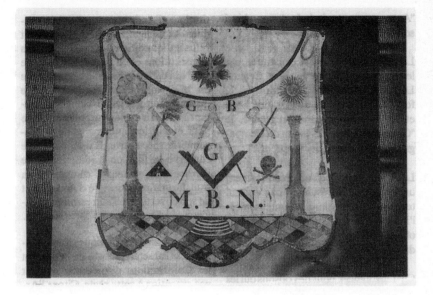

Fig. 35. Masonic apron. Note 'G' in blazing star.

this star with Isis, whom the Greeks called Sothis. This identification can be traced to the earliest epoch of Egyptian history, where numerous lines in the Pyramid Texts leave us in no doubt that the celestial form of the great Virgin-mother Isis was none other than the star Sirius-Sothis.[104] Ovason thus writes:

> The importance of the Egyptian star was recognised by Masons, who introduced its symbolism into its rituals, first in France and then into the United States. The American Freemason John Fellows wrote of Sirius as the 'radiant star', which was so widely used in the Masonic symbolism of America: 'The Blazing Star is Anubis, the Dog-Star; whose rising forewarned the Egyptians of the approach of the overflowing of the Nile.' It was scarcely surprising that the most sacred star of the Egyptians should have found its way into the Masonic mysteries, for the speculative Masons who sought out the origins of their craft seemed always to perfect their studies in Egypt. There may be little doubt that this Masonic transmission explains why Sirius should have become important for the United States of America. The new world was tied to the hermetic ancient world by several symbols, but the most secret of these was the Egyptian star, the flaming star which the Mason Napoleon Bonaparte had emblazoned on his apron.[105]

Another prominent Mason and contemporary of Napoleon who also had the blazing star put on his Masonic apron was Marie Joseph Paul

Yves Roch Gilbert Motier, better known as the Marquis de La Fayette.[106] Lafayette's apron can be seen today at the Washington Masonic Memorial in Alexandria, Washington DC.[107] La Fayette had played a pivotal part in both the French Revolution and the American Revolution alongside George Washington, with whom he struck up a close and noble brotherly friendship.[108] The prolific number of regions, streets and buildings in the USA that today bear his name is a token of the huge reverence that the American people bear towards this intrepid Frenchman. And none more so than the American Freemasons, to whom La Fayette represents the ideals of chivalry and is regarded as second only to George Washington. On 4th July 1917, for example, on Independence Day, General John J. Pershing, Commander-in-chief of the American Forces in France during World War I, headed a huge procession to the small cemetery of Picpus in Paris where La Fayette was buried and, in the presence of hundreds of Masons and also of Marshal Jules Joffre, the French hero of the war, uttered the famous words: 'La Fayette we are here' ('La Fayette nous voici').[109] With America helping to liberate France from the Germans, Perching was paying his nation's great debt of gratitude to the Frenchman who had, back in 1776, helped them in their struggle for independence from the English.[110]

The common denominator between La Fayette, Washington, Pershing and Joffre was the fact that they were all Freemasons. Pershing held the highest rank as a 33rd Degree Mason of the Supreme Council for the Ancient and Accepted Scottish Rites, sometimes also known as the Supreme Council of the 33rd Degree. The same title, incidentally, was held by the Marquis de La Fayette.[111] The Supreme Council of the 33rd Degree was founded in 1801 in Charleston, South Carolina, USA. It has its headquarters in Washington DC and it is from there that all other Supreme Councils around the world are regulated.[112] It offers thirty extra initiation degrees over and above the three standard degrees of craft or 'regular' Freemasonry,[113] and only a very elite handful are bestowed at any one time the much coveted 33rd Degree.[114] The emblem of the Supreme Council is, not unexpectedly, a triangle within which is the number 33. This number, it has often been pointed out, may refer to the final 'age' of Jesus who, according to Christian tradition, died at the age of thirty-three.[115]

It is obvious from the transposition of Masonic symbols that the number 33 has a deep mystical value associated with the letter G or the 'eye of God' also found in the glowing triangle or pyramid. Oddly, the Supreme Council also uses the double-headed eagle symbol, which has its origins in Christian iconography of the seventeenth century when it

Fig. 36. Symbol of the Qabalistic Order of the Rosy Cross.

was extensively used to denote the seal of the Hapsburg Holy Roman Emperor.[116] There is a curious seventeenth-century depiction of the capstone of an Egyptian obelisk which shows an 'eye' within the capstone which is surmounted by the double-eagle symbol.[117] This telling motif was designed by the Jesuit monk and celebrated Hermeticist, Athanasius Kircher, for the Hapsburg German Emperor Ferdinand III. There can be no doubt that it is this same symbol that is picked up, two centuries later, by the Supreme Council of the 33rd Degree. This motif can be seen quite plainly in a commemorative medal of the Supreme Council of the 33rd Degree in Germany dating to 1980.[118]

The connection between La Fayette and Washington in this Masonic context is most interesting. Ovason argues with much cogency that the Egyptian symbolism of the five-pointed star motif is very much an

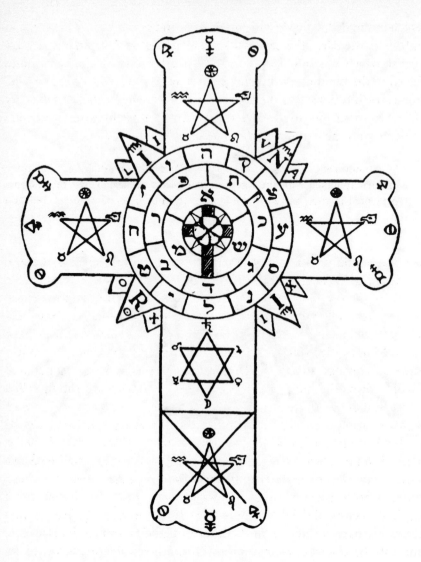

Fig. 37. Symbol of the Hermetic Order of the Golden Dawn.

integral part of the strange esoteric planning of the federal city of Washington DC.[119] Although the full evidence and arguments that Ovason puts forward are beyond the scope of this book,[120] his conclusions are worth noting, for they dovetail most eerily with a similar thesis concerning the city of Paris which I have been working on since 1988.[121] In brief then, Ovason shows how the layout and planning of the federal city was based on ancient Egyptian and Hermetic stellar lore and 'magic' which is mingled with Masonic mythology and symbolism. This, Ovason says, is particularly the case with the Washington Monument, a huge obelisk which was built between 1848 and 1885. In all the ceremonies linked to the building of this monument, from the laying of the corner-stone on 4th July 1848 to the final dedication ceremony on 21st February 1885, Ovason demonstrates how these events were deliberately chosen to coincide with the motions of the star Sirius[122]:

> The extraordinary truth is that the very existence of the Washington Monument is intimately linked with the Egyptian star Sirius, the Sihor that the ancients represented in their sacred hieroglyphics as an obelisk-like form as well as a star . . .[123]

For example, on 4th July 1848 when the cornerstone was laid, the sun, according to Ovason, was in '12.45 Cancer', which meant that in the course of the ceremony 'the star Sirius would have been on the eastern horizon. It would have been rising over the Capitol building, to the east of the monument.'[124] Apparently a five-pointed star had also been intended to be placed near the top of the Washington obelisk,[125] but this idea was later abandoned.[126] The thirteen tiers that make up the pyramid which crowns the huge obelisk were clearly modelled on the so-called Great Seal of the United States, where a thirteen-tier pyramid is shown with a glowing capstone and within it the 'eye of providence' – a well-known Masonic symbol which has also found its way on to the one-dollar bill.[127] But the solar-stellar Egyptian symbolism – apart from the obelisk itself – comes strong in the telling motif that was placed above the eastern entrance of the monument: a large winged solar disc (the Ureus) with a star in the centre of the disc. Oddly this star, however, is not five-pointed but rather has six sides, as in the 'Star of David' motif. This, I believe, can only be understood in the powerful Gnostic-Hermetic beliefs of speculative Freemasonry that the highest degree of initiation was achieved by Jesus at the age of thirty-three, i.e. the final death-resurrection ritual of a messianic king of solar pedigree. In Revelation 22:16 there is an extraordinarily relevant statement attributed to Christ which reads:

> I, Jesus, have sent my angels to you with this testimony for the churches. I am the scion of David, the Bright Star of Dawn . . .[128]

This statement, which is found on the very last page of the Bible, comes in the context of the prophetic return of the Holy City, the heavenly Jerusalem, which will mark the beginning of the new age of the Christ or the new order of the ages:

> Then I saw a new Heaven and a new Earth, for the first Heaven and the first Earth had vanished . . . I saw the holy city, New Jerusalem, coming down out of Heaven from God, made ready like a bride adorned for her husband. I heard loud voices proclaiming from the throne: 'Now at last God has his dwelling place among men! He will dwell among them and they shall be his people . . .'[129]

The 'Star of David' *is*, symbolically speaking, Jesus. It is the dawn star that mingles its light with that of the sun and, unquestionably, is the star Sirius. The esoteric aspect of the design of the 'Star of David' is the interlocking two pyramids, implying that the apex of the visible material world has its counterpart in the invisible, priestly, astral or 'angelic'

Fig. 38. The Mystical Union or 'Triangle' formed by the Solar King,
the Lunar Queen and the Dove of the Spirit (star).

world. The 'sending of the angels' in Revelations placed in the context of the establishment of a magical–holy city linked to the 'stars' is pure Hermetic astral magic which, the reader will recall, was extensively discussed in Chapter 6 in connection with the magical Hermetic city of Adocentyn in the Picatrix and the city of the sun' in the Hermetica manuscripts. This same 'astral magic' theme in connection with Masonic rituals is noted by Ovason, who writes:

> When the ancient Egyptians oriented their temples towards specific stars, they were not dealing with abstractions – they were literally inviting the stellar gods to participate beneficially in their earthly life. The same idea lies behind hundreds of foundation charts which have survived from the mediaeval period . . .[130]

> The designer (of Washington) intended this union of earth and skies to remain a secret. He knew how mysteries work. He recognised that it did not matter a great deal whether anyone who lived in his city discovered the meaning of his mystery; it was sufficient that he had bridged the material with the spiritual. He knew that the power born of this connection between earth and skies would continue to beneficially influence the souls of those who lived in the city, even if they did not know, with their conscious minds, whence this power came. His whole city was a Mystery, and he felt no need to explain it. He had taken for granted that the planner of a city should ensure that it was well designed on the earth, and that it was harmoniously linked with the skies. A city which is laid out in such a way that it is in harmony with the heavens is a city in perpetual prayer. It is a city built on the recognition that every human activity is in need of the sanctification of the spiritual world, of which the symbol is the light of the living stars.[131]

A full study on this strange and fascinating theme of the idea of 'Hermetic' city plans based on the stars is the subject of a book which I am writing with Graham Hancock.[132] However, in view of the connections that have been made between the Masons of France and the USA during the times of the 1776–1789 revolutions, a few words on the Masonic-Hermetic plan of the city of Paris must not go amiss here – especially as it relates directly to Isis and indirectly, as we shall now see, to the ceremony that is planned at Giza for the end of the millennium.

THE CITY OF ISIS

Since the fourteenth century AD, there has been a persistent belief among certain esoteric groups, especially the Freemasons, that the city of Paris owes its name to the Egyptian goddess Isis.[133] As strange as this may seem, this belief has a kernel of truth.[134] In ancient times, when France was a province of the Roman empire, it seems that on the site where today stands the abbey of St Germain-des-Pres had once existed an ancient Roman temple dedicated to the cult of Isis.[135] In fact the cult of this goddess, along with that of Serapis, was widespread in the Mediterranean world and was one of the most important cults in the Roman empire, especially among the soldiers. Temples of Isis were to be found everywhere: in Rome, Athens and as far as England.[136] The ancient name of Paris was Lutece, but because of the Temple of Isis nearby, the Romans apparently referred to the area as 'Juxta Isis' or 'Par Isi' which in Latin means 'near Isis', i.e. near the temple of Isis.[137] This lore was commonly quoted in historical books up to the nineteenth century and was the subject of an extensive study by the scholar Jurgis Baltrusaitis, *La Quete D'Isis*, in 1985.[138] Baltrusaitis discovered that in 1811, a few years after his disastrous expedition to Egypt, Napoleon Bonaparte set up a special commission to verify the claim which linked Paris to the Egyptian Virgin-Mother star-goddess Isis.[139] The commission, which seems to have been composed of Masonic historians, authenticated the story which immediately prompted Napoleon to issue a formal order to have the image of Isis sitting on her throne, as well as her 'star', included on the coat-of-arms of the city of Paris. This is a five-pointed star and we can safely assume that it was intended to represent Sirius. In fact we can accept this as certainty, for it is known that the famous astronomer Joseph-Jerome Lalande, who was a contemporary of Napoleon as well as a prominent Freemason and Grand Master of the celebrated Nine Sisters Lodge, seems to have made this association between Isis and Sirius often in his works.[140] At any rate, the original document which was drafted and signed by Napoleon can be examined today in the Bibliothèque Nationale in Paris. It reads:

> We have authorised and authorise again by this letter signed by our hand, that our good city of Paris will carry a coat-of-arms in the manner it is depicted and coloured in the attachments and which are: as seen from the front, an ancient ship, the prow carrying the seated figure of Isis in silver held on a sea of the same colour, and preceded in the front by a star, also in silver . . .[141]

During the Egyptian expedition Napoleon had taken with him a group of scientists, artists and men-of-letters to study the ancient monuments and people of Egypt. Their findings were published in 1810 in a multi-tome work, *La Description de l'Egypte*, which became an instant bestseller.[142] The frontispiece of this important work shows an ancient

Egyptian rectangular archway with the solar-winged Ureus above the lintel, much the same as the eastern entrance of the obelisk of the Washington Monument. As in Washington, the centre of the solar disc is emblazoned with a six-pointed star, but in this case the star, as was the case for Washington, was intended to represent Napoleon. Elsewhere in the artwork of the frontispiece is depicted the five-pointed star, particularly in combination with the symbol of an eagle. Napoleon had acquired two nicknames, one being 'L'Aigle' (the Eagle) and the other being 'L'Etoile' (the Star). That 'his star' was Sirius, the star of Isis, is not only made obvious by the coat-of-arms which he chose for Paris but, in a more arcane manner, it seems to have been linked to Napoleon's most famous monument, the Arc de Triomphe, also known as the Place de L'Etoile (the Place of the Star), located on the western side of the so-called Historical Axis of Paris, better known as the Champs-Élysées. This axis, which starts in the east at the Louvre Palace, first goes through the Arc de Triomphe du Cartousel, then through the capstone of the Egyptian obelisk at the Place de la Concorde, followed by the Arc de Triomphe at the Place de L'Etoile, and today extends far to the west to the Grande Arc of La Défense.[143] But the axis, curiously enough, is not straight. As it leaves the Louvre Palace, it deviates precisely twenty-six degrees north of west (azimuth 296 degrees). It has often been remarked by historians of the city that on 8th May, which is the feast of the apparition of the archangel St Michael, the sun sets twenty-six degrees north of west in alignment with the axis. Interestingly, St Michael, in Masonic lore, is associated with the notion of a New Order for the Ages.[144] But there is, perhaps, an additional explanation for the twenty-six degrees deviation. The star Sirius, as seen from the latitude of Paris, rises twenty-six degrees south of east. In consideration of the alleged connection between Paris and the goddess Isis, and of Napoleon's preoccupation with her 'star', this would be an unlikely coincidence.[145]

In 1822, a year after Napoleon's death, the scholar Champollion deciphered Egyptian hieroglyphs. Five years later, in 1827, King Charles X, who was a Freemason,[146] sent Champollion, apparently also a Freemason, to Egypt in order to arrange for the transportation to France of one of the obelisks outside the great temple of Luxor in Upper Egypt. The operation took several years and the obelisk was finally raised at the Place de la Concorde in 1836. The obelisk, too, was placed in alignment with the axis, roughly between the Louvre and Napoleon's Place de L'Etoile. The ceremony was presided over by King Louis-Philippe I, whose father, the Duc D'Orleans, had been Grand Master of the Masonic order of the Grand Orient from 1772 to 1793.[147] Two centuries

Fig. 39. The frontispiece of the 'Description de L'Egypte'.
Note the Star of Napoleon inside the solar disk of the Ureus.

later, in 1984, two new monuments were added to the axis: the Glass Pyramid in the Louvre courtyard and the Grande Arche de la Fraternité (Grand Arch of the Brotherhood) at La Défense. Both projects were directly commissioned by President François Mitterrand, whose brother, Jacques Mitterrand, was Grand Master of the Grand Orient of France. These two monuments were completed for the Bicentennial of the French Revolution which took place on 14th July 1989. The musician, Jean-Michel Jarre, was selected to organise the musical part of the celebration. For this occasion a huge metal pyramid was raised on the western end of the Historical Axis under the Grande Arche of La Défense. Oddly, the so-called Masonic 'eye of providence' was projected several times with laser lights on to the nearby buildings.[148] Nine years later, in May 1998, an unusual celebration took place in Paris near the Luxor obelisk at the Place de la Concorde. The mayor of the city of Paris unveiled a new gilded capstone on top of the obelisk. Present at the ceremony were Egypt's President Hosni Mubarak, Culture Minister Farouk Hosni, and Chief of Antiquities Dr Ali Gaballa. During the ceremony Farouk Hosni announced that a gilded capstone would also be placed on top of the Great Pyramid at midnight on 31st December 1999 to celebrate the new millennium. It was also announced that composer Jean Michel Jarre had been selected to conduct the celebrations in the same manner as he had done for Paris in 1989.[149]

STRANGE SYNCHRONICITY . . .

At the stroke of midnight on that special night of 31st December 1999, at the very moment that a military helicopter will lower in place the gilded capstone on top of the Great Pyramid, the star Sirius will cross the meridian and, as if by magic, will align itself with the axis of the Pyramid. As the astral Hermetic magicians of old would have said, the energy and 'spirit' of that star – along with all the powerfully symbolic connotations that it is charged with – will 'flow' into the gilded capstone, and possibly the most powerful talisman for the new age will thus have been created. Author and historian Jeremy Naydler, in his book *Temple of the Cosmos*, after a discussion on the Freemasons and the design of a glowing capstone and eye symbol on the one-dollar note, commented:

> . . . there is a story behind this mysterious design. Originally the Great Pyramid of Khufu had its capstone in place. It was gold-plated, and on each of its four sides a blue eye of Horus was painted. When the sun struck the pyramid, a beam

of light was reflected from this golden blue eye that could be seen for miles around. As the age of Egypt came to a close, the priesthood removed the capstone and buried it secretly. No one knows where. But according to the story, it will one day be rediscovered, and will be replaced on top of the pyramid. When that day comes, a 'new order of the ages' will be established, which will correspond to a general spiritual reawakening. It is just a story . . .[150]

But is it just a story? Perhaps. But on the eve of the new millennium, with Sirius merging with the gilded capstone on the Great Pyramid, and with hundreds of television cameras broadcasting this dramatic sky/ground, star/triangle connection to the far corners of the globe, right into the living rooms of hundreds of millions of viewers in Europe, Asia, Africa, America and Australia, an age-long quest reaches its climax through some weird and strange synchronicity. The ancient Hermetic prediction of Monte Libyco may, after all, still come to pass. And as for the ancient astronomer-priests of Heliopolis, those magicians and masters of the Hermetic Gnosis, they may have pulled off their game of age long prophecy after all.

The story that I have told is as strange as it is controversial. It is the story of an age-long mystery. A mystery which has haunted the imagination of seekers from generation to generation . . . To some it is a figment of the imagination, a myth and nothing else. To others it is an obvious possibility, a near-certain historical reality, a fact that will soon be confirmed at the turn of a spade. For deep inside the oldest, the largest, the tallest, the most massive and sacred monument on this planet, is a heavily guarded secret. Inside the Great Pyramid of Giza, wrapped in unearthly darkness and standing in hallowed stillness, could lie a secret chamber, waiting any minute now to be opened . . . And not far from the Great Pyramid, in a shallow enclave to the east, is the Great Sphinx. It, too, may be guarding the ultimate treasure-trove under its belly: a 'Hall of Records' of a civilisation long lost in the mists of time . . .

Robert Bauval
August 1999

Appendix 1

Original Articles by Robert Bauval from *Discussions in Egyptology* Journal, Oxford 1989–1990

A MASTER-PLAN FOR THE THREE PYRAMIDS OF GIZA
BASED ON THE CONFIGURATION OF THE THREE STARS
OF THE BELT OF ORION

Robert.G. Bauval

The Pyramid Texts embody the remnants of a well-structured star-cult, the main theme of which was the transfiguration of the dead pharaohs into stars <1>. Examination of the Pyramid Texts reveals that the dominant stars of this cult were those of the constellation of Orion. The special attention given to Orion can be understood in several ways: it is the most striking of the constellations; in the archaic Period, it happened to rise in midsummer at dawn (c.2600 BC), as though a celestial herald of the forthcoming yearly nilotic flood. Consequently, the appearance of Orion after a prolongued period of 'invisibility' was taken as the celestial event preluding a new season of rejuvenation and growth of nature as a whole. Mythologically, Orion was thus seen as the celestial representation of Osiris, the god of rebirth/resurrection, and with whom all the dead pharaohs, as star-gods, were identified <2>. Thus the Pyramid Texts proclaim: 'Behold, he has come as Orion, behold Osiris has come as Orion...O king, the sky conceives you with Orion, the dawn-light bears you with Orion, you will regularly ascend with Orion from the eastern region of the sky, you will regularly descend with Orion into the western region of the sky...' (pyr.820-822). 'O king, you are this great star, the companion of Orion, who traverses the sky with Orion, who navigates the Netherworld with Osiris, you ascend from the east of the sky, being renewed in your due season, and rejuvenated in your due time.' (pyr.882). 'Live, be alive! Be young beside your father, beside Orion in the sky...' (pyr. 2180).<3>.

The Egyptian knew Orion under the name of 'Sah'. They imagined 'Sah' as a male anthropomorphic figure undoubtedly representing Osiris. Several drawings of 'Sah' dating from the New Kingdom are known, notably from the tomb of Senmut (south hall ceiling), where 'Sah' is depicted as a man standing on a boat, holding the Ankh symbol in one hand and a staff in the other; above his head are three large stars in a row, the topmost star slightly deviated to the left (see plates)<4>. There can be little doubt that these three stars are Zeta, Epsilon and Delta Orionis -the Belt Of Orion- which form the same characteristic pattern at the centre of the constellation <5>. It is to be noted that this pattern has not perceptibly changed since the time of the Pyramid Age (c.2700 BC-2150 BC). This is because these three stars are well-over 1000 light-years away, and consequently no proper motion is normally registered for them. In any case, any undetected annual proper motion would probably be below the 1/1000th of a second level, thus far too small for the span of time considered to cause any perceptible change in the pattern of the three stars <6>. In short, the characteristic pattern formed by the three stars of the Belt Of Orion appears the same to us as it did to the Egyptians who built the Great Pyramid (c.2600 BC).

However, due to a planetary motion known as the 'precession of the equinoxes' the apparent position of the Belt Of Orion relative to the horizon and the equinoxes has changed since 2600 BC, such that the Right Ascension has increased by about three hours (about 45°), and the Declination south of the celestial equator has decreased by about 14°<7>. Table 1 shows the change of Declinations between the two epochs considered.<8>

Declinations

	1987 AD	2600 BC
Zeta Orionis	-1°56'	-15°33'
Epsilon Orionis	-1°12'	-15°16'
Delta Orionis	-0°17'	-14°45'

Table 1.

The Great Pyramid is sited at Latitude North 29°58', and the celestial equator, as seen from this latitude, crosses the meridian at an altitude of 60°02' above the southern horizon. Looking south, the three stars of the Belt Of Orion would have intersected the meridian at the following altitudes above the southern horizon in 2600 BC:

Zeta Orionis 44°29'; Epsilon Orionis 44°46'; Delta Orionis 45° 17'.

Virginia Trimble and Alexander Badawy have highlighted the fact that the southern 'ventilation' shaft in Cheops' pyramid, which is inclined 44°30' to the horizontal, would have pointed to one of the stars of the Belt Of Orion when it culminated at the meridian about the epochs 2800-2600 BC <9> (see fig.). In view of the religious association between the dead pharaoh and Orion in the Pyramid Texts, both Trimble and Badawy convincingly argued that the southern shaft had a symbolic significance <10>, and suggested it was intended as a means for the pharaoh's 'soul' to reach the place of Orion-Osiris in the sky.

The above calculations show that in 2600 BC the star closest to the line projected by the southern shaft was Zeta Orionis. Could the shaft have been specifically intended to point at Zeta Orionis ?

In 1983 the present writer drew attention <11> to the fact that the characteristic pattern of the three stars of the Belt Of Orion matched, with striking similarity, the pattern defined by the three

Great Pyramids of Giza. Apparently such a correlation had hitherto
escaped notice. In such a correlation, Zeta Orionis links up with
Cheops' pyramid (see fig. and plates). The pattern of the three
stars and the three pyramids compare as follows:

Belt Of Orion	Giza Pyramids
1. The three stars are aligned in a southwesterly direction as they cross the meridian.	The three pyramids are aligned in a southwesterly direction and are each orientated meridionally.
2. The uppermost star, Delta Orionis, however, is offset slightly to the east of the diagonal line projected by the two other stars.	The southernmost pyramid, Mycerinus', is offset slightly to the east of the diagonal line projected by the two other pyramids.
3. Delta Orionis is also much less bright than the other two stars which are of quasi-similar magnitude (magn. 2.20 compared to 1.70 & 1.79)	Mycerinus' pyramid is also much smaller than the other two pyramids which are of quasi-similar heights (65 m. compared to 146 m. & 143 m.)
4. The middle star, Epsilon, is almost equidistant the two other stars.	The Middle pyramid, Chephren's, is almost equidistant to the two other pyramids. <12>

Table 2.

A Masterplan with intent to correlate the Great Pyramids of Giza
with the pattern of the Belt Of Orion appears very likely indeed. A
question which must follow is: does this Masterplan include a wider
correlation between the geomorphy of the sky landscape about Orion
and the landscape about the Giza Necropolis ? Raising this question
is justified, for the Pyramid Texts indeed confront us with a
complete celestial topography onto which actual terrestial natural
and man-made features are imagined to exist. There is a major river
called the 'Winding Waterway'(pyr.340,600,802,1253), several
waterways (pyr.1102,1084,1716), Canals (Pyr. 1141, 1293, 1634),
lakes (pyr.519, 885, 1704), swamps (pyr. 130,340,1475), islands
(265,1216), mounds (574,915,1364) and pastures (910,1035), all
seemingly relate to earthly counterparts. Even some major cities,
such as Abydos (pyr.794,1716), Heliopolis (pyr.14, 207, 318) and
Busiris(pyr.288,2010), are mentioned in passages having
astronomical connotations. This celestial and mythological
landscape of the royal dead appeared so real to the ancient
Egyptians that they readily intermingled fantasy with reality when

reading the funerary texts, almost giving a tangible nature to both.

A most sacred location in the Afterworld was 'Rostau', the dominion of a mortuary deity called Sokar who, during the Pyramid Age, was assimilated to Osiris as Osiris-Sokar<13>. In later times, Rostau was believed to be the 'Gates of the Afterworld', a sort of cosmic access to the star-world, and was closely associated to a strip of land in the western desert on the fringe of the Nile Valley near Giza which, undoubtedly, had the Giza Necropolis as its epicentre <14>. In short, a cosmic counterpart of the burial zone originally reserved for royalty was a vivid reality in the minds of the Egyptians of later epochs.

A major feature of the Afterworld often mentioned in the Pyramid Texts is the 'Winding Waterway', which was, in all probability, seen as a celestial counterpart of the Nile:'I ferry across on the Winding Waterway... I am ferried over to the eastern side of the sky...' pyr.340. 'The Winding Waterway is flooded.' pyr.343,352. 'Hail to you, O Ra (the sun-god), you who traverse the sky and cross Nut, having traversed the Winding Waterway...' pyr.543. 'I travel the Winding Waterway.' pyr.1138. 'He goes aboard the bark like Ra at the banks of the Winding Waterway.' pyr. 1345. '...Osiris the king, the Winding Waterway is flooded...Awake, stand up at yonder eastern side of the sky at this place where the gods are born...the king will be born on yonder eastern side where the gods are born...' pyr. 1182-3. 'may you lift me and raise me up to the Winding Waterway, may you set me among the gods the imperishable stars...' pyr.1759. '...be firm O king, on the underside of the sky with the beautiful star upon the bends of the Winding Waterway...' pyr. 2061.

The 'winding' characteristic of this celestial-Nile perfectly describes the gyrations of the Milky Way about the earth, surely the only feature of the sky which can be regarded as a 'winding waterway'<15>. It is worth noting, therefore, that the relative position of the Belt Of Orion to the Milky Way also correlates to the relative position of the Giza pyramids to the Nile. Both triads are immediately west of their corresponding 'Niles'. Indeed, the 'southwesterly' alignment of the three stars relative to the Milky Way's axis matches the 'southwesterly' alignment of the three pyramids relative to the Nile's axis. Even the 'distance' of the stars to the Milky Way's axis can be said to matched -on an equal scale- the distance of the pyramids to the Nile's axis (see plates).

The above strongly points towards a deliberate correlation between the central stars of the Orion-Osiris sky-figure and the Giza Pyramids... and, consequently, the existence of a Masterplan for the Necropolis instigated by Cheops and his architects. Irrespective of the prevailing wariness the Egyptological profession has of new 'theories' on the pyramids, such a conclusion cannot be ignored, for it dovetails with smooth precision into the astronomical matrix of the Pyramid Texts and the astronomical features of the pyramids themselves.

It cannot be denied that monumental pyramids are proof that human capacity was strained to its very limits in order to satisfy the egocentric desire of pharaohs to 'establish' themselves after death as 'star-gods' near Orion-Osiris. Clearly the pyramids bear witness to an epoch when the conviction in such a transfiguration was thought of in tangible and real terms when assisted by magical rites performed in an symbolic setting. All the extant funerary paraphernalia -mummies, artifacts, statues, furnitures, drawings, texts and, of course, the huge stone monuments themselves- emphatically attest to the existence of this conviction. Thus a Masterplan for Giza based on the pattern of the Belt Of Orion and its relation to the Milky Way, when allocated to pharaohs who believed in a stellar transfiguration after death near Orion-Osiris, is a very real possibility indeed <16>.

notes:

1.Faulkner, R.O: 'The King And The Star-religion In The Pyramid Texts', in Journal Of Near Eastern Studies, 1966, pp.153-161. Selim Hassan also discussed the stellar destiny of the kings in the Pyramid Texts in much detail as early as 1946 (Excavations At Giza, Vol.6, part 1, Egyptian Gouvernment Press, 1946).
2. Rundle Clark, R.T, Myth & Symbol In Ancient Egypt, London 1978, pp.122-3.; Hart, G., A dictionary Of Egyptian Gods And Godesses, London 1986 ed., p. 153.
3.Quotations here are as translated by R.O.Faulkner (The Ancient Egyptian Pyramid Texts. Aris & Philips. Wiltshire.).
4.Neugebauer, O. & Parker R: Egyptian Astronomical Texts. Vol.1. Brown University Press. Providence 1964, p. 25 for the identification of Sah with Orion. See Vol.111, Plates 4,6,8,9,14,19,21,24 (Senmut).
5. See V. Trimble's paper reference in footnote 9 herebelow.
6.Sky Catalogue 2000 Vol.1 (Cambridge University Press 1982) gives the proper motion adjustment coefficients for RA and Declination of the Belt stars as 0.000".Astronomer Dr. J. Obyrne of the University Of Sydney (see fn.8 below) informed me that even if one assumes a small value of proper motion, rather than zero, the result would not be greater than 65 seconds of arc (just under 2 percent of a degree), which, in his opinion, is probably unrealistically large.
7.The coordinates of stars viz. their Right Ascensions and Declinations, perceptibly change from century to century (as a 'rule of thumb', the RA increases by 5' per century) due to this planetary motion. This motion is a slow gyration of the earth -a full cycle takes about 26000 years- which causes the earth's polar axis to define a circle about a fixed point (the ecliptic pole) in the sky. This, of course, is an 'apparent' motion as opposed to a 'proper' motion of the stars in space.
8. Precessional calculations were done on Casio Scientific Calculator Fx-8000G. Also A sample-result for 2500 BC was provided by Dr. J. O'Byrne of the Chatterton Department Of Astronomy,

University Of Sydney, NSW. The modern 'rigorous' formula for such calculations can be found in Sky Catalogue 2000.0 Vol.1, op. cit., p. xiii.

9.Badawy, A: 'The Stellar Destiny of Pharaoh and the so-called Air-Shafts of Cheop's Pyramid', in Mitteilungen der Instituts Fur Orientforschung (Akademie der Wissenschaften zu Berlin) Band 10, 1964, pp.189-206.; Trimble V:'Astronomical Investigations concerning the so-called Air-Shafts of Cheop's Pyramid', ibid., pp.183-7. There is also a northern shaft alledgedly pointing to the then-polar star Alpha Draconis which Badawy and Trimble relate to the so-called 'circumpolar' destiny of the pharaohs. I have dealt with the polar shafts in detail in an article (yet unpublished) entitled "The seeding of the star-gods" -hopefully to appear in print during the latter part of 1989.

10.Previously discussed by Steindorff G., Egypt (Baedeker), 1929, p.140.; Capart J., Etudes Et Histoire, I, Brussels 1924, p.182.; and Edwards I.E.S., The Pyramids Of Egypt, Pelican Books, 1961, p. 126. Edwards also discussed the Cheops shafts in 'The Air-channels in Chephren's Pyramid', in Studies in Honor of Dows Dunham, Boston, 1981, in which the unfinished shafts in the second pyramid are discussed. The present writer draws attention to the observation that the causeway of Chephren's pyramid is directed to about azimuth 73°30', which was the rising point of the Belt Of Orion in 2600 BC -a fact unnoticed so far.

11. A paper (unpublished) was circulated to several authorities in Egyptology during 1983-86.

12.Petrie, Sir W.M.F, The Pyramids And Temples Of Gizeh, London 1883, p.125.

13. Edwards, op. cit., p. 27.

14. Lichtheim, M., Ancient Egyptian Literature vol. 1, UCLA 1975 ed., p. 204, note 2.; Hart, G., A Dictionary Of Egyptian Gods And Goddesses, London 1986, p. 152.; Erman, A., A Handbook of Egyptian Religion, London 1907, p. 15. In New Kingdom depictions of 'Rostau', a curious subterranean zone is shown surmounted by a 'pyramid' and protected by two gigantic sphynxes, the latter appearing half-covered in sand; a depiction very reminiscent of the Giza plateau and the Great Pyramid as seen from the south of the great sphynx.

15. Faulkner (see footnote 1 above. p. 154, fn.7) briefly linked the Milky Way with the 'Winding Waterway'; this was also discussed by V. L. Davis of Yale University (Davis, V.L, ' Identifying Ancient Egyptian Constellations' in 'Archeoastronomy' Vol. No. 9, JHA, xvi 1985, p.S102). Many other ancient races saw the Milky Way as a celestial-River: the Chinese 'Silver River', the Akaddian 'River Of The Divine Lady', the Arab 'Al Nahr' (river), the Hebrew 'River of Light' (see Allen, R.H: Star Names -Their Lore & Meaning, Dover Publ. New York, 1963, p. 474).

16. I have refrained from discussing the symbolism embodied in the shape of the pyramids and their capstones, as this is discussed in length in my forthcoming article in DE 14 "Investigation On The Benben Stone: was it an iron meteorite ?".

Plate 1: Aerial View Of The Giza Necropolis

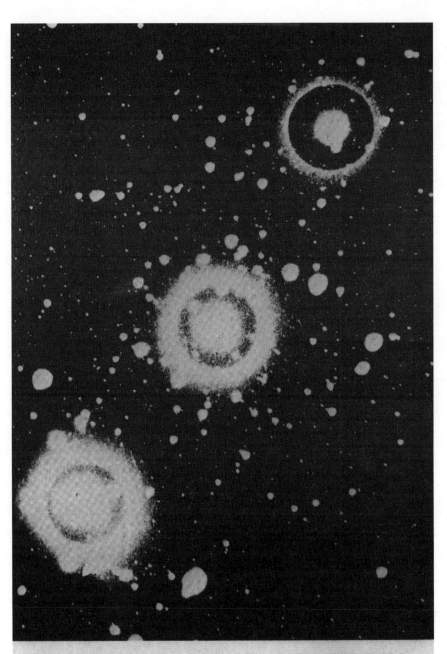

Plate 2: The Belt Of Orion. By courtesy of DOVER PUBLICATIONS Inc.
From Burnham's Celestial Handbook, by Robert Burnham Jr.
Vol. ii -1978 (sheet 1304).

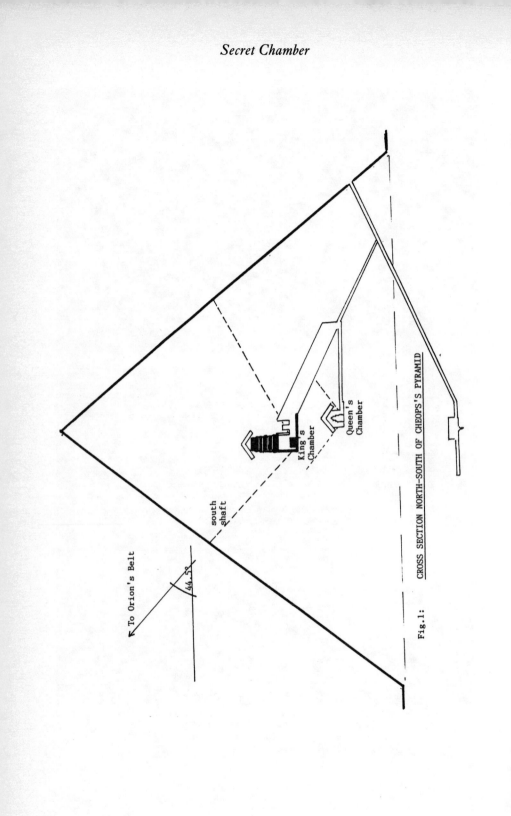

To Orion's Belt

south shaft

44.5°

King's Chamber

Queen's Chamber

Fig.1:   CROSS SECTION NORTH–SOUTH OF CHEOPS'S PYRAMID

INVESTIGATION ON THE ORIGINS OF THE BENBEN STONE:
WAS IT AN IRON METEORITE ?

Robert G. Bauval

The prevailing theory on the design of monumental true pyramids is that their shape was modelled on the Benben: a conical-shaped stone venerated in the 'Mansion Of The Phoenix' at Heliopolis (pyr.1652). The 'Mansion Of The Phoenix' was presumably within the precinct of the Great Sun Temple of Heliopolis, but there is evidence, however, that the Benben was worshipped there well before the sun cult of Ra (Baines, Orientalia 39, 1979, p. 391). The stone was probably originally associated to Atum, a much older deity who was mainly identified with the act of Creation via his masturbation (Baines, ibid., p.391, fn.2). Atum was later assimilated to Ra, as Ra-Atum. Though it is often recognized that the older, step pyramid design is the product of a predominant star cult <Edwards, p.292; Badawy, p. 205>, it is nevertheless widely advocated that the 'true pyramid' design which succeeded the 'stepped pyramid' design reflects the solar ideas induced by the powerful sun cult favoured in the Pyramid Age. The solar ideas supposedly dominated the stellar and Osirian cults as from the 4th Dynasty, when the true pyramid design was introduced <Breasted, pp. 101-2>. Many have therefore claimed that the Benben stone was symbolic of the sun. James H. Breasted, an instigator of such claims, noted the similarity of the word 'Benben' with the word 'Benbenet'(the pyramid-shaped apex of an obelisk) and accordingly declared that "an obelisk is simply a pyramid upon a lofty base which has become a shaft." Breasted also syllogised that because "the obelisk, as is commonly known, is a symbol sacred to the Sun-god...[it followed that] the king was burried under the very symbol of the Sun-god which stood in the holy of holies in the Sun-temple at Heliopolis" <Breasted, pp.70-3>. This, perhaps too hasty, conclusion inevitably extended the solar symbolism to the whole bulk of the monument below the pyramidion/capstone. Breasted ideas were later supported and expanded by I.E.S. Edwards, who also proposed that the occasional sight of an immaterial triangle afforded by the sun's rays striking downwards through the clouds at sunset could have been the origin of the Benben's shape "and its architectural derivative, the true Pyramid" <Edwards, pp.290-1>. Edwards looked for textual evidence in the Pyramid Texts, and quoted passages 1108 and 1231: "I have laid down for myself this sunshine of yours as a stairway under my feet ..." and : " May the sky make the sunlight strong for you, may you rise up to the sky..." (I have used Faulkner's more recent translation here). Edwards thus added that "the temptation to regard the true Pyramid as a material representation of the sun's rays and consequently as a means whereby the dead king could ascend to heaven seems irresistible." True , the sun's rays are said to be a means for the dead pharaoh to ascend to the sky; but several other 'means' for precisely the same purpose are also mentioned in the Pyramid Texts. These are: On a ladder (R.O. Faulkner titled Utterance 304 'The king climbs to the sky on a ladder'); on the wind: "the king is bound for the sky on the wind" (pyr. 309); on a storm-cloud/Thunderbolt: "The king is a flame (moving) before the wind...there is brought to him a way of ascent to the sky" (Ut. 261); on a hailstorm: "the hailstorms of the sky have taken me" (pyr. 336); on a reed-float/boat: "the reed-floats of the sky are set in place for me...I am ferried over to the eastern sky" (Ut. 263); by climbing a rope:"set the rope aright, cross the Milky Way..."(Ut.254); on the thighs of Isis: "I ascend [to the sky] upon the thighs of Isis" (pyr. 379).

Evidently, climbing on the sun's rays was not the only means, but yet another cosmic one made available for the celestial ascent of the departed king. Giving preference to any one of them for having influenced the shape of the true pyramid/Benben is unwarranted, especially when neither are specifically mentioned in the passage in question. There is, however, a passage which does directly equate the pyramid construction to Osiris: "This king is Osiris, this pyramid of the king is Osiris, this construction of his is Osiris, betake yourself to it, do not be far from it in its name of pyramid..." (pyr. 1657). Osiris in the Old Kingdom was primarily a star-god, whose soul was identified to the constellation of Orion:"Behold Osiris has come as Orion" (pyr.820). Furthermore the dead king was mostly identified with Osiris, and his star-soul is usually paired with Orion: "O king, you are this Great Star, the companion of Orion" (pyr. 882). On account of this, it would seem apt to examine the possibility of a stellar symbolism for the Benben and, consequently, the true pyramid's shape.

Though the 'Mansion Of The Phoenix' in which stood the Benben many have been linked to the Sun Temple of Ra in the latter part of the Pyramid Age, an association of the Benben with the sun does not necessarily follow. For one, no satisfactory explanation has yet been given why a conical stone would be venerated as a solar symbol (the solar symbol is often a disc, as would normally be expected). Supporters of the Benben solar symbolism offer, as one explanation, that the Benben was representative of the Primeval Mound on which the first sunrise took place. This would imply that also the pyramid had a similar correlation. This hypothesis is justifiably rejected by Edwards <Edwards, p. 287>, for though the Primeval Mound is perhaps indirectly linked to the much older 'Mastaba' tomb structure of the first three Dynasties, extending this association to the pyramidal-tomb is certainly stretching this possible correlation too far. In any case, the Mastaba tomb ideology may not be only solar, for A. Badawy seems to have found strong stellar symbolism in its orientation and design (JNES, vol.xv,1956, p.183). The radical change of the tomb design into monumental pyramids is likely due to a new interpretation by the clergy for the skywards ascent of the departed pharaohs, and possibly on new 'evidence' of his posthumous form which was, for some hitherto unexplained reason, now believed to be conical or pyramidal.

It is also often argued that the phoenix, a mythical bird which was said to appear at dawn perched on a pole extending from a benben, was representative of the sun-god's self-creating power <Breasted, p.72>. But the phoenix's cosmic identification was by no means exclusive to the sun. In the Middle Kingdom, for example, the phoenix was also said to be the soul of Osiris, aswell as the moon and sometimes the 'morning star' i.e. Venus <Rundle Clark, p.246-9>. The phoenix thus was symbolic of the rebirth at dawn not only of the sun-god but of cosmic beings in general. In The Book Of The Dead, Chapter 83 entitled 'Spell For Becoming The Phoenix (Bennu) Bird', the phoenix claims: " I am the seed corn of every god..."<Rundle Clark, p. 249>. His power of self-creation clearly symbolized the emerging (rebirth) of celestial bodies (gods) at dawn from the underworld, the tenebrous land of the dead below the horizon.

It is known that a sacred pillar was worshipped at Heliopolis before the Benben <Edwards, p.24>. The phallic symbolism of a pillar is of course obvious, and its association to the phallus of Atum seems almost a certainty, for in the Pyramid Texts we read: "Atum is he who once came into being, who masturbated in On (Heliopolis). He took his phallus in his grasp that he might creat orgasm by means of it..." (pyr. 1248); "O Atum-khoprer (as the Beetle or rising sun), you became high on the heights (pillar/mound?), you rose as the Benben stone in the Mansion Of The Phoenix in On..." (pyr. 1652). H. Frankfort suggested that the combination of the Benben with a pillar -later stylized perhaps into an obelisk with a Benbenet- may thus represent the semens or seed being ejaculated from a cosmic phallus associated to Atum <Frankfort, p. 153,380 & note 26>. Later, this fetish was probably considered sacred to Ra or Atum-Ra. In the Pyramid Texts, it is said: "O Ra, make the womb of Nut pregnant with the seed of the spirit which is in her".(pyr.990). "Pressure is in your womb, O Nut, through the seed of the god which is in you; it is I [the king] who am the seed of the god which is in you..." (pyr. 1416-7). "...the king is an imperishable star, son of the sky-goddess..." (pyr. 1469). "The king was fashioned by his father Atum..." (pyr.1466). "O Ra-Atum, this king comes to you, an imperishable spirit (star?)...your son comes to you, this king comes to you" (pyr.152). Judging from these passages, it is evident that Nut was imagined to be the mother of the king in his star form, the latter sired by Ra/Atum. A pillar surging skywards atop of which is placed a fetish representing a star-seed and offered to the sky-goddess for gestation in her womb, very much appears to be the intented symbolic function of the pillar/Benben combined fetish at Heliopolis (see plate 1 for a possible example of this). In consideration of the above, it is indeed significant to note that the word 'Benben' means 'to copulate' (to seed a womb ?) when followed by the determinative of an erect phallus ejaculating semens <Wallis Budge, p.217>. Several words containing the root 'Ben' also have sexual meanings (Baines, Orientalia 39, 1970, p. 389-395).

In the Pyramid Texts, the astronomical/mythological scenario which must be considered is that the departed pharaoh becomes a 'seed' to be reborn as a star. This 'seed' is sired by Ra/Atum and gestated in the womb of Nut: "The king is your seed, O Ra" (pyr.1508). "the king comes to you, O mother of the king, he has come to Nut, that you may bring the sky to the king and hang the stars for him.." (pyr.1516). "the sky concieves you with Orion..." (pyr. 820). "Recitation by Nut, the greatly beneficent: the king is my eldest son who splits open my womb..." (pyr.1). "...O King, you are this Great Star, the companion of Orion...the sky has borne you with Orion..." (pyr. 882-3). "The King is a star brilliant....the King appears as a star..." (pyr.262/3). " For you belong to the stars that surround Ra" (pyr.412). " You [Nut] have set this King as an imperishable Star who is in you..." (pyr.782). "The King is a star" (pyr. 1470). "The King is a star in the sky among the gods" (pyr. 1583). "I [the king] am a soul ...a star of gold..." (pyr. 887-9). "I sit among you, you stars of the Netherworld(pyr. 953). "I am a star which illumines the sky..." (pyr. 1455). "I am a nhh-star; the companion of a nhh-star, I become a nhh-star..." (pyr.909). "O Ra, for which you have said, O Ra, O for a Son!..he having a soul and being mighty and strong...Here I am, O Ra; I am your Son, I am a soul... I row Ra when traversing the sky, even I a star of gold" (pyr. 886-9). "I row Ra to the West...I am a Nhh-Star" (pyr.Ut. 469). "my star is set on high with Ra..." (pyr. 698).

In consideration of this, it is justified to assume that the predominant symbolism for the pyramid would be stellar, for this monument undoubtedly was considered the agency of the king's astral rebirth. The contemporary names of several monumental pyramids indeed attest to such a stellar symbolism: 'Djedefra is a Sehetu star'; 'Nebka is a star'; 'The soul (ba) of Sahura gleams'; 'Sneferu gleams'; 'Neferirkare has become a soul (ba)' <Edwards, The Pyramids, pp. 295-8; Badawy, JEA 63, p.58>. The compounding of the pharaoh's name with that of his pyramid is also significant, for it implies that the monument (or mainly it capstone, as we shall later see) was regarded as being the transfigured form of the departed pharaoh viz. a star-soul. Retaining the hypothesis that the Benben did inspire the designers of the true pyramid, then in what manner can this sacred stone's conical shape be related to the imagined shape of a star? Taking into account the stellar destiny of the dead pharaoh and his astral 'iron-bones' (see below), the Benben stone's supposedly cosmic origin and most particularly its 'conical' shape, it is justified to conjecture that this sacred stone was an 'oriented' (conical) iron-meteorite.

The idea in antiquity that meteorites were 'shooting stars' or 'falling stars' need no further emphasis. Factually, meteorites are debris from space -mostly from broken up asteroids- which fall on our planet, and which can be recovered (as opposed to meteors which completely burn up during atmospheric transit). Meteorites are classified into three main groups: iron-meteorites (usually 90 pc. iron/10-12 pc. nickel), stony/iron-meteorites, and stone-meteorites. The largest known are the iron-meteorites as these tend to survive the impact with the ground more easily than the other types for obvious reasons. Most meteorites are in fact very small. Occasionally, however, a large meteorite enters our atmosphere. If it is very large (the famous 1.2 km. wide Arizona meteor crater was caused by a lump of iron 25 meters across), it will retains most of its original velocity and usually explodes with dramatic effect just before hitting the ground, its mass breaking up into thousands of minute fragments (the Arizona meteor caused a blast equivalent to a 4-megaton nuclear explosion). Not all large meteorites, however, break up so easily. The largest single known meteoritic mass is the 'Hoba' iron-meteorite, and still lies in the place where it fell near Grootfontein farm in Southwest Africa. This meteorite is estimated to be a 60 tons chunk of iron. Most meteorites with a mass of 1000 to 15000 kg. usually have their velocity dampened by the atmosphere, causing them to free fall for the last 20 km. and thus strike the earth at about 0.1 km. per second. In the case of an iron-meteorite, the odds of survival with minimal damage in such cases is good. Also, many meteorites often retain their orientation in the direction of flight; this causes the front part to melt and flow towards the rear. The result -especially for the iron variety- is a meteorite having the characteristic shape of a rough cone. These are known as 'oriented' meteorites. Several oriented iron-meteorite weighing from 5 to 15 tons are known <Buckwald, chap.6>. The best examples are 'Morito' (10 tons) and 'Willamette' (14 tons -the names are usually of the places the meteorites were found). Morito is a well-preserved conical iron-meteorite, and is displayed in Mexico City. It measures about 110 cm in height and the base is about 150 cm. and does indeed look eerily like a pyramidal-cone. Willamette is displayed in the American Museum Of Natural History, New York (see plates 2 & 3).

There was a widespread belief among ancient Mediterranean people -including the Egyptians- that iron actually came from heaven; clearly here an allusion to its meteoritic origin. Today, the average number of meteorite finds is only 5 meteorites per year. Such scarcity is in spite of our sophisticated communication systems and greater scientific interest. A low number such as this could hardly have caused the widespread belief in antiquity that iron came from the sky, and many scientists are of the opinion, therefore, that meteorite falls Occured more frequently in the past - an hypothesis apparently supported by astrophysics research. The probability, therefore, of observing the fall of a large iron-meteorite and also recovering it was higher in our remote past than it is today. Indeed many sacred stones which were believed to have 'fallen from heaven', and accordingly worshipped in temples or shrines, were surely meteorites. The Ephesians (Acts xix-35), for example, are said to have worshipped in the temple of Diana 'that symbol of her which fell from heaven'. In the temple of Apollo in Delphi a stone <Roux, p.130>, probably shaped like an ovoid/cone (later to be replaced by the well-known Omphalos) was believed to have come from Cronnos the sky-god, and was the object of much veneration. This 'stone of Cronnos' was most likely a meteorite (Wainwright, Annal. Serv. xxviii, p. 185). A conical iron-meteorite is said to have also been worshipped by the Phrygian in the 7th century BC <McCall, p.17>. The conical blackstone known as Elagalabus was worshipped in Emessa and was a meteorite <Daremberg & Sangrio, p.529>. Not far from Emessa, in the temple of Heliopolis-Baalbek, were venerated black, conical stones <Hitti, p.312>. The Nabataean god, Dushara, was worshipped in the form of an obelisk or 'an unhewn four cornered blackstone' <ibid. p.385>. Indeed, a modern example of such stone-worship is the much venerated blackstone kept in the Ka'aba shrine in Mecca, Western Saudi Arabia, which is thought by geologists to be a meteorite recovered in antiquity (A further discussion on sacred meteorites will be found in my forthcoming article "The Fetish Of Ammon and Alexander The Great: an investigation on the meteoritic connexion").

British Egyptologist G.A. Wainwright has convincingly argued that iron in the Old Kingdom Period was mostly obtained from iron-meteorites (Wainwright, JEA 18, p.3). It seems that man-made iron from terrestial ores rarely contains nickel, whereas meteoritic-iron contains a high proportion of this element, on average 12 percent. Wainwright states that ornamental beads made of iron dating as far back as Pre-Dynastic times have been analyzed and shown to contain high levels of nickel, confirming their meteoritic origin (for a counterview see Dunham, JEA 28,p.57). Significantly the word 'Bja' meaning iron in ancient Egyptian also meant the 'material of which heaven was made' <1>. It is therefore highly likely that meteoritic-iron was also imagined the stuff from which were made the reborn kings as star-gods (Wainwright, JEA 18, p.11). Certain passages in the Pyramid Texts are indeed very suggestive of such a concept: "The king's bones are iron and the king's members are the imperishable stars..." (pyr.2051). "I [the king] am pure, I take to myself my iron bones...my imperishable limbs are in the womb of Nut" (pyr.530). "my bones are iron and my limbs are the imperishable stars" (pyr.1454).

It is also likely that chunks of iron-meteorite -which generally have a lustred, black appearance- were associated or even confused with black hardstones such as diorite, basalt and dark-grey granite found in Upper Egypt. To a primitive mind unfamiliar with iron and its chemical properties, the resemblance can be uncanny. Not suprisingly, black basalt was called 'Bja-Kam' meaning 'black iron' <Wallis Budge, p. 210>, suggesting that basalt, and possibly similar black hardstones viz. diorite and dark granite, were associated to meteoritic ironstone, and consequently to the 'bones' of star-gods. Most capstones of monumental pyramids were probably made of granite <Edwards, pp.118,151>. The almost-black granite capstone of the pyramid of Amenemhet III in the Cairo museum is a fine example of this (see plate 4). It was discovered in 1902 by Maspero, who remarked that its surface had been 'mirror' polished ("poli a miroir..." -Maspero, Annal.Serv. iii, p.206). Such a description is typical for the appearance of a freshly fallen iron-meteorite. Amenemhet III's capstone could well be the stylized man-made version of an oriented iron-meteorite symbolizing his materialized star-soul. The two lines of carved hieroglyphic inscriptions ornating the base of the capstone were first discussed by Maspero (Maspero, Annal.serv. iii, p.206), and later by Breasted <Breasted, p. 73> and Piankoff <Piankoff, p.5>. In the inscriptions several deities are evoked, among them supposedly the sun-god (as 'The Lord Of The Horizon') and Orion-Osiris, the great star-god of astral rebirth, depicted as a striding man holding a staff in one hand, and cupping a large star in the other. On one side of the capstone are carved two large eyes surmounted by a disc with feathered-wings; the inscription below states that "the face of Amenemhet is open, he sees the Lord Of The Horizon as he sails in the sky" (incidently, this curious winged-face/head is also depicted in the Pyramid Texts in conjunction with 'iron': "He has appeared upon the Stone (?), upon his throne, he has sharpened the iron by means of it...raise yourself, O king, gather your bones, take your head...O king, raise yourself as Min [the Phallic/fertility God] fly up to the sky and live with them, cause your wings to grow with your feathers on your head..." pyr. 1945-8). Another inscription on the Amenemhet III capstone states:"...the soul of king Amenemhet is higher than the heights of Orion...". Breasted's view that the inscritions proves the solar symbolism of the capstone is surely incorrect, for it is fairly evident from such inscriptions that we are to consider the capstone not as the material representation of the sun-god but rather that of the king's star-soul, a proginy of Ra, not Ra himself. It is in this capacity that the soul of the king, now established as a star-object high above the base of the pyramid, does indeed participate in the eternal cycles of the sun-god and the ancestral star-gods as they sail across the sky each day.

The hieroglyphic sign for the word 'pyramid' was sometimes depicted as a pyramid with a yellow apex, suggesting that the granite capstones of pyramids may have been gilded <Edwards, p.276>. An inscription found by Jequier at the pyramid of a queen called Udjebten supports this hypothesis, for it speaks of the gilded capstone of her pyramid <ibid.>. A quasi-black granite capstone, the stylized representation of an oriented iron-meteorite, finely polished and covered with a gold skin would certainly bear potent symbolism associated to a primitive concept of a 'living star' i.e. a star-soul shining in the sky, the bones of which were imagined to be made of iron or bja-kam, and the 'flesh' of gold. Evidence of this idea may be in these passages: "O King, raise yourself upon your iron bones and golden members, for this body of yours belongs to a god ... may your flesh be born to life and may your life be more than the life of the stars in their season of life..." (pyr.2244). "I [the king] row Ra when traversing the sky, even I a star of gold..." (pyr.886-9); and pyr.904 instructs the dead king to "be a soul like a living star".

Summary and Conclusion:

Similar to many other cases of meteoritic worship by ancient peoples, it is also likely that the Benben stone once worshipped in the 'Mansion Of The Phoenix' was a meteorite. Its conical shape, and its association with the pyramid's capstone -the latter a likely symbol of the star-soul of the departed pharaoh made of 'iron bones'- is very suggestive of an oriented iron-meteorite, possibly a mass within the 1 to 15 ton range. Such objects fallen from heaven were generally representative of 'fallen stars', and likely provided the Egyptian clergy with a tangible sample of a star-object, a 'seed' of Ra-Atum. It is recognized by many that the whole business of the rebirth rites performed for dead pharaohs was intensely, if not mainly, stellar. The well-known archeoastronomer E.C. Krupp rightly noted that "the language of the stellar cycles appears to be interchangeable with the language of funeral rites"<Krupp, p.216>. It is also generally accepted that the essense of the royal funerary rites was the re-enactment of the resurrection of Osiris, the latter having been revived after death by the magical rites of 'mummification' performed by Isis, thus becoming the first royal mummy. But this resurrection of Osiris as a 'mummy' is but an initial, partial stage of the magical rites, for the second and final stage was his self-transfiguration into a star-god, Sahu-Orion, in the form of which he becomes ruler of the Duat, a star-world for the souls <Hassan, p.286; Mercer, p.34>. This second cosmic transfiguration is not often appreciated <Rundle Clark,p.122>, nor is its stellar implication properly understood. All the rituals, ceremonies and litany for the royal funeral, however, are implicit of such a two-step transfiguration of the dead king. The fundamental point to be appreciated here is that both transfigurations i.e. corpse to 'Osiris', and 'Osiris' to 'star-god', were deemed to be materially possible. Firstly the dead king was made into a 'dead Osiris' <Champdor,p.69>, then followed his transfiguration into a 'star-soul'. To achieve the first transfiguration i.e. a 'dead Osiris', the corpse was actually ornated in the image of Osiris via a complex preparation which today is somewhat loosely termed 'mummification'. Then the 'Osirianized' corpse i.e. the mummy, through its own latent power, and also aided by magical spells recited by the clergy, was expected to self-transfigure into a 'Sahu', or spiritualized body <pyr. 1716; Wallis Budge BOD,lix; Hassan, p.314>. That no connection or word-play was intended between Sah (Orion, soul of Osiris) and Sahu (spiritual body of the dead Osiris-king) appears very unlikely. In the Pyramid Age, this second stage viz. the self-transfiguration into a 'star', was conveniently left in the charge of the pyramid itself, the latter proclaimed by the clergy as a monument endowed with the power to induce the metamorhosis of a 'dead Osiris' into a 'living star' <Bauval DE 13>. This was probably imagined to happen by the upwards transmittal of the soul of the entombed Osiris-king into his star-soul 'seed' i.e. the capstone/star-object crowning the pyramid. Thus the 'seed' of Ra-Atum was thrust skywards into the custody of the cosmic mother, the sky-goddess Nut, to be gestated and reborn at dawn as an 'established' star in the firmament. In the Pyramid Texts we read: " Nut has laid her hands on you, O King, even she whose hair is long and whose breasts hang down; she carries you for herself to the sky, she will never cast the king down to earth. She bears you, O King, like Orion..." (pyr.2171-2). "The King has come to you, O Mother of the king, he has come to Nut, that you may bring the sky to the king and hang up the stars for him, for his savour is the savour of your son who issued from you, the king's savour is that of Osiris your son who issued from you" (pyr.1516). If we link up these passages with passage 1657 "this king is Osiris, this pyramid of the king is Osiris" then much sense is made of, and modality given to this esoteric litany.

Notes:

1. A few Egyptologists have recently questioned the Bja = iron for the Old Kingdom epoch, suggesting 'copper' instead; see A. Nibbi, JARCE xiv, 1977, p.59; C. Lalouette, BIFAO 79, p.67. Nonetheless, Bja is widely accepted as being iron, and especially meteoritic iron in archaic times.

References:

BADAWY, A. in 'The Stellar Destiny of Pharaoh and the so-called Air-Shafts of Cheops Pyramid', in Mitteilungen der Instituts Fur Orientforschung (Akademie der Wissenschaften zu Berlin) Band 10, 1964 BAUVAL, R.G. in 'A Master-plan for the three Pyramids Of Giza based on the Configuration of the three Stars Of The Belt Of Orion', in Discussions In Egyptology, DE 13, 1988.; see also Trimble, V. in ' Astronomical Investigation concerning the so-called Air-Shafts of Cheop's Pyramid', in Mitteilungen der Instituts Fur Orientforschung (Akademie der Wissenschaften zu Berlin) Band 10, 1964, pp.183-7. BREASTED , J.H: Development Of Thought And Religion In Ancient Egypt. University Of Pennsylvania Press. Philadelphia, 1972 BUCKWALD, V.F: Handbook on Iron Meteorites, UCLA Press 1975. See also Brian Mason, Meteorites, New York 1962 CHAMPDOR, A: The Book Of The Dead, Garrett Publ. New York 1966 DAREMBERG Ch. & Saglio Edm.: Dictionnaire Des Antiquites Grecques et Romaines. See under 'elagalabus' and 'baetylia' EDWARDS, I.E.S.: The Pyramids Of Egypt, Penguin ed. 1979 FAULKNER, R.O: The Ancient Egyptian Pyramid Texts, Oxford 1969 FRANKFORT, H: Kingship And The Gods. Chicago 1978 HASSAN, S.: Excavations At Giza. Vol.vi, part i. Cairo 1946 HITTI, P.K.: History Of Syria, London 1951 KRUPP, E.C: In Search Of Ancient Astronomies, Chatto & Windus, London. Krupp is here mainly alluding to the cosmology of Seti I and Ramses IV (see Neugebauer O. & Parker R., Egyptian Astronomical Texts, vol. I, London 1960, pp. 36-94) MCALL, G.J.H:

Meteorites And Their Origins, Wren publ. 1973 MERCER, S.: The Pyramid Texts, Toronto 1952 PIANKOFF A: The Pyramid Of Unas, Princeton University Press, Bollingen Series XL.5 ROUX, G.: Delphes, son Oracle et ses Dieux, Paris 1976 RUNDLE Clark, R.T: Myth & Symbol In Ancient Egypt, London 1978 WAINWRIGHT, G.A. in Iron In Egypt, in The JEA, vol.XVIII, 1931, pp.3-15.; see also JEA XVII pp.185-195 & JEA XXI pp.152-170 for the meteoric links of Min. WALLIS Budge, E.A: A Egyptian Hieroglyphic Dictionary, Dover Publ.,New York, 1978; The Book Of The Dead -Papyrus of Ani in the British Museum, London, 1895. Preface.

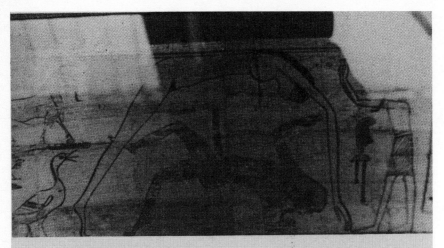

Plate:1
The Sky-goddess, NUT, arching her nude body over GEB, the
earth-god, whose oversized phallus is directed skywards.
This New Kingdom illustration is suggestive of a quasi-
similar concept for the 'seeding' of NUT by Atum-Ra's
cosmic phallus, whose original representation may have
been the sacred Pillar and Benben monument of Heliopolis.

Plate:2
Iron meteorite "MORITO". Photograph by courtesy of Vagn
Buchwald, Instituttet For Metallaere, Lyngby, Denmark.
"Morito" is here seen nose down, as displayed in Mexico City.

Plate: 3
Iron meteorite "WILLAMETTE". Reproduction by courtesy of Brian Mason,
Smithsonian Institution, Washington DC. "Willamette" is a fine 'oriented'
meteorite, here seen -- nose up on this old photograph. Today it rests
on its side as displayed in the American Museum Of Natural History in NY.

Plate: 4
The black-grey granite pyramidion from the pyramid of Amenemhet III.
Photograph by Robert G. Bauval of original monument in the Cairo Mus.

THE SEEDING OF THE STAR-GODS:
A Fertility Rite Inside Cheops's Pyramid ?

By Robert G.Bauval

Introduction

In two articles recently published, I have argued that the
'true' pyramids were originally star-symbols, with those of
Giza bearing a special correlation with the three stars of
Orion's Belt (1). Such a correlation led to the conclusion that
the three great pyramids at Giza were constructed in accordance
with a masterplan, probably one instigated by the Heliopolitan
clergy during the reign of Cheops (2). It was also recalled
that the narrow shafts which emanate from the king's chamber in
Cheops's pyramid were directed to regions of the sky vault
having great religious importance for the ancient Egyptians:
the northern shaft pointing towards the circumpolar region, and
the southern shaft pointing to the place where Orion's Belt
culminated in c.2750-2600 BC (3) [see diagram 1]. In this
present article it is now proposed to examine the astronomical
setting of yet another pair of shafts, namely those which
emanate from the so-called 'queen's chamber' (4), and also
suggest an appropriate ritualistic function for them as well as
for those of the king's chamber which were only briefly
discussed in the preceding articles.

The Astronomical Setting Of The Shafts Of The Queen's Chamber

These shafts are architecturally similar to those of the king's
chamber except that they do not pierce the pyramid right
through but stop somewhere within the core of the masonry. Also
when discovered in 1872, their openings were concealed by
plates of stone (5). Their mean slope to the horizontal were
measured by Petrie and given as $37°38'$ for the northern shaft,
and $38°28'$ for the southern shaft.

The shafts in question -unlike their counterparts of the king's
chamber- have received but little attention, probably because
of a widespread opinion that the queen's chamber was abandoned
before it could be completed -a hypothesis partly supported by
the rough condition of the flooring, and partly by the fact
that the shafts, as we have said, do not pierce the pyramid to
the outside (6). Even so, the fact remains that these shafts
must have been drilled before a decision to abandon the chamber
was made, for why would the builders bother otherwise ? It is
therefore reasonable to suppose that the slopes of the shafts
were chosen to express astro-mythological connotations -as was
to be the case with the slopes of their counterparts in the
king's chamber.

The Polar (northern) Shafts

The northern shaft in the queen's chamber is sloped at 37°38' to the horizontal, thus directing it well-into the circumpolar region of the sky. This setting was most certainly deliberately chosen for the same reason that the northern shaft of the king's chamber was aimed at the centre of the celestial polar region: to direct an observer towards the circumpolar constellations. The slope of the polar shaft of the king's chamber is 31°, and thus probably deliberately directed at the upper culmination of Alpha Draconis, the then-polar star in c.2600 BC (7)).

Now the circumpolar region of the sky as viewed from Giza (latitude 30°north) is defined by a circle with a radius of 30° of arc and with its centre the celestial pole (at 30°above the horizon). In c.2750-2600 BC could be found therein the constellations Draconis, Ursa Major and Ursa Minor. The Egyptian paid special attention to the circumpolar region for various reasons:

It would appear that they imagined it to be the gravid region of the sky and that in it dwelt Rer (or Tuart), the great Hippopotamus-goddess, protectress of pregnancy and childbirth. Her constellation was very likely Draconis (8). Also in the Pyramid Texts the dead king is often related to the 'imperishable' (stars), the name generally taken to be implicit of the circompolars (9). Ursa Major, the so-called 'Thigh' constellation, was sometimes associated to the 'four sons of Horus' (10), a set of minor stellar-divinities who were identified to the grandsons of the dead king and whose task during the rebirth rites were to assist the dead king in his heavenly ascent (11). There are, too, many passages in the Pyramid Texts which confirm that the dead king was imagined to be conceived again, this time by the sky-goddess, Nut, in order to be reborn as a star (pyr.1.828.990.1416-7.1469.1516.2171), and it is Atum or Ra who, for this purpose, makes Nut pregnant (pyr.152.990.886-9). In consideration of this, it would appear that the polar shafts in Cheops's pyramid were somehow thought to connect the king's mummified body with the 'womb' of the sky wherein he could be gestated as a cosmic-foetus and be reborn as a star (pyr.820-2).

The Southern Shafts

It is generally accepted that the southern shaft in the king's chamber was aimed at Orion's Belt as it reached the meridian. Orion's Belt is formed by three bright stars at the centre of this familiar constellation. Orion was identified to a deity called Sahu who appears to have been the counterpart of Osiris in the sky (pyr.820, 882).

As far as I know no equivalent 'stellar' analysis has been proposed for the southern shaft in the queen's chamber.

Now the stellar partner of Sahu (Orion-Osiris) was the goddess Sothis, identified with Sirius the brightest star in the sky (Alpha in Canis Major). Not surprising therefore, Sothis was considered the stellar counterpart of the goddess Isis, the sister-wife of Osiris.

Calculations using the rigorous precessional formulae reveal that the declination of Sirius was about -21° 34' (south of the celestial equator) at the epoch C.2750 BC. This means that when observed from Giza, the star would culminate some 38°28' above the southern horizon -an elevation which corresponds to the slope of the southern shaft in the queen's chamber (12). Coincidence must be ruled out when we consider the powerful mythological connexion of Sothis (Sirius-Isis) to Sahu (Orion-Osiris), and that the latter was not only the target of the southern shaft which emanate from the king's chamber but, as we shall see, had special associations to the dead kings (1).

The Osirian Aspect Of The Royal Funeral And The Birth Of Horus

The concensus among scholars is that the royal funerary rites as from very early' times were based on the mythological resurrection of Osiris:

Osiris was the eldest son of Nut and Geb, the sky-goddess and the earth-god. The other children were Isis, Seth and Nephtys. Osiris took as consort his sister, Isis, and together they ruled Egypt. While still in his prime, and still without a heir for his throne, Osiris was murdered by his brother Seth, who cut up his corpse and threw the various pieces all over Egypt. Isis, in an epic search, managed to recover all but one piece: the phallus. She then went about the task of joining the pieces together using the magical rites of mummification which brought Osiris back to life. It would seem that Isis managed to provide Osiris with an artificial phallus (13), for we are to understand that he copulated with her and made her pregnant, afterwhich he departed forever into the cosmic world of the dead (the Duat). The outcome of this supernatural sexual union was Horus, 'son of Osiris'. Horus grew up to avenged his father by defeating Seth, thus becoming king of all Egypt.

Horus was the prototype of pharaonic kingship and ancient

Egyptian theocracy rested on the belief that the pharaoh was the reincarnated 'Horus'. However when a pharaoh died he was subjected to the rites of 'mummification' and thus was converted into an 'Osiris', leaving his earthly throne and the Horus-title to his son/successor the same way the original Osiris had done.

Since the two southern shafts, one aimed at Orion's Belt and the other at Sirius, create, as it were, a 'link' with these stars and the king and queen chambers in Cheops's pyramid, we are compelled to suppose that the shafts were used in a procreational or 'seeding' ritual related to the sexual union of Osiris and Isis and, consequently, the procreation of a 'Horus' i.e. a ne earthly king. The ritual would have been intensely 'stellar', wherein the congregation imagined a merging of the dead king with Osiris-Orion. There is a passage in the Pyramid Texts which is indeed very suggestive of such a ritual:

"Your sister (wife) Isis comes to you rejoicing for love of you. You have placed her on your phallus and your seed issues into her, she being ready as Sothis (Sirius), and Horus-Sopd (a star) has come forth from you as 'Horus who is in Sothis' " (Pyr. 632).

Even though this passage does not actually name the deity evoked, there can be little doubt that it is Osiris-Orion –and by necessity the mummified king as well, for now he was considered transformed into an 'Osiris'.

The god Osiris, as is most evident from the funerary texts of all periods, was not only the god of rebirth but also the ruler of the Duat, the kingdom of the blessed dead. The ultimate aspiration of all Egyptians was that after death they could join Osiris in the Duat. The 'soul' of Osiris was, as many would agree, in the constellation of Orion, and to become one with his 'soul' was the main objective of the ancient Egyptian funerary rites. This, says Rundle Clark (14) " is what is meant by becoming 'an Osiris' ". Pyramid Text 882 makes this quite clear: " O king, you are this great star, the companion of Orion". Indeed in many other passages of the Pyramid Texts the name of the departed king is often compounded with the name of Osiris as if both are now merged into one cosmic being. The emphasis of the funerary rites, however, was on the act of 'mummification', the vehicle through which 'stellar' rebirth could be achieved. The culmination of this rite was the 'seeding' of Isis's womb by the 'dead' Osiris...or the womb of Sothis by Orion in a stellar context. The nature of the funerary rites quite clearly then was intensely stellar as well as intensely procreational.

The 'Function' Of The Shafts

Returning to the physical features of the shafts in Cheops's pyramid: other than their astronomical aspect, there is, too, the architectural and constructional design features to be considered. The shafts were very clearly not intended as sighting contraptions, for this function is made invalid by the fact that they were drilled first horizontally then sloped upwards (see note 15). A. Badawy has also argued against them being intended for ventillation (see note 3). Now in cults heavily imbued with fertility rites, elongated shafts within an intensely religious monument –and having no apparent <u>practical</u> function– would likely have been thought to have phallic or vaginal connotations. This hypothesis seems to be supported by yet another constructional feature of the shafts, namely that their openings in the chambers are positioned about 90 centimeters above the floor (15), making them conspicuously level with the reproductive parts of an adult person who may stand in front of an opening (diagram 2 a & b). Thus the 'stellar' and 'procreational' design aspects tempts us to conclude that some sort of fertility ritual took place inside the chambers of Cheops's pyramid. It is not difficult to imagine an ithyphallic statue of the king, or perhaps even the anthropomorphic coffin containing his mummy, placed upright and facing the shafts's openings for the purpose of symbolically linking the dead king with Osiris–Orion and Isis–Sirius, and also to link him with the gravid (circumpolar) region of the sky.

Although no graphic depiction of such a 'seeding' ritual has reached us from the Pyramid Age, ancient Egyptian funerary art from the New Kingdom onwards provides many examples showing the embalmed Osiris–king with his phallus erect and ready to inject his semens into Isis, her celestial nature represented as a kite hovering above the king–mummy's phallus. It is true that in these drawings the embalmed king lies on his back, but it is quite possible that in the ritual here suggested, an anthropomorphic/ithyphallic coffin of the dead king may have been stood temporarily in the manner so common to the god Min of Koptos (16) (diagram 2 c).

The 'New Year' Festivals And Fertility Rites

It is perhaps of some relevance to point out that such 'seeding' ritual involving an earthly monarch and a celestial 'consort' were not uncommon in other parts of the ancient world, notably in Mesopotamia at about the same epoch of the Old Kingdom in Egypt. I am making reference, of course, to the ritual performed in the Akitu festival of the "New Year' during which the monarch was united in marriage to a priestess of royal blood who personified the goddess Inanna–Ishtar (17). In this context the monarch personified the god Mardouk–Tamuz who, interestingly, resembled Osiris in many ways and who, too, was sometimes identified to the constellation of Orion (18).This ceremony took place in a chamber which was raised for the occasion on top of a Ziggurat, a temple shaped like a stepped pyramid. This ceremony undoubtedly had a great astral undertone, for Ishtar was a star-goddess identified to the 'Morning Star' (Venus/Sirius ?). In Egypt it was also on the day of the religious 'New Year' that the heliacal (first dawn rising) of Sirius took place, marking the start of the annual Innundation of the Nile and a rejuvenation and rebirth of Nature. Orion -whose rising precedes Sirius by about one hour- would thus dominate the eastern sky in the pre-dawn, heralding the great moment of cosmic and terrestial rebirth.

The design of the ziggurats, like the Egyptian pyramids, embodies many astronomical features. There are, too, striking engineering and architectural similarities between Zigurrats and the olde: stepped pyramids of Egypt, such as the so-called accretion method of construction, that lead the well-known architect-archeologist A. Badawy to suggest that the "pyramid would have been to pharaoh what the Ziggurat was for the mesopotamian gods" (19). Since the consensus is that the stepped pyramids of Egypt were constructed mostly under the influence of stellar ideas (20), and that the true-pyramids which followed embodied a stepped pyramid within their cores (21), the contents of this present article should compel us to suppose that a fertility rite not unlike the one performed in the Ziggurats of Mesopotamia may also have been performed inside Cheops's pyramid and possibly in other pyramids as well.

Reference & Notes:

(Abreviations: Pyr. = Pyramid Texts passage number).

1)Bauval, R.G., in Discussions In Egyptology vol.13, 1989, pp.7-18. Ibid., vol.14, 1989, pp.5-16.
2) Using a measurement surveying analysis, J.Legon arrives at a somewhat similar conclusions (Discussions In Egyptology, vol.10,1988,pp.33-40,vol.12,1988,pp.41-44,vol.14,1989,pp.53-60).
3) See A.Badawy's article 'The stellar destiny of pharaoh and the so-called airshafts in Cheops's pyramid', in Mit.Inst.fur Orient.(Akad.Wissen.Zu Berlin), Band 10, 1964, pp.189-206. Also by V. Trimble in Ibid.pp.183-187.
4)The name 'queen's chamber' was given by the Arabs; in fact nothing suggests that a queen was also entombed in Cheops's pyramid (Edwards I.E.S., The Pyramids Of Egypt, Pelican ed.1982, p.122).
5) Petrie, Sir W.M.F., The Pyramids And Temples Of Gizeh, London 1883, p.70-71.
6)Edwards I.E.S. op.cit.,p.123.
7) A full discussion by J.Ph.Lauer, BIFAO LX, 1960, p.176.
8) K.Locher, Archeoastranomy vol.9 (JHA,xvi,1985) p.S 152-3.
9) See R.O. Faulkner in JNES vol.25, 1966, p.153-61.
10) The 'sons of Horus' are often related to the adze-instrument, a little hook made of iron used in the ceremony of 'the opening

Appendix 2

The Giza Star-Correlation Theory and 10,500 BC

AN UPDATE

By Robert G. Bauval

Note: In order to avoid repeating the arguments that I have often previously used to prove that the similarity between the pattern formed by the three Pyramids of Giza is a deliberate attempt to reproduce on the ground the pattern formed by the three stars in Orion's belt, I have decided to reproduce in Appendix 1 the original article that appeared in 1989 in the journal Discussions in Egyptology. Readers who are unfamiliar with the theory are invited to consult Appendix 1 first before proceeding with Appendix 2.

Since *The Orion Mystery* was first published in February 1994 and *Keeper of Genesis* in May 1996, there has been a string of hostile opposition to the idea that the date of 10,500 BC could be at all linked to the Giza necropolis. This, in many ways, is understandable. For the possibility that there could be a connection between such a remote date and the Giza monuments would de facto bring about a complete re-think of the origin of Egyptian civilisation and, along with it, a total reconsideration of the origin of civilisation as a whole. For it is a deeply entrenched conclusion among the academics that the ancient Egyptian civilisation began c. 3000 BC and that the Giza necropolis is the product of the Fourth Dynasty of pharaohs who ruled in c. 2500 BC. And although it is generally admitted that Egypt was inhabited by primitive people prior to 3000 BC, few academics would be open to the suggestion that these people were able to plan the Giza necropolis, let alone build it. This last, however, is still an unresolved problem and not part of my argument. My argument is straightforward and simple: the Giza monuments were designed along astronomical principles; and when one examines these design principles devoid of bias and preconceived ideas about the capabilities of the culture involved, the date of 10,500 BC appears to be 'printed' on the layout of the site.

A LOGICAL SEQUENCE

It is important to properly realise how the date of 10,500 BC cropped up in my research in the design layout of the Giza necropolis. When I was completing *The Orion Mystery* in late 1993, I was intrigued by the emphasis laid by the ancient Egyptians on a concept they called Zep Tepi, which means 'The First Time'. Zep Tepi was believed to have been a Golden Age when the celestial gods had come down in the land of Egypt and had set in place the conditions and system of law and order to serve the pharaonic civilisation that sprung from them. It was the 'Time of Osiris', the husband-brother of Isis and father of Horus. Osiris, from the earliest times, was identified with the sky-god 'Sah' who was the constellation of Orion. In view of the intense astronomical quality of the Pyramids as well as in the Pyramid Texts, I wondered whether the epoch known as 'The First Time' could not, perhaps, be dated using the stars of Orion. My reasoning is this: the stars perform a slow, circular cycle lasting 26,000 years known as precession around the pole of the ecliptic like the dial on a watch; this cycle could be perceived as having itself a 'First Time'.

But where on the precessional circle of Orion could this be marked?

The reader will recall from Appendix 1 that the principal axis of the Great Pyramid runs from north to south, i.e. along the meridian. It is also along that axis that run the four 'star-shafts' emanating from the chambers. In c. 2500 BC the southern shaft of the King's Chamber pointed to Zeta Orionis, the lower (southernmost) star in Orion's belt as the latter crossed the south meridian. Using the versatile Skyglobe 3.6 programme to simulate the effect of precession on Orion's belt for the full 26,000 years cycle, it is easy to demonstrate that it will reach a high and low point along the line of the meridian – just like the upward and downward swing of a seesaw or pendulum. The low point or nadir of this precessional swing could, without stretching the imagination too far, be considered the 'beginning' or 'First Time' of the cycle. According to Skyglobe 3.6 this low point was reached in c. 10,500 BC when Orion's belt was about 10 degrees above the horizon, as opposed to nearly 60 degrees at the high point (to be fully reached in c. AD 2400).

When I looked at the pattern of Orion's belt at that remote date it was then that another unexplained aspect of the correlation which had been nagging me for years was suddenly clarified. This was the problem. In the epoch c.2500 BC the angle which the three stars of Orion's belt made with the meridian was about 73 degrees measured clockwise from the meridian. The angle that the three pyramids made with the meridian, however, was 45 degrees. So although there was an uncanny similarity between the sky image of the three stars in Orion's belt and the ground image of the three Pyramids at Giza, the correlation was not 'mirrored'. In order for both sky and ground image to match, the stars needed to be 'turned' anticlockwise some 28 degrees. You can do that with precession, for it's a fact that as the altitude of these three stars change due to precession, so does the angle they make with the meridian. I noted that c. 10,500 BC the angle was very near 45 degrees. Had the Pyramid builders used the phenomenon of precession to 'fix' in time the idea of Zep Tepi?

What added much cogency to this hypothesis was the astronomical alignment of another important monument at Giza: the Great Sphinx. On the ancient stele that was placed between the paws of the Sphinx, there is an inscription which states that the very place where stands the Sphinx was known as the 'place of the First Time'. Could the Sphinx also be a marker of '10,500 BC'? The Sphinx gazes due east at the place where the sun rises each year at the time of the equinoxes. This made me suddenly realise that Zeta Orionis in Orion's belt crossed the meridian in 10,500 BC with a right ascension of nearly 18 hours (actually 17 hours 58 minutes), which meant that as this star crossed the meridian in c. 10,500 BC, the vernal point – the spot in the sky which the sun occupies at the spring equinox – would have been on the horizon due east and thus in perfect alignment with the Sphinx. Also at this moment the zodiacal constellation of Leo would be located due east. It was well-known that the ancients from many cultures around the world commonly used the 26,000 years cycle rotation of the spring equinox along the circle of the zodiac to denote the 'time' of an age. The 'time' when the Great Sphinx was gazing at Orion's belt when it was at its low point at the south meridian was 10,500 BC, the 'Age of the Lion'. A celestial mythological figure called 'Horus of the Horizon' appears in the Pyramid Texts in conjunction with the rising of the sun. The same name is also known to have been used for the Great Sphinx of Giza. Such perfect interlocking of ground and sky imagery and symbolism could not, in my view, be simply attributed to 'coincidence'. Too many complex factors dovetailed neatly into one another for mere coincidence to be at play. I was, and still am, convinced that the ancients who designed Giza intended to lock a date to commemorate the 'First Time' or 'Age of Osiris', and that this date is around 10,500 BC.

ATTACK

In the June 1999 issue of the *Journal of the Royal Astronomical Society, Astronomy and Geophysics*, the well-known South African astronomer Anthony Fairall published an article on this issue entitled 'Precession and the Layout of the Ancient Egyptian Pyramids'. Although Fairall found my arguments 'ingenious' he nonetheless remained unconvinced about the Orion-Giza correlation theory and, more specifically, the links between the Giza monuments and the date of 10,500 BC. This was because the sky-ground image was not perfectly matched, but exhibited a deviation of some 3 to 5 degrees. In his own words:

> Precession . . . changes the angle that the belt (of Orion) makes in the sky. Bauval claims that by going back to 10,500 BC gives a perfect 'match'. Or does it? My own investigation showed that, while the line of the two outer pyramids is set 38 degrees from north, the angle of Orion's belt to north in 10,500 BC is close on 50 degrees! Hardly an exact match. I calculated that circular precessional motion would give 47 degrees, whereas including nutational terms makes it slightly higher. Bauval, on the other hand, uses computer programs. He implies that only with modern sophisticated computers can we examine the ancient skies! . . .

Fairall's article was, in fact, brought to my attention by the Scottish astronomer Mary Bruck. She offered to do the calculations to verify Fairall's claim, and confirmed Fairall's conclusions that the angle that Orion's belt formed with the meridian as measured from north was between 47 and 50 degrees, depending on whether nutational effects were taken into account or not. Neither of us, however, could understand how Fairall had worked out that the angle formed by the Pyramids was 38 degrees. The angle, in fact, is close to 45 degrees as can be seen quite clearly by the diagonal alignment of the two larger pyramids. Fairall did agree that in 10,500 BC the position of Orion's belt is 'furthest south in its precessional cycle' (i.e. it is at its lowest altitude as seen on the meridian) but saw no significance in that at all. At any rate, Fairall is right to point out that, according to calculations, there was a variation of 3 to 5 degrees between the angle formed by the three stars in Orion's belt and that formed by the Three Pyramids. This, Fairall says, invalidates the star-correlation theory. It certainly does not. Fairall's findings simply mean that according to his calculations there is a variation of 3 to 5 degrees, yet the similarity between the images is still there and valid. First the lay reader must be aware that precessional calculations over such a vast period of time are not 100 percent certain. For example, when in 1996 I had asked the astronomer Arthur Trew of the Computer Science Department at Edinburgh University to help me work out the position of Orion's belt for 10,500 BC, he declined. This was because Dr. Trew, quite correctly, felt that there was no 100 percent reliable mathematical model that could be used, and that the results would, therefore, always be subject to a degree of doubt []. And since no one can travel back in time to verify the calculated angle, then there is no way we can be proof-positive as to what the angle really was. Nonetheless, even if we fully accept the variation of 3 to 5 degrees calculated by Fairall, we need to see what this really means when Orion's belt is actually viewed with the naked eye at the meridian in 10,500 BC. The apparent angular size of Orion's belt as seen with the naked eye is about 1.5 degrees, roughly the width of an A4 size sheet, say 25 cm. By transferring this scale onto a photograph of Orion's belt, we can observe the effect. It is evident that we are splitting hairs here, and that the 'error 'is not significant to the naked eye. The fact is that scientists like Anthony Fairall fail to comprehend that when we are considering the ancient astronomer priests of Egypt who were not only subjugated to religious ideologies but also expressed what they saw in symbolic terms, then the accuracy of the correlation, in terms of symbolism, is pretty good indeed. But let me give a recent example to illustrate this point.. In early September 1999 I visited the well-known psychic Uri Geller at his home in Berkshire, England. Uri offered to perform a little telepathic experiment for me. He asked me to draw something on a sheet of paper while he went out of the room. I drew a star with a black felt pen and then turned the sheet face down. Uri came into the room and asked me to concentrate on the picture I had drawn while looking into his eyes. He then took a piece of paper and the same black felt pen and, amazingly, drew the very same star. Well, actually it was not *exactly* the same. Mine had the spokes of the star a little twisted to the left. But Uri had successfully made his point; and it was not necessary for his drawing to mirror mine *perfectly* in for me to concede that he had reproduced what I had in my thoughts even though what the star he had drawn did not have exactly the same angle with the vertical!

The point about Giza and the date of 10,500 BC is this: whether it pleases us or not, it cannot be denied that there is an uncanny, almost but not quite exact correlation between the imagery in the sky and the imagery on the ground at Giza at the epoch 10,500 BC when the vernal point is precisely on the rise. This is perfectly expressed in the Hermetic doctrine of 'As Above, So Below' that constitutes the cornerstone of all esoteric traditions that emanate out of Egypt. When all is considered – the meridional astronomical alignment of the Great Pyramid and its four star-shafts, the equinoctial alignment of the Sphinx, the many passages in the Pyramid Texts that identified the pharaohs with Orion and Leo, the statement on the Stele of the Sphinx and so forth – then it is my conviction that coincidence cannot be the cause of this design. Something else must be considered. And it is that 'something else' which is, I believe, what the quest for the Hall of Records is all about.

Appendix 3

Cosmic Ambience Revisited

Let us admit what all idealists admit that the nature of the
world is hallucinatory. Let us do what no idealist has done: let
us look for the unrealities that confirm that nature.

Luis Borges, *Avatars of the Tortoise*[1]

I THE RESURRECTION OF MATTER

In September, 1939, four years into the cycle of the Ninth Hell by Aztec
reckoning, as Hitler invaded Poland and plunged the world into war,
renegade psychologist Wilhelm Reich was observing the Aurora Borealis
in Norway. His reflections on that spectacular light-show may presage
the enlightenment we seek for the millennial outlook of humanity.[2]

Continued throughout the war in New York state and Rangeley,
Maine, Reich's little-known studies of the Northern Lights were
summarized in a book entitled *Cosmic Superimposition* which was found,
open, on Einstein's desk after he died. It is not surprising that Reich's
theory of 'orgone physics' would have been of keen interest to Einstein in
his last years. For one thing, Reich disputed the 'proof' of the non-
existence of a cosmic ether, widely believed follow from the Michelson-
Morley experiment of 1887. As the story goes, the fall of the ether led
directly to the formulation of Special Relativity in 1905. True enough
perhaps. hut Einstein reserved his doubts, because eliminating the
cosmic ether left an unacceptable void of 'empty space'. Technically, he

overcame this dilemma by positing the relativistic universe where space and time are merged in a gravitational mesh. Yet he continued to ponder the ether as he mused on the fabled grand synthesis, the Unified Field Theory.

One of Einstein's colleagues, Hermann Weyl, believed the UFT was possible on relativistic terms: because 'general relativity re-endows the metric world structure with the capacity of reacting with the forces of matter' and in that case 'ether' has now become synonymous with 'field' in the sense of a unified electromagnetic and metrical field.' In such a field, which exhibits 'a granular structure' of 'knots of energy' configured by momentum, 'no empty space exists.'[3] Weyl maintained that the field (*aka* ether) is not empty, therefore there is no empty space in the field. The argument is obviously circular, and Einstein would not be convinced.

Weyl does not really solve the dilemma, but Reich did, on two counts. First, he reinstated the ether as an omnipresent life-force called *orgone*. Second, he argued that 'light does not move at all but it is a *local effect of orgone lumination.*'[4] Both notions might well have captured the attention of Einstein, but especially the latter. Special Relativity posits the invariance of the speed of light relative to all phenomena. To say that 'light does not move at all' is, in effect, another way of asserting its invariance, a most intriguing way. Reich had cleverly resurrected ether theory on entirely new grounds. Moreover, his way of thinking had a universalizing flair that must have appealed to a generalist like Einstein. It's a great pity they were never able to collaborate.

Reich correlated orgone physics in microorganisms to human sexual coupling and 'cosmic superimposition' of celestial vortices, all on empirical terms. He described galaxies entwining each other like copulating dragons, the component stars pulsating with the universal life-force that surges through every cell in our bodies. In this view cellular pulsation, human heart-beat and wave-motion in the 'quantum foam' of the cosmos are one and the same activity.[5] For Reich, , the cosmic ground-force is bio-energetic. 'Orgone penetrates all space, including space occupied by physical matter.' The dynamic identity of organic life with atomic structure, on the one hand, and the Einsteinian curvature of space/time on the other, is possible because 'mechanical and chemical laws originated from the functional processes in the mass-free primordial energy ocean.'[6]

The interest of these ideas for Einstein must have been immense. Not only do they resolve the ether question, but they also verge on the fundamental problem of thermodynamics (heat-theory) which had so troubled Einstein after the suicide of Ludwig Boltzmann. In short, they open the way to framing the structure and dynamics of the universe within a comprehensive science of life- energies. Orgone physics is the resurrectional theory of matter.

Reich's leads have been largely abandoned since his premature death in a US federal prison in 1957. So far no work has gone into delineating the clear and strong parallels between his discoveries and Hermetic theory. With the current revival of Hermetics, Reich may show up again in contemporary discourse. If so, we might come to understand for the first time what really constituted the 'metaphysics' of the Ancients; or even to recapture the experiences from which it derived. Upon close study, the way Reich's discoveries recapitulate sacred science is astonishing. Unlike any other 20th century scientific visionary, he provides the basis for experimental work with cosmic ambience.

II LIVING IN THE AMBIENT

In the presence of the Northern Lights, Reich perceived '*the effect of orgonotic lumination at the outer fringes of the orgone energy envelope of the earth.*'[7] Thinking like a true Hermeticist, he associates auroral excitation with the earth-sun circuit and then extrapolates it to cosmic-scale interactions: 'The sun and the planets move in the same plane and revolve in the same direction due to the movement and direction of the cosmic orgone energy stream in the galaxy. Thus, the sun does not "attract" anything.'[8] Reich's language here comes across as a paraphrase of the few *genuine* Hermetic elements that survive in Ptolemy's resume of ancient celestial theory. Ptolemy uses the tertn 'Ambient' for what Reich calls the 'orgone energy envelope of the earth.' In Chapter II of the *Tetrabiblos*, he asserts 'that a certain power, derived from the aethereal nature, is diffused over and pervades the whole atmosphere of the earth.'[9] It makes the weather happen, so all astrological theory in the Greco-Latin idiom concerns itself extensively with meteorology. 'Subject to the motion of the stars,' the Anibient does not merely support life: it is itself inwardly alive. Hence, 'the impregnation and growth of the seeds from which all bodies proceed, are framed and moulded by the quality existing in the Ambient at the time of such impregnation and growth. [10]

Volumes are condensed in these pithy phrases. Unfortunately, Ptolemy's better ideas have been subsumed under the swampy notion of celestial influence and enshrined as astrological dogma. More sophisticated inquiries regarding the 'constitution of the Ambient' as an instrument of cosmic timing are lacking, but Reich's theories go a long way in that direction.[11] Moreover, Reichian bio-physics links Hermetics to Tantric emanational physics, the most reliable and best documented remnant of ancient metaphysical science. Three primary points of correlation can be noted:

First, orgone is sensorial. In Hermetics, the 'effects' of the planets are said to be deposited in human sense-impressions.[12] This parallels the Tantric teaching that *Cit-Akasha*, the ether of pure consciousness, pervades the realm of the senses and grounds our sense-organs directly in the cosmic continuum.[13]

Second, orgone pervades all space including the space occupied by solid objects. Hermetical alchemy identified the inner space of the psyche as coextensive with the space occupied by material forms, hence the 'paradoxical ubiquity and inaccessibility of the Philosopher's Stone'.[14] In Hindu Tantra the basis of materiality is *adrista*, the dusty residue of past universes. Pictured as coral in alchemical manuals, it is like a diffuse sponge that floats in the radiant plenum of *Akasha*, the *aqua permanens* of the Great Work.

Third, orgone is the cosmic life-force, known as *prana* in Hindu Tantra and the six Yoga schools. Prana at the solar level is called *Fohat* in theosophical argot. In Hermetics it is represented by the Green Lion. The image of the Green Lion eating the sun represents chlorophyll operating in photosynthesis, as well as the adept's ability to live directly off pranic emanations in the Ambient.

III MYSTERY CENTRES

The modern mind is largely baffled, if not boggled, by the evidence of ancient science and sacred technology in sacred monuments around the world. Our incomprehension of how and why these structures were erected is perhaps due less to our minds than to our bodies

In *Quicksilver Heritage*, intuitive scholar Paul Screeton states that 'the earth's magnetic field is estimated to have been 50 percent stronger in AD 500, and could have been even greater in megalithic times.'[15] This raises a basic conundrum concerning geomagnetism. Obviously, it exists, but no one in the scientific world is clear on how it works. Measurements suggests that 'the earth's magnetic field strength is approaching zero and may reverse as early as AD 2030,' but no one knows what this might portend.[16] All we can do is assume that geomagnetism features in the vital dynamics of our planet. If it does shift radically through the ages, we can suppose that it must have profound effects upon the Ambient, the atmospheric sheath we inhabit.

It has been argued that sacred sites around the world were designed to regulate or accumulate a range of geophysical forces essential to the well-being of the communities who constructed them. As Merlin said to Aurelius, 'In these stones is a mystery and a healing virtue against many ailments.'[17] Many sites are thought to have been located on the campuses of the great spiritual universities known as the Mystery Schools. This is logical and eminently sane, but it is only admissible if we pre sume that the Ancients had a respect for their terrestrial and cosmic environment that puts us to shame. According to French scholar, Jean-Louis Bernard, invocation of benefic effects in the Ambient 'was apparently done with megaliths and ultrasonics. The repercussion by stones of the ultrasonic waves causes a vibration in the cerebral-spinal column, and especially at the nape of the neck, which made it very easy to go into trance.'[18] Peter Tompkins suggests that 'sacred centers, by their accumulation of what Wilhelm Reich called orgone, may have helped to produce mass orgasms, therapeutic' for the entire community.[19]

Imagine the campus of a modern university stretched over some hundred acres of green, wooded and well-watered landscape. Imagine the entire setting regulated by a system of caretully designed avenues, obelisks, pools, pyramids and courts constructed on the principles of sacred geometry. Finally, imagine arriving at the site, partially ruined, three thousand years after school is out. The enlightened tourist to Giza or Avebury routinely performs this exercise. The fact is, sensitive people who visit such sites become automatically entranced, if not plunged into orgasm, mystical or otherwise. It comes with the territory. This alone is enormous proof of an original intent to optimize the Ambient.

Resonance is the term most often applied to these experiences. Inside the King's chamber one registers a certain resonance, different from the Hypogeum of Hal Saflieni on Malta, and different again from, say, Chartres cathedral. In each place, each setting, the resonance is quite particular and precise. A lot depends on the receiver, of course. israeli scientist Itzhak Bentov identified five different 'resonating systems' in the human body: the heart-aorta, the skull, the third and lateral ventricles, the sensory cortex and the two hemispheres of the brain 'where pulsating magnetic fields of opposite polarities are set up, these being very sensitive to environmental fields and providing a possible mechanism by which the brain picks up information from the environment through 'resonant feedback'.[20] Such feedback as it occurs in nature is an on-going miracle. In the sacred space of the Mystery Centres it was carefully managed (not controlled) via geometric norms such as the Golden Measure (1:: 1.618), said to correspond musically to the major sixth (8:5).[21] To date the musical and psycho-acoustical properties of sacred sites have been poorly researched and sparsely reported.

In Reich's theory, the supreme mark of orgone is the pulsating wave-motion evident all through nature from gamete to galaxy, but he warned of the blockage of the supreme life-force by 'character armouring' (of which, more below). Although we may all be designed to resonate to the Mystery Centres, some of us may be constitutionally incapable of resonant feedback.

As the millennium dawns, people are flocking to the ruins of the Mystery Centres in unprecedented numbers. At the same time, the planet is, day by day, immersed in a mounting wave of electromagnetic pollution - from cell phones, for instance. Science is baffled by the components of the Ambient: solar plasma filtered through the ozone screen, geomagnetism, the electromagnetic spectrum. Our ignorance of how this ensemble works does not prevent us from loading the atmosphere with human-made radiations, not the least of which is horrific noise. While the Ancients concentrated on the salubrious adaptation of the community to the Ambient, we seem intent on using it to drive ourselves insane. We might be alerted by the Sumerian myth that recounts how the Annunaki caused the Deluge to annihilate the human race *because we were making too much noise.* 'And the population soared, as the land like a roaring bull sent out its cry. The earth-dwelling gods were overwhelmed by the riotous din . . . and Enlil addressed the council of elders, saying, 'The commotion of these humans has become too strong. I can no longer rest for all their noise. Let us then command the Plague upon them.'[22]

If the ruins at Teotihuacan, Luxor, Easter Island and Newgrange were built as outposts by the Atiantean diaspora, survivors of an antediluvian civilization, it may be fatidic that we are powertully attracted to these sites at an historical moment when our own civilization is ending, one way or another.

IV HERMETICS FOR OUR AGE

To reclaim the Mystery Centres as heritage sites for a planetary culture due to emerge in the next Zodiacal Age is perhaps an overweening goal. Nevertheless, this intent is now calling the hearts and minds of millions of people. In the pitch of these aspirations, business goes on as usual and business, of course, is all about co-optation and commercialization. The prospect of a Messianic scam timed to the millennium is so obvious it hardly needs elaboration. This would be a serious departure from planetary enlightenment and, quite possibly, a nasty jolt back into the Dark Ages. Everything may depend on how we view the Ambient. And beyond that, on how we encounter the Ambient.

Cosmic ambience has a lot to do with timing. Lama Govinda phrased it brilliantly when he stated that 'we do not live *in* time, but time lives *within us*. Space is externalized, objectivated time, time projected outward. Time is internalized, subjectivated space.'[23] Thus, time and space are related to each other as inside and outside of a single reality, precisely as Einstein proposed in General Relativity. *As without, so within* is probably the best progressive formulation of Hermetic theory, preferable to 'as above, so below', which is a hierarchal notion, rather than a holistic one. If Reich were aligned with General Relativity, Einsteinian theory could be applied to our understanding of the Mystery Centres known to be informed by sacred geometry and geodetics. As noted above, General Relativity states that the metric (i.e., mensural) properties of the world are interactive with its material properties. This is the single most sophisticated idea in modern physics. It alone confirms that sacred engineering was a science of adaptation to the planetary Ambient through geometric/geodetic design. If 'the world is sound' as Tantra affirms, the design would include a range of fully demonstrable acoustic features.

In *Sacred Science*, R. A. Schwaller de Lubicz treats cosmic ambience in relation to Egyptian calendrics and the Zodiacal Ages. He ignores the particulars of teliuric and psycho–acoustical technology in the Mystery Centres, and there is some indication that he was notably inept with resonance and aural principles.[24] A traditionalist and obscurantist, Schwaller was sorely hampered by his elitism and seemingly unaware of the unwritten rule which requires Hermetics to be periodicaHy revised to compensate for the mental bias of each Zodiacal Age. He blindly repeats the law of correspondences: 'There exists a cosmic functional prototype for each organic specificity, the totality of which makes for the human body.' Thus, 'the doctrine of anthropocosmos which takes man as model in the study of All.'[25] This is not Hermetics for our Age, it is merely the vanishing point of the precedent style of Hermetic thinking.

V HIGH ANOMALY

Claiming the millennium is a feat of enlightenment open to any and all. The dawning moment defined as the cal endric limit of 2000 AD, based on Christian conventions, means nothing, but the internal timing is crucial. Terence MeKenna has proposed that the Mayan end-time of December 22, 2012 is like a temporal vortex, a 'strange attractor' in the space/time continuum. His graph of the infrastructure of historical time implies 'a possible ecological crisis within the community of species that may make access to the shamanic dimension a fact of historical "fatedness" of unique importance for humankind.'[26] Here at last is the genuine promise of the millennial moment. McKenna's efforts to explore the 'bioelectrical constellation of mind' exemplify Reichian principles that can guide us sanely and safely into the temporal vortex. A true Hermeticist, Reich affirmed the 'rooting of reason in nature.' Among five principles for scientific integrity proposed in *Ether, God and Devil*, he listed this point:

> The scientist will increase his errors in proportion to ihe neglect of his own system of sensory perception and awareness, He must know how be himself functions when he perceives and thinks.[27]

In other words, through our own organisms, our sensory instrumentation, we can recapture the intimate power of the Mysteries. 'Sensation', Reich insisted, 'is the greatest mystery of natural science.'[28] This is wholly consistent with the Tantric teaching that *Maya-Shakti*, the power of materialization, 'projects [the universe] from itself in a manner conformable to our own psychological experience, the object of *its* experience.'[29] In Tantra the five senses (*jnanaindrivas*) are integral to our psychological equipment, rather like sensors on the instrument panel of the nervous system. In revised or progressive Hermetics, the cosmos would not be modelled archetypally on 'MAN' but actually, dynamically configured with the human body/mind, so that it shape-shifts as we do. Tantra denies that primary properties (weight, mass, extension) are somehow more real than secondary properties (smell, taste, touch), for *Maya* is not illusion. It is the dimensional projection of Infinity into the human mind and senses and, as Reich suspected, it configures atomic and cellular activity with the same pervasive wave-motion (orgonotic radiation) that beats in our hearts.[30]

In *The Invisible Landscape*, Terence McKenna wrote:

The theory of shared genetic memory and DNA bioelectronic reflection in its environment may yet yield sufficient data for a relatively clear understanding of humanity's (and the shaman's) persistent intuition of an afterlife and the collective transformation which we suspect is iminanent and is creating the present shock of chaos at the end of history.[31]

As the moment arrives, the Ambient shivers around us, inviting 'a rupture of plane' as McKenna calls it, using a classical term from the study of mysticism. Since we commune with the cosmos primarily through our bodies, and not through our minds independent of our bodies, access to the Ambient can be impeded by the 'character armour' of the body, so Reich taught. He wrote that 'God' as the representation of the natural forces of life, of the bio–energy of man, and 'devil' as the representation of the perversion and distortion of these forces, appear as the ultimate results of character–analytic study.'[32] Were he present today, he would surely observe that 'God' more than the 'Devil' has become the primary pretext for the taboo on body/mind illumination.

In our time, religion is the main agent for the perversion of human bioenergetics. The mystico-fascist temperament, as Reich called it, is dangerously aroused by millennial tensions. An apocalyptic showdown by or before 2012 is likely to occur between opposing factions in the taboo-ridden, Fundamentalist cabals. Other minds will see the opportunity for a body-positive, scientifically enlightened plunge into the Ambient, rather than a salvationist crusade. Classical astrology was right on one point. Our character is our fate. Even more so, our character-structure (emotional armouring) is the judge of our fate.

The limit of inherited Hermetic theory can only be surpassed in certain moments, in certain settings. In his sly and idiosyncratic way, Borges gives the nod to this challenge. Today we know that monuments of cosmic ambience that embody the principle *as above/so below* affirm the static eminence of a vast range of correspondences (organic, geodetic, celestial). These sacred spaces were designed for optimum homeostasis, but not just for that. Among the Ancients profound conservatism (so strong in the Egyptians) was combined with immense daring. Every secret chamber of initiation was custom-made for the rupture of plane. The homeostatic setting of crypts and courtyards, pyramids and obelisks, provided a safe and sane environment for exploring the 'unrealities' that confirm the 'hallucinatory' nature of the world. In short, they were and still are places of *high anomaly*. In those settings, just at the right moment (which differed with each individual, for we carry time internally as the most subjective wave-form in the cosmic continuum), those who dared could plunge freely into the triple mystery of time, space and matter and, momentarily, reconfigure it.

Borges spoke ironically, knowing that the 'unrealities' he invoked were higher-dimensional realities. 'True hallucinations' (McKenna's term) require a stamina based on enormous resources for sanity. The Egyptians insisted on strict morality by adherence to *Ma'at*, the principle of reciprocity, because they knew that psychosomatic initiation, which advances the species on its learning curve, periodically requires the rupture of ordinary reality. The same sites that safeguarded the harmony of communal life supported the psychedelic plunge into chaos, the adventure of non-ordinary reality. As Michael Harner observed, 'Nature itself has made a decision that an altered state of consciousness is sometimes superior [for adaptive learning] than an ordinary state.'[33]

The Mystery Schools were the spiritual universities of antiquity. The common aim of their multi-disciplinary educational program was to guide and heal the human race. On the ancient campus at Giza and elsewhere, 'graduate work' was always done in altered states. At the millennial threshold, our age-old responsibilities are perhaps becoming clear once again. And not a moment too soon. The shift we face depends on reaching non-ordinary reality and not just remaining sane, but becoming more sane. The challenge to rediscover and revive cosmic ambience is the near, trembling focal point of the Mysteries to come.

John Lash, July 1999, Oudenaten

Appendix 4

A Sanctuary for Sokar

SIMON COX

As has been shown in previous books[1] the area known to the Ancient Egyptians as Rostau (or Rosetau) is the place we now know as Giza[2] and the deity associated with the environs of Rostau (by the Old Kingdom) was Osiris. One important fact that we know about the worship of Osiris was that in archaic times (First and Second Dynasties), and indeed up until about the Fourth Dynasty, Osiris seems to have been nothing more than an agricultural deity, possibly a corn god, as can be seen from his later association with the colour green, standing for growth and fertility.[3] It wasn't until Osiris usurped the role of the god Sokar that he became associated with the realm of the dead. However, for now we will concentrate on Osiris, moving on to Sokar shortly. At the early mortuary complex of Abydos, in lower middle Egypt, Middle Kingdom and New Kingdom pilgrims would journey to leave offerings and Ushabti figures at the site of the so-called hill of Heqreshu, close to the tomb of the first dynasty king Djer,[4] for they believed this place to be the tomb of Osiris. Petrie commented on this:

> At that time, with the revived interest in the kings' tombs, this rise (i.e. the hill of Heqreshu) became venerated: very possibly the ruins of the mastaba of Emzaza (on the hill) were mistaken for a royal tomb. It was the custom for persons buried elsewhere – probably at Thebes – to send down a very fine ushabti to be buried here, often accompanied by bronze models of yokes and baskets and hoes for the ushabti to work in the kingdom of Osiris.[5]

As has been stated previously, in the archaeological season 1906/7, Sir William Flinders Petrie was digging in the desert between Giza and

Zawiyet el-Aryan, about a mile and a half south of the plateau, when he discovered a hoard of Ushabti figures. The exact spot is hard to pinpoint as Petrie only states that he found the figures in the plain beyond a rocky ridge that rose half a mile south of the Great Pyramid.[6] The Ushabti figures were found in pits about ten feet deep that were filled with sand and rubbish. To all intents and purposes, these figures were what are known as extrasepulchral Ushabtis, in other words, they were left by pilgrims who were unrelated to any original tomb or burial,; many of these extrasepulchrals were also found by Mariette in the Serapeum at Saqqara, many of them bull-headed.[7] More of these figures were excavated in 1919 by an antiquities inspector called Tewfik Boulos, on a small hill about six kilometres south of the Petrie find. Some of the Ushabtis found by Petrie belonged to an individual called Khamwase, a son of Rameses II; at the spot Petrie found no tomb as such, but he did find some limestone building blocks that he couldn't explain.[8]

Why were the extrasepulchral Ushabtis left at Giza? Is there a correlation between these figures and the extrasepulchral finds at Abydos?

Was there a 'tomb of Osiris' at Giza/Rostau?

To answer these questions we must take a closer look at the deity that predates even Osiris and whom Osiris actually assimilates in the late Old Kingdom. That deity is Sokar.

The falcon-headed deity Sokar has gained popular notoriety because of his place in the Fourth and Fifth Hours (or houses) of the Duat. Many researchers and authors have assumed that this figure is just another side of Osiris and have therefore ignored him altogether. Sokar, however, merits closer attention. In my opinion, Sokar could possibly be the oldest deity known in Egypt, far older than Osiris and responsible for many of the later god figures of dynastic times. Sadly, textural and archaeological evidence for the cult of Sokar is sparse, but from what we have we can piece together a picture of how the deity was revered and worshipped not only in archaic and dynastic Egypt, but quite probably pre-dynastic times also. By the time of the new kingdom, the cult of Sokar, who it seems was a god of the Memphite necropolis, had appropriated many of the ritual, mythological, and ideological elements of the cult of Osiris.[9] But who was Sokar?

There is no doubt that Sokar was originally a god of the Memphite necropolis, indeed his name is echoed in the place today called Saqqara and his sanctuary was at Rostau, which as we shall demonstrate was at south Giza where certain parts of his festival were held. The primary objects of his cult were a mound and his sacred boat, the Henu-barque.

It is the Henu-barque that carries the dead king to heaven.[10] During the Old Kingdom, Sokar is seen as a patron of craftsmen, specifically of metal workers, and in the book of the Am-Duat, Sokar inhabits a strange land of the dead, a land that even Ra has no access to. This fact alone attests to his importance. Sokar can be seen in the representations of the Fourth and Fifth Hours of the Duat, standing upon his mound within what seems to be a hill topped by a black conical symbol of some sort, possibly a stone.[11] In this place the barque of the sun god Ra assumes the form of a snake in order to crawl along the sand and so traverse the realm of Sokar safely, whilst the souls of the dead cry out from the darkness around him. This echoes the Henu-barque of Sokar, which is also pulled along the ground and is placed atop a sled. The realm of Sokar is guarded by the two Aker lions and by a plethora of snakes and strange deities. The realm of Sokar certainly qualifies as a 'secret chamber', so secret in fact that, as we have noted, the sun god himself is denied access. It is interesting to note here that an unnamed official of Pepi I was known as 'master of secrets of the chamber of Sokar'.[12]

Having ascertained that the character of Osiris in the context of the late Old Kingdom texts (i.e. as a god of the dead) was based upon and assimilated with the earlier god Sokar, where does this leave us? Firstly, we must re-evaluate the idea that we stated previously of a tomb of Osiris at Giza mirroring the tomb of Osiris at Abydos. Surely, our references must now be to the tomb (or Shetayet as it is known from the texts) of Sokar, and the knock-on effect of this is that the Abydos pilgrimage site becomes the secondary site and the Giza site the primary. In other words, the archetype. Sokar is also assimilated with the Memphite god Ptah by the time of the Old Kingdom and it would seem that his assimilation had been going on for some time. Further evidence of his assimilation with Osiris can be seen in certain similarities between some of the ceremonies enacted in Sokar's festival and some episodes in the Khoiak festival of Osiris at Abydos.[13] As we have seen, the character of Sokar is intimately associated with his Henu-barque, possibly echoed by the various boat burials found within the pyramid fields.[14] In the festival of Sokar, besides the circumambulation of the walls of Memphis, there were at some point in the ten-day festival ceremonies at a Sokar-Osiris tomb, known as the Shetayet, in the Memphite necropolis, specifically at Rostau.[15]

The French Egyptologist C.M. Zivie believes that Rostau is located in the region of Gebel Gibli, about half a mile south of the Great Pyramid and the site of the so-called southern hill at Giza. This prominent hill is the only point on the plateau from which all nine pyramids can be seen. It is interesting to note therefore concerning this area that Petrie found 'many pieces of red granite, and some other stones scattered about the west side of the rocky ridge, as if some costly building had existed in this region'.[16] This would place a possible structure just to the west of the southern hill, in direct line with a most intriguing feature of the plateau, the Wall of the Crow. Could it be that Howard-Vyse was right in thinking that the wall was indeed a causeway, leading from an as yet undiscovered structure?[17] If not a causeway, then maybe an enclosure wall for the Shetayet of Sokar and the Henu-barque sanctuary. Egyptologist Mark Lehner has stated that the Wall of the Crow is quite possibly the oldest structure on the plateau[18] and a close inspection of this feature reveals it to be of cyclopean construction, with huge blocks used in the body of the wall and three truly enormous limestone blocks used to form the roof of the tunnel that runs through it from north to south (or vice versa). It is also interesting to note that the name Rostau was applied to an ancient village, later known as Busiris, which stood approximately on the site of the modern village of Nazlet-Batran.[19] It was in the desert to the west of this village that Petrie found the extrasepulchral Ushabtis mentioned above. It is tempting to speculate that these pieces of granite could have belonged to the Henu-barque sanctuary of Sokar; if this were the case, then the tomb of Sokar (Osiris) could not be far away. As we have previously stated, this tomb was known in the festival of Sokar as the Shetayet. The eminent British Egyptologist I.E.S. Edwards states that the Shetayet must have been a separate edifice, though undoubtedly close to the sanctuary of the Henu-barque.

So, let's review the situation. We have ascertained that an original tomb of Osiris would be seen as a very sacred and mysterious place, with pilgrims venerating and leaving offerings at the site, that it is very probable that such a tomb did exist at Giza and that this tomb was originally known as the Shetayet of Sokar and was therefore the original and archetypal tomb in Egypt, predating the tomb at Abydos. We have also pointed out that Rostau was located at Giza and specifically in an area known as Gebel Gibli, that the remains of a substantial and costly building has been found in this area and that pilgrims from at least the time of Rameses II left Ushabti figures here as offerings. Could it be that the way we see the Giza plateau today is only three quarters complete? Was an ancient structure in place in the area of the main wadi and the southern hill?

Did the Wall of the Crow form part of this structure?

Standing between the forepaws of the brooding Sphinx of Giza, the Dream Stele of Thutmose IV is largely disregarded by most visitors to this amazing place. Approximately seven feet tall and about three feet wide, originally a granite door lintel from the mortuary temple of Khafre, the stone was used to commemorate a special event in the life of a young prince.

The young prince Thutmose had been out hunting in his favourite location, a place we know as Giza. Whilst out with his companions, he decided to rest awhile in the scorching sun, beneath the Sphinx, which was at this time buried up to its neck in sand. As soon as the young prince had fallen asleep the Sphinx, in the form of Hor-em-akhet, spoke to him in his dream. He proclaimed that if Thutmose cleared the sand from his body, he would make the prince a king.

He was true to his word.

The most telling part of the tale comes halfway through. It describes the area where Thutmose is resting as the 'Setepet', or the sanctuary of Hor-em-akhet, which he details as being 'beside Sokar in Rostau'. Sokar, as we have seen, is an early Egyptian god of the dead and an integral figure to our whole quest for the 'secret chamber', Rostau, again as we have pointed out, being the ancient name of the Giza Plateau. Thus, the stele intimates that the Setepet, or the sanctuary of the Sphinx, was 'beside' Sokar, but where? The next few lines of the stele hold the answer.

The text describes the goddess Neith as 'mistress of the southern wall'. Again, we are being given geographical references to what can only be the Wall of the Crow. It continues: 'Sekhmet, presiding over the mountain, the splendid place of the beginning of time.'[20] Could it be that the 'mountain' was in fact our southern rocky hill? Was this 'the splendid place of the beginning of time'? And what was meant by 'beginning of time'? It is also interesting that it is the goddess Sekhmet that 'presides over the mountain', as in the various Eighteenth Dynasty tomb depictions of the Fourth and Fifth hours of the Duat it is a female figure that seems to encompass the hill of Sokar. Again we can see clues that are pointing to a specific geographical location: southern Giza, around the rocky knoll above the two modern cemeteries (one Muslim, one Coptic), just to the south of the Sphinx.[21]

As well as the straight archaeological and historical research that points to a hidden location on the plateau, I have, along with my co-authors David Ritchie and Jacqueline Pegg, put forward two further arguments that are just as compelling, if not more so. These revolve around the use of sacred geometry and astronomy. The astronomical argument is too long and complex to enter into in this short space, but I will let my co-author, David Ritchie, introduce you to the geometrical argument we hope to bring forth some time in the future.

There is one truth that still remains. It endures even though Man has done his best to obliterate and destroy it, because its language humbled even the greatest conquerors. I'm talking about the mathematics of the Giza Pyramids. The only language which cannot be corrupted, wherever, or whenever, you are. Mathematics was the original language of nature and the only way the Pyramid builders could send the message they so desperately wanted us to find, the location of Sokar in 'The Splendid Place of the Beginning of Time'.

The Giza Pyramids serve one ultimate purpose to indicate the Gateway to the Underworld by pure geometry. The number system that is encoded in the dimensions and positions of the pyramids of Khufu, Khafre and Menkaure, their satellites, temples and enclosure walls, form a geometrical picture that ties together the geometries of the pentagon, hexagon and heptagon, in other words, five, six and seven. Sacred geometry was the fundamental of Egyptian mathematics. The hieroglyphic symbol for the Duat is a five-pointed star enclosed within a circle. The 'hidden circles of the Duat' and the constructs that can be formed within them comprise 'the many paths of Rostau'.

'Rostau' is a 4000 cubit diameter circle and square centred on the Great Pyramid. 'Sokar' (the names we have given these constructs) is another, interlocking, 4000 cubit diameter circle and square that creates a 'Vesica Piscis', or the 'Eye of Horus'. Together they comprise the Duat. The centre of this second circle is a very precise location, exactly 800 royal cubits south of the north-east corner of the Sphinx temple. It is at the base of the vertical northern face of a hill called Gebel Gibli; this hill we believe to be the original 'mound of creation'. The 'Wall of the Crow', or 'Southern Causeway', leads to this place. The measurements from this point offer overwhelming evidence that there is something to be found beneath the sand and debris that has accumulated at the base of the hill over several millennia. The Giza Pyramids form a mnemonic computer, where the placement of every structure indicates the next step to be taken in a sequence that harmonises and integrates the different geometries.

At the spring equinox sunset of 1998 I stood at the 'Gateway' and watched the shadow of G3A, the easternmost of the three satellites of Menkaure's pyramid, touch my feet as the sun disappeared over the western horizon. That shadow has a measure: it is 1881 cubits long. The length of the Grand Gallery in the Great Pyramid is 1881 inches. The vertical angle of the Grand Gallery is 26.33 degrees; the angle from the Gateway to the Great Pyramid is 26.33 degrees. It is the angle generated by the ratio 1:2, or the angle across a double square. The floor of the King's Chamber is a double square which measures 10 x 20 royal cubits.

Endnotes

PROLOGUE

1. See Lynn Picknett and Clive Prince, *The Stargate Conspiracy*, Little Brown & Co. UK 1999.
2. In several Egyptian and international newspapers, magazines and television programmes as from May 1998. See the *Guardian* 4 June 1999 p. 17; also the *Al Ahram* 3–9 June 1999 p. 4.
3. This was also announced several times by Dr Hawass. The opening of the 'door', however, has been subjected to many previous announced dates which have been postponed since 1993. The latest is that the opening will take place in May 2000 (see Chapter 12 and Epilogue).
4. *The Trends Journal*, Winter Issue 1998, p. 1.
5. A. Robert Smith, *Hugh Lynn Cayce: About my father's business*, The Donning Company 1988, pp. 249–250.
6. Ibid. p. 249–250.
7. For example on the John Robbie Show on Radio 702, South Africa, in June 1996.
8. Letter from John West to Sphinx Project investors dated 30 January 1996.
9. Letter from Dr Hawass to John West dated 8 September 1996.
10. Published by the ARE Press, 1994. For the reference to the Second Coming of Christ and the Great Pyramid and the 'records', see pp. 74–93.
11. Degn-Film of Salzburg, Austria. The director-producer was Peter Beringer. I was also interviewed in this film as was Rudolf Gantenbrink.
12. Kirk Nelson, *The Second Coming 1998: Edgar Cayce's Earth-Change Prophecies*, ARE Press, 1998, p. 128.
13. *Al Ahram*, 5 November 1998.
14. This symbol is very old, probably harking back to ancient Egypt. It first appears in Freemasonry in the early eighteenth century. The 'eye' in the pyramid is also known as the 'Eye of Providence' but probably comes from the Egyptian idea of the 'Eye of Horus' (see Chapters 5 and 6).
15. The original capstone of this obelisk was a roughly cut irregular pyramid and an integral part of the obelisk. The new gilded capstone is a perfectly stylised pyramid, with a rather acute angle of slope.
16. Paul Naudon, *Histoire Générale de la Franc-Maconnerie*, Office du Livre, Paris 1987, p. 78.
17. Martina D'Alton, *The New York Obelisk*, The Metropolitan Museum of Fine Arts, NY 1993, p. 67.
18. Especially in Germany. See the magazine *2000 Plus* of February 1999. The story was also on several websites on the Internet.
19. *Arizona Daily Star*, 3 January 1989. The Millennium Society has its headquarters in Washington DC and describes itself as 'the world's oldest and largest organisation aiming at commemorating the year 2000'. The main emphasis is on

the celebration that will take place at the Great Pyramid of Giza which will be the 'cornerstone site of the World Millennium celebrations'. Its founder and first chairman is Edward E. Mcnally, a member of President George Bush's White House administration and who wrote the speeches for ex-President Bush and Mrs Barbara Bush. Mcnally also served under the Reagan administration. He is currently with the law firm of Alteimer & Gray in Chicago. He was educated at Yale University. Other members of the board include Michael P. Castine who served under the Reagan administration and was the director of the National Security Council Office of Private Sector Initiatives. An advisor to the board is the Duchess of York. Apparently ex-Presidents Ronald Reagan and Mikhail Gorbachev will also attend the millennium celebrations at Giza.

20. In the 3rd Degree of craft Freemasonry, also known as the Master Mason Degree, the initiate is placed on a symbolic coffin – usually a rug on which a coffin is drawn – at the centre of which is the skull and crossbones. The same insignia is found in Templar iconography and tombstones. Interestingly, several of the founding members of the Millennium Society in Washington DC are graduates from Yale University, home of the Skull & Bones secret society. For more information on the Skull & Bones secret society consult *Skull & Bones: A short history* in the *Executive Intelligence Review*, 30 January 1980. See also Anthony Sutton's *America's Secret Establishment: An Introduction to the Order of the Skull & Bones*, Billings Mt. Liberty Press House, 1986.

21. Former members of the Skull & Bones who also held responsible positions with the CIA were: William F. Buckley Jr., former CIA official in Mexico; William P. Bundy, former CIA official; George Bush, former Director of the CIA; Hugh Cunningham, former CIA official; Henry P. Davison, former CIA director of Personnel; Winston Lord, former CIA official in Asia; Dino Pionzio, former CIA deputy chief in Chile. US Presidents who were Freemasons were: George Washington; James Monroe; Andrew Jackson; James Polk; James Buchanan; Andrew Johnson; James Garfield; Theodore Roosevelt; William Taft; Warren Harding; Franklin D. Roosevelt; Harry Truman; Lyndon B. Johnson; Gerald Ford. I have not been able to ascertain whether more recent leaders of the White House were in the Brotherhood. Fifty of the fifty-six signatories of the Declaration of Independence in 1776 were Freemasons.

22. This symbol, with the words 'New World Order' attached to it, appears on top of a truncated pyramid on the reverse of the Great Seal of the United States. How exactly this design came to be adopted for the reverse of the Great Seal is still a matter hotly debated. It should come as no surprise that it has strong Masonic undertones, in view of the large number of Freemasons involved in the formation of the United States in 1776. The Great Seal Design First Committee was set up in 1776, and was headed by Benjamin Franklin, a prominent Freemason of Philadelphia and member of the famous Nine Sisters Lodge in Paris. It probably was Franklin who introduced the eye in the triangle into the Great Seal. The truncated thirteen-tier pyramid was first proposed in early 1782 by William Barton, and approved by Congress in June that same year, along with the Final Design of the Great Seal proposed by Charles Thompson. The idea of the truncated pyramid probably came from an earlier motif printed on the fifty-dollar note of 1778 designed by Francis Hopkinson. Opponents of the Masonic influence on this design argue that the various committees and the Masons took their ideas from 'parallel sources'.

23. See *George Bush: The Unauthorized Biography*, by Webster C. Tapley & Anton Chaitkin, 1992, Chapter 24, 'The New World Order'.

24. Broadcast live from Giza on 2 March 1999 at 8 p. m. ET in the USA and also satellite linked to various countries around the world. Graham Hancock, John West and Robert Bauval were invited by Dr Hawass also to take part in the programme.

25. I have no evidence of this and the connection may be superficial.
26. Kirk Nelson op. cit. p. 119.
27. See note 19 above.
28. Peter Tompkins, *The Secrets of the Great Pyramid*, Allen Lane 1971 p. 38. The idea of the phoenix for the Great Seal was introduced by William Barton in 1782 but was rejected by Charles Thompson, who insisted on the native American bald eagle.
29. See a study on this subject by Armand Bedarride, *Le Livre d'Instruction du Rose-Croix*, Demeter Paris 1987. The Rose-Croix 18th Degree in Freemasonry is laden with Christian mysticism based on the sacrificial death and resurrection of Jesus. According to Bedarride, 'The Phoenix is the magical formula I.N.R.I (the letters on top of Jesus's cross) come alive and active, and showing the fire, physical, intellectual, moral and spiritual in its eternal role of agent of transformation. The rising of the mystical phoenix from the ashes of the sacrificial fire is a powerful symbol of resurrection associated with Christ. In Rose-Croix Freemasonry the phoenix is sometimes replaced by the symbol of the pelican cutting its own chest to feed his blood to his offspring. Most insignia of the pelican also bear the I.N.R.I logo.'
30. The name 'Egyptian' derives from the Greek 'Aikoptos' or 'Aigyptos', meaning the inhabitants of Koptos, an ancient town in the Delta region of Lower Egypt reputed to have been the birthplace of Osiris. The name was automatically transferred to the Christian converts who were native Egyptians. It is still widely used today to denote a Christian of Egyptian origin.
31. Joseph Jochmans, *Time Capsule: The Search for the Hall of Records in Ancient Egypt*, in two volumes, Alma Tara Publishing, South Carolina, USA 1996. The quote is from an article by Jochmans in *Atlantis Rising* issue 4, 1995.
32. James J. Hurtak, *The Book of Knowledge: The Keys of Enoch*, The Academy For Future Science, Los Gatos, California, USA 1976.
33. According to Hurtak, he met Lehner in the mid-1970s at Giza, during the SRI exploration at the Sphinx.
34. A. Robert Smith op. cit. p. 193.
35. Bertram A. Tomes, transcript of speech given to the Swansea Lodge in 1922, p. 3.
36. Richard H. Drummond, Ph.D, *A Life of Jesus the Christ: from Cosmic Origins to the Second Coming*, St Martin's Paperbacks, NY, 1996, p. 32. See also Edgar Cayce Reading 5748–5.

CHAPTER ONE
1. A full discussion on this matter is given in Robert Schoch and Robert McNally's *Voices of the Rocks*, Crown Publishing Inc. New York 1999.
2. See *Keeper of Genesis*, William Heinemann Ltd. 1996.
3. See the *Daily Mail* 2 May 1996, pp. 50–1.
4. Interview on Radio 702 Johannesburg by John Robbie, June 1996.
5. Fox TV live from Giza: Opening of the Lost Tomb, 2 March 1999.

CHAPTER TWO
1. The Kore Kosmou (the Eye-pupil of the World) is a tract attached to the philosophical Hermetica. See Walter Scott's *Hermetica*, Shambala ed. Boston 1993, p. 457. Scott labels it 'Excerpt xxiii Isis to Horus'. Also sometimes known as 'The Virgin of the World', the Kore Kosmou has Isis revealing 'secret doctrines' and teachings to Horus, her son, which she has heard from 'Hermes (Thoth) the writer of records at the time he initiated me into the rites, and which you shall hear now' (Scott, p. 457).
2. Scott op. cit. p. 461. For quotes see Garth Fowden, *The Egyptian Hermes*, Princeton University Press, 1993, p. 33.
3. Garth Fowden op. cit. p. 40.

4. Ibid.
5. Ibid.
6. I.E.S. Edwards, *The Pyramids of Egypt*, Penguin ed. 1982, p. 53.
7. Robert Bauval and Adrian Gilbert, *The Orion Mystery*, William Heinemann Ltd. 1994, p. 24.
8. George Hart, *A Dictionary of Egyptian Gods and Goddesses*, Routledge & Kegan Paul, London 1988, p. 62.
9. Ibid.
10. I.E.S. Edwards op. cit. 1993 ed., p. 284.
11. G.Hart op. cit. p. 64.
12. For a full discussion see Selim Hassan, *Excavations at Giza*, vol.VI Part I, Government Press, Cairo 1946. For specific reference to the Fifth Division, Rostau and Monte Libyco see ibid. pp. 263–5.
13. Ibid.
14. Ibid.
15. Ibid.
16. Garth Fowden op. cit. p. 40.
17. Walter Scott op. cit. Intro. B.
18. Garth Fowden op. cit. pp. 4–5.
19. Walter Scott op. cit. p. 15.
20. Ibid. p. 5.
21. Ibid. p. 3.
22. George Hart op. cit. pp. 214–5.
23. Ibid. p. 216.
24. Ibid.
25. Lucy Lamie, *Egyptian Mysteries*, Thames & Hudson, London 1986, p. 72.
26. John Anthony West, *Serpent in the Sky*, Quest Books, 1993, p. viii.
27. Fragments circulated as early as the eleventh century among Neo–Platonic scholars, and the Corpus Hermetica that reached the Medicis in 1460 may have been compiled by Michael Psellus of Byzantium around 1050 AD. Earlier scholars refer to some of the Libelli of the Corpus Hermetica, such as the well-known fourth-century alchemist Zosimos, but there is no evidence that it was known as a complete corpus before the twelfth century, although it is possible that its compilation long predates Michael Psellus.
28. The Italians referred to Cosimo de Medici as 'Pater Patria', Father of Italy', and it is recognised by many that his role in the great Italian artistic and intellectual revival was paramount.
29. Frances A. Yates, *Giordano Bruno and the Hermetic Tradition*, The University of Chicago Press, 1991 ed. pp. 1–2.
30. Michael Baigent and Richard Leigh, *The Elixir and the Stone*, Viking, London 1997, pp. 112–3.
31. Walter Scott op. cit. pp. 35–40. The Hermetica was a source of almost total fascination among scholars during the Renaissance and the Enlightenment eras – a fascination that has not abated to this day with philosophical and esoteric seekers.
32. Walter Scott op. cit. p35.
33. Ibid.
34. Frances Yates, *Bruno* . . . op. cit. p. 182.
35. Ibid. p. 183.
36. Ibid. p. 113.
37. In the Old Charges of Freemasonry the 'seven liberal arts' constitute the opening statement of the historical account of the craft (see Fred Pick &. G. Norman Knight's *The Pocket History of Freemasonry*, Frederick Muller Ltd., London 1983 ed., p. 31). These are still referred to in the 2nd Degree of Freemasonry as part of the ritualistic liturgy. In Freemasonry 'Geometry' is considered supreme among all the arts and sciences, hence the quasi-veneration of the letter 'G' in Masonic

regalia and iconography.

38. Frances Yates, *Bruno* . . . op. cit. p. 115–6.
39. Ibid. p. 399.
40. Ibid. p. 400.
41. Ibid. p. 398.
42. Fowden, op. cit. p. 29.
43. Ibid. p. 30.
44. Ibid.
45. Plato, *Timaeus and Critias*, Penguin Classics, London 1977.
46. Fowden op. cit. p. 30.
47. Ibid.
48. Ibid.
49. Lewis Spence, *Egypt*, Bracken Books, London 1985 pp. 265-7.
50. Ibid.
51. Ibid. p. 51.
52. Ibid.
53. Dimitri Meeks & Christine Favard-Meeks, *Daily Life of Egyptian Gods*, London, Pimlico, 1993.
54. Fowden op. cit. p. 28.
55. Ibid. p. 32.
56. Ibid.
57. Peter Kingsley, *Poimandres: The Etymology of the name and the origins of the Hermetica*, Journal of the Warburg and Courtauld Institutes, vol. 56, 1993, p.2.
58. Scott op. cit. p. 29.
59. Fowden op. cit. p. 35.
60. Scott op. cit. p. 10.
61. Kingsley op. cit. p. 5.
62. Ibid. p. 6.

CHAPTER THREE
1. Miriam Lichtheim, *Ancient Egyptian Literature*, vol.1, University of Calif. Press, 1975, p. 215.
2. George Hart, *Egyptian Myths*, p. 69.
3. Christian Jacq, *Magic & Mystery in Ancient Egypt*, Souvenir Press, London 1998, p. 15.
4. Murry Hope, *The Sirius Connection*, Element Books,1990, p. 44.
5. Wallis Budge, *The Gods of the Egyptians*, vol. I, Dover Publication, NY 1969, p. 401.
6. Christian Jacq, *Magic & Mystery in Ancient Egypt*, p. 13.
7. See *The Jesus Mysteries* by Timothy Freke and Peter Gandy, Thorsons, London 1999.
8. Naydler, *Temple of the Cosmos*, Inner Traditions, Vermont 1996, p. 122.
9. Ibid.
10. A.H. Gardiner, *Egyptian Magic* in *Hastings 'Encyclopedia of Religion and Ethics'* – Edinburgh 1973, p. 263.
11. Naydler, op. cit., p. 125.
12. See Fred L. Pick & G. N. Knight's *The Pocket History of Freemasonry*, Frederick Muller Ltd. London 1983.
13. Wallis Budge, *An Egyptian Hieroglyphic Dictionary*, Dover Publications NY 1978. p. 886.
14. Brigadier General Albert Pike was the Supreme Commander of the Supreme Council of the 33rd Degree (Southern Jurisdiction) in the late 1880s and was reputed (unjustly) to wield enormous occult powers.
15. Thoth was often called the 'recorder of time' or 'the recorder of the stars'.
16. See John West's *Serpent in the Sky*, Quest Books, Wheaton Ill. 1993.

17. J. West, *Serpent in the Sky*, pp. 129–30.
18. Lewis Spence, *Egypt*, p. 252.
19. Jane B. Sellers, *The Death of Gods in Ancient Egypt*, Penguin Books, London 1992, p. 8.
20. The term 'magical device' for the shafts was coined by French engineer/ Egyptologist Jean Kerisel on the BBC 2 documentary *The Great Pyramid*, 6 February 1994.
21. www.cheops.org
22. See *The Orion Mystery*, William Heinemann ed. 1994, pp. 97–104.
23. You cannot compare the design criteria for a 'modern town house' which is purely on practical principles with an intensely sacred and esoteric monument such as the Great Pyramid. Chartres Cathedral or the Taj Mahal would be much better choices.
24. Walter Scott, *Hermetica*, Shambhala ed. Boston 1993, p. 127.
25. J.S. Gordon, *Land of the Fallen Gods*, Orpheus Publ. House, Surrey, England, 1997, p. 140.
26. George Hart, *Dictionary*, op. cit. p. 214.
27. Ibid. p. 215.
28. Observations of the stars over a few years determines the yearly cycle. A few months' observation of the moon will determine the monthly cycle. The annual Nile flood was matched to the observation of the stars, with Sirius marking the beginning of the flood season around end June.
29. Christian Jacq, op. cit. p. 13.
30. Ibid. p. 85.
31. Ibid. p. 84.
32. Manly P. Hall, *Freemasonry of the Ancient Egyptians*, Philosophical Research Society Inc. Los Angeles Calif. 1965, p. 131.
33. Moses, being a 'son of pharaoh', would certainly have been initiated into the mysteries of Heliopolis.
34. Plato, *Phaedrus*, 274D–275A.
35. Christian crosses worn on chains were also discouraged. No Christian priest was allowed to conduct mass. But most expatriate companies 'smuggled' a priest in at Christmas, and Santa Claus desert parties were a source of great amusement and tolerance to the foreign population.
36. There is an 'Arcadia' (Arkadhia) in Greece, but this is not the mythical one intended. The latter has its origins in a pastoral poem of c. 1503 inspired by Latin classics and, mostly, from Virgil.
37. M. Baigent, H. Lincoln and R. Leigh, *The Holy Blood and the Holy Grail*, Corgi Books, 1982, p. 40.
38. Ibid.
39. Ming Pei is a Chinese architect born and raised in the city of Philadelphia, USA. His reputation is world-wide, but the Louvre Pyramid got his name in the public domain.
40. Charles X who commissioned the obelisk was a Freemason. It was eventually dedicated to Louis-Philippe, king of France, whose father, Philippe-Egalité, was the first Grand Master of the Masonic Order of the Grand Orient.
41. See Picknett and Clive Prince, *The Templar Revelation*, Corgi Books 1998, p. 296; they also report a possible strange association between François Mitterrand and the Prière de Sion.
42. Jean Kerisel, *La Pyramide à travers les ages*, Presse Ponts et Chaussées 1991, p. 157.
43. Ibid, p. 161.
44. *JEA*, vol. XI, pp. 2–5, 1925.
45. *JEA*, vol. XI, p. 2–5, 1925.
46. Gardiner, *JEA*, vol. II, 1925.
47. Robert Bauval and Adrian Gilbert, *The Orion Mystery*, William Heinemann Ltd.

London 1994, p. 265.
48. Ibid., p. 269.
49. JEA, vol. XVI, 1930, p. 33–4.
50. Ibid.
51. I.E.S. Edwards, *The Pyramid of Egypt*, Penguin Books 1982 ed., p. 171.
52. *The Orion Mystery* op. cit, pp. 65–66.
53. See *The Orion Mystery*. See also *Keeper of Genesis*, William Heinemann Ltd. 1996.
54. See *The Orion Mystery*.
55. Green, *JEA*, XVI, 1930, p. 34.

CHAPTER FOUR
1. Memphite Theology c. 2000 BC, Shabaka Stone, British Museum
2. E.A. Budge, *Osiris and the Egyptian Resurrection*, vol.1, Dover Publ. NY, 1973, p. 10.
3. Although Budge covers the whole of the pharaonic era and up to the fifth century AD, the cult of Osiris probably stems from much older sources. Budge wrote: 'The Egyptian texts now available enable us to trace the history of the cult of Osiris from the Archaic to the Roman Period with tolerable completeness, but its beginning is hopelessly lost in obscurity.'
4. By the orders of the Christian emperor Theodocius.
5. Herodotus, *The Histories*, Book II.
6. Herodotus is reputed to have been the first man to have decided to record historical events for the sake of posterity. This honour is not entirely deserved. Historical records were kept by temple priests in Egypt, Sumer and Judea long before Herodotus.
7. Herodotus, *The Histories*, Book II, p. 124.
8. This was in 1998. Kerisel lives in Paris near the Trocadero and still, at the age of 90, acts as a consultant for special engineering works such as the Tower of Pisa. Dr Hawass has publicly (and very unfairly in my opinion) criticised Kerisel, implying he has joined ranks with the 'Pyramidologists' (ARE Conference 20 August 1999).
9. Conversations with Kerisel, Paris, July 1999.
10. *The Great Pyramid: Gateway to the Stars*, BBC2 *Everyman* Special 6 February 1994.
11. Produced by Jean-Claude Bragard of the BBC's *Ancient Voices* series.
12. Kerisel was President of the Soil Studies Institute in Paris, and has served on many engineering committees.
13. Andrew Collins, *Gods of Eden*, Headline Books 1998, p. 224.
14. Ibid., Chapter 13.
15. Ibid.
16. *New Humanist*, Dec. 1990.
17. I.E.S. Edwards, *The Pyramids of Egypt*, op. cit. p. 42.
18. Ibid., p. 104.
19. Simon Cox has researched Egyptological subjects for various authors, including Andrew Collins, David Rohl, Graham Hancock and Lynn Picknett.
20. Simon Cox, *The Makers of Time*, unpublished manuscript.
21. *Keeper of Genesis*, op. cit. p. 149.
22. Selim Hassan, *Excavations at Giza*, vol.VI, part I, Cairo Government Press 1946, p. 265.
23. Mark Lehner was much of the same opinion: see Chapter 8.
24. It is tempting to see in the name of 'Sokar' a link with the 'Aker'. Sokar's name is usually followed by an ideogram of a boat on which is seen a falcon perched on a rounded object – an omphalos – very similar to the one seen often on the back of the Aker lion.
25. Hassan, op. cit. p. 265.
26. For full discussions see *Keeper of Genesis*, Mandarin 1997, p. 189.

27. It was taken out of Egypt during the British invasion of Egypt in 1801 against the French occupation.
28. The originals were either carved on wooden tablets or written on papyrus.
29. Translation by Miriam Lichtheim, *Ancient Egyptian Literature*, vol.1, p. 52.
30. Op. cit., p. 51.
31. Ibid.
32. See *Keeper of Genesis*, pp. 143–4.
33. Miriam Lichtheim, op. cit. p. 52.
34. Hassan, *Excavations at Giza*, op. cit.
35. Hassan, *Excavations at Giza*, op. cit., p. 184.
36. Adolf Erman, *A Handbook of Egyptian Religion*, 1907, p. 15.
37. For an in-depth look at this area, see Appendix 4 by Simon Cox.
38. Pyramid Text (PT) 445.
39. PT 1256–7.
40. M. Lichtheim, op. cit., p. 204.
41. Suggestive, of course, of an underground system at Giza.
42. R.O. Faulkner, *The Ancient Egyptian Book of the Dead*, edited by Carol Andrews, British Museum Press, London 1990, p. 192.
43. Rundle Clark, *Myth and Symbol in ancient Egypt*, op. cit., p. 108.
44. James H. Breasted, *Ancient Records II*, Histories & Mysteries of Man Ltd., London 1988, p. 323, also line 7 on the stela itself.
45. Written on coffins of the Middle Kingdom Period c. 2100 BC – 1750 BC.
46. Coffin Texts, spell 1080.
47. A detailed study of the Duat and all its meanings is given in Hassan's *Excavations at Giza* op. cit. There is a great deal of confusion among Egyptologists as to whether the the Duat is an 'underworld' or whether it is in the sky. The correct way to see the Duat, I think, is that it was a cosmic world which could be accessed from inside the Earth and also from the sky.
48. A full discussion in *Keeper of Genesis*, Chapter 8.
49. E.A. Wallis Budge, *Egypt Heaven and Hell*, Martin Hopkinson, London 1905, three Vols in one, 1925, p. 62.
50. Hassan, *Excavations at Giza*, op. cit., p. 265.
51. Peter Tompkins, *Secret of the Pyramid*, Allen Lane, London, 1973, p. 298.
52. Robert Temple, *The Sirius Mystery*, Destiny Books ed. 1987, pp. 130–1.
53. *Keeper of Genesis*, ill.39 and pp. 146–7.
54. Ibid., pp. 156–7.
55. Ibid., pp. 144–7.
56. *The Orion Mystery*, Mandarin ed., 1998, p. 188.
57. *The Orion Mystery*, Mandarin ed., 1998, p. 226.
58. Coffin Text Spell 236.
59. Coffin Text Spell 241.
60. Coffin Text Spell 314.
61. Coffin Text Spell 571.
62. Coffin Text Spell 1018.
63. Coffin Text Spell 1035.
64. Coffin Text Spell 1072.
65. *The Orion Mystery*, Mandarin ed. 1998, p. 124–5.
66. This region of the sky is contained by the ecliptic and the horizon at the time of the rising of Sirius, making a rough triangle with Sirius, Taurus and Leo.
67. Sellers uses the equinox rising of Orion, whereas I use the meridian during the precessional cycle. The meridional alignment of the shafts in the pyramid, one of which points to Orion, makes the latter approach more likely. See *The Orion Mystery*, Heinemann ed, op. cit. p. 146.
68. It is possible that his earlier name was *Sokar*, but this is not generally accepted by Egyptologists.

69. I.E.S. Edwards, *The Pyramids of Egypt*, 1982 ed., p. 27.
70. Edwards, op. cit., p. 24.
71. For a general discussion, see *Keeper of Genesis*.
72. Pyramid Text (PT): 1652–1657.
73. R.Clark, *Myth & Symbol*, p. 246.
74. 'Vital essence' could also mean 'efflux', the material aspect of the spiritual being.
75. R. T. Rundle Clark, *Myth & Symbol in Ancient Egypt*, p. 247.
76. R. Clark, *Myth & Symbol in Ancient Egypt*, p. 249.
77. R.O. Faulkner, *The Ancient Egyptian Coffin Texts*, vol. I, Aris & Phillips, Warminster, England, 1978, pp. 138–150.
78. The Bennu is sometimes described as a 'Heron' by Egyptologists.
79. Herodotus, *Histories* II, p. 73.
80. R.T. Rundle Clark, *Myth & Symbol in Ancient Egypt*, p. 246.
81. R. Clark, *Myth & Symbol*, p. 39.
82. *Discussions in Egyptology*, vol.14, 1989.
83. Ibid.
84. This 'stone' is said to have been brought down from heaven by an angel and given to Ismail, the son of Haggar and Abraham, and the 'Patriarch' of Islam.
85. For photographs of these meteorites, see *The Orion Mystery*, plates 14a & 14b.
86. PT 530.
87. PT 1454.
88. PT 2051.
89. PT 1583.
90. PT 262.
91. PT 347.
92. PT 904.
93. PT 886–9.
94. *The Orion Mystery*, pp. 92–4.
95. Ibid. p. 214.
96. PT 1657.
97. I.E.S. Edwards, op. cit., p. 276.
98. Ibid.
99. PT 2244.
100. Shirley Moskow, 'Ancient Ambassadors to the Modern World', *Horus* magazine, April/June 1999, p. 14.
101. PT 887–889.
102. *Annales du Services des Antiquités*, Note sur le Pyramiion d'Amennemhat III à Dachour, tome iii, 1903 p. 206.
103. The steel ruler belonged to Chris Dunn.
104. Thus described by Maspero when discovered. *Annales du Services* op. cit.
105. Ibid.
106. James H. Breasted, *Development of Religion and Thought in Ancient Egypt*, University of Pennsylvania Press, 1972, pp. 70–3.
107. E.A. Wallis Budge, *The Gods of the Egyptians*, vol. I, op. cit., p. 189, fig.
108. R.T. Rundle Clark, *Myth & Symbol*, pp. 171–2.
109. Today it is often seen drawn on doors of homes and on the backs of cars and buses.
110. R.T. Rundle Clark, *Myth & Symbol*, p. 219.
111. Ibid.
112. Ibid., pp. 220–5. The components of the symbols that make the eye sum up to 63 parts in 64; with one part 'missing'.
113. R. Clark, *Myth & Symbol*, p. 225.
114. R. Clark, *Myth & Symbol*, p. 109.
115. Ibid, also see Shabaka texts.
116. PT 1792–8.
117. PT 55.

118. PT 1004–7.
119. PT 1016.
120. PT 1686.
121. R.T. Rundle Clark, op. cit., p. 287.
122. R.T. Rundle Clark, op. cit., p. 39.
123. I.E.S. Edwards, op. cit., 91.
124. Ibid., I.E.S. Edwards, op. cit., pp. 288–9.
125. Ibid., p. 293.
126. PT 1123–4.
127. PT 1016.
128. PT 800–803.
129. For full discussion, see *Keeper of Genesis*, Chapter 8.
130. E.A. Wallis Budge, *Osiris and the Egyptian Resurrection*, vol. II, p. 55.
131. Ibid., p. 53.
132. Miriam Lichtheim, op. cit., p. 53.
133. The kites are also geodetic markers of the cardinal directions.
134. Hart, *Egyptian Myths*, p. 53.
135. R. Clark, *Myth & Symbol*, p. 39, fig.2.
136. Hart, *Egyptian Myths*, p. 53.
137. Hart, *Egyptian Myths*, p. 53.
138. *The Orion Mystery*, p. 216.
139. Known also as *Sekhem* and *Mekhem* in ancient times. See Budge, *Dict.* 1032a. Letopolis was named by the Greeks after Leto, the mother of Apollo, who was often identified with Horus, suggesting that they might have seen this place as sacred to Isis, mother of Horus.
140. R.T. Rundle Clark, op. cit. p. 187.
141. *The Orion Mystery*, fig.22, p. 216.
142. Ibid.
143. Coffin Text Spell 236.
144. PT 800–803.
145. *The Orion Mystery*, p. 217.
146. *The Orion Mystery*, p. 217.
147. *The Orion Mystery*, Appendix 4.
148. *The Orion Mystery*, p. 262.
149. On the star Zuben El Ganoub which defines the pivot of the celestial scales, i.e. Libra.
150. *Keeper of Genesis*, Appendix 1.
151. Shown graphically in the BBC 2 *Everyman* Special *The Great Pyramid: Gateway to the Stars*, 6 Feb.1994.
152. Ibid.

CHAPTER FIVE
1. William Kingsland, *The Gnosis*, Solos Press, 1993 ed.
2. For a full discussion see R.T. Rundle Clark, op. cit. p. 263.
3. Papyrus BM 10371/10435.
4. Budge, *Dict.* I, p. 271a.
5. Budge, *The Gods of the Egyptians*, vol.I, p. 400.
6. Also the Papyrus of Hunefer at the BM.
7. *The Orion Mystery*, p. 214.
8. Matthew 5: 1–16.
9. Matthew 5: 17–20.
10. W. Kingland, *The Gnosis*, Solos Press, 1993, p. 21.
11. Ibid. back cover.
12. Ibid. p. 92.
13. Ibid. p. 93.

14. Plutarch, *Lives: Alexander*.
15. Eratosthenes was born in c. 276 BC in the Greek colony of Cyrene, on the Libyan coast, near Siwa. He died in Alexandria in c. 194 BC. Writer, poet and astronomer, Eratosthenes loved to make observations of nature and the stars. Afflicted by blindness in his old age, he committed suicide by starving himself.
16. Paul Faure, *Alexandre*, ed. Fayard 1985, p. 348.
17. See website http://projectequinox2000.com.
18. J.C. Fuller, *The Generalship of Alexander the Great*, A Da Capo Press NY 1960, p. 58.
19. Paul Faure, *Alexandre*, p. 391.
20. Ibid. p. 391.
21. Running north to south and known as the Soma (the body) in ancient times. It formed a cross with the Canopus Way, which ran east to west.
22. Paul Faure, *Alexandre*, p. 392.
23. The route, of course, was mostly via Greece.
24. Michael Baigent and Richard Leigh, *The Elixir and the Stone*, Viking, London 1997, p. 11.
25. Ibid., p. 12.
26. Carl Sagan, *Cosmos*, Book Club ed., London 1981, p. 333.
27. Geraldine Pinch, *Magic in Ancient Egypt*, BM Press 1994, p. 61.
28. S. Mayassis, *Mystères et Initiations de l'Ancienne Egypte*, Athenes 1957, pp. 3–4.
29. The main theme of *Keeper of Genesis*.
30. Clement of Alexandria, *Stromata*, V–7. Clement (AD 150–215) was canonized by the Catholic Church; his feast day is on 23rd November. The leading Christian 'apologist' of his times.
31. Plutarch, *Iside et Osiride*, 3 – v.
32. Synesius, *De Provid*. I, 6.
33. The precise conjunction with the summer solstice occurred in c. 3400 BC. It shifted by about 7 days for each thousand years, so that today the heliacal rising (dawn rising) of Sirius, as seen from Cairo, occurs on 4th August.
34. D. Jason Cooper, *Mithras*, Samuel Weiser Inc. 1996, p. 155.
35. The term 'Christian' came much later and is derived from the Greek 'Christos', i.e. 'the anointed one'.
36. It is closed, and in dire need of repair.
37. Robert Lomas & Christopher Knight, *The Hiram Key*, Century 1996, p. 67.
38. Ibid.
39. See *Encyclopaedia Britannica*: Nero.
40. Robert Lomas & Christopher Knight, *The Hiram Key*, p. 68–69.
41. Ibid.
42. Ibid., p. 70.
43. Mark 14:51–52.
44. *The Hiram Key*, op. cit., p. 70.
45. 'Apocalypse of Peter' in the Nag Hammadi Codex.
46. *The Jesus Mysteries*, op. cit., p. 191–202.
47. Ibid., p 244.
48. *Cosmos*, op. cit., p. 446.
49. Y. Stoyanov, *The Hidden Tradition*, Penguin Books, 1995.
50. *The Hiram Key*, op. cit.
51. *The Elixir and the Stone*, op. cit., p. 40.
52. Ibid. p. 41.
53. *The Hiram Key*, pp. 38–43; for a full discussion see *The Temple and the Lodge* by Michael Baigent, Richard Leigh and Henry Lincoln, Jonathan Cape, London 1989. Also Lynn Picknett and Clive Prince, *The Templar Revelation*, Corgi Books 1998.
54. James M. Robinson, the Nag Hammadi Library, p. 22.

55. Also known as a Dishdash in the Arab world. A long, flowing robe worn by men.
56. We were researching for *Keeper of Genesis* at the time, and had to go to Amsterdam to complete a film based on the book made for Dutch and European television and also the Discovery Channel (Histories Mysteries series).
57. Telephone conversation with Joseph Ritman on 30.12.1994.
58. See Chapter 9.

CHAPTER SIX
 1. Cosimo de Medici 'Pater Patriae' died in 1464 in Careggi, near Florence. Also known as Cosimo the Elder (il Vecchio), he died a depressed man, having lost most of his family through illness. A huge crowd accompanied his funeral to the tomb of S. Lozenzo. He is regarded as one of the backbones of Humanism.
 2. Also known as the Larentian Library, in honour of his grandson, Lozenzo the Magnificent.
 3. Various allusions to the so-called books of Thoth or Hermetic writings, the celebrated Corpus Hermeticum as Cosimo and his contemporary would call it, are found in medieval writings, and incomplete copies are known to have been circulated in Europe since the twelfth century. See Yates, *Bruno*, p. 13.
 4. Frances A. Yates, *Giordano Bruno and the Hermetic Tradition*, Univ. of Chicago Press, 1991, p. 13.
 5. Clement, *Stromata*, VI, iv, xxxv–xxxviii.
 6. S. Mayassis, *Mystères*, p. 7.
 7. Peter Kingsley, *Journal of the Warburg and Courtauld Institutes*, vol. 56, 1993.
 8. Corpus Hermeticum, Libellus I, 6.
 9. *Myth & Symbol*, op. cit., pp. 35–39.
10. Yates, *Giordano Bruno . . .*, op. cit., p. 26.
11. Ibid., p. 20.
12. *The Elixir and the Stone*, p. 23.
13. Tat is clearly a derivative of Thoth. Fowden, op. cit., p. 33.
14. Walter Scott, for example, felt that the Egyptian influence was minimal, if at all. Scott, *Hermetica*, p. 6.
15. *Magic in Ancient Egypt*, p. 167.
16. Yates, *Bruno*, pp. 62–83; 144–56.
17. *The Elixir and the Stone*, p. 23.
18. Ibid., p. 19.
19. It was a must to have a copy of the Hermetica among the educated. It is said that even the great Copernicus quoted from the Hermetica in support of his helio-centric theory.
20. Even today, the Hermetica has a tremendous influence on free-thinkers, and probably constitutes the most potent strain in the modern occult and esoteric movements.
21. Yates, *Bruno*, p. ix–xii.
22. Ibid., p. x.
23. Ibid., p. 192.
24. Ibid., p. 204.
25. Calendar of State Papers, foreign, Jan-June 1583, p. 214.
26. Yates, *Bruno*, pp. 215, 223–5, 239.
27. Ibid. pp. 194–203.
28. Ibid., p. 263.
29. No one in Bruno's time could 'read' hieroglyphs. But being symbols, Bruno must surely have been receptive to some of their meaning.
30. Ibid., p. 211.
31. Ibid., p. 209. For a counter view see Paolo Rossi, *Francis Bacon: from Magic to Science*, the Uni. Of Chicago Press 1968, p. 40.
32. Yates, Giorgio de Santillana, *The Age of Adventure*, Mentor Books, pp. 245–9.

33. Yates, *Bruno*, p. 211.
34. Bruno, Giordano, *Spaccia della Bestia Trionfante*, dialogue 3; F. Yates, *Bruno*, p. 212.
35. The most active of thought manipulators using the Hermetic lore were the Jesuits, headed by Athanasius Kircher (1602–1680) at the Roman College of the Vatican. For a good study on Kircher, see Jocelyn Godwin, *Athanasius Kircher: A Renaissance Man and the Quest for Lost Knowledge*, Phanes Press. 1980.
36. J. Dagens, *L'Hermetisme et Cabale en France, de Lefevre d'Etaples à Bossuet*, in the Revue de la litérature comparée, Jan-March 1961, p. 6.
37. Christopher McIntosh, *The Rosicrucians*, Samuel Weiser Inc., Maine, 1997, pp. 13–18.
38. Ibid. p. 17.
39. Ibid., pp. 19–30.
40. Corpus Hermeticum, Asclepius III, 24b.
41. The 'call' for people of the world to unite at Giza to herald the 'new age' beginning on 1st January 2000, oddly, has been given by the Egyptian authorities.
42. Asclepius III 27 d.
43. Frances A. Yates, *The Art of Memory*, Pimlico, London 1994, p. 212.
44. Yates, *Bruno* . . . , p. 49.
45. *The Elixir and the Stone*, p. 38.
46. David Pingree, 'Some of the sources of the Ghayat El Hakim', *Journal of the Warburg Inst.*, vol.43, 1981, p. 1.
47. Ibid., p. 2.
48. David Pingree, 'Picatrix: the Latin version of the Ghayat El Hakim', *Journal of the Warburg Inst.* 1986.
49. David Pingree, *Journal of the Warburg Inst.*, vol.43, p. 1.
50. A talisman can be any object. Think of a wedding ring to get the basic idea of powerful ideas and feeling 'locked', as it were, inside an object. Ancient Egyptian statuary is mostly talismanic, i.e. they were intended not for aesthetics purposes but to be 'inhabited' by a 'god' or 'spirit'. An obelisk is probably one of the most potent talismanic monuments from ancient Egypt, with one towering over the Vatican's Piazza St Peter atop of which is placed a crucifix.
51. David Pingree, *Journal of the Warburg Inst.* vol. 43, p. 4.
52. Yates, *Bruno*, p. 54.
53. Picatrix, Lib. IV, cap. 3.
54. Ibid.
55. German translation of the Picatrix, *Studies of the Warburg Inst.*, vol.27, 1962.
56. Yates, *Bruno*, pp. 49, 55–56.
57. The Memphite necropolis proper extends from Dashur to Abu Roash, with Giza roughly at its mid-point. As such, it covers an area some forty miles long and two miles wide. But most observers would generally not include Dashur and Abu Roash, but define it as being only from Giza to the south of Saqqara, thus reducing its overall length to about ten miles.
58. Genesis 12:11.
59. Walter Scott, *Hermetica*, p. 100, fn 1.
60. This was written by a Christian Arab named Abu Youssef Abshaa Al Qathii, AD c. 900.
61. Peter Tompkins, *Secrets of the Great Pyramid*, pp. 6–8.
62. Walter Scott, *Hermetica*, p. 101.
63. Walter Scott, *Hermetica*, p. 102, fn.2.
64. Yates, *Bruno*, p. 60.
65. 'Star religion', of course, is precisely what the ancient Pyramid builders practised. See *The Orion Mystery*, Chapter 4 for a full discussion.
66. Walter Scott, *Hermetica*, p. 99, fn.1.
67. Vol 3, p. 457, Cairo Ed.

68. Hassan, *Excavations at Giza*, vol. VI part I, p. 45.
69. Ibid.
70. Budge, *Dict.* II, p. 656.
71. Ibid.
72. Walter Scott, *Hermetica*, p. 98, fn.2.
73. Hassan, op. cit., p. 45, fn.
74. W.R. Fix, *Pyramid Odyssey*, Mercury Media Inc. 1978, p. 52.
75. Idris (from the noun *moudaress*, 'teacher') appears in the Koran as an immortal figure and a prophet. Like Thoth, Hermes Trismegistus, and the Biblical Enoch, Idris transmitted to mankind divine revelations which he also inscribed in books.
76. Christopher McIntosh, *The Rosicrucians*, p. 25.
77. Yates, *Bruno*, p. 352.
78. Ibid., p. 352.
79. Walter Scott, *Hermetica*, excerpt xxiv.
80. Ibid., excerpt xxiv, p. 503.
81. The Great Pyramid is not only a perfectly orientated monument, but happens to lie at the centre of the land masses of the Earth.
82. E.M. Antoniadi, *L'Astronomie Egyptienne*, Paris 1934, p. 119.
83. *The Times*, 30 page supplement 'Introducing Time', May 1999.
84. See Appendix 2.
85. Yates, *Bruno*, p. 274.
86. Ibid., pp. 274, 414–5.
87. Christopher McIntosh, *The Rosicrucians*, pp. 13–18.
88. Ibid.
89. Ibid., p. 18.
90. Ibid.
91. Known as the 'Tubingen Group'. The idea of an 'Invisible College' was also entertained in England a little while later by scholars and learned men of the Oxford circle just prior to the 1660 Restoration of Charles II. See Yates, *The Rosicrucian Enlightenment*, Ark, London 1986, pp. 171–192.
92. Christopher McIntosh, *The Rosicrucians*, p. ix.
93. Ibid., p. 1.
94. Yates, *Bruno*, p. 414–5.
95. Christopher McIntosh, *The Rosicrucians*, pp. 19–30.
96. Ibid. p. 17.
97. *Fama Fraternitatis*, appendix to F. Yates, *The Rosicrucian Enlightenment*, p. 249.
98. McIntosh, *The Rosicrucians*, p. 19.
99. Ibid. pp. 30; 41;43; 48.
100. Ibid., p. 50. See alsoYates, *The Rosicrucian Enlightenment*, p. 200.
101. Yates, ibid., pp. 206–219.
102. I visited the Evreux centre in 1993. The building is a typical French chateau with magnificent gardens. I did not manage to see anyone, as the centre was closed at the time. The San Jose centre is in the style of an ancient Egyptian temple.
103. From the AMORC official Website.
104. Paul Naudon, *Histoire generale de la Franc-Maconnerie*, Office d Livre 1981 ed., p. 224.

CHAPTER SEVEN
1. Paul Naudon, op. cit., p. 64.
2. *The Pocket History of Freemasonry*, op. cit., p. 326. The Duke of Kent was one of the recent Grand Masters of the Order.
3. Paul Naudon, op. cit., pp. 63–112; 113–131.
4. Pick & Knight, *The Pocket History of Freemasonry*, pp. 13–14; C.W. Leadbeater, *The Hidden Life in Freemasonry*, The Theosophical Publishing House, London 1988, pp. 1–6.

5. Martin Short, *Inside the Brotherhood*, Grafton, 1989, p. 115.
6. Naudon, op. cit., p. 181.
7. Ibid.
8. Official website of the University of Philadelphia.
9. Dr Hawass officially denies this allegation.
10. See David Ovason, *The Secret Zodiacs of Washington DC*, Century 1999.
11. Ibid.
12. I have visited this monument several times. It dominates the district of Alexandria in Washington DC, and from its top one can see the Pentagon and the Obelisk in alignment.
13. Pick & Knight, op. cit., p. 275.
14. See note 21 to Prologue above.
15. William A. Brown, *History of the George Washington Masonic National Memorial*, 1980.
16. See official website of Shriner.
17. Gerard Galtier, *Maconnerie Egyptienne, Rose Croix and Neo-Chevalerie*, Ed. du Rocher 1989, p. 36.
18. Ibid.
19. Ibid. See also Manly P. Hall, *Freemasonry of the Ancient Egyptians*, Philosophical Research Society 1965 ed., p. 73.
20. Today called Mit Rahin, a small village some twelve miles south of Cairo.
21. *Les dossiers de l'Histoire Mystérieuse*, F. Carbonnel editeur, Album 7 DHM.2112 RD7, Paris, p. 111.
22. *Freemasonry in Egypt from Bonaparte to Zaghloul* by Karim Wissa, Turcica Tome xxiv, 1992.
23. Gerard Galtier, op. cit. p. 40.
24. See Francois Collaveri, *La Franc-Maconnerie des Bonaparte*, Payot, Paris 1982.
25. Galtier, op. cit., p. 139.
26. Jean Andre Faucher, *Les Francs Macons et le Pouvoir*, Ed. Perrin, Paris 1986, p. 54. See also Paul Naudon, *Histoire Générale de la Franc Maconnerie*, Office du Livre 1981, p. 97.
27. Jean Andre Faucher, *Les Francs Macons et le Pouvoir*, pp. 53–56.
28. Paul Naudon, p. cit., p. 229.
29. Jean Andre Faucher, op. cit., p. 58.
30. Paul Naudon, op. cit., p. 224.
31. Laura Foreman and Ellen Blue Phillips, *Napoleon's Lost Fleet*, Roundtable Press 1999.
32. Pick & Knight, op. cit. pp. 327–8.
33. Gerard Galtier, op. cit., p. 149.
34. Ibid.
35. Ibid.
36. Ibid.
37. Ibid.
38. Today only one obelisk stands at Heliopolis, that of Sesortis I. In ancient times dozens graced this city, but all have either been taken to Europe or destroyed. For a full account, see Labib Habachi's *The Obelisks of Egypt*, The American University in Cairo Press, 1988.
39. The obelisk was originally the belonging of Thothmoses. Thothmoses means 'son of Thoth', a name adopted by four pharaohs who reigned from c. 1500 BC to c. 1402 BC.
40. The story is reported in John Butler's *The Arab Conquest*, London.
41. Aubrey Noakes, *Cleopatra's Needles*, Witheby 1962, p. 2.
42. Ibid. p. 10.
43. Ibid., p. 10.
44. Pick & Knight, p. 326.

45. Ibid.
46. Noakes, op. cit., p. 18.
47. Masonic Memorial no. 19.
48. Ibid.
49. Ibid.
50. Ibid.
51. Gerard Galtier, op. cit., p. 151.
52. Pick & Knight, op, cit., p. 331; G. Galtier, op. cit., p. 153.
53. Noakes, op. cit., p. 26–7.
54. See *The Life and Works of Sir William James Erasmus Wilson* by R.M. Hadley, *Medical History*, vol. III, 1959.
55. Noakes, op. cit., pp. 26–27.
56. Ibid.
57. Mary Brück and Herman Brück, *The Peripatetic Astronomer*, Adam Hilger, Bristol 1988, pp. 133.
58. Ralph Orr, *How Anglo-Israelism Entered the Church of God: A history of the Doctrine from John Wilson to Joseph W. Tkach*. See also Worldwide Church Website (at www. wcg. org). See also The Identity Movement Website.
59. Ibid.
60. Ibid.
61. Ibid.
62. Ibid.
63. Ibid.
64. Ibid.
65. Ibid.
66. Piazzi Smyth, *The Great Pyramid*, Bell Publ. 1990 Ed.pp. 614–5. See also Mary and Herman Bruck, *The Peripatetic Astronomer*, Adam Hilger, Bristol 1988, pp. 132–3
67. Ibid.
68. See Worldwide Church official website (www.wcg.org).
69. Brück and Brück, op. cit.
70. See *The Orion Mystery*, Epilogue.
71. Ibid.
72. Ibid.
73. Ibid.
74. Ibid.
75. Ibid.
76. The relics were found in late December 1993. They had been given to the British Museum in 1972 by Mrs Beth Porteous, a great-grandaughter of John Dixon, but were placed in a drawer and forgotten.
77. Piazzi Smyth, *The Great Pyramid*, op. cit. p. 553.
78. *Newcastle Daily Chronicle*, 1 February, 1878.
79. *The Orion Mystery*, Epilogue.
80. *The Graphic*, 7 December 1872 pp. 530–45.
81. See Peter Tompkins' *The Secret of the Great Pyramid*, op. cit., pp. 70–94. See also Sir Isaac Newton's Dissertation on Cubits in Piazzi Smyth's *Life and Work at the Great Pyramid* vol. II, Edinburgh 1867.
82. Ibid.
83. *The Peripatetic Astronomer*, pp. 132–3.
84. Ibid.
85. For example Lord James Kitchener, General Charles Warren and Charles Wilson.
86. *The Peripatetic Astronomer*, p. 50.
87. *Ars Quator Coronatorum*, transactions, vol. 1886–1888.
88. *The Survey of Western Palestine*, by Col. Sir Charles Warren K.C.M.G, R.E. and Capt. Claude Reigner Conder, R.E., The Committee of the Palestine Exploration

Fund, Inc., 1 Adam Street, Adelphi, London WC, England 1884.

89. *Square*, September 1991, p. 139.
90. *Ordinance Survey of Jerusalem*, by Captain Charles W. Wilson, R.E., 1886.
91. Egypt Exploration Fund, *Report of the first general meeting*, July 1883.
92. Ibid, p. 4.
93. Ibid.
94. R.M. Hadley, *Medical History*, Vol III, 1959, p. 238.
95. Ibid, p. 238.
96. Ibid, p. 240.
97. Ibid, p. 242.
98. Noakes, op. cit. p. 15. For the connection between Bonomi and Piazzi Smyth, see *The Peripatetic Astronomer*, p. 136.
99. See also 'Builder' no. 1330, 1868, p. 575.
100. See Epilogue.
101. See Epilogue.
102. The latitude of central London is closer to 51 degrees 30 minutes, and the angle of the Great Pyramid is 51 degrees 51 minutes. Still, this *almost* correlation is intriguing, especially when the connection is made with Sirius/'Star of the East'. As David Ovason has shown (see *The Secret Zodiacs of Washington DC*), the Masons are rather fond of astrological associations with the placing of their monuments and buildings.
103. *Square*, September 1991, p. 139.
104. *Memorial*, no.19, p. 67.
105. Ibid, pp. 57–58.
106. *Insight Magazine*, Cairo 1.3.1999.
107. Ibid, p. 67.
108. *Memorial* no.7, 1905.
109. *Dedication of New Masonic Lodge*, *Memorial* no. 7, 1905, pp. 9–18.
110. 'Freemasonry in Egypt: is it still around?' by Samir Rafaat, *Insight* magazine, Cairo 1.3.1999.
111. No doubt, however, that ex-members of Masonic Lodges still live in Egypt today.
112. Samir Rafaat, op. cit.
113. Ibid.
114. Susanl.avi@www.sis.gov.eg
115. Samir Rafaat, op. cit.
116. Wissa, op. cit.
117. Ibid.
118. Ibid.
119. Ibid.
120. Ibid.
121. Samir Rafaat, op. cit.
122. Ibid.
123. A short statement made by Lord Balfour to the effect that Her Majesty's Government favoured the establishment of a Jewish homeland in Palestine.
124. *Les Dossiers de l'Histoire Mystérieuse*, Album No. 6, p. 172.
125. Samir Rafaat, op. cit.
126. Ibid.
127. Ibid.
128. Ibid.
129. Ibid.
130. Informal discussion with Samir Rafaat and Karim Wissa on 3rd August 1999.
131. This notion was instigated by the Catholic Church in the aftermath of the French Revolution. Freemasonry was an act short of excommunication until not long ago. For a full discussion (although somewhat biased) on this subject, see John Lawrence's *Freemasonry: A Religion?* Kingsway Publications, Eastbourne,

England 1991.
132. My next book, to be co-authored with Graham Hancock, will delve in much greater depth into this subject.
133. Christopher McIntosh, *The Rosicrucians*, p. 137.
134. AMORC 'tours' to Egypt and Giza are organised on a regular basis by US-based operators. Meditation sessions in the Great Pyramid cost approximately $50 per person.
135. AMORC official website.
136. Christopher McIntosh, op. cit., p. 127.
137. Ibid.
138. Galtier, op. cit., pp. 348; 415.
139. AMORC official website.
140. H. Lewis Spence, *The Symbolic Prophecy of the Great Pyramid*, 1936 H.C.
141. H.C.Randall-Stevens, *Atlantis to the Latter Days*, 1981, plates vi and vii.
142. Ibid.
143. Ibid.
144. See Chapters 9 and 10.
145. Ibid, pp. 55–64.

CHAPTER EIGHT
1. A. Robert Smith, *Hugh Lynn Cayce*, p. 30.
2. A. Robert Smith, *The Lost Memoirs of Edgar Cayce: Life as a Seer*, ARE Press 1997, p. 56.
3. Harmon H. Bro, *A Seer out of Season*, Signet, NY, 1990, p. 272.
4. Ibid. p. 269.
5. Ibid. p. 277.
6. Ibid. p. 278.
7. Ibid. p. 279.
8. Ibid. p. 284.
9. Ibid. p. 286.
10. Ibid. p. 293.
11. *Bowler Green Times Journal*, 22 June 1903.
12. *New York Times*, 10 October 1910.
13. For a full discussion, see Thomas Sogrue's *There is a River*, ARE Press 1997.
14. *A Seer out of Season*, op. cit., pp. 270–7.
15. Ibid. p. 284.
16. A. Robert Smith, *Hugh Lynn Cayce*, pp. 19, 25.
17. Kevin J. Todeschi, *Edgar Cayce on the Akashic Records*, ARE Press 1998, pp. xi–xii.
18. Ibid, p. 2.
19. Revelations 20: 12.
20. Edgar Evans Cayce, Gail Cayce Schwartzer, Douglas G. Richards, *Mysteries of Atlantis Revisited*, Harper & Row, San Francisco, 1988, p. xiii.
21. Ibid. p. xiii.
22. Mark Lehner, *The Egyptian Heritage*, ARE Press 1974, p. v.
23. *Mysteries of Atlantis Revisited*, p. 49. See also *The Egyptian Heritage*, p. 5.
24. *Mysteries of Atlantis*, p. 125.
25. Reading 294–151.
26. Reading 5748–5.
27. Reading 294–151.
28. Reading 5748–5.
29. Reading 5748–5.
30. Reading 281–42.
31. Reading 5748–6.
32. *The Egyptian Heritage*, pp. 91–2.
33. Reading 5749–7.

34. Reading 5749–7.
35. Reading 2067–11.
36. Reading 5748–5.
37. Reading 2067–7.
38. Reading 5748–5.
39. Reading 5749–2.
40. Reading 2823–1.
41. Reading 5749–2.
42. Kirk Nelson, *The Second Coming 1998*, ARE Press, pp. 58–9.
43. Reading 294–151.
44. Reading 5748–6.
45. Reading 378–16.
46. Kirk Nelson, *The Second Coming 1998*, pp. 112–128.
47. Robert O. Clapp, *Archaeology: Egypt Gobi: 10,500 BC*, ARE Press, pp. 46–7.
48. *Mysteries of Atlantis Revisited*, p. 127.
49. Reading 900–275.
50. Reading 5748–6.
51. Reading 378–16.
52. Reading 2329–3.
53. See Chapter 7.
54. Virginia, the state of George Washington and many of the founders of the United States, is deemed to be one of the regions where Freemasonry first took hold in America, particularly in Norfolk (Naudon, op. cit., p. 183).
55. This is still a very popular book, and was almost certainly stocked in the bookshops where Edgar Cayce had worked.
56. Ignatius Donelly, *Atlantis the Antediluvian World*, Dover publication 1976 ed., pp. 139, 331, 317–42.
57. Donelly, op. cit., p. 331.
58. Gerald Massey, *Ancient Egypt, the Light of the World*, 1907, p. 339.
59. Peter Tompkins, *Secrets of the Great Pyramid*, pp. 256–9.
60. Ibid.
61. Charles J. Ryan, *Helena Blavatsky and the Theosophical Movement*, Point Loma Publ. Ed. 1976, p. 29.
62. Reading 5748–6.
63. Charles J. Ryan, op. cit., p. 1.
64. Ibid. p. 24.
65. C. G. Harrisson, *The Transcendental Universe*, c. 1890.
66. For example, the Minister of Culture, Dr Farouk Hosni, to whom the Supreme Council of Antiquities is directly responsible.
67. Edgar Evans Cayce et al., *Mysteries of Atlantis*, p. 18.
68. This is evident from the many books published by the ARE. I have visited the ARE headquarters in Virginia Beach many times, and I am always baffled as to the many members who are convinced that they have lived in ancient Egypt.
69. All of the 'expeditions' that took place at Giza were financed from donations by members and supporters. See Chapters 9 and 10.

CHAPTER NINE
1. Edgar Evans Cayce, Gail Cayce Schwartzer, Douglas G. Richards, *Mysteries of Atlantis Revisited*, Harper & Row Publishers, San Francisco 1988, p. 131.
2. A. Robert Smith, *Hugh Lynn Cayce: About my Father's Business*, The Donning Company, Virginia Beach 1988, p. 243.
3. *Mysteries of Atlantis Revisited*, op. cit. p. 130.
4. After the 1956 Suez War Egypt put a tight restriction on the use of hard currencies in the country. The only source of US dollars was through the black market where they could fetch several times their official value fixed by the Egyptian Central

Bank.

5. A. Robert Smith op. cit. p. 243.
6. Ibid.
7. The sewage is still operational today. When in 1995 the Supreme Council of Antiquities cleared the area in front of the Sphinx to build a new parking zone, I examined the sewer level and estimated that it flowed some ten feet below ground level.
8. *Mysteries of Atlantis Revisited* p. 131.
9. Ibid.
10. Peter Tompkins, *The Secret of the Great Pyramid*, Allen Lane, Penguin Books 1973. See also Peter Lemesurier, *The Great Pyramid Decoded*, Element Books, Devon 1977.
11. I speak, of course, from personal experience. When the Orion-correlation theory came out in the open in 1994 in the BBC documentary *The Great Pyramid: Gateway to the Stars* (it was published in *DE* vol. 13 in 1989, but without much response) the proverbial Egyptological ton of bricks fell on my head. Even such a well-reasoned and scientifically based theory was quickly branded 'Pyramidology' and 'Pyramidiocy' by the Egyptological profession.
12. An interview with Mark Lehner, *ARE News* 12, 1982.
13. A. Robert Smith, op. cit. p. 244.
14. Interview: Mark Lehner, *Venture Inward* magazine, ARE Press Jan/Feb. 1985, p. 7.
15. Mark Lehner, *The Egyptian Heritage*, ARE Press 1974, p. v.
16. A. Robert Smith, op. cit. p. 244.
17. Ibid. p. 245.
18. Ibid. p. 256.
19. Ibid. p. 246.
20. I met Rufus Mosely for the first time at Virginia Beach in 1996. He is an extremely friendly and helpful person, and provided me with photographs and documents for my research. Rufus has known Dr Hawass since the early 1970s, and at the 1999 ARE Conference was selected to introduce Dr Hawass to the audience. Both men have clearly a warm affection and much respect for each other. I often meet Rufus in Cairo, where he flies his TWA commercial flights quite regularly. Rufus acts as an unofficial ARE representative, having been a member of the Edgar Cayce Foundation for several decades now.
21. Ibid. p. 247.
22. Ibid. p. 248.
23. Edgar Cayce Foundation Egypt/Sphinx Research Project Report 1976–1982, ARE Press 1983.
24. I met Ingo Swann in September 1998 in New York. A gentle, very cordial man, Ingo now devotes his time to painting. He had 'remote viewed' the Sphinx in the 1970s with the author Peter Tompkins during the SRI project at Giza. Ingo felt that no underground chamber such as that described by Cayce existed, but there were, in his view, many underground tunnels and passageways linking the monuments.
25. I had the pleasure of meeting Geller in August 1999 on the day of the total solar eclipse. We were guests of *Quest for Knowledge* magazine on the Channel ferry *Pride of Le Havre*. Yuri, of course, bent a spoon for me and, as much as I wanted to stay sceptical, I was utterly convinced that his powers are genuine. It has to be seen to be believed.
26. *Mysteries of Atlantis Revisited*, op. cit. p. 133.
27. Ibid.
28. Ibid. See also Peter Tompkins, op. cit. pp. 270–5.
29. Ibid. p. 273.
30. *Geophysics & the Temple Mound*, by Lambert Dolphin, 1995.

31. Lynn Picknett and Clive Prince, *The Stargate Conspiracy*, Little Brown & Co. UK, 1999, p. 85.
32. Ibid. p. 83.
33. *New Haven Connecticut Register* 30 October 1983. See also *Herald & News*, Klamath Falls, Oregon, 31 October 1983.
34. Bechtel, the giant management consultant contractor, was run, in the 1980s, by an ex-CIA boss during the phase of mega-contracts management of ARAMCO in the eastern province of Saudi Arabia and the construction of Riyadh University and airport.
35. *Jerusalem Post*, article by Louis Rappaport, June 1983.
36. *Geophysics & the Temple Mound*, op. cit.
37. Ibid.
38. *A Very Brief Resumé*, by Lambert Dolphin, 1 February 1996.
39. See
40. Interview: Mark Lehner, on 8 mm film, ARE 1978 Sphinx Project.
41. ECF Egypt/Sphinx Research Project Report, op. cit. p. 2.
42. 1977 Report by joint team, NSF Grant GF-38767, SRI International, 333 Ravenswood Avenue, Menlo Park, CA 94025.
43. Ibid. pp. 64–5.
44. Among those who formally asked Lambert Dolphin to present his report in July 1999 were, as far as I know, Chris O'Kane of the ex-UK Mars Project and myself. Emails were sent to Dolphin to which he responded that he intended to provide a report on this affair shortly. The report, put on the Internet on 21 July 1999, *Geophysics Studies around the Sphinx 1978*, is scant and very subjective. Most of it comprises a letter he wrote in January 1992 to Dr Robert Schoch regarding the dating of the Sphinx. Dolphin exhibits some rather unorthodox ideas of Biblical dating and Egyptian chronology in this correspondence. On first seeing this letter, I was immediately struck by the opening statement of the letter to Schoch: 'Last week my friend and colleague of many years, Dr James Hurtak . . .' The relationship with Hurtak, in many ways, is an eye-opener to Dolphin's Biblical slant to his scientific work. I met James Hurtak in 1996, and although he comes across as a polite and friendly man, it is very difficult for me to reconcile his scientific education and background with the material he writes. His most popular work – and which apparently has a huge following – is a book entitled *The Book of Knowledge: The Key of Enoch* (The Academy for Future Science, California 1977) which is a 600 page opus where the Bible, Cabala and Science are intermingled into impenetrable mumbo jumbo. The first few paragraphs of the book tell it all:

> While I was in the act of prayer calling upon the name of the Father, asking how to know the meaning of life and for what reason I was called into the world, my room suddenly became full of a different type of light. And in the presence of this 'Light' a great being stood before me who announced he was Master Ophanim Enoch. The being had so much Love and Light, I felt as if I were a child in the presence of this divine Master Ophanim. The being asked if I were ready to go with him into the Father's midst, and I said I was. And with that a great field of light was placed around my body and I sped upwards into the heavens; first into a region of stars called Merak and Muscida . . .

I have quoted these lines because it is fairly obvious, at least to me, that Hurtak attempts to present himself as a Hermes-like prophet by virtually paraphrasing the opening lines of the Hermetica:

> Once on a time, when I had begun to think about the things that are, and my thoughts had soared high aloft, while my bodily senses had been put under restraint by sleep – yet not such sleep as that of men weighed down by fullness of food or by bodily weariness – methought there came to me a Being of vast and boundless magnitude, who called me by my name and said to me 'what do you wish to hear and see and to learn and come to know by thought?' . . . And I

beheld a boundless view; all was changed into Light . . .

The rest of Hurtak's book is, quite frankly, incomprehensible. Here's a sample:

The *'Kodoish, Kodoish, Kodoish Adonai Tsebayoth'* ties together all biorhythms of the body with the spiritual rhythms of the Overself body, so that all circulatory systems operate with one cosmic heart beat. The *'Kodoish, Kodoish, Kodoish Adonai Tsebayoth'* is given within the fifth socket of the Great Pyramid which aligns the heart vibratory beat with the five bodies of vibration operating within the biochemical shell of man. Furthermore it is the Light energy created by this 'holy code' that enables the body vehicle to experience the direct energy of the Masters of Light serving YHWH . . . [*The Keys of Enoch*, p. 388]

On his website, Lambert Dolphin exhibits – admittedly in a much more rational way – the same need to merge bible jargon with his scientific work. This idiosyncrasy comes across in his 1992 letter to Dr Schor where, for example, he states:

In contrast with fuzzy notions about the actual origin of Egyptian civilisations among most Egyptologists, Genesis 10–11 is clear in ascribing the repopulation of the world after the flood to the three sons of Noah: Shem, Ham and Japheth. Mizraim, a son of Ham, is the ancestor of the Egyptians (Misr is still one of the names for Egypt in use today, for example there is a Bank Misr). Some Bible scholars in fact believe Mizraim is identical with Menes Narmer. Egypt is the subject of many prophetic passages in the Bible, because of Egypt's past, present and future relationship with the people of Israel. The Egyptians are not really Arabs, for example, and that helps to explain why many Egyptians today consider Islam a foreign, imported religion in their modern restlessness to seek out their own ancient roots amongst the pharaohs. The rapid emergence of ancient Egyptian civilisation migrating out of ancient Babylon is therefore Biblically reasonable if the dating for early Egyptian dynasties is placed at about 3000 BC at the earliest . . . [Letter to Dr Robert Schoch dated 21 January 1992]

Dolphin's 'Biblical' view of the world stems, perhaps from his tragic background. His parents divorced when he was a child of twelve, and his mother died two years later. After obtaining his Ph.D. in physics at Stanford University, he began to be disillusioned with the scientific outlook of existence. Alcohol and LSD led him 'by the age of thirty to despair . . . [and] . . . suicide seemed a good way out'. In 1962 he read the Book of Revelations which began what he calls 'My Search' when he was 'overwhelmed with God's Love'. He immediately converted to Christianism. Dolphin has published a booklet called 'My Search' which can be ordered on the Internet. My impression of Dolphin (although I have not met him personally) is that he is an honest man who is utterly devoted to 'Jesus' and his 'Return' as well as the rebuilding of 'The Temple of Solomon'. An odd candidate, however, for exploratory work at Giza in an intensely dominant Muslim country.

45. *Geophysical Studies Around The Sphinx* 1978, by Lambert Dolphin, p. 1.
46. Ibid.
47. Ibid. pp. 2–3.
48. A. Robert Smith, op. cit. p. 249.
49. Ibid.
50. This was during the ARE 1997 Egypt Conference at Virginia Beach. Rufus also kindly provided me with some photographs of the ARE expeditions.
51. See *Keeper of Genesis*, Appendix 3.
52. These were provided by a friend in New York who had had contacts with the ARE's archives department. Copies and full transcripts of the sound tapes are in my possession.
53. *Venture Inward*, Jan/Feb. 1985, p. 9.
54. The SRI has never acknowledged their participation in the ARE's hunt for the Hall of Records, except recently in July 1999 when Lambert Dolphin published a short report on the Internet. The impression that was always given from these quarters

was that they were conducting a purely scientific 'resistivity' survey without clearly stating the motives.

55. Tapes and filmed interview with Mark Lehner, March 1978.
56. For more details and depictions see E.A. Wallis Budge's *The Book of the Dead*, Arkana Ed. 1989.
57. A. Robert Smith, op. cit. p. 249.
58. ECF Egypt/Sphinx Research Project Report 1976–1982, p. 4.
59. See *Keeper of Genesis* p. 92.
60. *Mysteries of Atlantis Revisited*, op. cit. p. 136.
61. The Supreme Council of Antiquities in Egypt may, perhaps, have files on this matter, but I have not been able to ascertain this.
62. See *Keeper of Genesis*, Appendix 1.
63. Telephone conversation between J. Jahoda and Graham Hancock, February 1995.
64. The husband and wife team may have been the owners of Carter Lord film co.
65. Letter from Mark Lehner to the author dated 15 October 1995.
66. Telephone conversation with J. Jahoda, 1998.
67. Ibid.
68. A. Robert Smith, op. cit. p. 249.
69. Letter from Mark Lehner op. cit.
70. A.Robert Smith op. cit. p. 249.
71. Ibid. p. 250.
72. Ibid.
73. A.Robert Smith op. cit. p. 248.
74. Ibid.
75. Ibid. p. 57. See also *The Egyptian Heritage*, op. cit. p. vii.
76. *The Egyptian Heritage* op. cit. p. vii.
77. Letter from Mark Lehner op. cit.
78. *Mysteries of Atlantis Revisited,* op. cit. p. 138.
79. Ibid.
80. ECF Egypt/Sphinx Research Project Report 1976–1982 p. 16.
81. *ARE News* No.12, 1982.
82. *ARCE Newsletter* 132, 1985, p. 44.
83. *Mysteries of Atlantis Revisited*, op. cit. p. 114. See also *Keeper of Genesis*, Appendix 5.

CHAPTER TEN
1. Schwaller de Lubicz, *Sacred Science*, p. 96.
2. *Boston Globe*, 23 October 1991.
3. Ibid.
4. *The New York Times National Sunday*, 9 February 1992.
5. Paul W. Roberts is also the author of award-winning books: *Empire of the Soul*; *River in the Desert; In search of the Birth of Jesus*. Published by Riverhead Books, NY.
6. *Saturday Night*, 11 March 1992.
7. *The New Times National Sunday*, p. 73.
8. John West, *Serpent in the Sky*, pp. 227–28. See also *Mystery of the Sphinx*, NBC documentary distributed by BC Video New York.
9. *Mystery of the Sphinx*, NBC documentary 1993.
10. John West, *Serpent in the Sky*, p. 228.
11. *Mystery of the Sphinx*, NBC documentary, interview with Dobecki.
12. List of funders/sponsors provided by J. West.
13. Ibid.
14. *Akhbar El Yom*, 8 January 1994.
15. West has coined the so–called 'A word': Atlantis. By this he means that as much as academics used the 'E word', i.e. Erich Von Daniken, to denigrate those with

controversial theories, so do the archaeologists and Egyptologists use the 'A word', as if it is the worst insult you can throw upon a fellow researcher. I often use the word 'Atlantis' in my articles and talks (indeed it is used in this book several times). But I use it in the generic sense, i.e. implying a lost civilisation. So do John West and Robert Schoch.

16. *Akhbar El Yom*, 8 January 1994.
17. See Prologue.
18. This was eventually confirmed by Joe Jahoda to me.
19. The library at the ARE is probably one of the best stocked with esoteric books of all kinds and a very good source of research.
20. Letter from author to Charles Thomas Cayce, dated 30 May 1994.
21. Letter from Douglas G. Richards to author, dated 29 July 1994.
22. See Chapter 11.
23. Telephone conversation between Jahoda and Graham Hancock, Feb. 1995.
24. I am not sure if it is just a paper company or it actually has a physical office and employees.
25. Letter from J. West to Joseph Schor, dated 15 December 1995 .
26. I have had the pleasure of meeting Brenda Dunne in September 1996 at the University of Delaware, Return at the Source Conference organised by the SSE.
27. Letter from Dr R. Schoch to Dr Mohammad Ibrahim Bakr, dated 5 April 1993.
28. Letter from the dean of Boston University to Dr Nureldin dated 1 July 1993.
29. Letter from Dr J. Schor to John West, dated 15 December 1995.
30. Letter from John West to the 'Investors', dated 30 January 1996.
31. Film produced by Paul Mason and presented by John Kunuoni.
32. *Secret Chamber*, promo Magic Eye Inc. 1996.
33. Ibid.
34. Fax from R. Bauval and Graham Hancock to Dr J.Schor, dated 13 March 1996.
35. Fax from Dr J. Schor to Graham Hancock, dated 15 March 1996.
36. Fax from Robert Bauval and Graham Hancock to Dr J. Schor, dated 15 March 1996.
37. Letter from Robert Bauval and Graham Hancock to Dr Abdel Halim Nureldin, dated 10 April 1996.
38. *Egyptian Gazette*, 14 April 1996.
39. Statement by D. Pullen of FSU, dated 28 August 1996.
40. Ibid.
41. Letter from Dr J. Schor to author, dated 10 November 1998.
42. Letter from Dr Schor to Gerry Cannon, dated 14 November 1996.
43. On the John Robbie Show, Radio 702 South Africa.
44. This proved to be a red herring. The rumour seems to have started with Boris Said, but I cannot confirm this.
45. One of these senators had read Hancock's books, and invited him to address a group of his friends and colleagues.
46. Most of the ARE members appeared to be unaware of these activities.
47. There is a confusion on this matter. Said claims that when Schor returned to Giza, he worked under Said's commercial filming licence.
48. *Carte Blanche*, M-Net TV South Africa, 29 December 1996.
49. I met Richard for the first time in May 1996 during his first visit to England, and spoke at two of his conferences in London and at Leeds.
50. The Art Bell Show, 26–27 September 1996.
51. The New Yorker, *Perils of the Sphinx*, by Alexander Stille p. 60.
52. 'Hawass Harassed by Pyramidiots', see *Quest for Knowledge* magazine, vol. 2, Issue 3, June/July 1998.
53. This was provoked, apparently, by the appearance of John West, Graham Hancock and myself on a live TV show in Rome at the RAI 3 studios.
54. *New York Times* 24 May 1997.

55. *Sunday Times* 22 June 1997.
56. Ibid.
57. I was seriously ill from March 1997 to May 1998 caused by a combination of over work, exhaustion, poor diet, and various liver, bladder and kidney infections, which in turn triggered an extended state of depression. I see it as my descent into the 'Duat' and have much learnt from this experience and emerged the wiser.
58. Boris Said later claimed that they used his commercial filming licence.
59. Going under the name 'The Hall of Record'. It is now off the air.
60. On EGYPTNEWS and SPHINXNEWS.
61. On Dr Hawass's official website 'Guardian'.
62. Amargi Hillier and Larry Hunter ended up 'splitting up' on account of this and other differences between them. Amargi runs a new website 'The Duat Project' from Giza.
63. The rumour started around the autumn of 1997.
64. See *Giza: The Truth* by Chris Ogilvie-Herald and Ian Lawton, Virgin 1999.
65. *Daily Telegraph*, 4 March 1935.
66. Ibid.
67. Film of the Schor Expedition (extended version of the promo *Secret Chamber*) provided to me by Richard Hoagland who got it from Boris Said.
68. Dr Hawass admitted this fact later on to the press, but he is still hailed as the 'discoverer' of the well-shaft.
69. Telephone conversation with Boris Said, 30 September 1998.
70. I have no idea what evidence Boris Said was talking about. Boris was clearly wounded and frustrated by the whole affair and put the blame fair and square on Dr Hawass.
71. This was lately seen as some bizarre 'plot' to usher in the 'ancient spacemen gods' of Egypt! See *Daily Mail*, 23 July 1999, p. 55.
72. A. Robert Smith, *Hugh Lynn Cayce*, p. 255.
73. A few minutes of the 'discovery' of the sarcophagus lid was shown on a large screen.
74. *Carte Blanche*, M-Net TV, 'Return to Keeper of Genesis', 5 December 1998.
75. Fox TV 'Opening of the lost tomb: Live from Egypt', 2 March 1999, 8pm ET.
76. See my statement on EGYPTNEWS August 1998.
77. Due out in 2001 and with working title *The Phoenix Unveiled*.

CHAPTER ELEVEN
1. See *The Orion Mystery*, Heinemann ed., 1994, pp. 125–7.
2. Ibid.
3. Ibid. p. 132.
4. Ibid. p. 227.
5. Ibid. p. 132.
6. Ibid. p. 131.
7. *The Pyramids of Egypt*, published by Penguin Books and reprinted nearly every year since 1946. Last reprint was in 1994.
8. Letter from Dr Edwards to author 23 January 1993.
9. Letter from the author to Dr Rainer Stadelmann 24.1.1993.
10. Letter from author to Dr Edwards 25.1.1993.
11. Letter from Dr Edwards to author 27.1.1993.
12. Copy of press release provided by R. Gantenbrink to author.
13. Letter from the author to Dr Edwards dated 9 March 1993.
14. Fax from author to Gantenbrink at Movenpick Hotel 16.3.1993.
15. Sent to Mr Sami (sic) Hosni and signed by J.B. Peitz on behalf of R. Gantenbrink
16. Reply came on 7 April 1993.
17. *The Stargate Conspiracy*, pp. 43–45.
18. *Giza: The Truth*, p. 407.

19. Ibid.
20. Fax from the author to Gantenbrink dated 4 April 1993.
21. Reported by Gantenbrink to me.
22. Filmed in May 1996 by Jochen Breitenstein.
23. The article mentions 'scattered fine black dust in front of the 2mm-wide gap between the stone door and the wall'. This is a fact that only Gantenbrink was aware of.
24. I was the only person who had publisheda scientific paper on the matter of the shafts since Trimble and Badawy's articles in 1964.
25. We arranged for all audio-visual equipment and viewing area.
26. This is on film, which I showed at the Questing Conference in October 1998.
27. Letters from author to Dr Davies, dated 24 April 1993. Letter from Dr Davies to author, dated 26 April 1993.
28. Reuters, 16 April 1993, JFX AM $NSM1, job 1023.
29. *The Times*, 17 April 1993.
30. The *Independent*, 17 April 1993.
31. Ibid.
32. *The Times*, 26 April 1993, p. 4.
33. Ibid.
34. *The Times*, 26 April 1993, p. 4.
35. *Egyptian Gazette*, 28 April 1993.
36. This is also explained on Gantenbrink's official website (cheops.org).
37. See *Keeper of Genesis*, Heinemann ed. 1996, p. 123.
38. See Gantenbrink's website.
39. These are really far too numerous to list here. After six years articles still appear here and there nearly every week.
40. *Stern,* July 1993, pp. 22–25.
41. *Ancient Skies* no.3/1993 17 Jahrgang; also no.4/1994 18 Jahrgang.
42. *GRAL* 5/94 Sept/Oct 1994, pp. 198–202. See also *GRAL* 1/95 Jan/Feb.; 2/95 Mar/Apr 1995; 3/96; *GRAL* Sonderband no.8 Mar. 1995.
43. See *Chauffage, Ventilation, Conditionement* vol. No. 12, December 1990.
44. Fax from BBC/John Blake to Olaf Schroter, dated 30 July 1993.
45. *The Times*, July 1993.
46. It is not clear whether it is Gantenbrink's film.
47. This was filmed also by the BBC crew with Chris Mann.
48. Ibid.
49. This angle was later published several times in German periodicals, including *GRAL*.
50. Documented in a letter by Gantenbrink to John Blake of the BBC.
51. Documented in a letter from Gantenbrink to Dr R. Stadelman dated 9 September 1993.
52. Documented.
53. Matters are not so clear as to who has the copyrights as opposed to commercial rights. I assume it is Gantenbrinks.
54. Letter to Chris Mann at BBC 1.2.1993.
55. This involved photographic material. Gantenbrink had provided me with a photo of the robot and his permission to use it.
56. Documented in communications with Gantenbrink and with the publishers.
57. Gantenbrink was in the habit of calling me at least once a day around that time. After the clash with the BBC, he cut all communication with me. We tentatively resumed contact several months later.
58. Roy Baker worked from the BBC White City offices.
59. Documented in many letters to and from the BBC.
60. Documented.
61. Documented in a letter by Gantenbrink to Dr Stadelmann 9.9.1993.

62. This does not apply for filming explorations and archaeological works, for which a special licence is required.
63. For example, on ABC *Prime Time Live* 1.3.1995.
64. This was done through a so-called Tomlins Order signed by the parties in June 1993.
65. Which I did at conferences and any other opportunity I got.
66. Fax to Dr Kerieleis dated 28 September 1995.
67. Copy of fax to Kerieleis, 28 September 1995.
68. I have stopped doing this since January 1999.
69. On the Art & Entertainment Channel, 8 January 1995, and many times since.
70. This was dispatched through the Egyptian embassy in Bonn in early April 1993.
71. Delivered personally by Gantenbrink in February 1994.
72. This matter has gone into the annals of history and needs to be corrected accordingly.
73. In fact several times in September 1995.
74. Faxed to Dr Stadelmann on 28.9. 1995.
75. This was faxed on 13.10.1995.
76. Fax from Gantenbrink to author, 28 December 1995.
77. Ibid.
78. Announced by Dr Hawass at the ARE Conference, 20 August 1999.
79. I presume that Dr Stadelmann, of course, assumed the same for Dr Hawass.
80. Actually at the moment of closing my manuscript (20.9.1999) I was on my way to Cairo to attend a conference where Gantenbrink will also be speaking.

CHAPTER TWELVE

1. Website: www.cheops.org
2. See full details on Farouk El Baz on Amargi Hillier's website (Projectduat).
3. Ibid.
4. Ibid.
5. *Egyptian Gazette*, 31 March 1993.
6. Fax from P.Z. to R.B. dated 11 October 1994.
7. Fax from P.Z. to R.B., 21 November 1994.
8. Undisclosed.
9. Fax from P.Z. to R.B., 20 March 1995 and 24 March 1995.
10. In a recorded telephone conversation.
11. Shown on Spiegel TV (Sat 1) in August 1995.
12. Fax from R.B. to P.Z., 30 April 1996.
13. See *Giza: The Truth*, p. 401.
14. Mostly by Larry Hunter.
15. Channel 4 *News at Seven*, 16 April 1993.
16. Ibid.
17. *The Orion Mystery*, pp. 224–5.
18. With Jean-Claude Bragard of the BBC *Ancient Voices* progamme.
19. Dr Hawass's official website (guardian.com).
20. Ibid.
21. Ibid.
22. See Chapter 4.
23. See *Keeper of Genesis*, Chapter 10.
24. Dr Hawass's official website.
25. *Keeper of Genesis*, Illustration 69.
26. As seen from the latitude of Washington DC.

EPILOGUE

1. Alan Moorhead, *The Blue Nile*, Penguin Book 1972, p. 65.
2. Gerard Galtier, op. cit., p. 139.

3. Alan Moorhead, op. cit., p. 67.
4. Also known as Joseph Balsamo. Said to be the principal instigator of 'Egyptian' Freemasonry and many other modern Rosicrucian movements (Galtier, op. cit., 26), Caliostro came from Italy into France in 1784 and set up Masonic lodges in Lyon. He eventually went to Paris where he set up 'women' lodges, which became the craze at the court of Louis XVI. He was accused of plotting against Queen Marie-Antoinette and was thrown in the Bastille just before the Revolution broke out. Many thought he was the reincarnation of the famous Count of St Germain.
5. Wissa, op. cit.
6. Gerard Galtier, p. 139.
7. *Kneph*, vol. III, no.6, June 1883, p. 45.
8. Expounded on Internet statements and at various meetings with me.
9. *Network* has become a cult film since its showing in the 1970s. It featured William Holden, Robert Duval, Faye Dunaway and Peter Finch.
10. These are above the roof of the King's Chamber. No one is sure about their purpose, but some have suggested they served to relieve the King's Chamber from the dead weight of the Pyramid, and the name stuck.
11. Copies available from Art Bell Program which can be mail ordered.
12. Organised by Vision Travel Inc. of Los Angeles owned by Abass Nadim, a close friend of Dr Hawass.
13. The Project Duat website.
14. See Chapter 10.
15. See Chapter 10.
16. He apparently now thinks there is another similar 'conspiracy' linked to the Miami Stone Circle controversy. Hoagland has a brilliant mind and has done much to draw attention to certain irregularities related to NASA. But whether these irregularities are 'conspiracies' is, of course, another matter altogether.
17. Filmed by Boris Said, but commercial rights belong to Dr Schor.
18. For difficulties, I think, with funding his trip.
19. Hosted by Omar Sharif as special guest of Dr Hawass.
20. Which also led Hancock to affirm that the 'conspiracy' of the graffiti reported by the author Zacharia Sitchin (*Stairway to Heaven*, Dell Books) was wrong. The graffiti were genuine and contemporary with the Pyramid.
21. *Sunday Times*, 10 August 1997.
22. Nigel Appleby, *Hall of the Gods*, Heinemann 1998, p. 13.
23. His 'theory' involves just about everything: sacred geometry, astronomy, Cabala, numerology etc . . . but little or no use of ancient Egyptian sources such as the Pyramid Texts.
24. See OPERATION HERMES website.
25. *Operation Hermes Newsletter*, vol. 1, Issue no. 6, December 1997. See also *Quest for Knowledge* magazine, Issue 7, 1997.
26. Ibid.
27. Ibid.
28. An advance of approx. £70,000 was agreed, of which Appleby received about a third on signature of the deal.
29. Also known as 'Ralph' Ellis for reasons unknown. I saw Ellis twice: once at my home in July 1998, and the other time during a tour in Egypt in November 1998.
30. House of Commons Debate for 20 May 1999 presented by Mr Christopher Chope to Mr John Morris, the Attorney-General.
31. See OPERATION HERMES website.
32. Ibid.
33. Ibid. They have apparently sent a 'reconnaissance' team to Tibet.
34. See Amazon UK website reviews on *The Stargate Conspiracy*.
35. *Turin Shroud: In Whose Image?* (1994) and *The Templar Revelation* (1998)
36. Scottish launch was organised by the Templar Lodge. See Templarlodge website.

37. Graham Hancock, Robert Temple, John Anthony West, Robert Bauval, James Hurtak and various others.
38. Lynn Picknett and Clive Prince, *The Stargate Conspiracy*, Little Brown & Co.UK 1999
39. Ibid.
40. Little Brown & Co. UK press release, 'The Stargate Conspiracy', June/July 1999 by Becky Shaw.
41. See ProjectEquinox2000 website.
42. Authors included Michael Baigent, Yuri Stoyanov, Robert Temple, Christopher Lomas and Robert Knight and John Lash.
43. The *Daily Mail*, 23 July 1999, p. 55.
44. See Templarlodge website.
45. By Daily Grail website.
46. Chris Ogilvie-Herald was one-time editor of the *Quest for Knowledge* magazine, a small circulation bimonthly issue owned by Roy Bird of Top Events. Ian Lawton is an accountant with an interest in car racing and Egyptology. I met Chris only once, when I invited him to my home in July 1998 (also present was Roger Ellis) to discuss the Appleby affair. Chris knew Appleby quite well and had useful information to give Ellis in his legal case against the former.
47. *Giza: The Truth*, op. cit.
48. It devotes a substantial part to an extensive critique and 'attack' on my 'integrity' as an author and researcher.
49. This was absolutely essential, as many 'verbal' statements were being constantly altered or adjusted to suit the circumstances.
50. I have personally met Gantenbrink on numerous occasions. Also Dr Rainer Stadelmann, Dr Hawass, Dr Nureldin, Jochen Breitenstein and Dr Ali Hassan.
51. Amargi Hillier and Larry Hunter get the No.1 prize, however, in the rumour and conspiracy game of Gizagate.
52. *The Stargate Conspiracy*, p. xv.
53. Apparently now in November 1999.
54. See *Keeper of Genesis*, pp. 152–66.
55. Ibid.
56. For detailed discussion see *Keeper of Genesis*, Chapters 8 & 9.
57. Graham Hancock and I, for example, have discovered on numerous occasions that our related actions often match an 'astronomical' counterpart, such as finding ourselves climbing the Great Pyramid and near the exit of the southern shafts on the day of the spring equinox in 1996.
58. Yuri Stoyanov and myself have 'played' a mythico-astrological game whilst in Alexandria in November 1998, where daily events were 'matched' to astrological and weather changes and the myth of Alexander's visit to this place. It is my own belief that the ancients did the same.
59. David Ovason, *The Secret Zodiacs of Washington DC*, Century Book 1999, p. 103
60. For a full discussion, see Robert Temple's *The Sirius Mystery*, Century 1998.
61. The three stars in a row forming the Belt of Orion act as a pointer towards Sirius which is south of Orion. These three stars rise almost due east and can be used for navigation.
62. 1.21 arc seconds per year.
63. R.A. Schwaller de Lubicz, *Sacred Science*, Inner Traditions International, New York 1982, pp. 174–5.
64. PT 632.
65. See *The Orion Mystery*, Heinemann ed. 1994, p. 80, quote from the astronomer E.C. Krupp at the top of Chapter 8. 'There may be no need to try to connect the Pyramid and the Benben to the sun, as much has been often done with unsatisfactory effect, for the pyramid may be the agency for the rebirth of kings, just as the decans (i.e. stars) . . .'. Krupp then points out that the sign for Sirius has

a Benben symbol, suggesting a link between the two ideas.

66. The name 'Sepdt', i.e. Sirius, is seen on an ivory tablet dated from the first Dynasty, some three centuries before the construction of Giza. See *Sacred Science*, p. 180.
67. 'The Seeding of the Star-Gods; a Fertility Ritual in Cheops' Pyramid?'. *DE* 16, 1990.
68. See Appendix 1.
69. *Discussions in Egyptology*, vol. 16, 1990.
70. Matthew 2:2–3.
71. Matthew 2:9.
72. Matthew 2:13–5.
73. Ian Wilson, *Jesus The Evidence*, Pan Books, London 1985, annotated map p. 6.
74. A stele dating from the Twenty-sixth Dynasty. Found in Alexandria in 1828 and donated by Muhamad Ali to Prince Metternich.
75. *The Gods of the Egyptians*, vol. 2, pp. 220–221.
76. For a full discussion, see D. Jason Cooper's *Mithras*, op. cit.
77. This was the feast of the Saturnalia in Rome, celebrated at the Winter Solstice from 17 to 23 December. People wished themselves a 'happy saturnalia' and exchanged gifts at midnight after a lavish banquet.
78. *Mithras*, pp. 9, 66–8.
79. Lewis Spence, *Egypt*, p. 287: 'The Apis, though dead, was even yet more powerful, for his soul became joined to that of Osiris . . .'.
80. *Mithras*, p. 66.
81. A soft felt cap, conically shaped, characterised by a pointed crown that is curled forward. Also worn by the Revolutionary mob in France, and has become a sort of emblem for 'Freedom' in France. Worn by the slaves of Rome (Christians) to show their defiance to the Romans. It was very popular in the twelfth century AD.
82. *Keeper of Genesis*, Appendix 1.
83. Peter Lemesurier, *The Great Pyramid Decoded*, p. 19.
84. *The Hiram Key*, p. 76.
85. Ibid, p. 77.
86. Ta-Meri was a name for the Land of Egypt or, in my view, the Land of Pyramids, since Mer or Meri stood for 'pyramid' (see Edwards, op. cit. p. 293).
87. *The Hiram Key*, pp. 239–40.
88. Published in 1965.
89. Still standing today. A church was built to mark the place where the Holy Family supposedly rested.
90. *Quest for Knowledge* magazine, autumn 1995.
91. See also Richard H. Allen, *Star Names: Their Lore and Meaning*, Dover Publ. NY 1963, p. 316.
92. *Keeper of Genesis*, Appendix 1.
93. *The Hiram Key*, p. 14.
94. Paul Naudon, op. cit., p. 14
95. Martin Short, *Inside the Brotherhood*, Grafton Books 1989, p. 93.
96. Ibid. p. 91.
97. Ibid. p. 104.
98. Ibid. p. 92.
99. Pick & Knight, op. cit., p. 31.
100. Ibid, p. 32.
101. David Ovason, op. cit., p. 4.
102. Ibid. p. 116.
103. Ibid. p. 118.
104. *The Orion Mystery*, pp. 76, 95–6. 136.
105. David Ovason, op. cit., p. 118.
106. Paul Naudon, op. cit., p. 188.

107. It is kept just outside Lodge 22, where George Washington was initiated.
108. Paul Naudon, op. cit., p. 198.
109. Ibid. p. 159.
110. Ibid.
111. Ibid.
112. Pick & Knight, op. cit., p. 231.
113. Available only to selected Master Masons.
114. About 700 in the UK.
115. The intensely 'Christian' 18th degree, with all its implications of self-sacrifice and spiritual transfiguration through the 'rosy cross' is very suggestive of this idea.
116. See *The Rosicrucian Enlightenment*, plates 14a & 14b.
117. Erik Iversen, *The Myth of Egypt and its Hieroglyphs*, GEG Gag Publ. Copenhagen 1961, plate xix, pp. 104–5.
118. Paul Naudon, op. cit., p. 122.
119. David Ovason, op. cit., Chaper 5.
120. These will be discussed in my forthcoming book *The Phoenix Unveiled*, with Graham Hancock.
121. Ibid.
122. David Ovason, op. cit., pp. 137–8.
123. Ibid. p. 138.
124. Ibid.
125. Ibid. p. 128.
126. Ibid.
127. See Prologue note 22.
128. Rev. 22:16.
129. Rev. 21:1–3.
130. David Ovason, op. cit., p. 361.
131. Ibid. p. 350.
132. *The Phoenix Unveiled*. It was contracted by William Heinemann Ltd. in 1995, but delayed to the publication of our other books. It will now be published by Penguin Books in c. autumn 2001.
133. Jurgis Baltrusaitis, *La Quete D'Isis*, Flammarion, Paris 1985, pp. 21–78.
134. Ibid. p. 70–1.
135. Ibid.
136. Ibid. p. 112.
137. Ibid. p. 58.
138. Ibid. p. 51–5.
139. David Ovason, op. cit., p. 117.
140. *Texte des Lettres Patentes de concession d'armoiries en faveur de la ville de Paris*, redige le 20 Janvier 1811, translated by the author.
141. *La Quete D'Isis*, p. 54.
142. Published by the order of Napoleon Bonaparte. *Description de L'Egypte ou Receuil des Observations et des Recherches qui on été faites en Egypte pendant l'expedition de l'armée Française*, Paris 1809.
143. The Arc de la Défense is also known as L'Arche de la Fraternité (Arch of the Brotherhood).
144. David Ovason, op. cit., p. 30.
145. The French author and historian Jean Duche reports a strange conversation between Napoleon and Cardinal Fesch: 'Do you see this star?' asked the Emperor. 'No,' replied the Cardinal. 'Well, as long as I will be the only one to see it, I will go toward my destiny and I will not suffer criticism.' (Duche, *L'Histoire de France racontée a Juliette*, Press Pocket, Paris 1954). Was Napoleon referring to the star of Egypt?
146. Paul Naudon, op. cit., p. 78.
147. Ibid. p. 74.

148. Apparently the same might be done on the Great Pyramid on 31 December 1999.
149. See Jean Michel Jarre's official website, 'The Twelve Dreams of the Sun'.
150. Jeremy Naydler, *Temple of the Cosmos*, Inner Traditions, Rochester Vermont 1996, p. 285.

APPENDIX 3: COSMIC AMBIENCE REVISITED BY JOHN LASH

1. Jorge Luis Borges, *Other Inquisitions, 1937–1953* (New York, 1965) Translated by Ruth L.C. Simms, p.114.
2. On the Nine Hells of 52 years each, reckoned from the Aztec Calender Stone, see Tony Shearer, *Beneath the Sun and Under the Moon* (Albuquerque, New Mexico, 1987), p. 153ff.
3. Hermann Weyl, *Philosophy of Mathematics and Natural Science* (New York, 1963), p. 172–6.
4. Wilhelm Reich, *Ether, God and Devil Cosmic Superimposition* (New York, 1979), p. 139.ff
5. Quantum foam is a term from the theoretical physics of superspace proposed by John A. Wheeler. It was unknown to Reich although it fits his thinking. See Michael Talbot, *Mysticism and the New Physics* New York, 1981), p. 116 where Talbot alludes to Tantric teachings on the *Akasha* or universal ether.
6. Reich, Ibid., p. 145, 190.
7. Ibid., p. 240. Reich's italics.
8. Ibid., p. 191.
9. *Tetrahiblos* translated by J.M Ashmand (North Hollywood, Ca., 1976), p. 2.
10. Ibid., p. 3.
11. In Chapter II, Ptolemy posits the general theory of astrological correspondence: the Ambient at any moment is configured with the temperament of the individual born at that moment. *How* this can be occur consistently on the level of psychological and moral behaviour remains the unsolved enigma of sun-sign astrology.
12. See my article, 'The Alchemical Tree and the Planetary Metals' in *The Golden Blade*, 1988, where I argue that 'the alchemists perceived that the planetary effluvia, though plant-like and ethereal in character, come to be converted into sense-impressions.'
13. On this theory, see the works of Sir John Woodruffe, especially *Shakti and Shakta, The World as Power* and *The Garland of Letters*,
14. Mircea Eliade, *The Forge and the Crucible* (New York, 1971), p. 165.
15. Cited in Peter Tompkins, *The Magic of Obelisks* (San Francisco, 1981), p. 376ff
16. John White, Ed., *Pole Shift* (Virginia Beach, 1980), p. 356.
17. Cited in Tompkins, Op. Cit., p. 377.
18. Ibid., p. 378. Tompkins cites Bernard's book, *Aux Origines de l'Egypte*.
19. Ibid., p. 376.
20. G. L. Playfair and Scoff Hill, *The Cycles of Heaven* (London, 1978)
21. H. E. Huntley, *The Divine Proportion* (New York, 1970), p. 55.
22. From *Atrahasis*, the Epic of the Supersage, Tablet VII, in Jean Boffero and Samuel Noah Kramer, *Lorsque les dieux faisaient l'homme*, p. 541. My translation.
23. Cited in Joachim-Ernst Berendt, *The World is Sound* (Rochester,Vermont, 1991), p. 95.
24. In his memoire of Schwaller, *Al-Kemi* (Great Barrington, 1987), Andre Vanderbroeck mentions that the master made some elementary mistakes in his treatment of harmonics in Le Temple de l'homme. P. 34ff
25. *Sacred Science* (New York, 1982), p. 180.
26. Terence McKenna, *The Invisible Landscape* (San Francisco, 1993), p. 6.
27. Reich, *Ether, God and Devil*, p. 20.
28. Ibid., p.96.
29. Sir John Woodruffe, *The Garland of Letters* (Madras, 1969), p. 124.

30. On a novel theory of 'heart waves,' see 'The Origin of Disease and Health, Heart Waves' by Irving I. Dardik in *Frontier Perspectives*, V.6, #2, Spring/Summer, 1997.
31. McKenna, Op. Cit., p. 156.
32. Reich, Op.Cit., p. 138.
33. Michael Harner, *The Way of the Shaman* (San Francisco, 1990), p. xxi.

APPENDIX 4: A SANCTUARY FOR SOKAR BY SIMON COX

1. See Bauval & Gilbert, *The Orion Mystery*, London, William Heinemann Ltd., 1994
2. See Zivie, C.M., *Giza au deuxième millenaire*, Cairo, 1976.
3. See Fraser, *The Golden Bough*
4. Petrie, W.M.F, *Royal Tombs I*, London, 1900
5. Ibid.
6. Petrie, W.M.F, *Gizeh and Rifeh*, London, 1907
7. Mariette, *Le Serapeum de Memphis*, Paris, 1857
8. Ibid.
9. Gaballa, G.A., and Kitchen, K.A., *The Festival of Sokar*, Orientalia 38, 1969.
10. Pyr. 138c
11. For a full discussion of this, see Cox, Pegg, Ritchie, *The Makers of Time*, unpublished manuscript
12. Ref from MDAIK 17, 1961
13. Gaballa & Kitchen, op. cit.
14. See Hassan, S., *Excavations at Giza*, vol VI – pt I, Cairo, Government Press, 1946.
15. Gaballa & Kitchen, op. cit.
16. Petrie, op. cit. p. 9
17. See Vyse and Perring, *Excavations at Giza*, 1842
18. Lehner, *The Complete Pyramids*, London, Thames and Hudson 1997.
19. So-called on a stela of Rameses III. See Zivie, op. cit. 1976.
20. See the translation of the Dream stela by Hassan, op. cit.
21. See Cox, Pegg, Ritchie, *The Makers of Time*, unpublished manuscript, for further discussions on this area, notably on the significance of the positioning of the two modern cemeteries and the fact that this low-lying area could, we believe, be the legendary 'Field of Reeds', as mentioned in the various funerary texts.

Index